International Handbook of Cognitive and Behavioural Treatments for Psychological Disorders

International Handbook of Cognitive and Behavioural Treatments for Psychological Disorders

Edited by

V.E. CABALLO

Faculty of Psychology
University of Granada
Granada, Spain

1998
PERGAMON
An imprint of Elsevier Science

ELSEVIER SCIENCE Ltd
The Boulevard, Langford Lane
Kidlington,Oxford OX5 1GB, UK

Library of Congress Cataloging-in-Publication Data

International handbook of cognitive and behavioural treatments for
   psychological disorders / edited by V.E. Caballo.
       p.   cm.
    Includes bibliographical references and index.
    ISBN 0-08-043433-9
    1. Cognitive therapy--Handbooks, manuals, etc. 2. Behavior
  therapy--Handbooks, manuals, etc.   I. Caballo, V. E. (Vicente E.)
  RC489.C63I58   1998
  616.89'142--dc21   98-42129
                                                              CIP

British Library of Cataloguing in Publication Data
A catalogue record from the Library of Congress has been applied for

First edition 1998

ISBN: 0-08-043433-9

⊗The paper used in this publication meets the requirements of ANSI/NISO Z39.48-199
(Permanence of Paper).
Printed in The Netherlands

Contents

Preface

VICENTE E. CABALLO

Universidad de Granada, Spain

The behavioural or cognitive-behavioural perspective in clinical psychology is more popular nowadays than it has ever been before. It appears that the vast majority of health professionals now recognize that cognitive-behavioural procedures are very useful these days in treating many "mental" disorders, even if certain disciplines continue to favour other kinds of treatment (psycho-analytical, pharmacological, etc.) often due to a profound ignorance of cognitive-behavioural interventions. This manual is an attempt to show the interested reader the wide perspective cognitive-behavioural treatment can now offer to health professionals. The descriptive basis and theoretical framework of the main psychiatric disorders in adults have already been explained and assessed in previous works.[1,2,3] The most commonly used intervention techniques within the cognitive-behavioural field, somewhat independent of their application to specific disorders have also been described in detail.[4] In order to round out this area of clinical-behavioural psychology, structured programmes for specific disorders are needed. This is the gap this book attempts to fill.

Nowadays, treatments are described for specific mental disorders (behavioural as well as pharmacological). So, for example, while the proposed treatment for bipolar disorder is lithium carbonate and for schizophrenia with positive symptoms, antipsychotics,[5] the preferred treatment for primary insomnia is stimulus control, for specific phobia desensitization and for obsessive-compulsive disorder exposure plus response prevention.[5] The development of structured cognitive-behavioural programmes for different "mental" disorders is a fast-growing trend today in the field of clinical psychology.

This *Handbook* offers a wide range of structured programmes for the treatment of various psychological/psychiatric disorders. The range of disorders included in this book has been mainly guided by the diagnostic classification of the DSM-IV.[6] As a result, the layout will be familiar to the majority of health professionals in the description of mental disorders and their later treatment.

The present manual has been divided into six sections which represent as many different kinds of groups as the DSM-IV,[6] such as anxiety disorders, sexual disorders, somatoform, impulse control disorders, emotional disorders and psychotic and organic disorders.

The section that deals with anxiety disorders is the most extensive in the book. Specific treatments for the different disorders in this group are brought together although some treatment strategies such as relaxation, exposure, desensitization or cognitive restructuring are used extensively for many of these disorders. Although all these strategies have already been described elsewhere[4] here treatment programmes are explained, in many cases step by step or technique by technique, so that professionals can deal with each one of the anxiety disorders. As Barlow and Lehman[7] point out, studies already exist which demonstrate the effectiveness of new psychosocial treatments when compared to lack of treatment, with a psychosocial "placebo" or even an alternative psychotherapeutic treatment. "For some disorders treatment is well-established, for others promising treatments exist, but are at the stage of early development" (p. 727).

Then two kinds of sexual disorders are dealt with. There is an explanation of sexual disorders (a relatively common problem nowadays) and paraphilias (with a very innovative programme aimed at this difficult problem that society presently punishes).

The third part of the book is dedicated to the treatment of somatoform disorders, specifically hypochondria and body dismorphic disorders, with very specific programmes for each one. Impulse control disorders are mainly represented by pathological gambling and trichotillomania. The fourth section includes treatment of emotional disorders with a chapter dedicated to bipolar disorders (where cognitive-behavioural therapy is beginning to be used with notable success) and two chapters to depression disorders, one from a behavioural and another from a cognitive perspective.

Finally in the last section we deal with problems which are considered psychotic or organically based. Although the latter term is unfortunate (in fact it has disappeared from the diagnostic classification of the DSM-IV), it is a way of grouping together disorders such as dementia or mental retardation.

We hope that throughout the twenty-two chapters in this book health professionals can have at their disposal a structured guide with which to start tackling a whole series of "mental" disorders. The use of other texts may be required when one wants to go into more depth about specific problems, and here the book provides guidelines as to where to look for more information. The tendency to develop structured treatment programmes has already been established. In the next few years we will see these suggestions come to fruition. We hope that these programmes will be more and more effective for more and more disorders with lower economic costs and time investment for both patient and therapist.

---

[1] Caballo, V. E., Buela-Casal, G., & Carrobles, J. A. (1995). *Manual de psicopatología y trastornos psiquiátricos, Vol. 1: Fundamentos conceptuales, trastornos por ansiedad, afectivos y psicóticos*. Madrid: Siglo XXI.

[2] Caballo, V. E., Buela-Casal, G., & Carrobles, J. A. (1996). *Manual de psicopatología y trastornos psiquiátricos, Vol. 2: Trastornos de personalidad, medicina conductual y problemas de relación.* Madrid: Siglo XXI.

[3] Buela-Casal, G., Caballo, V. E., & Sierra, J. C. (1996). *Manual de evaluación en psicología clínica y de la salud.* Madrid: Siglo XXI.

[4] Caballo, V. E. (1991). *Manual de técnicas de terapia y modificación de conducta.* Madrid: Siglo XXI.

[5] Acierno, R., Hersen, M., & Ammerman, R. T. (1994). Overview of the issues in prescriptive treatments. In M. Hersen & R. T. Ammerman (Eds.), *Handbook of prescriptive treatments for adults.* New York: Plenum Press.

[6] APA (1994). *Diagnostic and statistical manual of mental disorders,* 4th edition (DSM-IV). Washington, DC: American Psychiatric Association.

[7] Barlow, D. H., & Lehman, C. L. (1996). Advances in the psychological treatment of anxiety disorders. *Archives of General Psychiatry, 53,* 727–735.

Foreword

According to Kuhn, science is characterized by long periods of "ordinary science", working along agreed and established paradigmatic lines, followed by "revolutions" which call in doubt the existing paradigm, and introduce a new paradigm. Problems often arise in that new definitions, new criteria and new methods render discussion and comparison between the old and the new paradigm difficult, if not impossible. The old paradigm is dethroned because too many anomalies have accumulated during its long reign; its explanatory rules have failed too frequently to account for well-authenticated facts; its predictions have been disconfirmed too frequently to make it acceptable. Scientists trained in the old tradition stubbornly cling to it, but the new generation enthusiastically embraces the new paradigm.

Paradigm shifts do not occur only in the hard sciences. One of the most remarkable such shifts has occurred in psychology. Freudian methods of psychotherapy had ruled the roost since the turn of the century, almost without any opposition, until the 1950s. Nobody seemed to be willing to ask the crucial question: Does psychoanalysis actually work? Freud himself frequently acknowledged both the existence of spontaneous remission, and the worrying lack of lasting success for psychoanalytic treatment, but his successors claimed that psychoanalysis, and only psychoanalysis, could really cure psychological disorders.

In the 1950s several doubters challenged this unsupported belief, and showed that the emperor had no clothes – there was no evidence that psychoanalysis produced better results than no treatment at all.[1] This is still the position, Svartberg & Stiles[2] have published a meta-analysis of 19 studies comparing the effectiveness of psychodynamic psychotherapy with "no treatment", without observing any difference in outcome. They also found that other methods of treatment did significantly better.

Other and better methods were already foreshadowed by Watson's theory of neurotic symptoms as conditioned emotional responses, leading to the view that therapy consisted in the extinction of these conditioned responses, in 1920. But the Zeitgeist resolutely resisted these theories, and even the demonstration by Mary Cover Jones that the deconditioning methods actually worked extremely well failed to impress. But gradually *behaviour therapy*, based on principles of learning theory, began its ascent, and the revolution gained momentum. We now know that these new methods are much more successful than any other; some 3000 comparative studies allow us to state with conviction that treatment of psychopathology is successful in proportion to the degree to which it incorporates these principles.[3]

Much has been learned in recent years about the best way of applying these new methods to all the different types of psychopathology, and it is with these specific applications that the Handbook is concerned. The methodologies in question should be familiar to every student involved with treatment, and students in particular will benefit from gaining familiarity with the methods and theories involved. Constant advances will no doubt soon call for a revision of this excellent textbook; an enormous amount of research is in constant progress, much of it reported in "Behaviour Research and Therapy", the leading research journal in this field.

Behaviour therapy has always contained cognitive elements as an important part of its basic theory; already Pavlov insisted on language as a "second signalling system" incorporating cognition in reflexology, and modern learning theory insists on the relevance of cognition even in the learning and conditioning processes of lowly animals. The term "cognitive-behavioural" is therefore somewhat redundant *all* behavioural treatments use *eo ipso* cognitive. But using this phraseology has the advantage that ignorant objections that our theories leave out essential cognitive elements are not likely to be taken seriously.

The revolution is still going on, and far from complete. Not all of the old guard has ceased to exist, and much remains to be done in the battle to establish successful for unsuccessful and even harmful methods of treatment. But scientifically the battle has been won.

All the evidence proclaims the superiority of the new theories and methods over the old. This book is testimony to that.

H.J. Eysenck
Institute of Psychiatry
University of London

[1] Eysenck, H. J. (1985). *Decline and fall of the Freudian empire*. London: Viking.
[2] Svartberg, M., & Stiles, T. (1991). Comparative effects of short-term psychodynamic psychotherapy: A meta-analysis. *Journal of Consulting and Clinical Psychology, 59*, 704-714.
[3] Grawe, K., Donati, R., & Bernauer, F. (1994). *Psychotherapie im Wandel*. Toronto: Hogrefe.

List of Contributors

V. Andres, Centro de Psicologia Bertrand Russell, c/ Marques de Urquijo, 10-1° Centro, 28008 Madrid, Spain

M.M. Antony, C. Psych., Department of Psychology, St. Joseph's Hospital, 50 Charlton Avenue East, Hamilton, Ontario L8N 4A6, Canada, email: mantony@stjosham.on.ca

M. Astin, Emory Clinic, Department of Psychiatry and Behavioral Sciences, 1365 Clifton Road, Atlanta, GA 30322, USA

D.H. Barlow, The Center for Anxiety and Related Disorders, Boston University, 684 Beacon Street, 6 Floor, Boston, MA 02215-2002, USA, email: dhbarlow@bu.edu

F. Bas, Centro de Psicologia Bertrand Russell, c/ Marques de Urquijo, 10-1° Centro, 28008 Madrid, Spain

M.R. Basco, University of Texa Southwestern Medical Center at Dallas, Division of Psychology, 5323 Harry Hines Blvd., Dallas, TX 75235-9044, USA, email: mbasco@email.msn.com

C. Botella, Dpto. de Psicología, Facultad de Ciencias Humanas y Sociales, Campus de Borriol, Apdo. de Correos 242, 12080 Castellón, Spain, email: botella@psb.uji.es

V.E. Caballo, Facultad de Psicología, Universidad de Granada, 18071 Granada, Spain, email: caballo@ibm.net

M.P. Carey, Department of Psychology, Syracuse University, 430 Huntington Hall, Syracuse, NY 13244-2340, email: mpcarey@syr.edu

P. Chadwick, All Saints Hospital, Dept. of Clinical Psychology, Lodge Road, Winson Green, Birmingham B18 5SD, UK

P. de Corral, Facultad de Psicologia, Universidad del Pais Vasco, Avda. de Tolosa, 70, 20009 San Sebastian, Spain, email: ptpodece@ss.ehu.es

M.G. Craske, Department of Psychology, University of California, Los Angeles, 405 Hilgard Ave, Los Angeles, CA 90095-1563, USA, email: craske@psych.ucla.edu

J.L. Deffenbacher, Department of Psychology, Colorado State University, Fort Collins, Colorado 80523-1876, USA, email: jld6871@lamar.colostate.edu

L. DelliCarpini, Department of Psychiatry, St. Lukes Roosevelt Hospital, New York, NY, USA

M. Dugas, Ecole de Psychologie, Universite Laval, Ste-Foy, Qc., Canada, G1K 7P4

E. Echeburua, Facultad de Psicologia, Universidad del Pais Vasco, Avda. de Tolosa, 70, 20009 San Sebastian, Spain, email: ptpodece@ss.ehu.es

B. Edelstein, Department of Psychology, West Virginia University, P.O. Box 6040, Morgantown, WV 26506-6040, USA, email: u21b4@wvnvm.wvnet.edu

Y.M. Fernandez, Department of Psychology, Queen's University, Kingston, Ontario, K7L 2N6, Canada, email: 3yml@qlink.queensu.ca

A. Freeman, 7914 Ivy Ln, Elkins Park, PA 19117, USA, email: artcbt@aol.com

M.H. Freeston, Centre de recherche Fernand-Seguin, 7331, rue Hochelaga, Montreal, Qc, H1N 3V2, Canada, email: freeston@microtec.net, mark.freeston@crfs.umontreal.ca

I.H. Gotlib, Department of Psychology, Building 420, Jordan Hall, Stanford University, Stanford, CA 94305, USA, email: gotlib@psych.stanford.edu

M. Hautzinger, Psychologische Institut, Saarstrasse 21/Staudingerweg 9, D-55099 Mainz, Germany

C. Jackson, Northern Birmingham, Mental Health NHS Trust, The Early Intervention Service, Harry Watton House, 97 Church Lane, Aston, Birmingham B6 5UG, UK, email: m.j.birchwood.20@bham.ac.uk

R. Ladouceur, Ecole de Psychologie, Université Laval, Ste-Foy, Qc., Canada, G1K 7P4, email: robert.ladouceur@psy.ulaval.ca

M.R. Lewin, California State University, San Bernardino, Department of Psychology, 5500 University Parkway, San Bernardino, CA 92407-2397, USA, email: mlewin@wiley.csusb.edu

P.M. Lewinsohn, Oregon Research Inst, 1715 Franklin Blvd., Eugene, OR 97403, USA, email: pete@ori.org

M.J. Lobato, Avda. de Marín, 29-3°C, 32001 Orense, Spain

W.L. Marshall, Department of Psychology, Queen's University, Kingston, Ontario, K7L 2N6, Canada

M.P. Martinez Narvaez, Facultad de Psicologia, Universidad de Granada, 18071 Granada, Spain

K.T. Mueser, New Hampshire-Dartmouth Psychiatric Research Center, 105 Pleasant Street, Main Building, Concord, NH 03301, USA, email: kim.t.mueser@dartmouth.edu

C.M. Nezu, Department of Clinical & Health Psychology, Allegheny University of the Health Sciences, MS 626, Broad & Vine, Philadelphia, PA 19102-1192, USA, email: nezuc@auhs.edu

A.M. Nezu, Department of Clinical & Health Psychology, Associate Dean for Research, School of Health Professions, Allegheny University of the Health Sciences, MS 626, Broad & Vine, Philadelphia, PA 19102-1192, USA

L. Northrop, 807 41st Avenue, San Francisco, CA 94121, USA, email: lynn.me.northrop @ncal.kaiperm.org

D. Opdyke, Clinical Team Supervisor, Catawba County Mental Health, Adolescents and Children in Treatment (ACT), 40 West Sixth Street, Newton, NC 28658, USA, email: opdyke@abts.net

C.L. Oster, Suite 220, 32-50 N Arlington Heights Road, Arlington Heights, IL 60004, USA

S. Rebolledo, Avda. de Marín, 29-3°C, 32001 Orense, Spain

P. Resick, Center for Trauma Recovery, Weinman Building, University of Missouri-St. Louis, 8001 Natural Bridge Rd., St. Louis, MO 63121, USA, email: resick@umsl.edu.

J.C. Rosen, University of Vermont, Dept. of Psychology, Burlingotn, VT 05405, USA, email: j.rosen@dewey.uvm.edu

B.O. Rothbaum, Emory University School of Medicine, Department of Psychiatry, 1365 Clifton Road, NE, Atlanta, GA 30322, email: brothba@emory.edu

L. Sharpe, Department of Psychology, West Middlesex University Hospital, Twickenham Road, Isleworth TW7 6AF, UK

N. Staats, 14 San Jose Avenue, Pacifica, CA 94044, USA email: staats.natalie_d@palo-alto. va.gov

M.E. Thase, University of Pittsburgh School of Medicine, 3811 O'Hara Street, Pittsburgh, PA 15213-2593, USA

1

Specific Phobia

MARTIN M. ANTONY[a] and DAVID H. BARLOW[b]

[a]St. Joseph's Hospital and McMaster University, Hamilton, ON, Canada; [b]Center for Anxiety and Related Disorders at Boston University, USA

Introduction

In DSM-IV (APA, 1994), a specific phobia is defined as a marked and persistent fear that is cued by the presence or anticipation of a specific object or situation. The fear must be recognized by the individual to be excessive or unreasonable, must be associated with functional impairment or subjective distress, and is typically accompanied by an immediate anxiety response and avoidance of the feared object or situation. In some individuals, phobic avoidance is minimal, although exposure to the situation reliably leads to intense levels of fear. Specific phobias may be differentiated from other phobic disorders based on the types of situations avoided as well as the associated features of the disorder. For example, individuals who avoid a range of specific situations typically associated with agoraphobia (e.g., crowds, driving, enclosed places) are likely to receive a diagnosis of panic disorder with agoraphobia, especially if the focus of apprehension in the feared situation is on the possibility of experiencing a panic attack. Similarly, a person who fears and avoids situations involving social evaluation (e.g., public speaking, meeting new people) is likely to receive a diagnosis of social phobia. In DSM-IV, a diagnosis of specific phobia is not assigned if the fear is better accounted for by another mental disorder.

DSM-IV includes five main specific phobia types: animal type, natural environment type, blood–injection–injury type, situational type, and other type. The introduction of these types was based on a series of reports to the DSM-IV Anxiety Disorders Work Group (e.g., Craske, 1989; Curtis, Himle, Lewis & Lee, 1989) showing that specific phobia types tend to differ on a variety of dimensions including age of onset, gender composition, patterns of covariation among phobias, focus of apprehension (i.e., anxiety over physical sensations), timing and predictability of the phobic response, and type of physical reaction during exposure to the feared object or situation.

Phobias from the animal type may include fears of any animal, although animals that are commonly feared include snakes, spiders, insects, dogs, cats, mice, and birds. Animal phobias typically begin in childhood and tend to have an earlier age of onset than other phobia types (Himle, McPhee, Cameron & Curtis, 1989; Marks & Gelder, 1966; Öst, 1987). In addition, they more common among women than men, with percentages of patients who are female ranging from about 75% in epidemiological studies (Agras, Sylvester & Oliveau, 1969; Bourdon, Boyd, Rae, Burns, Thompson & Locke, 1988) to 95% or more in studies of clinical patients (Himle et al., 1989; Marks & Gelder, 1966; Öst, 1987). Among women, animal phobias are the most common type of specific phobia (Bourdon et al., 1988).

Natural environment phobias include fears of storms, water, and heights. These fears are quite common; in fact, among men, height phobias are the most commonly reported specific phobia (Bourdon et al., 1988). Natural environment fears tend to begin in childhood, although there is some evidence that height phobias begin later than other phobias from this type (Curtis, Hill & Lewis, 1990). Large epidemiological studies have found that storm and water phobias are more common among women than men. For example, anywhere from 78% (Bourdon et al., 1988) to 100% (Agras, Sylvester & Oliveau, 1969) of individuals with storm phobias tend to be female. With respect to sex ratio, height phobias appear to be different than other natural environment phobias in that only 58% of individuals with height phobias tend to be female (Bourdon et al., 1988). These data, as well as other recent findings (e.g., Antony, Brown & Baldwin, 1997a,b) suggest that height phobias may not be typical of the natural environment type.

Blood–injection–injury phobias include fears of seeing blood, receiving injections, watching or undergoing surgical procedures, and other related medical situations. They tend to begin in childhood or early adolescence, and are more common in females, although sex differences are less pronounced than for animal phobias (Agras et al., 1969; Öst, 1987, 1992). Unlike other phobias, blood–injection–injury phobias are often associated with a diphasic physiological response during exposure to the feared situation. This response begins with an initial increase in arousal which is subsequently followed by a sharp drop in heart rate and blood pressure, often leading to fainting. Approximately 70% of individuals with blood phobia and 56% of those with injection phobias report a history of fainting in the feared situation (Öst, 1992). As discussed in a later section, the tendency for individuals with blood and injection phobias to faint has led to the development of specific treatment strategies for preventing fainting in this group.

Situational phobias include specific phobias of situations that are often feared by individuals with agoraphobia. Typical examples include enclosed places, driving, elevators, and airplanes. Situational phobias tend to have a mean age of onset in the twenties (Himle et al., 1989; Öst, 1987); and tend to be more common in women than men. Situational phobias are more likely to be associated with delayed and unpredictable panic attacks in some studies (Antony et al., 1997a; Ehlers, Hofmann, Herda & Roth, 1994), although other studies have found contradictory results (e.g., Craske & Sipsas, 1992).

Finally, an "other type" was included in DSM-IV to describe phobias not easily classified using the four main specific phobia types. Examples of phobias from the "other type" include fears of choking, vomiting, and balloons, although any phobia not easily classified as one of the other four types would be classified in this category.

Overall, specific phobia is the most prevalent anxiety disorder diagnosis and is among the most prevalent of all psychological disorders. Lifetime prevalence estimates for specific phobia are in the range of 14.45 to 15.7 percent for women and 6.7 to 7.75 percent for men (Eaton, Dryman & Weissman, 1991; Kessler et al., 1994). Despite their prevalence, there is still much to learn about the nature and treatment of specific phobias. Although subclinical fears among college students have been studied extensively by investigators seeking to understand the nature of fear and methods of fear reduction, few studies have examined the psychopathology and treatment of specific phobias in clinical patients. Furthermore, the studies that have been conducted tend to focus on a relatively small range of phobias, have small sample sizes, and have not examined differences in treatment response among specific phobia types. Nevertheless, there is increasing evidence that specific phobias are among the most treatable of all disorders. In as little as one session of systematic exposure to the feared situation, the majority of individuals with phobias of animals, blood, and injections are able to overcome their phobias (Öst, 1989).

Theoretical Foundations of Exposure-Based Treatment

Exposure to the feared object or situation is believed to be an essential component of any successful treatment for specific phobia (Marks, 1987), although the mechanisms by which exposure exerts its effects are unclear. Barlow (1988) summarized some of the major theories to explain the process of fear reduction. First, *habituation* was proposed by Lader & Wing (1966) to explain the therapeutic effects of systematic desensitization. Habituation is the process of becoming familiar with and thereby responding less to a particular stimulus over time (e.g., as when one becomes less aware of a particular odor after prolonged exposure). This process typically leads to only short term changes in responding and appears to affect physiological responses (e.g., galvanic skin response) more than subjective feelings. The role of learning in habituation is presumed to be minimal. Evidence for the role of habituation in fear reduction is mixed (Barlow, 1988).

A more popular model for explaining the therapeutic effects of exposure has been the process of *extinction*. Extinction involves the weakening of a conditioned response by discontinuing reinforcement. According to Mowrer's (1960) two-stage model of fear development, a fear (e.g., a dog phobia) begins when a neutral stimulus (e.g., a dog) is paired through classical conditioning with an aversive unconditioned stimulus (e.g., being bitten). According to Mowrer, fear is maintained by negative reinforcement resulting from avoidance of the conditioned stimulus. In other words, avoidance prevents the aversive symptoms associated with the feared object from occurring and is thereby reinforced operantly. In theory, exposure puts an end to the negative reinforcement associated with avoidance and thereby leads to extinction of the fear. Extinction is presumed to involve new learning (i.e., changes in the way information is processed), and tends to have lasting effects, relative to habituation. Nevertheless, there exists evidence that calls into question the value of extinction as a model of fear reduction. For example, some studies (e.g., Rachman, Craske, Tallman & Solyom, 1986) have shown that exposure appears to be effective for decreasing fear in the long term even when an individual escapes from the situation before reaching the maximum level of anxiety. However, contrary to this finding and consistent with extinction theory, several studies have shown that exposure of longer durations is more effective for decreasing fear than exposure of shorter durations (Marks, 1987).

Consistent with modern theories of conditioning (e.g., Rescorla, 1988), *cognitive factors* may play an important role in fear reduction. Data are beginning to converge to suggest that variables such as perceived control (Sanderson, Rapee & Barlow, 1989), presence of safety signals such as a spouse (Carter, Hollon, Carson & Shelton, 1995), and predictability of exposure (Lopatka, 1989) all affect levels of fear during exposure to a feared situation.

In addition, theories of *emotional processing* (e.g., Foa & Kozak, 1986; Rachman, 1980) have been proposed to explain the process of fear reduction using an emotion theory framework (e.g., Lang, 1985). According to Foa & Kozak (1986), exposure to a feared situation provides information that is inconsistent with that previously stored in emotional memory. For example, habituation within a given session demonstrates that fear does not last forever and that it is possible to be in the presence of a previously feared object without feeling frightened. Similarly, repeated exposure teaches an individual that the probability of danger in the feared situation is low. In theory, emotional processing depends on the activation of appropriate anxiety structures stored in memory. Variables that are proposed to interfere with emotional processing include distraction, autonomic arousal that is too high (so that within-session habituation cannot occur), and autonomic arousal that is too low (reflecting incomplete activation of the anxiety structure).

As with the other models discussed, evidence supporting emotional processing as a model of fear reduction is mixed (Barlow, 1988). For example, studies examining the effects of distraction on fear reduction during exposure have yielded contradictory results (Rodriguez & Craske, 1993b). Similarly, Holden & Barlow (1986) found that the relationship between arousal and anxiety is more complicated than theories of emotional processing might predict. Specifically, Holden and Barlow (1986) had individuals with agoraphobia and with no mental disorder undergo a standard behavioral approach test involving walking away from a safe place. Both groups began with elevated heart rates and showed similar gradual decreases in heart rate during the behavioral test. This finding occurred despite the fact that subjects with no mental disorder reported no anxiety during the behavioral test.

It is too soon to say exactly how exposure leads to fear reduction. Furthermore, it is possible that the theories mentioned above are not mutually exclusive explanations. Although none of these theories fully explains the process of fear reduction, each may explain some small part of the story. For example, habituation and extinction may both be involved in within-session reductions in fear, whereas extinction may be more relevant for explaining between-session decreases in fear. Variables such as perceived control, perceived safety, predictability, and emotional processing may partially mediate the changes that occur during habituation and extinction. Finally, repeated exposure may have an impact on certain physiological variables that appear to be related to the experience of fear. As reviewed by Barlow (1988), chronic exposure to fearful stimuli can lead to overall decreases in norepinephrine, which tend to be associated with certain behavioral changes consistent with the process of "toughening up" or developing greater tolerance for aversive stimuli (Gray, 1985). In summary, the mechanisms by which exposure leads to decreases in fear are most likely determined by multiple factors. Unidimensional theories are likely to be inadequate for explaining the process of fear reduction. To the extent that investigators begin to examine how cognitive, behavioral, and physiological variables interact to produce changes in fear during treatment, we may begin to develop an understanding of how exposure works.

Empirical Findings on the Treatment of Specific Phobias

Numerous studies have demonstrated that exposure-based treatments are effective for decreasing specific fears. Specifically, exposure has been shown to be effective for phobias of blood (Öst, Lindahl, Sterner & Jerremalm, 1984), injections (Öst, 1989), dentists (Liddell, Ning, Blackwood & Ackerman 1991; Jerremalm, Jansson & Öst, 1986), animals (Foa, Blau, Prout & Latimer, 1977;

Muris, de Jong, Merckelbach & van Zuuren, 1993; O'Brien & Kelley, 1980; Öst, 1991; Öst, Salkovskis & Hellström, 1991b), enclosed places (Booth & Rachman, 1992; Öst, Johansson & Jerremalm, 1982), flying (Denholtz & Mann, 1975; Howard, Murphy & Clarke, 1983; Solyom, Shugar, Bryntwick & Solyom, 1973), heights (Baker, Cohen & Saunders, 1973); Bourque & Ladouceur, 1980; Marshall, 1988), and choking (Ball & Otto, 1993; McNally, 1986).

The way in which exposure is conducted can have an impact on its effectiveness in many cases. Exposure-based treatments can vary on numerous dimensions including the degree of therapist involvement, the duration of exposure, the inclusion of additional treatment strategies (e.g., cognitive restructuring, relaxation), the intensity of exposure, the frequency of sessions, the number of sessions, the cues to which the individual is exposed (e.g., external situation vs. internal sensations), and the degree to which the situation is confronted in real life vs. in imagination.

In addition, the relationship between these variables and treatment success may vary depending on the phobia type, the nature of the fear reaction, and other variables that differ across patients. For example, Öst et al. (1982) demonstrated that individuals with claustrophobia who were primarily behavioral responders (i.e., for whom avoidance was the principal pattern of responding) benefited more from exposure than from applied relaxation training. In contrast, patients with claustrophobia who were primarily physiological responders (i.e., principal response was increased arousal upon exposure to the situation) responded most to applied relaxation. However, this finding was not confirmed in a group of individuals with dental phobias (Jerremalm et al., 1986).

Spacing and Duration of Exposure Sessions

It appears that longer exposure sessions are more effective than shorter sessions in most studies (Marks, 1987). In addition, exposure appears to work best if sessions are spaced close together rather than far apart. For example, Foa, Jameson, Turner & Payne (1980) found that treatment of agoraphobia was more effective with 10 daily exposure sessions than with 10 weekly sessions. However, the applicability of this finding to specific phobias is unclear, especially in light of the fact that as many at 90% of individuals with animals and injection phobias can be successfully treated (i.e., much improved or completely cured) in one treatment session of exposure and therapist modeling (Muris et al., 1993; Öst, 1989).

Models of fear reduction predict that exposure should work best when patients are prevented from escaping before their fear has decreased. Studies examining this variable have yielded mixed results. For example, de Silva and

Rachman (1984) and Rachman, Craske, Tallman and Solyom (1986) found that escaping before the fear peaks had no effect on the efficacy of exposure for agoraphobia. In contrast, Marks (1987) reviewed numerous studies showing that prolonged exposure is more effective than exposure of shorter durations. But at what point should exposure be terminated? Gauthier and Marshall (1977) examined several criteria by which a clinician might decide to terminate exposure sessions for snake phobias. Specifically, they examined treatment efficacy when termination of exposure sessions was determined by return to baseline on each of the following measures: heart rate, patient's self-reported anxiety, patient's anxiety according to two independent observers, and a combination of using all three measures. Terminating sessions based on reductions in observer-rated anxiety led to the greatest therapeutic gains, relative to the other methods.

Degree of Therapist Involvement

Findings have been inconsistent with respect to the importance of having a therapist present during exposure sessions. Marks (1987) reviewed numerous studies showing that self-exposure is effective for treatment of a variety of phobic disorders including agoraphobia, social anxiety, and obsessive compulsive disorder. However, for specific phobias, it seems that some therapist involvement may be better than no therapist involvement. Öst, Salkovskis & Hellström (1991b) found that 71% of individuals with spider phobia were clinically improved following therapist-assisted exposure, whereas only 6% were improved following self-directed exposure. Similarly, O'Brien & Kelley (1980) found that exposure sessions that were mostly therapist-assisted were significantly more effective for decreasing snake phobias relative to sessions that were mostly or exclusively self-directed and slightly better than sessions that were entirely therapist-assisted. These data suggest that therapist involvement is important for overcoming animal phobias, although patients should eventually be taught to confront the situation on their own as well. Bourque & Ladouceur (1980) found no differences between exposure conducted with and without a therapist present for treatment of height phobia. However, the number of patients per group in this study was small and patients met with the therapist before and after the exposure session in all treatment conditions. In other words, even for conditions in which the therapist was not present during the exposure, sessions were not completely self-directed. Clearly, more studies are needed to examine the benefits of self-exposure for other specific phobia types.

Distraction during Exposure Sessions

Although most models of fear reduction predict that distraction should interfere with the effectiveness of exposure, studies on the effects of distraction have yielded contradictory results. Rodriguez & Craske (1993a) reviewed the literature on distraction during exposure to phobic stimuli and concluded that the specific effects of distraction may depend on a number of variables including the way anxiety is measured (e.g., physiological arousal vs. subjective anxiety), the type of distraction (e.g., perceptual vs. cognitive), focus of distraction (e.g., away from stimulus or situation vs. away from response or physical sensations), affective quality of the distracter, and intensity of fear. Rodriguez & Craske (1993b) found that distraction was most likely to undermine the effects of exposure under conditions of high intensity exposure for animal phobias. In addition, Muris et al. (1993) suggested that certain differences in coping style may predict the effects of distraction for a given individual. Specifically, they found that individuals with spider phobias who were "monitors" (i.e., tended to seek out threat-relevant information) responded less to focused exposure than did individuals who were "blunters" (i.e., tended to avoid threat-related information). They suggested that monitors might benefit more from treatment if they were distracted from time to time, although this hypothesis has yet to be tested.

Imaginal Versus In Vivo Exposure

Exposure may be conducted in a variety of ways. Although imaginal exposure can be an effective method of fear reduction (e.g., Baker et al., 1973; Foa et al., 1977), it is generally accepted that live exposure is more effective than exposure in fantasy (Marks, 1987). Of course, *in vivo* exposure is not always possible when confronting the feared situation is dangerous (e.g., phobia of being attacked), impossible (e.g., phobia of monsters), or difficult (e.g., phobias of storms, airplanes). In such cases, imaginal exposure can be an effective adjunct or substitute for *in vivo* or live exposure.

Combining Other Strategies with Exposure

Finally, certain phobia types may benefit from specialized treatment strategies. The best example is the treatment of blood phobia by applied tension (Kozak & Montgomery, 1981; Öst & Sterner, 1987). Because such a high percentage of individuals with blood phobias faint in the phobic situation, strategies for preventing fainting have been developed and tested in people with blood phobias. Fainting tends to occur when an individual experiences a sudden drop in blood pressure upon exposure to a situation involving blood. Therefore, investigators have studied the use of applied tension (a method of temporarily increasing blood pressure) for the treatment of blood phobia. Applied tension has repeatedly been shown to be an effective treatment for blood phobia (Öst et al., 1984; Öst & Sterner, 1987). In fact, applied tension may be a more effective treatment than exposure alone (Öst, Fellenius & Sterner, 1991a).

In addition, other strategies have been used alone and in conjunction with *in vivo* exposure, including cognitive restructuring, interoceptive exposure (i.e., exposure to feared sensations), applied relaxation. Very little is known about whether these strategies add anything to *in vivo* exposure for the treatment of specific phobias, although there is some evidence that they may have at least a limited impact on fear reduction (Booth & Rachman, 1992; Öst, Sterner & Fellenius, 1989).

A Cognitive-Behavioral Treatment Program for Specific Phobia

In this section, we describe a treatment program for specific phobias. For a more detailed description of this treatment, the reader is referred to our treatment manual, Mastery of your specific phobia (Antony, Craske & Barlow, 1995; Craske, Antony & Barlow, 1997). This manual includes general information on the nature and treatment of specific phobias, as well as detailed chapters on the treatment of the most common specific phobia types (e.g., heights, animals, blood/injections, claustrophobia, etc.).

Initial Assessment and Presentation of the Treatment Rationale

Although the distress and functional impairment associated with specific phobias typically is not as severe as that associated with other anxiety disorders, the desire to avoid the phobic situation is usually as strong or stronger than that for other types of phobic disorders. It is not unusual for individuals initially to refuse to be exposed to the phobic object or situation or even to discuss the object of their fear. Therefore, presenting the rationale for treatment in a clear and convincing manner is essential for the successful treatment of specific phobias. The first part of the initial session is spent defining the parameters of the individual's phobia, providing a framework for understanding the nature and possible causes of the phobia and discussing how treatment will help the patient to overcome his or her fear.

In our program, the first session begins with a brief discussion about the nature of anxiety and fear. Specifically, patients are taught that fear is a normal and adaptive emotion and that most everyone has situations that they find threatening. In addition, possible etiological factors for the patient's phobia are discussed (e.g., direct conditioning, observational learning, misinformation about the feared situation). Because many people with phobias cannot remember how their fear began, patients are reassured that it is not necessary to discover the initial cause of a phobia to overcome the fear. Rather, treatment addresses the current factors that maintain the fear (e.g., avoidance, inaccurate information about the feared object, etc.).

Patients are encouraged to think of their phobia in terms of the associated *feelings*, *thoughts* and *behaviors*. With respect to feelings experienced during exposure, patients are asked to describe the intensity and nature of their emotional reaction (e.g., crying, screaming, terror, etc.). In addition, they are helped to generate a list of physical symptoms (e.g., racing heart, breathlessness, "wobbly legs," dizziness, shaking, sweating, fainting) experienced during typical exposures.

Next, patients examine the specific thoughts, predictions, and expectations that help to maintain their fear. Anxious thoughts are often related to the feared situation (e.g., being bitten by a snake, struck by lightening, falling from a high place, etc.), although many patients report apprehension over the symptoms associated with the fear as well (i.e., anxiety over how they might react in the situation). As an example, Table 1.1 lists some of the anxious thoughts often reported by individuals with specific phobias of driving.

Next, the therapist assists the patient to identify the anxious behaviors associated with the feared object or situation. In most cases, these behaviors have the function of helping an individual manage his or her fear by avoiding the phobic object or situation. Avoidance may be overt or more subtle. Examples of overt avoidance strategies include refusing to enter the situation

Table 1.1. Anxious Thoughts often Reported by Individuals with Driving Phobias

Thoughts about the Feared Situation:	Thoughts about the Anxious Reaction
I will get into an accident.	I will lose control over the car.
I will be injured.	I will get distracted.
Other drivers are not paying attention.	My mind will go blank.
I am not a skilled driver.	Anxiety will impair my driving.
Other drivers are not competent.	I will have a heart attack or stroke.
Other drivers will become angry with me.	I will embarrass myself.
Other drivers will think I am incompetent.	I will die.
I will get lost.	My physical sensations will be too strong
I will get into a traffic jam.	I will faint.
My car will break down.	My fear will be overwhelming.
The road conditions are dangerous.	I won't be able to react quickly.
I will hit a pedestrian or animal.	
My actions will confuse other drivers.	

Adapted from Antony, Craske & Barlow, 1995. Copyright © 1995 by The Psychological Corporation. Reprinted by permission. All rights reserved.

and escaping from the situation when one's fear becomes too overwhelming. Subtle forms of avoidance may include distraction, the use of medication or drugs, and other subtle coping strategies. For example, an individual with a height phobia may avoid looking down from a high place or insist on holding a railing. A person who fears spiders may sit on the side of the room farthest from a spider that he or she notices in the corner. Someone who fears driving might be sure to drive only in certain lanes or at certain times.

In addition, many people with phobias rely on *safety signals* when confronting the phobic object or situation. Safety signals are stimuli that provide a sense of safety or security in a feared situation. For example, an individual who fears elevators might only use an elevator when accompanied by a friend or relative so that help would be available in the event of an emergency. Finally, individuals with specific phobias often engage in behaviors that are excessively protective. One of the most common behaviors of this type is checking. A person with a snake phobia is likely to check the grass for snakes before sitting down at a picnic. People with storm phobias often report spending excessive amounts of time watching weather reports before planning their daily activities.

Although avoidance, distraction, overreliance on safety signals, and other related behaviors are effective methods of managing anxiety in the short term, patients are taught that these behaviors are counterproductive in the long term. First, these behaviors are negatively reinforced by the relief that is experienced when an individual escapes or avoids, thereby making it more difficult to enter the situation in the future. Second, avoidance prevents the individual from learning that the situation is not dangerous and that his or her anxious predictions are unlikely to come true.

Next, systematic exposure to the phobic situation is introduced as the principal method by which the specific phobia will be treated. At this point, patients are sometimes quick to express doubt that they will be able to confront the situation or that exposure can help them. After all, an individual who fears spiders might have encountered spiders frequently during their daily life without any relief. In fact, exposure might have led to increased fear in the past. Such concerns are addressed in a discussion of how therapeutic exposure is different than the type of exposure that tends to occur naturally in the patient's life.

Specifically, therapeutic exposure is prolonged and includes repeated practices spaced close together. In contrast, the exposure that occurs in everyday life is typically brief (i.e., patients tend to escape quickly) and as infrequent as possible. Second, therapeutic exposure is predictable and under the patient's control. Patients are told what to expect, are never surprised, and must give their permission before any steps are taken to increase the intensity of exposure. In contrast, exposure in everyday life is often perceived as unpredictable and out of the patient's control. Finally, patients are provided with a variety of adaptive coping strategies to replace the strategies previously used. These strategies are discussed in a later section.

Preparing for Exposure Practices

To maximize the effectiveness of exposure practices, it is important to determine the specific parameters that affect an individual patient's fear. For example, some people with height phobias are most frightened standing on the edge of an unprotected drop. Others report the greatest fear when driving in high places (e.g., bridges, elevated roads). Some people are more anxious when alone; some feel worse when accompanied. Identifying the variables that influence an individual's fear will help in the development of relevant practices and the identification and prevention of subtle avoidance behaviors (e.g., looking away) during the practices. Table 1.2 lists variables that might influence fear levels in people with specific phobias. Examples are provided for a spider phobia and a flying phobia.

Because patients tend to avoid the situations that they fear, it may be difficult to identify all of the variables that influence an individual's fear. Therefore, a behavioral approach test (BAT) may be helpful. During the BAT, the patient is exposed to the feared object or situation and asked to report his

Table 1.2. Variables that Might Influence Fear for Individuals with Specific Phobias

Example: flying phobia	Example: spider phobia
Size of airplane	Shape of spider
Sounds on the airplane	Color of spider
Number of passengers; crowdedness	Size of Spider
Delayed flight; reason for delay	Hairiness of spider
Bad weather (e.g., rain, fog)	Potential for being bitten
Time of day (light vs. dark)	Presence of another person
Seating (aisle, window, etc.)	Location (e.g., backyard vs. in bed)
Hearing safety information before take off	Whether spider is restrained (e.g., in jar)
Turbulence	Form of exposure (e.g., imagining spiders,
Snow or ice on the ground	talking about spiders, looking at cartoons,
Surface down below (e.g., water vs. land)	toys, photos, watching videotaped spiders
Taking off	watching live spiders)
Landing	Distance from spider
Duration of flight	Speed of movement
Altitude of airplane (e.g., above clouds)	Unpredictability of movement
Presence of friend or relative	Type of movement (e.g., jumping)
Amount of stress in patient's life	
Size of airport	

Adapted from Antony, Craske & Barlow, 1995. Copyright © 1995 by The Psychological Corporation. Reprinted by permission. All rights reserved.

Table 1.3. Exposure Hierarchy for a Spider Phobia

Look at a picture of a distant spider
Look at a close-up picture of a spider
Watch a film of a moving spider
Stand 10 feet from a live spider in a tank
Stand 5 feet from a live spider in a tank
Stand 1 foot from a live spider in a tank
Touch the tank containing a live spider
Use a piece of paper and glass bottle to capture a spider
Have a spider crawl on one's hand
Have a spider crawl on ones' arm

or her experiences. BATs can be a useful tool to help patients identify anxious thoughts, behaviors and sensations. By manipulating specific parameters, the therapist can examine the effect of these variables on the patient's fear. For example, when treating an injection phobia, the therapist can assess whether the point of needle insertion affects a patient's fear by holding a syringe to various locations (e.g., upper arm, inner elbow, etc.). If the patient is too anxious to undergo a BAT before treatment, many of these questions can be answered as treatment progresses.

Before beginning exposure, the therapist should have an idea of the types of situations that are avoided and the relative difficulty of these situations. Once such situations are identified, an exposure hierarchy should be developed. The hierarchy should include ten to fifteen feared situations listed in order of difficulty. Table 1.3 is an example of an exposure hierarchy developed for an individual with a spider phobia.

Finally, before beginning exposure practices, the therapist and client should generate a list of ways to create the feared situation. In many cases, the patient will not be able to provide stimuli for exposure practices because of his or her anxiety over encountering these stimuli. Therefore, it will often be up to the therapist or the patient's family and friends to locate the stimuli for exposure sessions. Antony, Craske & Barlow (1995) list ways to obtain phobic stimuli for most common specific phobias.

Conducting Exposure Practices

The ideal number and duration of exposure sessions depends on the individual patient's needs as well as the stamina of the patient and therapist. For some phobia types (e.g., animals, injections), a single session of treatment may be enough to achieve long lasting results. For other phobia types (e.g., driving), the specific phobia triggers (e.g., poor weather, being cut off by another driver, etc.), may be more difficult to produce during practices and more sessions may be necessary. In any case, sessions should last 1–3 h, until the patient has experienced a decrease in fear or is able to complete more difficult tasks (e.g., approach a feared animal more closely) than when the session began. Most specific phobias can be treated in one to five sessions, especially if the patient practices on his or her own between sessions.

Practices should begin with easier items on the hierarchy and should progress through the items until the highest item is practiced successfully. The rate at which more difficult items are attempted depends on how much anxiety the patient is willing to tolerate. Moving more quickly through the hierarchy items will lead to a quicker reduction in fear, although the intensity of fear experienced during the practices will be greater. Moving more slowly will make the practices less aversive, although overcoming the phobia will take longer. Typically, we recommend that patients progress through the hierarchy items as quickly as they are willing.

Eventually, patients should reach a point at which they can do more than most people who have no fear might be willing to do in the phobic situation. For example, an individual with a snake phobia should reach a point at which she can hold a live snake comfortably. A person with claustrophobia should reach a point at which he can stand in a small, dark closet for an extended period. By taking exposure practices to these extremes, the types of situations encountered in the patient's everyday life will be that much easier. Of course, patients should never be asked to do anything that is unsafe (e.g., picking up a live snake in the wild).

Several methods can be used to help patients take increasingly difficult steps during exposure practices. First, the therapist should continually model non-fearful behavior for the patient. For example, during the initial stages of exposure to a high ledge, the therapist may stand with the patient near the ledge. If working with a patient who fears birds, the therapist should be able to demonstrate how to hold and handle birds. It is not unusual for the therapist to need practice before working with the patient. In addition, the therapist should remain calm despite the patient's discomfort. Patients should be encouraged to experience their feelings rather than to fight them, distract, or escape. Patients should be reassured that their responses (e.g., crying screaming) are a normal part of overcoming a phobia. The therapist should prepare the patient to feel intense discomfort and explain that the discomfort will eventually subside. Patients should be encouraged to measure their success by their achievements rather than by the way they feel in the situation. A successful session is one in which the patient confronts a feared situation despite the fear. With each step that is endured without catastrophic consequences, the patient's trust will increase.

If a patient refuses a particular task, it is the therapist's job to find a creative way to help the patient continue to move forward. One way of doing this is by making the steps smaller. For example, a patient with a driving phobia may reach a point at which he or she can drive accompanied but still refuse to try driving alone. One solution is to have the patient drive with the therapist following immediately behind. Driving while followed might be the intermediate step needed to help the patient to be able to drive alone. Gradually, the distance between therapist and patient can be increased until the patient is essentially driving alone.

Between-Session Practices

Patients should be encouraged to conduct exposure practices between sessions. Typically, exposure to the feared situation is more frightening when the therapist is absent and patients may be unwilling to conduct practices that are as difficult as those that were conducted in session. To the extent that between-session practices can be structured (e.g., planning a specific number of practices and specifying the times for these practices), patients will be more likely to complete homework assignments. The therapist should anticipate possible reasons why homework might not be completed and attempt to generate solutions to increase the likelihood that the patient will complete his or her practices. One of the most common reasons for not completing homework is excessive anxiety about the homework task. Therefore, patients may be given alternative suggestions for practices in the event that they find the primary task too difficult. For example, a patient might be instructed to practice standing in a small closet with the door closed when nobody is at home to overcome a fear of enclosed places. However, if this practice proves to be too difficult, the patient may decrease the intensity of the exposure by having the closet door opened slightly or by conducting the practice when a family member is home. The more difficult practice may be saved for another day. Conducting an easier practice is better than conducting no practice.

Involving the patient's family or friends in exposure practices may be helpful. Family members can provide encouragement and model non-fearful behavior in the phobic situation. However, the therapist should be sure that the family member or friend fully understands the rationale for exposure and is able and willing to be supportive and coach the patient during practices. In addition, he or she should observe some of the therapist-assisted exposure sessions to be familiar with the patient's reaction and how to respond to the patient's fear. Eventually, the patient should be able to conduct practices without help from significant others.

Other Treatment Strategies

Cognitive strategies. In addition to exposure, two main approaches may be used to help correct misinformation about the phobic object or situation. First, patients should be instructed to seek out information about the feared object or situation. For example, if an individual fears snakes, he or she should learn as much as possible about snakes. If a snake's movement is particularly frightening, the patient should read about how snakes move and spend time watching snakes move.

Second, patients should be taught to identify unrealistic anxious thoughts and consider more realistic, alternative predictions regarding the phobic situation. The first type of anxious thought that is frequently associated with specific phobias is *probability overestimation*. Probability overestimation involves overestimating the likelihood that some predicted event will occur, for example, patients who fear flying often overestimate the chances of crashing on an airplane. To change this pattern of thinking, patients should be taught to evaluate the evidence for and against their anxious beliefs. For example, in addition to noting occasional news stories about plane crashes, patients who fear flying should be taught to examine evidence contrary to their anxious predictions (e.g., each day many thousands of airplanes take off and land safely) and to evaluate the realistic probability of having their predictions come true.

The second main type of anxious thought that tends to occur in individuals with specific phobias is *catastrophic thinking*, which involves overestimating the negative impact of an event if it were to occur. For example, patients with spider phobias often believe that it would be awful and unmanageable to have a spider touch them. Catastrophic predictions can be challenged by changing the focus of one's thoughts from how terrible an encounter might be with the phobic object to how one might cope with such an encounter. One way of doing this is to ask oneself questions such as, "Realistically, what is the worst thing that might happen?", "Why would it be so terrible if I encountered the object or situation?" or "How could I cope with the situation?"

Exposure tends to work very well on its own. However, for some patients, cognitive restructuring may be a valuable adjunct to exposure. Furthermore, these strategies can be useful methods of helping a patient to engage in a difficult exposure practice that he or she might avoid otherwise.

Interoceptive exposure. Recall that some patients report anxiety over the physical sensations associated with fear, in addition to their anxiety over the phobic object or situation. For example, although individuals who fear heights may be anxious about accidentally falling or being pushed from a high place, they often report anxiety over losing control because of the intense physical symptoms that they feel as well. In addition to exposure to the feared situation, exposure to the feared sensations may be helpful for some individuals. This is particularly true for phobias that are associated with heightened interoceptive anxiety (e.g., claustrophobia). For such patients, interoceptive exposure

Table 1.4. Exercises for Inducing Feared Sensations During Interoceptive Exposure Practices

1. Shake head from side to side for 30 s
2. Hold breath for as long as possible
3. Breath through a straw for 2 min
4. Overbreath for 60 s
5. Spin in a swivel chair for 90 s
6. Tense every muscle in your body for 1 min

exercises may be added to situational exposure practices in a systematic way. Antony et al. (1995) describe how to conduct such exercises. As with situational exposure, interoceptive exposure exercises should be conducted repeatedly until they no longer create anxiety. Examples of exercises used to induce feared sensations are listed in Table 1.4.

Applied muscle tension. As mentioned earlier, applied muscle tension has been used very effectively for the treatment of blood phobia. Applied tension involves teaching patients to tense the muscles of their body in order to raise their blood pressure and thereby prevent fainting during exposure to situations involving blood. This technique was originally developed by Kozak & Montgomery (1981) and expanded upon by Öst & Sterner (1987). The specific steps involved in using applied tension are listed in Table 1.5.

Table 1.5. How to Conduct Applied Muscle Tension for Blood and Injection Phobias Involving Fainting

1. Sit in a comfortable chair and tense the muscles of your arms, torso, and legs. Hold the tension for 10 or 15 seconds. You should hold the tension long enough to feel a warm feeling in your head. Release the tension and let your body return to normal for 20 or 30 seconds. Repeat the procedure 5 times. If you want to demonstrate to yourself that tensing increases your blood pressure, try measuring your blood pressure with a home blood pressure kit before and after tensing.
2. Repeat step 1 five times per day (a total of 25 tension cycles per day) for about a week. Practice will help you to perfect the technique. If you develop headaches, decrease the strength of your tension or the frequency of your practices.
3. After practicing the tension exercises for a week, start to use the applied tension techniques during your exposure practices as described in the remainder of this chapter. Note, if you are afraid of needles, it will be important for you to keep your "needle arm" relaxed during the insertion of the needle. You can incorporate this into your practices by tensing all of your muscles except for those in one arm.
4. After you can practice exposure with minimal anxiety, discontinue the tension exercises. After the fear has decreased, many individuals are able to be in situations involving blood and needles without fainting. If you still feel faint, begin using the applied tension exercises during exposures again.

Maintaining treatment gains. Success following exposure based treatments for specific phobia tends to be long lasting (Öst, 1989). Nevertheless, patients should be prepared to cope with possible setbacks. In our program, patients are warned about several factors that may lead to increased fear in the future. The first of these factors is heightened stress. Patients are warned that general life stress (e.g., losing one's job, marital problems) may increase the difficulty of confronting a situation that was previously feared. Second, a traumatic experience in the feared situation (e.g., a car accident by an individual who has overcome a phobia of driving) may make future exposures more difficult. Finally, long periods without exposure to the feared situation may lead to some return of fear for a small percentage of patients. If an individual notices that his or her fear is returning, we recommend that they begin systematic exposure to the situation again. In addition, to prevent a return of fear, patients should be encouraged to engage in occasional exposure practices when the opportunities arise. For example, patients who fear spiders should spend some time looking at and perhaps catching spiders that they find in their home before releasing them outside. Occasional exposure to the feared situation will make setbacks less likely.

Conclusions and Future Directions

Specific phobias are among the most common and the most treatable of all anxiety disorders. Up to 90% of individuals with phobias of animals or injections are much improved or cured following one session of exposure therapy. Nevertheless, individuals with specific phobias are among the least likely to seek treatment for their anxiety disorder. Possible reasons for their tendency to avoid treatment may include the relatively small degree of distress and functional impairment experienced by people with specific phobias and perhaps a lack of awareness (on the part of patients and mental health professionals) that effective treatments exist.

An area of research that has just begun is the exploration of differences among specific phobia types. To date, most treatment studies have focused on a relatively small number of specific phobias. Although a single session of treatment is often enough for animal phobias, little is known about the effectiveness of single session treatments for other common phobias (e.g., heights, driving, storms, claustrophobia). Future studies will need to take into account differences among phobias with respect to rates of habituation, the importance of cognitive factors (e.g., misinformation about the feared situation), focus of apprehension (e.g., on situational vs. interoceptive cues), and the possible roles of negative responses other than fear (e.g., disgust, startle, fainting, etc.).

References

Agras, S., Sylvester, D., & Oliveau, D. (1969). The epidemiology of common fears and Phobias. *Comprehensive Psychiatry, 10,* 151–156.

APA (1994). *Diagnostic and statistical manual of mental disorders,* 4th edition (DSM-IV). Washington, DC: American Psychiatric Association.

Antony, M. M., Brown, T. A., & Barlow, D. H. (1997a). Heterogeneity among specific phobia types in DSM-IV. *Behaviour Research and Therapy, 35,* 1089–1100.

Antony, M. M., Brown, T. A., & Barlow, D. H. (1997b). Response to hyperventilation and 5.5% CO_2 inhalation of subjects with types of specific phobia, panic disorder, or no mental disorder. *Americal Journal of Psychiatry, 154,* 1089–1095.

Antony, M. M., Craske, M. G., & Barlow, D. H. (1995). *Mastery of your specific phobia (client manual).* San Antonio, TX: The Psychological Corporation.

Baker, B. L., Cohen, D. C., & Saunders, J. T. (1973). Self-directed desensitization for acrophobia. *Behaviour Research and Therapy, 11,* 79–89.

Ball, S. G., & Otto, M.W. (1993). *Cognitive-behavioral treatment of choking phobia: Three case studies.* Paper presented at the annual convention of the Association for Advancement of Behavior Therapy, Atlanta, GA.

Barlow, D. H. (1988). *Anxiety and its disorders: The nature and treatment of anxiety and panic.* New York: Guilford Press.

Booth, R., & Rachman, S. (1992). The reduction of claustrophobia-I. *Behaviour Research and Therapy, 30,* 207–221.

Bourdon, K. H., Boyd, J. H., Rae, D. S., Burns, B. J., Thompson, J. W., & Locke, B. Z. (1988). Gender differences in phobias: Results of the ECA community study. *Journal of Anxiety Disorders, 2,* 227–241.

Bourque, P., & Ladouceur, R. (1980). An investigation of various performance-based treatments with acrophobics. *Behaviour Research and Therapy, 18,* 161–170.

Carter, M. M., Hollon, S. D., Carson, R., & Shelton, R. C. (1995). Effects of a safe person on induced distress following a biological challenge in panic disorder with agoraphobia. *Journal of Abnormal Psychology, 104,* 156–163.

Craske, M. G. (1989). *The boundary between simple phobia and specific phobia* (Report to the DSM-IV Anxiety Disorders Work-group). Albany, NY: Phobia and Anxiety Disorders Clinic.

Craske, M. G., & Sipsas, A. (1992). Animal phobias versus claustrophobias: Exteroceptive versus interoceptive cues. *Behaviour Research and Therapy, 30,* 569–581.

Craske, M. G., Antony, M. M., & Barlow, T. A. (1997). *Mastery of your specific phobia, Therpaist guide.* San Antonio, TX: Psychological Corporation.

Curtis, G. C., Himle, J. A., Lewis, J. A., & Lee, Y. (1989). *Specific situational phobias: Variant of agoraphobia?* (Report to the DSM-IV Anxiety Disorders Work-group). Ann Arbor, MI: University of Michigan.

Curtis, G. C., Hill, E. M., & Lewis, J. A. (1990). *Heterogeneity of DSM-III-R simple phobia and the simple phobia/agoraphobia boundary: Evidence from the ECA study.* (Report to the DSM-IV Anxiety Disorders Work-group). Ann Arbor, MI: University of Michigan.

Denholtz, M. S., & Mann, E. T. (1975). An automated audiovisual treatment of phobias administered by non-professionals. *Journal of Behavior Therapy and Experimental Psychiatry, 6,* 111–115.

de Silva, P., & Rachman, S. (1984). Does escape behavior strengthen agoraphobic avoidance? A preliminary study. *Behaviour Research and Therapy, 22,* 87–91.

Eaton, W. W., Dryman, A., & Weissman, M. M. (1991). Panic and phobia. In L. N. Robins &

D. A. Regier (Eds.), *Psychiatric disorders in America: The Epidemiological Catchment Area Study.* New York: The Free Press.

Ehlers, A., Hofmann, S. G., Herda, C. A., & Roth, W. T. (1994). Clinical characteristics of driving phobia. *Journal of Anxiety Disorders, 8,* 323–337.

Foa, E. B., & Kozak, M. S. (1986). Emotional processing of fear: Exposure to corrective information. *Psychological Bulletin, 99,* 20–35.

Foa, E. B., Jameson, J. S., Turner, R. M., & Payne, L. L. (1980). Massed versus spaced exposure sessions in the treatment of agoraphobia. *Behaviour Research and Therapy, 18,* 333–338.

Foa, E. B., Blau, J. S., Prout, M., & Latimer, P. (1977). Is horror a necessary component of flooding (implosion)? *Behaviour Research and Therapy, 15,* 397–402.

Gauthier, J., & Marshall, W. L. (1977). The determination of optimal exposure to phobic stimuli in flooding therapy. *Behaviour Research and Therapy, 15,* 403–410.

Gray, J. A. (1985). Issues in the neuropsychology of anxiety. In A. H. Tuma & J. D. Maser (Eds.), *Anxiety and the anxiety disorders.* Hillsdale, NJ: Erlbaum.

Himle, J. A., McPhee, K., Cameron, O. J., & Curtis, G. C. (1989). Simple phobia: Evidence for heterogeneity. *Psychiatry Research, 28,* 25–30.

Holden, A. E., & Barlow, D. H. (1986). Heart rate and heart rate variability recorded *in vivo* in agoraphobics and nonphobics. *Behavior Therapy, 17,* 26–42.

Howard, W. A., Murphy, S. M., & Clarke, J. C. (1983). The nature and treatment of fear of flying: A controlled investigation. *Behavior Therapy, 14,* 557–567.

Jerremalm, A., Jansson, L., & Öst, L.-G. (1986). Individual response patterns and the effects of different behavioral methods in the treatment of dental phobia. *Behaviour Research and Therapy, 24,* 587–596.

Kessler, R. C., McMonagle, K. A., Zhao, S., Nelson, C. B., Hughes, M., Eshleman, S., Wittchen, H.-U., & Kendler, K. S. (1994). Lifetime and 12-month prevalence of DSM-III-R psychiatric disorders in the United States: Results from the National Comorbidity Study. *Archives of General Psychiatry, 51,* 8–19.

Kozak, M. J., & Montgomery, G. K. (1981). Multimodal behavioral treatment of recurrent injury-scene elicited fainting (vasodepressor syncope). *Behavioural Psychotherapy, 9,* 316–321.

Lader, M. H., & Wing, L. (1966). *Physiological measures, sedative drugs, and morbid anxiety.* London: Oxford University Press.

Lang, P. J. (1985). The cognitive psychophysiology of emotion: fear and anxiety. In A. H. Tuma & J. D. Maser (Eds.), *Anxiety and the anxiety disorders.* Hillsdale, NJ: Erlbaum.

Liddell, A., Ning, L., Blackwood, J., & Ackerman, J. D. (1991). Long term follow-up of dental phobics who completed a brief exposure based behavioral treatment program. Paper presented at the annual convention of the Association for Advancement of Behavior Therapy, New York.

Lopatka, C. L. (1989). *The role of unexpected events in avoidance.* Unpublished master's thesis, University at Albany, State University of New York.

Marks, I. M. (1987). *Fears, phobias, and rituals.* New York: Oxford University.

Marks, I. M., & Gelder, M. G. (1966). Different ages of onset in varieties of phobia. *American Journal of Psychiatry, 123,* 218–221.

Marshall, W. L. (1988). Behavioral indices of habituation and sensitization during exposure to phobic stimuli. *Behaviour Research and Therapy, 26,* 67–77.

McNally, R. J. (1986). Behavioral treatment of choking phobia. *Journal of Behavior Therapy and Experimental Psychiatry, 17,* 185–188.

Mowrer, O. (1960). *Learning theory and behaviour.* New York: Wiley.

Muris, P., de Jong, P. J., Merckelbach, H., & van Zuuren, F. (1993). Is exposure therapy outcome affected by a monitoring coping style? *Advances in Behaviour Research and Therapy, 15,* 291–300.

O'Brien, T. P., & Kelley, J. E. (1980). A comparison of self-directed and therapist-directed practice for fear reduction. *Behaviour Research and Therapy, 18,* 573–579.

Öst, L.-G. (1987). Age of onset of different phobias. *Journal of Abnormal Psychology, 96,* 223–229.

Öst, L.-G. (1989). One-session treatment for specific phobias. *Behaviour Research and Therapy, 27,* 1–7.

Öst, L.-G. (1992). Blood and injection phobia: Background and cognitive, physiological, and behavioral variables. *Journal of Abnormal Psychology, 101,* 68–74.

Öst, L.-G., & Sterner, U. (1987). Applied tension: A specific behavioral method for treatment of blood phobia. *Behaviour Research and Therapy, 25,* 25–29.

Öst, L.-G., Johansson, J., & Jerremalm, A. (1982). Individual response patterns and the effects of different behavioral methods in the treatment of claustrophobia. *Behaviour Research and Therapy, 20,* 445–460.

Öst, L.-G., Lindahl, I.-L., Sterner, U., & Jerremalm, A. (1984). Exposure *in vivo* vs. applied relaxation in the treatment of blood phobia. *Behaviour Research and Therapy, 22,* 205–216.

Öst, L.-G., Sterner, U., & Fellenius, J. (1989). Applied tension, applied relaxation, and the combination in the treatment of blood phobia. *Behaviour Research and Therapy, 27,* 109–121.

Öst, L.-G., Fellenius, J., & Sterner, U. (1991a). Applied tension, exposure *in vivo,* and tension-only in the treatment of blood phobia. *Behaviour Research and Therapy, 29,* 561–574.

Öst, L.-G., Salkovskis, P.M., & Hellström, K. (1991b). One-session therapist directed exposure vs. self-exposure in the treatment of spider phobia. *Behavior Therapy, 22,* 407–422.

Rachman, S. J. (1980). Emotional processing. *Behaviour Research and Therapy, 18,* 51–60.

Rachman, S. J., Craske, M. G., Tallman, K., & Solyom, C. (1986). Does escape behavior strengthen agoraphobic avoidance? A replication. *Behavior Therapy, 17,* 366–384.

Rescorla, R. A. (1988). Pavlovian conditioning: It's not what you think it is. *American Psychologist, 43,* 151–160.

Rodríguez, B. I., & Craske, M. G. (1993a). The effects of distraction during exposure to phobic stimuli. *Behaviour Research and Therapy, 31,* 549–558.

Rodríguez, B. I., & Craske, M. G. (1993b). *Distraction during high and low intensity in vivo exposure.* Paper presented at the annual convention of the Association for Advancement of Behavior Therapy, Atlanta, GA.

Sanderson, W. C., Rapee, R. M., & Barlow, D. H. (1989). The influence of perceived control on panic attacks induced via inhalation of 5.5% CO_2-enriched air. *Archives of General Psychiatry, 46,* 157–162.

Solyom, L., Shugar, R., Bryntwick, S., & Solyom, C. (1973). Treatment of fear of flying. *American Journal of Psychiatry, 130,* 423–427.

Further Reading

Antony, M. M., & Barlow, D. H. (1997). Social and specific phobias. In A. Tasman, J. Kay & J. A. Lieberman (Eds.), *Psychiatry.* Philadelphia, PA: W. B. Saunders Company.

Antony, M. M., Craske, M. G., & Barlow, D. H. (1995). *Mastery of your specific phobia.* Albany, NY: Graywind Publications.

Craske, M. G., Antony, M. M., & Barlow, D. H. (1997). *Therapist guide for mastery of your specific phobia.* San Antonio, TX: Psychological Corporation. In Canada, 1-800-387-7278.

Davey, G. C. L. (1997). *Phobias: A handbook of theory research and treatment.* New York: Wiley.

Hagopian, L. P., & Ollendick, T. H. (1993). Simple phobia in children. In R. T. Ammerman & M. Hersen (Eds.), *Handbood of behavior therapy with children and adults.* Boston, MA: Allyn and Bacon.

Öst, L.-G. (1996). Long-term effects of behaviour therapy for specific phobia. In M. R. Mavissakilian & R. F. Prien (Eds.), *Long-term treatments of anxiety disorders.* Washington, DC: American Psychiatric Press.

Rachman, S. (1990). The determinants and treatment of simple phobias. *Advances in Behaviour Research and Therapy, 12,* 1–30.

Stanley, M. A., & Beidel, D. C. (1993). Simple phobia in adults. In R. T. Ammerman & M. Hersen (Eds.), *Handbood of behavior therapy with children and adults.* Boston, MA: Allyn and Bacon.

Taylor, C. B., & Arnow, B. (1988). *The nature and treatment of anxiety disorders.* New York: The Free Press.

Thyer, B. A., Baum, M., & Reid, L. D. (1988). Exposure techniques in the reduction of fear: A comparative review of the procedure in animals and humans. *Advances in Behaviour Research and Therapy, 10,* 105–127.

2

Social Phobia

VICENTE E. CABALLO[a], VERANIA ANDRÉS[b] and FRANCISCO BAS[b]

[a]Universidad de Granada, Spain; [b]Centro de Psicología Bertrand Russell, Madrid, Spain

Introduction

Only a few years ago it was said that social phobia was the most neglected of anxiety disorders (Liebowitz, Gorman, Fyer & Klein, 1985) and for several years it has been the least understood and researched of such disorders (Herbert, Bellack & Hope, 1991; Judd, 1994; Turner, Beidel, Dancu & Stanley, 1989). Social phobia was not officially recognised as a diagnostic entity until the publication of the DSM-III in 1980 (APA, 1980), although it had previously been described clinically (e.g., Marks, 1969; Shaw, 1976). However, this outlook has changed considerably in recent years, resulting in a huge increase in interest and research in social phobia and its treatment (see, for example, Salaberría, Borda, Báez & Echeburúa, 1996). Even the World Psychiatric Association has created a Task Force for the study of social phobia which recently presented some of its findings (Montgomery, 1996).

However, although it is true that systematic investigation into social phobia, as diagnosed by the classification system of the American Psychiatric Association (APA, 1980, 1987, 1994) and by the World Health Organization (WHO, 1992), started to have relevance from the end of the 1980s, we should not overlook the fact that research into social anxiety and its treatment had previously been important, especially in the United States, during the 1970s and 1980s. A large part of the research into areas which were then known as "assertiveness" and "social skills" is valid in the study of social phobia, its assessment and treatment (see Caballo, 1993). Moreover, it is likely that a large part of subjects treated under "assertion training" and/or "social skills training" during these years would have been diagnosed as suffering from social phobia nowadays. The *Zeitgeist* in these days is to begin with a diagnosis of every psychological disorder and continue with a search for specific treatments for each one of them, first and foremost of a cognitive/behavioural and/or pharmacological kind. Although the 1970s are hardly mentioned when it comes to beginning the task of studying social phobia, the research carried out during these years is nowadays importantly reflected in the assessment and the psychosocial treatment of this disorder.

A number of reasons have been given to explain why it took so long to recognise social phobia as an important health problem. Various reasons were proposed such as inadequate information about the lack of treatment for social phobia, the reluctance to interact with strangers (and as a result with a therapist) inherent in this disorder, its frequent comorbidity with other disorders (such that social phobia was considered a secondary condition), the scant attention paid to this disorder by the medical class until recently, or the problem of finding ways in which to confront individuals with social phobia who often adopt their lifestyle around their disorder (Montgomery, 1995).

Another noted reason has been the universal nature of many of the experiences of social anxiety (Hazen & Stein, 1995a; Uhde, 1995). Who has not felt anxious about having to speak in public, in striking up a conversation with a member of the opposite sex we do not know, or in engaging in conversation with a superior to ask them something? A common aspect of these situations which explains, at least in part, the anxiety we experience is fear of negative evaluation by others. This fear is a basic characteristic of individuals with social phobia when they find themselves in feared situations. It has even been said that the term "social phobia" is perhaps not appropriate to describe the clinical syndrome it defines (Stein, 1995). This author also points out that the latter term implies that the individual fears social situations, when what they really fear is being *negatively* evaluated by others. Taking into account the universality of this fear, it has also been argued that human beings have possibly been prepared by evolution to fear scrutiny and evaluation by others (Rosenbaum, Biederman, Pollock & Hirshfeld, 1994).

Although feeling anxiety in certain social situations is something relatively common in people, such anxiety does not tend to reach such a high intensity that it interferes with the person's ability to function adequately in these situations. So, the question is not whether one experiences social anxiety, but how much anxiety is experienced, how long the episode lasts, how frequently the anxiety recurs, how much dysfunctional avoidance behaviour is caused by the anxiety, and how the anxiety is evaluated by the individual experiencing it (Falcone, 1995; Walen, 1985).

Definition and Epidemiological and Clinical Characteristics

Social phobia is defined in the DSM-IV (APA, 1994) as "A marked and persistent fear of one or more social or performance situations in which the person is exposed to unfamiliar people or to possible scrutiny by others. The individual fears that he or she will act in a way (or show anxiety symptoms) that will be humiliating or embarrassing" (APA, 1994, p. 416). The individual has to be *doing* something whilst they *know* that others are watching and, to a certain extent, *evaluating* their behaviour. The distinctive characteristic of individuals with social phobia is fear of scrutiny by others (Heimberg, Dodge & Becker, 1987; Taylor & Arnow, 1988). Generally, individuals with social phobia fear that this scrutiny could be embarrassing, humiliating, could make them look stupid or be judged in a negative way. This is clearly "social" phobia because these individuals do not experience difficulty when they carry out the same tasks in private. "Only when others are watching does the behaviour deteriorate" (Barlow, 1988, p. 535).

The DSM-IV (APA, 1994) also indicates, within the diagnostic criteria for social phobia, that exposure to the feared situation almost invariably provokes anxiety in individuals with social phobia and that they recognise that their fear is excessive or unreasonable. Also, social situations or performance situations are avoided or endured with intense anxiety, the symptoms of the disorder interfere significantly with the person's normal functioning in one or more areas and/or there is a marked distress about having the phobia.

The most frequently feared social situations in individuals with social phobia include (Hazen & Stein, 1995a; Hope, 1993; Schneier, Spitzer, Gibbon, Fyer & Liebowitz, 1991; Turner et al., 1992):

- Initiating and/or maintaining a conversation.
- Meeting (having a date) with someone
- Going to a party.
- Behaving assertively (e.g. expressing disagreement or rejecting a request).
- Telephoning someone (especially people they do not know well).
- Talking with authority figures.
- Returning goods to a store.
- Making eye contact with unfamiliar people.
- Giving and receiving compliments.
- Attending meetings, social gatherings.
- Speaking in public (e.g., large or small groups).
- Performing in public.
- Being the centre of attention (e.g. going into a room when everyone else is already seated).
- Eating/drinking in public.
- Writing/working when others are observing.
- Using public bathrooms.

Individuals with social phobia will try to avoid these situations, but on occasion will have to put up with them with marked anxiety. The most frequent somatic symptoms in response to fear in these individuals are (Amies, Gelder & Shaw, 1983): palpitations (79%), trembling (75%), sweating (74%), muscle tension (64%), sinking feeling in stomach (63%), dry mouth (61%), feeling hot/cold (57%), blushing (51%) and pressure in head/headaches (46%).

The most usual behavioural symptom of social phobia is avoidance of the feared situations. By definition, individuals with social phobia fear or avoid situations in which they might be observed by others (Caballo, 1995; Echeburúa, 1993). The cognitive factors that may be involved in the maintenance or worsening social phobia are fairly numerous. Amongst them are over-evaluation of the negative aspects of behaviour, excessive self-consciousness, fear of negative evaluation, excessively high standards of evaluation of behaviour, perceived lack of control over one's own behaviour, etc. (Caballo, 1995).

Although the DSM-IV (APA, 1994) only recognises (specific) social phobia and generalized social phobia, other sub-types of social phobia have been put forward. Thus, for example Heimberg (1995) proposes the existence of a *discrete* (or circumscribed) *social phobia* is experienced when the individual fears only one or two situations, a *non-generalised social phobia*, when a selection of situations are feared and *generalised social phobia*, which is diagnosed when the subject fears most social situations. It has been argued that *avoidant personality disorder* would be a more severe psychopathological problem than social phobia (e.g., Marks, 1985; Turner, Beidel, Dancu & Keys, 1986) and even in many cases we will see a comorbidity of generalised social phobia and avoidant personality disorder (the percentages found range from 25 to 89%), which would be the most serious condition. We doubt, based on the diagnostic criteria of the DSM-IV, that it is possible to distinguish between generalized social phobia and avoidant personality disorder (see Caballo, 1995). Until the diagnostic criteria is more refined for both disorders we do not consider it appropriate or scientifically correct to consider them two separate disorders.

The Social Phobia Work Group of the DSM-IV considered the possibility of adopting a classification system of three subtypes of social phobia, *performance type*, *limited interactional type* and *generalised type*, although it was finally decided to include the latter only (Hazen & Stein, 1995b). Some authors have proposed the inclusion of *fear of public speaking* as a specific sub-type of social phobia (Stein, Walker & Forde, 1994), mainly due to the large prevalence of this kind of social phobia over others.

Although it is difficult to establish the average age of the onset of social phobia due to our excessive dependence on retrospective reports, it does seem clear that it is a disorder that begins at an early age. Apparently, a critical period for the onset of the disorder is adolescence (APA, 1994; Kendler, Neale, Kessler, Heath & Eaves, 1992; Schwalberg, Barlow, Alger & Howard, 1992; Turner, Beidel and Townsley, 1992), especially the first teen years (Schneier, Johnson, Hornig, Liebowitz & Weissman, 1992); however, we should also pay important attention to childhood, since the latter authors found that 33% of subjects had showed the first signs of the disorder between the ages of 0 and 10 years. Once developed, the disorder tends to be chronic and lasts a lifetime (see Caballo, 1995).

The prevalence of social phobia varies notably according to the various studies, although it is considered one of the most common "mental" disorders, with percentages varying from 3 to 13% (APA, 1994). These percentages can be higher, such as 14.4% (in France) found by Weiller, Bisserbe, Boyer, Lepine & Lecrubier (1996) or lower, such as 2.6% (in the United States), 1% (in Puerto Rico) and 0.5% (in Korea) found by Weissman, Bland, Canino, Greenvald, Lee, Newman, Rubio-Stipec & Wickramaratne (1996), depending on the culture where the study was carried out and upon the authors themselves. Distribution according to sex is basically the same in clinical samples (see Caballo, 1995), whilst in the general population, the percentage of women appears to be higher than men, consisting of 59 to 72% of people with social phobia (Davidson, Hughes, George & Blazer, 1993; Kessler, McGonagle, Zhao, Nelson, Hughes, Eshleman, Wittchen & Kendler, 1994; Myers, Weissman, Tischer, Holzer, Leaf, Orvaschel, Anthony, Boyd, Burke, Kramer & Stoltzman, 1984). A possible explanation of this discrepancy between data from clinical and non-clinical samples could be found in the different strategies used by men and women to cope with their problem, being more probable that men will use alcohol or drugs as a means of dealing with it. The comorbidity of social phobia with other disorders of the *Axis I* is common, especially with anxiety problems such as specific phobia, agoraphobia, obsessive-compulsive disorder or generalised anxiety disorder (Davidson et al., 1993; Sanderson, Rapee & Barlow, 1987). Also, it is sometimes accompanied by alcohol or drug problems which tend to serve as an (inadequate) method of coping with social phobia. The personality disorders which most frequently accompany social phobia (without considering avoidant personality disorder due to the impossibility of distinguishing it from generalised social phobia) are obsessive compulsive disorders, dependent, and histrionic personality disorders (Jansen, Arntz, Merckelbach & Mersch, 1994; Turner et al., 1992).

Although there is not much information about the impairment of normal functioning due to social phobia, it has been indicated that it can have a very important impact on the lifestyle of the subject (Montgomery, 1995). Thus, it has been found that it is more likely that people with social phobia, when compared to a control group (Davidson et al., 1993; Schneier et al., 1992): (a) are single; (b) have a lower socio-economic status; (c) are less educated; (d) are financially dependent; (e) have lower incomes; (f) suffer from other psychological disorders; (g) have suicidal thoughts; (h) have suicidal attempts; (i) change jobs more frequently; (j) do not do well at work; (k) are socially isolated; and (l) have a lack of social support.

Theoretical Foundations of the Treatment of Social Phobia

Social phobia can be effectively treated nowadays through cognitive-behavioural interventions. Although there remain many problems to be solved, we can point out that the cognitive-behavioural approach consists of empirically validated treatments for social phobia. In the following section, we present some of the theoretical bases upon which applications of different treatments for social phobia are supported.

Classical, Operant, and Vicarious Conditioning

Although the precise cause of phobias is unknown, it is usually considered learned fear, acquired by means of direct conditioning, vicarious conditioning (when fear is learned by observing others), or by the transmission of information and/or instructions (Caballo, Aparicio & Catena, 1995).

However, it is not very usual for an individual with social phobia to describe a single traumatic event as the onset of the phobia. The fear gradually increases as a result of repeated fear-producing experiences or as a result of social learning. Sometimes this happens during a period of stress or high stimulation, when fearful responses are easily learned.

A comprehensive interpretation of Mowrer's two-factor theory explains the acquisition and maintenance of phobic reactions. Symptoms of social phobia are a conditioned response acquired via the association between the phobic object (the conditioned stimulus) and an aversive experience. Once the phobia has been acquired, avoidance of the phobic situation avoids or reduces the conditioned anxiety, consequently reinforcing avoidance behaviour. This avoidance maintains the anxiety since it makes it difficult to learn that the feared object or situation are not in fact dangerous, or not as dangerous as the patient believes or anticipates. Thoughts can also maintain fear, such as thoughts about somatic symptoms, about the possible negative consequences of performance, etc.

Öst & Hugdahl (1981) found that 58% of individuals with social phobia acquired their phobias as a result of a direct experience. Turner et al. (1992) report that after interviewing a sample of 71 patients with social phobia, approximately 50% recounted what appeared to be an experience of conditioning. The latter authors also indicate that a large percentage of patients reported a premorbid "shyness" and go on to say that for many individuals there are other important factors, besides the conditioning experience, including biological as well as not biological variables.

Another way of acquiring social fears is vicarious conditioning. According to this paradigm, observing others experiencing anxiety in social situations can lead to the observer fearing these situations. Bruch, Heimberg, Berger &

Collins (1988) found that parents of individuals with social phobia themselves avoided social situations, but Öst & Hugdahl (1981) found that in only 12% of individuals with social phobia was vicarious conditioning responsible for the development of the phobia. It should be pointed out, however, that a relationship between the fears of the parents and the children may also be as a result of other kinds of processes than vicarious conditioning, such as information processes, genetic influences or similar traumatic experiences for example.

Public Self-Consciousness

Some authors (e.g. Buss, 1980) suggest that socially anxious people may be high on the dimension of "public self-consciousness". This is defined as awareness of oneself as a social object (Heimberg et al., 1987). Public self-consciousness suggests that the social-evaluative stimuli may be more salient and that the individual may be more reactive to the outcomes of social events.

Self-Presentation

Social anxiety is defined here as anxiety derived from the prospect or presence of personal evaluation in real or imagined social situations. Schlenker & Leary (1982) point out that such anxiety occurs when a person has the goal of creating a particular impression on others, but *doubts* that his/her own ability will succeed in creating this impression, anticipating a negative reaction instead. According to this approach, people experience social anxiety when two necessary and sufficient conditions are met. First, the person must be motivated (or have the objective) to make a particular impression on others. The second condition necessary for producing anxiety is that the individual does not believe he or she will be successful in conveying the impressions they wish to make and, as such, expect to be regarded in the fashion they desire.

Vulnerability

Beck & Emery (1985) have presented a model of anxiety where the concept of the cognitive *schema* plays a basic role. Schemas are cognitive structures which are used to label, classify, interpret, evaluate and assign meanings to objects and events. They help the individual to orient to the situation, selectively recall relevant details from memory and pay attention only to the most important aspects of the situation. Schemas are the basic structural components of cognitive Organization and they are organised into coherent groupings labelled *modes*. A mode imposes a general bias on the persons that influences the type of attitudes they select as they moves from one situation to another (Heimberg, Dodge & Becker, 1987). In anxiety disorders, it is possible to describe the individual as functioning in the *vulnerable mode*. Vulnerability is defined by Beck and Emery as "a person's perception of himself as subject to internal or external dangers over which his control is lacking or is insufficient to afford him a sense of safety" (p. 67). When the vulnerable mode is active, incoming information is processed in terms of weakness instead of strength and the person finds him/herself more influenced by past events that emphasise their failures than by factors that may predict success. The feeling of vulnerability in the individual is maintained by excluding or distorting contradictory data by means of predominant cognitive schemes: minimisation of personal strengths, magnification of personal weaknesses, selective attention to weaknesses, dismissal of past achievements, and so on.

The individual with social phobia is hypervigilant to social threats, constantly evaluating the severity of a potential threat and their ability to cope with it. Cognitive distortions prevent the individual reaching a reasonable estimate of either threat or coping means. Beck and Emery (1985) point out that the socially anxious individual fears social consequences which, to a large degree, seem plausible and can really happen. The person who anticipates feeling uncomfortable on a first date, in a job interview or who finds it difficult to say something when they try to talk to a person he or she finds attractive, will occasionally be correct. However, the individual with social phobia is unique among victims of anxiety disorders because the fear to the consequences of the phobia may actually bring them about. According to Beck and Emery (1985) automatic inhibition of speech, thinking, and recall are "primal" responses to anxiety, powerful enough to distract the person from the social task, contributing additional evidence for negative self-evaluation and maintaining the primacy of the vulnerability mode (Heimberg et al., 1987).

A Model for the Acquisition of Social Phobia/Anxiety

The acquisition of social phobia can happen in several ways (direct contact with the fear-inducing situation, learning through observation, information), but other factors have an important influence. For example, a biological vulnerability may exist, named *behavioural inhibition* (Kagan, Snidman & Arkus, 1993), or *spontaneous emotional expression* (Buck, 1991), or anything else which establishes a basis for a possible social phobia/anxiety disorder. Apart from this biological beginning, the first learning experiences are crucial in favouring and reinforcing biological predispositions or, on the contrary, reducing or discouraging them. After a certain time, the individual already possesses an initial repertoire of behaviours and cognitions regarding situations and social interactions. This first repertoire can be adequate and adaptive or

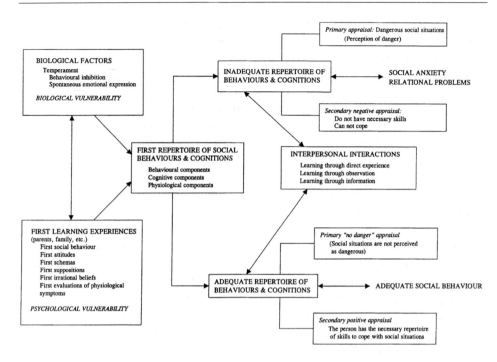

Figure 2.1. A model for the acquisition of social phobia/anxiety and other adequate/inadequate behaviours.

inadequate and maladaptive. Such a repertoire is modified or maintained through the daily interpersonal interactions the individual experiences, learning by direct contact, by observation, or by information. The interaction between the behavioural/cognitive repertoire of the individual and social interactions defines an adequate or inadequate repertoire. In the first case (adequate repertoire), the subject will not see social interactions as dangerous and will think he or she has enough resources to cope with situations they may encounter, which in turn will strengthen and improve their repertoire. In the second instance, the inadequate repertoire makes social situations seem dangerous and impossible to cope with successfully, causing interaction problems which, in turn, maintain or impair further the already inadequate repertoire.

Figure 2.1 shows a graphic representation of the model we have just described for the acquisition of social phobia/anxiety.

Empirical Results on the Effectiveness of Cognitive-Behavioural Treatments for Social Phobia

From the beginning of the 1980s, more and more attention has been paid to the effectiveness of cognitive- behavioural treatments for various psychological disorders. In the case of anxiety disorders there are studies which have shown the effectiveness of new cognitive behavioural treatments, comparing them with the lack of treatment, with a believable psychosocial "placebo", or even with other alternative psychotherapeutic alternatives. Nowadays well-established treatments exist for almost all the disorders previously mentioned. Although such treatments differ depending upon the specific disorder, most of them involve procedures based upon exposure, some type of cognitive therapy or attention to cognitive and emotional factors, even those outside the patient's consciousness. Coping strategies or problem-solving, as well as non-specific factors are also used (Barlow & Lehman, 1996). These authors point out that these treatments tend to pay more attention to the interpersonal system of the patient and to incorporate such an approach to the group formats.

Traditionally, cognitive-behavioural treatment of social phobia has been divided into four kinds of procedures: relaxation strategies, social skills training, exposure and cognitive restructuring (Heimberg & Juster, 1995; Schneier, Marshall, Street, Heimberg & Juster, 1995), although, quite often, the intervention package includes several of these procedures. *Social skills training* is a set of techniques which attempt to teach interpersonal skills and strategies with the intention of improving the interpersonal competence of individuals in specific types of social situations. Its application to social phobia is based on the idea that people with social phobia lack appropriate social skills, both verbal and non-verbal (Schneier et al., 1995). Is it assumed that the anxiety reactions are secondary to these deficits and improved behavioural skills should result in anxiety reduction. The application of *relaxation* strategies to social interaction is based on the notion that these techniques will give the patient a means of coping with anxiety. *Exposure* to real-life feared situations has long been acknowledged as a basic component of effective fear reduction (Mattick, Page & Lampe, 1995; Schneier et al., 1995).Its goal is to extinguish the conditioned response (CR) of fear when faced with the conditioned stimulus (CS) (or social situations) by repeated exposure to these conditioned situations without the occurrence of an aversive unconditioned stimulus (US) (see Caballo, Aparicio & Catena, 1995). Finally, it has been suggested that cognitive factors are more important in the development of social phobia than in the case of other anxiety disorders (Butler, 1985). Fear of scrutiny or negative evaluation by others, which is a basic characteristic of social phobia, is a problem in the perception of behaviour and the motives of others. As such, interventions which deal with perceptions and distorted thoughts can be especially important in the treatment of social phobia. Heimberg & Juster (1995) and Mattick et al. (1995) have reviewed the effectiveness of cognitive behavioural procedures for the treatment of social phobia. Their revisions reveal that the most frequently used procedure is *exposure,* followed by *social skills training* and some kind of *cognitive restructuring* (rational-emotive behaviour therapy, Beck's cognitive therapy, self-instructional training). In some other studies there were also used, although much less frequently, *systematic desensitisation* and some kind of *relaxation*. Analysed in general, most of cognitive behavioural techniques used for the treatment of social phobia/anxiety seem to produce effective results, at least to a certain degree, inducing us to seriously consider the availability of cognitive-behavioural procedures appropriate for the disorder with which we are concerned (e.g., Hope, Heimberg & Bruch, 1995; Turner, Beidel & Cooley-Quille, 1995). However, we believe more research is necessary to clarify difficulties and gaps which still exist in this field.

First of all, many of the works reviewed by the former authors did not include any control group but only compared different treatment procedures against one another, questioning the possible effectiveness they could have. Secondly, a large number of studies used patients' self-reports as their only measure of the results. (Mattick et al., 1995). We need to consider if the changes in the self-report instruments and even the behavioural measures used in some of the studies imply clinically significant changes (Kazdin, 1977). It does not appear that we have advanced very much in this respect, although important efforts have been made in recent years to find standardized measures to evaluate the final functioning state of the individual treated for their social phobia (e.g., Turner, Beidel, Long, Turner & Townsley, 1993; Turner, Beidel and Wolff, 1994a). Studies evaluating changes that have taken place in the "real life" of the patient due to treatment (e.g., Cape and Alden, 1986) can shed more light on the true effectiveness of treatment, other than simply trusting in self-reports measures filled out by the subjects themselves. Finally, attempts should be made to try and determine why the same procedure works well in some cases, but not in others. What changes from one study to another? The experience of the therapist, non-controlled variables of the patients, researchers' sympathies for one procedure or another, the type of phobia (circumscribed versus generalised), the number of sessions devoted to the procedure in question, could be some of the reasons to take into consideration when coming to explain these contradictory results. Although we are on the right way, the next few years will be critical in determining which procedures are the most simple and effective for which kind of person with which type of social phobia.

Assessment

The assessment of social phobia, as well as other phobias, should be structured by asking systematically about physiological, behavioural and subjective symptoms and about reactions to them. The severity of the phobia can be estimated by finding out to what extent it interferes with daily life, including the ability to work and have normal relationships. It may be useful to ask the patient (Butler, 1989a): "What does the phobia prevent you doing?" "If you no longer had this problem, what differences would it make to your life?" (p. 103).

A detailed history about the origin of the phobia is not necessary. It is more important to identify the factors maintaining it because they may interfere with progress. Avoidance is usually the maintaining factor, although cognitive factors also tend to play an important role.

In the next section, we will briefly describe some of the most used techniques for the assessment of social phobia.

Semi-Structured Interviews

The *Anxiety Disorders Interview Schedule, ADIS*, (DiNardo, Barlow, Cerny, Vermilyea, Himadi & Waddell, 1985) has been the most commonly used interview format for anxiety disorders in general. The present version of the ADIS follows the criteria laid out in the DSM-IV (APA, 1994). The *Structured Clinical Interview for DSM-III-R, SCID,(* Spitzer, Williams, Gibbon & First, 1992) has been also used frequently, with the DSM-IV (First, Spitzer, Gibbon & Williams, 1995) having already appeared. Nevertheless, the latter interview format explores all the disorders of the *Axis I*, making it much less specific when it comes to anxiety disorders, including social phobia. Finally, the *Entrevista dirigida para habilidades sociales* (Caballo, 1993) ("Structured interview for social skills") is also very useful in sampling the social relationships of the patients, including evaluation of their specific behaviour (by means of molecular components) during the interaction with the interviewer. Such an interview can gather detailed information about the situations, activities and people the patient avoids and also to know how the patient interprets the situations which cause anxiety to him/her.

Self-Report Questionnaires

Research into social phobia has used self-report questionnaires which can be divided into four main categories (Glass and Arnkoff, 1989), according to their measure of (a) Fear and anxiety, (b) Social anxiety, (c) Shyness, and (d) Social skills (see Caballo, 1995, for a list of these instruments). Those most relevant to social phobia are the following:

Liebowitz Social Anxiety Scale, LSAS (Liebowitz, 1987). Contains 24 items which assess anxiety regarding social interaction and public performance, as well as avoidance of such situations.

The *Social Phobia Scale, SPS* and the *Social Interaction Anxiety Scale, SIAS* (Mattick & Clarke (1988). Both contain 20 items each. The SPS assesses fear of being observed during daily activities, whilst the SIAS assesses more general fears of social interaction.

The *Social Phobia and Anxiety Inventory, SPAI;* (Turner et al., 1989). This scale comprise two subscales, one devoted to social phobia (32 items) and the other to agoraphobia (13 items). Data on the psychometric properties of the scale with Spanish samples can be found in Caballo & Alvarez-Castro (1995).

The *Social Avoidance and Distress Scale, SAD* and the *Fear of Negative Evaluation, FNE* (Watson and Friend (1969). Theses two scales have been perhaps the most used in the field of social anxiety. The SAD contains 28 items regarding anxiety and avoidance associated to social interaction, whilst the FNE contains 30 items and assesses self-expectations of being negatively evaluated by others. Data with Spanish samples on these scales can be found in Caballo (1993).

Self-Monitoring

Self-monitoring is a very practical and effective method to assess the social behaviour of an individual in his/her natural environment, outside the clinic or laboratory (McNeil, Ries & Turk, 1995). Self-monitoring is a regular component of most cognitive-behavioural programmes, including those focusing on social phobia. The therapist may assess the frequency of social contact, its antecedents and consequences, the range or number of different people with whom the patient interacts, duration of the interactions, topics of conversation or types of interactions, and self-assessment of anxiety and social skill. Likewise, anticipated anxiety can be assessed separately from the real anxiety experienced during the situation, as well as various physiological symptoms, negative thoughts, avoidance behaviours, etc.

Behavioural Measures

Tests generated and used for the assessment of social skills (e.g., the *Simulated Social Interaction Test, SSIT,* Curran, 1982; see Caballo, 1987, for a modified version of this instrument) have been used as assessment methods for individuals with social phobia (e.g., Mersch, Breukers & Emmelkamp, 1992). McNeil et al. (1995) also mention the usefulness of tests originated in the analysis of social skills to assess the behaviour of individuals with social phobia (e.g., *Heterosocial Adequacy Test,* Perry & Richards, 1979; *Taped Situation Test,* Rehm & Marston, 1968; *Social Interaction Test,* Trower, Bryant & Argyle, 1978). A more detailed review of these instruments can be found in Caballo (1993). Similar strategies are the Tests for Behavioural Assessment, where it can be measured situations such as starting a conversation with a unknown member of the same sex, with an unknown member of the opposite sex or giving a talk in front of a small group of people. Other tests have included interacting in a group conversation or beginning a conversation with someone attractive in whom one is emotionally interested (McNeil et al., 1995).

Physiological Measures

Physiological measures have shed little light on differential characteristics of individuals with social phobia, at least until recently. However, there appears to be a rebirth of interest in using this kind of measurement in anxiety disorders in general (McNeil et al., 1995). However, unlike these authors, we do not think that reliable data exist on the relevance of physiological measures in the investigation of social phobia.

Development of a Programme for the Cognitive-Behavioural Treatment of Social Phobia

Before describing the treatment programme for social phobia, we should distinguish between discrete social phobia (one or two social situations) and generalized social phobia (most social situations). In the first type of phobia, exposure is usually a highly recommendable and effective technique, with rates that can occasionally reach 100% efficiency (e.g., Turner, Beidel & Jacob, 1994b). However, in individuals with generalised social phobia it is a good idea to add elements of cognitive restructuring and social skills training (Caballo & Carrobles, 1988; Echeburúa, 1995).

Our treatment is in group format, with 6–8 people, and, if possible, with an equal number of both sexes. Sessions take place once a week, and last 2.5 h. each. The programme is fourteen sessions long, plus follow-up and booster sessions (once a month for 6 months these last kind of sessions). However, the number of sessions can be extended depending on how the group moves along and on the therapist's judgement. An atmosphere of unconditional acceptance and support for members of the group should be developed, with empathic listening, reinforcing successive approximations to target behaviour, and the practice of this behaviour. The goals of therapy should be clearly explained to the group, what they can and cannot expect from it, the importance of motivation to transfer to real-life what had been learned in the sessions and the central role of self-control of one's own behaviour at the end of therapy.

Many individuals with social phobia expect that therapy will provide them with clear rules about how they should behave in social situations. Although treatment can give them some direction, particularly social skills training, it should be made clear from the beginning, that it is difficult to give such clear rules, partly because social situations are unpredictable, and because people may have different opinions about what reactions are most appropriate. Instead of searching for rules, patients should better learn to accept and handle their uncertainty, by observing how other people behave, paying attention to relevant environment stimuli, asking other people for information when they need it or learning to see the relativity of consequences (Scholing, Emmelkamp & Van Oppen, 1996).

The treatment programme basically includes procedures such as education techniques, relaxation, cognitive restructuring, exposure and social skills training. The rest of the chapter will be devoted to explain the cognitive-behavioural programme for the treatment of social phobia session by session.

First Session

1. Introduction of the therapist(s) and group members
2. Explanation of some of the basic rules of how the group works
3. Explanation of social phobia/anxiety
4. Explanation of the foundations of treatment
5. Explanation of the goals, frequency, duration, etc., of the treatment programme
6. Evaluation of motivation and expectations regarding the programme
7. Training in Jacobson's progressive relaxation
8. The importance of homework is emphasised and the first assignments are established.

Introduction of the therapist(s) and group members. The therapist(s) introduces him/herself to the group, followed by the rest of the group. In this introduction they may give their name, what they do (work, study, etc.) and some of the things they find enjoyable.

Explanation of some of the basic rules of the how group works. Some of the basic rules of how the group works are presented to the group members, such as the confidentiality of what is dealt with in the group, regular attendance, punctuality, active participation in the group, the importance of doing the homework, etc.

Explanation of social phobia/anxiety. Give an up-to-date explanation of the nature of social phobia/anxiety. This explanation usually includes a definition of social phobia, its clinical characteristics (behavioural, cognitive, physiological), its subtypes, frequently feared situations, the influence of genetics, epidemiology and course of the disorder, and its possible etiology (from a cognitive-behavioural perspective) (see Caballo, 1995, for a detailed information about this question). Insist upon the fact that social phobia is a learned behaviour and, as such, can be unlearned. Explain how phobias are acquired and maintained (e.g., using Mowrer's two-factor theory) and the need for the patient to become actively involved in order to break the vicious circle that maintains the phobia.

Explanation of the foundations of treatment. The foundations of the treatment programme are explained, and so are the basis of different techniques, such as relaxation, exposure, cognitive restructuring and social skills training for the treatment of social phobia. Also comment upon the tested effectiveness of this kind of systematic treatment of the disorder, that some elements may seem similar to others the patient may have used formerly to deal with their symptoms, but that when carried out in a systematic way and directed by a professional have a much greater probability of succeeding.

Explanation of the goals, frequency, duration, etc. of the treatment programme. The goals that the treatment is attempting to reach are explained, the frequency of the sessions is established, as is the approximate length of the programme and any doubts that group members may have over these issues are clarified.

Evaluation of motivation and expectations regarding the programme. Many patients have already tried different ways of dealing with their social anxiety/phobia problem with little success and may have reservations about using similar methods during treatment. For instance, an individual with social phobia often maintains social contact because they have to go to work, they have to use public transport and buy food and clothes, yet they frequently report that this continuing exposure is not helpful to them (Butler, 1989b). The therapist can attempt to understand why the method has not been effective so far; for example, if the patient continues to avoid important aspects of the situation in a subtle way, if they focus on their negative thoughts and expectations when in the situation, if they do not persist when feeling uncomfortable, or may try to deal with the most difficult situation without having first practised easier tasks, etc.

Training in Jacobson's progressive relaxation. Relaxation is a way of eliminating tension. When a person is stressed over long periods of time, their muscles have little chance to relax. This causes discomfort in the individual, continuous apprehension, people may feel irritated, tired, etc. Furthermore, anxiety may hinder or inhibit many forms of social behaviour.

Individuals are taught Jacobson's progressive relaxation. Lying on mattresses on the floor, group members tense and relax different muscle groups in their body. Once they have finished relaxing, it should be clear to the subject how to carry out the task by themselves, because it would be the first homework assignment (see Caballo, 1993, for a detailed description of the Jacobson method)

The importance of homework is emphasised and the first assignments are established. The patient needs to use behaviours learned in treatment sessions in real-life situations, so that learning can be transferred to real life. The use of practice is the same as when learning a new skill, that is, it is useful for its own sake and not for some wider purpose (Butler, 1989a).

For homework, it is assigned daily relaxation according to the Jacobson method and some readings on social phobia/anxiety. The patient is given a self-monitoring form so he/she can write down some social situations they find difficult.

Second Session

1. Review of homework
2. Practice of rapid relaxation
3. Analysis of anxiety in social situations
4. Cognitive restructuring: explanation of the A-B-C model of the REBT
5. Homework assignment

Review of homework. Approximately 20 min of each session should be devoted to review homework assignments of the previous week. It is described what each individual did, homework done correctly is reinforced and any difficulties the patients has had are clarified.

Rapid relaxation practice. Teach group members how to relax in a shorter period of time. Muscles are not tensed anymore, but only relaxed. The sequence of relaxation is similar to the previous session.

Analysis of anxiety in social situations. Go over some possible "myths" about anxiety that the therapist may need to correct. For example (Walen, 1985):
a. Anxiety is dangerous: I could have a heart attack
b. I could lose control or blow up in some way
c. It is a sign of weakness
d. The anxiety attack will never pass
Explain to the patient that anxiety has a "lifecycle" and that after reaching its peak, it will begin to subside. Furthermore, a little anxiety can be good in some situations. However, a large part of daily tension is unnecessary.

In order to recognise tension more easily, the patient may be aware of certain "symptoms" which may indicate the presence of anxiety. Table 2.1 lists some of these symptoms which are indicators of the presence of anxiety.

Table 2.1 Possible Symptoms of Expression of Anxiety or Nervousness

1. Trembling knees
2. Stiff arms
3. Self-manipulations (scratching, rubbing, etc)
4. Limited hand movement (in pockets, behind back, clasped together)
5. Trembling hands
6. No eye contact
7. Tense facial muscles (grimaces, tics etc.)
8. Inexpressive face
9. Pale face
10. Flushing
11. Licking lips
12. Swallowing saliva
13. Breathing difficulties
14. Slower or faster breathing
15. Sweating (face, hands, armpits)
16. Letting out a squawk
17. Stammering or incomplete sentences
18. Faster or slower steps
19. Rocking
20. Dragging one's feet
21. Clearing one's throat
22. Dry mouth
23. Pain or acid stomach
24. Increased heart rate
25. Swinging legs/feet when sitting down with one leg crossed over the other
26. Biting one's nails
27. Biting one's lips
28. Feeling nauseous
29. Feeling dizzy
30. Feelings of suffocation
31. Frozen to the spot
32. Not knowing what to say

Then the group is taught how to use the Subjective Units of Disturbance Scale (SUDS) in the following way (Cotler & Guerra, 1976; Galassi & Galassi, 1977).

The SUD scale is used to communicate the level of anxiety subjectively experienced. In using the scale, you will have to rate your anxiety level from 0, completely relaxed, to 100, a state of panic.

Imagine when you are completely relaxed and calm. For some people this occurs whilst resting, taking a nice warm bath, or reading a good book. For others, it happens when they are walking on the beach or floating in the water. Give a "0" rating for how you feel when you are at your most relaxed.

Next, imagine a situation in which you experience extreme anxiety, a state of panic. Imagine feeling extremely tense and nervous. Maybe in this situation your hands feel cold and tremble. You may feel dizzy or flushed, or you may feel awkward. For some people, the situations in which they feel most nervous may be when a person close to them has had an accident, when there is excessive pressure on them (exams, work, etc.); or when they speak in front of a group. Give a rate of "100" for how you feel in this situation. You have already identified the two poles of the SUD Scale. Imagine the entire scale (like a ruler) that goes from "0" SUDS, completely relaxed, to "100" SUDS, very nervous, in panic.

0	5	10	15	...	50	...	85	90	95	100

Completely   State
relaxed   of panic

Now you are familiar with the entire scale so that you can rate your level of anxiety. To practice using this scale, write down your SUDS rating right now.

You can use the SUDS rating to evaluate social situations that you encounter in real life. The relaxation method that you are learning will help to reduce your SUDS rating. Experiencing high levels of anxiety is uncomfortable to most people. Also, anxiety can prevent you from saying something you want to and can interfere with the way in which you get your message across.

The extent to which you will feel capable of reducing your SUDS scores in any kind of situation will depend upon a series of factors, including the level of anxiety which you generally experience, the SUDS rating you initially had, what type of behaviour is required, and the person to whom you direct your comment. We do not think that your goal should be to reach a 0 or 5 in every situation. Your goal will be to reduce your SUDS level to a point where you feel comfortable enough to express yourself.

To practice using the SUD scale, a series of situations can be described. For each situation, listen to the description of the scene and then imagine what is happening to you in this situation. After imagining the situation, write down the amount of anxiety (SUDS level) that you feel. Finally, if you were nervous or tense whilst imagining the scene, try concentrating on the parts of your body where you feel most anxiety (see Table 2.1). Did your stomach feel tense? Did you have a knot in your throat? Did you have cold or sweaty hands? Did you have a headache? Did your eyelids twitch? If you locate the area or areas where you feel most tense, you can use relaxation methods better.

For homework, the subject is given a self-report form where they have to identify and register a brief description of the situations which take place in their life and which cause them different levels of relaxation and anxiety. Along with the brief description of the situation, the patient is asked to describe their physical symptoms (see Table 2.1). The SUD ratings are already marked down on the page in increments of 10 points, so that the patient uses the whole scale, to 100 points. During the time they use the self-report sheet, the patient has to describe a situation which causes 0 to 9 anxiety and another which falls within the 10–19 range, etc. (see Table 2.2)

The evaluation of the different levels of anxiety produced by different situations can serve several purposes. For example, asking individuals to register their anxiety level during interactions makes them think and concentrate. Thinking and concentrating is, in part, incompatible with anxiety. As such, it is likely that the person's anxiety level will be reduced. Also, constantly checking the SUD rating during interpersonal interactions makes the subjects more aware of situations in which they repress their emotions and do not say or do anything about it.

It is explained to the patients that symptoms of anxiety are a consequence of negative cognitive stimulation and of avoidance behaviours, as well as subjective interpretation of the latter. It is explained to them that sometimes even using relaxation, some anxiety symptom(s) will occur (e.g. blushing, sweating, etc.). In these cases, they should stop fearing these responses and learn to tolerate them in order to eliminate them. Tell them that, paradoxically, to pass an exam we have to stop worrying about failing, to stop anxiety we have to stop worrying about anxiety and put up with it... Understanding of these facts is a great help in general for increasing tolerance and, as a result, diminishing the frequency of the appearance of these physiological responses.

Cognitive restructuring: introducing the REBT fundamentals. One way of introducing the individual to the rational emotive behaviour therapy (REBT), discovering defence mechanisms, showing how feelings are influenced by thinking, realising that a large part of these thoughts is automatic, is the following task: Ask groups members to sit down, to close their eyes, take deep breaths through their nose, hold it for a while and slowly breathe out through their mouth. Then give them the following instructions (Wessler, 1983):

Table 2.2. Self-Monitoring Form of Subjective Units of Disturbance (SUDS)

Name:			Period:
Day and Time	SUDS	Describe the situation	Describe the anxiety/ relaxation responses
	0–9		
	10–19		
	20–29		
	30–39		
	40–49		
	50–50		
	60–69		
	70–79		
	80–89		
	90–100		

I'm going to ask you to think of some secret, something about yourself that you normally wouldn't tell to anyone else. It might be something you've done in the past, something you are doing now in the present. Some secret habit or physical characteristic *(Pause)*. Are you thinking about it?*(Pause)* Good. Now I'm going to ask someone to tell the group what they have thought of... to describe it in some detail *(Short pause)* But since I know that everyone would want to do this, and we don't have enough time to get everyone in, I'll select someone *(Pause – looking around the group)* Yes, I think I have someone in mind *(Pause)*. But before I call on that person, let me ask, what are you experiencing right now? (p. 49).

Usually people feel a high level of anxiety (if they have really gone through the exercise), which can be quantified by asking the subjects their SUDS rating. At this moment, the therapist shows the group that it is thinking *about doing* something, not doing it, what leads up to their feelings. Then, the therapist asks about the kinds of thoughts that led up to these feelings.

This exercise can be used to introduce individuals to the fundamentals of rational emotive behaviour therapy. For Ellis, anti-scientific or irrational thought is the main cause of emotional disturbance, since, consciously or unconsciously, the person chooses to become neurotic, with their unrealistic and illogical way of thinking (Ellis & Lega, 1993; Lega, Caballo & Ellis, 1997). Socially inadequate behaviour may stem from irrational or incorrect thought, from excessive or deficient emotional reactions to specific stimuli, and from patterns of dysfunctional behaviour. What we usually point out as our emotional reactions in certain situations are mainly caused by our conscious and/or automatic evaluations and suppositions. So, we feel anxiety not at the objective situation, but at our own interpretation of the situation. The ABC model of rational emotive behaviour therapy (see Figure 2.2) works in the following way (Lega, 1991; Lega et al., 1997): The **A** or *activating event* (specific activity or situation) does not directly and automatically produce **C** or *consequences* [which can be *emotional* (**eC**) and/or *behavioural* (**bC**)], otherwise, everyone would react identically to the same situation. "C" is caused by an interpretation of "A", that is, by beliefs (**B**) which we generate about the situation. If "B" is functional, logical and empirical, it is considered "rational" (**rB**). If, on the other hand, it hampers normal functioning of the individual it is "irrational" (**iB**). The main method of replacing irrational beliefs (**iB**) with rational ones (**rB**) is called *dispute or debate* (**D**) and, basically, is an adaptation of the scientific method to daily life, a method through which hypothesis and theories are questioned to determine their validity. Science is not simply the use of logic and data to verify or reject a theory. Its most important aspect consists of constant revision and change of theories and the attempt to replace them with more valid ideas and useful conjectures. It is flexible

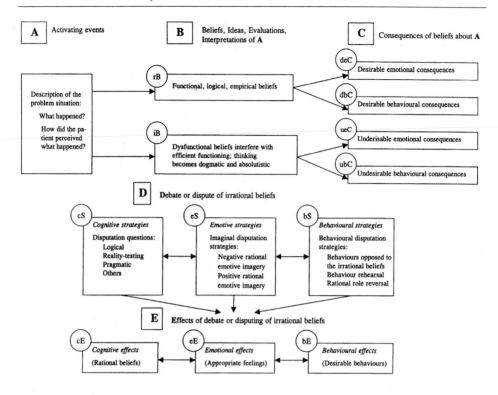

Figure 2.2. ABC model of rational emotive behaviour therapy (from Lega, Caballo & Ellis, 1997).

rather than rigid, open-minded instead of dogmatic. It strives for a greater truth, but not for a perfect or absolute truth. It sticks to data and real facts (which can change at any moment) and to logic thought (which does not contradict itself by simultaneously upholding two opposite points of view). It also avoids rigid thinking patterns, such as "all-or-nothing" or "one or the other", and accepts that, in general, reality has two sides and is made up of contradictory events and characteristics. Irrational thinking is dogmatic and dysfunctional and the individual evaluates him/herself, others, and the world in a rigid way (Ellis & Lega, 1993; Lega, 1991; Lega et al., 1997). These evaluations are couched via absolutistic demands, in the form of dogmatic *"musts"*, *"shoulds"*, and *"have to's"* (instead of using probable or preferential concepts), generating dysfunctional emotions or behaviours which interfere with the successful pursuit of personal goals. From these absolutistic thinking, three conclusions are derived: (1) *Awfulizing*, which is the tendency to focus excessively on the negative nature of an event; (2). *Low frustration tolerance* or "I cant-stand-it-itis", which is the tendency to exaggerate the discomfort of a situation and (3) *Damnation* which is the tendency to evaluate oneself or others as "totally bad", compromising their value as people due to their behaviour. Ellis & Lega (1993) point out that learning to think rationally consists of applying the main rules of the scientific method to the way of seeing oneself, others and life. These rules are:

1. It is better to accept what is going on in the world as "reality", even if we do not like it and try to change it.
2. In science, theories and hypothesis are postulated in a logical and consistent way, avoiding important contradictions (as well as false or unrealistic "data".)
3. Science is flexible, nonrigid. It does not uphold something in an unconditional or absolute way.
4. Science does not include the concept of "deservingness" or "undeservingness", nor deifies people (or things) for their "good" acts or damns them for their "bad" behaviour.
5. Science has no absolute rules about behaviour and human affairs, but it can help people to reach their goals and to be happy *without* offering any guarantees (Ellis & Lega, 1993).

Some of the most common irrational thoughts in human beings which Ellis recently summarised into the three conclusions we have just pointed out (e.g., Lega, 1991; Lega et al., 1997; Ellis, 1994), are the following (Ellis & Harper, 1975):

1. I *must* have love and approval from all the people significant to me.
2. I *must* prove thoroughly competent, adequate and achieving, or at least, must have competence or talent in some important area.
3. When people act obnoxiously and unfairly, they *must* be blamed and damned, and be considered as bad, wicked, or rotten.
4. It is *awful* and *catastrophic* when things do not go the way I would like them to.
5. Emotional misery comes from external pressures and people have little ability to control or change their feelings.
6. If something seems dangerous or fearsome, I *must* preoccupy myself with and make myself anxious about it.
7. It is easier to avoid confronting many life difficulties and responsibilities than undertake more rewarding forms of self-discipline.
8. People and things *should* turn out better than they do and I must view it as *awful* and *horrible* if I do not find good solutions to life's hard realities
9. I can achieve happiness by inertia and lack of action or by passively and uncommittedly "enjoying myself".

The application of the rules of the scientific method to challenge irrational thoughts is one of the key points of rational-emotive behaviour therapy. For instance, a patient with generalised social phobia thinks his co-workers "do not like him"; after being trained in the detection and analysis of these ideas (see later), they are able to recognise that the first irrational idea underlies this irrational thought ("I must be loved and approved by all the people significant to me"). Disputing such an idea could have the following steps (Ellis & Lega, 1993):

1. Conclusion ("awfulizing")
2. Is this belief realistic and factual? (No, since there is no law which states that I *have to be* approved by people whom I find important;
3. Is this belief logical? (No, just because I find certain people important it does not follow that they *must* approve of me).
4. Is this belief flexible and unrigid (No, because it holds that under *all* conditions and at *all the time* people whom I find *must* approve of me, which is quite inflexible;
5. Do this belief prove that I "deserve" something? (No. It cannot prove that there is a rule of the universe they *ought to*, *have to*, and *must* approve of me even if I act nicely towards them; and
6. Does this belief show that I will be happy, I will act properly and will obtain good results? No, to the contrary. It does not matter how hard I try to get people to approve of me, I can easily fail – and if I then think that they *have to* like me, *I will* probably feel depressed).

Thinking about "always trying to get along with everyone", of "having to always be approved of in an unconditional way by those around you" is very typical of individuals with generalised social phobia, so that any kind of minor criticism from others can cause anxiety symptoms to appear. These individuals are particularly sensitive to any kind of situation or commentary involving discomfort, disapproval or disagreement by others. These individuals tend to exaggerate and dramatise these comments, eliciting a maladaptive behavioural reaction, being aggressive or defensive, or clumsy (as Trower & Turland, 1984, describe it) or using avoidance or escape behaviours.

Homework Assignment. With the self-monitoring form of Table 2.2 group members have to select situations which have a subjective level of anxiety and which fall into everyone of the intervals indicated on the self-monitoring sheet. Each individual practices rapid relaxation every day at home. They also learn more about REBT with the appropriate reading (e.g., Lega et al., 1997).

Third Session

1. Review of homework
2. Practice of differential relaxation
3. Cognitive restructuring: Identification of automatic thoughts
4. Cognitive restructuring: Determining if thoughts are rational
5. Cognitive restructuring: the challenging of thoughts
6. Assignment of new homework

Review of homework. Approximately the first 20 min of each session are devoted to reviewing homework assigned during the previous week. It is described what each individual did, give positive reinforcement for correctly completed tasks and clarify any difficulties.

Practice of differential relaxation. Group members are taught differential relaxation. So, once they have carried out rapid relaxation in the group, they are taught how to use (and tense) certain muscle groups whilst they relax others.

Cognitive restructuring: identification of automatic thoughts. Once the individual understands the REBT fundamentals and the importance of thoughts in producing emotional consequences, they should also learn how to identify what things are going on in their head to make them feel anxious. If irrational or dysfunctional thought is common, it may be difficult to identify it. It is not easy to figure out what one is thinking in a specific situation. A reason for this is that many thoughts are automatic in response to situations which one finds worrying. However, the more one practices, the easier it is to detect these thoughts.

One way to get started is to use any feelings of anxiety, fear, or discomfort and work backwards. That is, when one feels uncomfortable, then there must be some underlying thought which caused the feeling. In any situation or interaction in which one feels anxious or distorted, one should ask oneself (Andrews, Crino, Hunt, Lampe & Page, 1994): (a) How do I feel?, (b) What situations have I been involved in recently?, (c) What do I think about myself?, (d) What do I think about the other people?, (e) What do I think about this situation? Subjects can also be made to close their eyes, vividly remember a real-life situation which may have caused them anxiety and concentrate on the sequence of thoughts, feelings and images which took place before, during and after the fantasy. It is important that patients express these aspects and that the therapist helps them to recognise their maladaptive images and/or cognitions. The patient has to learn to identify negative self-verbalisations, and, later on, to re-evaluate these verbalisations more carefully and rationally. Beck, Rush, Shaw & Emery (1979) also mention four methods of eliciting self-verbalisations: (1) Assigning half an hour a day to reflect upon these thoughts; (2) Monitoring the negative thoughts which go along with an important negative emotion; (3) Gathering thoughts associated to negative feelings and to the precipitating environmental events; and (4) Key words for identifying maladaptive thoughts during the interview are: "I should", "I have to"", "I can't stand it", "I don't have the right", "It's unfair", "Terrible", "Awful", "Catastrophic", "Always", "Never", etc

Andrews et al. (1994) also point out several characteristics of maladaptive thoughts which can help to identify them. Such thoughts are: (1) Automatic, that is, they come to mind without any effort from the individual, (2) Distorted, they do not fit all of the facts, (3) Unhelpful, keeping the subject anxious, making change difficult and preventing them from getting what they want out of life, and, (4) Involuntary, that is, the individual does not choose to have them and, moreover, can find it very difficult to get rid of them.

Cognitive restructuring: determining if thoughts are rational. Once internal dialogues have been identified, it has to be determined if they are rational or irrational. *What a person says to him/herself* (e.g., self-verbalisations, images, self-evaluations, attributions) before, during and after an event is an important determinant of what kind of behaviour they will demonstrate. For instance, people sometimes start to concentrate on their own behaviour (excessive self-consciousness) to such an extreme that they lose all perception of what the other person is saying, doing or, perhaps, feeling. People tend to experience anxiety in social situations because they focus on negative thoughts and self-verbalisations, such as fear of looking foolish, fear of what others might think, fear of not being liked, not knowing what to say, etc. The other person does not make us feel this way, it is our own negative self-verbalisations. It is not true that the other person is making us feel nervous. It is more likely that what we are telling ourselves is making us nervous.

Common patterns of irrational thoughts are also known as cognitive distortions. Some typical ones are (Beck et al., 1979; Freeman & Oster, 1997):

1. Coming to conclusions when there is a lack of evidence or even when it is contradictory *(arbitrary inference)*.
2. Concentrating on a specific detail, taken out of context, without taking into account other aspects of the situation which are more relevant *(Selective abstraction)*.
3. Drawing conclusions from an isolated incident *(Overgeneralization)*.
4. Exaggerating or playing down the significance of an event *(Maximising and Minimising)*.
5. A tendency to attribute external phenomena to oneself *(Personalization)*.
6. Classifying all experiences in opposing categories *(Dichotomous thinking)*.

Explanation of these and other cognitive errors can help the patient even more in identifying their maladaptive cognitions and working on changing them to more suitable and facilitating cognitions of more socially appropriate behaviour.

Cognitive restructuring: the challenging of thoughts. Once people know how to distinguish rational thoughts from irrational ones, the latter can be challenged. In the debate, patients confront their irrational philosophy and are asked to examine them, piece by piece, so that they can see if they are useful and make any sense. Disputing is a logical and empirical process in which the patient is helped to stop and think. Its basic objective is to help the patient internalise a new philosophy, reflected in expressions such as "It would be a big disappointment if I don't get it, but I can stand it. I just can fail and that's not so terrible."

Strategies employed in disputing irrational thoughts can be of cognitive, behavioural or imaginal nature (Lega et al., 1997; Walen et al., 1992) (see Figure 2.2). *Cognitive debates* are an attempt to change the patient's erroneous beliefs through philosophical persuasion, didactic presentations, Socratic dialogue, vicarious experiences and other forms of verbal expression. One of the most important tools in cognitive debate is the use of *questions*. Some of those which can ask for logic consistency or semantic clarity in the patient's thinking are: Is that good logic? Is that true? Why not? Why is that so? How do you know? What do you he mean by that term? Why does it have to be so?

A second group of questions requires the patients to determine whether their beliefs are consistent with empirical reality. For example, most demanding beliefs ("I have to", "I must") are inconsistent with reality. It can be shown that patients who endorse low frustration tolerance beliefs and they can not stand the occurrence of **A**, they have, in fact, stood it again and again. "Catastrophizing" beliefs can be challenged by pointing out that a negative **A** did not have a 100% bad effect. Likewise, it can be shown that self-downing beliefs are wrong because everyone does something good and is important to someone else in the world. Examples of questions from this second group are: What is the proof? What would happen if...? Can you stand with it? Let's be scientific, what do the facts reveal? Why do you have to do this? If this were true, what would be the worst thing that could happen? What if that happens? In what way would it be so terrible? (Walen et al., 1992)

A third group of questions attempts to persuade patients of the hedonic value of their belief system. Rational beliefs help us to reach our own objectives, so that beliefs can be evaluated according to this functional criteria. For example, do they help the patient to solve their personal problems? To reduce their emotional difficulties? Examples of questions are: is it worth it? When you think this way, how do you feel?

Through *behavioural debate* the individual questions their irrational thoughts, behaving in a contrary way to them. Behavioural debate gives patients experiences which go against their irrational ideas. For example, if they believe they cannot stand rejection, they are encouraged to seek it out. Behavioural debates are usually carried out outside the clinic and are frequently given as homework. However, it is often useful to use behaviour strategies during the session, such as *role-playing* or *rational role reversal* (the patient plays the rational role) (Walen et al., 1992)

Finally, a third strategy is *imaginal debate*. In this procedure, after a verbal debate, the therapist might ask patients to imagine themselves again in the problematic situation; this may allow the therapist to see if emotions have changed. If they have, the therapist can ask the patients what they are now saying to themselves as a way to rehearse more rational thoughts. If the emotions have not changed, more irrational thoughts may be present and the imagery exercise might allow them to emerge. The therapist may use one of the following kinds of rational-emotive images (Maultsby, 1984).

In *negative rational-emotive images* patients close their eyes and imagine themselves in a difficult situation (**A**), trying to experience their normal emotional problems (**C**). Wait until the patient experiences **C** and then ask them to focus on their internal dialogue which seems related to these emotional consequences. Then, instruct patients to change the feeling of a disturbed emotion to a more constructive negative emotion (e.g. from anxiety to worry). Patients must be reassured that this can be done, even if it is only during a fraction of a second. Tell the patient that as soon as the task is over they are to open their eyes. When they give this sign, simply ask, How were you able to you do it? Almost always the answer will demonstrate a cognitive change; usually patients reply that they have stopped catastrophizing (Walen et al., 1992).

In *positive rational emotive images* (Maultsby, 1984; Maultsby & Ellis, 1974), patients imagine they are in a difficult situation, but see themselves behaving and feeling differently. For example, patients anxious about speaking in public imagine themselves speaking in class or at a meeting and feeling relatively relaxed as they do it. As soon as the patient signals they have had this image, the therapist asks, "And what did you say to yourself to do this?" This technique is useful because it allows patients to practice a positive plan and to develop a group of coping skills (Walen et al., 1992).

Homework assignments. Homework assignments use differential relaxation techniques in previously-selected real-life situations. The subject also practices identifying dysfunctional thoughts, differentiating them from rational ones and challenging them in anxious social situations. Behaviour experiments are programmed to test the irrationality of certain of the subject's thoughts.

Fourth Session

1. Review of homework
2. Review of differential relaxation
3. Cognitive restructuring: the three column technique and testing the hypothesis
4. Cognitive restructuring: false attributions and self-control
5. Introduction to basic human assertive rights
6. Introduction of the multimodal self-monitoring form
7. Homework assignment

Review of homework. Approximately the first 20 min of each session are dedicated to reviewing homework assigned during the last week.

Review of differential relaxation. Differential relaxation is reviewed in the group, imagining anxious social situations and using this relaxation method.

Cognitive restructuring: the three column technique and testing the hypothesis. Once the subject has learned to identify irrational thoughts, the double or three column technique can also be used to change irrational thinking to a rational one. So, in the left column they write the automatic negative thought and in the right column they write various positive alternative responses. They can also make use of a third column in which the environmental event is re-interpreted. A use of the double and triple column would be the following:

Irrational Thought	*Rational thought*	*Re-interpretation*
If I am quiet, people will think I am strange, but if I speak, they will think I am stupid and that would be terrible.	People will not necessarily think I am strange if I am quiet; they might not even take notice of how much time I spend speaking.	People like superficial conversation. It doesn't make sense that every comment should be intelligent.

Patients have to learn to discriminate between perception and reality and to change their analysis from deductive to inductive, to consider thoughts as theories or hypothesis that have to be contrasted, instead of factual affirmations (Caballo, 1993; Lega et al., 1997). Most of patients with social phobia perceive problems before they happen; likewise, when they really have a problem they exaggerate its importance, they dramatise and avoid the situation, giving an unrealistic significance to the behaviour of others. So, the hypothesis has to be empirically contrasted, looking for facts which confirm or invalidate it.

Adjustment contrast is also used to help us make the patient understand the negative consequences of dysfunctional thinking: these thoughts only increase the possibility of creating what is most feared, i.e., rejection from others. An analysis of the positive and negative consequences in the short, medium and long term helps the patient to realise the dysfunctionality of these thoughts and that they are not justified even when others do criticise him/her. Becoming depressed is not the answer to this problem, neither is becoming angry or becoming nervous, since these responses only contribute to more social problems. At this point we teach the patient that even when their negative thoughts have an empirical basis, they are not justified. We give patients examples such as the following: if a patient is objectively overweight, worrying and continually repeating that they are fat, this will be more likely to lead them to eat excessively than to control their diet. The patient must understand that negative thinking stems from their learning history, where they learned to mistrust their social skills and their ability to be socially attractive to others. However, the continued presence of their negative evaluations is not justified, since maintaining these expectations only increases negative consequences: decreasing mood, increase in anxiety and awkward behaviour, avoidance or escape from social situations. Not contrasting these expectations with reality only perpetuates the vicious circle of believing more and more in them.

The patient is also helped to look for more realistic expectations, more adjusted to reality, undistorted, not irrational and adaptive, so they can try them out in conflict situations. We explain to them that initially the expectations will not have a high degree of credibility but, when rehearsing emotionally load in troublesome situations, the level of self-confidence will continue to increase gradually. As negative expectations decrease, emotional well-being increases, anxiety and worry diminish and socially adjusted behaviour is more frequently carried out.

Cognitive restructuring: false attributions and self-control. The patient tends to attribute others' negative behaviour to his/her own actions or presence, in a generalised and negative way. For example, if a colleague at work is in a bad mood and say hello to Him/her improperly, it is because "s/he has bothered them without realising it". If a neighbour does not greet them on the street, it is because "the patient has done something wrong". If a girl/boy they like does not take any notice of them, it is because "they are unattractive and nobody is interested in them". We often hear how the behaviour of others is personalised by the patient who, occasionally, believes they are doing it on purpose ("they are doing it to annoy me". "they're behaving like that to bother me", etc.); sometimes the patient considers him/herself to be the centre of everyone's attention ("everyone was watching me at then disco when I asked him/her to dance and they said no"). The patient with social phobia can be completely controlled by these attributions, maintaining these negative intentions and showing a picture as a socially isolated individual impair his/her mood and contributes significantly to the presence of serious depressive symptoms which, in turn, aggravates the phobic symptoms.

In discussing these attributions, we found the *explanation of the model of helplessness* (Abramson, Seligman & Teasdale, 1978) very useful. Particularly in its discussion of the depressogenic attributional style which conforms *internal, stable* and *global* attributions for his/her failures. Introduction and discussion of this style, in line with the educational background of the patient, helps the latter to realise how he/she arrive to biased and generalised attributions, without being able to discriminate between their own and others' responsibilities and the different contributions to the conflict with the other (Bas & Andrés, 1993).

For individuals with social phobia, too much self-observation and the bias of this process tends to be important. The patient selectively scrutinises their inadequate social behaviour, blowing out of proportion and dramatising the negative consequences, which causes an increase in the physiological responses to anxiety and, as a result, an increase in awkward behaviour. The control of this variable is of great importance, since we have often concluded that as long as the patient observes him/herself in the social situation their behaviour will be inappropriate. Some of the strategies we use in these cases are: explanation of the phenomenon, how it becomes a self-fulfilling prophecy with negative consequences, stressing the contribution this variable makes to the increase in physiological anxiety and awkward behaviour; discussion of the cognitive distortions already mentioned which justify, according to the patient, the need to be completely attentive to the negative aspects of his/her social behaviour; the introduction and critique of Ellis's irrational idea which states "if something is dangerous or fearsome one should be continually worried about it, focusing on the possibility that it may occur", since this belief once again justifies the patient's need to keep self-monitoring; control of obsessive thoughts with strategies such as thought detention or cognitive satiation, in cases where the patient has little control over these obsessions; training in distraction techniques, which can be used at the time of social interaction, so that the patient does not focus on themselves. Finally, in the case of *in vivo* exposure, as a reality test which is carried out first in the office, we have a good opportunity to make the patient see the immediate negative consequences of this excessive self-observation, which, as we have already mentioned, will be related to the patient's inappropriate social behaviour when role-playing the simulated situation. All in all, there are three major modalities for working with self-observation: managing external attention (distraction), self-attention (satiation, etc.), or working with the negative scheme which controls self-attention (cognitive restructuring, etc.), as we have shown in other studies (Bas, 1991, 1997). Likewise, excessive self-evaluation is common in these patients. They use rigid and perfectionistic criteria, coupled with a lack of self-reinforcement of their social behaviour and excessive self-inflicted punishment for their inadequate behaviour, all of which grow worse when depressive symptoms are added to the phobia. *In vivo* exposure, as a reality test, works with these variables, adjusting the perfectionist, demanding and unrealistic criteria, paying attention to cognitive distortions and encouraging the practice of more adjusted and adaptive self-evaluations. Training in the observation of positive behaviours and self-reinforcement for these are useful strategies in changing the negative cognitive style. On the other hand, a discussion of the dysfunctional consequences of self-punishment helps to decrease the negative influence of this variable, especially when one explains to the patient how self-punishment has a negative effect upon mood and, as such, increases the probability of avoidance behaviour as well as his/her trust in negative beliefs about their social interest to other people, increasing his/her discomfort and anxiety.

Introduction of basic human assertive rights. Our human rights come from

Table 2.3. Sample of Basic Human Assertive Rights

1. The right to maintain your dignity and respect by behaving in a skilled or assertive way- even if a person feels hurt- whilst not violating the basic human rights of others.
2. The right to be treated with respect and dignity.
3. The right to reject requests without feeling guilty.
4. The right to experience and express your own feelings.
5. The right to stop and think before you act.
6. The right to change your mind.
7. The right to ask for what you want (all the while realizing that the other person has the right to say no).
8. The right to do less than you are humanly capable of doing.
9. The right to be independent.
10. The right to decide what to do with your own body, time and property.
11. The right to ask for information.
12. The right to make mistakes – and to be responsible for them.
13. The right to feel good about oneself.
14. The right to have your own needs and to be as important as the needs as others. Also, we have the right to ask (not demand) others to respond to our needs and to decide if we satisfy the needs of others.
15. The right to have opinions and to express them.
16. The right to decide if you satisfy the expectations of others or of if you behave according to your interests – always without violating the rights of others.
17. The right to talk about the problem with the person involved and clarify it, in extreme cases where rights might not be clear.
18. The right to obtain what you pay for.
19. The right to choose not to behave in an assertive or socially-skilled way.
20. The right to have rights and to defend them.
21. The right to be listened to and taken seriously.
22. The right to be alone when you choose it.
23. The right to do anything as long as you don't violate the rights of another person.

the idea that we are all born equal, in a moral sense, and, that certain rights are deemed necessary to all human beings to live a decent life. In social relations between two people neither person has exclusive privileges because the needs and objectives of each person have to be equally valued. A basic human right in the context of social skills is something that everyone has the right to be (i.e. be independent), to have (i.e. have their own thoughts and feelings) or to do (i.e. ask for what they want) in virtue of their existence as human beings.

One kind of right that is often confused with basic human assertive rights is role rights. Human assertive rights apply to everyone, whilst *role* rights are those a person possesses because of a formal or informal contract to perform certain responsibilities or use certain skills.

Since not everyone recognises the same basic human assertive rights, conflict may arise. Lange & Jakubowski (1976) give four reasons for the importance of developing a belief system which helps people to uphold and justify their socially appropriate behaviour: (1) the person may continue to think that they have the right to behave as they think they should, even when they are unjustly criticised for such behaviour; (2) they may challenge any kind of irrational guilt which may occur later, as a result of having behaved the way they did; (3) they may be proud of their behaviour even when no one else appreciates it; and (4) it will be more likely that they will behave the way they want to

To illustrate the importance of believing in the basic human assertive rights we all have, the following exercise can be carried out. From the form with the basic human assertive rights (see Table 2.3) group members are asked to choose a right from the list which is important to them, but which does not normally apply to their lives, or even one which is difficult for them to accept. Then, they are given the following instructions: "Close your eyes...Get comfortable...Breathe in deeply, hold the air inside as long as you can, then let it out slowly...Now imagine you have the right you chose from the list...imagine how your life has changed in accepting this right...How would you act?...How would you feel about yourself?...about other people?...". This fantasy goes on for 2 min, after which the therapist goes on to say: "Now imagine you no longer have this right...Imagine how your life has changed compared to just a few minutes ago...How would you act now...and how to you feel about yourself...and about other people...". This fantasy goes on for 2 min. Then, in pairs, the following questions are discussed: which right they chose, how they acted and felt when they had and did not have the right and what the exercise taught them (Kelley, 1979; Lange & Jakubowski, 1976).

Introduction of the multimodal self-monitoring form. Group members are introduced to the multimodal self-monitoring form, where they will write

Table 2.4. Multimodal Self-Monitoring Form to use in the Assessment of Social Behaviour (From Caballo, 1993)

Name:					Period:	
Time and day of occurrence	Situation	Evaluation of anxiety (0–100)	Irrational thoughts	Rational thoughts	Evaluation of anxiety (0–100)	Open social behaviour

down their behaviour, degree of anxiety and thoughts which occurred in the target situation from the homework (see Table 2.4).

Homework assignment. Homework is assigned which mainly consists of entering situations which cause some degree of anxiety (behavioural exercises of hypothesis testing) agreed upon in advance by the therapist and group members. Patients are reminded to use differential relaxation and to identify and challenge dysfunctional thoughts which come to mind. Likewise, they have to identify the rights present in each of the situations confronted.

The multimodal self-monitoring form is used to record the level of anxiety the situation causes, dysfunctional thoughts which were experienced, counter-acting rational thoughts, the level of anxiety after these rational thoughts and the open performed behaviour. (Table 2.4).

Fifth Session

1. Review of homework
2. Gradual exposure
3. Homework assignment

Review of homework. Approximately the first 20 min of each session are dedicated to reviewing homework assigned during the last week.

Gradual exposure. The acquisition of fears based on Mowrer's two factor theory can be explained once again at the beginning of this section on gradual exposure therapy (a basic intervention strategy for patients with social phobia). It is explained to the patient that instead of escaping from the feared situation, which does not solve anything, it is better to expose them to the situation until anxiety notably diminishes or disappears. Likewise, *in vivo* exposure is used as a *reality test* for feared situations.

The objective of treating people with social phobia is to overcome avoidance and break the association between anxiety and specific social situations. This is carried out gradually. A typical hierarchy of feared social situations that the patient avoids or endure with marked distress and awkward behaviour is created. We start by rehearsing this behaviour in the clinic with previous analysis of negative expectations: we ask the patient what his/her expectations are of carrying out the appropriate social behaviour and he/she will report the content of their fears. For example, the patient will say, "I'm not going to do it well". Our first task consists of making an operative description of this belief so that it can be contrasted, since such an abstract verbalisation is difficult to contrast with reality. After several questions, we will specify the contents of the fear: "No words will come out, I won't be able to say a single word, I'll stammer, I'm not going to look them in the eye, etc". These expectations can indeed be contrasted. Then, we will ask him/her how strongly he/she believe this will definitely be the case and then we will rehearse the situation (from the hierarchy) associated to the lowest level of anxiety. We will record the patient's behaviour on videotape so they can objectively see how appropriate their behaviour has been. In general, we find that in patients with an adequate repertoire of social skills, the completion of the social task is only inadequate if they are thinking negatively; negative expectations act as a self-fulfilling prophecy, contributing to the appearance of physiological discomfort which is immediately perceived by the patient and labelled in an irrational way ("I'm blushing, it's awful, I can't stand it"), favouring the appearance of awkward behaviours (stammering, lack of eye contact, too much talking or keeping quiet, etc.). On the other hand, if the patient controls these negative expectations, this vicious circle can be broken and they will be able to act naturally and spontaneously, without the expression of physiological responses due to anxiety and the feared awkward behaviour.

Later, after the patient has evaluated the extent he/she believes in their expectations and has carried out the planned social behaviour, they are once again asked how they perceived their behaviour. Often patients with social phobia are clearly biased in the evaluation of their social behaviour due to cognitive distortions. Thus, we find that his/her judgement of the situation is more negative than expected and, surprisingly to him/her, does not agree with the opinion of the rest of the group members who give a better rating to his/her behaviour. For example, before they watch their behaviour on video, the patient is asked to evaluate to what extent his/her negative expectations were fulfilled (on a subjective scale between 0 and 100) and to rate the way in which s/he carried out the task (0 = completely inappropriate behaviour and 100 = completely appropriate behaviour). Their group mates carry out the same evaluation so that the patient can contrast it with their own. Then, the video is shown so that the patient can contrast their evaluation criteria with reality and see if their negative expectations were true and to what extent. If the patient has been controlled by their negative expectations throughout the performance, s/he will see them fulfilled to a large extent, confirming the initial hypothesis; the patient is then shown how the problem starts by thinking in such a negative way. If the patient does not see him/herself controlled by these expectations and has remained calm, they are able to confirm that their judgement of their behaviour was incorrect and, in general, their expectations have not come true to the extent they feared and that their behaviour has been better than they had expected. At this point, the degree he/she believe in the fulfilment of their expectations and in the right performance of his/her behaviour, is contrasted with the group average of appropriate behaviour to confirm their distortions. It is at this moment that the patient realises that his/her evaluative criteria are distorted and more demanding and inflexible than those of the rest of the group. Surprisingly, the members of the group will make the same errors when submitted to the same contrast, but whilst serving as objective evaluators of the social behaviour of their mates in the group, will not fall into the same cognitive distortions and will present a judgement more in line with reality.

After this test, the patient is asked to generate self-reinforcement for the socially appropriate behaviour, and the rest of the group and the therapist also reinforce the socially effective behaviour and the more objective evaluations that the patient starts to make about their behaviour after this discussion. Then, another behaviour (from the hierarchy) eliciting higher anxiety is rehearsed.

The criteria for stopping to rehearse these situations are determined by the scores the patients reach (in the control assessments presented after every performance after every performance), particularly the degree of subjective anxiety they feel when role-playing these situations and the degree of adjustment of their objective evaluations, as well as the management of self-observation.

Specifically, the following records are used for each patient and each tested behaviour: (a) degree of subjective anxiety during the performance (SUD scale, from 0 to 100); (b) level of fulfilment of negative expectations previous to the performance; (c) level of the effectiveness of performance on a subjective scale from 0 to 100 (0 = completely incompetent and 100 = completely competent); (d) level of effectiveness of the performance according to the members of the group, and (e) Adequacy of verbal and non-verbal skills relevant to the task (on a scale from 1 to 5, where 3 represents normal adequacy, 1= lack of adequacy and 5= total adequacy) according to external observers (see Caballo, 1993).

Carrying out such an exhaustive control, even when it is complicated in real clinical practice, is incredibly useful in getting patients to understand their evolution and in contrasting their opinions with the objective reality others observe, motivating them to keep working on therapy and becoming more involved in it. We have been able to appreciate, throughout our clinical experience, how the control of the process of evolution through relevant recording of patient's behaviour lessens the probability of them dropping treatment, motivates them to carry out therapeutic tasks and, as a result, promote recovery.

As we said before, managing self-observation is a critical point. If the patient watches him/herself while performing his/her social behaviour will be inadequate and awkward. If the patient focuses on the situation controlling their inappropriate and excessive self-observation, it is more likely that their social behaviour will be adequate. For the patient, it will always be a big challenge to lower his/her self-scrutiny which is a great disadvantage for their social behaviour. Later, we will comment on the importance of managing this variable.

These rehearsals take place before the patient tries to practice his/her behaviour in real situations, increasing the probability that the patient will behave adequately and efficiently in real life.

Some social situations can also be experienced via imagination, making the subject think about the situations after having gone through rapid relaxation. The level of anxiety felt by patients can be measured using the SUD scale already seen in a previous session. If the anxiety level of the patient is too high, the scene is ended and the subject relaxes again. The same situations the patient has imagined can be given as homework, divided into small steps if they are complex. For example, in the case of an individual with a fear of eating in public, the behaviour could be divided into more specific tasks (Andrews et al., 1994):

1. Have a coffee in the morning in the cafeteria
2. Have a soft drink about ten
3. Have a soft drink and some snacks at noon
4. Have a full meal for at least 20 min. in the afternoon
5. Have a full meal, finish it and ask for a tea, staying for at least 15 min afterwards, the next day.

The SUD scale can be used to evaluate the level of anxiety produced by each step. Likewise, dysfunctional thoughts at each step are recorded.

Homework assignment. The multimodal self-monitoring form is used to record different social situations in which the subject will be involved throughout the week. Several situations from the hierarchy established in the session are planned in order that the subject can be exposed to them using differential relaxation and challenging of maladaptive thoughts.

Sixth Session

1. Review of homework
2. Introduction to the field of social skills
3. Brief talk and explanatory exercises about the molecular components of social skills
4. Differences between assertive, non-assertive and aggressive behaviour
5. Homework assignment

Review of homework. Approximately the first 20 min of each session are dedicated to reviewing homework assigned during the last session.

Introduction to the field of social skills. The group is given a general idea of what social skills are. The concept of social skills is introduced, the different dimensions of social skills are presented and all this is integrated into the problem of social phobia (Caballo, 1991, 1993).

Brief talk and explanatory exercises on the molecular components of social skills. Basic information is given to patients on the most important non-verbal, paralinguistic and verbal components of socially skilled behaviour (see Caballo, 1993). So, first of all a general view of non-verbal communication is given and the most important characteristics of certain elements are described, such as:

Gaze. Gaze is defined as "looking at another person in or between the eyes", or more generally, the upper half of the face. Mutual gaze implies that "eye contact" is made with another person (Cook, 1979). Almost all human being's interactions rely upon reciprocal gaze.

Some of the significance and functions of the gaze patterns are: (a) *Attitudes.* People who look more are seen as more pleasant, but extreme staring is seen as hostile and/or dominant. Certain interaction sequences have further meaning, e.g. looking away first is a sign of submission. Pupil dilation signal interest for another person; (b) *More looking* intensifies the impression of some emotions, such as anger, whilst *less looking* intensifies others, such as shame; (c) *Speech accompaniments.* Gaze is used, along with conversation, to synchronize, accompany or comment upon the spoken word. In general, more listener looking produces more speaker response; more speaker looking is seen as more persuasive and confident (Trower, Bryant & Argyle, 1978).

Facial expression. The face is our principal means of expressing emotion. There are six main emotional expressions: happiness, surprise, sadness, fear, rage, and disgust/dislike. Socially appropriate behaviour should have a facial expression which corresponds with the message. If a person has an expression of fear or anger whilst s/he is trying to start a conversation with someone, they probably will not be successful.

Gesture. A gesture is any action that sends a visual signal to an observer. To become a gesture, an act has to be seen by someone else and convey some piece of information to them. Gestures are basically cultural. Hands and, to a lesser degree, the head and feet can produce a wide variety of gestures, which are used for a variety of different purposes. Gestures provide a second channel, in addition to the vocal channel, which is are very useful for synchronisation and feedback. Gestures which match the spoken words emphasise the message adding emphasis, sincerity and liveliness. Uninhibited movements may also suggest honesty and self-confidence (unless the gesture is erratic or nervous) and spontaneity on the part of the speaker.

Posture. The position of the body and limbs, the way a person feels, how they stand and walk, reflects their attitude about him/herself and their relation with others. Some postures give the following messages: (a) *Attitude.* A group of postures position which reduce the distance and increase the openness to another are warm, friendly, intimate, etc. While the reverse positions are seen as cold, unfriendly, etc. Warm positions include leaning forward, open arms and legs, and hands extended towards other. (b) *Emotions.* There is evidence that posture can communicate specific emotions (such as being tense or re-laxed). For instance, shoulders shrug, arms raised, hands outstretched indicate indifference; various pelvic movements, crossing and uncrossing legs (in women) indicate flirting; (c) *Accompaniment of speech.* Important changes in posture are used to mark of larger units of speech, as in change of topic.

Orientation. The degree of orientation indicates the degree of inti-macy/formality in the relationship. The more face-to-face the orientation, the more intimate the relationship and *vice versa.* The bodily orientation which seems most appropriate for many situations is a modified version of being head-on, in which those who are communicating are slightly at an angle of about 10 to 30 degrees. This position clearly suggests a high degree of in-volvement, allowing the patient to occasionally avoid complete eye contact.

Distance/physical contact. Within any culture there is a set of implicit norms concerning distances between two people who are talking. The degree of proximity clearly expresses the nature of any kind of interaction and varies according to social contexts. For example, being very close to a person or even touching them suggests an intimate quality to the relationship, unless they take place in a crowded situation. Within bodily contact, there are different degrees of pressure and different points of contact which can point out emotional states, such as fear, impersonal attitudes, or a desire for intimacy.

Personal appearance. Personal appearance refers to how a person looks on the outside. Although some traits are innate, such as the shape of the face, body structure, eye colour, hair colour, etc., nowadays, a person's personal appearance can be totally changed. Besides plastic surgery and medical inter-vention, it is possible to change almost every observable aspect of a person. From dying hair, making yourself look taller with heels, even changes in your eye colour with contact lenses.

Clothes and accessories also play an important role in forming the impres-sion others have of us. Components upon which attractiveness and the percep-tion of others are based are clothing, physique, face, hair and hands. "The main way of manipulating one's appearance is self-presentation which indi-cates how one sees oneself and how one would like to be treated" (Argyle, 1978, p. 44). People take care of their appearance with a little or a lot of care and it has a powerful effect on other's perceptions and reactions (and some effect upon the person who is doing the wearing) (Argyle, 1975). Aspects of personal appearance offer impressions to others about the attractiveness, status, degree of conformity, intelligence, personality, social class, style and taste, sexuality and age of the individual. "You might think that people who respond for these outward signs are not worth knowing, since they are ignor-ing the "person inside". However, people might never get a chance to know the person inside if they are turned off by outward appearance" (Gambrill & Richey, 1985, p. 215). Presentation of a self-image to others is an essential part of social behaviour, but it has to be used properly.

Voice volume. The most basic function of volume is to carry a message to a potential listener and an obvious deficit is a volume level too low to serve this function. A high volume level may indicate security and dominance. However, speaking too loud (which suggests aggressiveness, anger or coarseness can also have negative consequences- people may leave or avoid future encounters. Changes in voice level can be used in a conversation to emphasise certain points. A voice which varies little in volume would not be very interesting to listen to.

Pitch. Pitch is a way of getting across feelings and emotions. The same words can express hope, affection, sarcasm, anger, excitement or disinterest, depending upon the pitch variation of the speaker. Low pitch with soft volume indicates boredom or sadness. A unvarying pattern can be dull and monotonous. People are perceived as more dynamic and extroverted when they change the pitch of their voices often during conversation. Variations in pitch can also regulate turn taking; a person can increase the pitch of his/her voice to indicate that he/she would like someone else to speak. A rising pitch is evaluated positively (that is, happy); a descending pitch, negatively (depressed); a constant note as neutral. Many times pitch of words is more important than the verbal message one is trying to communicate.

Fluency. Hesitations, false starts and repetitions are fairly common in daily conversations. However, excessive nonfluencies of speech can give an impression of insecurity, incompetence, little interest, or anxiety. Too many silent periods could be interpreted negatively, especially as anxiety, anger and even contempt. Expressions with an excess of "filler words" during pauses, such as "you know", "well", or sounds like "eer" or "ah" give the impression of anxiety or boredom. Other kind of disturbance includes repetitions, stammers, mispronunciation, omissions and nonsense words (Gambrill & Richey, 1985)

Length of speaking. This element refers to the time the individual spends speaking. The time of conversation can be deficient on both extremes, that is, hardly speaking or speaking a lot. The most appropriate behaviour is to have a reciprocal exchange of information.

Content. Speech is used for a variety of reasons, e.g. to communicate ideas, to describe feelings, to reason and argue. The words used depend upon the situation, the role of individuals in this situation and what they are trying to achieve. The topic or content of the speech may vary greatly. It may be intimate or impersonal, simple, abstract or technical. Some important verbal elements which have been found important in socially skilled behaviour have been, for example, expressions of personal attention, positive comments, asking questions, verbal reinforcement, the use of humour.

Differences between assertive, non-assertive and aggressive behaviour. An initial distinction between assertive, non-assertive and aggressive behaviours can be made using a bidimensional model of assertiveness, where one dimen-

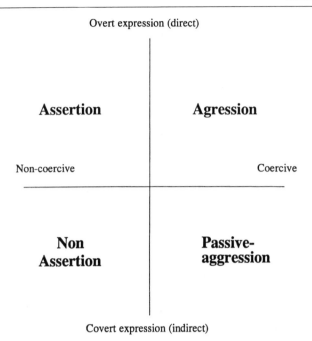

Figure 2.3. A bidirectional model of assertiveness to explain differences between assertive, nonassertive and aggressive behaviours (according to Del Greco, 1983).

sion refers to the style of expression, *overt/covert*, and the other dimension to the behaviour style *coercive/non-coercive* (a coercive behaviour style uses punishment and threat to reach its objective). In "assertion" the behaviour is expressed in an open way, without coercing the other person, whilst "aggressive" behaviour is overt, but coercive. In "non-assertion", either there is a lack of expressive behaviour or it is indirect, but without intimidating the other person. "Passive-aggressive" behaviour is expressed indirectly, but by coercing the other person, that is, trying to control their behaviour in an indirect or subtle way (e.g., with a threatening gaze). Figure 2.3 is a graphic representation of these four styles of response (Del Greco, 1983).

Table 2.5 introduces a series of differences on both verbal and non verbal levels and the consequences of these three styles of response. Later in the session, different examples of assertive, non-assertive and aggressive behaviour are introduced. This can be done in several ways (video, role-playing, verbal explanation, etc.).

Homework assignment. The multimodal self-monitoring form is used to record different social situations in which the subject has been involved throughout the week. Various situations (from the hierarchy established in the session) are planned so that the subject can be exposed using differential relaxation and challenging of maladaptive thoughts.

Seventh Session

1. Review of homework
2. Introduction to behaviour rehearsal test as part of social skills training
3. Role-playing of a situation by each member of the group
4. Homework assignment

Review of homework. Approximately the first 20 min of each session are dedicated to reviewing homework assigned during the last session.

Introduction to behaviour rehearsal as part of social skills training. The rehearsal of necessary basic social skills, without self-observation or negative self-evaluation and without perfectionist criteria, is necessary so that the patient realises they can behave successfully in social situations. In this case, the process of *in vivo* exposure as a reality test which takes place in the clinic, as we have already indicated, is very useful, since it helps the patient to successfully practice the appropriate skills and become aware of them. When they see themselves on video and contrast their evaluation with other group members, they begin to evaluate their behaviour in a more objective way. If there is no self-observation, the patient behaves normally and spontaneously and, in general, their behaviour is adequate. If they are self-evaluating as they behave, they focus on their physiological anxiety responses, labelling them in a dramatic and irrational way, so that their clumsy behaviour will appear almost immediately. Focusing on this inadequate behaviour will increase their desire to flee and will contribute to avoidance behaviour, appearing negative mood and, in serious cases, a huge discouragement which will only perpetuate their avoidance. If, when anxiety is increasing, the patient gives self-instructions such as "relax", "calm down", "breathe deeply", etc., dedramatises the importance of the situation and his/her behaviour, stop self-scrutiny and focus on the social task, the likelihood that the feared behaviour will appear is considerably lessened. These behaviours are very important in understanding how the environment reacts to patients with this disorder. We have often heard that awkward behaviour of patients usually takes place with people who are most important to them. When the patient does not want the other persons to realise that he/she is interested in them, he/she may act in an open hostile way or try to pass unnoticed, so the likelihood is high that the other people does not react in an appropriate way and does not relate to the patient. This situation is interpreted as one more fact which shows how others reject them, without realising that their own behaviour is, for the most part, responsible of others' lack of attention. So we can see that management of aggressive, concealed or awkward behaviours in front of others is very important for the patient to be able to cope with social situations, so that the probability of getting social reinforcement from significant others increases.

Table 2.5. Three Styles of Response (From Caballo, 1993)

Non-assertive	Assertive	Aggressive
Too little, too late Too little, never	Sufficient appropriate behaviour at the right time	Too much, too soon Too much, too late
Non-Verbal Behaviour Downcast eyes; soft voice; hesitation; helpless gestures; slumped posture; no eye contact; not listening	**Non-Verbal Behaviour** Direct eye contact; conversational voice level; fluent speech; firm gestures; Erect posture; Listening; loose hands	**Non-Verbal Behaviour** Glaring; loud voice; fluent/fast speech; confrontation; threatening gestures; intimidating posture/ dishonest
Verbal Behaviour "Perhaps"; "I suppose;" "I wonder if"; "Would it bother you much?"; "It's just"; "Don't you think that?"; "Really, it's not important"	**Verbal Behaviour** "I think"; "I feel"; "I want"; "Let's"; "How could we solve this?"; "What do you think?"; "How does it look to you?"	**Verbal Behaviour** "You would be better to"; "Do"; "You must be joking"; "If you don't do it"; "You don't know"; "You should", "Bad"
Effects Interpersonal conflicts Depression Helplessness Poor self-image Hurt to themselves Loses opportunities Tension Feels out of control Loneliness Dislikes themselves and others Feels angry	**Effects** Feels at ease with others Feels satisfied Feels at ease with themselves Relaxed Feels in control Creates most opportunities Likes themselves and others Is good to themselves and others	**Effects** Interpersonal conflicts Blame Frustration Poor self-image Hurts others Loses opportunities Tension Feels out of control Loneliness Dislikes others Feels angry

Deficits in social skills, verbal (stuttering, inability to say something, etc.) and non-verbal (lack of visual contact, no smiles, etc.) are corrected in the rehearsal sessions of feared situations. Patients are very afraid of behaving inappropriately, when in fact their behaviour is a lot more appropriate than they think. However, as we have already pointed out, they need to watch themselves on videotape to adjust their observational criteria and be aware of his/her observational bias and their distortions. Once again, the control of other group members will help the patient to realise that their judgement is always more severe than that of outside observers. In more serious cases, others' opinions are dismissed by the patient who does not believe they are true, saying things like "well, of course that's what they're going to say", "they're not going to destroy me by telling me that I really did it badly", "they're only saying it to encourage me", etc. In these cases it is useful to point out that when they judge others and reinforce them for their appropriate behaviour, it is not to encourage them, to trick them or lie to them: he/she is just telling them the truth, as they do when they judge him/her. The patient with a more severe disorder may resist accepting that their skills are sufficient and, occasionally, quite appropriate to the demands of the situation. In any case, some less-skilled patients need more rehearsals of the feared situations with more practice of the verbal and non-verbal skills they are lacking. To do this, behaviour rehearsal is used.

During behaviour rehearsal, the patient plays short scenes analogous to situations from real life. The main actor – the patient – is asked to briefly describe a real problem situation. Questions such as *who, what, when, where* and *how* are useful for setting up the scene, as well as determining the specific way in which the individual wants to behave. The question "why" should be avoided. The actor/s of the other role/s should be given names of significant people in the patient's real life. Once the scene starts to be played out, it is the responsibility of trainers to make sure that the main actor plays his/her role and attempts to follow to behavioural steps as they act. If they "come out of their role" and start to make comments explaining past facts or other topics, the trainer firmly points out that they need to put themselves in their role again.

If the patient has difficulty with a scene, it should be stopped and discussed. Continuing when someone is anxious or distressed, or is showing inappropriate or dysfunctional behaviour is not constructive. On the other hand, if the subject only shows slight hesitation or is getting close to the desired behaviour, he/she can be "prompted" by given him/her support and encouragement. "Prompting" may be "any kind of direct instruction, indication or sign to the subject given during a scene rehearsal, either verbal or non-verbal". If the chosen situation for the behaviour rehearsal proves very difficult, the role-player should be guided to rehearse an easier version of the same situation.

An appropriate number of behaviour rehearsals for a segment or situation varies from 3 to 10. Unless the situation rehearsed is short, it should be divided into segments to be practised in the order in which they occur.

Although the sequence of each role play (that is, the behavioural steps) is always the same (there may be small variations), the content of the situations played changes in accordance with what happens or could happen to subjects in real life. We will describe a typical sequence for carrying out behaviour rehearsal in group format. Many steps are listed to give a good idea of how a complete sequence of behaviour rehearsal might be performed (with the use of other procedures), although it is not always necessary to run through all the steps. These are the following:

1. *Description* of the "problem" situation.
2. *Role playing* of what the patient usually does in this situation.

3. Identification of the possible *dysfunctional cognitions* influencing the socially inappropriate behaviour of the patient.

4. Identification of the *basic human assertive rights* involved in the situation.

5. Identification of an *appropriate objective* to the patient's response. Patient's evaluation of short and long-term goals (*Problem solving*).

6. Suggestion of alternative responses by other group members and the trainers/therapists, focusing on the *molecular* elements of the behaviour.

7. Demonstration of one of these responses by one of the group members for the role player (*modelling*).

8. Using differential relaxation, the patient *covertly* practices the behaviour he/she is going to play as a preparation for the role-playing.

9. *Role-playing* by the patient of the chosen response, taking into account the behaviour of the model they have just witnessed and the *suggestions* from other group members/therapist of the modelled behaviour. The patient does not have to mimic exactly the modelled behaviour, but should integrate it into their response style.

10 *Assessment of the effectiveness* of the response:

   a. By the role player, based on the level of anxiety present and how effective he/she felt their response was.

   b. By other group members/trainers, based on the criteria of skilled behaviour. *Feedback* should be specific, highlighting positive traits and pointing out inappropriate behaviour in a friendly, not punitive way. A way of doing this is that the therapist asks other group members "What could be improved?", taking into account that they should refer to concrete and observable "molecular" elements. Furthermore, therapist(s) should reinforce improvements using a shaping strategy.

11 Taking into account the assessment done by the patient and the rest of the group, the therapist or other group member role plays once again *(model)* the behaviour, incorporating some of the suggestions made in the previous step. It is not appropriate to try to improve more than one or two verbal/non-verbal elements at a time.

12 Steps 8–11 should be repeated as many time as necessary, until the patient (mainly) and the other group members/therapist think that the response has reached an *appropriate level* to be carried out in real life. It should be pointed out that the modelling of the step 11 does not need to be repeated each time the scene is rehearsed. The patient directly incorporates suggestions which have been made of their new role-playing.

13 The whole scene is replayed when all the improvements have been progressively incorporated to behaviour.

14 The patient is given final instructions about applying learned behaviour to real life, about the positive and/or negative consequences which he/she might be encountered, and that the most important aspect is to try, not to be successful *(homework)*. It is also pointed out that, in the next session,

both the way in which the behaviour was carried out and the obtained results will be analysed.

If the patient is unable to complete the rehearsal satisfactorily, then the role-played scene should be broken down into smaller units and rehearsed tried step by step. "It could also be broken down into verbal and non-verbal behaviour and practised non-verbally before adding the words" (Wilkinson & Canter, 1982, p. 47). These authors also point out that group members can also be given the opportunity to practice, before the role-play is enacted in front of a group, for a few minutes in groups of two or three, etc. (depending on the situation). This enables the trainer to go round the group and make suggestions before it is performed "in public".

Rehearsal of each group member's scene. Each group member presents a situation to illustrate the usual behaviour rehearsal.

Homework assignment. The scene from the session is carried out in real life, recording it on the multimodal self-monitoring form. Some situations are chosen from the hierarchy of situations feared by each patient and the subject exposes him/herself to them in real life, taking into account all that they have learned up until this point.

Sessions 8–13

1. Review of homework
2. Role-playing situations with relaxation and cognitive restructuring
3. Real-life exposure
4. Homework assignment

Sessions 8–13 begin and end revising and assigning the homework, respectively. These sessions are devoted to the main techniques of treatment, that is, relaxation, cognitive restructuring and exposure plus social skills training, along with homework. Each patient presents one situation which is role-played in the group. Examples of these situations are: initiating a conversation with an unknown person of the opposite sex, speaking in small groups, etc. Then exposure to the same situations in real life is carried out. Group members are asked about their worst fears about the situation and these fears are incorporated into the simulated exposures. In this way, if a patient fears public ridicule whilst speaking in a group, the participants are asked to do it, even when the possibility of occurrence is very low. During the simulations, individuals do regular assessments of their anxiety on the SUD scale previously described.

For the rest of the treatment, hierarchical and gradual *in vivo* exposure is carried out, but previously the feared situations are rehearsed in the office. It is highly recommended that this exposure be undertaken in a prolonged and repetitive way, carrying out the greatest number of exposures in the least time possible. In this way the patient will see how their anxiety will disappear more quickly and their expectations of self-efficacy will increase, whilst subjective discomfort decreases when exposure is repeatedly carried out.

The order of intervention tends to be the following: (a) exposure to feared situations in the clinic as a reality test; (b) training in rejection; (c) controlled in vivo exposure with therapist(s) and member of the group in real-life situations, and (d) exposure to feared situations in natural contexts, looking for a generalisation of responses in a variety of situations.

We have already talked about the first two steps of this procedure. We would now like to point out that the third step is directed towards the probability of the patient exposing only to feared situations. Occasionally, this intermediate step cannot be undertaken due to the nature of the problem but, in many cases, situations such as greeting, starting conversations with unknown, attractive or interesting people, or expressing negative or positive feelings, as well as asking to meet up again, or inviting someone out for a drink, etc. can be practised (in group and with the therapist present) in real situations outside.

In these cases it is common practice, first of all, for the therapist to carry out the specific behaviour and for the patient to observe, so that they can learn via modelling and realise that the consequences of this behaviour are not as negative as they had expected. It is common for these patients to think that others are inevitably going to react in a very negative way when faced with their social initiatives.

Secondly, the patient carries out the behaviour whilst being observed by the therapist(s) who, in a concealed way, takes note of the appropriateness of their behaviour so that they can give him/her specific feedback about their skills.

Thirdly, the patient listens the comments by the therapist(s) and by the other patients who have been present, starting a discussion about his/her behaviour and the others' who were interacting with him/her. Social and self-reinforcement is given for the performance. It is assessed if negative expectations were present, if the patient focused his/her attention on him/herself whilst interacting with the other person, and their degree of anxiety during the social interaction.

The presence of a patient who acts as a "model", who finished the treatment, and who has suffered and overcome the same symptoms as the patient, is of great help in cases where, working outside, the patient wants to avoid the situation and show resistance behaviours to performance, trying to manipulate the therapist by crying, depressive feeling, etc.

The therapist of a group of patients with social phobia should be assertive and know how to manage the reinforcement of the patient's dysfunctional behaviours, who may attempt to avoid their performance, even when they have successfully rehearsed in the office on several occasions. Even under these conditions, a patient with social phobia has a significant avoidance tendency when the behaviour has to be performed outside. The therapist should be prepared for this eventuality and have negotiated, ahead of time, the practice of a *response cost* which will be applied for avoidance behaviours. It is interesting not to allow much time to pass after is has been decided which item from the hierarchy is going to be performed until it is carried out. The more time a patient has the chance to say things like "I can't do it", "I'm not prepared", "I don't feel very well", "Let's leave it for another day", etc., the more fear they generate and the more credible the negative expectations seem to them, increasing the possibility that, at the end of this process, the patient will avoid confronting the feared situation. If the therapist allows avoidance to happen, the patient's anxiety will immediately be alleviated, being once again negatively reinforced for their avoidant behaviour and decreasing the possibility of a new exposure. We should not forget that even when the patient feels better just after avoidance, they will soon feel discouraged, their helplessness will increase, thinking more and more that their problem has no solution. We have repeatedly observed in our work outside that the patient is considerably encouraged when they carry out the exposure, decreasing helplessness and depressive feelings, and increasing their expectations of self-efficacy.

Another issue we should take into account in these practice is that patients should not drink alcohol before or during social interaction, since, in the past, some patients only have been able to socially interact under the influence of this substance, which has acted as uninhibitor of their social behaviours.

In any case, the therapist should be sensitive to special difficulties the patient may present occasionally (separation of couple, death of a loved one, etc.) and not put excessive pressure on the patient if he/she is severely affected, stopping temporarily the role-playing.

We should also not forget that the other person may react negatively to the initiation of the interaction by the patient. In this case, the latter should behave in the way he/she practised when training in rejection, where it was foreseen what could be done when the other person reacts aggressively or indifferently. It is of great interest that others react in an inappropriate way, so that the patient can practice their skills in coping with others' negative behaviour and increase their expectations of self-efficacy in relation to problematic people. Occasionally, and as a final part of training in rejection in real life, we provoke others to respond in an inappropriate way with the presence of confederates (that the patient does not know) who have been asked to react in a definitely negative way, even when our patient's behaviour be correct. Other times, we expose the patient in a premeditated way to interact with people we know in advance will give them a negative response (waiters, shop assistants, etc., who we are familiar with because of previously work with them).

All the feared situations are tried in real life (we are obviously talking about all those distressing situations to the subject and that can be worked on outside) until the patient's anxiety is considerably decreased (assessed in SUD units). Also, occasionally we take the patient's pulse before and after their interaction to see the evolution of their tachycardia. All this data are recorded in a graphic format that the patient him/herself can control and which are very useful for them to observe their gradual progress, promoting self-reinforcement and encouraging them to continue with their exposure.

After this work in real life, we consider the patient ready to expose by themselves alone to feared situations. Control of anxiety responses continues to exist throughout this time, registering their degree of anxiety of the SUD scale (from 0 to 100). We ask the patient to carry out successive exposures until his/her anxiety is at a minimum, he/she considers it manageable and non distressing and does not prevent them from performing spontaneously and unawkwardly.

Throughout the treatment the importance of exposing to anxiety-producing situations is stressed and so are the use of relaxation and cognitive skills in real life. Homework is assigned during the treatment to facilitate this process and is kept in association, as much as possible, with the simulated exposures plus behaviour rehearsals.

Some of the topics commonly covered in these sessions are the following:

1. *Establishment and maintenance of social relationships.* Group members suggest possible situations for initiating and maintaining conversations (in class, at a party, at a bus stop, etc.). How and when to start a conversation is rehearsed, and which elements (mainly non-verbal) to pay attention to start a conversation. Basic strategies are used to maintain a conversation, such as open-ended questions, free information, self-disclosure, active listening, etc. The patient also learn to maintain a relationship by asking for someone's telephone number, calling now and again when appropriate, maintaining the conversation for a certain amount of time, etc. (see Caballo, 1993).

2. *Public speaking.* Situations which frequently cause anxiety to group members are speaking in public, in front of small groups of people, etc. Depending on the kind of problem situation, a gradual approach from easy situations to more difficult ones is taken (e.g., asking a question in class, asking and making comments, giving a brief talk, etc.). It is first rehearsed in the office, with the other group members and therapist(s) acting as the audience. Situations are made more difficult in the sessions within the office than they probably would be in real life.

3. *Writing in front of others.* This situation, less frequent than the previous ones, may need to be carried out by some group members. It can be ap-

proached starting with small steps which work towards the final goal.

4. *Expressing justified annoyance and displeasure.* When role-playing this kind of behaviour, the DESC (*Describe, Express, Specify and Consequences*) scripts could be used (Bower & Bower, 1976).

Other situations that can be dealt with during social skills training are the following:

5. Performing some activity whilst others are observing
6. Interacting with people in authority
7. Joining conversations which are already taking place
8. Giving and receiving compliments
9. Refusing requests
10. Making mistakes in front of others
11. Disclosing personal information
12. Expressing opinions
13. Coping with criticism

Session 14

In this last session, homework done during the last week is revised. Each group member's progress is also revised and new long and short-term goals are planned for each individual, and the next booster session is arranged (approximately a month later). Some tasks for each member to carry out during this month are also planned, taking in to account what has been learned in the sessions.

Conclusions and Future Directions

We now need more research to determine what the best set of procedures are for the treatment of social phobia. Exposure and cognitive restructuring seem to be basic components of treatment, but relaxation and social skills training also seem to be important elements. However, not all treatment packages seem to agree on the same strategies for treatment. So, whilst some intervention programmes encourage exposure and social skills training as basic procedures for treatment of social phobia (e.g., Turner, Beidel & Cooley, 1994), others favour cognitive restructuring as an essential element along with exposure (Heimberg, Juster, Hope & Mattia, 1995; Scholing et al., 1996). All these procedures are probably useful if the patient is motivated enough to do the homework and exposure to real-life situations.

Social phobia can be limited to one or two situations or it can be generalised. The impairment of the individual's life due to generalised social phobia and the amount of time needed to treat it must be taken into account, especially if onset was in childhood. In this case, the patient may have adopted thinking and behaviour patterns that restrict their social relations, showing also poor social skills. Intervention will require gradual modification of these patterns, using cognitive and behavioural procedures, with the duration of intervention being much longer.

The next few years will see the refinement of cognitive-behaviour treatment for social phobia (discrete and generalised). It is probable that more will be known about the contribution of the procedures involved in this kind of intervention, including the addition of some new treatment strategy not commonly used today. However, apparently we are on the right way and future research will bring the necessary elements to improve and increase the efficiency of cognitive-behavioural intervention.

References

Abramson, L. Y., Seligman, M. E. P., & Teasdale, J. D. (1978). Learned helplessness in humans: critique and reformulation. *Journal of Abnormal Psychology, 87,* 49–74.

APA (1980). *Diagnostic and statistical manual of mental disorders*, 3rd edition (DSM-III). Washington, DC: American Psychiatric Association.

APA (1987). *Diagnostic and statistical manual of mental disorders*, 3rd edition revised (DSM-III-R). Washington, DC: American Psychiatric Association.

APA (1994). *Diagnostic and statistical manual of mental disorders*, 4th edition (DSM-IV). Washington, DC: American Psychiatric Association.

Amies, P. L., Gelder, M. G., & Shaw, P. M. (1983). Social phobia: a comparative clinical study. *British Journal of Psychiatry, 142,* 174–179.

Andrews, G., Crino, R., Hunt, C., Lampe, L., & Page, A. (1994). *The treatment of anxiety disorders*. New York: Cambridge University Press.

Argyle, M. (1975). *Bodily communication*. London: Methuen.

Argyle, M. (1978). *Psicología del comportamiento interpersonal*. Madrid: Alianza.

Barlow, D. H. (1988). *Anxiety and its disorders*. New York: Guilford Press.

Barlow, D. H., & Lehman, C. L. (1996). Advances in the psychosocial treatment of anxiety disorders. *Archives of General Psychiatry, 53,* 727–735.

Bas, F. (1991). *Hacia un modelo cognitivo-conductual del cambio*. Doctoral thesis, Universidad Autónoma de Madrid.

Bas, F. (1997). Hacia una conceptualización cognitivo-conductual de los paradigmas de aprendizaje cognitivo: el caso de la autoatención. *Psicologia Conductual, 5,* 27–54.

Bas, F., & Andrés, V. (1993). *Terapia cognitivo-conductual de la depresión: un manual de tratamiento*. Madrid: Fundación Universidad-Empresa.

Beck, A. T., & Emery, G. (1985). *Anxiety disorders and phobias*. New York: Basic Books.

Beck, A. T., Rush, A. J., Shaw, B. R., & Emery, G. (1979). *Cognitive therapy of depression*. New York: Guilford Press.

Bower, S. A., & Bower, G. H. (1976). *Asserting yourself: A practical guide for positive change*. Reading, MA: Addison-Wesley.

Bruch, M. A., Heimberg, R. G., Berger, P., & Collins, T. M. (1988). Social phobia and perceptions of early parental and personal characteristics. Unpublished manuscript.

Buck, R. (1991). Temperament, social skills, and the communication of emotion: A developmental-interactionist view. In D. G. Gilbert & J. J. Connolly (Eds.), *Personality, social skills, and psychopathology*. New York: Plenum Press.

Buss, A. H. (1980). *Self-consciousness and social anxiety*. San Francisco, CA: Freeman.

Butler, G. (1985). Exposure as a treatment for social anxiety: some instructive difficulties. *Behaviour Research and Therapy, 23*, 651–657.

Butler, G. (1989a). Phobic disorders. In K. Hawton, P. M. Salkovskis, J. Kirk & D. M. Clark (Eds.), *Cognitive behaviour therapy for psychiatric problems*. Oxford: Oxford University Press.

Butler, G. (1989b). Issues in the application of cognitive and behavioral strategies to the treatment of social phobia. *Clinical Psychology Review, 9*, 91–106.

Caballo, V. E. (1987). *Evaluación y entrenamiento de las habilidades sociales: una estrategia multimodal*. Doctoral thesis, Universidad Autónoma de Madrid.

Caballo, V. E. (1991). El entrenamiento en habilidades sociales. In V. E. Caballo (Ed.), *Manual de técnicas de terapia y modificación de conducta*. Madrid: Siglo XXI.

Caballo, V. E. (1993). *Manual de evaluación y entrenamiento de las habilidades sociales*. Madrid: Siglo XXI.

Caballo, V. E. (1995). Fobia social. In V. E. Caballo, G. Buela-Casal & J. A. Carrobles (Eds.), *Manual de psicopatología y trastornos psiquiátricos, vol. 1*. Madrid: Siglo XXI.

Caballo, V. E., & Carrobles, J. A. (1988). Comparación de la efectividad de diferentes programas de entrenamiento en habilidades sociales. *Revista Española de Terapia del Comportamiento, 6*, 93–114.

Caballo, V. E., & Alvarez-Castro, S. (1995). Some psychometric properties of the Social Phobia and Anxiety Inventory (SPAI) in a Spanish sample. Paper presented at the *I World Congress of Behavioural and Cognitive Therapies*, Copenhagen.

Caballo, V. E., Aparicio, C., & Catena, A. (1995). Fundamentos conceptuales del modelo conductual en psicopatología y terapia. In V. E. Caballo, G. Buela-Casal & J. A. Carrobles (Eds.), *Manual de psicopatología y trastornos psiquiátricos*, Vol. 1. Madrid: Siglo XXI.

Cape, R. F., & Alden, L. E. (1986). A comparison of treatment strategies for clients functionally impaired by extreme shyness and social avoidance. *Journal of Consulting and Clinical Psychology, 54*, 796–801.

Cook, M. (1979). Gaze and mutual gaze in social encounters. In S. Weitz (Ed.), *Nonverbal communication: Reading with commentary*, 2nd edition. New York: Oxford University Press.

Cotler, S. B., & Guerra, J. J. (1976). *Assertion training: A humanistic-behavioral guide to self-dignity*. Champaign, IL: Research Press.

Curran, J. P. (1982). A procedure for the assessment of social skills: The Simulated Social Interaction Test. In J. P. Curran & P. M. Monti (Eds.), *Social skills training: A practical handbook for assessment and treatment*. New York: Guilford Press.

Davidson, J. R. T., Hughes, D. L., George, L. K., & Blazer, D. G. (1993). The epidemiology of social phobia: findings from the Duke Epidemiological Catchment Area Study. *Psychological Medicine, 23*, 709–718.

Del Greco, L. (1983). The Del Greco Assertive Behavior Inventory. *Journal of Behavioral Assessment, 5*, 49–63.

DiNardo, P. A., Barlow, D. H., Cerny, J., Vermilyea, B. B., Himadi, W., & Waddell, M. (1985). *Anxiety Disorders Interview Schedule-Revised* (ADIS-R). Albany, NY: State University of New York at Albany.

Echeburúa, E. (1993). *Fobia social*. Barcelona: Martínez Roca.

Echeburúa, E. (1995). *Tratamiento de la fobia social*. Barcelona: Martínez Roca.

Ellis, A. (1994). *Reason and emotion in psychotherapy: Revised and updated.* New York: Birch Lane.

Ellis, A., & Harper, R. A. (1975). *A new guide to rational living.* North Hollywood, CA: Wiltshire Books.

Ellis, A., & Lega, L. (1993). Cómo aplicar algunas reglas básicas del método científico al cambio de ideas irracionales sobre uno mismo, otras personas y la vida en general, *Psicologia Conductual, 1*, 101–110.

Falcone, E. (1995). Fobia social. In B. Rangé (Ed.), *Psicoterapia comportamental e cognitiva de transtornos psiquiátricos.* São Paulo: Psy.

First, M. B., Spitzer, R. L., Gibbon, M., & Williams, J. B. W. (1995). *Structured Clinical Interview for DSM-IV Axis I Disorders.* New York: New York State Psychiatric Institute, Biometrics Research Department.

Freeman, A., & Oster, C. L. (1997). Terapia cognitiva de la depresión. In V. E. Caballo (Ed.), *Manual para el tratamiento cognitivo-conductual de los trastornos psicológicos, vol. 1.* Madrid: Siglo XXI.

Galassi, M. D., & Galassi, J. P. (1977). *Assert yourself! How to be your own person.* New York: Human Sciences Press

Gambrill, E. D., & Richey, C. A. (1985). *Taking charge of your social life.* Belmont, CA: Wadsworth.

Glass, C. R., & Arnkoff, D. B. (1989). Behavioral assessment of social anxiety and social phobia. *Clinical Psychology Review, 9*, 75–90.

Hazen, A. L., & Stein, M. B. (1995a). Social phobia: Prevalence and clinical characteristics. *Psychiatric Annals, 25*, 544–549.

Hazen, A. L., & Stein, M. B. (1995b). Clinical phenomenology and comorbidity. In M. B. Stein (Ed.), *Social phobia: Clinical and research perspectives.* Washington, DC: American Psychiatric Press.

Heimberg, R. G. (1995). Cognitive-behavioral treatment of social phobia. Workshop given at the World Congress of Behavioural and Cognitive Therapies, Copenhagen.

Heimberg, R. G., & Juster, H. R. (1995). Cognitive-behavioral treatments: Literature review. In R. G. Heimberg, M. R. Liebowitz, D. A. Hope & F. R. Schneier (Eds.), *Social phobia: Diagnosis, assessment, and treatment.* New York: Guilford Press.

Heimberg, R. G., Dodge, C. S., & Becker, R. E. (1987). Social phobia. In L. Michelson & L. M. Ascher (Eds.), *Anxiety and stress disorders.* New York: Guilford Press.

Heimberg, R. G., Juster, H. R., Hope, D. A., & Mattia, J. I. (1995). Cognitive-behavioral group treatment: Description, case presentation, and empirical support. In M. B. Stein (Ed.), *Social phobia: Clinical and research perspectives.* Washington, DC: American Psychiatric Press.

Herbert, J. D., Bellack, A. S., & Hope, D. A. (1991). Concurrent validity of the Social Phobia and Anxiety Inventory. *Journal of Psychopathology and Behavioral Assessment, 13*, 357–368.

Hope, D. A. (1993). Exposure and social phobia: assessment and treatment considerations. *the Behavior Therapist, 16*, 7–12.

Hope, D. A., Heimberg, R. G., & Bruch, M. A. (1995). Dismantling Cognitive-Behavioral Group Therapy for social phobia. *Behaviour Research and Therapy, 33*, 637–650.

Jansen, M. A., Arntz, A., Merckelbach, H., & Mersch, P. P. A. (1994). Personality disorders and features in social phobia and panic disorder. *Journal of Abnormal Psychology, 103*, 391–395.

Judd, L. L. (1994). Social phobia. A clinical overview. *Journal of Clinical Psychiatry, 55(6, suppl.)*, 5–9.

Kagan, J., Snidman, N., & Arcus, D. (1993). On the temperamental categories of inhibited and uninhibited children. In K. H. Rubin & J. B. Asendorpf (Eds.), *Social withdrawal, inhibition, and shyness in childhood*. Hillsdale, NJ: Erlbaum.

Kazdin, A. E. (1977). Assessing the clinical or applied importance of behavior change through social validation. *Behavior Modification, 1*, 427–452.

Kelley, C. (1979). *Assertion training: A facilitator's guide*. San Diego, CA: University Associates.

Kendler, K. S., Neale, M. C., Kessler, R. C., Heath, A. C., & Eaves, L. J. (1992). The genetic epidemiology of phobias in women: The interrelationship of agoraphobia, social phobia, situational phobia, and simple phobia. *Archives of General Psychiatry, 49*, 273–281.

Kessler, R. C., McGonagle, K. A., Zhao, S., Nelson, C. B., Hughes, M., Eshleman, S., Wittchen, H. U., & Kendler, K. S. (1994). Lifetime and 12-month prevalence of DSM-III-R psychiatric disorders in the United States. *Archives of General Psychiatry, 51*, 8–19.

Lange, A., & Jakubowski, P. (1976). *Responsible assertive behavior*. Champaign, IL: Research Press.

Lega, L. (1991). La terapia racional emotiva: Una conversación con Albert Ellis. In V. E. Caballo (Ed.), *Manual de técnicas de terapia y modificación de conducta*. Madrid: Siglo XXI.

Lega, L., Caballo, V. E., & Ellis, A. (1997). *Teoría y práctica de la terapia racional emotivo conductual*. Madrid: Siglo XXI.

Liebowitz, M. R. (1987). Social phobia. *Modern Problems in Pharmacopsychiatry, 22*, 141–173.

Liebowitz, M. R., Gorman, J. M., Fyer, A. J., & Klein, D. F. (1985). Social phobia: review of a neglected anxiety disorder, *Archives of General Psychiatry, 42*, 729–736.

Marks, I. M. (1969). *Fears and phobias*. New York: Academic Press.

Marks, I. M. (1985). Behavioral treatment of social phobia. *Psychopharmacology Bulletin, 21*, 615–618.

Mattick, R. P., Page, A., & Lampe, L. (1995). Cognitive and behavioral aspects. In M. B. Stein (Ed.), *Social phobia: Clinical and research perspectives*. Washington, DC: American Psychiatric Press.

Mattick, R. P., & Clarke, J. C. (1988). *Development and validation of measures of social phobia scrutiny fear and social interaction anxiety*. unpublished manuscript, University of South Wales, Sydney.

Maultsby, M. C. (1984). *Rational behavior therapy*. Englewoods Cliffs, NJ: Prentice-Hall.

Maultsby, M. C., & Ellis, A. (1974). *Technique for using rational-emotive imagery*. New York: Institute for Rational-Emotive Therapy.

McNeil, D. W., Ries, B. J., & Turk, C. L. (1995). Behavioral assessment: Self-report, physiology, and overt behavior. In R. G. Heimberg, M. R. Liebowitz, D. A. Hope & F. R. Schneier (Eds.), *Social phobia: Diagnosis, assessment, and treatment*. New York: Guilford Press.

Mersch, P. P. A., Breukers, P., & Emmelkamp, P. M. G. (1992). The Simulated Social Interaction Test: a psychometric evaluation with Dutch social phobic patients. *Behavioral Assessment, 14*, 133–151.

Montgomery, S. A. (Ed.) (1995). *Social phobia: A clinical review*. Basle: Hoffman-La Roche.

Montgomery, S. A. (Ed.) (1996). *Prontuario de fobia social*. London: Science Press.

Myers, J. K., Weissman, M. M., Tischer, G. L., Holzer, C. E., Leaf, P. J., Orvaschel, H., Anthony, J. C., Boyd, J. H., Burke, J. D., Kramer, M., & Stoltzman, R. (1984). Six-month prevalence of psychiatric disorders in three communities. *Archives of General Psychiatry, 41*, 959–967.

Organización Mundial de la Salud (1992). *Trastornos mentales y del comportamiento*. Madrid: Meditor.

Öst, L. G., & Hugdahl, K. (1981). Acquisition of phobias and anxiety response patterns in clinical patients. *Behaviour research and Therapy, 16,* 439–447.

Perry, M. G., & Richards, C. S. (1979). Assessment of heterosocial skills in male college students: Empirical development of a behavioral role-playing test. *Behavior Modification, 3,* 337–354.

Rehm, L. P., & Marston, A. R. (1968). Reduction of social anxiety through modification of self-reinforcement: An instigation therapy technique. *Journal of Consulting and Clinical Psychology, 32,* 565–574.

Rosenbaum, J. F., Biederman, J., Pollock, R. A., & Hirshfeld, D. R. (1994). The etiology of social phobia. *Journal of Clinical Psychiatry, 55(6, suppl.),* 10–16.

Salaberría, K., Borda, M., Báez, C., & Echeburúa, E. (1996). Tratamiento de la fobia social: un análisis bibliométrico. *Psicologia Conductual, 4,* 111–121.

Sanderson, W. C., Rapee, R. M., & Barlow, D. H. (1987). *The DSM-III-R revised anxiety disorders categories: Descriptors and patterns of comorbidity.* Paper presented at the annual convention of the Association for Advancement of Behavior Therapy, Boston, MA.

Shaw, P. M. (1976). The nature of social phobia. Paper presented at the annual convention of the British Psychological Society, York.

Schlenker, B. R., & Leary, M. R. (1982). Social anxiety and self-presentation: a conceptualization and model. *Psychological Bulletin, 92,* 641–669.

Schneier, F. R., Spitzer, R. L., Gibbon, M., Fyer, A. J., & Liebowitz, M. R. (1991). The relationship of social phobia subtypes and avoidant personality disorder. *Comprehensive Psychiatry, 32,* 496–502. .

Schneier, F. R., Johnson, J., Hornig, C. D., Liebowitz, M. R., & Weissman, M. M. (1992). Social phobia: comorbidity and morbidity in an epidemiologic sample. *Archives of General Psychiatry, 49,* 282–288.

Schneier, F. R., Marshall, R. D., Street, L., Heimberg, R. G., & Juster, H. R. (1995). Social phobia and specific phobias. In G. O. Gabbard (Ed.), *Treatment of psychiatric disorders,* Vol. 2. Washington, DC: American Psychiatric Press.

Scholing, A., Emmelkamp, P. M. G., & Van Oppen, P. (1996). Cognitive-behavioral treatment of social phobia. In V. B. Van Hasselt & M. Hersen (Eds.), *Sourcebook of psychological treatment of adult disorders.* New York: Plenum Press.

Schwalberg, M. D., Barlow, D. H., Alger, S. A., & Howard, L. J. (1992). Comparison of bulimics, obese binge eaters, social phobics, and individual with panic disorder on comorbidity across DSM-III-R anxiety disorders. *Journal of Abnormal Psychology, 101,* 675–681.

Spitzer, R. L., Williams, J. B., Gibbon, M., & First, M. B. (1992). Structured Clinical Interview for DSM-III-R (SCID): History, rationale, and description. *Archives of General Psychiatry, 49,* 624–629.

Stein, M. B. (1995). Introduction. In M. B. Stein (Ed.), *Social phobia: Clinical and research perspectives.* Washington, DC: American Psychiatric Press.

Stein, M. B., Walker, J. R., & Forde, D. R. (1994). Setting diagnostic thresholds for social phobia: Considerations from a community survey of social anxiety. *American Journal of Psychiatry, 151,* 408–412.

Taylor, C. B., & Arnow, B. (1988). *The nature and treatment of anxiety disorders.* New York: Free Press.

Trower, P., Bryant, B., & Argyle, M. (1978). *Social skills and mental health.* London: Methuen.

Trower, P., & Turland, D. (1984). Social phobia. In S. M. Turner (Ed.), *Behavioral thories and treatment of anxiety.* New York: Plenum Press.

Turner, S. M., Beidel, D. C., Dancu, C. V., & Keys, D. J. (1986a). Psychopathology of social phobia and comparison to avoidant personality disorder. *Journal of Abnormal Psychology*, 95, 389–394.

Turner, S. M., Beidel, D. C., Dancu, C. V., & Stanley, M. A. (1989). An empirically derived inventory to measure social fears and anxiety: the Social Phobia and Anxiety Inventory, *Psychological Assessment*, 1, pp. 35–40.

Turner, S. M., Beidel, D. C., & Townsley, R. M. (1992a). Behavioral treatment of social phobia. In S. M. Turner, K. S. Calhoun & H. E. Adams (Eds.), *Handbook of clinical behavior therapy*, 2th edition. New York: Wiley.

Turner, S. M., Beidel, D. C., & Townsley, R. M. (1992b). Social phobia: A comparison of specific and generalized subtypes and Avoidant Personality Disorder. *Journal of Abnormal Psychology*, 101, 326–331.

Turner, S. M., Beidel, D. C., Long, P. J., Turner, M. W., & Townsley, R. M. (1993). A composite measure to determine the functional status of treated social phobics: the Social Phobia Endstate Functioning Index. *Behavior Therapy*, 24, 265–275.

Turner, S. M., Beidel, D. C., & Wolff, P. L. (1994a). A composite measure to determine improvement following treatment for social phobia: the Index of Social Phobia Improvement. *Behaviour Research and Therapy*, 32, 471–476.

Turner, S. M., Beidel, D. C., & Jacob, R. G. (1994b). Social phobia: A comparison of behavior therapy and atenolol. *Journal of Consulting and Clinical Psychology*, 62, 350–358.

Turner, S. M., Beidel, D. C., & Cooley, M. R. (1994c). *Social Effectiveness Therapy*. Charleston, SC: Turndel Press.

Turner, S. M., Beidel, D. C., & Cooley-Quille, M. R. (1995). Two-year follow-up of social phobics treated with Social Effectiveness Therapy. *Behaviour Research and Therapy*, 33, 553–555.

Uhde, T. W. (1995). Foreword. In M. B. Stein (Ed.), *Social phobia: Clinical and research perspectives*. Washington, DC: American Psychiatric Press.

Walen, S. R. (1985). Social anxiety. In M. Hersen & A. S. Bellack (Eds.), *Handbook of clinical behavior therapy with adults*. New York: Plenum Press.

Walen, S. R., DiGiuseppe, R., & Dryden, W. (1992). *A practitioner's guide to rational emotive therapy*. New York: Oxford University Press.

Watson, D., & Friend, R. (1969). Measurement of social-evaluative anxiety. *Journal of Consulting and Clinical Psychology*, 33, 448–457.

Weiller, E., Bisserbe, J. C., Boyer, P., Lepine, J. P., & Lecrubier, Y. (1996). Social phobia in general health care: An unrecognised undertreated disabling disorder. *British Journal of Psychiatry*, 168, 169–174.

Weissman, M. M., Bland, R. C., Canino, G. J., Greenvald, S., Lee, C. K., Newman, S. C., Rubio-Stipec, M., & Wickramaratne, P. J. (1996). The cross-national epidemiology of social phobia: a preliminary report. *International Clinical Psychopharmacology*, 11 (3, Suppl.), 9–14.

Wessler, R. L. (1983). Rational-emotive therapy in groups. In A. Freeman (Ed.), *Cognitive therapy with couples and groups*. New York: Plenum Press.

Wilkinson, J., & Canter, S. (1982). *Social skills training manual: Assessment, programme design and management of training*. Chichester: Wiley.

Further Reading

Caballo, V. E. (1997). *Manual de evaluación y entrenamiento de las habilidades sociales* (2nd ed.). Madrid: Siglo XXI.

Echeburúa, E. (1995). *Tratamiento de la fobia social.* Barcelona: Martínez Roca.

Heimberg, R. G., Liebowitz, M. R., Hope, D. A., & Schneier, F. R. (Eds.) (1995). *Social phobia: Diagnosis, assessment, and treatment.* New York: Guilford Press.

Scholing, A., Emmelkamp, P. M. G., & Van Oppen, P. (1996). Cognitive-behavioral treatment of social phobia. In V. B. Van Hasselt & M. Hersen (Eds.), *Sourcebook of psychological treatment of adult disorders.* New York: Plenum Press.

Stein, M. B. (Ed.) (1995). *Social phobia: Clinical and research perspectives.* Washington, DC: American Psychiatric Press.

Turner, S. M., Beidel, D. C., & Cooley, M. R. (1994). *Social Effectiveness Therapy.* Charleston, SC: Turndel Press.

3

Psychological Treatment of Agoraphobia

ENRIQUE ECHEBURÚA and PAZ DE CORRAL

Universidad del País Vasco, Spain

Introduction

Agoraphobia consists of a *group of fears* of public places – especially when the patient is alone – such as going outside, using public transport and being in public places (supermarkets, cinemas, churches, football stadia, etc.), which cause serious interference in daily life. Other *external fears* may spring from this core phobia, such as using lifts, going through tunnels, crossing bridges, etc., as well as other *internal fears*, such as excessive worry about physical sensations (palpitations, vertigo, dizziness, etc.) or an intense fear of panic attacks, including fear of social interaction (Echeburúa & Corral, 1995). However, the patognomonic symptom of agoraphobia – and predictor of the appearance of the conditions described – is fear of public places, which is not manifest in specific phobias. The diagnostic criteria of this behavioural disorder according to the DSM-IV (APA, 1994) appear in Table 3.1.

The first panic attack can occur unexpectedly in any kind of agoraphobic situation (bus, shop, church, etc.) when the subject finds him/herself in a heightened state of unspecified stress (disgust, sickness, persistent worry). Once this crisis has occurred, the patient tends to avoid the situation and, from then on, this avoidance carries over into other situations. Indeed, avoidance of public places in order to reduce fear or panic becomes the main cause of incapacity in patients, who, in more serious cases, end up confined to their homes. As such, psychopathological symptoms associated with depression,

Table 3.1. Diagnostic Criteria for Agoraphobia Without History of Panic Disorder According to the DSM-IV (APA, 1994)

A.	The presence of agoraphobia – that is, anxiety about being in places or situations from which escape might be difficult (or embarrassing) or in which help may not be available in the event of having an unexpected or situationally predisposed Panic Attack or panic-like symptoms. Agoraphobic fears typically involve characteristic clusters of situations that include being outside the home alone; being in a crowd or standing in a line; being on a bridge; and travelling in a bus, train or automobile
B.	The situations are avoided (e.g., travel is restricted) or else endured with marked distress or with anxiety about having a panic attack, or panic-like symptoms, or require the presence of a companion
C.	The patient does not meet any of the diagnostic criteria for Panic Disorder
D.	If an associated general medical condition is present, the fear described in Criterion A is clearly in excess of that usually associated with the condition
E.	The Panic Attacks are not better accounted for by another mental disorder, such as Social Phobia (e.g. occurring on exposure to feared social situations), Specific Phobia (e.g., on exposure to a specific phobia situation), Obsessive-Compulsive Disorder (e.g., on exposure to dirt in someone with an obsession about contamination), Post-traumatic Stress Disorder (e.g., in response to stimuli associated with a severe stressor), Separation Anxiety Disorder (e.g., in response to being away from home or close relatives)
F.	The agoraphobia is not due to the direct physiological effects of a substance (e.g., a drug of abuse, a medication) or a general medical condition

general anxiety and hypochondria are not infrequent, neither are obsessive thoughts.

The course of agoraphobia fluctuates, with increases in severity and partial remissions. Nevertheless, spontaneous remission is very uncommon. The fluctuation of this clinical state can depend on psychological factors (emotions, stressful events, etc.), on physical aspects (fatigue, illness, etc.) and even on environmental variables (heat and excessive light aggravate symptoms) (Bados, 1993, 1995).

Agoraphobia is the main research field of behavioural therapy nowadays in the area of anxiety disorders. Part of the reason for this is the severe nature of the disorder and the debilitating effect it has on patients. In fact, agoraphobia has a prevalence rating of 1.2–3.8% of the general population (Weissman, 1985). Although lower than that of specific phobias or that of generalized anxiety disorders, it nevertheless poses a much greater clinical problem because of the degree of interference that it causes in daily life. As such, this behavioural disorder represents between 50 and 80% of the phobic population seeking therapy.

Assessment

Self reports lack the necessary contextual specifications and detail of re-

Table 3.2. Principal Inventories and Questionnaires in the Assessment of Agoraphobia (Echeburúa, 1996)

Tool	No. of items	Authors	Year
FQ[a]	5	Marks and Mathews	1979
MI	29	Chambless et al.	1985
BSQ	17	Chambless et al.	1984
ACQ	15	Chambless et al.	1984
SPAI[1]	13	Turner et al.	1989
IA	69	Echeburúa and Corral	1992

[a]The number of items for these tools which appear in the corresponding column, only refer to the subscale for agoraphobia.

sponse, but are, without doubt, the most useful evaluation tools in clinical practice for determining, on the one hand, the intensity of the symptoms, and, on the other hand, for quantifying changes which have taken place after therapeutic intervention.

In the following paragraphs we present a summarized description of the principal ways of evaluating of agoraphobia presently available (Table 3.2). A more detailed description of these, with the corresponding psychometric properties, can be found in Echeburúa (1996).

The Fear Questionnaire (FQ) (Marks & Mathews, 1979) consists of a sub-scale of agoraphobia, which has only five items and is limited to the evaluation of motor behaviour. An additional limitation to this subscale is that the content of the items does not allow the patient to specify if avoidance takes place when alone or accompanied. We should remember that companionship is a critical factor in the mobility of agoraphobics.

The Mobility Inventory (MI) (Chambless, Caputo, Jasin, Gracel & Williams, 1985), which consists of 29 items, attempts to evaluate the severity of avoidance behaviour and the degree of discomfort in agoraphobics. It consists of three measures: avoidance when alone; avoidance when accompanied and frequency of panic attacks. Unlike the *FQ*, this inventory covers a much wider range of situations and distinguishes between the measures of avoidance when the subject is alone and when accompanied.

The *Body Sensations Questionnaire (BSQ)* and the *Agoraphobic Cognition Questionnaire (ACQ)* (Chambless, Caputo, Bright and Gallagher, 1984) – the first with 17 items and the second with 15 – evaluate cognitive changes (especially the so-called *fear of fear*) (Table 3.3) and psychosomatic changes. They are, from this point of view, complements of the inventory previously mentioned. The patients have to indicate the amount of fear which they experience when faced with the signs of automatic arousal (such as tachycardia or sweating, for example) and with what frequency they have negative thoughts when they are anxious, such as "I'm going to die," "I'm going to go crazy", etc.

Table 3.3. Most Frequent Kinds of Cognitive Alterations in Agoraphobia (Chambless and Goldstein, 1983, modified)

1.	Anticipation of negative consequences *"If I go outside, I'm going to faint"*
2.	Negative evaluation of personal abilities *"I'm not going to be able to put up with an hour in the hairdressers and I'm going to make a spectacle of myself in front of others."*
3.	Constant self-scrutiny and faulty evaluation of somatic symptoms *"With all this pressure on my chest I'm going have a heart attack."* *"These fainting spells and shaking are sign that I'm going crazy"*
4.	Thoughts of escape/avoidance *"I need to run out of this shop, otherwise something is going to happen to me."*

The Social Phobia and Anxiety Inventory (SPAI) (Turner, Beidel, Dancu & Stanley, 1989) consists of a subscale of agoraphobia containing 13 items, which attempt to determine if the social discomfort experienced is due to fear of negative evaluation (social phobia) or fear of a panic attack (agoraphobia). As such, this instrument is interesting from the perspective of differential diagnosis. The content of the items of the *SPAI* tends to be more concrete than is usual in other inventories of a similar kind.

The Inventory of Agoraphobia (IA) (Echeburúa, Corral, García, Páez & Borda, 1992) – the only one detailed enough and validated in the Spanish context – consists of 69 items and in the first part measures different kinds of responses from the patient (motor, psychosomatic and cognitive), according to criteria of being alone or accompanied in the most common situations. In the second part, the variability of responses according to factors which cause an increase or decrease in anxiety is measured, thus allowing for an individualized analysis of each patient. The possibility of carrying out a functional analysis of behaviour and of paying particular attention to the contextual specifications does not appear in any of the previously mentioned questionnaires.

The proposed cut-off rate for distinguishing the sane population from that suffering from agoraphobia is from 176 on the global scale and from 96, 61 and 30 on the Motor, Psychosomatic and Cognitive Subscales, respectively. The *IA* is particularly sensitive at detecting therapeutic change with exposure therapy (Echeburúa, Corral, García & Borda, 1991, 1993).

In short, structured interviews/tests and subjective measurements (self reports and diaries), especially when they take the form of Likert-type scales, allow for a much wider exploration of behaviours – many of which are not possible with direct observation- in a relatively short period of time. A critical research goal for the next few years is to design long and short-term research protocols consisting of instruments with good psychometric properties which do not overlap one another, are validated with Spanish samples and are sensitive to early detection of agoraphobia, as well as therapeutic changes.

Exposure Therapy

Regular in vivo exposure to the feared stimuli is the most effective psychological treatment available these days to confront avoidance behaviours in phobic disorders. Careful evaluation of the *objectives* and *tasks* is a fundamental process in the therapeutic application of this technique. The *objectives* are things which the patient fears or avoids and which create difficulty in their daily life. The *tasks* are the concrete steps needed to reach each one of these objectives.

Self-Exposure

In this technique, the therapist shows the patients that avoidance perpetuates the agoraphobia, that it is the main source of the disorder and that it can be overcome with the help of regular exposure to feared situations. The therapist explains to the patient the way in which they carry out exposure, draws up target-behaviours and helps them to gradually carry out established tasks and to evaluate their own progress. Planning of these sessions extends over a week-long period initially, diminishing as the therapy moves along.

Description of the technique. Present methods of treatment tend to reduce the number of therapeutic sessions and to show the patient ways of *in vivo* self-exposure. This diminishes the therapy time, reduces dependency on the therapist and makes it easier to maintain therapeutic achievements. Self-exposure is most effective when used in conjunction with a self-help manuals (such as Marks, 1978, chapter 12; Mathews, Gelder & Johnston, 1981),[1] with the collaboration of a family member/friend as co-therapist in the initial sessions and with the use of structured diary entries – supervised by the therapist- about exposure therapies (Marks, 1987) (Appendix 1). In any case, the presence of a co-therapist is not strictly necessary (Emmelkamp, Van Dyck, Bitter & Heins, 1992), even though it does seems to reduce the percentage of drop-outs (Bados, 1993).

Patients are encouraged to remain daily in the phobic situation until the attack or discomfort disappear or, at least, until they are considerably reduced, which tends to occur regularly in a period of 30–45 min. In this way, patients learn not to escape in order to feel better, since the discomfort might disappear if they remain long enough in the place where it occurred.

---

[1] The appendix of the original text (i.e. the self-help manual) has been translated into Spanish with the title *Práctica programada para la agorafobia. Manual del paciente*, by the Central Publications Service of the Basque Government (Vitoria, 1986). Also listed is the translated self-help manual for the family member with the same bibliographical reference.

Patients should continue with each task until at least a 25% reduction in anxiety has taken place (which is a measurement of habituation). Useful confrontational methods for overcoming discomfort experienced during exposure-including panic – vary a great deal from one person to another: taking long and deep breaths, relaxation, positive self-reinforcement, etc. The diary of exposure tasks is revised at the beginning of each session and new exposure tasks are continually set. A help guide to exposure handed to patients appears in Table 3.4.

The effectiveness of therapy depends on repeated and prolonged exposure to as many as possible of the components of the group of anxiety-producing stimuli, as well as keeping the patient interested and attentionally involved in exposure therapy (Echeburúa & Corral, 1991, 1993; Marks, 1992).

Table 3.4. Help Guide for Exposure

The golden rules of exposure are:
  (a) The greater the fear of something, the more frequent exposure should be.
  (b) The key to success is regular and prolonged exposure to previously-planned tasks, with a growing degree of difficulty.

In planning the adequate kind of exposure for each case, the following steps can be useful:
  (a) Making a list of situations that you avoid or cause you anxiety. The objectives should be clear and precise. For example "meet new people" is not a good objective; however "invite the new neighbours over on Friday night" is.
  (b) Put the situations in order of difficulty.
  (c) Confront the situation over and over so that you can handle it without difficulty.
  (d) Go on to the next situation on the list.
  (e) Do not underestimate your achievements. Demeaning successes makes you feel bad and is an obstacle to keep on trying. In conquering several small achievements, you can achieve the larger ones.

The success of exposure can be increased in the following way:
  (a) Plan exposure activities without particular haste and without added impeding factors (hunger, lack of sleep, illness, PMT, etc.).
  (b) Breathe long and deeply before and during exposure exercises. Breathe in deeply, hold the breath (counting to three) and breathe out, so that 8–12 complete breaths are produced each minute. Thus substituting a short and gasping breath for one which is slower and more relaxed.
  (c) Abandon the exposure task (or distract yourself from it) for a few brief moments if you feel bad, and immediately return to it once you feel a little better.

The degree of the exposure tasks can be carried out according to the following variables:
  (a) Difficulty of the task.
  (b) Companionship of the co-therapist or not.
  (c) Duration of the task.
  (d) Number of people present.
  (e) Hierarchical or emotional importance of the interlocutor.
Relax and enjoy a task well done.

Table 3.5. Summary Table of Exposure Techniques

Variables	Alternatives		Maximum effectiveness
Modality	Imagination	In vivo	In vivo
Exposure agent	Self-exposure	With therapist present	Self-exposure
Intensity	Gradual	Abrupt	As abrupt as the patient can cope with
Interval between tasks	Short	Long	Short (daily)
Duration of tasks	Short	Long	Long enough to facilitate habituation (30–120 min on average)
Arousal in front of the task	High degree of anxiety	Low degree of anxiety	Not important
Attentional implication	Attention to the task	Cognitive distraction	Attention to the task
Helpful tools	Self-help manual	Help of a co-therapist	Both
Coping strategies	Self-instruction	Long and deep breaths	Varies from one patient to another
Medication	Anti-depressants	Tranquilizers	None (except anti-depressants in cases of a depressive state)

If there are no complications, the initial evaluation can last an hour and later sessions (from 6 to 10) half an hour. The average amount of therapist-patient clinical contact is approximately 7 h in total.

The main significant parameters of exposure therapy appear in Table 3.5. The specific programme of self-exposure laid out by the authors (Echeburúa et al., 1993) appears in Appendix 2. At the same time, a detailed description of the application of self-exposure in a clinical case of agoraphobia can be seen in Borda & Echeburúa (1991).

Therapeutic limits of exposure therapy. Exposure therapy acts specifically upon avoidance behaviours and, more generally, upon autonomic arousal, panic and social and labour limitations. Improvements can be seen after the first few treatment sessions, however completion of the entire programme can require many months, especially to resolve social and labour problems. This is due to the fact that the ability to generalize exposure to non-treated behaviours is poor.

Exposure mainly affects avoidance, but can also have an effect on panic. Besides the majority of cases labelled *panic disorder* fear public places (Echeburúa & Corral, 1995), exposure treatment can reduce both unexpected and situational panic (Klosko, Barlow, Tassinary & Cerny, 1988; Michelson, 1988).

Exposure also has an effect on cognitive distortions. In fact, reduction of fear during exposure has much wider effects and leads to improvements in: avoidance, panic, catastrophic thoughts and physiological changes, such as palpitations and sweating. However, some aspects may improve more quickly than others. Thus, for example, avoidance and tachychardia may diminish before cognitive distortions (Clark, 1989; Echeburúa & Corral, 1993).

Effectiveness of self-exposure. The success rates obtained through exposure techniques in the treatment of agoraphobia vary between 65% and 75% of treated cases (Echeburúa & Corral, 1993; Öst, 1989; Öst, Westling & Hellstrom, 1993), but in some cases these figures are reduced to 50% if drop-outs are taken into account as well as long-term follow ups (Michelson, Mavissakalian & Marchione, 1988).

The usual sequence is that the improvements tend to increase gradually during the first months of follow up and from then on remain stable (Echeburúa et al., 1993). Improvements as a result of exposure therapy are maintained for at least a period of 1–8 years (Table 3.6), whilst non-treated patients do not experience any therapeutic change over a 5-year period (Agras, Chapin & Oliveau, 1972). These assertions can be made with some consistency because the loss of patients in follow-up, after controls of 1–2 years, does not tend to exceed 10% (Cohen, Monteiro & Marks, 1984).

The success of self-exposure – also carried out in the subject's natural environment, not in hospital or an outpatients' clinic – lies in the patient adopting a main role and attributing the success to their own efforts.

Therapeutic failures are fundamentally related to the incompletion of therapeutic prescriptions (Emmelkamp & Van den Hout, 1983). In other cases, the failure of success is associated with the difficulty the patient has in growing accustomed to the feared stimuli, which, in turn, is related to the alcohol

Table 3.6. Results of Exposure Therapy in the Treatment of Agoraphobia

Country	Authors	Years of follow-up	N	Results
Germany	Hand (1986)	6	75	Stable improvement
Spain	Echeburúa et al. (1991)	1	31	Stable improvement
Great Britain	Marks (1971)	4	65	Stable improvement
Great Britain	Munby and Johnston (1980)	7	65	Stable improvement
Great Britain	McPherson et al. (1980)	4	56	Stable improvement
Great Britain	Burns et al. (1986)	8	18	Stable improvement
Great Britain	Lelliott et al. (1987)	5	40	Stable improvement
Holland	Emmelkamp and Kuipers (1979)	4	70	Stable improvement

consumption or the use of tranquilizers, or with specific adaptation problems to feared stimuli. Finally, therapeutic failure can be related to a high level of depression.

Self-Exposure with the Help of Drugs

The limitations of exposure therapy presented, as well as psychological changes present in agoraphobia (especially panic and feeling depressed), have led to the study of the possible improvement of this technique with drugs.

Tricyclical antidepressants, especially imipramine (commercial name: *Tofranil*), and benzodiazepines, especially alprazolam (commercial name: *Trankimazín*), are the most studied drugs in the treatment of agoraphobia. The interest in combined treatment derives from the possible synergistic effect of therapy directed specifically towards behavioral objectives – exposure therapy – and of another – medication – directed towards changes in emotions (dread, depression, panic or both) (Cox, Endler, Lee & Swinson, 1992; Mavissakalian & Michelson, 1983; Telch, 1988).

Self exposure and anti-depressants. Side effects of antidepressants (dryness of the mouth, constipation, difficulty with visual accommodation, urinary retention, sweating, etc.) begin immediately, yet therapeutic effects are only manifest after 2–3 weeks of regular administration and require the maximum therapeutic potency after 12 weeks.

The ways and means of interaction between antidepressants and exposure are still under investigation. Although the results are far from clear, antidepressant drugs have a *global* effect on panic, depression and anxiety; exposure techniques, however, have an *earlier* effect and *specifically* effect phobic avoidance, playing a less significant role in the emotions of the subject (Marks & O'Sullivan, 1992) (Table 3.7).

The prescription of antidepressants (imipramine) in therapeutic doses (range: 75–300 mg/day) in the treatment of agoraphobia is compatible with exposure therapy and tends to make it more effective (Mavissakalian, Michelson & Dealy, 1983; Telch, Agras, Taylor, Roth & Gallen, 1985), even if there are some studies (Marks, Gray, Cohen, Hill, Mawson, Ramm & Stern, 1983) in which imipramine only increases the benefits of self-exposure in cases where the patient is depressed. In fact, impipramine ceases to have an anti-phobic effect (but without losing its anti-depressant effects) if patients are given instructions contrary to exposure (Telch et al., 1985).

Side effects of anti-depressant drugs lead to a larger drop-out of treatment (around 30–35%) compared to exposure therapy (10–15%). Likewise, there is a greater amount of relapses after suspension of medication use, in treatment with imipramine (33%) (Mavissakalian, 1982) and in combined treatment

Table 3.7. Recent Studies with imipramine in the Treatment of Agoraphobia

Authors	Without exposure	Instructions about self-exposure	Exposure guided by a therapist
Sheehan et al. (1980)		+	
Zitrin et al. (1980)			+
Zitrin et al. (1983)		+	
Marks et al. (1983)		−	−
Mavissakalian et al. (1983)	¿+		
Ballenger et al. (1984)		+	
Garakani et al. (1985)			
Telch et al. (1985)	¿+		
Munjack et al. (1985)	¿+		+
Mavissakalian and Michelson (1986)	¿+	+	+
Cox et al. (1988)		+	

+, With a therapeutic effect from imipramine; −, without a therapeutic effect from imipramine; ¿, without placebo control group.

(exposure plus imipramine) (around 25–30%) than in exposure treatment by itself, perhaps because of the attribution of therapeutic effects to the medication.

Self-exposure and tranquilizers. The immediacy of the therapeutic effect and the relative absence of side effects of tranquilizers have led to the development of alprazolam (range: 3–6 mg/day) like a benzodiazepine that has specific anti-panic properties in the treatment of agoraphobia.

In a multicentre study on panic disorder with 526 patients – the majority of them agoraphobic-, alprazolam has proven to be more effective than a placebo in several measures (panic attacks, avoidance behaviours, phobias and anxiety), but this superiority levels out and even decreases in relation to the placebo when medication is interrupted (Ballenger, Burrows & Dupont, 1988).

In the study carried out by Echeburúa et al. (1991, 1993) with 31 agoraphobics, alprazolam had a very weak therapeutic effect, easily decreased over time and which was completely inferior to self-exposure (Table 3.8).

The effect of alprazolam is different to anti-depressants in two ways: (a) it causes a short-term improvement in anxiety and panic in the first phase, and in depression and avoidance in the second; and (b) it tends to produce an almost immediate relapse once medication is stopped (Marks & O'Sullivan, 1992).

Tranquilizers and exposure interact in a negative way. Agoraphobics expose themselves more easily to feared situations under the influence of tranquilizers, but what they experience under the effects of anxiety reducers does not continue when the effects have worn off (Marks & O'Sullivan, 1992). This kind of drug can interfere with long-term memory processes, and finally, can make the habituation process between sessions difficult.

Table 3.8. Recent Studies with Alprazolam in the Treatment of Agoraphobia/Panic Disorder

Authors	N	Comparison between	Results
Ballenger et al. (1988)	52	1. Alprazolam 2. Placebo	1 > 2 post-treatment 1 = 2 follow-ups
Echeburúa et al. (1991)	63	1. Self-exposure 2. Alprazolam 3. Self-exposure + placebo 4. Self-exposure + Alprazolam	1,3 and 4 > 2 post-treatment 1 and 3 > 2 and 4 follow-ups
Klosko et al. (1988)	160	1. Alprazolam 2. Placebo 3. CBT 4. Control group	1 > 4 1 = 3 3 > 2 and 4
Rizley et al. (1986)	44	1. Imipramine 2. Alprazolam	1 = 2 Action of 2 faster than 1

CBT, cognitive behaviour therapy; >, greater than.

Self-exposure and placebo. A recent study (Echeburúa et al., 1991, 1993) demonstrated the positive long-term interaction between self-exposure and placebos. After the follow-up controls of 1, 3, 6 and 12 months, the self-exposure group + placebo clearly tended to get better after a time, whilst the exposure group tended to maintain the therapeutic results.

Even if the placebo can have positive effects in and of itself in the treatment of agoraphobia (Klosko et al., 1988; Mavissakalian, 1987), the positive interaction between self-exposure and the placebo can be related on the one hand, to the efficacy of exposure therapy, and, on the other, the patient attributing the huge therapeutic success to a complete and double treatment (one psychopharmacological and the other psychological) (Echeburúa et al., 1991).

Medication or Exposure?

The attraction of oral medication derives from the facility with which it can be prescribed by the doctor and taken by the patient, with very little dedication on the therapist's part (Table 3.9).

However, relapse after suspension of medication and secondary long-term effects, (which, although unknown, should not be underestimated) do not make it advisable to use medication as the principal means of treatment for agoraphobia. Exposure, on the other hand, is a more effective and durable

Table 3.9. Effects of Medication on Agoraphobia and Panic Disorder (Marks and O'Sullivan, 1989)

*	The effects cover *a wide spectrum* (patholithic), not specifically anti-phobic. Phobic symptoms improve, *but also* depression, panic, anxiety and irritability
*	With anti-depressants, the majority of symptoms get better *at the same time*
*	With alprazolam anxiety and panic improve *before* avoidance and depression

therapeutic alternative, which saves time and energy for the therapist from what can be made of present self-exposure programmes and which has hardly any secondary effects (Basoglu, 1992).

As far as the patient's perception is concerned, psychological treatment (exposure and cognitive) are more acceptable and useful, especially long-term, than those based on the administration of drugs (Norton, Allen & Hilton, 1983). In fact, the rejection rate of pharmacological treatment can oscillate at around 20% of cases (Telch et al., 1985).

From the perspective of combined treatments, tranquilizers and alcohol interact negatively with exposure if they exceed the equivalent of 10 mg a day for diazepam or two glasses of wine daily. Even small amounts below these limits can interfere negatively if consumed over a course of 4 h before treatment. On the contrary, antidepressants are compatible with exposure and can be useful (even before committing to an exposure programme) if the patients are very depressed (Marks & O'Sullivan, 1992).

Likewise in the treatment of agoraphobia , benzodiazepines require large doses over a long period of time (Tyrer, 1989). These are factors which predispose dependency. In fact, after a short treatment of eight weeks, close to one third of patients treated with alprazolam for agoraphobia with panic, developed an abstinence syndrome once medication was stopped (Pecknold, Swinson, Kuch & Lewis, 1988).

Cognitive and Coping Techniques to Improve Exposure Therapy

The presence of cognitive changes in agoraphobia, such as anticipatory anxiety, the negative evaluation of one's own abilities and the inadequate evaluation of somatic symptoms (Table 3.3) has made it advisable to add cognitive techniques to exposure and/or extend exposure to internal stimuli (Hoffart, 1993; Michelson & Marchione, 1991).

Cognitive techniques have more or less consisted of rational-emotive therapy, cognitive restructuring, problem solving and training in self-instructions without there being any clear demonstration of superiority of some techniques over others. The empirical evidence on the effectiveness of these techniques is contradictory (for example, Beck, Sokol, Clark & Berchik, 1992; Chambless & Gillis, 1993).

The most up-to-date cognitive therapeutic focus of Clark (1989) and Barlow (1993) consists, in the first place, of inducing symptoms (palpitations, dizziness etc.) of a panic attack by means of voluntary hyperventilation; and in the second place, in demonstrating mistaken beliefs about the catastrophic results of such symptoms by Socratic methods and other techniques used in cognitive therapy for depression; and in the third place, in encouraging the patient to follow through with planned behaviours to test their previous beliefs along with reinforcing more realistic thought systems related to the symptoms.

The therapeutic investment in the application of these techniques does not correspond with the results obtained (Marks, 1987). We should remember that exposure in and of itself also has an effect on cognitive changes, above and beyond the fact that the improvement of these symptoms is not synchronous with that of motor behaviour.

A more adequate alternative to structured cognitive therapy is to combine exposure with simple cognitive methods, such as giving a clear explanation to the patient of the normality of the panic attacks and showing them some simple methods for controlling anxiety, such as breathing techniques, relaxation and self-instructions (Mathews et al., 1981).

Some recent therapeutic programmes have been specifically geared towards retraining the patient to breathe to cope with the problem of involuntary hyperventilation (Van der Molen, Van den Hout, Merckelbach, Vandieren & Griez, 1989). However, it is still unknown what percentage of anxiety patients encounter hyperventilation problems and how many people, as such, can benefit from breathing training (Table 3.10). It is still premature to systematically recommend deep breathing exercises in exposure therapy for agorapho-

Table 3.10. Breathing re-training as a means of controlling involuntary hyper-ventilation

When one encounters the first signs of involuntary hyperventilation, one should follow these steps:

1. Stop what you are doing and sit down, or, at least, concentrate on the following instructions
2. Hold your breath without taking any deep breaths and count to 10
3. When you get to 10, exhale and keep saying the word "calm down" in a soothing way
4. Breathe in and out in cycles of 6 s (3 for inhalation and 3 for exhalation), saying the word "calm down" each time you exhale. As such, there will be 10 breathing cycles a minute
5. At the end of each minute (after 10 breathing cycles), hold your breath again for 10 s. As you continue, resume the six-second breathing cycles
6. Continue breathing in this way until all symptoms of involuntary hyperventilation have disappeared

bics. The obtained results are still not conclusive (Marks, 1987; Rijken, Kraai-maat, De Ruiter & Garssen, 1992).

Biofeedback techniques (at least those concerned with heart rate and skin conduction) do not increase the specific value of exposure (Marks, 1987). However, investigation into applied biofeedback techniques applied to agoraphobia has come up with interesting ways – in the first place, because the improvement of subjective feelings tends to lag behind that of improvement of avoidance and heart rate, and, in the second place, because relapse is more probable if the patient no longer avoids phobic situations, but still shows a high level of autonomic arousal (Barlow & Mavissakalian, 1981). In this case, the application of biofeedback techniques can be of interest.

Many of the therapeutic programmes presently in use (Bados, 1993; Barlow, 1993; Botella, 1991; Clark, 1989) use multiple cognitive and psychophysi-ological strategies to improve the results of exposure, but the specific benefits of each one is not known, neither is there a clear justification from the perspective of therapeutic efficiency (costs and benefits). In short, the effectiveness of the many confrontational strategies- breathing training, relaxation, positive self- reinforcement, etc.- in the strengthening of exposure is not at all well-researched and probably depends on different individuals. That is to say, hyperventilatory agoraphobics can benefit from breathing and relaxation techniques (Öst, 1988); on the contrary, agoraphobics suffering from an intense anticipatory anxiety can react positively to training in self-instructions. Yet even these affirmations require further investigation.

Conclusions

From a psychiatric perspective, panic has been conceptualized as a reaction to a chemical imbalance. According to this focus, medication must be the first line in the treatment of agoraphobia/panic disorder and exposure should be, in any case, a mere complement of the drugs (Sheehan, Coleman & Greens-blatt, 1984). On the contrary, it can be concluded from the present investigation that exposure modifies physiological changes (with changes even at a synaptic level), as well as avoidance and cognitive alterations, and that medication is only a secondary option in some cases (Echeburúa et al., 1993; Marks & O'Sullivan, 1992).

Side effects, especially from anti-depressants, and relapses after the drop-out of medication make it advisable to use exposure therapy as a first line of therapeutic treatment. Tranquilizers should not be used. Only in cases where there is a lack of adequate therapeutic response does it seem advisable to use antidepressants as a complement to exposure, especially if the patient is in a depressed state.

Exposure treatment is, in conclusion, a powerful therapy in the control of agoraphobia, but it still presents unresolved problems. In the first place, rejection or drop-out of therapy, although lower than that of pharmacological therapies, can affect up to 25% of patients. In the second place, elimination of avoidance behaviours allows for a substantial improvement in the patient, but it does not always lead to a total clinical improvement in all patients. And, in the third place, the tendency to experience depression continues in phobic patients with a previous history of depression, even though exposure therapy has been successful.

The predictable power of variables implied in exposure therapy varies greatly from one study to another. However, in general, they are good indicators of therapeutic success in clearly showing avoidance behaviours, feeling emotionally stable, following therapeutic prescriptions and not undergoing exposure therapy when under the effect of alcohol or tranquilizers. On the contrary, the age or intensity of the problem do not constitute a reliable predictor of the therapeutic result. During therapy, the best indicator of therapeutic success is progress during the first sessions. Patients who initially obtain large therapeutic benefits are those who are more likely to maintain it on a long-term basis and those who are less likely to experience bouts of depression (Echeburúa et al., 1991, 1993; Lelliott, Marks, Monteiro & Tsakiris, 1987).

Likewise, it is difficult to place a value on the usefulness of cognitive techniques in relation to exposure, since all them include components of exposure. Thus, in Mark's (1987) study cognitive techniques are, on the one hand, inferior to exposure and on the other, have not brought any added component to exposure in and of itself in the case of cognitive-behavioural therapy. Their value, however, cannot be underestimated. In the early stages of treatment, they can act as motivational strategies for treatment; during therapy, as a way of observing therapeutic prescriptions and as preparatory cognitive exercises for the therapeutic method of exposure (Salkovskis & Warwick, 1985); and finally, as a way of increasing the expectancy of self-effectiveness and, in the last place, as a way of preventing relapses (Butler, 1989).

Finally, there are still various technical problems of great therapeutic significance in exposure programmes which have not been resolved, such as the role of covert and open avoidance, the way of obtaining faster habituation and wider generalization, the determination of the optimum amount of exposure and its duration, as well as the possibility of increasing the potency of exposure with the addition of cognitive techniques and/or exposure to internal stimuli which are precipitators of anxiety (cognitive and physiological).

References

Agras, S., Chapin, H. N., & Oliveau, D.C. (1972). The natural history of phobia: Course and prognosis. *Archives of General Psychiatry, 26,* 315–317.

APA (1994). *Diagnostic and statistical manual of mental disorders*, 4th edition. Washington, DC: American Psychiatric Association.

Bados, A. (1993). Tratamiento en grupo de la agorafobia. In D. Macià, F.X. Méndez & J. Olivares (Eds.). *Intervención psicológica: programas aplicados de tratamiento*. Madrid. Pirámide.

Ballenger, J. C., Burrows, G. D., & Dupont, R. L. (1988). Alprazolam in panic disorder and agoraphobia: I. Efficacy in short-term treatment. *Archives of General Psychiatry, 45*, 413–422.

Ballenger, J. C., Peterson, G. A., Laraia, M., & Hucek, A. (1984). A study of plasma catecholamines in agoraphobia and the relationship of serum tricyclic levels to treatment response. In J. C. Ballenger (Ed.), *Biological aspects of agoraphobia*. Washington, DC: American Psychiatric Association.

Barlow, D. H. (1993). Avances en los trastornos por ansiedad. *Psicología Conductual, 1*, 291–300.

Barlow, D. H., & Mavissakalian, M. (1981). Directions in the assessment and treatment of phobia: The next decade. In M. Mavissakalian & D. H. Barlow (Eds.), *Phobia: Psychological and pharmacological treatment*. New York: Guilford Press.

Basoglu, M. (1992). Pharmacological and behavioural treatment of panic disorder. *Psychotherapy and Psychsomatics, 58*, 57–59.

Beck, A. T., Sokol, L., Clark, D. A., & Berchik, R. (1992). A crossover study of focused cognitive therapy for panic disorder. *American Journal of Psychiatry, 149*, 778–783.

Borda, M., & Echeburúa, E. (1991). La autoexposición como tratamiento psicológico en un caso de agorafobia. *Análisis y Modificación de Conducta, 17*, 993–1012.

Botella, C. (1991). Tratamiento psicológico del trastorno de pánico: adaptación del paquete cognitivo-comportamental de Clark. *Análisis y Modificación de Conducta, 17*, 871–894.

Burns, L. E., Thorpe, G. L., Cavallaro, A., & Gosling, J. (1986). Agoraphobia 8 years after behavioral treatment. *Behavior Therapy, 17*, 580–591. .

Butler, G. (1989). Phobic disorders. In K. Hawton, P.M. Salkovskis, J. Kirk & D.M. Clark (Eds.), *Cognitive behaviour therapy for psychiatric problems: A practical guide*. Oxford: Oxford University Press.

Chambless, D. L., & Goldstein, A. J. (1983). *Agoraphobia: Multiple perspectives on theory and treatment*. New York. Wiley.

Chambless, D. L., & Gillis, M. M. (1993). Cognitive therapy of anxiety disorders. *Journal of Consulting and Clinical Psychology, 61*, 248–260.

Chambless, D. L., Caputo, G. C., Bright, P., & Gallagher, R. (1984). Assessment of fear of fear in agoraphobics: the body sensations questionnaire and the agoraphobic cognitions questionnaire. *Journal of Consulting and Clinical Psychology, 52*, 1090–1097.

Chambless, D. L., Caputo, G. C., Jasin, S. E., Gracel, E. J., & Williams, C. (1985). The movility inventory for agoraphobia. *Behaviour Research and Therapy, 23*, 35–44.

Clark, D. M. (1989). Anxiety states. Panic and generalized anxiety. In K. Hawton, P. M. Salkovskis, J. Kirk & D. M. Clark (Eds.), *Cognitive behaviour therapy for psychiatric problems. A practical guide*. Oxford. Oxford Medical Publications. .

Cohen, S., Monteiro, W., & Marks, I. M. (1984). Two-year follow-up of agoraphobics after exposure and imipramine. *British Journal of Psychiatry, 144*, 276–281.

Cox, B. J., Endler, N. S., Lee, P. S., & Swinson, R. P. (1992). A meta-analysis of treatments for panic disorder with agoraphobia: Imipramine, alprazolam, and in vivo exposure. *Journal of Behavior Therapy and Experimental Psychiatry, 23*, 175–182.

Cox, D. J., Ballenger, J. C., Laraia, M., & Hobbs, W. R. (1988). Different rates of improvement of different symptoms in combined pharmacological and behavioral treatment of agoraphobia. *Journal of Behavior Therapy and Experimental Psychiatry, 19*, 119–126.

Echeburúa, E. (1996). Evaluación psicológica de los trastornos de ansiedad. In G. Buela-Casal, V.E. Caballo & J. C. Sierra (Eds.). *Manual de evaluación en psicología clínica y de la salud*. Madrid: Siglo XXI.

Echeburúa, E., & Corral, P. (1991). Eficacia terapéutica de los psicofármacos y de la exposición en el tratamiento de la agorafobia/trastorno de pánico. *Clínica y Salud, 2,* 227–241.

Echeburúa, E., & Corral, P. (1993). Técnicas de exposición: variantes y aplicaciones. In F. J. Labrador, J. A. Cruzado & M. Muñoz (Eds.), *Manual práctico de modificación y terapia de conducta*. Madrid: Pirámide.

Echeburúa, E., & Corral, P. (1995). Agorafobia. In V. E. Caballo, G. Buela-Casal & J. A. Carrobles (Eds.), *Manual de psicopatología y trastornos psiquiátricos*, Vol. 1. Madrid: Siglo XXI.

Echeburúa, E., Corral, P., García, E., & Borda, M. (1991). La autoexposición y las benzodiazepinas en el tratamiento de la agorafobia sin historia de trastorno de pánico. *Análisis y Modificación de Conducta, 17,* 969–991.

Echeburúa, E., Corral, P., García, E., Páez, D., & Borda, M. (1992). Un nuevo inventario de agorafobia (IA). *Análisis y Modificación de Conducta, 18,* 101–123.

Echeburúa, E., Corral, P., García, E., & Borda, M. (1993). Interactions between self-exposure and alprazolam in the treatment of agoraphobia without current panic: an exploratory study. *Behavioural and Cognitive Psychotherapy, 21,* 219–238.

Emmelkamp, P. M., & Kuipers, A. C. (1979). Agoraphobia: A follow-up study 4 years after treatment. *British Journal of Psychiatry, 134,* 352–355. .

Emmelkamp, P. M. G., & Van den Hout, A. (1983). Failure in treating agoraphobia. In E. B. Foa & P. M. G. Emmelkamp (Eds.), *Failures in behavior therapy.* New York: Wiley.

Emmelkamp, P.M.G., Van Dyck, R., Bitter, M., & Heins, R. (1992). Spouse-aided therapy with agoraphobics. *British Journal of Psychiatry, 160,* 51–56.

Garakani, H., Zitrin, C. M., & Klein, D. F. (1985). Treatment of panic disorder with imipramine alone. *American Journal of Psychiatry, 141,* 446–448.

Hand, I. (1986). Exposure in-vivo with panic management for agoraphobia: Treatment rationale and long-term outcome. In I. Hand & H. U. Wittchen (Eds.), *Panic and phobias.* Berlin: Springer-Verlag.

Hoffart, A. (1993). Cognitive treatments of agoraphobia: A critical evaluation of theoretical basis and outcome evidence. *Journal of Anxiety Disorders, 7,* 75–91.

Klosko, J. S., Barlow, D. H., Tassinari, R. B., & Cerny, J. A. (1988). Alprazolam versus cognitive behaviour therapy for panic disorder: A preliminary report. In I. Hand & H. U. Wittchen (Eds.), *Panic and phobias.* New York: Springler-Verlag.

Lelliott, P. T., Marks, I. M., Monteiro, W. O., Tsakiris, F., & Noshirvani, H. (1987). Agoraphobics 5 years after imipramine and exposure. Outcome and predictors. *Journal of Nervous and Mental Disease, 175,* 599–605.

Marks, I. M. (1971). Phobic disorders: four years after treatment. *British Journal of Psychiatry, 118,* 683–688.

Marks, I. M. (1978). *Living with fear.* New York: McGraw-Hill.

Marks, I. M. (1987). *Fears, phobias, and rituals.* New York: Oxford University (translation, Martínez Roca, 2 vols., 1991).

Marks, I. M. (1992). Tratamiento de exposición en la agorafobia y el pánico. In E. Echeburúa (Ed.), *Avances en el tratamiento psicológico de los trastornos de ansiedad.* Madrid: Pirámide. .

Marks, I. M., & Mathews, A. M. (1979). Brief standard self-rating for phobic patients. *Behaviour Research and Therapy, 17,* 263–267.

Marks, I. M., & O'Sullivan, G. (1992). Psicofármacos y tratamientos psicológicos en la agorafobia/pánico y en los trastornos obsesivo-compulsivos. In E. Echeburúa (Ed.), *Avances en el tratamiento psicológico de los trastornos de ansiedad*. Madrid: Pirámide.

Marks, I. M., Gray, S., Cohen, D., Hill, R., Mawson, D., Ramm, E., & Stern, R.S. (1983). Imipramine and brief therapist-aided in agoraphobics having self-exposure homework. *Archives of General Psychiatry, 40,* 153–162.

Mathews, A. M., Gelder, M. G., & Johnston, D. W. (1981). *Agoraphobia. Nature and treatment.* New York: Guilford Press.

Mavissakalian, M. (1982). Pharmacological treatment of anxiety disorders. *Journal of Clinical Psychiatry, 43,* 487–491.

Mavissakalian, M. (1987). The placebo effect in agoraphobia. *Journal of Nervous and Mental Disease, 175,* 95–99.

Mavissakalian, M., & Michelson, L. (1983). Self-directed in vivo exposure practice in behavioral and pharmacological treatments of agoraphobia. *Behavior Therapy, 14,* 506–519.

Mavissakalian, M., & Michelson, L. (1986). Two-year follow-up of exposure and imipramine treatment of agoraphobia. *American Journal of Psychiatry, 143,* 1106–1112. .

Mavissakalian, M., Michelson, L., & Dealy, R. S. (1983). Pharmacological treatment of agoraphobia: imipramine versus imipramine with programmed practice. *British Journal of Psychiatry, 143,* 348–355.

McPherson, F. M., Brougham, L., & McLaren, S. (1980). Maintenance of improvement in agoraphobic patients treated by behavioural methods -a four-year follow-up. *Behaviour Research and Therapy, 18,* 150–152.

Michelson, L. (1988). Cognitive, behavioral, and psychophysiological treatments and correlates of panic. In S. Rachman & J. D. Maser (Eds.), *Panic: Psychological perspectives.* New York: Lawrence Erlbaum.

Michelson, L., & Marchione, K. (1991). Behavioral, cognitive and pharmacological treatments of panic disorder with agoraphobia. Critique and synthesis. *Journal of Consulting and Clinical Psychology, 59,* 100–114. .

Michelson, L., Mavissakalian, M., & Marchione, K. (1988). Cognitive, behavioral and psychophysiological treatments of agoraphobia: A comparative outcome investigation. *Behavior Therapy, 19,* 97–120.

Munby, M., & Johnston, D. W. (1980). Agoraphobia: The long-term follow-up of behavioural treatment. *Bristish Journal of Psychiatry, 137,* 418–427.

Munjack, D. J., Rebal, R., & Shaner, R. (1985). Imipramine versus propanolol for the treatment of panic attacks: A pilot study. *Comprehensive Psychiatry, 26,* 80–89.

Norton, G. R., Allen, G. E., & Hilton, J. (1983). The social validity of treatments for agoraphobia. *Behaviour Research and Therapy, 21,* 393–399. .

Öst, L. G. (1988). Applied relaxation versus progressive relaxation in the treatment of panic disorder. *Behaviour Research and Therapy, 26,* 13–22.

Öst, L. G. (1989). One-session treatment for specific phobias. *Behaviour Research and Therapy, 21,* 393–399.

Öst, L. G., Westling, B. E., & Hellstrom, K. (1993). Applied relaxation, exposure in vivo and cognitive methods in the treatment of panic disorder with agoraphobia. *Behaviour Research and Therapy, 31,* 383–394.

Pecknold, J. C., Swinson, R. P., Kuch, K., & Lewis, L. P. (1988). Alprazolam in panic disorder and agoraphobia: results from a multicenter trial: III. Discontinuation effects. *Archives of General Psychiatry, 45,* 429–436.

Rijken, H., Kraaimaat, F., De Ruiter, C., & Garssen, B. (1992). A follow-up study on short-term treatment of agoraphobia. *Behaviour Research and Therapy, 30,* 63–66.

Rizley, R., Kahn, R. J., McNair, D. M., & Frankentheler, L. M. (1986). A comparison of alprazolam and imipramine in the treatment of agoraphobia and panic disorder. *Psychopharmacological Bulletin, 22,* 167–172. .

Salkovskis, P. M., & Warwick, H. M. C. (1985). Cognitive therapy of obsessive-compulsive disorder. Treating treatment failures. *Behavioral Psychotherapy, 13,* 243–255.

Sheehan, D. V., Ballenger, J., & Jacobsen, G. (1980). Treatment of endogenous anxiety. *Archives of General Psychiatry, 37,* 51–59.

Sheehan, D. V., Coleman, J. H., & Greensblatt, D. J. (1984). Some biochemical correlates of panic attacks with agoraphobia and their response to a new treatment. *Journal of Clinical Psychopharmacology, 4,* 66–75.

Telch, M. J. (1988). Combined pharmacological and psychological treatment. In C.G. Last & M. Hersen (Eds.), *Handbook of anxiety disorders.* New York: Pergamon Press.

Telch, M. J., Agras, W. S., Taylor, C. B., Roth, W. T., & Gallen, C. C. (1985). Combined pharmacological and behavioral treatment for agoraphobia. *Behaviour Research and Therapy, 23,* 325–335.

Turner, S. M., Beidel, D. C., Dancu, C. V., & Stanley, M. A. (1989). An empirically derived inventory to measure social fears and anxiety: the Social Phobia and Anxiety Inventory. *Psychological Assessment, 1,* 35–40.

Tyrer, P. (1989). *Classification of neurosis.* Chichester: Wiley (traducción, Díaz de Santos, 1992).

Van der Molen, G. M., Van den Hout, M. A., Merckelbach, H., Vandieren, A. C., & Griez, E. (1989). The effect of hypocapnia on extinction of conditioned fear responses. *Behaviour Research and Therapy, 27,* 71–77.

Weissman, M. M. (1985). The epidemiology of anxiety disorders: Rates, risks and familial patterns. In H. Tuma & J. Maser (Eds.). *Anxiety and anxiety-related disorders.* Hillsdale, NJ: Lawrence Erlbaum.

Zitrin, C. M., Klein, D. F., & Woerner, M. G. (1980). Treatment of agoraphobia with group exposure in vivo and imipramine. *Archives of General Psychiatry, 37,* 63–72.

Zitrin, C. M., Klein, D. F., Woerner, M. G., & Ross, D. (1983). Treatment of phobias: I. Comparison of imipramine hydrochloride and placebo. *Archives of General Psychiatry, 40,* 125–138.

Further Reading

Agras, S. (1989). *Pánico. Cómo superar los miedos, las fobias y la ansiedad.* Barcelona: Labor (Original, 1985).

Bados, A. (1993). Tratamiento en grupo de la agorafobia. In D. Macià, F.X. Méndez., & J. Olivares (Eds.). *Intervención psicológica: Programas aplicados de tratamiento.* Madrid: Pirámide.

Bados, A. (1995). *Agorafobia* (2 Vols.). Barcelona: Paidós.

Echeburúa, E., & Corral, P. (1992). *La agorafobia. Nuevas perspectivas de evaluación y tratamiento.* Valencia: Promolibro.

Marks, I. M. (1991). *Miedos, fobias y rituales* (2 Vols.). Barcelona: Martínez Roca (Original, 1987).

Mathews, A. M., Gelder, M., & Johnston, D. W. (1985). *Agorafobia. Naturaleza y tratamiento.* Barcelona: Fontanella (Original, 1981).

Peurifoy, R. Z. (1993). *Venza sus temores. Ansiedad, fobias y pánico.* Barcelona: Robinbook (Original, 1992).

Appendix 1. Diary of exposure tasks (Echeburúa and Corral, 1991)

Date	Time		Exposure tasks	Maximum anxiety (0–10)		Alone or with co-therapist	Coping strategies
	Begin	End		Before	After		
			2nd behaviour-objective: To go with friends to the cinema or a play on the weekend.				
19/11	19:30	21:30	* To go with my sister one Monday afternoon to watch a film and to sit right at the back at the end of the row.	7	3	Co-therapist	Positive self-instructions: "I'm going to enjoy this film; my sister is right next to me."
23/11	22:30	00:30	* To go with my sister to the cinema with my sister on a Friday night and sit in the centre at the end of the row. My sister will sit somewhere else nearby.	8.5	4	Co-therapist	Positive self-instructions: "I am capable of doing what others do; I'm no different"
26/11	19:30	21:30	* To go alone to the cinema in the afternoon and sit in the centre at the end of the row.	9	4.5	Alone	Deep breaths. Positive Self-instructions: "I'm going to breathe well; that way I feel capable."

Appendix 2. Self-exposure therapy in Agoraphobia (Echeburúa et al., 1991)

1. General Aspects
Requirements for self-exposure
* Manuals (for patient and therapist)
* Diary of exposure tasks
* Presence of a co-therapist
* Number of sessions with a co-therapist: 7

Structure of the Self-Exposure Programme
* Active Participation: gradual and continuous
* Frequency: 6 days/week
* Duration: 2 h/day
* Daily diary of exposure tasks.

Therapist's Function
* To explain the exposure programme
* To explain precisely what needs to be done.
* To actively involve the patient.
* To not speak about the problem but the programme.
* Principal objective: to direct the patient towards behaviour objectives by means of suitable tasks.

Patient's Function
* To strictly follow the therapists rules.
* To expose themselves to the necessary tasks (which they now avoid) in each one of the behaviour objectives.
* Reinforce to themselves that they are capable of confronting such tasks and that nothing bad happens to them as a result.

Co-Therapist's Function
* To serve as a support model, as well as giving positive reinforcement to the patient to try and eliminate avoidance behaviour.
* To accompany the patient according to the schedule:
  – 1st week :   100% of the task time
  – 2nd week :   80% of the task time
  – 3rd week :   60% of the task time
  – 4th week :   40% of the task time
  – 5th week :   20% of the task time
  – 6th week :   0% of the task time
  To be available the rest of the time.

2. Content of the Sessions With the Therapist
1st Session (45 min)
* Introduce the hypothesis of the problem
* Explain the active role of the patient and the therapeutic necessity of breaking avoidance behaviours.
* Describe self-exposure according to the behavioural objectives.

* Mention self-help manuals.
* Show the diary and make reference to the importance of filling it out
* Give the patient instructions about how to control panic.
* Explain in detail the role of the therapist.
* Stress the importance of the role of the co-therapist as a model.
* Point out the suitable use of reinforcement and self-reinforcement
* Prepare the tasks to be carried out between the first and second session. As a minimum, two objectives should be worked on per week.
* Make a calendar of the sessions.

2nd session (45 min)
* Review the patient's diary entries.
* Reinforce the patient and co-therapist for the tasks that have been carried out.
* Deal with the difficulties that have emerged during exposure therapy.
* Work on questions which have been raised by the patient and co-therapist about the self-help manual.
* Prepare the tasks for the following week.

3rd session (30 min)
* Review the patient's diary entries.
* Reinforce the patient and co-therapist for the tasks that have been carried out.
* Deal with the difficulties that have emerged during exposure therapy
* Check how the patient is dealing with anxiety.
* Analyse adaptive behaviours (social, free time etc.)
* Prepare the tasks for the following week.

4th session (30 min)
* Review the patient's diary entries.
* Reinforce the patient and co-therapist for the tasks that have been carried out.
* Deal with the difficulties that have emerged during exposure therapy.
* Explain the concept of generalization: incorporation of alternative behaviours, spontaneous tasks, etc.
* Prepare the tasks for the following week.

5th session (30 min)
* Review the patient's diary entries.
* Reinforce the patient and co-therapist for the tasks that have been carried out.
* Deal with the difficulties that have emerged during exposure therapy
* Discuss long-term plans: a) continued practice; b) establishment of new objectives; c) increase in social activities; d) anticipation of relapses; and e) re-reading the self-help manuals to help solve problems.
* Prepare the tasks for the following week.

6th session (30 min)
* Review the patient's diary entries.
* Reinforce the patient and co-therapist for the tasks that have been carried out.
* Deal with the difficulties that have emerged during exposure therapy
* Stimulate the patient and the pair to establish objectives that go beyond the daily routine (shopping in a department store, long-distance journeys and holidays, etc.)
* Explain the prevention of relapse: early-warning signs of relapse, immediate strategies of

intervention, reconditioning sessions, etc.
* Prepare the tasks for the following week.

7th session (45 min)
* Review the patient's diary entries.
* Reinforce the patient and co-therapist for the tasks that have been carried out.
* Deal with the difficulties that have emerged during exposure therapy
* Carry out a global assessment of the tasks that have been carried out.
* Review the programme's value in relation with other behaviour objectives: confidence, security, self-control, etc.
* Record the re-reading of the manual.
* Instill in the patient that continuing these practices is key for future success.
* Prepare a follow-up programme.
* Thank the patient and co-therapist for their participation and let them know you are available should any setback occur in the future.

4

Cognitive-Behavioral Treatment of Panic Disorders

MICHELLE G. CRASKE and MICHAEL R. LEWIN

University of California at Los Angeles, USA

Introduction

Significant advances have been made in recent years with respect to cognitive-behavioral treatment of panic disorders (with and without agoraphobia). As reviewed in this and other recent chapters (e.g., Craske & Barlow, 1993), the results from these newly developed treatments are very promising. Cognitive-behavioral approaches are considered among treatments of choice for individuals afflicted with panic disorder (NIMN, 1993). These developments are particularly important given the frequency with which panic disorder is experienced (3.5% of the general population; Kessler, McGonagle, Zhao, Nelson, Hughes, Eshleman, Wittchen & Kendler, 1994), and the seriousness of the social and personal repercussions, including substance abuse, depression, and suicidal tendencies (e.g., Markowitz, Weissman, Ouellette, Lish & Klerman, 1989). Advances in cognitive-behavioral treatment approaches were prompted largely by advances in conceptualizations of panic disorder. These conceptual developments recognize the role of specific internal triggering cues and cognitive attributional factors for panic. An update of cognitive-behavioral interventions for panic disorder, and their efficacy, is provided in this chapter. The treatment for agoraphobia is not covered in detail. Theoretical bases for these treatment procedures are also presented.

According to DSM-IV (APA, 1994), panic disorder primarily involves the experience of discrete periods of abrupt intense fear or discomfort (i.e., panic).

The panic is characterized by a cluster of physical and cognitive symptoms, occurs unexpectedly (on at least some occasions) and recurrently, and is distinct from gradually building anxious arousal and from phobic reactions to clearly discernible, circumscribed stimuli. Also, pervasive apprehension about panic attacks develops in the form of persistent worry about future attacks, worry about the perceived physical, social or mental consequences of attacks, or major changes in behavior in response to attacks.

The ubiquity of panic attacks across the anxiety disorders has been recognized in DSM-IV (APA, 1994); a panic attack is described as an emotional state that may be associated with any anxiety disorder. Specifically, panic attacks are differentiated into three types: (1) unexpected (uncued) panic attacks, where no situational cue is identified, (2) situationally bound (cued) panic attacks, where a specific situational cue is invariably identified, or (3) situationally predisposed panic attacks, where a specific situational cue is likely, however not invariably identified as a precursor to the panic attack. Although no absolute diagnostic rules exist, unexpected panic attacks are most often associated with panic disorder, situationally bound panic attacks are most often associated with more circumscribed phobic disorders (e.g., specific and social phobias), and situationally predisposed panic attacks occur most often in panic disorder with agoraphobia (especially later in the course of the disorder), but can occur in more circumscibed phobias also. Delineation of panic attacks in this way is intended to aid the differential diagnosis of panic disorder from other anxiety disorders where panic attacks may occur but where the focus of apprehension is not upon the panic attack itself (e.g., social phobias, specific phobias, obsessive-compulsive disorder).

Agoraphobia is described separately from panic disorder in the DSM-IV to highlight the occurrence of agoraphobic avoidance/distress in individuals with or without a history of panic disorder. Nevertheless, panic has been found to precede agoraphobia in the majority of persons seeking treatment (e.g., Craske, Miller, Rotunda & Barlow, 1990).

Rarely does the diagnosis of panic disorder/agoraphobia occur in isolation. Commonly co-occurring Axis I conditions include simple (specific) phobia, social phobia, generalized anxiety disorder, substance abuse, major depressive disorder and dysthymia (Sanderson, DiNardo, Rapee & Barlow, 1990; Goisman, Warshaw, Peterson, Rogers, Cuneo, Hunt, Tomlin-Albanese, Kazim, Gollan, Epstein-Kaye, Reich & Keller, 1994). Several independent investigations have shown that from 25 to 60% of persons with panic disorder with/without agoraphobia meet criteria for a personality disorder, particularly avoidant and dependent personality disorders (Chambless & Renneberg, 1988; Mavissakalian & Hamman, 1986; Reich, Noyes & Troughton, 1987). However, the nature of the relationship between panic disorders and personality disorders remains unclear. For example, comorbidity rates are highly dependent on the method used to establish Axis II diagnosis (Chambless

& Renneberg, 1988) as well as the co-occurrence of depressed mood (Alnaes & Torgersen, 1990), and some personality "disorders" remit with successful treatment of panic and agoraphobia (Mavissakalian & Hamman, 1987; Noyes, Reich, Suelzer & Christiansen, 1991).

Theoretical and Emipirical Foundations of Treatment

Recently, several highly convergent conceptualizations of panic have been proposed, differing in their points of emphasis only. For example, some emphasize cognitive misappraisal (Beck, 1988; Clark, Salkovskis, Gelder, Koehler, Martin, Anastasiades, Hackmann, Middleton & Jeavons, 1988), some emphasize associative learning and emotional processing (Barlow, 1988; Wolpe & Rowan, 1988), and others emphasize physiological sensitivities (Ehlers & Margraf, 1989). In this section, an overview of the recent conceptualizations is provided, since these form the theoretical bases for the newer cognitive-behavioral treatments for panic disorder.

The initial panic attack has been conceptualized by Barlow (1988) as a misfiring of the "fear system," under stressful life circumstances, in physiologically vulnerable individuals. (A physiological vulnerability factor accounts for the strong familial concordance for panic disorder (Crowe, Noyes, Pauls & Slyman, 1983; Moran & Andrews, 1985; Torgersen, 1983)). However, an isolated panic attack does not necessarily lead to the development of panic disorder, as evidenced by the discrepancy between prevalence estimates for an unexpected panic attack in the past 12 months (ranging from 10 to 12%: e.g., Telch, Lucas & Nelson, 1989) and for panic disorder with/without agoraphobia in the past 12 months (ranging from 2 to 3%: Kessler et al., 1994).

Barlow and others (e.g., Clark et al., 1988) speculate that a psychological vulnerability accounts for the development of anxious apprehension about the recurrence of panic, which in turn, leads to the development of panic disorder. The psychological vulnerability is conceptualized as a set of danger-laden beliefs about the symptoms of panic (i.e., "I am losing control") and about the meaning of panic attacks in relation to the individual's conceptualization of themselves and their world (i.e., "Events are proceeding uncontrollably and unpredictably; I am too weak to control my emotions"). These beliefs are presumed to accrue from various life experiences, including vicarious and informational transmission from significant others about physical and mental dangers associated with certain bodily symptoms (Ehlers, 1993), as well as life stressors proximal to the first panic attack. In support, Maller & Reiss (1992) found that 75% of individuals who experienced panic attacks for the first time between 1984 and 1987 scored on the Anxiety Sensitivity Index (a measure of misappraisals of bodily sensations as being harmful) in 1984. Also, in a one-year follow-up study, anxiety sensitivity predicted maintenance of panic disorder in an untreated panic disorder group, and panic attacks in a non-clinical panic group (Ehlers, 1995). Finally, anxiety sensitivity predicted the development panic attacks 5 weeks after an acute military stressor (Schmidt, Lerew & Jackson, 1997).

Given the traumatic nature of the initial panic(s), it is proposed (Barlow, 1988) that classically conditioned fearful associations develop with various aspects of the context in which the panic occurred, including the situational environs and the symptoms of arousal. Learned fearfulness of arousal cues is akin to Razran's (1961) description of "interoceptive conditioning": a form of conditioning that is relatively resistant to extinction and is non-conscious. That is, interoceptive conditioned fear responses are not dependent on conscious awareness of triggering cues. According to this model, panics may seem to be uncued, or to occur from out of the blue, because they are triggered by subtle alterations in physical state, of which the individual is not fully aware.

Furthermore, cognitive misappraisals of danger (such as fears of dying or losing control) are likely to increase fearful arousal, which, in turn, intensifies the arousal cues that are feared. Consequently, a vicious cycle of "fear of fear" (or fear of sensations) is sustained, until the physiological arousal system is exhausted or until disconfirming evidence is obtained (Clark et al., 1988).

Hence, panic disorder is viewed essentially as a phobia of internal bodily cues. However, in contrast to external feared stimuli, internal feared cues are generally less predictable, and less escapable, leading to more intense fear, more abrupt fear, less predictable fear, and greater anticipatory anxiety about the recurrence of fear (Craske, 1991; Craske, Glover & DeCola, 1995). Moreover, as Barlow (1988) proposes, anxious anticipation of panic may increase the likelihood of its occurrence, since anxious arousal is likely to increase symptoms that have become conditioned cues for panic, and/or increase the degree of attentional vigilance for such cues. In this manner, a maintaining cycle is established between anxious apprehension about panic and panic itself.

The empirical evidence in support of this conceptualization continues to grow. For example, persons who panic have stronger beliefs and fears of physical or mental harm arising from specific bodily sensations associated with panic attacks (Chambless, Caputo, Bright & Gallagher, 1984; Clark et al., 1988; Holt & Andrews, 1989; McNally & Lorenz, 1987; van den Hout, van der Molen, Griez & Lousberg, 1987). Also, there is partial evidence for heightened awareness of, or ability to detect, bodily sensations of arousal (Antony, Brown, Craske, Barlow, Mitchell & Meadows, 1995; Ehlers, Brever, Dohn & Fiegenbaum, 1995; Ehlers & Margraf, 1989; van den Hout, Albus, Pols, Griez, Zahn, Breier & Uhde, 1988), presumably due to an attentional vigilance mechanism. In addition, persons with panic disorder are fearful of procedures that elicit bodily sensations similar to the ones experienced during panic attacks, including benign cardiovascular, respiratory, and audiovestibular exercises (Jacob, Furman, Clark & Durrant, 1992; Zarate, Rapee, Craske &

Barlow, 1988). Further support derives from studies showing that correction of danger-misappraisals about certain bodily sensations seems to lessen fearfulness. For example, considerably less panic is reported when subjects perceive that hyperventilation and carbon dioxide inhalations (which produce strong panic-like physical symptoms) are safe and controllable (Rapee, Mattick & Murrell, 1986; Sanderson, Rapee & Barlow, 1989) or when accompanied by a safe person (Carter, Hollon, Carson & Shelton, 1995), or after cognitive behavioral treatment that reduces fears of bodily sensations (Schmidt, Trakowski & Staab, 1997). The role of cognitive appraisal may extend to nocturnal panics, or panic attacks that occur from a state of deep sleep (Craske & Freed, 1995; Craske & Rowe, 1997).

Individuals with agoraphobia who seek treatment usually report a history of panic that preceded development of avoidance (Craske et al., 1990; Noyes et al., 1986; Pollard, Bronson & Kenney, 1989; Swinson, 1986; Thyer, Himle, Curtis, Cameron & Nesse, 1985). However, not all persons who panic develop agoraphobic avoidance, and the extent of avoidance that does emerge is highly variable. The reasons for these individual differences are not clear (see Craske & Barlow, 1988, for a review). Although more agoraphobic individuals tend to have experienced panic over longer durations, the relationship with chronicity is relatively weak, since a significant proportion panic for many years without developing an agoraphobic style. Nor is agoraphobic avoidance related to age of onset, proportions of different types of attacks (i.e., cued/uncued, and expected/unexpected), panic frequency, fearfulness of bodily sensations, or degree of apprehension about panicking overall (Adler, Craske, Kirschenbaum & Barlow, 1989; Craske & Barlow, 1988). Data regarding intensity of panic attack symptoms is also contradictory (e.g., De Jong & Bouman, 1995 versus Cox, Endler & Swinson, 1995). Although agoraphobic individuals may be more concerned with the social consequences of panicking (e.g., De Jong & Bouman, 1995; Amering et al., 1997).

On the other hand, females increasingly predominate the sample as degree of agoraphobic avoidance becomes more severe (Reich et al., 1987; Thyer et al., 1985). Possibly, sex-role behaviors and expectations influence the degree to which apprehension about panic leads to agoraphobic avoidance (Barlow, 1988). Furthermore, it is speculated that individual styles of coping with aversive or stressful situations in general (i.e., approach versus withdrawal) may moderate the degree to which panic apprehension leads to agoraphobic avoidance (Craske & Barlow, 1988). In summary, agoraphobic avoidance is viewed as one style of coping with the apprehension of panic. It is noteworthy that another style of coping which may be more common for males who panic is to confront anticipated situations with the aid of alcohol or drugs (Barlow, 1988).

One implication of this conceptualization of panic and agoraphobia is that direct treatment of panic may enhance the treatment of agoraphobic avoid-

ance. Traditionally, agoraphobic avoidance was the primary target of behavioral interventions, leaving panic to diminish as a function of increased
mobility and approach behavior, or to be controlled by medication. However,
many individuals who learn to be less agoraphobic continue to panic (Arnow,
Taylor, Agras & Telch, 1985; Michelson, Mavissakalian & Marchione, 1985;
Stern & Marks, 1973). Futhermore, the continuance of panic has been linked
with the possibility of agoraphobic relapse (Craske, Street & Barlow, 1989;
Arnow et al., 1985). Therefore, the value of cognitive-behavioral treatments
that target panic directly is important for individuals with and without agoraphobia.

Cognitive-Behavioral Treatment Approaches

Several earlier studies demonstrated the effectiveness of a combination of
behavioral treatment strategies for panic attacks, including relaxation, assertiveness training, in vivo exposure, biofeedback training, and cognitive
restructuring (e.g., Gitlin, Martin, Shear, Frances, Ball & Josephson, 1985;
Shear, Ball, Fitzpatrick, Josephson, Klosko & Frances, 1991). The effects of
similar multicomponent treatments were shown to be superior to the passage
of time alone (Waddell, Barlow & O'Brien, 1984). The more recent treatment
components include breathing retraining, applied relaxation, vagal innervation
techniques, cognitive restructuring, and exposure to feared bodily sensations.

Breathing retraining

Several researchers have examined the efficacy of breathing retraining (i.e.,
training in slow, diaphragmatic breathing), given that 50–60% of panickers
describe hyperventilatory symptoms as being very similar to their panic attack
symptoms (deRuiter, Garssen, Rijken & Kraaimaat, 1989). Although, it is
noteworthy that recent research has shown that report of hyperventilatory
symptoms does not accurately represent hyperventilatory physiology (Holt &
Andrews, 1989); most patients tend to over-report symptomatology of this
nature.

In the conception of panic attacks that emphasizes hyperventilation, panic
attacks are viewed as stress-induced, respiratory changes that either provoke
fear because they are perceived as frightening, or augment fear already elicited
by other phobic stimuli (Clark, Salkovskis & Chalkley, 1985; Ley, 1991).
Kraft & Hoogduin (1984) found that six, bi-weekly sessions of breathing
retraining and progressive relaxation reduced frequency of panic attacks from
10 to 4 per week. However, the treatment was no more effective than either
repeated hyperventilation and control of symptoms by breathing into a bag or

identification of life stressors and problem solving. Two case reports have described the successful application of breathing retraining in the context of cognitively-based treatments, where patients are taught to reinterpret sensations as harmless (Rapee, 1985; Salkovskis, Warwick, Clark & Wessels, 1986). Clark et al. (1985) reported a larger scale, although uncontrolled, study in which 18 panickers received two weekly sessions of respiratory control and cognitive reattribution training. Panic attacks were reduced markedly in that brief period of time, especially in subjects who were not significantly agoraphobic. Salkovskis et al. (1986) gave nine panic patients four weekly sessions of forced hyperventilation, corrective information, and breathing retraining, after which in vivo exposure to agoraphobic situations was provided if necessary. Panic frequency reduced, on average, from 7 to 3 per week after respiratory control training. Although these studies demonstrate impressive results from brief therapuetic interventions, there are several concerns. First, participants are usually selected on the basis of exhibiting hyperventilatory symptoms and, therefore, generalizability to subjects who do not report hyperventilatory symptoms is unclear. Second, de Ruiter, Rijken, Garssen, and Kraaimaat (1989), using similarly selected subjects, did not replicate the efficacy of a combination of breathing retraining and cognitive restructuring. Third, breathing retraining protocols typically include cognitive restructuring and interoceptive exposure which, as will be described, have been shown to be very effective treatments for panic attacks. Therefore, it is difficult to attribute the results primarily to respiratory control. Fourth, the extent to which brief breathing retraining interventions reduce anticipatory anxiety and other indices believed to underly panic disorder (e.g., attentional vigilance to symptoms of arousal etc.) is not known. Finally, success of breathing retraining is unlikely to be directly attributable to changes in actual breathing (Garssen, de Ruiter & van Dyck, 1992); distraction and/or enhanced perceived control are offered as possible mechanisms underlying the efficacy of breathing retraining.

Relaxation

A form of relaxation known as applied relaxation has shown promising results as a treatment for panic attacks. Applied relaxation entails training in progressive muscle relaxation (PMR), until skilled in the use of cue-control procedures, at which point the relaxation skill is applied to practice of items from an hierarchy of anxiety provoking tasks. A theoretical basis for the use of relaxation for panic attacks has not been elaborated beyond the provision of a somatic counter response to the muscular tension that is likely to occur during anxiety and panic. However, evidence from other sources does not lend support to this notion (Rupert, Dobbins & Mathew, 1981). It is suggested that fear and anxiety are reduced to the extent that relaxation provides a sense of control or mastery (Bandura, 1977, 1988; Rice & Blanchard, 1982). The procedures and mechanisms accountable for therapeutic gains are further clouded in the case of applied forms of PMR, given the involvement of exposure procedures.

Ost (1988) reported very favorable results from applied PMR. One-hundred percent of an applied PMR group ($n = 8$) were panic-free after 14 sessions, in comparison to 71.7% of a nonapplied PMR group ($n = 8$). Furthermore, the results of the first group were maintained at follow-up (approximately 19 months after treatment completion), while maintenance occurred for 57% of the second group. All of the applied PMR group were classified as high end-state at follow-up, in comparison to 25% of the PMR group. In contrast, Barlow et al. (1989) found that applied PMR was relatively ineffective for the control of panic attacks. This discrepancy may be due to different types of tasks to which cue controlled relaxation was applied. Ost's (1988) applied PMR condition included exposure to interoceptive cues (i.e., feared bodily sensations), whereas Barlow et al. (1989) limited their PMR condition to external situation tasks. More recently, Michelson Marchione, Geenwald, Glanz, Testa, & Marchione (1990) combined applied PMR with breathing retraining and cognitive training for 10 patients with panic disorder. By treatment completion, all subjects were free of "spontaneous" panics, all but one were free of panic attacks altogether, and all met criteria for high end-state functioning. However, the specific contribution of applied PMR to these results is not known.

Vagal innervation

Vagal innervation is a less researched somatic control technique. Control of heart rate is taught through massaging the carotoid, by pressing on one eye during expiration, or by exerting pressure on the chest. Preliminary results suggest some success with this procedure (Sartory & Olajide, 1988).

Cognitive restructuring

Cognitive strategies for panic disorder were spearheaded by Beck's (1986) extension of his cognitive model of depression to anxiety and panic. Cognitive treatment focuses upon correcting misappraisals of bodily sensations as threatening. The cognitive strategies are conducted in conjunction with behavioral techniques, although the effective mechanism of change is assumed to lie in the cognitive realm. In an uncontrolled study, Sokol and Beck (1986; cited in Beck, 1988) treated 25 patients with cognitive techniques in combination with interoceptive and in vivo exposure for an average of 17 individual sessions. Panic attacks were eliminated in the 17 patients who did not have additional diagnoses of personality disorder, at post and twelve-month assessments. In a more recent, very well controlled study, Clark, Salkovskis, Hackmann, Middleton, Anastasiades & Gelder (1993) compared cognitive therapy (which included self-exposure) to applied relaxation and imipramine. After an average of 10 treatment sessions, 18 of 20 patients who completed cognitive therapy were panic-free, as were 17 at a 1-year follow-up assessment. While these results are impressive, it is difficult to attribute the outcome specifically to cognitive strategies given their combination with behavioral strategies.

On the other hand, a preliminary report from Margraf, Gobel & Schneider (1989) suggests that cognitive strategies conducted in isolation from exposure procedures are highly effective means of controlling panic attacks. Also, Salkovskis, Clark & Hackmann (1991) reported results from a single case multiple baseline replication design, which examined the effects of two weeks of focussed cognitive therapy with anti-exposure instructions. Panic attacks reduced or ceased in all but one of the 7 patients. Although these results are promising, caution is advised as this study has been criticized on methodological grounds (Acierno, Hersen & Van Hasselt, 1993). Overall, these results contribute to the growing evidence in support of cognitive techniques. However, as Salkovskis et al. (1991) point out, behavioral strategies may remain the most effective means for accomplishing cognitive modification. Furthermore, measurement of change is usually limited to panic frequency. As noted with the studies evaluating breathing retraining, the extent to which primarily cognitive strategies reduce attentional vigilance for symptoms of arousal, level of chronic arousal, and anticipation of the recurrence of panic requires more complete examination.

Interoceptive exposure

The purpose of interoceptive exposure, as in the case of exposure to external phobic stimuli, is to disrupt or weaken associations between specific bodily cues and panic reactions. The theoretical basis for interoceptive exposure is one of fear extinction, given the conceptualization of panic attacks as "conditioned" or learned alarm reactions to salient bodily cues (Barlow, 1988). Interoceptive exposure is conducted through procedures that induce panic-like sensations reliably, such as cardiovascular exercise, inhalations of carbon dioxide, spinning in a chair, and hyperventilation. The exposure is conducted using a graduated format. In early studies, Bonn, Harrison & Rees (1971) and Haslam (1974) observed successful reduction in reactivity with repeated infusions of sodium lactate (a drug that produces panic-type bodily sensations, as do other chemical substances such as caffeine and yohimbine). However, panic was not monitored in these investigations. Griez and van den Hout

(1986) compared six sessions of graduated carbon dioxide inhalations with a treatment regimen of propranolol (a beta blocker chosen because it suppresses symptoms that are induced by carbon dioxide inhalations), both conducted over the course of 2 weeks. Such inhalation treatment resulted in a mean reduction from 12 to 4 panic attacks, which was superior to the results with propranalol. In addition, inhalation treatment resulted in significantly greater reductions in reported fear of sensations. A 6-month follow-up assessment suggested maintenance of treatment gains, although panic frequency was not reported.

In the first controlled study of behavioral treatments for panic disorder, Barlow et al. (1989) compared the following four conditions: applied PMR; interoceptive exposure plus breathing retraining and cognitive restructuring; their combination; and a wait-list control. Interoceptive exposure entailed repeated exposures using induction techniques, such as forced hyperventilation, spinning, and cardiovascular effort. The two conditions involving interoceptive exposure and cognitive restructuring were significantly superior to applied PMR and Wait-List conditions, in terms of panic frequency. Fully 87% of those two treatment groups were free of panic at post-treatment. Similar rates of success were reported by Klosko, Barlow, Tassinari & Cerny (1990) who used the combined treatment approach described by Barlow et al. (1989). Furthermore, the results from the Barlow et al. (1989) study maintained up to 24 months following treatment completion for the group receiving interoceptive exposure and cognitive restructuring without PMR, while the combined group tended to deteriorate over the follow-up (Craske, Brown & Barlow, 1991). This study demonstrates the superiority of interoceptive exposure and cognitive procedures in the short-term and long-term, for the control of panic attacks. However, PMR was as effective as the exposure and cognitive strategies for general anxiety reduction. Moreover, only 50% of each treatment condition was classified as high-end state functioning. That is, despite the elimination of panic, a large portion of subjects continued to experience anxiety, distress, and/or interference with functioning. More specific measures of attentional vigilance for arousal symptoms or anticipation of the recurrence of panic may have highlighted the sources of the continued distress. Telch, Lucas, Schmidt, Hanna, LaNae Jaimez, and Lucas (1993) reported higher rates of overall success from a group treatment approach that emphasized cognitive therapy and interoceptive exposure. After 12 treatment sessions, 64% achieved high end-state functioning status at post-treatment, as did 63% at a 6-month follow-up assessment. We found that group treatment of cognitive motivating, interoceptive exposure and in vivo exposure was slightly more effective than group treatment of cognitive restructuring, breathing retraining and in vivo exposure (Craske, Rowe, Lewin & Noriega-Dimitri, 1997).

Cognitive-Behavioral Treatment Protocol

Overview

The following protocol was developed at the Center for Stress and Anxiety Disorders (Craske, Rapee & Barlow, 1988) and is available as a detailed treatment manual (Barlow & Craske, 1984). In research protocols, the treatment is typically conducted in 11 1-h individual sessions, although group formats have been implemented also. The sessions are typically scheduled weekly, although intensive daily treatment is possible also.

The treatment protocol aims to influence directly the cognitive, misinterpretational aspect of panic attacks and anxiety, the hyperventilatory response and conditioned reactions to physical cues. This is done firstly through the provision of accurate information as to the nature of the physiological aspects of the fight/flight response. Second, specific techniques for modifying cognitions are taught, including identifying and challenging aberrant beliefs. Next, specific information concerning the effects of hyperventilation and its role in panic attacks is provided with extensive practice of breathing retraining. Finally, repeated exposure to feared internal cues is conducted to "decondition" fear reactions.

Session 1

The goals of Session 1 are to describe anxiety, provide a treatment rationale and description, and emphasize the importance of self-monitoring and homework practices between treatment sessions. Therapy begins with identifying anxiety patterns and the situations in which anxiety and panic attacks are likely to occur. Many clients have difficulty identifying specific antecedents, reporting that anxiety can occur at almost any time. Special emphasis is given to internal cues that may trigger anxiety and fear, particularly negative verbal cognitions, catastrophic imagery, and physical sensations.

Clients are instructed in the three response-system model for describing and understanding anxiety and panic, so that they develop an alternative non-threatening conceptualization of anxiety and panic and an objective self-awareness. Clients are asked to describe cognitive, physiological, and behavioral aspects to their responding: to identify what they *feel, think,* and *do* when they are anxious and panicky. Differences between the response profiles of anxiety and panic are highlighted. For example, the cognitive component in general anxiety may involve worrying about future events, whereas the cognitive component in panic-fear may involve worrying about immediate danger; the behavioral component in general anxiety may consist of agitation and fidgeting, whereas the behavioral component in panic-fear may involve escape or avoidance; the physiological component in general anxiety may involve muscular tension whereas the physiological component in panic-fear may involve palpitations. Interactions among the response systems are described also (e.g., the exacerbation of physiological arousal by fearful cognitions).

Next, clients are informed that understanding the reasons for which they began to experience panic attacks is not necessary in order to benefit from the treatment, because factors involved in onset are not necessarily the same as factors involved in the maintenance of a problem. Nevertheless, the initial panic attack is viewed as a manifestation of anxiety/stress. The stressors surrounding the time of the first panic attack are explored with the client, particularly in terms of how they may have increased levels of physiological arousal, and primed certain danger-laden cognitive schemata.

The first session ends with a full treatment rationale and description. The homework entails self-monitoring of each panic attack, including measures of intensity and triggering cues as well as daily records of depression, anxiety, and worry about panic. Clients are asked to monitor their fear and anxiety in the format of the three response-system described in this session.

Session 2

The goals of this session are to describe the physiology underlying anxiety and panic and the concepts of hypervigilance and interoceptive conditioning. Clients are given a detailed handout which summarizes the didactic portion of the session.

The main concepts covered in this educational phase are (1) survival value or protective function of anxiety and panic, (2) physiological basis to the various sensations experienced during panic and anxiety, and (3) role of specific learned and cognitively mediated fears of certain bodily sensations. The model of panic that was described earlier in this chapter is explained. In particular, the concept of interoceptive conditioning is explained to account for panic attacks that seem to occur for no apparent reason; such panic attacks are viewed as occurring in response to very subtle internal cues or physical sensations.

The homework is to continue the development of an alternative conceptual framework and an objective versus subjective self awareness. This is achieved through self-monitoring of panics, keeping in mind the principles discussed to date, and re-reading of the handout.

Session 3

The primary goal of the third session is corrective breathing training. Clients are asked to voluntarily hyperventilate by standing and breathing fast and deep, as if blowing up a balloon, for 1.5 min. The experience is discussed in terms of the degree to which it produced symptoms similar to those that occur naturally during anxiety or panic. Often, similarity of the symptoms is confused with similarity of the anxiety. Because the exercise is conducted in a safe environment, and the symptoms have an obvious cause, most clients rate the experience as less anxiety provoking than if the same symptoms had occurred naturally. This distinction is important to make, because it demonstrates the significance of perceptions of safety for the degree of anxiety experienced. The hyperventilatory experience is discussed in terms of the three response systems and the role of misappraisals and interoceptive conditioning described last session.

Next, clients are educated about the physiological basis of hyperventilation. As before, the goal of the didactic presentation is to allay misinterpretations of the dangers of overbreathing, and to provide a basis of information upon which to draw when actively challenging misinterpretations as the therapy progresses.

Breathing control begins by emphasizing diaphragmatic muscle involvement versus over-reliance on thoracic muscles. In addition, clients are instructed to concentrate on their breathing, by counting on their inhalations, and thinking the word "relax" on exhalations. [Slow breathing is introduced in the next session]. Therapists model the suggested breathing patterns, and provide corrective feedback to clients while they practice in the office setting.

Breathing control is a skill that requires considerable practice before it can be successfully applied to manage episodes of high anxiety or panic. In addition, initial reactions to the exercise can be negative for clients who are afraid of respiratory sensations (as the exercise entails concentration upon breathing), or for clients who are chronic overbreathers and for whom the interruption of habitual breathing patterns initially increases overbreathing symptomatology. In both cases, continued practice is advisable, with reassurance that sensations such as shortness of breath or lightheadedness are not harmful.

Finally, the integration of breathing control techniques and cognitive strategies is emphasized. On occasion, clients mistakenly view breathing control as a way of relieving themselves of terrifying symptoms, thus falling into the trap of fearing dire consequences should they not succeed in changing their breathing. The homework for this session entails continued self-monitoring, and practice of diaphragmatic breathing at least two times a day, at least 10 minutes each time.

Session 4

The goals of this session are to develop breathing control, and to begin active cognitive restructuring. The therapist models and then provides corrective feedback for slowing the rate of breathing (to span a full inhalation and exhalation cycle over 6 s). Clients are instructed to practice slow breathing in "safe" or relaxing environments over the coming week. They are discouraged from applying slow breathing to the management of anxiety until fully skilled in its application.

Cognitive restructuring is introduced by explaining that errors in thinking occur naturally during heightened anxiety, thus preparing the client to gain an objective self awareness and expectation that their thinking is distorted. Concepts of automatic thinking and discrete predictions are explained to encourage becoming an astute observer of one's own habitual self-statements in specific situations. Recognition of the thought "I feel terrible - something bad could happen" is insufficient, nontherapeutic, and may serve to intensify anxiety by virtue of its global and nondirective nature. Instead, recognition of the thought "I am afraid that if I get too anxious while driving then I'll lose control of the wheel and drive off the side of the road and die" allows for very constructive questionning to challenge the series of misassumptions.

Two main types of errors in cognitions are described. The first is overestimation, or, jumping to negative conclusions and treating negative events as probable when in fact they are unlikely to occur. The client is asked to identify overestimations from the anxiety and panic incidents over the last couple of weeks: "Can you think of events that you felt sure were going to happen when you were feeling anxious, only to find out in the end that they did not happen at all".

Reasons why overestimations persist despite repeated disconfirmation are explored. Typically, the absence of danger is misattributed to external safety signals or behaviors (e.g., "I only made it because I managed to find help in time", "If I had not taken Xanax last week when I panicked in the store, I'm sure I would have passed out" or "I wouldn't have made it if I hadn't pull off the road in time"), or to "luck", instead of realizing the inaccuracy of the original prediction. Similarly, clients may erroneously assume that the only reason why they are still alive, sane, etc., is because the "big panic" has not happened yet. In this case, it is mistakenly assumed that more intense panic attacks increase risks for dying, losing control, etc.

The method for countering overestimation errors is to question the evidence for probability judgements. The general format is to treat thoughts as hypotheses or guesses rather than facts and examine the evidence for predictions, while considering alternative, more realistic predictions. This is best done in a socratic style so that clients examine the content of their statements and reach alternatives. Questionning of the client's specific logic (e.g., "How does a racing heart lead to heart attack"), or the bases from which judgments are made (e.g., misinformation from others, unusual sensations) are useful in this regard.

The homework assignment for this session is to practice breathing control, monitor examples of overestimation and challenge errors in thinking by questionning the odds and examining the evidence more realistically.

Session 5

The goals of this session are application of breathing control, and extension of cognitive restructuring to the second type of cognitive error, which is catastrophizing. Clients are asked to practice breathing control in demanding environments, such as while sitting at a desk at work, or while waiting at a stop light in the car. They are encouraged to do "mini-practices" often throughout the day.

The second type of cognitive error arises from misinterpreting events as "dangerous", "insufferable", or "catastrophic". Hence, typical kinds of catastrophic errors are "If I faint people will think that I'm weak and that would be unbearable", or "Panic attacks are the worst thing I can imagine", and "The whole evening is ruined if I start to feel anxious". Decatastrophizing means to realize that the occurrences are not as "catastrophic" as stated, which is achieved by considering how negative events are managed versus how "bad" they are. For example, for the person who states that negative judgements from others is unbearable, it is important to discuss what he/she would do to cope should someone else make an explicit negative judgement. Similarly, for the person who states that the physical symptoms of panic are intolerable, the discussion can focus on coping with symptoms and realistic outcomes based upon previous experiences.

The homework is applied breathing control, and identification and challenging of overestimations and catastrophic styles of thinking.

Session 6

The main goal of this session is to begin interoceptive exposure. The rationale for interoceptive exposure is very important for facilitating generalization from in-session practices to daily experiences. The concept of interoceptive conditioning is reviewed, and the way in which avoidance of feared sensations serves to maintain fearfulness is explored. Avoidance of physical sensations may not be immediately obvious to the client, but activities that are typically avoided for these reasons include physical exercise, emotional discussions, suspenseful movies, steamy rooms (e.g., shower with doors and windows closed), certain foods, or stimulants. The purpose of interoceptive exposure is to repeatedly induce the sensations that are feared, and weaken fear through habituating and learning that no actual danger results. In addition, the repeated inductions allow practice with cognitive and breathing strategies. As a result, fear of physical sensations that occur naturally is significantly reduced.

The procedure begins by assessing the client's response to a series of standardized exercises. The therapist models each exercise first. Then, after the client has completed the exercise, the sensations, anxiety level (0–8), sensation intensity (0–8), and similarity to naturally occurring panic sensations (0–8) are recorded. The exercises include: shaking the head from side to side for 30 s; placing the head between the legs for 30 s and lifting the head to an upright position quickly; running on the spot for 1 min, holding one's breath for 30 s or for as long as possible; complete body muscle tension for 1 min or holding a pushup position for as long as possible; spinning in a swivel chair for 1 min; hyperventilating for 1 min; breathing through a narrow straw (with closed nasal passages) for 2 min; and staring at a spot on the wall or at one's mirror image for 90 s. If none of these exercises produce sensations at least moderately similar to those that occur naturally, other individually tailored exercises are generated. For example, if chest pain is the primary feared sensation, tightness around the chest can be induced by taking in a deep breath before hyperventilating.

If clients report little or no fear because they feel safe in the presence of the therapist, they are asked to attempt each exercies alone while the therapist leaves the office, or at home. For a minority of clients, the known cause and course of the sensations overrides the fear response. For the majority of clients, at least several of the list of exercises are feared despite knowing the cause of the sensations and their controllability.

Exercises rated as producing at least somewhat similar sensations (at least 3 on the 0–8 point similarity scale) are selected for repeated exposure in the next session. From the selected exercises, an hierarchy is established according to the anxiety ratings. Homework entails continued cognitive monitoring and challenging.

Session 7

The primary goal of this session is to conduct repeated interoceptive exposure. But first, breathing control is reviewed. Clients are encouraged to apply breathing control at times of anxiety or uncomfortable physical sensations from this point on. Also, hypothesis testing is introduced to facilitate cognitive restructuring. Hypothesis testing involves identifying overestimations or catastrophic predictions about situations that are likely to be encountered in the near future. The likelihood of the prediction coming true is rated in this session. At the next session, the client and therapist examine the evidence that either supports or refutes the predictions that were made the week prior. In this manner, the client obtains more concrete evidence that few if any of his/her dire predictions come true.

A graduated approach is used for interoceptive exposure, beginning with the lowest item on the hierarchy established last session. For each trial of exposure, the client is asked to begin the induction, indicate when the sensations are first experienced, and continue the induction for at least 30 s longer to prevent the tendency to escape from the sensations. After terminating the induction, anxiety is rated, and cognitive and breathing management strategies are applied. Finally, the therapist reviews the induction experience and the application of management strategies with the client. During this review, the therapist emphasizes the importance of experiencing the sensations fully during the induction, of concentrating objectively on the sensations versus distracting from them, and the importance of identifying specific cognitions and challenging them by considering all of the evidence. In addition, the therapist asks key questions to help the client realize his/her safety (e.g., "what would have happened if you had continued spinning for another 60 s"), and to generalize to naturally occurring experiences (e.g., "how is this different from when you feel dizzy at work"). In other words, cognitive challenging extends the cognitive reprocessing already taking place as a result of repeated interoceptive exposure. The trials are repeated enough times until anxiety levels for a given exercise are no greater than 2 (or mild). Then, the procedure is repeated for the next exercise on the hierarchy, progressing up the hierarchy until all items are completed.

Homework practice is very important, as safety signals present in the clinic setting or deriving from the therapist per se may limit generalizability to the natural setting. Clients are instructed to practice the interoceptive items conducted in session on a daily basis.

Session 8

The goals of this session are to continue the hypothesis testing and interoceptive exposure from the preceding session. It is especially important to review daily practice of interoceptive exposure. The possibility of avoidance should be evaluated; either overt failure to practice, or covert avoidance by minimizing the intensity or duration of the sensations induced, or by limiting practices to the presence of a safety signal (such as a significant other) or to times when the client does not feel anxious. The reasons for avoidance include continued misinterpretation of the dangers of bodily sensations (i.e., "I don't want to hyperventilate because I'm afraid that I won't be able to stop overbreathing and no-one will be around to help me"), or the misperception that anxiety levels will not reduce over repetition of the exercise. Avoidance-motivations are best addressed cognitively, using the priniciples described in the previous sessions. The homework from this session is to continue progressing up the interoceptive exposure hierarchy, hypothesis testing, and cognitive restructuring when anxious.

Session 9

The primary goal of this session is to extend interoceptive exposure to naturalistic tasks. In addition, cognitive restructuring is continued through hypothesis testing, and monitoring and challenging of negative cognitions as anxiety arises.

Naturalistic interoceptive exposure refers to exposure to daily tasks or activities that have been avoided or endured with dread because of the associated sensations. Typical examples include aerobic exercise or vigorous physical activity, running up flights of stairs, eating foods that create a sensation of fullness or are associated with sensations of choking, standing quickly from a seated position, saunas or steamy showers, driving with the windows rolled up and the heater on, caffeine consumption, and so on. [Of course, these exercises may be modified in the event of actual medical complications, such as asthma or high blood pressure]. From a list of typically feared activities, and generation of items specific to the individual's own experience, an hierarchy is established. Each item is ranked in terms of anxiety level. Clients are instructed to identify maladaptive cognitions and rehearse cognitive restructuring before beginning each activity. In-session rehearsal of the cognitive preparation allows therapists to provide corrective feedback. It is important to identify and remove (gradually, if necessary) safety signals or protective behaviors such as portable phones, lucky charms, and staying in close proximity to medical facilities. Clients are asked to practice two items from their hierarchy at least three times each before the next treatment session, scheduled for two weeks in advance.

Sessions 10–11

Sessions 10–11 review practices of naturalistic interoceptive exposure, and check cognitive monitoring and breathing control strategies. These last two sessions are scheduled biweekly to to enhance generalization from the treatment setting. The last treatment session reviews all of the principles and skills learned, and provides clients with a template of coping techniques for potential high risk situations in the future.

Conclusions and Future Directions

In summary, procedures of cognitive restructuring, breathing retraining, applied relaxation, and interoceptive exposure have been shown to control panic attacks for the majority of individuals, with results lasting for up to 2 years following treatment completion. However, even though panic ceases, a significant proportion may continue to experience anxiety or distress (Brown & Barlow, 1995). Given the relative lack of construct-based outcome measurement (e.g., measurement of attentional vigilance for symptoms of arousal and anticipation of recurrence of panic), the nature of that anxiety has not been fully assessed. Also, several studies have shown that agoraphobic avoidance may continue despite elimination of panic attacks (Clark et al., 1985; Craske et al., 1991; Salkovskis et al., 1991), suggesting that the most effective treatment combines panic-control procedures with agoraphobia-control procedures.

It remains to be seen whether panic-control strategies such as interoceptive exposure enhance the efficacy of in vivo exposure for agoraphobia. Some research suggests panic-control methods may minimize relapse after invivo exposure treatment. Conceivably, panic-control might reduce attrition and enhance reduction of agoraphobic avoidance as well. The combined effect of panic-control strategies and in vivo exposure is currently under investigation in several clinical research centers.

Another area in need of research is the combination of cognitive-behavioral treatment for panic with pharmacotherapy. Most studies to date have examined the combination of drug therapies and in vivo exposure therapy for agoraphobia (e.g., Marks, Grey, Cohen, Hill, Mawson, Ramm & Stern, 1983; Mavissakalian & Michelson, 1986; Mavissakalian, Michelson & Dealy, 1983; Zitrin, Klein & Woerner, 1980; Zitrin, Klein, Woerner & Ross, 1983; Telch, Agras, Taylor, Roth & Gallen, 1985). A large collaborative project recently investigated the singular and combined effects of impramine and exposure/cognitive procedures for panic attacks in individuals without severe levels of agoraphobic avoidance (see Barlow & Lehman, 1996).

Finally, individual differences that may impede success with cognitive-behavioral treatment for panic are yet to be fully identified. For example, personality characteristics, severe depression and/or substance abuse (all of which are relatively comorbid with panic disorder) warrant further investigation as potential obstacles to treatment success.

References

Acierno, R. E., Hersen, M., & Van Hasselt, V. B. (1993). Interventions for panic disorder: A critical review of the literature. *Clinical Psychology Review, 13,* 561–578.

Alneas, R., & Torgersen, S. (1990). DSM-III personality disorders among patients with major depression, anxiety disorders, and mixed conditions. *The Journal of Nervous and Mental Disease, 178,* 693–698.

Amering, M., Katschnig, H., Berger, P., Windhaber, J., Baischer, W., & Dantendorfer, K. (1996). Embarrassment about the first panic attack predicts agoraphobia in panic disorder patients. *Behaviour Research and Therapy, 35*, 517–521.

APA (1994). *Diagnostic and statistical manual of mental disorders*, 4th edition (DSM-IV). Washington, DC: American Psychiatric Press.

Antony, M., Brown, T. A., Craske, M. G., Barlow, D. H., Mitchell, W. B., & Meadows, E. (1995). Accuracy of heart beat perception in panic disorder, social phobic, and nonanxious subjects. *Journal of Anxiety Disorders, 9*, 355–371.

Arnow, B. A., Taylor, C. B., Agras, W. S., & Telch, M. J. (1985). Enchancing agoraphobia treatment outcome by changing couple communication patterns. *Behavior Therapy, 16*, 452–467.

Bandura, A. (1977). Self-efficacy: Toward a unifying theory of behavioral change. *Psychological Review, 84*, 191–215.

Bandura, A. (1988). Self-efficacy conception of anxiety. *Anxiety Research, 1*, 77–98.

Barlow, D. H. (1988). *Anxiety and its disorders: The nature and treatment of anxiety and panic*. New York: Guilford Press.

Barlow, D. H., Cohen, A., Waddell, M., Vermilyea, J., Klosko, J., Blanchard, E., & DiNardo, P. (1984). Panic and generalized anxiety disorders: Nature and treatment. *Behavior Therapy, 15*, 431–449.

Barlow, D. H., & Craske, M. G. (1994). *Mastery of your anxiety and panic II*. San Antonio, TX: Harcourt Brace & Co.

Barlow, D. H., Craske, M. G., Cerny, J. A., & Klosko, J. S. (1989). Behavioral treatment of panic disorder. *Behavior Therapy, 20*, 261–282.

Barlow, D. H., & Lehman, C. L. (1996). Advances in the psychosocial treatment of anxiety disorders. *Archives of General Psychiatry, 53*, 727–735.

Beck, A. T. (1988). Cognitive approaches to panic disorder: Theory and therapy. In S. Rachman & J. D. Maser (Eds.), *Panic: Psychological perspectives*. Hillsdale, NJ: Erlbaum.

Bonn, J. A., Harrison, J., & Rees, W. (1971). Lactate-induced anxiety: Therapeutic application. *British Journal of Psychiatry, 119*, 468–470.

Brown, T. A., & Barlow, T. A. (1995). Long-term outcome in cognitive-behavioural treatment of panic disorders: Clinical predictors and alternative strategies for assessment. *Journal of Consulting and Clinical Psychology, 63(5)*, 754–765.

Carter, M. M., Hollon, S. D., Carson, R., & Shelton, R. C. (1995). Effects of a safe person on induced distress following a biological challenge in panic disorder with agoraphobia. *Journal of Abnormal Psychology, 104*, 156–163.

Chambless, D. L., & Renneberg, B. (1988). *Personality disorders of agoraphobics*. Paper presented at the World Congress of Behavior Therapy, Edinburgh.

Chambless, D. L., Caputo, G., Bright, P., & Gallagher, R. (1984). Assessment of fear in agoraphobics: The Body Sensations Questionnaire and the Agoraphobic Cognitions Questionnaire. *Journal of Consulting and Clinical Psychology, 52*, 1090–1097.

Clark, D., Salkovskis, P., & Chalkley, A. (1985). Respiratory control as a treatment for panic attacks. *Journal of Behavior Therapy and Experimental Psychiatry, 16*, 23–30.

Clark, D. M., Salkovskis, P., Gelder, M., Koehler, C., Martin, M., Anastasiades, P., Hackmann, A., Middleton, H., & Jeavons, A. (1988). Tests of a cognitive theory of panic. In I. Hand & H. Wittchen (Eds.), *Panic and phobias II*. Berlin: Springer-Verlag.

Clark, D. M., Salkovskis, P., Hackmann, A., Middleton, H., Anastasiades, P., & Gelder, M. (1994). A comparison of cognitive therapy, applied relaxation, and imipramine in the treatment of panic disorder. *British Journal of Clinical Psychology, 164*, 759–769.

Cox, B. J., Endler, N. S., & Swinson, R. P. (1995). An examination of levels of agoraphobic severity in panic disorders. *Behaviour Research and Therapy, 33*, 57–62.

Craske, M. G. (1991). Phobic fear and panic attacks: The same emotional state triggered by different cues? *Clinical Psychology Review, 11,* 599–620.

Craske, M. G., & Barlow, D. H. (1988). A review of the relationship between panic and avoidance. *Clinical Psychology Review, 8,* 667–685.

Craske, M. G., & Barlow, D. H. (1993). Panic disorder and agoraphobia. In D.H. Barlow (Ed.), *Clinical handbook of psychological disorders* (2nd edition). New York: Guilford Press.

Craske, M. G., & Freed, S. (1995). Expectations about arousal and nocturnal panic. *Journal of Abnormal Psychology, 104,* 567–575.

Craske, M. G., & Rowe, M. K. (1997). Nocturnal panic. *Clinical Psychology: Science and Practice, 4,* 153–174.

Craske, M. G., Rapee, R. M., & Barlow, D. H. (1988). *Manual for panic control treatment.* Unpublished manuscript.

Craske, M. G., Street, L., & Barlow, D. H. (1989). Instructions to focus upon or distract from internal cues during exposure treatment for agoraphobic avoidance. *Behaviour Research and Therapy, 27,* 663–672.

Craske, M. G., Miller, P. P., Rotunda, R., & Barlow, D. H. (1990). A descriptive report of features of initial unexpected panic attacks in minimal and extensive avoiders. *Behaviour Research and Therapy, 28,* 395–400.

Craske, M. G., Brown, T. A., & Barlow, D. H. (1991). Behavioral treatment of panic disorder: A two-year follow-up. *Behavior Therapy, 22,* 289–304.

Craske, M. G., Glover, D. A., & DeCola, J. (1995). Predicted versus unpredicted panic attacks: Acute versus general distress. *Journal of Abnormal Psychology, 104,* 214–223.

Craske, M. G., Rowe, M., Lewin, M., & Noriega-Dimitri, R. (1997). Interpoceptive exposure versus breathing retraining within cognitive-behavioural therapy for panic disorder with agoraphobia. *British Journal of Clinical Psychology, 36(1),* 85–99.

Crowe, R. R., Noyes, R., Pauls, D. L., & Slymen, D. J. (1983). A family study of panic disorder. *Archives of General Psychiatry, 40,* 1065–1069.

de Jong, G. M., & Bouman, T. K. (1995). Panic disorder: A baseline period. Predictability of agoraphobic avoidance behaviour. *Journal of Anxiety Disorders, 9(3),* 185–199.

deRuiter, C., Rijken, H., Garssen, B., & Kraaimaat, F. (1989). Breathing retraining, exposure and a combination of both, in the treatment of panic disorder with agoraphobia. *Behaviour Research and Therapy, 27,* 647–656.

Ehlers, A. (1993). Somatic symptoms and panic attacks: A retrospective study of learning experiences. *Behaviour Research and Therapy, 31,* 269–278.

Ehlers, A. (1995). A 1-year prospective study of panic attacks: Clinical course and factors associated with maintenance. *Journal of Abnormal Psychology, 104,* 164–172.

Ehlers, A., & Breuer, P. (1996). How good are patients with panic disorder at perceiving their heartbeats? *Biological Psychology, 42,* 165–182.

Ehlers, A., & Margraf, J. (1989). The psychophysiological model of panic attacks. In P. M. G. Emmelkamp (Ed.), *Anxiety disorders: Annual series of European research in behavior therapy,* Vol. 4. Amsterdam: Swets.

Garssen, B., de Ruiter, C., & Van Dyck, R. (1992). Breathing retraining: A rational placebo. *Clinical Psychology Review, 12,* 141–154.

Gitlin, B., Martin, M., Shear, K., Frances, A., Ball, G., & Josephson, S. (1985). Behavior therapy for panic disorder. *Journal of Nervous and Mental Disease, 173,* 742–743.

Goisman, R. M., Warshaw, M. G., Peterson, L. G., Rogers, M. P., Cuneo, P., Hunt, M. F., Tomlin-Albanese, J. M., Kazim, A., Gollan, J. K., Epstein-Kaye, T., Reich, J. H., & Keller, M. B. (1994). Panic, agoraphobia, and panic disorder with agoraphobia: Data from a multicenter anxiety disorders study. *Journal of Nervous and Mental Disease, 182(2),* 72–79.

Griez, E., & van den Hout, M. A. (1986). CO_2 inhalation in the treatment of panic attacks. *Behaviour Research and Therapy, 24,* 145–150.

Haslam, M. T. (1974). The relationship between the effect of lactate infusion on anxiety states and their amelioration by carbon dioxide inhalation. *British Journal of Psychiatry, 125,* 88–90.

Holt, P., & Andrews, G. (1989). Hyperventilation and anxiety in panic disorder, agoraphobia, and generalized anxiety disorder. *Behaviour Research and Therapy, 27,* 453–460.

Jacob, R., Furman, J., Clark, D., & Durrant, J. (1992). Vestibular symptoms, panic and phobia: Overlap and possible relationships. *Annals of Clinical Psychiatry, 4,* 163–174.

Kessler, R. C., McGonagle, K. A., Zhao, S., Nelson, C. B., Hughes, M., Eshleman, S., Wittchen, H. U., & Kendler, K. S. (1994). Lifetime and 12-month prevalenceof DSM-III-R psychiatric disorders in the United States. *Archives of General Psychiatry, 51,* 8–19.

Klosko, J. S., Barlow, D. H., Tassinari, R., & Cerny, J. A. (1990). A comparison of alprazolam and behavior therapy in treatment of panic disorder. *Journal of Consulting and Clinical Psychology, 58,* 77–84.

Kraft, A. R., & Hoogduin, C. A. (1984). The hyperventilation syndrome: A pilot study of the effectiveness of treatment. *British Journal of Psychiatry, 145,* 538–542.

Ley, R. (1991). The efficacy of breathing retraining and the centrality of hyperventilation in panic disorder: A reinterpretation of experimental findings. *Behavior Research and Therapy, 29,* 301–304.

McNally, R., & Lorenz, M. (1987). Anxiety sensitivity in agoraphobics. *Journal of Behaviour Therapy and Experimental Psychiatry, 18,* 3–11.

Maller, R. G., & Reiss, S. (1992). Anxiety sensitivity in 1984 and panic attacks in 1987. *Journal of Anxiety Disorders, 6,* 241–247.

Margraf, J., Gobel, M., & Schneider, S. (1989). *Comparative efficacy of cognitive, exposure, and combined treatments for panic disorder.* Paper presented at the annual meeting of the European Association for Behavior Therapy, Vienna.

Marks, I., Grey, S., Cohen, S. D., Hill, R., Mawson, D., Ramm, E., & Stern, R. (1983). Imipramine and brief therapist-aided exposure in agoraphobics having self-exposure homework: A controlled trial. *Archives of General Psychiatry, 40,* 153–162.

Markowitz, J. S., Weissman, M. M., Ouellette, R., Lish, J. D., & Klerman, G. L. (1989). Quality of life in panic disorder. *Archives of General Psychiatry, 46,* 984–992.

Mavissakalian, M., & Hamman, M. (1986). DSM-III personality disorder in agoraphobia. *Comprehensive Psychiatry, 27,* 471–479.

Mavissakalian, M., & Michelson, L. (1986). Two-year follow-up of exposure and imipramine treatment of agoraphobia. *American Journal of Psychiatry, 143,* 1106–1112.

Mavissakalian, M., Michelson, L., & Dealy, R. (1983). Pharmacological treatment of agoraphobia: Imipramine versus imipramine with programmed practice. *British Journal of Psychiatry, 143,* 348–355.

Michelson, L., Marchione, K., Geenwald, M., Glanz, L., Testa, S., & Marchione, N. (1990). Panic Disorder: Cognitive-behavioral treatment. *Behavior Research and Therapy, 28,* 141–151.

Michelson, L., Mavissakalian, M., & Marchione, K. (1985). Cognitive-behavioral treatments of agoraphobia: Clinical, behavioral, and psychophysiological outcome. *Journal of Consulting and Clinical Psychology, 53,* 913–925.

Moran, C., & Matthews, G. (1985). The familial occurance of agoraphobia. *British Journal of Psychiatry, 146,* 262–267.

Myers, J., Weissman, M., Tischler, C., Holzer, C., Orvaschel, H., Anthony, J., Boyd, J., Burke, J., Kramer, M., & Stoltzam, R. (1984). Six-month prevalence of psychiatric disorders in three communities. *Archives of General Psychiatry, 41,* 959–967.

NIMH (1993). *Understanding panic disorder*. Washington, DC: U.S. Department of Health and Human Services.

Noyes, R., Crowe, R. R., Harris, E. L., Hamra, B. J., McChesney, C. M., & Chaudhry, D. R. (1986). Relationship between panic disorder and agoraphobia: A family study. *Archives of General Psychiatry, 43,* 227–232.

Noyes, R., Reich, J., Suelzer, M., & Christiansen, J. (1991). Personality traits associated with panic disorder: Change associated with treatment. *Comprehensive Psychiatry, 32,* 282–294.

Öst, L.-G. (1988). Applied relaxation vs. progressive relaxation in the treatment of panic disorder. *Behaviour Research and Therapy, 26,* 13–22.

Pollard, C. A., Bronson, S. S., & Kenney, M. R. (1989). Prevalence of agoraphobia without panic in clinical settings. *American Journal of Psychiatry, 146,* 559.

Rapee, R. M. (1985). A case of panic disorder treated with breathing retraining. *Behavior Therapy and Experimental Psychiatry, 16,* 63–65.

Rapee, R. M., Mattick, R., & Murrell, E. (1986). Cognitive mediation in the affective component of spontaneous panic attacks. *Journal of Behavior Therapy and Experimental Psychiatry, 17,* 245–253.

Razran, G. (1961). The observable unconscious and the inferable conscious in current soviet psychophysiology: Interoceptive conditioning, semantic conditioning, and the orienting reflex. *Psychological Review, 68,* 81–147.

Reich, J., Noyes, R., & Troughton, E. (1987). Dependent personality disorder associated with phobic avoidance in patients with panic disorder. *American Journal of Psychiatry, 144,* 323–326.

Rice, K. M., & Blanchard, E. B. (1982). Biofeedback in the treatment of anxiety disorders. *Clinical Psychology Review, 2,* 557–577.

Rupert, P. A., Dobbins, K., & Mathew, R. J. (1981). EMG biofeedback and relaxation instructions in the treatment of chronic anxiety. *American Journal of Clinical Biofeedback, 4,* 52–61.

Salkovskis, P., Clark, D., & Hackmann, A. (1991). Treatment of panic attacks using cognitive therapy without exposure or breathing retraining. *Behaviour Research and Therapy, 29,* 161–166.

Salkovskis, P., Warwick, H., Clark, D., & Wessels, D. (1986). A demonstration of acute hyperventilation during naturally occurring panic attacks. *Behaviour Research and Therapy, 24,* 91–94.

Sanderson, W. S., Rapee, R. M., & Barlow, D. H. (1989). The influence of an illusion of control on panic attacks induced via inhalation of 5.5% carbon dioxide enriched air. *Archives of General Psychiatry, 48,* 157–162.

Sanderson, W. S., DiNardo, P. A., Rapee, R. M., & Barlow, D. H. (1990). Syndrome comorbidity in patients diagnosed with a DSM-III-Revised anxiety disorder. *Journal of Abnormal Psychology, 99,* 308–312.

Sartory, G., & Olajide, D. (1988). Vagal innervation techniques in the treatment of panic disorder. *Behaviour Research and Therapy, 26,* 431–434.

Schmidt, N. B., Lerew, D.R., & Jackson, R. J. (1997). The role of anxiety sensitivity in the pathogenesis of panic: Prospective evaluation of spontaneous panic attacks during acute stress. *Journal of Abnormal Psychology, 106,* 355–364.

Schmidt, N. B., Trakowski, J. H., & Staab, J. P. (1997). Extinction of panicogenic effects of a 35% CO_2 challenge in patients with panic disorder. *Journal of Abnormal Psychology, 106(4),* 630–638.

Shear, M. K., Ball, G., Fitzpatrick, M., Josephson, S., Klosko, J., & Francis, A. (1991). Cognitive-behavioral therapy for panic: An open study. *Journal of Nervous and Mental Disease, 179,* 467–471.

Stern, R. S., & Marks, I. M. (1973). Brief and prolonged flooding: A comparison of agoraphobic patients. *Archives of General Psychiatry, 28,* 270–276.

Swinson, R. (1986). Reply to Kleiner. *The Behavior Therapist, 9,* 110–128.

Telch, M. J., Agras, W. S., Taylor, C. B., Roth, W. T., & Gallen, C. (1985). Combined pharmacological and behavioral treatment for agoraphobia. *Behaviour Research and Therapy, 21,* 505–527.

Telch, M. J., Lucas, J. A., & Nelson, P. (1989). Nonclinical panic in college students: An investigation of prevalence and symptomatology. *Journal of Abnormal Psychology, 98,* 300–306.

Telch, M. J., Lucas, J. A., Schmidt, N. B., Hanna, H. H., LaNae Jaimez, T., & Lucas, R. A. (1993). Group cognitive-behavioral treatment of panic disorder. *Behaviour Research and Therapy, 31,* 279–288.

Thyer, B. A., Himle, J., Curtis, G. C., Cameron, O. G., & Nesse, R. M. (1985). A comparison of panic disorder and agoraphobia with panic attacks. *Comprehensive Psychiatry, 26,* 208–214.

Torgersen, S. (1983). Genetic factors in anxiety disorders. *Archives of General Psychiatry, 40,* 1085–1089.

van den Hout, M. A., van der Molen, G. M., Griez, E., & Lousberg, H. (1987). Specificity of interoceptive fear to panic disorders. *Journal of Psychopathology and Behavioral Assessment, 9,* 99–109.

Waddell, M. T., Barlow, D. H., & O'Brien, G. T. (1984). A preliminary investigation of cognitive and relaxation treatment of panic disorder: Effects on intense anxiety vs. "background" anxiety. *Behaviour Research and Therapy, 22,* 393–402.

Wolpe, J., & Rowan, V. (1988). Panic disorder: A product of classical conditioning. *Behaviour Research and Therapy, 26,* 441–450.

Zarate, R., Rapee, R. M., Craske, M. G., & Barlow, D. H. (1988). *Response norms for symptom induction procedures.* Paper presented at the 22nd Annual AABT convention, New York.

Zitrin, C. M., Klein, D. F., & Woerner, M. G. (1980). Behavior therapy, supportive psychotherapy, imipramine, and phobias. *Archives of General Psychiatry, 37,* 63–72.

Zitrin, C. M., Klein, D. F., Woerner, M. G., & Ross, D. C. (1983). Treatment of phobias I. Comparison of imipramine hydrochloride and placebo. *Archives of General Psychiatry, 40,* 125–138.

Further Reading

Barlow, D. H. (1988). *Anxiety and its disorders: The nature and treatment of anxiety and panic.* New York: Guilford Press.

Barlow, D. H., Craske, M. G., Cerny, J. A., & Klosko, J. S. (1989). Behavioral treatment of panic disorder. *Behavior Therapy, 20,* 261–282.

Barlow, D. H., Brown, T. A., & Craske, M. G. (1994). Definition of panic attacks and panic disorder in the DSM-IV: Implications for research. *Journal of Abnormal Psychology, 103,* 553–564.

Craske, M. G. (1998). *Anxiety disorders: psychological approaches to theory and treatment.* Boulder, CO: Westview Press/ Basic Books.

Craske, M. G., Brown, T. A., & Barlow, D. H. (1991). Behavioral treatment of panic disorder: A two-year follow-up. *Behavior Therapy, 22,* 289–304.

Pastor, C., & Sevillá, J. (1995). *Tratamiento psicológico del pánico-agorafobia.* Valencia: Centro de Terapia de Conducta.

5

The Cognitive-Behavioral Treatment of Obsessions

MARK H. FREESTON and ROBERT LADOUCEUR

Université Laval, Québec, Canada

Introduction

Up until the mid-1980s and the advent of the Epidemiological Catchment Area Survey (Myers, Weissman, Tischler, Holzer, Leaf, Orvaschel, Anthony, Boyd, Burke, Kramer & Stoltzman, 1984; Robins, Helzer, Weissman, Orvaschel, Gruenberg, Burke & Regier, 1984) and other broadly based community studies, OCD was considered to be a rare disorder with estimates of the order of 0.05% (see Rasmussen & Eisen, 1992). Further, although there have always been reports of patients suffering from "ruminations", "pure obsessions" and similar phenomena where no overt compulsions are present (e.g., Rachman, 1971, 1976), this group has traditionally been considered rare among OCD patients with estimates of 20–25% of all cases of OCD (Emmelkamp, 1982; Marks, 1987; Rachman, 1985). More importantly, it was widely believed that this variant of OCD was highly resistant to treatment (see Beech & Vaughn, 1978; Foa, Steketee & Ozarow, 1985; Greist, 1990; Jenike & Rauch, 1994).

During the last 10 years there have been a number of significant breakthroughs. First, data from the US (Karno, Golding, Sorenson & Burnam, 1988) and now cross national epidemiological data from six countries have shown that Obsessive-Compulsive Disorder is much more prevalent than previously thought: recent estimates place the 1 year prevalence of OCD between 1.1 and

1.8% and the lifetime rate between 1.9 and 2.5% (Weissman, Bland, Canino, Greenwald, Hwu, Lee, Newman, Oakley-Browne, Rubio-Stipec, Wickramarathe, Wittchen & Yeh, 1994). Second, the same authors reported that the proportion of OCD cases not reporting compulsions (i.e., reporting obsessions only) may be as high as 50–60% although the structured interview used in these community studies may be overinclusive for obsessions. Third, Salkovskis (1985) working from the earlier description, analysis and treatment recommendations for obsessional thoughts by Rachman and colleagues (Rachman, 1971, 1976, 1978; Rachman & de Silva, 1978; Rachman & Hodgson, 1980) provided a comprehensive model of obsessional thoughts and outlined a treatment approach (Salkovskis & Westbrook, 1989). Fourth, a number of case reports and single case studies describing the successful treatment of obsessions using some form of exposure appeared in the literature (Headland & McDonald, 1987; Himle & Thyer, 1989; Hoogduin, de Haan, Schaap & Arts, 1987; Ladouceur, Freeston, Gagnon, Thibodeau & Dumont, 1993, 1995; Martin & Tarrier, 1992; Moergen, Maier, Brown & Pollard, 1987; Milby, Meredith & Rice, 1981; Salkovskis, 1983; Salkovskis & Westbrook, 1989). These findings have changed the status of pure obsessions from a rare, treatment refractory variant of OCD, to a relatively prevalent form with interesting treatment possibilities.

Diagnostic Issues

Differential Diagnosis

The DSM-IV (APA, 1994) criteria for Obsessive-Compulsive Disorder retain many of the classical features of OCD described in the psychopathological literature. Obsessive-Compulsive Disorder can be diagnosed by the presence of either obsessions or compulsions. There are several important changes from DSM-III-R. (APA, 1987). First, obsessions are now defined as "recurrent and persistent thoughts, impulses, or images that are experienced, at some time during the disturbance, as intrusive and inappropriate, and cause marked anxiety or distress" (p. 422). The word "senseless" has been replaced by "inappropriate" and the criteria of initial insight has been replaced with "at some time". Second, obsessions are "not simply excessive worries about real-life problems", thus trying to distinguish OCD from GAD (however some worries are not about real-life problems, see Dugas & Ladouceur, this volume). As before, although a diagnosis of OCD does not require compulsions to be present, it is required that "the person attempts to ignore or suppress such thoughts or impulses or to neutralize them with some thought or action". The requirement that the thoughts are seen as being of internal origin remains unchanged. A third improvement is that the definition of compulsions explicitly includes mental acts: compulsions are "repetitive behaviors (...) or mental acts (...) that the person feels driven to perform in response to an obsession, or according to rules that must be applied rigidly" that "are aimed a preventing or reducing distress or preventing some dreaded event or situation; however these behaviors or mental acts are not connected in a realistic way with what they are designed to neutralize or prevent, or are clearly excessive" (p. 423). Finally, an important precision is that the degree of insight is more clearly recognized as being highly variable: "At some point during the course of the disorder, the person has recognized that obsessions or compulsions are excessive or unreasonable. Note: this does not apply to children" (p. 423). In fact a subtype of OCD is also defined, Poor Insight Type, when insight is lacking in the current episode.

Comorbidity

Before treatment it is important to establish that the obsessional disorder is not complicated by the existence of other Axis 1 or Axis 2 disorders: it is normal to expect a certain degree of co-morbidity. The recent cross national epidemiological study showed lifetime median comorbidity rates of 27% for major depression and 52% for another anxiety disorder (Weissman et al., 1994) and figures may be even higher in clinical samples, especially for major depression (see Rasmussen & Eisen, 1992). In some cases cognitive-behavior therapy of obsessional thoughts should either be delayed or is contra-indicated. For example, with comorbid Panic Disorder or Post-Traumatic Stress Disorder, it may be indicated to treat the comorbid disorders first as effective exposure to obsessional stimuli may be difficult. Likewise, severe depression may require treatment before targeting the obsessional thoughts (see also Steketee, 1993; Riggs & Foa, 1993). Cormorbid substance abuse or psychotic disorders present particular treatment problems and treating obsessional thoughts with cognitive-behavioral techniques may be contra-indicated. There are no figures available for personality disorders among this subgroup of patients, but eleven studies with systematic assessment of DSM-III and DSM-III-R Personality Disorders reported that a median of 52% of OCD patients have one or more personality disorders (see also Molnar, Freund, Riggs & Foa, 1993; Steketee, 1993). Personality traits may interfere with treatment, particularly schizotypic features that may contribute to poor insight, and borderline features may prevent exposure (Steketee, 1993).

A Clinical Model of Obsessional Thoughts

The model presented below (Freeston & Ladouceur, 1994a) is a synthesis of earlier cognitive-behavioral models (e.g., Rachman & Hodgson, 1980; Salkovskis, 1985) and our own clinical and research experience with obsessions without overt compulsions.

Obsessions

The themes reported by patients commonly refer to aggression and loss of control, harming, negligence, dishonesty, accidents, sexuality, religion, contamination, and illness. However there are occasionally obsessions referring to minor ambiguities in everyday life (e.g., Did I step on the crack, or just before, or just after?), existential questions (e.g., When does the spirit enter the body?), and otherwise apparently neutral thoughts. In most cases, the individual generally recognizes the ego dystonic and irrational aspects of its content. But in some cases patients are not convinced that the thoughts are irrational (for a discussion see Kozak & Foa, 1994). As treatment progresses, patients gradually recognize the inappropriate, non-realistic or excessive aspects of the thought.

Current accounts of OCD generally agree that the thought content as such is less important than the meaning that the patient ascribes to it. Thus obsessions are conceptualized as an internal stimulus that are subject to further processing. They may occur spontaneously or be triggered by either external or internal stimuli. Internal stimuli include physical sensations, emotional states, and cognitive events whereas external stimuli include objects, situations, and people (Figure 5.1).

Appraisal and Perception of Threat

In line with other cognitive models of anxiety (e.g., Beck & Emery, 1985; Clark, 1986), appraisal is a process by which the individual attaches meaning to the thought in terms of its value, its importance, or its implications. If the thought is adequately appraised (e.g., "this is strange thought but it doesn't mean anything"), in that the individual treats the thought as a cognitive event that does not necessarily have any real life referents, then the thought is judged as having little importance, no particular value, or no particular personal implications. On the other hand, if the thought is inadequately appraised as having negative implications for the individual (e.g., "this thought might mean that I really could attack someone") then some type of further processing will occur. Thus, through the process of appraisal, an intrusion will acquire personal significance and, in the case of negative appraisal, will result in the perception of threat.

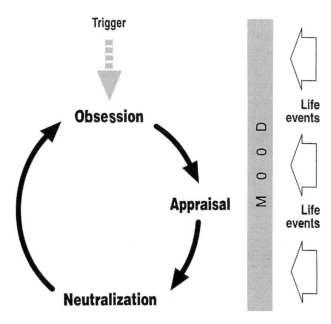

Figure 5.1. Cognitive-behavioral model of intrusive thoughts.

Cognitive Rituals, Coping, and Neutralization

We strongly believe that the key to the successful cognitive-behavioral treatment of obsessive thoughts with exposure and response prevention is to understand neutralization. Historically cognitive rituals have typically been defined in quite a narrow way. For example, "A cognitive ritual is defined as a mental act carried out in a specific fashion and consisting of a number of discrete steps" (Turner & Beidel, 1988, p. 3). Rachman & de Silva (1978) distinguished between neutralization and coping mechanisms. The former, referring to "attempts at putting right" (Rachman, 1976), are acts intended to enable escape from or avoid the obsession. Neutralization in this narrower sense referred to any act that may be "amendatory, neutralizing, reparative, corrective, preventive, or restorative" (Rachman & Hodgson, 1980, p. 273). Coping strategies were not defined but some examples were given: saying "stop", distraction by singing, counting, or praying, physical avoidance, and reassurance seeking was also included among the coping mechanisms. We have conducted an extensive program of studies on what normal subjects and patients do with their intrusive thoughts and obsessions using both question-naires and structured interviews (Freeston, Ladouceur, Gagnon & Thibodeau, 1991a,b, 1992; Freeston & Ladouceur, 1997; Freeston, Ladouceur, Provencher & Blais, 1995). The overall picture emerging from these studies may be sum-marized as follows:

1. Most individuals use a variety of different responses to intrusive thoughts, including doing nothing, some form of self-reassurance, thinking the thought through, seeking reassurance, replacing the thought with another, performing a mental or concrete action to remove the thought, using a distracting activity, distracting oneself with surroundings, and thought stopping. They may use different strategies with different thoughts and different strategies to deal with a given thought.
2. The choice of response depends on a variety of factors such as the thought, its appraisal, situational context, others strategies, and mood state.
3. No strategy is consistently more efficient than another, although specific strategies may be relatively efficient for some people. Some people report great variability in the efficiency of a given strategy.
4. Although activities meeting the narrow definition of cognitive rituals and neutralization presented above were reported by many obsessional patients, all used a wide range of coping strategies to deal with their thoughts.

Based on this knowledge we have adopted a very wide definition of neutralization that englobes cognitive rituals, attempts at putting right, and coping strategies: *neutralization is defined as anything that is voluntary and effortful directed at removing, preventing, or attenuating the thought.* Thus, many forms of neutralization may not meet the DSM-IV (APA, 1994) definition of a cognitive compulsion in that they may not be repetitive, "driven to perform.. or according to rules (p. 423)". This does not prevent a diagnosis of OCD as the various forms of neutralization are attempts to ignore, suppress, or neutralize thoughts as stipulated by the DSM-IV criteria for obsessions.

Mood and Life Events

Mood is conceptualized as playing a modulating role in obsessive-compulsive disorder (see Freeston & Ladouceur, 1994a). Specifically, it is postulated that negative mood states (1) increase the frequency and duration of obsessions (Rachman, 1981), (2) increase the likelihood of inadequate appraisals with, inflated subjective probabilities, extreme consequences etc., while decreasing the likelihood of adequate appraisals (Freeston & Ladouceur, 1994b), (3) decrease the efficacy of neutralization (Freeston et al., 1998), (4) increase hypervigilance for triggering stimuli (Mathews, 1990), and (5) decrease motivation or ability to engage in the strategies learnt during therapy.

Although major life events may be associated with the onset of OCD or with the start of the current episode (McKeon, Roa & Mann, 1984; Khanna, Rajendra & Channabasavanna, 1988), minor life events or hassles are believed to be responsible for the typical fluctuations involved in symptoms levels (Freeston & Ladouceur, 1994b; Rasmussen & Eisen, 1991). They may be seen as indirect triggers linked to worsening symptoms and among the most common reported by patients are being criticized, being ill, insufficient rest, insufficient sleep, fear of rejection, difficulty making decisions, unable to relax, stupid mistakes, too much responsibility, illness of a family member, noise, losing things, social obligations, thinking about the future, unexpected visits, too many things to do, not enough time, conflicts, and for women, menstrual problems (Freeston & Ladouceur, 1994b).

Assessment

Successful cognitive-behavior therapy depends on accurate behavioral analysis. The following instruments have proven useful in the treatment of obsessive thoughts.

General Psychopathology

The *Yale-Brown Obsessive-Compulsive Scale* (Goodman, Price, Rasmussen, Mazure, Delgado, Heniger & Charney 1989a; Goodman, Price, Rasmussen, Mazure, Fleischmann, Hill, Heniger & Charney, 1989b) is a clinician rating scale that is widely used in recent therapy trials of cognitive, behavioral, and pharmacological methods. The symptom checklist preceding the Y-BOCS is particularly helpful in providing an overall picture of current and previous obsessive-compulsive symptomatology. The obsession subscale and general assessment items are also useful in assessing the current severity of OCD, although the compulsion subscale may not always be easy to apply to neutralization strategies.

For general OCD and related symptoms, three self-report measures are also recommended. The *Padua Inventory* (Sanavio, 1988) is a comprehensive 60-item inventory of OC symptomatology with four subscales: Loss of Mental Control, Contamination, Checking, and Impulses and Worries about Loss of Control. An abridged 40-item version also exists (Freeston et al., 1998). The *Beck Depression Inventory* and *Beck Anxiety Inventory* (Beck, Epstein, Brown & Steer, 1988; Beck, Rush, Shaw & Emery, 1979) are useful brief measures of depressive and anxious symptomatology.

Self-Monitoring Diary

The self-monitoring diaries that we use measure discomfort associated with the thoughts, thought frequency, and total duration of the thoughts on a 9-point scale in notebooks adapted from Marks and colleagues (Marks, Stern,

Mawson, Cobb & McDonald, 1980). Discomfort is the easiest variable to compare across subjects for two principal reasons. First, thought frequency or thought duration is difficult to compare across subjects: some subjects may report only two or three thoughts per day, but engage in two hours of rumination for each thought whereas other subjects report literally hundreds of brief "flashes" that last a few seconds at most. Second, the intrusive thought literature (see Freeston et al., 1991a) has established that obsession-like intrusive thoughts are an almost universal experience that vary widely in frequency and duration. Thus, a normal response (i.e., decreased discomfort) to obsessions seems a more obvious outcome variable until clear target parameters are established for frequency and duration. Self-monitoring is conducted throughout treatment. It is important to make sure that patients use the scales in a realistic way so that the maximum score is defined as the worst that symptoms have been in the last month and not the worst that they have ever been.

Cognitive Assessment

The *Cognitive Intrusions Questionnaire* (CIQ, Freeston et al., 1991a; Freeston & Ladouceur, 1993) is a highly specific measure of the formal characteristics of the most troublesome thought, reactions to the thought, and appraisal of the thought. The CIQ first identifies the target obsessive thought which is then evaluated on a series of different items using 9 point likert-type scales: frequency, worry, sadness, difficulty to remove, guilt, probability, disapproval, perceived responsibility, triggers, avoidance of triggers, effort to counter, relief from countering, and success in removing the thought. Patients then indicate whether the intrusive thought took the form of an idea, image, impulse, doubt, or feeling. They also indicate which of 10 strategies they use to counter the thought when it occurs. We have used the CIQ extensively in both clinical and nonclinical samples and have demonstrated adequate reliability and validity (Freeston et al., 1991a; Freeston & Ladouceur, 1993).

The *Structured Interview on Neutralization* (Freeston et al., 1995) assesses strategies used to counter the most troublesome thought identified in the Cognitive Intrusions Questionnaire (CIQ) as the target thought (Freeston et al., 1991a; Freeston & Ladouceur, 1993). Subjects are asked to form the thought clearly at the start of the interview. The interviewer then uses 10 probe questions to elicit examples of strategies. Sub-questioning continued until operational descriptions are obtained and further similar examples are sought. Once the repertoire has been established, each strategy is then analyzed according to the following parameters: specific context where it is used, specific sequence, the probability that the thought would come true in real life, the intensity of the intrusion, the mood state, the mood intensity, and the immediate efficiency of the strategy, and the number of times that the strategy is repeated. Probability, thought intensity, mood intensity, and efficiency are rated on a five-point likert scale (0, *not at all,* to 4, *extremely*).

The *Inventory of Beliefs Related to Obsessions* (IBRO, Freeston, Ladouceur, Gagnon & Thibodeau, 1993) is a 20-item measure of dysfunctional beliefs related to obsessive thoughts that we have developed and validated sequentially on six independent samples. The IBRO is reliable (test-retest, $r = 0.70$; Cronbach's alpha = 0.82). Criterion (known groups) validity has been shown by contrasting both clinical patients with matched controls and subjects highly troubled by intrusive thoughts with less troubled subjects. Factor analysis revealed factors measuring Responsibility, Overestimation of Threat and Intolerance of Uncertainty respectively.

As well as calculating total scores for questionnaire measures, it is important to follow up with specific questions about symptoms, appraisals, and beliefs. Items with extreme ratings or unexpectedly high or low ratings (i.e., when a checked item is in disagreement with interview data or the clinician's working hypotheses) should be investigated to see what the patient means by the rating.

Treatment

The most successful current treatments are various developments of exposure methods first described by Rachman and colleagues as satiation training or habituation training. Although there are several case studies, a few case series, and some single-case designs (Headland & McDonald, 1987; Himle & Thyer, 1989; Hoogduin et al., 1987; Ladouceur et al., 1993, 1995; Martin & Tarrier, 1992; Moergen, Maier, Brown & Pollard, 1987; Milby, Meredith & Rice, 1981; Salkovskis, 1983; Salkovskis & Westbrook, 1989), there is, at the time of writing, only one controlled study with a waiting list control group (Ladouceur, Freeston, Rhéaume, Letarte, Thibodeau, Gagnon, & Bujold, 1994). The treatment package presented below was systematically evaluated on 28 patients. In all we have treated more than 45 patients with these methods.

Treatment Characteristics

The goal of the treatment is to change the patient's understanding of obsessions, prevent neutralization and thus enable patients to habituate to the obsessional thoughts. The thought frequency and duration and the distress caused by the thoughts will then decrease. The specific objectives are: (1) to provide an adequate explanation of obsessions, (2) to enable the patient to understand the role of neutralization in the maintenance of obsessional thoughts; (3) to prepare the client for exposure to the thoughts and to the situations which trigger the obsessions; (4) to correct when necessary the overestimation of the power and the importance of thoughts; (5) to expose the client to the thoughts and to implement response prevention (i.e., stop neutralizing activity); (6) to correct when present the exaggeration of specific fear consequences associated with the though; (7) to correct when present exaggerated responsibility and perfectionism; (8) to make the patient aware of situations in which he or she is more vulnerable to relapse and (9) to prepare the strategies to use when relapse occurs. The program is standardized in the sense that each patient receives all treatment components. It is individualized in the sense that the type of exposure, the targets for response prevention and the targets for cognitive correction will vary according to the individual characteristics of each patient. The format that we used to deliver the treatment was based on one and a half hour sessions for the first two-thirds of therapy. There were normally three to four assessment sessions followed by two sessions a week until exposure to target thoughts and response prevention was mastered, with decreasing session length and frequency in the later stages and gradual fade-out. Patients typically receive four to five months of treatment with about three months at two sessions a week.

Assessment Sessions

Once a diagnosis has been established assessment typically takes at least three sessions. The first normally addresses major symptoms identifying obsessive thoughts, neutralizing responses, situations that are avoided etc. The Yale-Brown Obsessive Compulsive Scale may be useful here and the BAI, BDI and Padua Inventory may be given as a homework task to complete a general picture of the principal and associated symptoms. The second may be used for general history taking, such as onset and course of the disorder, previous treatment (psychological or pharmacological), exacerbations with stress, social functioning, and knowledge about OCD. The cognitive questionnaires (CIQ, IBRO) may be given as a homework task. The third session can focus on the strategies used and on some aspects of appraisal.

Self-Monitoring

Self-monitoring should be introduced as soon as possible, for example, once target symptoms have been identified. Some clients are apprehensive about self-monitoring and believe that their obsessions will increase and they will become more preoccupied. It is important to establish with the client that this does not happen very often and that there are numerous advantages in self-monitoring for the successful application of the treatment. For instance, self-monitoring enables the client and the therapist to discover what may be modulating the variability and symptom severity (e.g., fluctuations linked to the menstrual cycle in women) and ultimately help in relapse prevention. Furthermore, it allows the client and the therapist to know when the therapy is working and why, and when it is not working and why not. It is very important to work closely with the patient at subsequent sessions until self-monitoring appears reliable and meaningful.

First Intervention Sessions

In all sessions the therapist first sets the agenda for the session and verifies self-monitoring and any other task that was assigned to the patient. Looking at homework reports increases the information available to the therapist and also shows the patient the importance of the assigned tasks. The first session has two main goals: to establish the therapeutic contract and to provide a model of obsessive thoughts that will be used throughout the treatment.

Establishing the therapeutic contract. The therapist states that he or she is ready to explain each step of the treatment in full, and to answer all valid questions. Patients are encouraged to ask questions so that each task may be successfully completed. The therapist explains that the goal of each exercise will be identified by the patient and the therapist together. When patients understand, they can actively participate in the process and adopt a problem-solving approach. Patients are actively involved in all decisions, for example exposure targets, and patients must indicate whether they think they are able to complete the exercise and to suggest changes in order to make the exercise more personally relevant. The therapist will encourage the patient very strongly to complete exercises but will never force the patient to do things against his or her will but will remind the patient of existing agreements. The therapist will seek feedback from the patient. Patients must report honestly whether exercises have been accomplished or not so that adjustments can be made for any difficulties that might arise.

Establishing a model. The model that is presented to the patient is adapted according to the patient's sophistication. In all cases the model is illustrated with the patients own obsessions, appraisals, beliefs, neutralization strategies etc.

The first step is to provide an account of intrusive thoughts.

Unpleasant thoughts come into people's mind against their will in about 99% of the population. We have studied these unpleasant thoughts among more than two thousand (2000) people of all ages and occupations and we found several common themes. They typically concern sexuality, religion, harm, disease, contamination, aggression, mistakes, dishonesty but may also involve order, symmetry, and minor unimportant details. The thoughts often seem to come out of nowhere although they maybe triggered by specific triggers. For example, thoughts about harming people may be triggered by seeing a large knife, etc.

At this point, the therapist gives the patient a list of thoughts reported by the general population and invites the patient to read the list. The therapist then helps the patient make the connection between the patient's own thoughts and thoughts reported by the population in general. There are sufficient examples in the list coming from the normal population that cover all major themes reported by patients. The goal is to establish that the thought content does not differ between thoughts reported by patients and thoughts reported by the general population.

There are very few differences in the content of the thoughts between the general population and people who consult for their obsessive thoughts. The differences lie in the frequency of the thoughts, the discomfort, the duration, the importance that the person attaches to the thoughts, and the effort that the person uses to deal with the thoughts. Strange intrusive thoughts are a normal experience which among about 2% of the population become problematic and are then called obsessions. As it is normal to have some unpleasant thoughts, the goal of the therapy is not to eliminate the thoughts because this would make you different from everybody else people. The goal is to change your reactions to the thoughts by changing the importance that you attached to the thoughts, to change the strategies that you use. Then the frequency and the duration of the thoughts will decrease together with the discomfort. The thoughts will become much less frequent and less disturbing and you will be able to deal with the thoughts when they occasionally come to mind.

At this point, patients often ask "Why do I have this type of thought?". At the moment, we do not unfortunately have totally convincing answers to this question. However, one explanation has proven satisfactory with patients follows.

We need the ability to have spontaneous thoughts in order to be able to solve problems and to be creative. This way, we may know how to act in a new situation or imagine new ideas or invent something new. Thus, we need a thought generator which can give us new ideas. However, this thought generator may also give us other types of thoughts, and we believe that these unpleasant thoughts also result from the idea generator.

We also have an ability to react to danger in useful ways, and to antici-pate danger. The danger detection system is there to protect us: this is the role of anxiety. For a number of different reasons, the idea generator and the danger detection system seem be more strongly associated in some people. The danger detection system seems to overreact by acting as though there is a tiger waiting around the corner when in fact its is only a pet cat. So when the idea generator and the danger detection system overreact together, obsessions are produced. Whatever the exact reasons, we know that we can learn to make the idea generator and the danger de-tection system react more appropriately so that the useful features remain while the overactive features associated with obsessions decrease greatly.

The next step in the model is the importance that the person attaches to the thoughts. Although this is technically referred to as *appraisal,* our experience with patients suggests that the "importance given to the thoughts" is a more accessible term, emphasizing the patient's active role in appraisal.

The reason why the same type of unpleasant thoughts causes a great deal of upset for some people but not for others is due to how the person in-terprets the thoughts or how much importance the person attaches to the thought. It is no coincidence that we typically see harming obsessions among gentle people, religious obsessions among religious people, thoughts about sexuality among highly moral people, and thoughts about mistakes among careful people: the more important something is, the worse it seems to have a bad thought about it.

The next step in the model is the idea of neutralization.

When someone attaches a great deal of importance to the thoughts, either its presence or its content, and that the person concludes that the thought is negative, dangerous, unacceptable etc., it is then normal to want to try to remove the thought, control the thought, or resolve it in one way or another. To give you an example we will do a short experiment. First close your eyes and try to think about a camel for 2 min. Each time that the camel disappears from your mind, indicate by lifting your finger. (The therapist records the number of times that the patient loses the thought.) How was that? Was it easy to keep the camel in mind? Now we will change things around. Close your eyes and try *not* to think about a camel for 2 min. Lift your finger each time that the thought appears. (The therapist records the number of times that the patient loses the thought.) What happened? Was it difficult to keep the thought away? What do these experiments tell you about trying to control our thoughts?

In all cases that we have seen, with both clinical and non-clinical subjects, keeping the thought present is difficult, and keeping the thought away totally is impossible! The therapist, by inviting the patient to comment on the experiment, leads the patient to conclude that our mental control, even for images or ideas that have no particular meaning, is much less than perfect. Even more important, the more that we try not to think about something, the more the thought comes to mind. It may be useful to suggest that the patient tries the same experiment with someone else who does not have obsessions. Most patients spontaneously make the link between this experiment and their own obsessions. The therapist can then formally define neutralization.

> All the strategies, which in the beginning may be very logical, eventually become part of the problem. All efforts to control, to remove or to avoid the thoughts are forms of what we call neutralization. (Particular examples from the patient's repertoire established during the structured interview are then added to the model.). How many different strategies have you tried? How many have worked? How many work all of the time?

The basic model has now been established and may be stated as follows:

> Obsessions may be thought of as a vicious circle where thoughts may be either triggered or occur spontaneously. You attach a particular importance to the thoughts, try to remove them or control them, and with the camel effect, the thoughts come back.

At this point, the critical distinction is made between the voluntary part of the model and the involuntary part of the model. The obsessional thought and the "camel effect" are both considered involuntary, whereas the importance attached to the thought and the neutralization are considered voluntary. With a little bit of prompting, the patient is led to establish that the two voluntary parts of the model, namely the importance given to the thoughts and neutralizing strategies, are the places where modification is possible.

The patient is invited to summarize the principle points of the model as a homework task. The patient is asked to note the types of interpretation or importance given to the thought.

Second and Third Intervention Sessions

The goal of the second treatment session is to check that the model is understood, add any further details, and prepare the patient for exposure and response prevention.

The role of anxiety. The therapist explains the role of anxiety (or other negative emotions reported by the patient such as discomfort, frustration, stress, or tension) in terms of the model.

> When the thought is given a lot of importance in terms of danger or harm, it is normal that anxiety increases. Anxiety is an unpleasant experience and it is normal that people try to do something with the thought to decrease the anxiety. Neutralization often but not always leads to a temporary and partial reduction in anxiety. Because it brings some relief, the reduction in discomfort increases the probability of neutralizing again (by negative reinforcement). Furthermore, as anxiety worsens, the frequency of the thought also increases.
>
> Although it is normal to want to avoid or to decrease anxiety, neutralizing means that because of the "camel effect" the thought will come back. Not only will anxiety be experienced again, but with a sense of losing control, the anxiety is often worse on each subsequent occasion. This is a bit like playing Monopoly; every time you pass go you collect another $200!

The therapist can then show an anxiety curve for neutralization and contrast it with a habituation curve (Figure 5.2).

> See how anxiety increases following the obsessional thought and decreases partially following neutralization, only to increase again with the next thought and go even higher! On the other hand, there is a natural habituation curve for anxiety which involves a first increasing phase, a second plateau phase, then a third decreasing phase. This type of curve has been studied in thousands of people with all types of anxiety, including the anxiety associated with obsessions. Thus, if we neutralize, we can never learn that anxiety will decrease by itself, even if we do nothing.

Avoidance. Although in most cases neutralizing means doing something to deal with the thought, there are some patients all of the time and many patients in some circumstances who also use passive avoidance to try to control the thoughts. Avoidance, by adding to the importance attached to the thought, maintains obsessions by increasing the range of potential stimuli. Avoidance prevents the patient from learning that anxiety provoked by the thoughts or by the stimuli will decrease, even when the stimulus is confronted.

Reassurance seeking. Reassurance seeking is identified as another form of neutralization. It may be necessary to explicitly make the link between certain features of reassurance seeking and other forms of neutralization, for example,

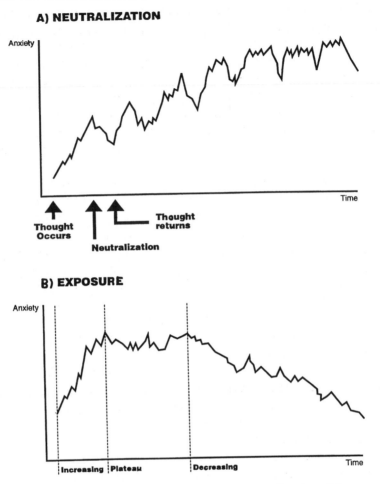

Figure 5.2. Anxiety associated with obsessions: (a) neutralization; (b) exposure.

the temporary effect, the need to repeat the demand, and the variability in the efficacy of reassurance.

Exposure. Now that the model has been fully established and illustrated with examples from the patient's own repertoire of thoughts, interpretations and strategies, it is shown that to break the vicious circle, it is then necessary to learn to tolerate the thought. This involves deliberately thinking the thought (exposure) without neutralizing (response prevention). When this has been achieved, anxiety will decrease, the importance given to the thought will decrease, any feared consequences will either happen or not happen with exactly the same probability as before, and the thoughts will gradually decrease in intensity, duration and frequency. It must be remembered that patients are normally looking for another trick, another strategy, or a new way of removing obsessions when they enter therapy. Thus exposure and response prevention may seem counter-intuitive. At this point, it may useful to use an example to illustrate the principle of exposure. For example, how the patient would help a child to overcome a fear (e.g., of dogs), or how the patient has already overcome a fear in the past. The idea of progressive exposure can also be introduced. The method described by the patient can then be reformulated in terms of exposure. The therapist can then show obsessions are like having a phobia to ones own ideas and that the same methods of treatment can be applied.

The main reason for using tape loops (as used in answering machines) for exposure is that they provide the therapist with some ability to manipulate an otherwise covert event: obsessional thoughts are much less predictable than sources of contamination or stimuli associated with checking found with the more common forms of OCD. The regular presentation of the thought on a tape loop enables the patient to repeatedly practice response prevention. Longer exposure sessions are easier with tape loops than with other techniques requiring repeated trials in imagination, speaking out loud, etc. We do not suggest that tape loop exposure is essential, nor is it necessarily the best way to proceed: the verbal presentation of the thought may interfere under some circumstances with successful image formation. However, we believe that tape loops provide a practical, effective means of training the patient in exposure and response prevention for covert events. As the patient masters exposure and response prevention, the tape may not always be necessary for items higher up the hierarchy. When there are several thoughts, the least anxiety provoking thought may be targeted first (Table 5.1).

However, if there is one major thought, it may not be possible to have a variety of exposure targets arranged hierarchically in terms of content. In this case, it is the context of exposure that will vary:
- With therapist in the office (anxiety 3);
- With therapist in the office with knife and picture of child (4);
- With therapist at home (5);
- Alone at home (7); and finally
- Alone at home while child is there (8).

Table 5.1. Hierarchy for different thoughts

Anxiety level	Thought
2	Shouting out rude words
3	Pushing someone when walking in the street
5	Punching someone in the face
7	Attacking someone with a knife
8	Going completely crazy, going on the rampage and killing a lot of people

Developing hierarchies may take some creativity but the use of a walkman will certainly facilitate exposure in specific physical contexts. We have no evidence that gradual exposure is superior to exposure to the worst thought right away. However, given the covert nature of obsessions and most neutralization strategies, functional exposure is often hard to achieve initially. So from a purely practical standpoint it may be advisable to start with less threatening thoughts or contexts until the techniques of exposure and response prevention have been fully mastered.

Once the first target has been identified mutually by the therapist and the client, the therapist then asks the client to describe the thought in detail. The therapist asks questions until there is sufficient detail, for example, precise words, colors, textures, sounds, smells, cognitive and emotional reactions to the thoughts, and any physical responses. Next, the therapist asks the patient to write the thought, using as much detail as possible. We agree with other sources (e.g., Riggs & Foa, 1993; Steketee, 1993) that it is not necessary to exaggerate or add additional consequences. However, we believe it is necessary for patients to expose themselves as far as the feared consequences go. For example, if the ultimate result of a harming obsession is arrest, trial, and incarceration for life in a mental institution, it is important to expose up until this point. It can be uncomfortable for therapists when they listen to the horrific scenarios reported by patients and the very distressing reactions that can occur during exposure. The technique is efficient when properly conducted and the therapist's discomfort will also decrease with habituation after several experiences with the technique.

An example of the text for exposure to the second thought for the previous example would be:

> I'm walking down the street, I see an old woman coming towards me. She looks frail and defenseless. All of a sudden I have the thought "What happens if I lose control and push her". My stomach tightens, my hands sweat and I have trouble breathing. The old woman is much closer. My fists clench and I struggle to keep control. She is almost up to me and I start to panic. She is quickly past me and I keep on walking. I wonder if I did push her. The doubt starts to grow. I see her lying in the street with broken bones. The ambulance comes. I feel terrible, I am a murderer and will be condemned.

The text may be very short or it may be a long evolved scenario. The therapist ensures that no neutralizing element (i.e., no anxiety decreasing element) is included in the sequence. The therapist then reads the thought out loud to the patient so that the patient can see if there are any parts missing. The patient then practices reading the thought out loud so that the therapist can time the text to choose a suitable length tape, and also to ensure that the thought is read with sufficient expression, at a suitable speed and leaving any pauses necessary to allow images to be formed. The patient is asked to read in a way that the therapist can experience what it is like to have the thought. Reading fast, mechanically, or with flat affect may be forms of cognitive avoidance. The thought is then recorded on a looped tape of appropriate length (e.g., 15 s, 30 s, 1 min, 3 min) with the number of repetitions necessary to fill the tape almost completely.

Once the thought has been recorded and verified, the exposure session can begin. The instructions are as follows.

> We will shortly begin the first exposure session. This will typically take 25 to 45 min, although it may be longer. We will continue until your anxiety level has decreased. Close your eyes and listen to the cassette without neutralizing, don't.. (name the specific strategies used by the patient). Stay with the thought, don't block it, filter it, or remove it. After each repetition of the thought, report your level of discomfort on the usual scale (typically the scale that is used for self-monitoring). Now please tell me what we are going to do.

If there is insufficient time to complete exposure during the session, (i.e., a minimum of 50 min), the exposure will be re-scheduled for the next session. The therapist asks the patient to complete a self-monitoring form before starting the exposure exercise. This typically consists of the current anxiety level, the expected maximum anxiety level during exposure, and the expected anxiety level after the exposure session. It is useful for the therapist to track anxiety ratings on a graph during the exposure session.

If the level of discomfort has not increased after several presentations, for example after 6–10 min, the therapist stops exposure in order to conduct a behavioral analysis of the situation. There are several possible reasons why the anxiety may not increase. First, the recording may be inadequate. For example, the words used may not be sufficiently representative of the actual thought or there is insufficient time to form images. Second, some patients do not have the ability to imagine the thought sufficiently clearly for functional exposure. If the person is unable after several attempts in using practice attempts on positive or neutral scenes to place themselves in the situation, other forms of exposure must be considered (see Ladouceur et al., 1993). Third, the patient may be neutralizing, either by using strategies that have already been identified or by using other previously unidentified strategies. If so, the therapist reiterates the importance of not neutralizing by referring to the model. The therapist should also investigate reasons for neutralizing in the case where the patient anticipates negative consequences. In this case, an intervention of a cognitive nature is necessary to explore, reformulate, or confront these anticipations.

Exposure continues if the anxiety increases. Note that increases and decreases in the level of anxiety are not necessarily uniform. The therapist watches the patient closely for any physical signs such as changes in breathing rate, trembling, facial expression, and to see if there are any signs that there is disagreement between the physical clues and the patient's verbal report. The exposure continues until the discomfort decreases below the starting point for at least two presentations, and if possible, until the level of anxiety has decreased much lower than the starting point. Once exposure has been completed, the therapist asks the patient to fill out the second part of the self-monitoring sheet rating the current anxiety and the maximum anxiety during exposure. The patient also notes whether neutralization occurred, and if so, what form was used and whether the patient re-exposed immediately to the thought.

The therapist then asks the patient to describe reactions to the experience. The reactions are then reframed in terms of the model and in terms of the patient's previous expectations. In our experience, it is rare that the first exposure session will be highly conclusive because of the difficulties in implementing response prevention to all forms of neutralization. For this reason, it is very important not to give exposure as homework until the patient has succeeded during the therapeutic session.

Once exposure has been successfully conducted in the office, exposure may be used at home. This is typically, but not invariably, after two exposure sessions. Our current recommendation is to listen to the cassette twice a day. It is important to identify the time and situation where it will possible to successfully complete exposure exercises.

Later Exposure Sessions

In all sessions where exposure has been given as homework, it is important to examine the exposure self-monitoring forms in detail at the start of each session. The duration, ratings and notes on neutralization should all be addressed.

When patients are able to complete exposure without neutralizing, they can start to conduct exposure when the thoughts occur spontaneously. The instruction here is as follows:

When the thoughts occur, just watch them. See them come and watch them go without reacting to them; just leave them where they are without trying to do anything in particular.

In order to increase generalization, the cassette can be modified when it provokes less anxiety (i.e., some between-session habituation has occurred). These modifications call on the patient's and therapist's creativity in order to find ways of creating optimal functional exposure and include varying the stimulus, the situation, the thought intensity, and the mood.

Cognitive Techniques

Cognitive techniques may target any one of a number of different themes that are commonly observed in patients with obsessional thoughts. These are:
(1) overestimating the importance of the thoughts and its derivatives such as fusion of thought and action and magical thinking;
(2) exaggerated responsibility,
(3) perfectionistic control over thoughts and actions and the closely related need for certainty,
(4) the consequences related to the thought's content which involve overestimations of the probability and the severity of the consequences of negative events,

The specific targets vary according to the patient and the types of appraisal made. The CIQ and the IBRO will give leads as to the specific dysfunctional appraisals and underlying beliefs.

We use cognitive techniques in two ways. In the first case they may be used as a means of facilitating exposure by first addressing patients' concerns such as the power of thoughts to cause actions, the nature of responsibility, and the consequences of anxiety. In this case they are a prerequisite or corequisite of effective exposure. In the second case they may be used as a supplement to exposure in order to fully integrate the new information generated by exposure, encourage generalization, and create conditions that will minimize the chances of relapse. Thus for some patients, some targets may be addressed very early in therapy whereas others will be addressed once the patient has mastered the basics of exposure.

Once target appraisals have been identified, a variety of techniques may be used limited only by the therapist's creativity and the patient's ability to actively participate. Once of the best ways of identifying underlying assumptions is to use the "downward arrow" (Burns, 1980) also known as the "so what?" technique where the original thought is examined sequentially for proximal and distal consequences. It is not uncommon in the course of this technique to find several types of underlying assumptions: for example, faulty appraisals of harm are often associated with faulty appraisals of the severity and probability of consequences as well as exaggerated responsibility. Faulty assumptions can be challenged by any appropriate technique, below are some examples of interventions that have proven useful with patients in our treatment program and private practices.

Over-estimation of the importance of thoughts. This occurs in several forms.

The first example relates to magical thinking, that thinking can lead to real events.

A married woman had horrific images of her husband in a car accident and used a prayer to counter the image each time. Here is the downward arrow associated with this thought.

If I keep on thinking about my husband having an accident
and don't pray each time, he will have an accident

⇓

It will be my fault

⇓

I could never forgive myself

⇓

I would become depressed and commit suicide

The key assumption here is that thoughts can cause actions although responsibility is also clearly present. One way that we have successfully challenged this type of belief is with behavioral experiments. For example, the patient buys a lottery ticket on Monday and imagines winning the jackpot for half an hour a day all week (chances are 1 in 14 000 000 for the most popular lottery in Quebec). Alternatively, a minor household appliance is identified that is known to be in good working order (e.g., a toaster). The patient thinks 100 times a day that the appliance will break down within the next week. The outcome is then compared to the prediction.

Exaggerated responsibility. A young university educated male was obsessed with the idea that by letting the water run while he brushed his teeth or rinsed dishes, he would be responsible for the installation of water meters on all houses.

If I let the water run while I am brushing my teeth,
I am wasting water

⇓

If I waste water then they will install water meters to
control the quantity of water that people use

⇓

That will cost a lot of money for everybody

⇓

Poor people will have even less money

⇓

It will be on my conscience

The key assumption here is inflated personal responsibility which operates at two levels. The first refers to the individual's use of water compared to everybody else in the town's use of water. In fact, if everybody in the region did stop running water while brushing teeth, the savings would be considerable, but one individual's role remains insignificant. Using a pie chart to determine the volume of water used by the individual while brushing teeth (which can be measured) compared to the volume used by industry, all the other households, watering gardens etc., will establish the respective contributions. The technique is to attribute responsibility to all other sources before looking at the individual's remaining responsibility. Thus the idea of pivotal power is clearly erroneous: How can the minute proportion of water used by the patient influence public policy?.

The second level is to address the individual's personal responsibility vs. the collective responsibility for rational water use: although his pivotal role was clearly erroneous, as a responsible citizen he has some degree of responsibility. However, rational water use is a collective responsibility and not an individual responsibility. Once again the pie-chart is used to accurately identify personal responsibility. Responsibility is attributed, for example, to the role of planners and policy makers (40%), the role of local government to educate people about responsible water use (15%), enforcing changes in industrial practises (25%), the role of environmental groups in raising public awareness (5%), the role of education in the schools (5%), and then finally to the 10 000 households in the town (10%) (see Figure 5.3). Thus as one of the 10 000 households and with 5 people in the household, the individual's personal responsibility is $10\% \times 1/10\ 000 \times 1/5 = 0.0002\%$.

An additional way to challenge this type of appraisal is for the patient to act as prosecuting attorney and/or defense attorney to argue the case. It is often more difficult for the patient to be the prosecuting attorney because usually the only evidence of guilt (i.e., responsibility) is, by emotional reasoning, their subjective feeling of guilt. The patient must instead prove his "guilt" by finding solid arguments with real empirical proof ("What are the facts?"). When the patient plays both roles, he can consider and compare two opposing points of view, thus highlighting the modifiable nature of the appraisal. The role of the therapist is to play the judge and "strike from the record" inadmissible evidence such as hearsay ("I once heard that..") or irrational arguments.

The key to challenging responsibility appraisals is to first establish an awareness (e.g., by self monitoring) of situations where the patient takes excessive responsibility. Emotional cues such as feeling guilty or uncomfortable about something are often the best way of detecting excessive responsibility. When patients take excessive responsibility for specific events, one way of exposing the excessive nature is to transfer responsibility (on a temporary basis) to the therapist through a contract for any harm that will occur during a specified period (see Rachman, 1993). Thoughts, behavior and reactions are

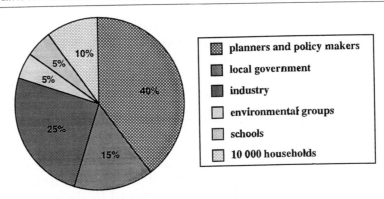

Figure 5.3. Adequate attribution of responsibility for water use.

then monitored and compared to a similar period when the responsibility is re-transferred to the patient. Another way of highlighting exaggerated responsibility is by predicting the patient's reactions (cognitive, emotional, or behavioral) when responsibility is transferred to someone else, for example, if someone is paid a large amount to take care of the situation. The patient is asked, "would you still neutralize if you had paid $30 000 to a person for driving behind you to make sure that you had not hit someone".

Exaggerated probability and consequences of a negative outcome. This type of appraisal is common across a number of anxiety disorders and there are a number of good examples in the literature (Beck & Emery, 1985; van Oppen & Arntz, 1994). The downward arrow is used to identify all the steps in the chain leading to the ultimate feared consequence. The subjective probability of each step is evaluated to then calculate the cumulative probability. Once all steps are identified, the logic of the consequence at each step and its probability can be challenged.

Perfectionism. Perfectionistic appraisals of thoughts exists in a number of forms. One form of perfectionism is the need for certainty or completeness (see Rasmussen & Eisen, 1991). A young male graduate student with a range of obsessions related to different ambiguities had repeated obsessions that he had not perfectly understood things he had read. His reading slowed, he took less pleasure in reading, and would become distracted in other tasks by trying to see whether he had understood what he had read by explaining the text to himself.

What if I didn't understand everything I read

⇓

It's as if I understood nothing

⇓

I won't know what I need to know

⇓

I'll end up knowing nothing

⇓

I'll fail

This was challenged in three ways. First, the dichotomous thinking ("If I didn't understand everything then its as if I understood nothing") was identified and challenged. Second, the advantages and disadvantages of trying to understand everything perfectly were exposed.

Advantages	Disadvantages
Knowing that I know	Self-doubt and frustration when I don't succeed (most of the time)
Certainty about a few things	Reading less
	Loss of pleasure in reading
	Preoccupation and distraction, fatigue

Once the advantages and disadvantages were established, the validity of the advantages was challenged. In this case the patient had to identify the number of times he was certain of what he had read. In fact, (as may be predicted) he admitted this happened extremely infrequently, if at all. Thus, not only was he (1) engaged in the fruitless pursuit of so-called advantages that almost never happened, but (2) he also suffered all the disadvantages of seeking perfect understanding. This opened the door to modify the underlying beliefs by a change in behavior.

To challenge the prediction ("If I don't understand everything that I read, I won't know what I need to know and will ultimately fail"), a behavioral experiment was devised. He first divided things to be read into three categories.
1. Things that only have to be read (publicity, brochures, junk mail, newspapers etc.)
2. Things that have to be read and understood in general terms (background reading, reading for pleasure)
3. Things that have to be read and well understood (exam material, job applications etc.).

In the first category things were to be read as fast as possible with no going back. In the second category, the first page was read at his normal speed, subsequent pages were to be read 1/3 faster. The third category remained unchanged for the time being. Not only was the prediction not true (that he would end up knowing nothing and fail), but the patient found that his pleasure increased, his speed increased, distraction decreased and he ended up knowing more because he read more and worried less. He was eventually able to take a third category text and read some parts faster than others according to their relative importance.

Behavioral experiments are useful for challenging both exaggerated responsibility and perfectionistic attitudes, for example, deliberately making a small error or changing a rigid habit, and then predicting the specific negative consequences and comparing them to the real outcome. When appropriately reframed, these experiments enable more accurate predictions to be made.

Relapse Prevention

The formal study of relapse and relapse prevention in OCD is still in its infancy, but recent texts (e.g., Emmelkamp, Kloek & Blaauw, 1992; Salkovskis, 1985; Steketee, 1993) are addressing the question more explicitly. There are no data on relapse for obsessional thoughts without overt compulsions, our own experience is that treatment is best faded out with increased spacing between sessions and occasional contact with the therapist for "fine tuning" and learning how to react adequately to new situations. Although much of the necessary information to deal with relapse is implicit throughout treatment, it should be explicitly identified in the later sessions and packaged together in a document that the patient can keep. The essential information in the kit includes:

- A clear understanding of the model and how mood and life events may modulate the model thus helping the patient to understand changes in residual symptom levels and identify early signs of relapse. The model and basic information should be put in writing. Relapse prevention sessions can also be taped.
- Clear expectations about residual symptoms. The patient expects to have some thoughts with occasional flare ups of more frequent and intense thoughts but will be able to cope with them. In particular, low frequency triggering situations are more difficult to adjust to because of the lack of practice and novelty. Thus, vacations, unforeseen life changes, "bad luck" situations are often associated with increases in obsessional symptoms.
- Written instructions about what to do in case of relapse. This may be reduced to the following but is better when presented with personalized detail and examples:
  1. Don't panic
  2. Revise the model
  3. Don't attach importance to the thought, don't catastrophize
  4. Don't neutralize, avoid, seek reassurance etc.
  5. Do exposure exercises
  6. Analyze key situations, apply restructuring techniques to re-evaluate probability, attribute responsibility, etc.

7. Identify stressors and apply problem solving, seeking aid when necessary
8. Identify what you were doing when things were going better and that you have stopped doing now
9. Look at relapses as a chance to put theory into practice and keep up to date, and not as a setback or failure.

It should be noted that other authors have discussed a variety of supplements that may be useful with OC patients to prevent relapse (Emmelkamp et al., 1992; Riggs & Foa, 1993; Steketee, 1993; Turner & Beidel, 1988; Warren & Zgourides, 1991). The general consensus is to develop ways of overcoming difficulties in normal day to day living. Supplements may include assertiveness training, marital or family therapy, stress management training, activity planning, problem solving training etc.

Combined Pharmacological and Cognitive-Behavioral Treatment

In recent years there has been increased interest in the combination of pharmacological and cognitive-behavioral therapies in the treatment of OCD. A recent meta-analysis of 87 OCD treatment studies (van Balkom, van Oppen, Vermeulen, Nauta, Vorst & van Dyck, 1994) found that behavior therapy was significantly superior to placebo on assessor ratings of OC symptoms. They also observed marginally significant results for cognitive therapy. On self-rated symptoms, behavior therapy appeared to be more effective than the antidepressants clomipramine, fluoxetine, or fluvoxamine combined together and there was no evidence that these antidepressants in combination with behavior therapy was superior to behavior therapy only. As there are no comparative studies on obsessional thoughts without overt compulsive rituals, it is not possible to provide empirically based recommendations. However, as we have stated elsewhere (Ladouceur, Freeston & Gagnon, 1996), our experience has shown that in some cases appropriate combinations of antidepressants and cognitive-behavior therapy may facilitate treatment by stabilizing the patient, improving depressive symptoms and establishing an initial sense of control, thus enabling the patient to commit more resources to cognitive-behavior therapy.

Close collaboration between the prescribing physician and therapist is necessary to allow appropriate fade-out and/or substitution of alternative medication (e.g., an antidepressant with no proven anti-obsessional effects) so that skills may be practised with appropriate symptom levels and permit adequate attribution of treatment gains to the new skills that have been learnt during cognitive-behavior therapy. This may decrease the likelihood of relapse when medication is withdrawn. We have observed that some patients with prior history of depression or relapse when previous trials of medication were withdrawn may particularly benefit from a continued low maintenance dosage of medication well below normal recommended levels while life-style changes are made following successful cognitive-behavior therapy. With a "safety-net" in place, the patient will feel more confident and more able to meet the challenges of learning to live without obsessions with less fear of relapse.

Efficacy of Cognitive Behavior Treatment

In addition to the successful cases already reported (Ladouceur et al., 1993; 1995), 28 patients recently participated a controlled outcome study. At post-test, there was significantly greater improvement in the treatment group than in the control group on the Yale-Brown Obsessive-Compulsive Scale as well as on measures of global functioning and self-report measures of anxiety, depression, obsessive symptoms and cognitive variables. The average treatment gain for all patients was a 57% mean reduction in the initial Yale-Brown score. For patients who completed treatment, 82% were much improved. Self-reported obsessive, depressive, and anxious symptoms as well as irrational beliefs and appraisal of target thoughts all decreased, with close to three-quarters of the patients' scores falling within the normal range after treatment. Six-month follow-up showed that gains remained stable. Follow-up on patients who completed treatment 2–3 years earlier shows that they are maintaining treatment gains although some remain vulnerable to mood disturbances and occasional flare-ups in response to stressful events. We are planning to adapt the package to treat adolescent OCD in the near future.

References

APA (1987). *Diagnostic and statistical manual of mental disorders*, 3th edition revised (DSM-III-R). Washington, DC: American Psychiatric Association.

APA (1994). *Diagnostic and statistical manual of mental disorders*, 4th edition (DSM-IV). Washington, DC: American Psychiatric Association.

Beck, A. T., & Emery, G. (1985). *Anxiety disorders and phobias: A cognitive perspective*. New York: Basic Books.

Beck, A. T., Epstein, N., Brown, G., & Steer, R. A. (1988). An inventory for measuring clinical anxiety: Psychometric properties. *Journal of Consulting and Clinical Psychology, 56*, 893–897.

Beck, A. T., Rush, A. J., Shaw, B. F., & Emery, G. (1979). *Cognitive therapy of depression*. New York: Guilford Press.

Beech, H. R., & Vaughn, M. (1978). *Behavioural treatment of obsessional states*. Chichester, UK: Wiley.

Burns, D. D. (1980). *Feeling good: The new mood therapy*. New York: New American Library.

Clark, D. M. (1986). A cognitive approach to panic. *Behaviour Research and Therapy, 24*, 461–470.

Emmelkamp, P. M. G. (1982). *Phobic and obsessive-compulsive disorders.* New York: Plenum Press.

Emmelkamp, P. M. G., Kloek, J., & Blaauw, E. (1992). Obsessive-compulsive disorders. In P. H. Wilson (Ed.), *Principles and practice of relapse prevention.* New York: Guilford Press.

Foa, E. B., Steketee, G. S., & Ozarow, B. J. (1985). Behavior therapy with obsessive compulsives. In M. Mavissakalian, S. M. Turner & L. Michelson (Eds.), *Obsessive-compulsive disorder.* New York: Plenum Press.

Freeston, M. H., & Ladouceur, R. (1993). Appraisal of cognitive intrusions and response style: Replication and extension. *Behaviour Research and Therapy, 31,* 181–190.

Freeston, M. H., & Ladouceur, R. (1994a). From intrusions to obsessions: An account of the development and maintenance of obsessive-compulsive disorder. Manuscript in preparation.

Freeston, M. H., & Ladouceur, R. (1994b). Mood, cognitive appraisal, daily life events and obsessional severity in OCD without overt compulsions. Manuscript in preparation.

Freeston, M. H., & Ladouceur, R. (1997). What do patients do with their obsessive thoughts? *Behaviour Research and Therapy, 35,* 335–348.

Freeston, M. H., Ladouceur, R., Gagnon, F., & Thibodeau, N. (1991a). Cognitive intrusions in a non-clinical population. I. Response style, subjective experience, and appraisal. *Behaviour Research and Therapy, 29,* 585–597.

Freeston, M. H., Ladouceur, R., Gagnon, F., & Thibodeau, N. (1991b). *Les intrusions cognitives: Implications pour le trouble obsessionnel-compulsif.* (Intrusive thoughts: Implications for obsessive compulsive disorder). Paper presented at the annual convention of the Société Québécoise pour la Recherche en Psychologie, Trois-Rivière, Québec.

Freeston, M. H., Ladouceur, R., Gagnon, F., & Thibodeau, N. (1992). *Intrusive thoughts, worry, and obsessions: Empirical and theoretical distinctions.* Paper presented at the World Congress of Cognitive Therapy, Toronto.

Freeston, M. H., Ladouceur, R., Gagnon, F., & Thibodeau, N. (1993). Beliefs about obsessional thoughts. *Journal of Psychopathology & Behavioral Assessment, 15,* 1–21.

Freeston, M. H., Ladouceur, R., Provencher, M., & Blais, F. (1995). Strategies used with intrusive thoughts: Context, appraisal, mood, and efficacy. *Journal of Anxiety Disorders, 9,* 201–215.

Freeston, M. H., Ladouceur, R., Letarte, H., Rhéaume, J., Gagnon, F., & Thibodeau, N. (1998). Measurement of obsessive-compulsive symptoms with the Padua Inventory: Replication and extension. Submitted.

Goodman, W. K., Price, L. H., Rasmussen, S. A., Mazure, C., Delgado, P, Heniger, G. R., & Charney, D. S. (1989a). The Yale-Brown Obsessive Compulsive Scale. II. Validity. *Archives of General Psychiatry, 46,* 1012–1016.

Goodman, W. K., Price, L. H., Rasmussen, S. A., Mazure, C., Fleischmann, R. L., Hill, C. L., Heniger, G. R., & Charney, D. S. (1989b). The Yale-Brown Obsessive Compulsive Scale. I. Development, use and reliability. *Archives of General Psychiatry, 46,* 1006–1011.

Greist, J. H. (1990). Treatment of obsessive compulsive disorder: Psychotherapies, drugs, and other somatic treatment. *Journal of Clinical Psychiatry, 51,* 44–50.

Headland, K., & McDonald, B. (1987). Rapid audio-tape treatment of obsessional ruminations. A case report. *Behavioural Psychotherapy, 15,* 188–192.

Himle, J., & Thyer, B. A. (1989). Clinical social work and obsessive-compulsive disorder. *Behavior Modification, 13,* 459–470.

Hoogduin, K., de Haan, E., Schaap, C., & Arts, W. (1987). Exposure and response prevention in patients with obsessions. *Acta Psychiatrica Belgica, 87,* 640–653.

Jenike, M. A., & Rauch, S. L. (1994). Managing the patient with treatment-resistant obsessive-compulsive disorder: Current strategies. *Journal of Clinical Psychiatry, 55,* 11–17.

Karno, M., Golding, J. M., Sorenson, S. B., & Burnam, M. A. (1988). The epidemiology of obsessive-compulsive disorder in five US communities. *Archives of General Psychiatry, 45,* 1094–1099.

Khanna, S., Rajendra, P. N., & Channabasavanna, S. M. (1988). Life events and onset of obsessive-compulsive disorder. *The International Journal of Social Psychiatry, 34,* 305–309.

Kozak, M. J., & Foa, E. B. (1994). Obsessions, overvalued ideas, and delusions in obsessive.compulsive disorder. *Behaviour Research and Therapy, 32,* 343–353.

Ladouceur, R., Freeston, M. H., Gagnon, F., Thibodeau, N., & Dumont, J. (1993). Idiographic considerations in the cognitive-behavioral treatment of obsessional thoughts. *Journal of Behavior Therapy and Experimental Psychiatry, 24,* 301–310.

Ladouceur, R., Freeston, M. H., & Gagnon, F. (1996). Cognitive and behavioral treatment of obsessive-compulsive disorder. *Canadian Family Physician, 42,* 1169–1178.

Ladouceur, R., Freeston, M. H., Rhéaume, J., Letarte, H., Thibodeau, N., Gagnon, F., & Bujold, A. (1994). *Treatment of obsessions: A controlled study.* Paper presented at the annual convention of the Association for the Advancement of Behavior Therapy, San Diego, CA.

Ladouceur, R., Freeston, M. H., Gagnon, F., Thibodeau, N., & Dumont, J. (1995). Cognitive-behavioral treatment of obsessions. *Behavior Modification, 19,* 247–257.

Marks, I. M. (1987). *Fears, phobias, and rituals.* New York: Oxford University Press.

Marks, I. M., Stern, R. S., Mawson, D., Cobb, J., & McDonald, R. (1980). Clomopramine and exposure for obsessive-compulsive rituals: I. *British Journal of Psychiatry, 136,* 1–25.

Martin, C., & Tarrier, N. (1992). The importance of cultural factors in the exposure to obsessive ruminations: A case example. *Behavioural Psychotherapy, 20,* 181–184.

Mathews, A. (1990). Why worry? The cognitive function of anxiety. *Behaviour Research and Therapy, 28,* 455–468.

McKeon, J., Roa, B., & Mann, A. (1984). Life events and personality traits in obsessive-compulsive neurosis. *British Journal of Psychiatry, 144,* 185–189.

Milby, J. B., Meredith, R. L., & Rice, J. (1981) Videotaped exposure: A new treatment for obsessive-compulsive disorders. *Journal of Behavior Therapy and Experimental Psychiatry, 12,* 249–255.

Moergen, S., Maier, M., Brown, S., & Pollard. C. A. (1987). Habituation to fear stimuli in a case of obsessive-compulsive disorder: Examining the generalization process. *Journal of Behavior Therapy and Experimental Psychiatry, 1,* 65–70.

Molnar, C., Freund, B., Riggs, D., & Foa, E. B. (1993). *Comorbidity of anxiety disorders and DSM-III-R axis II disorders in obsessive-compulsives.* Paper presented at the annual convention of the Association for the Advancement of Behavior Therapy, Atlanta, GA.

Myers, K., Weissman, M., Tischler, L., Holzer, E., Leaf, J., Orvaschel, H., Anthony, C., Boyd, H., Burke, D., Kramer, M., & Stoltzman, R. (1984). Six-month prevalence of psychiatric disorders in three communities: 1980–1982. *Archives of General Psychiatry, 41,* 959–967.

Rachman, S. J. (1971). Obsessional ruminations. *Behaviour Research and Therapy, 9,* 229–235.

Rachman, S. J. (1976). The modification of obsessions: A new formulation. *Behaviour Research and Therapy, 14,* 473–443.

Rachman, S. J. (1978). An anatomy of obsessions. *Behavior Analysis and Modification, 2,* 255–278.

Rachman, S. J. (1981). Part I. Unwanted intrusive cognitions *Advances in Behaviour Research and Therapy, 3,* 89–99.

Rachman, S. J. (1985). An overview of clinical and research issues in obsessional-compulsive disorders. In M. Mavissakalian, S. M. Turner & L. Michelson (Eds.), *Obsessive-compulsive disorder: Psychological and pharmacological treatment*. New York: Plenum Press.

Rachman, S. J. (1993). Obsessions, responsibility and guilt. *Behaviour Research and Therapy, 31*, 149–154.

Rachman, S. J., & de Silva, P. (1978). Normal and abnormal obsessions. *Behaviour Research and Therapy, 16*, 233–248.

Rachman, S. J., & Hodgson, R. J. (1980). *Obsessions and compulsions*. Englewood Cliffs, NJ: Prentice Hall.

Rasmussen, S., & Eisen, J. L. (1991). Phenomenology of OCD: Clinical subtypes, heterogeneity and coexistence. In J. Zohar, T. Insel & S. Rasmussen (Eds.), *The psychobiology of obsessive-compulsive disorder*. New York: Springer-Verlag.

Rasmussen, S. A., & Eisen, J. L. (1992). Epidemiology of obsessive-compulsive disorder. *Journal of Clinical Psychiatry, 53*, 4–10.

Riggs, D. S., & Foa, E. B. (1993). Obsessive compulsive disorder. In D. H. Barlow (Ed.), *Clinical handbook of psychological disorders*. New York: Guilford Press.

Robins, L. N., Helzer, J. E., Weissman, M. M., Orvaschel, H., Gruenberg, E., Burke, J. D., & Regier, D. A. (1984). Lifetime prevalence of specific psychiatric disorders in three sites. *Archives of General Psychiatry, 41*, 949–959.

Salkovskis, P. M. (1983). Treatment of an obsessional patient using habituation to audiotaped ruminations. *British Journal of Clinical Psychology, 22*, 311–313.

Salkovskis, P. M. (1985). Obsessional-compulsive problems: A cognitive-behavioral analysis. *Behaviour Research and Therapy, 23*, 571–583.

Salkovskis, P. M. (1989). Cognitive-behavioral factors and the persistence of intrusive thoughts in obsessional problems. *Behaviour Research and Therapy, 27*, 677–682.

Salkovskis, P. M., & Westbrook, D. (1989). Behaviour therapy and obsessional ruminations: Can failure be turned into success? *Behaviour Research and Therapy, 27*, 149–160.

Sanavio, E. (1988). Obsessions and compulsions: The Padua Inventory. *Behaviour Research and Therapy, 26*, 169–177.

Steketee, G. S. (1993). *Treatment of obsessive compulsive disorder*. New York: Guilford Press.

Turner, S. M., & Beidel, D. C. (1988). *Treating obsessive-compulsive disorder*. New York: Pergamon Press.

van Balkom, A. J. L. M., van Oppen, P., Vermeulen, A. W. A., Nauta, M. M.C, Vorst, H. C. M., & van Dyck, R. (1994). A meta-analysis on the treatment of obsessive-compulsive disorder: A comparison of antidepressants, behavior and cognitive therapy. Manuscript in preparation.

van Oppen, P., & Arntz, A. (1994). Cognitive therapy for obsessive-compulsive disorder. *Behaviour Research and Therapy, 32*, 79–87.

Warren, R., & Zgourides, G. D. (1991). *Anxiety disorders: A rational-emotive perspective*. New York: Pergamon.

Weissman, M. M., Bland, R. C., Canino, G. J., Greenwald, S., Hwu, H.-G., Lee, C. K., Newman, S. C., Oakley-Browne, M. A., Rubio-Stipec, M., Wickramarathe, P. J., Wittchen, H. U., & Yeh, E. K. (1994). The cross national epidemiology of obsessive-compulsive disorder. *Journal of Clinical Psychiatry, 55*, 5–10.

Further Reading

Mavissakalian, M., Turner, S. M., & Michelson, L. (Eds.) (1985). *Obsessive-compulsive disorder: Psychological and pharmacological treatment*. New York: Plenum Press.

Rachman, S. J., & Hodgson, R. J. (1980). *Obsessions and compulsions*. Englewood Cliffs, NJ: Prentice Hall.

Riggs, D. S., & Foa, E. B. (1993). Obsessive compulsive disorder. In D. H. Barlow (Ed.), *Clinical handbook of psychological disorders*. New York: Guilford Press.

Steketee, G. S. (1993). *Treatment of obsessive compulsive disorder*. New York: Guilford Press.

Turner, S. M., & Beidel, D. C. (1988). *Treating obsessive-compulsive disorder*. New York: Pergamon Press.

6

Cognitive-Behavioral Treatment of Posttraumatic Stress Disorder

MILLIE C. ASTIN and PATRICIA A. RESICK

University of Missouri, St. Louis, USA

Introduction

Posttraumatic stress disorder (PTSD) describes a pattern of symptoms that may develop in individuals who have experienced traumatic stressors. PTSD became an official diagnosis in 1980 with the advent of the DSM-III (APA, 1980), although many of the symptoms of PTSD had been previously recognized. Criteria were largely derived from the study of combat veterans, but since then PTSD has been applied to a wide range of trauma groups including survivors of rape, childhood sexual abuse, physical abuse (including battering), criminal victimization, as well as natural and manmade disasters.

To qualify for a diagnosis of PTSD according to DSM-IV (APA, 1994), the individual first of all must have experienced, witnessed, or otherwise been confronted with an event which involved actual or threatened death, serious injury, or threat to physical integrity. Second, the individual's response to the event must include intense fear, helplessness, or horror. Thus, an event is defined as traumatic when it has involved death or serious injury or the threat of death or injury and the individual experiences strong negative affect in response to the event. In earlier versions of the DSM (APA, 1980; 1987), a traumatic stressor was defined as an event outside the range of usual human experience which almost anyone would find markedly distressing. Unfortunately, this technically eliminated relatively common traumatic experiences such as childhood abuse, domestic violence, and sexual assault because of their high frequency. The DSM-IV definition eliminates this problem and emphasizes that the direct or indirect threat to life or well-being and how an individual responds to that threat are specifically what makes a given event traumatic. This was derived from numerous research studies which found that the experience of life threat was a significant predictor of PTSD development (Blank, 1993; Davidson & Smith, 1990; Kilpatrick & Resnick, 1993; March, 1993).

Symptom manifestations fall into three broad categories. These include intrusive memories, avoidance and numbing symptoms, and physiological hyperarousal. Intrusive memories are considered the hallmark of PTSD and consist of the traumatic event being reexperienced in some fashion. Memories of the trauma may intrude into consciousness repetitively, without warning, seemingly "out of the blue," without triggers or reminders to elicit them. Other memories experienced in the waking state include "flashbacks" or intensely vivid reenactment experiences in which the original traumatic fear and psychological distress are also reactivated and relived. Intrusive memories may also occur during the sleeping state in the form of thematically related nightmares. Additionally, when faced with cues associated with the traumatic event, whether actual or symbolic, the individual may exhibit intense psychological reactions (terror, disgust, depression, etc.) and/or physiological responses (increased heart rate, perspiration, and rapid breathing, etc.). Cues are sometimes obvious like the combat veteran who ducks in fear when a car backfires because it sounds like gunfire. However, sometimes the relationship between the trauma and the cue is not immediately clear. For example, one rape victim became fearful of the ceiling fan in her bedroom. It was not until she began to deal with the trauma memory in therapy that she connected the fan with the sensation she had prior to the rape of someone approaching her from behind. All of these phenomena are generally experienced as distressing and intrusive because the individual has no control over when or how they occur and because they elicit the negative emotions associated with the initial trauma (Janoff-Bulman, 1992; Resick & Schnicke, 1992).

The trauma victim may also experience symptoms of increased physiological arousal. This suggests that the individual is in a constant state of "fight or flight" which is similar to how the individual's body responded during the actual traumatic event. In this constant state of alert, the individual is primed to react to new threats of danger in even relatively "safe" situations. During a crisis, this is adaptive because it facilitates survival. However, as a steady state, hyperarousal interferes with daily functioning and leads to exhaustion. In this state, the individual spends a great deal of energy scanning the environment for danger cues (hypervigilance). The individual is likely to experience sleep disturbance, decreased concentration, irritability, and an overreactivity to stimuli (exaggerated startle response). There is evidence to suggest that this constant state of tension has deleterious effects on overall physical health (Kulka, Schlenger, Fairbank, Hough, Jordan, Marmar & Weiss, 1990).

Avoidance and numbing symptoms reflect the individual's attempt to gain psychological and emotional distance from the trauma. Some have suggested that avoidance symptoms are a response to intrusive symptomatology (Creamer, Burgess & Pattison, 1992). As traumatic memories intrude into consciousness, so do the painful negative emotions associated with the original trauma. Thus, the individual may avoid thoughts and feelings about the trauma, avoid situations and events reminiscent of the trauma, or may actually forget significant aspects of the trauma. Avoidance of the trauma memory leads to a temporary decrease in painful emotions which increases avoidance behavior. Similarly, detachment or numbing symptoms are an attempt to cut off the aversive feelings associated with intrusive memories (Astin, Foy, Layne & Camilleri, 1994; Resick & Schnicke, 1992). This may become generalized resulting in detachment from all emotions, both positive and negative. Trauma victims commonly state that they no longer have strong feelings or feel numb. This sort of pervasive detachment may interfere profoundly with the individual's ability to relate to others, enjoy daily life, remain productive, and plan for the future. Trauma victims have frequently reported highly constricted lifestyles after the traumatic experience due to the need to avoid reminders of the traumatic memory and associated emotions.

These symptoms must be experienced for at least 1 month in order to receive a diagnosis of PTSD. A substantial proportion of trauma survivors exhibit full symptoms of PTSD immediately after the traumatic event. However, these rates drop almost by half within 3 months post-trauma, but then tend to stabilize. For example, rape survivors assessed at 2 weeks, 1 month, 3 months, 6 months, and 9 months exhibited PTSD rates of 94, 65, 47, 42, and 42% respectively (Rothbaum & Foa, 1993). Thus, after 3 months, PTSD rates did not drop substantially. If symptoms do not remit within this time frame, PTSD tends to persist over time and may worsen without appropriate intervention. Several studies of trauma survivors have demonstrated the presence of diagnosable PTSD many years after the trauma (Kilpatrick, Saunders, Veronen, Best & Von, 1987; Kulka et al., 1990). In a national (U.S.) random probability sample of 4008 women, Resnick, Kilpatrick, Dansky, Saunders & Best (1993) found the following lifetime PTSD rates: completed rape, 32%; other sexual assault, 31%; physical assault, 39%; homicide of family or friend, 22%; any crime victimization, 26%; noncrime trauma (natural and manmade disasters, accidents, injuries, etc.), 9%.

While high rates of PTSD have been found among trauma survivors, individuals with PTSD are also at higher risk for developing disorders of depression, anxiety, suicidal ideation, and substance abuse (Helzer, Robins & McEnvoy, 1987; Kessler, Sonnega, Bromet, Hughes & Nelson, 1995; Kilpatrick, Edmunds & Seymour, 1992; Kulka et al., 1990; Resick et al., 1992). However, data suggest that at least some comorbid conditions may be directly related to the presence of PTSD. Increased substance abuse has been well-documented in trauma survivors and may represent another form of avoidance or numbing. Research on depression in persons with PTSD has demonstrated different biophysiological responses than those found in individuals with depression alone. This may suggest that the depression that accompanies PTSD has a different biological base than depression not associated with PTSD (Pitman, 1993; Yehuda, Southwick, Krystal, Bremner, Charney & Mason, 1993). Thus, while it can be argued that trauma survivors may need to be treated for more than PTSD, it may also be the the that treatment of PTSD can be crucially linked to the resolution of comorbid conditions.

In addition to formal disorders, the trauma victim may develop cognitive distortions which reflect the severe disruption that has occurred in the victim's worldview (Janoff-Bulman, 1992; Resick and Schnicke, 1993). Extreme self-blame, inability to trust others, constant fear for personal safety, disruptions in interpersonal relationships, and low self-esteem may develop in response to the trauma and are significant to the resolution of PTSD symptoms (McCann & Pearlman, 1990).

Learning Theory

Most behavioral and cognitive-behavioral treatments of PTSD are grounded in behavioral learning theory. Following Mowrer's Two Factor Theory (1947), numerous authors have proposed that PTSD can be explained via classical and operant conditioning (Becker, Skinner, Abel, Axelrod & Cichon, 1984; Holmes & St. Lawrence, 1983; Keane, Zimering & Caddell, 1985; Kilpatrick, Veronen & Best, 1985; Kilpatrick, Veronen & Resick, 1982). First of all, classical conditioning has been used to explain the development of PTSD symptoms, especially high levels of distress and arousal symptoms. In this model, the trauma is the unconditioned stimulus (UCS) which evokes extreme fear, the unconditioned response (UCR). The trauma (UCS) becomes associated with a trauma memory which then becomes the conditioned stimulus (CS). Thus, any time the trauma is remembered, the memory (CS) evokes extreme fear which now has become the conditioned response (CR). Then, via stimulus generalization and higher order conditioning, not only the trauma memory, but also cues associated with the memory and neutral cues reminiscent of those triggers become conditioned stimuli which elicit extreme fear (CR). For example, if a woman in a grocery store parking lot is abducted at gunpoint by a man with a beard who throws her into a van and dumps her in an open field after raping her, many previously neutral stimuli may become conditioned stimuli that elicit anxiety. Although the memory of the abduction and rape is not dangerous in and of itself, it represents the traumatic event and thus becomes conditioned to elicit anxiety whenever the trauma is remembered. Other neutral stimuli may also elicit anxiety, such as men with beards, vans, open fields, grocery stores, and parking lots (Foa, 1995).

Normally, in a classical conditioning model, one would expect that this link between the CS and CR to extinguish over time if the original UCS is not repeated. Therefore, operant conditioning is used to explain the development of PTSD avoidance symptoms and maintenance of symptoms over time despite the fact that the UCS or traumatic stressor does not reoccur. Because the trauma memory (CS) elicits extreme anxiety (CR), the trauma memory (CS) is avoided and the result is a reduction in anxiety (CR). In this manner, avoidance of the trauma memory (CS) is negatively reinforced which prevents extinction of the link between the trauma memory (CS) and anxiety (CR) which would normally be expected without repetition of the trauma itself (UCS). Using the example above, the woman who was raped may become highly anxious whenever she thinks of the abduction and rape. Additionally, she may feel equally distressed every time she sees a man with a beard, or has to park in a lot, or has to buy groceries, because they all remind her of the trauma memory. Thus, she may avoid both the trauma memory and anyone or anything which reminds her of that memory such as bearded men, grocery stores, or parking lots. This, unfortunately, prevents her from learning that these situations and even the memory of the rape are not truly dangerous and PTSD symptoms may become chronic.

Anxiety Management Techniques

Stress inoculation training (SIT) is a cognitive-behavioral technique based on learning theory and originally developed by Meichenbaum (1974) for the management of anxiety. Subsequently, SIT was adapted for use with rape victims in individual and group formats (Kilpatrick et al., 1982; Resick & Jordan, 1988; Veronen & Kilpatrick, 1983). The primary goal of SIT is to help clients understand and manage their trauma-related fear reactions. The SIT protocol consists of three phases: education, skill-building, and application. SIT protocols range from 8 to 20 sessions depending on the needs of the client, but all versions use essentially the same techniques.

The first few sessions are devoted to the educational phase. This includes an overview of treatment, information about the development of fear responses based on learning theory, and education about sympathetic nervous system arousal. Additionally, the client is taught progressive muscle relaxation and asked to practice this in session and for homework. The therapist also helps the client identify cues that trigger fear reactions. In subsequent session(s), this information is reviewed and more detailed information about specific fear responses is given as manifested across three channels: the body (physiological responses), the mind (cognitive responses), and actions (behavioral responses).

For homework, the client is to practice progressive muscle relaxation and identify cues that trigger fear responses.

In the second phase of treatment, the client learns a set of coping skills to manage the identified fear responses across the three response channels. These usually include diaphragmatic breathing, thought stopping, covert rehearsal, guided self-dialogue, and role playing (Kilpatrick et al., 1982; Resnick & Newton, 1992; Resick & Jordan, 1988). Other techniques included in some protocols are a relaxation technique called the quieting reflex (Stroebel, 1983) and problem-solving skills (Resick & Jordan, 1988). Progressive muscle relaxation and diaphragmatic breathing are aimed at helping the client relax across a variety of anxiety-provoking situations. This is based on the notion that anxiety and relaxation cannot occur at the same time. Thought stopping (Wolpe, 1958) is used to manage intrusive or obsessional thoughts that promote anxiety. Guided self-dialogue and cognitive restructuring both help the client identify irrational, faulty, or maladaptive thinking patterns and replace them with more positive and adaptive cognitions. Problem-solving skills help clients to generate and evaluate potential options. Finally, role playing and covert modeling (in which the client imagines the therapist and later herself successfully resolving a specific problem) addresses behavioral avoidance. Both teach the client how to communicate effectively and resolve problems using appropriate social skills.

In the third phase of treatment, the client learns how to apply these coping skills in daily situations which provoke anxiety, step-by-step. The steps of stress inoculation include: (1) assessing the probability of the feared event; (2) managing avoidance behavior with thought stopping and quieting reflex; (3) controlling self-criticism with guided self-dialogue and cognitive restructuring; (4) engaging in the feared behavior using problem-solving skills and skills learned via role-playing and covert modeling and (5) reinforcing self for using skills in feared situation. Before ending treatment, the therapist helps the client generate a fear hierarchy of events not addressed directly in therapy which the client is assigned to continue working on with these skills afterwards.

Foa, Rothbaum, Riggs & Murdock (1991) compared 45 rape victims who were randomly assigned to SIT, Prolonged exposure (PE), supportive counseling, and no treatment controls and found SIT and PE clients significantly improved on measures of PTSD, depression, and anxiety. However, scores for SIT clients were the most improved at post-treatment, while there was a trend for PTSD scores to be the most improved at 3 months follow-up for PE clients. It should be noted, however, that clients in the SIT condition did not confront feared situations as described earlier because this PE protocol also uses this technique (graded *in vivo* exposures). However, when Foa, Freund, Hembree, Dancu, Franklin, Perry, Riggs & Moinar (1994) compared SIT, PE, and combined SIT/PE, PE clients showed the most improvement in PTSD symptoms. Using group therapy formats, Resick, Jordan, Girelli, Hunter & Marhoefer-

Dvorak (1988) compared SIT, assertion training, supportive psychotherapy, and a no-treatment control group. They found that all three treatments significantly reduced symptoms of PTSD, depression, self-esteem, rape-related fears, and social fears compared to controls, but at 6 month follow-up, only improvements in rape-related fears were maintained. In non-controlled studies, SIT has been effective in reducing PTSD-related symptoms of anxiety, fear, and depression in rape victims (Veronen & Kilpatrick, 1982, 1983).

SIT has primarily been used and studied with rape victims. Biofeedback coupled with progressive muscle relaxation was found to reduce symptoms in 6 combat veterans (Hickling, Sison & Vanderploeg, 1986). However, there was no control group and physicians referred only those patients whom they thought would benefit from this treatment. Biofeedback techniques were also effective in decreasing symptoms of tachycardia in rape victims, but again, no control group was included (Blanchard & Abel, 1976).

Emotional Processing Theory

While learning theory accounts for much of the development and maintenance of PTSD, it does not really explain intrusion symptoms, i.e., the repetitive memories of the trauma which intrude into the victims's thoughts in both conscious and unconscious states. Some have proposed that individuals who have experienced traumatic stressors develop fear structures which contain memories of the trauma event as well as related emotions and escape plans. Based on Lang's (1977) concept of anxiety development, Foa, Steketee & Rothbaum (1989) suggest that PTSD emerges due to the development of an internal fear structure which elicits escape and avoidance behavior. Anything associated with the trauma may elicit the fear structure or schema and subsequent avoidance behavior. Chemtob, Roitblat, Hamada, Carlson & Twentyman (1988) propose that these structures are constantly activated in individuals with PTSD and guide their interpretation of events as potentially dangerous. According to emotional processing theory, repetitive exposure to the traumatic memory in a safe environment will result in habituation of the fear and subsequent change in the fear structure. As emotion decreases, clients with PTSD will begin to modify their meaning elements spontaneously and will change their self-statements and reduce their generalization.

Exposure Techniques

A number of related behavioral techniques have been used successfully with various trauma groups based on both learning theory and emotional processing theory. These include, flooding, or prolonged exposure (also called direct therapeutic exposure), and variants of systematic desensitization. All of these techniques involve confrontation of feared stimuli until previously conditioned fear responses diminish. In the case of trauma victims, the trauma memory and cues associated with the trauma memory constitute these stimuli. Flooding or prolonged exposure involves prolonged, repeated exposures to the trauma memory either directly (also known as in vivo flooding) or indirectly via imagination (also known as in vitro flooding or imaginal exposure.) For example, a combat veteran with PTSD might be shown videos of combat with combat sounds and images, taken on helicopter rides, etc. Alternatively, a combat veteran might be asked to generate an account of his combat experiences and then be exposed to this account over and over. Systematic desensitization, originally developed by Wolpe (1958) can also be accomplished directly (in vivo) or indirectly (in vitro), but is a more gradual form of exposure technique in which the client is presented with a graded series of anxiety-provoking stimuli until anxiety is extinguished.

Foa & Kozak (1986) have argued that exposure techniques are actually based on both learning theory and emotional processing theory because once the client is processing trauma-related emotions by allowing them to habituate, the client is also able to process the trauma memory that had previously been avoided. Through repeated exposure to the trauma memory, Foa et al. (1995) suggest that a more accurate memory record is generated which allows the client to reevaluate the meanings attached to the trauma memory and integrate them more easily with existing cognitive schemata.

Originally used extensively with combat veterans, prolonged exposure (PE) has been applied more recently to rape victims and victims of violent crime (Foa et al., 1991). PE, as developed by Foa and colleagues, is designed as a 9–12 session treatment that incorporates both imaginal exposure and graded in vivo exposures (a type of systematic desensitization). The core components include: education about PTSD and the treatment rationale (Session 1); normalization of reactions to trauma and development of fear hierarchy for in vivo exposure homework assignments (Session 2), and repeated exposure to feared stimuli during therapy sessions (Sessions 3–9). (Additional exposure sessions may be added if the therapist determines that more exposures are necessary for adequate processing of the trauma memory and related emotions.)

During therapy sessions, the client is asked to close her eyes, and to relive what happened to her by using the present tense to relate the details of the rape as if it were happening currently. The client is asked to provide as much detail as possible including sensory details such as smells, sounds, what she saw, etc., as well as emotions or physical sensations experienced. This is done for 60 min in Session 3 and for about 45 min in subsequent sessions. Usually, the account is repeated 2–3 times in each session depending on the length of the account. Sessions are audiotaped and the client listens to these between sessions, again keeping a record of her anxiety levels using Subjective Units of Distress (SUDS) ratings. During initial exposures, anxiety is expected to be high. With repeated exposures in a safe setting, anxiety diminishes. The link between the trauma memory (conditioned stimulus) and fear (conditioned response) is broken.

As noted before, when Foa et al. (1991) compared PE with Stress Inoculation Training (SIT), supportive counseling, and a no treatment control group in a sample of 45 rape victims, they found that only PE and SIT were significantly effective in reducing symptoms of PTSD, depression, and anxiety compared to controls. At immediate post-treatment, SIT clients had improved the most, but at a 3.5 month follow-up, there was a trend for PE clients to have fewer symptoms of PTSD than other clients. Foa et al. (1991) argue that this is because SIT provides short-term relief from anxiety via anxiety management whereas PE may provide more long-term relief because the emotional and cognitive processing that occurs during exposures may result in permanent changes in the traumatic memory.

In an effort to discriminate the differential effects of SIT and PE, Foa et al. (1994) randomly assigned rape victims to three treatment conditions: PE alone, SIT alone, and a combined SIT/PE protocol. On a composite measure of psychological functioning, they found greater improvement in clients who received PE alone rather than SIT alone or the combined SIT/PE treatment. Additionally, a greater range of symptoms improved with PE (intrusion, avoidance, arousal, and depression severity) than with SIT which was only associated with lower levels of avoidance severity. However, Foa concedes that these results may reflect that by combining SIT and PE, but keeping the total treatment time equivalent to SIT alone or PE alone, that the treatment time devoted to either treatment may not have been sufficient to be effective. In a case study utilizing an expanded version of the SIT/PE protocol with a rape victim with a complicated prior trauma history, Nishith, Hearst, Mueser & Foa (1995) found significant reductions in PTSD symptoms across all domains as well as anxiety and dissociative symptoms at post-treatment. These improvements were maintained at 3-month follow-up and depressive symptoms were significantly reduced from post-treatment to 3-month follow-up. For extremely anxious clients, the coping skills training of SIT may not be sufficient alone, but may help the client manage anxiety enough to tolerate treatment with PE.

In a study of 24 Vietnam War veterans with PTSD, Keane, Fairbank, Caddell & Zimering (1989) compared flooding combined with relaxation to waitlist controls. Subjects who received treatment reported significantly less depression, anxiety, fear, hypochondriasis, and hysteria at both post-treatment and at 6 month follow-up assessments. Therapists' ratings on intrusion symptoms, startle reactions, amnesia, concentration problems, impulsivity, and irritability were also significantly lower for the treatment group than the control group.

In other non-controlled trials and case studies, several researchers have reported flooding to be effective in reducing symptoms in sexual and physical assault victims, (Haynes & Mooney, 1975), incest survivors (Rychtarik, Silverman, Van Landingham & Prue, 1984), combat veterans (Fairbank, Gross & Keane, 1983; Fairbank & Keane, 1982; Johnson, Gilmore & Shenoy, 1982; Keane & Kaloupek, 1982; Schindler, 1980) and in accident victims (McCaffrey & Fairbank, 1985).

Systematic desensitization or in vivo exposure has also been found to be effective in reducing specific symptoms of PTSD, especially intrusion and arousal symptoms. Peniston (1986) randomly assigned 16 combat veterans to a no treatment condition or a 4-month, 48 session protocol using EMG biofeedback-assisted desensitization. The treatment group reported significantly less muscle tension, nightmares, and flashbacks than the no-treatment group. In a noncontrolled trial with 10 combat veterans, Bowen and Lambert (1986) also found systematic desensitization to be effective in reducing arousal symptoms. In other non-controlled studies and case studies, systematic desensitization has been found effective in reducing fear, anxiety, depression, and PTSD symptoms, and improving social adjustment in rape victims (Frank & Stewart, 1984; Turner, 1984; Wolff, 1977), and in accident victims (Fairbank, DeGood & Jenkins, 1981; Muse, 1986).

Information Processing Theory

Resick & Schnicke (1992, 1993) have argued that post-trauma affect is not limited to fear and that individuals with PTSD may be just as likely to experience a range of other strong emotions, such as shame, anger, or sadness. These emotions emanate directly from the trauma, but also from interpretations individuals make regarding the traumatic event and their role in it. While also based in learning theory, they have proposed a more cognitive theory of PTSD based on information processing theory. Information processing theory has to do with how information is encoded, organized, stored, and retrieved in memory (Hollon & Garber, 1988). People develop cognitive schemas or generic maps to aid in this process. Therefore, information is usually interpreted in terms of cognitive schemas. New information which is congruent with prior beliefs about self or world is assimilated quickly and without effort because the information matches the schema and little attention is needed to incorporate it. On the other hand, when something happens which is schema discrepant, individuals must reconcile this event with their beliefs about themselves and the world. Their belief systems, or their schemas, must be altered or accommodated to incorporate this new information. However, this process is often avoided because of the strong affect associated with the trauma and frequently, because altering beliefs may in fact leave persons feeling more vulnerable to future traumatic events. For example, many people believe that bad things happen to bad people and good things happen to good people. This belief would need to be altered after something traumatic happened. However, even when victims accept that bad things can happen to them that they aren't responsible for, they may be more anxious about the possibility of future harm. Thus, rather than accommodating their beliefs to incorporate the trauma, victims may distort (assimilate) the trauma to keep their beliefs intact.

In the case of strong affect, it may be that cognitive processing does not occur because trauma victims avoid the strong affect and subsequently never accommodate the information because they never completely remember what happened or think through what it means (i.e., process the event). Some people are raised believing that emotions are a sign of weakness or that they should be avoided. While people may be able to distract themselves or deflect normal affective experience, traumatic events are associated with much greater emotion which cannot be avoided entirely. Individuals with PTSD may have to work hard to shut down their affective response. Moreover, because the information about the traumatic event has not been processed, categorized, and accommodated, the trauma memories continue to emerge during the day as flashbacks or intrusive reminders or at night in the form of nightmares. The emotional responses and arousal which are part of the trauma memory emerge as well, which triggers further avoidance.

Given this information processing model, affective expression is needed, not for habituation, but in order for the trauma memory to be processed fully. It is assumed that the affect, once accessed, will dissipate rather quickly, and that the work of accommodating the memory with schemas can begin.

Cognitive Processing Therapy

Cognitive processing therapy (CPT) was developed in order to facilitate the expression of affect and the appropriate accommodation of the traumatic event with more general schemas regarding oneself and the world (Resick & Schnicke, 1993). Developed originally for use with rape and crime victims, CPT was adapted from basic cognitive techniques explicated by Beck & Emery (1985). After an educational component in which the symptoms of PTSD are described and explained with information processing theory, the clients are asked to consider what it means to them that the event happened. The client is then taught to identify the connection between events, thoughts and feelings. The next phase of therapy is for the client to recall the trauma in detail. In this particular therapy, the client is asked to write an account of the event including thoughts, feelings, and sensory details. The client reads the account to the therapist and rereads it daily. After rewriting the account, the therapy moves into the cognitive challenging phase. The therapist teaches the client to ask questions regarding his or her assumptions and self-statements in order to begin challenging them. Clients are then taught how to use worksheets to systematically challenge and replace maladaptive thoughts and beliefs.

Resick & Schnicke (1992) compared rape victims who received cognitive processing therapy with a waiting-list comparison sample and found CPT to be highly effective. There was a significant reduction in symptoms of PTSD and depression and significant improvement in social adjustment. At 6 months post-treatment, none of the women treated were diagnosed with PTSD. In the preliminary findings of a controlled trial comparing CPT and PE, Resick, Astin & Nishith (1996) have found that CPT and PE are equally and highly effective in treating PTSD, but CPT appears superior in reducing symptoms of depression and guilt (Resick, Nishith & Austin, 1998). In neither study did the nontreatment comparison samples report any improvement. General Beckian cognitive therapy has also been compared to systematic desensitization to address depression in rape victims (Frank, Anderson, Stewart, Dancu, Hughes & West, 1988) and no differences between treatments were found. However, no control group was included. Additionally, PTSD symptoms were not assessed. Resick and Schnicke (1993) have noted that one reason that so many treatment comparison studies for PTSD have not found differences among treatments may be due to the fact that almost all of the treatments include, either formally or informally, corrective information which may facilitate information processing.

The following section describes the therapy in greater detail. Examples from rape victims are used. However, CPT has been adapted for a number of trauma populations including crime victims, combat veterans, bank robbery victims, and disaster victims. A formal adaptation for childhood sexual abuse survivors has also been developed (Chard, Weaver & Resick, 1996) which has demonstrated significant improvements in PTSD, depression, and overall distress symptoms. Controlled trials of this adaptation are currently underway.

Cognitive processing therapy session by session: Session 1
   I.   Overview of Treatment
   II.   Education: PTSD and Maintenance of Symptoms
   III. Information Gathering: The client's PTSD and Related Symptoms
   IV.   Education: Information Processing Theory
   V.   Information Gathering: The Client's Sexual Assault
   VI.   Presentation of Treatment Goals and Rationale
   VII. Assignment of Homework: Impact Statement

The main goals of Session 1 are education, information gathering, and rapport building. The client is presented with information about PTSD, information processing theory (including assimilation and accommodation), why PTSD develops, and how it is maintained. The therapist invites the client to discuss the symptoms that are most problematic for her and emphasizes that it is common for individuals who have experienced traumas to experience such symptoms. In the context of this information, the therapist gives an overview of the treatment components, states the primary goals of the treatment, and provides a rationale for the treatment. (See theory and rationale for CPT above.)

The purpose of this is to help the client understand what the treatment will involve and to emphasize the importance of treatment compliance. Since avoidance behavior is a primary component of PTSD and may interfere with treatment, the client is alerted to this and is encouraged to be aware of the desire to skip treatment sessions or not complete homework assignments. Usually by anticipating avoidance behavior and labeling any subsequent efforts to avoid as avoidance, most clients comply sufficiently with the treatment protocol. Another important function of this is to invite the client to view the treatment as a collaboration between client and therapist and understand that success depends on the client's efforts as well as those of the therapist.

Additionally, the therapist will ask the client to relate briefly what happened to her. Most of our clients have already gone through an extensive assessment, so there is no need to go into depth at this point, neither regarding the trauma specifics nor the client's symptoms. However, by asking about the trauma, the therapist is able to set a nonjudgmental tone for the treatment protocol, and can convey that the focus of treatment will be directly on the trauma experience. This also allows therapist and client to become acquainted with one another and for the therapist to begin to anticipate the client's stuck points. At the end of the session, the client is instructed to write at least one page on what the trauma means to her with regard to her beliefs about herself and others.

Session 2
I.   Review Homework: Client Reads Impact Statement
II. Identify Stuck Points
III. Introduce Connection Between Thoughts and Feelings
IV. Introduce A-B-C Sheets
V.   Assign Homework: A-B-C Sheets

The goal of this session is to begin identifying the client's stuck points. Initially, the therapist asks the client about what it was like to write the impact statement and what she learned from it. This is processed briefly and the client is praised for her efforts to begin thinking about her trauma experience. Then, the client is asked to read the impact statement out loud. The therapist's task is to listen for stuck points that are evident in the statement. When the client is finished, the therapist helps the client to identify the stuck points and explore some of them briefly.

No real challenging is attempted at this point. Occasionally, the therapist may explore a stuck point further to determine how entrenched the belief is. For example, for a client who states that she doesn't think any man can be trusted, the therapist might ask, "There aren't *any* men who you trust? Not even one?" Most clients can think of at least one or two men they trust and this may help them to realize that this belief is not absolute. Others may staunchly maintain that they've never met a man who was trustworthy. This gives the therapist an idea of how flexible the client is and the work ahead. This process also introduces the idea to the client that other perspectives may be possible.

Most clients complete this assignment. However, when avoidance behaviors are strong, some clients may arrive at the session without having completed their homework. In such cases, it is essential that the therapist gently label this as avoidance (whatever the client's excuse) and then proceed to have the client to do the homework in the session with the therapist and the homework is reassigned. This presents the message that homework is important and avoidance will not be rewarded.

Afterwards, the connection between thoughts and feelings is introduced. In other words, what we think affects how we feel and vice verse. For example, a student fails an exam. He tells himself, "I'm stupid." This thought leads to feelings such as sadness and anger (at self). If, however, he tells himself, "You didn't study very much; you need to study for the next test," the student is more likely to feel minor irritation that he didn't study and determination to do better next time. Accurate thoughts or self-statements lead to appropriate feelings, whereas inaccurate or faulty self-statements generate invalid and unnecessary feelings. Stuck points are a form of inaccurate or maladaptive self-statements that are a result of faulty assimilation and overaccommodation. Understanding this connection becomes crucial later in the treatment when the client is taught how to challenge stuck points.

In order to teach the client how to sort out thoughts and feelings, A-B-C sheets are introduced (Figure 6.1). Column A is for events; Column B is for thoughts; and Column C is for feelings. In the example above, "I failed my exam" would be written in Column A; "I am stupid" would go under Column B, and "I feel sad and angry" would go under Column C. Sometimes we place the words, 'I feel' in front of a thought (e.g., "I *feel* stupid") and consider it a feeling when it is really a thought, ("I am stupid") that generates feelings (sad, angry, etc.) Therefore, the client is presented with four basic emotions: angry, sad, glad, and scared. Each of these can vary in intensity and each can be combined with other feelings to create new feelings. Thus, the client is asked to focus on these four feelings in order to identify feelings. For homework, the client is assigned to do at least two A-B-C sheets a day. One should be on a thought about the rape and one can be on an everyday event, positive or negative. Since most people find it easier to identify events and/or feelings, the client is instructed to begin with Column A or C.

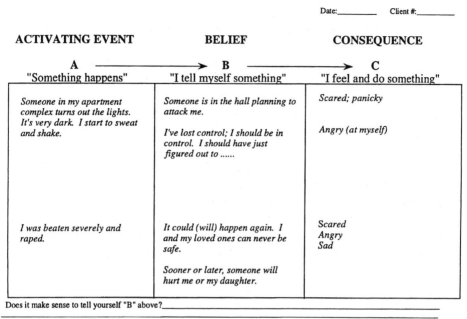

Figure 6.1. A-B-C Sheets.

Session 3

I.   Review and Clarify Homework: A-B-C Sheets
II. Assign Homework: Written Account of Rape; Continue A-B-C Sheets

The majority of this session is spent going over the client's A-B-C sheets with her. The therapist makes sure that thoughts and feelings are placed correctly in their respective columns, that thoughts are not being confused with feelings and vice verse, and that appropriate feelings are connected to the correct thoughts. With respect to the latter, clients often write several thoughts and several feelings without indicating which go together. One thought may generate one feeling or.several. Similarly, several thoughts may generate the same feeling. However, whenever there are multiple thoughts or multiple feelings, the therapist should probe to find out the connections and whether other thoughts or feelings exist. This is important because often a more problematic belief or self-statement underlies the belief that the client has identified. If the underlying thought is not identified, the associated feelings will continue to be generated.

For homework, the client is asked to write out the account of the rape. She is to write down what happened to her in as much detail as possible. She is to include sensory details (what she saw, heard, felt, smelled, tasted, etc.) and what she was thinking and feeling at the time. The client is instructed to begin this assignment immediately and not to wait until the evening before the next session. If she needs to stop due to being overwhelmed by emotions, she is to draw a line where she stops, and come back to finish later. Often, the points at which a client has to stop provide important clues to the therapist about the client's stuck points. The client is encouraged to allow herself to feel her feelings as they emerge. The therapist should emphasize that this surge of emotions is normal and is an indication of emotional processing. Emotions related to the trauma need to be processed and once she begins this, the emotions rise in intensity and then subside. It is also helpful to advise the client that she may experience physiological symptoms (e.g., nausea, rapid heartbeat, etc.) while writing about the rape and that this is a normal part of processing trauma-related emotions also. Additionally, the client is instructed to read her account at least once before the next session. The client is also asked to continue filling out A-B-C sheets in order to solidify the connection between thoughts and feelings.

Session 4
  I. Review and Clarify A-B-C Sheets
 II. Client Reads Written Rape Account
III. Challenging of Stuck Points
IV. Assign Homework: Second Written Rape Account; Continue A-B-C Sheets

In the beginning of this session, the therapist and client review A-B-C sheets and clarify any remaining problems. Then the focus turns to the written rape account. The therapist discusses how this assignment was experienced by the client, what kinds of emotions were felt, and whether there were any surprises. Then the client is asked to read the account out loud and slowly. Again, the client is encouraged to allow herself to feel any feelings that arise during the reading of the account. The purpose of this task is twofold. First of all, it serves as an exposure component which allows the client to process the traumatic memory and related affect. Secondly, it provides the therapist (and eventually the client) with essential information about the sequence of events within the traumatic experience and further information about the client's stuck points. For instance, the account usually contains information that the client did not cause the trauma even though she may believe that she did. The therapist will use this when she begins to challenge stuck points about self-blame.

Ideally, the client's account of the trauma will be rich in details and she will be able to express considerable affect during the exposure reading. However, it is fairly common for clients to hold back somewhat the first time that they write the account and the resulting account may be brief or what Resick & Schnicke (1992) refer to as the "police-blotter" version of the trauma, i.e., the minimal basic facts of the trauma without essential emotions or details. After the reading, the therapist will help the client process what she has just read, especially in terms of affect. What kinds of emotions did she feel? How intense were they? Did she feel physiological changes as she read (rapid heartbeat, etc.)? If she did not appear to be expressing emotion, what was going on? With respect to content or sequence, were there any surprises? All of this is processed in the context of the treatment rationale, i.e., that the painful emotions associated with the traumatic memory must be felt and allowed to run their course in order for the connection between the traumatic memory and the emotions to be broken and for these emotions to diminish in intensity. In other words, it is normal for the client to feel intense negative emotions as she/he approaches the trauma memory, but if she allow herself to feel and process these feelings, they will diminish over time. This rationale must be emphasized, especially if the client is reluctant to feel the trauma-related feelings because this is essential to the recovery process.

At this point, the therapist begins to challenge the client's assimilation errors (self-blame, denial, and minimization) gently, but more systematically. This is usually accomplished indirectly via socratic questioning and the therapist expressing confusion. Thus, the therapist does not tell the client that she is not to blame because there is no way she could have known what was going to happen. Instead, the therapist might ask the client to explain why it was her fault. For example, the therapist might say, "I'm not sure I understand. You were attacked by a man with a gun, but you have said that the rape was your fault because she didn't fight enough. Tell me again what it is that you were supposed to do and when you had an opportunity to do something other than what you did? Often the therapist will refer the client back to her account and have her walk through the sequence of events to find evidence for her claims. At this stage, the client usually begins to develop some insight that the trauma event really was a rape and that it not was caused by her.

For homework, the client is asked to start over and rewrite the rape account. This time, she is asked to add more detail and sensory experiences as well as her thoughts and feelings as she is writing it. As before, she is to read this account at least once before the next session, but preferably every day. The purpose of this second exposure is to ensure adequate emotional processing has occurred. Also, because some formal challenging of assimilation errors has taken place, the client now has the opportunity to begin developing new, more accurate perspectives about the rape as she processes the trauma memory. If the client's trauma has consisted of multiple events, the therapist may also ask the client to write an account of another salient trauma event. Again, the client is asked to continue with A-B-C sheets.

Session 5
  I.   Review and Clarify A-B-C Sheets
  II. Client Reads Second Written Rape Account
  III. Challenging of Stuck Points

IV.   Introduce Challenging Questions
V.   Assign Homework: Challenging Questions

The structure and goals of this sessions are similar to those of Session 4. A-B-C sheets are reviewed briefly and clarified if necessary. The therapist and client discuss the experience of writing the account a second time. If the client wrote a very detailed account the first time and was able to feel the related emotions, commonly she will report that it did not seem nearly so overwhelming the second time. This is explained in the context of the treatment rationale, i.e., when she adequately processes her emotions, they diminish in intensity over time. If the client wrote an account without much detail or avoided feeling the associated emotions the first time, she will often report that the second account was harder to do and she felt worse. Again, this is explained in terms of the treatment rationale, i.e., the first time the client was not adequately processing emotions, but now that she is not avoiding the process, the painful negative emotions are being elicited, which is a sign of processing. As the client continues to not avoid these emotions, they will diminish over time. Then, the client reads the second account out loud, and again, is encouraged to feel her feelings. Depending on how well the client has processed these emotions by the end of this session, the therapist may choose to assign the client to continue reading the account in between sessions.

Afterwards, the therapist systematically challenges stuck points, especially assimilation errors including self-blame. Once again, the therapist professes confusion about how the actual event and the client's beliefs fit together logically. Usually, by the end of this session, the client has some understanding that they don't make sense and is no longer as convinced that her beliefs about the rape are accurate.

At this point, the therapist introduces the Challenging Questions Sheet adapted from Beck & Emery (1985). These twelve questions (Figure 6.2) are designed to help the client to begin challenging her stuck points on her own. The therapist explains what each one means and goes over an example stuck point with her. For homework, the client is asked to use these questions to challenge two of her stuck points. The therapist will help the client choose two of the stuck points, usually around self-blame to make sure that these stuck points have been challenged adequately. It is generally helpful for the therapist to help the client generate a written list of her stuck points at this time. Challenging these stuck points, and any others added later, will be the primary focus for the rest of the treatment.

Session 6
  I.   Review Homework: Challenging Questions on Stuck Points
 II.   Introduce Faulty Thinking Patterns
III.   Assign Homework: Faulty Thinking Patterns

Below are a list of questions to be used in helping you challenge your maladaptive or problematic beliefs. Not all questions will be appropriate for the belief you choose to challenge. Answer as many questions as you can for the belief you have chosen to challenge below.

Belief:
1. What is the evidence for and against this idea?
2. Are you confusing a habit with a fact?
3. Are your interpretations of the situation too far removed from reality to be accurate?
4. Are you thinking in all-or-none terms?
5. Are you using words or phrases that are extreme or exaggerated? (i.e., always, forever, never, need, should, must, can't and every time).
6. Are you taking selected examples out of context?
7. Are you making excuses? (e.g., I'm not afraid, I just don't want to go out; other people expect me to be perfect; or I don't want to make the call because I don't have time).
8. Is the source of information reliable?
9. Are you thinking in terms of certainties instead of probabilities?
10. Are you confusing a low probability with a high probability?
11. Are your judgments based on feelings rather than facts?
12. Are you focusing on irrelevant factors?

Figure 6.2. Challenging questions sheet.

Session 6 is spent reviewing, correcting, and clarifying the client's challenging of her stuck points. The therapist continues to challenge any resistant stuck points on self-blame. Then the therapist introduces Faulty Thinking Patterns (Figure 6.3) also adapted from Beck & Emery (1985). The seven patterns

Listed below are several types of faulty thinking patterns that people use in different life situations. These patterns often become automatic, habitual thoughts that cause us to engage in self-defeating behavior.

Considering your own stuck points, find examples for each of the patterns. Write in the stuck point under the appropriate pattern and describe how it fits that pattern. Think about how that pattern affects you.
1. Drawing conclusions when evidence is lacking or even contradictory.
2. Exaggerating or minimizing the meaning of an event (you blow things way out of proportion or shrink their importance inappropriately).
3. Disregarding important aspects of a situation.
4. Oversimplifying events or beliefs as good/bad or right/wrong.
5. Overgeneralizing from a single incident (you view a negative event as a never-ending pattern of defeat).
6. Mind-reading (you assume that people are thinking negatively of you when there is no definite evidence for this).
7. Emotional reasoning (you reason from how you feel).

Figure 6.3. Faulty thinking patterns.

overlap considerably with the Challenging Questions, but represent more global types of thinking errors. The therapist goes through each of these and provides examples of each type of faulty thinking pattern. For homework, the client is asked to consider which type of faulty thinking pattern is represented by each of her stuck points. She is asked to write these down and the reason(s) she believes they represent that pattern.

Session 7
I.   Review Homework: Faulty Thinking Patterns and Stuck Points
II. Introduce Challenging Belief Worksheets
III. Introduce Safety Issues
IV. Assign Homework: Challenging Belief Worksheets on Safety

The therapist and client review and discuss the client's homework on Faulty Thinking Patterns. Some clients' stuck points will be limited to only a few patterns while others' will cover most of the patterns. The therapist helps the client to focus on the types of faulty thinking patterns that are most problematic for her and discusses how this has impeded her recovery from the rape. The therapist continues to challenge stuck points. However, by now, clients usually are able to do much of the challenging on their own, with guidance from the therapist.

At this point, the therapist introduces the Challenging Belief Worksheets (Figure 6.4). This worksheet pulls together all of the techniques that the client has learned up to this point including: A-B-C sheets (Columns A & B); Challenging Questions (Column C); and Faulty Thinking Patterns (Column D). In addition, these worksheets have added columns to help the client replace automatic thoughts or stuck points with new, more accurate alternative thoughts based on the evidence that the client is able to find through the process of challenging each stuck point. The therapist explains each column and works through an example with the client.

For the next five sessions (Sessions 8–12), stuck points of overaccommodation regarding the five themes of safety, trust, power/control, esteem, and intimacy are explored and challenged. Because the themes are interwoven, clients sometimes jump ahead to other themes. Following the order in which they are presented is preferable because each one tends to build on the last one. These five themes are generally pertinent to most victims of interpersonal traumas (rape, domestic violence, child abuse, etc.) and some may also be salient for survivors of other types of traumas such as combat or natural disasters. We find that this covers most areas of cognitive disruption for rape survivors. However, other areas prone to overaccommodation may be unique to certain traumas and the therapist should consider these when treating other types of trauma. For instance, childhood sexual abuse survivors may need to deal with specific developmental issues which have been distorted as a result

Column A	Column B	Column C	Column D	Column E	Column F
Situation	**Automatic Thoughts**	**Challenging Your Automatic Thoughts**	**Faulty Thinking Patterns**	**Alternative Thoughts**	**Decatastrophizing**
Describe the event(s), thought(s), or belief(s) leading to the unpleasant emotion(s).	Write automatic thought(s) preceding emotion(s) in Column A. Rate belief in each automatic thought(s) below from 0-100%.	Use the **Challenging Questions** sheet to examine your automatic thought(s) from Column B.	Use the **Faulty Thinking Patterns** sheet to examine your automatic thought(s) from Column B.	What else can I say instead of Column B? How else can I interpret the event instead of Column B? Rate belief in alternative thought(s) from 0-100%.	What's the worst that could ever realistically happen? *People will continue to think they can hurt me throughout my life.*
I perceive myself to be damaged in some way.	*Something must be wrong with me that he thought he could rape me in the first place.* 60%	*Little factual evidence except the way I feel about myself, "allowing" myself to be betrayed and tricked into thinking he would not hurt me.* *Confusing a habit of thinking about myself as being damaged because of what others have done throughout my lifetime. Reality states it had nothing to do with anything about me that I was raped.* *Judgment of being damaged is based on feelings, therefore, the source is unreliable.*	*Drawing conclusion - Men rape for reasons to do with themselves, not with women.* *Exaggerating an event - It means that he was violent, not that there's something wrong with me.*	*I was not raped because there was something wrong with me, but because there was something wrong with him.* 75%	Even if that happened, what could I do? *They can only do that if I let them.*
					Outcome
Emotion(s)					Rerate belief in automatic thought(s) in Column B from 0-100%.
Specify sad, angry, etc., and rate the degree you feel each emotion from 0-100%.					30%
					Specify and rate subsequent emotion(s) from 0-100%.
Sad - 75% *Frightened - 50%*					*Sad - 25%* *Frightened - 25%*

Figure 6.4. Challenging Beliefs Worksheet.

of the abuse. For example, such a survivor might adopt the cognition, "Sex means love. The only way I will be loved is via sex."

In the latter part of this session, the therapist introduces safety issues. The client receives a handout on typical stuck points that develop around self-safety and other- safety after a rape and a sample challenging belief worksheet which illustrates how a safety stuck point might be challenged. The therapist reviews these with the client. Self-safety has to do with what the client believes about her ability to keep herself safe. Other-safety relates to the client's beliefs about the safety or dangerousness of others. If the client had general positive beliefs about either type of safety prior to the rape, these beliefs may be disrupted and the client may assume that she can never be safe, either because of her own inability to make her environment safe or the ability of dangerous others to invade her life. If her views prior to the rape were unrealistically negative, the rape may seem to confirm these beliefs. The therapist helps the client to establish whether her beliefs about safety were positive or negative prior to the rape and which stuck points about trust are most salient for her. For homework, the client is assigned to complete at least two challenging belief worksheets, one of which should be on a safety issue.

The client is asked to do two Challenging Belief Worksheets on two stuck points for homework, at least one on safety and one on another stuck point. Often, it is helpful to have the client do a worksheet on one of her most significant self-blame stuck points that she has previously challenged so that she has a complete worksheet on it that includes alternative thoughts.

Session 8
  I.   Review and Work Through Challenging Belief Worksheets on Safety
 II.   Review other Challenging Belief Worksheets as needed
III.   Introduce Trust Issues
 IV.   Assign Homework: Challenging Beliefs Worksheets on Trust

In this session, the therapist and client review the Challenging Belief Worksheets which the client has completed about stuck points on safety (and any other worksheets such as on self-blame). The therapist and client go over the worksheets together. The therapist's job is to make sure that the client has accurately identified stuck points and emotions, and has adequately challenged the stuck point using the challenging questions and faulty thinking patterns. Thus, the therapist may add more material to bolster the challenging of the stuck point which the client may not have taken into consideration. Some clients have difficulty eliciting alternative statements. The therapist and client will examine the client's alternative statements to ensure that they are realistic and accurate. For example, a client whose stuck point is "Everyone is dangerous," might develop an alternative statement which is the complete opposite – "There's no reason to think others are dangerous." This alternative statement does not take the reality into account that there are some people who are dangerous or do not have your best interest in mind. Therefore, the therapist would help the client incorporate this reality and develop another alternative statement. For example, "There are many people who are safe (and I can think of specific examples of such persons) and others who are dangerous. It's OK for me to take a neutral stance and watch for evidence that a particular person is dangerous or not."

In the latter part of this session, the therapist introduces trust issues. The client receives a handout on typical stuck points that develop around self-trust and other-trust after a rape and a sample challenging belief worksheet which illustrates how a trust stuck point might be challenged. The therapist reviews these with the client. Other-trust has to do with the trustworthiness of others. Self-trust relates to how much the client trusts her own judgment. If the client had generally positive beliefs about either type of trust prior to the rape, these beliefs may be disrupted and the client may assume that no one can be trusted or that she can no longer trust her own judgment. If her views prior to the rape were unrealistically negative, the rape may appear to confirm these beliefs. The therapist helps the client to establish whether her beliefs about trust were positive or negative prior to the rape and which stuck points about trust are most salient for her. For homework, the client is assigned to complete at least two challenging belief worksheets one of which should be on a trust issue.

Session 9
I. Review and Work Through Challenging Belief Worksheets on Trust
II. Review other Challenging Belief Worksheets as needed
III. Introduce Power/Control Issues
IV. Assign Homework: Two Challenging Beliefs Worksheets on Power/Control Issues

The therapist and client review the Challenging Belief Worksheets which the client has completed about stuck points on trust. By this point, clients usually are able to challenge stuck points on their own and may need only minor guidance and refinements from the therapist. Trust is conceptualized as existing on a continuum. In others words, some people can be trusted completely, others can be trusted with some things, but not others, and some people cannot be trusted at all. In order to find out the difference, the client is encouraged to take a neutral stance with others, not trusting or distrusting, but waiting for evidence which suggest which is appropriate with that individual.

In the latter part of this session, the therapist introduces power and control issues. The client receives a handout on typical stuck points that develop around power and control. Again, the client is provided with a sample challenging belief worksheet which illustrates how power and control issues might be challenged. The therapist reviews these with the client. Power and control issues regarding self and others have to do with perceptions of having no power or control while others have all power and control. If the client held positive beliefs about power and control prior to the rape, these beliefs may be shattered and the client may respond to these stuck points by becoming overly passive, setting herself up for further victimization. Alternatively, she may seek to control all facets of her life which may interfere with interpersonal relationships. If her views prior to the rape were unrealistically negative, the rape may appear to confirm these beliefs. The therapist helps the client to establish whether her beliefs about power and control were positive or negative prior to the rape and which stuck points are most important to her. For homework, the client is assigned to complete at least two challenging belief worksheets, one of which should be on a power and control issue.

Session 10
   I. Review and Work Through Challenging Belief Worksheets on Power and Control
  II. Review other Challenging Belief Worksheets as needed
 III. Introduce Esteem Issues
  IV. Have client complete Identifying Common Assumptions Sheet
   V. Assign Homework

The therapist and client review the Challenging Belief Worksheets which the client has completed about stuck points on power and control. A relevant issue for many clients, depending on the culture and family environment in which they were raised, is whether emotions are permissible and whether emotions must be controlled at all times. This is usually evident from the manner in which the client responded to the therapist's encouragement to feel her feelings during earlier sessions and may need to be addressed in this session as a power/control stuck point. Clients often hold dichotomous beliefs regarding control (e.g., "If I'm not completely in control, then I am out of control"). Also, it may become clear to clients that while they didn't have control over the traumatic experience, that doesn't mean that they have no control over the events in their lives.

In the latter part of this session, the therapist introduces esteem issues. The client receives a handout on typical stuck points that develop around esteem. The client is provided with a sample challenging belief worksheet which illustrates how an esteem issue might be challenged. The therapist reviews these with the client.

Self-esteem issues have to do with perceptions of the self as worthy and good. Other-esteem has to do with the client's perceptions of others as good and worthy or bad and evil. If the client held positive beliefs about self and others prior to the rape, these beliefs may be shattered. If her views prior to the rape were unrealistically negative, the rape may seem to confirm these beliefs.

Listed below are beliefs that some people hold. Please circle the number next to the beliefs that are *true for you*.

A. *Acceptance*
1. I have to be cared for by someone who loves me.
2. I need to be understood.
3. I can't be left alone.
4. I'm nothing unless I'm loved.
5. To be rejected is the worst thing in the world.
6. I can't get others mad at me.
7. I have to please others.
8. I can't stand being separated from others.
9. Criticism means personal rejection.
10. I can't be alone.

B. *Competence*
1. I am what I accomplish.
2. I have to be somebody.
3. Success is everything.
4. There are winners and losers in life.
5. If I'm not on top, I'm a flop.
6. If I let up, I'll fail.
7. I have to be the best at whatever I do.
8. Others' successes take away from mine.
9. If I make a mistake, I'll fail.
10. Failure is the end of the world.

C. *Control*
1. I have to be my own boss.
2. I'm the only one who can solve my problems.
3. I can't tolerate others telling me what to do.
4. I can't ask for help.
5. Others are always trying to control me.
6. I have to be perfect to have control.
7. I'm either completely in control or completely out of control.
8. I can't tolerate being out of control.
9. Rules and regulations imprison me.
10. If I let someone get too close, that person will control me.

Figure 6.5. Identifying assumptions.

The therapist helps the client to establish whether her esteem beliefs were positive or negative prior to the rape and which stuck points are most relevant to her. Additionally, the client is presented the Identifying Common Assumptions Sheet and is asked to mark which she perceives to be true for her (see Figure 6.5). These may help the client clarify which areas of control and self-esteem are problematic for her. For homework, the client is assigned to complete at least two challenging belief worksheets one of which should be on an esteem issue. Additionally, the client is assigned to practice giving and receiving compliments everyday, to do one nice thing for herself every day without having to earn it, and to write these down. These latter exercises are to assist her in reengaging interpersonally and to assist with self-esteem.

Session 11
I. Review and Work Through Challenging Belief Worksheets on Esteem
II. Review other Challenging Belief Worksheets as needed
III. Introduce Intimacy Issues
IV. Assign Homework: Challenging Belief Worksheets on Intimacy; Second Impact Statement

The therapist and client review the Challenging Belief Worksheets which the client has completed about stuck points on esteem. Any remaining issues regarding self-blame may need to be addressed with respect to self-esteem. Additionally, the therapist and client discuss other homework assignments (receiving compliments and doing nice things for herself) and their connection to self-esteem. For example, feeling uncomfortable or suspicious when complimented or feeling guilty when doing nice things for yourself suggest an underlying stuck point regarding self-esteem, i.e. "I'm not worthy to do this for myself."

In the latter part of this session, the therapist introduces intimacy issues. The client receives a handout on typical stuck points that develop around intimacy. The client is provided with a sample challenging belief worksheet which illustrates how an intimacy issue might be challenged. The therapist reviews these with the client.

Intimacy issues regarding others have to do with the client's perceptions of what it means to be close or intimate with others. Self-intimacy issues have to do with the client's ability to use internal resources to self-soothe when feeling distressed. If the client held positive beliefs about relating to others and her own ability to give herself comfort prior to the rape, these beliefs may be disrupted. If her views prior to the rape were unrealistically negative, the rape may confirm these beliefs. The therapist helps the client to establish whether her beliefs about intimacy were positive or negative prior to the rape and which stuck points are most relevant to her.

For homework, the client is assigned to complete at least two challenging belief worksheets one of which should be on an intimacy issue. The client is asked to continue giving and receiving compliments every day and doing one nice thing for herself every day without having to earn it. The client is also asked to write a second impact statement in which she states what it means to her at this point that she was raped. As before, she is asked to write about how it has affected her view of herself, of others, and of the world, and how it has affected the five areas of focus during treatment: safety, trust, power/control, esteem, and intimacy.

Session 12
 I. Review and Work Through Challenging Belief Worksheets on Intimacy
 II. Review other Challenging Belief Worksheets as needed
 III. Read and Review Second Impact Statement
 IV. Review Gains and Future Goals; Termination

The therapist and client review the Challenging Belief Worksheets which the client has completed about stuck points on intimacy. Then the client is asked to read her new statement on what it means to her that she was raped. Afterwards, the therapist and client discuss how the client's view of herself, others, and the world has changed during the course of treatment. At this point, the therapist may read the client's old impact statement (from Session 2) and draw comparison and contrasts with the client. (If time is short, the therapist may choose to give the old statement to the client and highlight the differences.) The purpose of this is to help the client see the gains and changes made over the course of therapy, to identify areas or stuck points that remain to be worked on, and deal with termination issues. Therapy is conceptualized as having started her on the road to recovery and providing her with a set of tools and skills with which to tackle remaining stuck points. The client is given feedback about current PTSD and depression scores on self-report measures. The client is reminded that recovery is a process and it is not unusual for some symptoms to wax and wane over time, especially when the client experiences stressors or experiences reminders of the trauma. If intrusive memories return, this is a sign that a little more processing is needed and the client is encouraged not to avoid, but to allow herself to think about the rape and feel associated feelings. If the client does this and continues to identify stuck points and challenge them as needed, symptoms will continue to diminish more and more over time.

Eye Movement Desensitization and Reprocessing

Eye movement desensitization and reprocessing therapy (EMDR) is the most recent technique to be applied to PTSD. As originally developed by Shapiro (1995), EMDR was not based on theoretical or empirical findings in the research literature, but on a chance observation that troubling thoughts were resolved when her eyes followed the waving of leaves during a walk in the park. Shapiro developed EMDR on the basis of this observation and argued that lateral eye movements facilitate the initiation of the client's cognitive processing of the trauma. Subsequently, EMDR was conceptualized as a cognitive-behavioral treatment aimed at facilitating information processing of traumatic events and cognitive restructuring of negative trauma-related cognitions.

EMDR is described as an eight-phase treatment which includes: history taking, client preparation, target assessment, desensitization, installation, body scan, closure, and reevaluation of treatment effects. In the basic EMDR protocol, the client is asked to identify and focus on the traumatic image or memory (target assessment phase). Next, the therapist elicits negative cognitions or belief statements about the memory. The client is then asked to assign a rating to the memory and negative cognitions on an 11-point SUDS (0 = no anxiety; 10 = highest anxiety possible) and to identify the physical location of the anxiety. Subsequently, the therapist elicits positive cognitions from the client which would be preferable to associate with the memory. These are rated on a 7-point Validity of Cognitions Scale (VoC; Shapiro, 1989) where 1 = completely false and 7 = completely true. Once the therapist has instructed the client in the basic EMDR procedure, the client is asked to do four things together (desensitization phase): (i) visualize the memory; (ii) rehearse the negative cognitions; (iii) concentrate on the physical sensation of the anxiety; and (iv) visually track the therapist's index finger. While the client does this, the therapist rapidly moves the index finger rapidly back and forth from right to left 30–35 cm from the client's face, with two back and forth movements per second. These are repeated 24 times. Then the client is asked to blank out the memory and take a deep breath. Subsequently, the client brings back the memory and cognitions and assigns a SUDS value. Sets of eye movements are repeated until the SUDS value equals 0 or 1. At this point, the client is asked about how they feel about the positive cognition and gives a VoC rating for it (installation phase).

EMDR has been controversial for numerous reasons including lack of theoretical foundation and lack of empirical data with sound methodology. In her own controlled study of EMDR, Shapiro (1989) reported that 22 combat veterans with PTSD were successfully treated with one 90 min session of EMDR. Unfortunately, she based this on highly subjective SUDS and VoC ratings rather than objective, standardized measures of treatment outcome. While a number of case studies, non-controlled studies, and anecdotal data have indicated improvement of PTSD symptoms with EMDR (Kleinknecht & Morgan, 1992; Lazgrove, Triffleman, Kite, McGlashan & Rounsaville, 1995; Lipke & Botkin, 1992; Marquis, 1991; McCann, 1992; Puk, 1991; Spector & Huthwaite, 1993; Wolpe & Abrams, 1991), empirical studies with adequate comparison groups have only recently begun to emerge in the literature.

Several of these have found significant reductions in symptoms of PTSD and related symptomatology such as depression or anxiety in subjects who received EMDR when compared to non-treatment controls (Rothbaum, 1995; Wilson, Becker & Tinker, 1995a). Others have found significant improvements in subjects who received EMDR and no outcome differences when compared to other treatments for PTSD (Boudewyns, Hyer, Peralme, Touze, Kiel, 1995; Carlson, Chemtob, Rusnak, Hedlund & Muraoka, 1995; Vaughan, Armstrong, Gold, O'Connor, Jenneke & Tarrier, 1994). Unfortunately, the majority of these studies have serious methodological shortcomings such as inclusion of stressors that do not meet the Criterion A definition of traumatic stressor (Wilson et al. , 1995a); inclusion of substantial numbers of subjects who did not meet diagnostic criteria for PTSD (Vaughan et al., 1994; Wilson et al., 1995a); and extremely small (less than 15 per cell) sample sizes (Carlson et al., 1995; Rothbaum, 1995; Vaughan et al., 1994).

However, in a sample of 61 combat veterans, all of whom met diagnostic criteria for PTSD, Boudewyns et al. (1995) found EMDR to be equally as effective as prolonged exposure in reducing symptoms of PTSD, depression, anxiety, and heart rate. In this study, subjects were randomly assigned to one of three groups. All three groups received the standard treatment at their facility which consisted of 8 group therapy sessions and a few spontaneous individual sessions. One received only this form of treatment; the second and third groups also received either 5–8 sessions of EMDR or 5–8 sessions of prolonged exposure. All three groups improved significantly on symptoms of PTSD. The group therapy only group did not improve on depression and showed increases in anxiety and heart rate, while the two other groups improved on all measures.

Two studies have found mixed or negative results for EMDR. Pitman, Orr, Altman, Longpre, Poire & Lasko's (1993) study of 17 combat veterans compared 12 sessions of EMDR to an eyes-fixed procedure in which the therapist alternately tapped each leg of the subject. The EMDR group reported significantly greater improvement on measures of subjective distress, self-report measures of PTSD intrusion and avoidance, and psychiatric symptoms. No effects were observed, however, on other standardized self-reports and structured interviews of PTSD. Jensen (1994) compared 2 sessions of EMDR with no treatment in 25 combat veterans and found no improvements in either group on standardized measures of PTSD. In both studies, concern was expressed about therapists' experience with EMDR.

While Shapiro maintains that lateral eye movements are an essential therapeutic component of EMDR, studies which have examined this have found mixed results. Renfrey & Spates (1994) treated a sample of 23 heterogeneous trauma victims with standard EMDR, a variant in which saccadic eye movements were engendered via a light tracking task, or another variant in which no saccadic eye movements were induced and subjects were instructed to fix their visual attention. All three groups improved significantly on measures of PTSD, depression, anxiety, heart rate, SUDs scores, and VoC scores at post-treatment and at 1–3 month follow-up. No differences were found among treatments. In contrast, Wilson, Silver, Covi & Foster (1995b) in 18 heterogeneous trauma victims found significant improvements in subjects who received EMDR, but not in subjects who were instructed to fix their visual attention, or in subjects who alternated tapping right and left thumbs to a metronome. Physiological measures, SUDS, and VoC, but no standardized distress measures were used to measure outcome. Pitman et al. (1993) as noted above, found mixed results.

Thus, it is not clear whether lateral eye movements are an essential component of EMDR or not. EMDR forces the client to think about the trauma, to identify the negative cognitions associated with the trauma, and to work toward positive cognitions as they process the traumatic memory. Without the saccadic eye movements, EMDR is quite similar to a form of cognitive processing therapy which facilitates the processing of the traumatic memory. Therefore, any efficacy demonstrated by EMDR is may be more attributable to engagement of the traumatic memory and the facilitation of information processing than to eye movements.

Future Directions

Since the inception of PTSD as a formal diagnosis in 1980, much has been learned about the etiology and treatment of PTSD among traumatized individuals. At least 3–4 types of cognitive-behavioral treatments have been developed which have been found to be effective in treating symptoms of PTSD. To date, however, no one treatment has been shown to be more effective overall than the others. This may be an artifact of small effect sizes and relatively small sample sizes in complex comparison studies or may simply reflect that each of these treatments is equally effective. Alternatively, this may reflect the overlap in treatment applications. Each of the treatments examined above is really a treatment package consisting of various components, some of which are similar across treatments. In other words, because all of the treatments may involve these elements to some degree, it is not clear whether emotional processing or information processing is the crucial element for resolution of PTSD symptoms or whether both are necessary for effective treatment. Understanding this will be important for the refinement of these existing techniques as well as the development of new treatments.

A related issue of concern is elucidating which types of individuals will benefit most from which type of treatment. Although, all appear effective at this point, we still do not know if one type of treatment may be preferable for particular individuals or particular comorbid disorders. For example, a victim whose primary trauma-related affect is fear may benefit best from exposure techniques. On the other hand, victims who are so anxious that they cannot function, may benefit more from anxiety management techniques. In contrast, victims with a complicated history of victimization who blame themselves for their traumas, may benefit more from cognitive processing therapy. Moreover, we do not yet know how much comorbid disorders such as personality disorders, substance abuse, depression, and other anxiety disorders will complicate treatment choice. While these examples are speculative, they illustrate the need to examine and refine our understanding of how PTSD symptoms are resolved.

Finally, more work is needed to adapt these treatments for more trauma populations. All three have been studied in rape victims and some portions of all three have been used with combat veterans. Cognitive-behavioral treatments for other groups such as abused children and battered women are just now beginning to be explored. While one might assume that little adaptation would be needed from one group to another, the most salient aspects of each trauma may be considerably different. For example, abused children frequently experience developmental disruptions that must be addressed by treatment. Moreover, the chronicity of the trauma experienced may require further protocol adaptations to be effective. Further research and clinical application is needed to accomplish these goals in the treatment of PTSD.

References

APA (1980). *Diagnostic and statistical manual of mental disorders*, 3th edition (DSM-IV). Washington, DC: American Psychiatric Association.

APA (1987). *Diagnostic and statistical manual of mental disorders*, 3th edition revised (DSM-III-R). Washington, DC: American Psychiatric Association.

APA (1994). *Diagnostic and statistical manual of mental disorders*, 4th edition (DSM-IV). Washington, DC: American Psychiatric Association.

Astin, M. C., Layne, C. M., Camilleri, A. J., & Foy, D. W. (1994). Posttraumatic stress disorder in victimization-related traumata. In J. Briere (Ed.), *Assessing and treating victims of violence*. San Francisco, CA: Jossey-Bass.

Beck, A. T., & Emery, G. (1985). *Anxiety disorders and phobias: A cognitive perspective*. New York: Basic Books.

Becker, J. V., Skinner, L. J., Abel, G. G., Axelrod, R., & Cichon, J. (1984). Sexual problems of sexual assault survivors. *Women and Health, 9*, 5–20.

Blanchard, E. B., & Abel, G. G. (1976). An experimental case study of the biofeedback treatment of a rape induced psychophysiological cardiovascular disorder. *Behavior Therapy, 7*, 113–119.

Blank, A. S. (1993). The longitudinal course of posttraumatic stress disorder. In J. R. T. Davidson and E. B. Foa (Eds.) *Posttraumatic stress disorder: DSM-IV and beyond*. Washington, DC: American Psychiatric Press.

Boudewyns, P. A., Hyer, L. A., Peralme, L., Touze, J., & Kiel, A. (1995). *Eye movement desensitization and reprocessing (EMDR) and exposure therapy in the treatment of combat-related PTSD: An early look*. Paper presented at the annual convention of the American Psychological Association, New York.

Bowen, G. R., & Lambert, J. A. (1986). Systematic desensitization therapy with post-traumatic stress disorder cases. In C. R. Figley (Ed.), *Trauma and its wake*, Vol. II. New York: Brunner/Mazel.

Carlson, J. G., Chemtob, C. M., Rusnak, K., Hedlund, N. L., & Muraoka, M. (1995). *Eye movement desensitization and reprocessing for combat-related posttraumatic stress disorder: A controlled study*. Paper presented at the 4th annual convention of the European Conference on Traumatic Stress, Paris.

Chard, K. M., Weaver, T. L., & Resick, P. A. (1996). Adapting cognitive processing therapy for work with survivors of childhood sexual abuse. Manuscript in preparation.

Chemtob, C., Roitblat, H. L., Hamada, R. S., Carlson, J. G., & Twentyman, C. T. (1988). A cognitive action theory of post-traumatic stress disorder. *Journal of Anxiety Disorders, 2,* 253–275.

Creamer, M., Burgess, P., & Pattison, P. (1992). Reactions to trauma: A cognitive processing model. *Journal of Abnormal Psychology, 101,* 452–459.

Davidson, J. R. T., & Smith, R. D. (1990). Traumatic experience in psychiatric outpatients. *Journal of Traumatic Stress, 3,* 459–476.

Fairbank, J. A., & Keane, T. M. (1982). Flooding for combat-related stress disorders: Assessment of anxiety reduction across traumatic memories. *Behavior Therapy, 13,* 499–510.

Fairbank, J. A., DeGood, D. E., & Jenkins, C. W. (1981). Behavioral treatment of a persistent post-traumatic startle response. *Journal of Behavior Therapy and Experimental Psychiatry, 12,* 321–324.

Fairbank, J. A., Gross, R. T., & Keane, T. M. (1983). Treatment of posttraumatic stress disorder: Evaluation of outcome with a behavioral code. *Behavior Modification, 7,* 557–568.

Foa, E. B. (1995). Cognitive-behavioral approaches to the treatment of PTSD. In J. Fairbank (Chair), *Psychodynamic and cognitive-behavioral approaches to the treatment of PTSD.* Plenary Symposium of the Annual Meeting of the International Society for Traumatic Stress Studies, Boston, MA.

Foa, E. B., & Kozak, M. J. (1986). Emotional processing: Exposure to corrective information. *Psychological Bulletin, 99,* 20–35.

Foa, E. B., Steketee, G., & Rothbaum, B. O. (1989).Behavioral/cognitive conceptualizations of post-traumatic stress disorder. *Behavior Therapy, 20,* 155–176.

Foa, E. B., Rothbaum, B. O., Riggs, D. S., & Murdock, T. B. (1991). Treatment of post-traumatic stress disorder in rape victims: A comparison between cognitive-behavioral procedures and counseling. *Journal of Counseling and Clinical Psychology, 59,* 715–723.

Foa, E. B., Freund, B. F., Hembree, E., Dancu, C. V., Franklin, M. E., Perry, K. J., Riggs, D. S., & Moinar, C. (1994). *Efficacy of short-term behavioral treatments of PTSD in sexual and nonsexual assault victims.* Paper presented at the 28th annual convention of the Association for the Advancement of Behavior Therapy, San Diego, CA.

Frank, E., & Stewart, B. D. (1984). Depressive symptoms in rape victims. *Journal of Affective Disorders, 1,* 269–277.

Frank, E., Anderson, B., Stewart, B. D., Dancu, C., Hughes, C., & West, D. (1988). Efficacy of cognitive behavior therapy and systematic desensitization in the treatment of rape trauma. *Behavior Therapy, 19,* 403–420.

Haynes, S. N., & Mooney, D. K. (1975). Nightmares: Etiological, theoretical, and behavioral treatment considerations. *Psychological Record, 25,* 225–236.

Helzer, J. E., Robins, L. N., & McEnvoy, L. (1987). Post-traumatic stress disorder in the general population: Findings of the Epidemiological Catchment Area Survey. *New England Journal of Medicine, 317,* 1630–1634.

Hickling, E. J., Sison, G. F. P., & Vanderploeg, R. D. (1986). Treatment of posttraumatic stress disorder with relaxation and biofeedback training. *Behavior Therapy, 16,* 406–416.

Hollon, S. D., & Garber, J. (1988). Cognitive therapy. In L. Abramson (Ed.), *Social cognition and clinical psychology: A synthesis.* New York: Guilford Press.

Holmes, M. R., & St. Lawrence, J. S. (1983). Treatment of rape-induced trauma: Proposed behavioral conceptualization and review of the literature. *Clinical Psychology Review, 3,* 417–433.

Janoff-Bulman, R. (1992). *Shattered assumptions.* New York: Free Press.

Jensen, J. A. (1994). An investigation of eye movement desensitization and reprocessing

(EMD/R) as a treatment for posttraumatic stress disorder (PTSD) symptoms of Vietnam combat veterans. *Behavior Therapy, 25,* 311–325.

Johnson, G. H., Gilmore, J. D., & Shenoy, R. Z. (1982). Use of a flooding procedure in the treatment of a stress-related anxiety disorder. *Journal of Behavior Therapy and Experimental Psychiatry, 13,* 235–237.

Keane, T. M., & Kaloupek, D. G. (1982). Imaginal flooding in the treatment of post-traumatic stress disorder. *Journal of Consulting and Clinical Psychology, 50,* 138–150.

Keane, T. M., Zimering, R. T., & Caddell, J. M. (1985). A behavioral formulation of posttraumatic stress disorder in Vietnam veterans. *Behavioral Therapist, 8,* 9–12.

Kessler, R. C., Sonnega, A., Bromet, E., Hughes, M., & Nelson, C. B. (1995) Posttraumatic stress disorder in the national comorbidity study. *Archives of General Psychiatry, 52,* 1048–1060.

Kilpatrick, D. G., Veronen, L. J., & Resick, P. A. (1982). Psychological sequelae to rape. In D. M. Doleys, R. L. Meredith & A. R. Ciminero (Eds.), *Behavioral medicine: Assessment and treatment strategies.* New York: Plenum Press.

Kilpatrick, D. G., Veronen, L. J., & Best, C. L. (1985). Factors predicting psychological distress among rape victims. In C. R. Figley (Ed.), *Trauma and its wake: Vol.1. The study and treatment of posttraumatic stress disorder.* New York: Brunner/Mazel.

Kilpatrick, D. G., Saunders, B. E., Veronen, L. J., Best, C. L., & Von, J. M. (1987). Criminal victimization: Lifetime prevalence reporting to police, and psychological impact. *Crime and Delinquency, 33,* 479–489.

Kilpatrick, D. G., Edmunds, C. N., & Seymour, A. K. (1992). *Rape in America: A report to the nation.* Arlington, VA: National Victim Center.

Kilpatrick, D. G., & Resnick, H. S. (1993). Posttraumatic stress disorder associated with exposure to criminal victimization in clinical and community populations. In J. R. T. Davidson & E. B. Foa (Eds.) *Posttraumatic stress disorder: DSM-IV and beyond.* Washington, DC: American Psychiatric Association.

Kleinknecht, R., & Morgan, M. P. (1992). Treatment of post-traumatic stress disorder with eye movement desensitization and reprocessing. *Journal of Behavior Therapy and Experimental Psychiatry, 23,* 43–49.

Kulka, R. A., Schlenger, W. E., Fairbank, J. A., Hough, R. L., Jordan, B. K., Marmar, C. R., & Weiss, D. S. (1990). *Trauma and the Vietnam War generation.* New York: Brunner/Mazel.

Lang, P. J. (1977). Imagery in therapy: An information processing analysis of fear. *Behavior Therapy, 8,* 862–886.

Lazgrove, S., Triffleman, E., Kite, L., McGlashan, T., & Rounsaville, B. (1995). *The use of EMDR as treatment for chronic PTSD: Encouraging results of an open trial.* Paper presented at the annual convention of the International Society for Traumatic Stress Studies, Boston, MA.

Lipke, H., & Botkin, A. (1992). Brief case studies of eye movement desensitization and reprocessing with chronic post-traumatic stress disorder. *Psychotherapy, 29,* 591–595.

March, J. S. (1993). What constitutes the stressor? The criterion A issue. In J. R. T. Davidson & E. B. Foa (Eds.), *Posttraumatic stress disorder: DSM-IV and beyond.* Washington, DC: American Psychiatric Association.

Marquis, J. N. (1991). A report on seventy-eight cases treated by eye movement desensitization. *Journal of Behavior Therapy and Experimental Psychiatry, 22,* 187–192.

McCaffrey, R. J., & Fairbank, J. A. (1985). Post-traumatic stress disorder associated with transportation accidents: Two case studies. *Behavior Therapy, 16,* 406–416.

McCann, D. L. (1992). Post-traumatic stress disorder due to devastating burns overcome by a single session of eye movement desensitization. *Journal of Behavior Therapy and Experimental Psychiatry, 23,* 319–323.

McCann, I. L., & Pearlman, L. A. (1990). *Psychological trauma and the adult survivor: Theory, therapy, and transformation.* New York: Brunner/Mazel.

Meichenbaum, D. (1974). *Cognitive behavior modification.* Morristown, NJ: General Learning Press.

Mowrer, O. H. (1947). On the dual nature of learning: A reinterpretation of "conditioning" and "problem solving." *Harvard Educational Review, 17,* 102–148.

Muse, M. (1986). Stress-related, posttraumatic chronic pain syndrome: Behavioral treatment approach. *Pain, 25,* 389–394.

Nishith, P., Hearst, D. E., Mueser, K. T., & Foa, E. B. (1995). PTSD and major depression: Methodological and treatment considerations in a single case design. *Behavior Therapy, 26,* 319–335.

Peniston, E. G. (1986). EMG biofeedback-assisted desensitization treatment for Vietnam combat veterans' posttraumatic stress disorder. *Clinical Biofeedback and Health, 9,* 35–41.

Pitman, R. K. (1993). Biological findings in posttraumatic stress disorder: Implications for DSM-IV classification. In J. R. T. Davidson & E. B. Foa (Eds.), *Posttraumatic stress disorder: DSM-IV and beyond.* Washington, DC: American Psychiatric Press.

Pitman, R. K., Orr, S. P., Altman, B., Longpre, R. E., Poire, R. E., & Lasko, N. B. (1993). *A controlled study of EMDR treatment for post-traumatic stress disorder.* Paper presented at the annual convention of the American Psychological Association, Washington, DC.

Puk, G. (1991). Treating traumatic memories: A case report on the eye movement desensitization procedure. *Journal of Behavior Therapy and Experimental Psychiatry, 22,* 149–151.

Renfrey, G., & Spates, C. R. (1994). Eye movement desensitization: A partial dismantling study. *Journal of Behavior Therapy and Experimental Psychiatry, 25,* 231–239.

Resick, P. A. (1996). *The sequelae of trauma: Beyond posttraumatic stress disorder.* Keynote address presented at the annual meeting of the British Association for Behavioural and Cognitive Psychotherapies, Southport, UK.

Resick, P. A., & Jordan, C. G. (1988). Group stress inoculation training for victims of sexual assault: A therapist manual. In P. A. Keller & S. R. Heyman (Eds.), *Innovations in clinical practice: A source book* (Vol. 7). Sarasota, FL: Professional Resource Exchange.

Resick, P. A., & Schnicke, M. K. (1992). Cognitive Processing Therapy for sexual assault victims. *Journal of Consulting and Clinical Psychology, 60,* 748–760.

Resick, P. A., & Schnicke, M. K. (1993). *Cognitive processing therapy for rape victims: A treatment manual.* Newbury Park, CA: Sage.

Resick, P. A., Jordan, C. G., Girelli, S. A., Hunter, C. K., & Marhoefer-Dvorak, S. (1988). A comparative outcome study of behavioral group therapy for sexual assault victims. *Behavior Therapy, 19,* 385–401.

Resick, P. A., Astin, M. C., & Nishith, P. (1996). Preliminary results of an outcome study comparing cognitive processing therapy and prolonged exposure. In P. A. Resick (chair), *Cognitive-behavioral treatments for PTSD: New findings.* Symposium conducted at the annual meeting of the International Society for Traumatic Stress Studies, San Francisco, CA.

Resick, P. A., Nishith, P., & Astin, M. C. (1998). *A controlled trial comparing cognitive processing therapy and prolonged exposure: Preliminary findings.* Paper presented at the Lake George Research Conference on Posttraumatic Stress Disorder, Lake george, NY.

Resnick, H. S., & Newton, T. (1992). Assessment and treatment of post-traumatic stress disorder in adult survivors of sexual assault. In D. W. Foy (Ed.), *Treating PTSD: Cognitive-behavioral strategies.* New York: Guilford Press.

Resnick, H. S., Kilpatrick, D. G., Dansky, B. S., Saunders, B. E., & Best, C. L. (1993).

Prevalence of civilian trauma and posttraumatic stress disorder in a representative national sample of women. *Journal of Consulting and Clinical Psychology, 61,* 984–991.

Rothbaum, B. O. (1995). *A controlled study of EMDR for PTSD.* Paper presented at the annual convention of the Association for the Advancement of Behavior Therapy, Washington, DC.

Rothbaum, B. O., & Foa, E. B. (1993). Subtypes of posttraumatic stress disorder and duration of symptoms. In J. R. T. Davidson & E. B. Foa (Eds.), *Posttraumatic stress disorder: DSM-IV and beyond.* Washington, DC: American Psychiatric Press.

Rothbaum, B. O., Foa, E. B., Riggs, D. S., Murdock, E. T., & Wayne, W. (1992). A prospective examination of posttraumatic stress disorder in rape victims. *Journal of Traumatic Stress, 5,* 455–475.

Rychtarik, R. G., Silverman, W. K., Van Landingham, W. P., & Prue, D. M. (1984). Treatment of an incest victim with implosive therapy: A case study. *Behavior Therapy, 15,* 410–420.

Schindler, F. E. (1980). Treatment of systematic desensitization of a recurring nightmare of a real life trauma. *Journal of Behavior Therapy and Experimental Psychiatry, 11,* 53–54.

Shapiro, F. (1989). Efficacy of the eye movement desensitization procedure in the treatment of traumatic memories. *Journal of Traumatic Stress, 2,* 199–223.

Shapiro, F. (1995). *Eye movement desensitization and Reprocessing: Basic principles, protocols, and procedures.* New York: Guilford Press.

Spector, J., & Huthwaite, M. (1993). Eye-movement desensitization to overcome post-traumatic stress disorder. *British Journal of Psychiatry, 163.* 106–108.

Stroebel, C. F. (1983). *Quieting reflex training for adults: Personal workbook (or practitioners guide).* New York: DMA Audio Cassette Publications.

Turner, S. M. (1979). *Systematic desensitization of fear and anxiety in rape victims.* Paper presented at the annual convention of the Association for the Advancement of Behavior Therapy, San Francisco, CA.

Veronen, L. J., & Kilpatrick, D. G. (1982, noviembre). *Stress inoculation training for victims of rape: Efficacy and differential findings.* Paper presented at the annual convention of the annual convention of the Association for the Advancement of Behavior Therapy, Los Angeles, CA.

Vaughan, K., Armstrong, M. S., Gold, R., O'Connor, N., Jenneke, W., & Tarrier, N. (1994). A trial of eye movement desensitization compared to image habituation training, and applied muscle relaxation in posttraumatic stress disorder. *Journal of Behavior Therapy and Experimental Psychiatry, 25,* 283–291.

Veronen, L. J., & Kilpatrick, D.G. (1983). Stress management for rape victims. In D. Meichenbaum & M. E. Jaremko (Eds.), *Stress reduction and prevention.* New York: Plenum Press.

Wilson, S. A., Becker, L. A., & Tinker, R. (1995a). Eye movement desensitization and reprocessing (EMDR) treatment for psychologically traumatized individuals. *Journal of Consulting and Clinical Psychology, 63,* 928–937.

Wilson, D. L., Silver, S. M., Covi, W. G., & Foster, S. (1995b). *Eye movement desensitization and reprocessing: Effectiveness and autonomic correlates.* Paper presented at the annual convention of the American Psychiatric Association, Miami, FL.

Wolff, R. (1977). Systematic desensitization and negative practice to alter the aftereffects of a rape attempt. *Journal of Behavior Therapy and Experimental Psychiatry, 8,* 423–425.

Wolpe, J. (1958). *Psychotherapy by reciprocal inhibition.* Stanford, CA: Stanford University Press.

Wolpe, J., & Abrams, J. (1991). Post-traumatic stress disorder overcome by eye movement desensitization: A case report. *Journal of Behavior Therapy and Experimental Psychiatry, 22,* 39–43.

Yehuda, R., Southwick, S. M., Krystal, J. H., Bremner, J. D., Charney, D. S., & Mason, J. W. (1993). Enhanced suppression of cortisol following dexamethasone administration in post-traumatic stress disorder. *American Journal of Psychiatry, 150*, 83–86.

Further reading

Davidson, J. R. T., & Foa, E. B. (1993). *Posttraumatic stress disorder: DSM-IV and beyond.* Washington, DC: American Psychiatric Press.

Foy, D. W. (1992). *Treating PTSD: Cognitive-behavioral strategies.* New York: Guilford Press.

Freedy, J. R., & Hobfoll, S. E. (1995). *Traumatic stress: From theory to practice.* New York: Plenum Press.

Resick, P. A., & Schnicke, M. K. (1993). *Cognitive processing therapy for rape victims: A treatment manual.* Newbury Park, CA: Sage.

Saigh, P. A. (1992). *Posttraumatic stress disorder: A behavioral approach to assessment and treatment.* Boston, MA: Allyn and Bacon.

7

Analysis and Treatment of Generalized Anxiety Disorder

MICHEL J. DUGAS and ROBERT LADOUCEUR

École de Psychologie, Université Laval, Canada

Introduction

Generalized Anxiety Disorder (GAD) is among the most frequent anxiety disorders. Using DSM-III-R diagnostic criteria, Breslau & Davis (1985) found a prevalence of 9% in the general population. However, two large-scale American studies yielded more modest rates. The National Institute of Mental Health (NIMH) multi-site study obtained a prevalence of 4% for GAD (cited in Barlow, 1988) and the National Comorbidity Survey (NCS) produced similar numbers, showing a 6-month prevalence of 3.1% and a lifetime prevalence of 5.1% (Kessler, McGonagle, Zhao, Nelson, Hughes, Eshleman, Wittchen & Kendler, 1994). The NCS also revealed a higher lifetime prevalence of GAD in women than in men, 6.6% and 3.6%, respectively.

Despite its prevalence, mental health professionals report that they seldom see GAD patients as compared to other anxiety disorder patients (Barlow, Blanchard, Vermilyea & Di Nardo, 1986; Bradwejn, Berner & Shaw, 1992). This apparent contradiction may be explained in two ways. First, individuals with GAD tend not to seek help for their problem. Compared to other anxiety disorders such as Panic Disorder, GAD is associated with less symptomatic distress and social impairment (Noyes, Woodman, Garvey, Cook, Suelzer, Clancy & Anderson, 1992). Therefore, GAD patients tend to wait many years before seeing a mental health professional (Rapee, 1991). Also, 80% of individuals with GAD do not remember their first symptoms and report having been worried and anxious all their life (Barlow, 1988; Rapee, 1991). For this reason, they often interpret their symptoms as unmodifiable personality traits and do not seek professional help. Second, when these individuals seek help, GAD may not be properly recognized. General practitioners are often seen first and they tend to limit their investigation to GAD somatic symptoms such as fatigue and insomnia (Bradwejn, Berner & Shaw, 1992). Further, GAD patients frequently become depressed, socially anxious and demoralized (Butler, Fennel, Robson & Gelder, 1991). If these consequences become sufficiently severe, they may be seen as the main problem and GAD will again remain undetected.

Classification

GAD was officially recognized in the third edition of the *Diagnostic and statistical manual of mental disorders* of the American Psychological Association (APA, 1980). It was originally considered a residual diagnostic category, which meant that it could not be diagnosed in the presence of another disorder. In 1987, DSM-III-R made GAD a primary diagnostic category and defined its main feature as unrealistic or excessive worry. The diagnosis also required 6 out of 18 somatic symptoms, which were divided into three categories, motor tension, autonomic hyperactivity, and vigilance and scanning. Although DSM-III-R improved the diagnostic reliability of GAD, it remained relatively weak as compared to other anxiety disorders (Di Nardo, Moras, Barlow, Rapee & Brown, 1993; Williams, Gibbon, First, Spitzer, Davies, Borus, Howes, Kane, Pope, Rounsaville & Wittchen, 1992).

In order to clarify the definition of GAD and improve its diagnostic reliability, DSM-IV (APA, 1994) made many significant changes. The first diagnostic criteria for GAD is now "Excessive anxiety and worry (apprehensive expectation), occurring more days than not for at least 6 months, about a number of events or activities (such as work or school performance)." (APA, 1994, p. 435). The worry must be difficult to control and lead to significant distress or impairment in important areas of functioning (e.g., social, occupational, etc.). To improve the diagnostic specificity of the somatic criterion, DSM-IV changed the diagnostic criterion from six out of 18 to three out of six symptoms: (1) restlessness or feeling keyed up or on edge, (2) being easily fatigued, (3) difficulty concentrating or mind going blank, (4) irritability, (5) muscle tension, and (6) sleep disturbance. Although studies of the diagnostic reliability of DSM-IV GAD have yet to appear, our clinical experience suggests that these changes in GAD criteria will lead to greater diagnostic agreement.

Comorbidity

Many studies report very high rates of comorbidity for patients with a principal diagnosis of GAD. Sanderson, Di Nardo, Rapee & Barlow (1990b) report that 91% of their GAD patient sample had an additional DSM-III-R diagnosis. In a similar study, de Ruiter, Ruken, Garssen, van Schaik & Kraaimaat (1989) report a comorbidity rate of 67% for GAD. In these studies, the most common additional diagnoses were Social Phobia, Panic Disorder, Dysthymic Disorder and Specific Phobia. When comparing GAD and Panic Disorder, Noyes and colleagues (1992) report that Specific Phobia was a more common secondary diagnosis for GAD subjects. In a large-scale study involving 468 anxiety disorder patients, Moras, Di Nardo, Brown & Barlow (1991, cited in Brown & Barlow, 1992) report that GAD and Panic Disorder with Agoraphobia were the principal diagnostic categories that had the highest comorbidity rates.

High rates of comorbidity for GAD as a secondary disorder have also recently been reported. In their extensive study, Moras et al. (1991, cited in Brown & Barlow, 1992) found that GAD was the most common additional diagnosis (23%) at the clinical level (at least moderate severity). In a study of patients with a principal diagnosis of Major Depression or Dysthymia, Sanderson, Beck and Beck (1990a) report that GAD and Social Phobia were the two most common additional diagnoses. Brown and Barlow (1992) suggest that further research on comorbidity is of the utmost importance for diagnostic classification and treatment outcome. Considering the high rate of comorbidity of GAD, these considerations become all the more important.

The Concept of Worry

The Penn State research team originally defined worry as "a chain of thoughts and images, negatively affect-laden and relatively uncontrollable. The worry process represents an attempt to engage in mental problem solving on an issue whose outcome is uncertain but contains the possibility of one or more negative outcomes." (Borkovec, Robinson, Pruzinsky & DePree, 1983a, p. 10). Following a series of empirical studies, Borkovec and colleagues now suggest that worry is primarily a verbal conceptual activity which may be used as a coping strategy (Borkovec & Lyonfields, 1993; Borkovec, Shadick & Hopkins, 1991; Roemer & Borkovec, 1993). In DSM-IV, worry is also referred to as apprehensive expectation which has been described by the Albany research group as "a future-oriented mood state in which one becomes ready or prepared to attempt to cope with upcoming negative events. Anxious apprehension is associated with a state of high negative affect and chronic overarousal, a sense of uncontrollability, and an attentional focus on threat-related stimuli (e.g., high self-focused attention or self-preoccupation and hypervigilance)" (Brown, O'Leary & Barlow, 1993, p. 139). In both these definitions, worry consists of repeated thoughts about future danger which are experienced as aversive and relatively uncontrollable. Borkovec (1985) also suggests that worry is best described by the phrase "What if...". Thus, high worriers are experts at identifying possible problems while being poor at generating effective solutions or coping responses.

Worry Themes

Sanderson & Barlow (1990) investigated worry themes in 22 GAD patients and found that they worried most about their family (79% of subjects), finances (50%), work (43%) and illness (14%). All worries that were subjected to interjudge reliability ratings were placed in one of these four categories. Interestingly, GAD patients reported more worry about minor matters than other clinically anxious groups included in the study (Social Phobia, Panic Disorder, Specific Phobia, and Obsessive-Compulsive Disorder).

Craske, Rapee, Jackel & Barlow (1989) compared the worry themes of 19 GAD patients with those of 26 normal subjects. Their results show that GAD subjects worry more about illness/health/injury and miscellaneous issues while worrying less about finances than normal subjects. Worries about family, home and interpersonal relationships were equally reported by both groups. The authors attempted to classify all worries using the four categories identified by Sanderson & Barlow (1990), but they only managed to place 74.8% of GAD worries and 84.8% of normal worries in the family, finances, work and illness categories. Craske et al. conclude that these four categories are clearly insufficient to account for the diversity of worry themes in individuals with GAD.

Shadick, Roemer, Hopkins & Borkovec (1991) assessed worry themes in 31 GAD patients, in 12 non-clinical university students who met GAD diagnostic criteria ("high worriers") and in 13 non-anxious subjects. For all three groups, the most common worry themes were family, home and interpersonal relationships. However, GAD patients and high worriers reported a higher percentage of worries about miscellaneous problems that could not be placed in one of the four pre-established categories (family, finances, work and illness). The authors conclude that GAD patients and high worriers worry about a greater variety of situations, including minor problems, and that these multiple situations must be investigated to better understand excessive worry.

The studies described above suggest that GAD and normal worry themes are relatively similar. These results have lead some researchers to claim that these groups do not differ substantially on the content of worry (e.g., Brown et al., 1993; Wells, 1994). However, two differences have emerged from the literature.

First, GAD patients worry about a greater diversity of situations than non-clinical subjects (Craske et al., 1989; Shadick et al., 1991). Second, they also worry more about minor matters than non-anxious subjects (Shadick et al., 1991) and other clinically anxious patients (Sanderson & Barlow, 1990). Indirect support for this claim was provided by Di Nardo (1991, cited in Brown et al., 1993) who showed that a negative response to the question "Do you worry excessively about minor matters?" can effectively rule out a diagnosis of GAD (negative predictive power of .94). Our research group has also shown that worry about minor matters is sensitive as 86% of subjects meeting GAD cognitive and somatic criteria reported worrying about minor things (Dugas, Freeston & Ladouceur, 1994b).

In more general terms, many authors suggest that worry themes have a social evaluative basis (e.g., Sanderson & Barlow, 1990; Borkovec et al., 1991; Eysenck & van Berkum, 1992). Lovibond & Rapee (1993) showed that feared social outcomes, and not feared physical outcomes, correlate with the Penn State Worry Questionnaire. Likewise, our research team found that public self and body consciousness were better predictors of scores on the Penn State Worry Questionnaire than private self and body consciousness (Letarte, Freeston, Rhéaume & Ladouceur, 1998). In other words, awareness of oneself as an object of public scrutiny is more closely related to worry than awareness of internal states. Recently, we have shown that social worry, as compared to physical or financial worry, is a stronger predictor of the general tendency to worry (Freeston, Dugas & Ladouceur, 1995). It remains to be established if GAD worry and normal worry differ in the degree to which they are rooted in social evaluation.

Worry and Problem Solving

Many studies point to an important relationship between worry and problem solving. Our research team obtained correlation coefficients ranging from 0.31 to 0.51 between measures of worry and problem solving in a non-clinical population (Dugas, Letarte, Rhéaume, Freeston & Ladouceur, 1995d). Subscales describing problem-solving skills explained very little or non-significant amounts of variance of worry scores whereas problem orientation subscales, which describe initial affective, cognitive and behavioral reactions to problem situations, were strong predictors of worry scores. These findings were replicated with a clinical sample as GAD patients and high worriers had poorer problem orientation scores than moderate worriers (Blais, Ladouceur, Dugas & Freeston, 1993). As predicted, all three groups were similar on measures of problem-solving skills. These studies suggest that GAD patients and high worriers do not lack knowledge about how to solve problems but have difficulty applying their knowledge because of counter-productive reactions to problem situations. For instance, one of our GAD patients worried a great deal that his girlfriend would leave him because of ongoing dissatisfaction with the relationship. During pre-treatment evaluation, he spontaneously described behaviors which he could adopt to improve the relationship. He clearly knew that if he could initiate more social activities, explore and pursue new mutual interests, and generally adopt a more proactive attitude, this would go a long way toward improving the quality of the relationship and increasing his girl-friend's satisfaction. Although the patient and therapist both realized that adopting these behaviors would greatly improve the relationship, the patient could not bring himself to act accordingly because of counter-productive reactions to the problem situation. In fact, he expressed great difficulty in perceiving his relationship problems as challenges to be met. As can be ex-pected, 2 months into therapy, the relationship had not changed and the patient's girlfriend decided to leave him.

In a related line of research, three studies have shown that high worriers are slower on categorization tasks when the stimuli are ambiguous and the correct response unclear (Metzger, Miller, Cohen, Sofka & Borkovec, 1990; Tallis, 1989; Tallis, Eysenck & Mathews, 1991). Tallis and colleagues (1991) suggest that worriers, when attempting to solve problems, are hindered by elevated evidence requirements. Our research group hypothesized that elevated evidence requirements may be a component of a cognitive vulnerability factor in high worriers and GAD patients, namely intolerance of uncertainty. In order to test the relationship between worry and intolerance of uncertainty, we devised the *Intolerance of Uncertainty* questionnaire which evaluates emotional, cognitive and behavioral reactions to ambiguous situations, implications of being uncer-tain, and attempts to control future outcomes. We then demonstrated that worry is highly related to intolerance of uncertainty and that the relationship is not simply a consequence of shared variance with negative affect (Freeston, Rhéaume, Letarte, Dugas & Ladouceur, 1994c). These findings were replicated with a clinical sample as GAD patients and high worriers were more intolerant of uncertainty than were moderate worriers (Ladouceur, Freeston & Dugas, 1993b). Thus, intolerance of uncertainty seems to be an important cognitive vulnerability factor in GAD patients and high worriers.

Worry as Approach-Avoidance Behavior

Although many recent findings concerning worry are compatible with each other, some are more difficult to reconcile. On the one hand, worry is associ-ated with approach behavior. Subjects report that worrying helps them find a solution or a better way of doing things and increases their feelings of control (Freeston et al., 1994c). Worry also leads to selective attention to threatening information (Macleod & Mathews, 1988) which can occur without the individual's knowledge (Mathews, 1990). On the other hand, worry is associated with different types of avoidance. GAD patients claim that worrying helps them avoid improbable negative outcomes (Brown et al., 1993; Roemer & Borkovec, 1993) and non-clinical subjects report that worrying distracts them from thinking about worse things (Freeston et al., 1994c). Worry is also related to avoidance of mental images associated with unpleasant somatic experience (Borkovec & Hu, 1990; Freeston, Dugas & Ladouceur,1994a) and to avoidance of threatening material (Roemer, Borkovec, Posa & Lyonfields, 1991a).

Recently, Krohne (1989, 1993) has proposed a general model of anxiety which may be helpful in integrating these findings and understanding worry. Krohne suggests that individual coping patterns are the result of dispositional preferences for vigilance (as a result of intolerance of uncertainty) and for avoidance (as a consequence of intolerance of emotional arousal). High-anxious individuals would have strong tendencies to approach and to avoid which would lead to fluctuating, anxiety-increasing coping behavior in threatening situations.

In order to test the suitability of Krohne's model specifically for worry, our research team examined the relationship between coping patterns on the one hand, and the tendency to worry and GAD somatic symptoms on the other (Dugas, Freeston, Doucet, Provencher & Ladouceur, 1995b). Subject groups were formed according to four types of behavior patterns: (1) high intolerance of uncertainty and high suppression (HU/HS), (2) high intolerance of uncertainty and low suppression (HU/LS), (3) low intolerance of uncertainty and high suppression (LU/HS), and (4) low intolerance of uncertainty and low suppression (LU/LS). As predicted, the HU/HS group scored higher than all other groups on the Penn State Questionnaire and reported more intense somatic symptoms. Therefore, GAD patients may be intolerant of both uncertainty and emotional arousal. As Krohne (1989, 1993) correctly points out, uncertainty and emotional arousal cannot be attenuated simultaneously as vigilance decreases uncertainty but increases emotional arousal whereas avoidance decreases arousal while increasing uncertainty. GAD patients would switch from one coping mode to the other in a futile attempt to deal with a perceived threat. Thus, worry would seem to be approach-avoidance behavior, resulting from the deployment of both vigilant and avoidant coping modes.

Clinical Conception of GAD Worry

Based on the empirical studies described above and our clinical experience with GAD patients, we have elaborated a specific clinical conception of GAD worry. Let us begin with the perception of threat. Considering that everyday life involves numerous ambiguous situations, individuals who are intolerant of uncertainty will perceive more threatening situations due to their vigilant mode of coping (Krohne, 1989, 1993). The perception of threat leads to worry and an increase in levels of anxiety (Macleod & Mathews, 1988) and depression (Dugas, Freeston, Blais & Ladouceur, 1994a). The individual will then be particularly attentive to threatening information (Mathews, 1990), detect subjective risk to a greater degree (Butler & Mathews, 1987), perceive ambiguous material as threatening (Eysenck, Macleod & Mathews, 1987; Eysenck, Mogg, May, Richards & Mathews, 1991; Mathews, Mogg, Kay & Eysenck, 1989) and overestimate the probability of negative outcomes (Macleod, Williams & Bekerian, 1991). In turn, this biased treatment of environmental information increases levels of worry and anxiety.

Even if worry involves a stream of negative thoughts, loss of mental control and is related to negative affect (Borkovec et al., 1983a; Brown et al., 1993), it may nonetheless be evaluated in positive terms. High worriers (Freeston et al., 1994c) and GAD patients (Ladouceur et al., 1993b) claim that worry helps them avoid negative events, find a better way to do things and increase their feelings of control. Further, GAD patients may view their worry as such an important part of them that they wonder how they will be if they no longer worry (Brown et al., 1993). Worry may thus be partially maintained by both positive and negative reinforcement although the benefits of worrying are often overestimated (e.g., high worriers often report that worrying helps them avoid events which are, in fact, highly unlikely). The following two examples illustrate how GAD patients may perceive worry as a way of preventing negative outcomes. First, a 24-year-old female student involved in our treatment program reported that she had always worried a great deal about school and had always succeeded in her courses. Not only did she believe that if she worried less she would not succeed, she observed that other students who did not seem to worry very much did not perform as well as she did in school, thus "confirming" her erroneous belief about the usefulness of worry. In the same perspective, a middle-aged woman being treated at our clinic worried about the health of her grandson during her three week vacation in Europe. Upon her return, she was relieved to find him in good health. Unfortunately, two weeks later, her grandson became ill. The patient interpreted this turn of events as follows: "This proves that my worries really did prevent him from becoming ill because when I stopped worrying, he became sick. I should have continued worrying!"

In addition to being intolerant of uncertainty, if an individual is also intolerant of emotional arousal, he will then be vulnerable to becoming excessively worried (Dugas et al., 1995b). Recall that uncertainty and emotional arousal cannot be attenuated simultaneously (Krohne, 1989, 1993). When the individual attempts to decrease uncertainty by using a vigilant coping style, he increases his emotional arousal. Further, when high worriers attempt to use problem solving to deal with the perceived threat, they have difficulty applying their problem-solving skills due to poor problem orientation (Blais et al., 1993; Davey, 1994; Dugas et al., 1995d).

On the other hand, attempts at decreasing emotional arousal by an avoidant coping mode will lead to increases in uncertainty. Instances of avoidant coping include the avoidance of mental imagery associated with worry. Worries are primarily made up of verbal-linguistic thought activity (Borkovec & Inz, 1990; Borkovec & Lyonfields, 1993; Freeston et al., 1994a) and often do not concern the individual's worst fears. Avoidance of mental images leads to a decrease in peripheral physiological activity (Borkovec & Hu, 1990; Borkovec, Lyonfields, Wiser & Deihl, 1993) and in emotional processing of the threatening material (Butler, Wells & Dewick, 1992; Foa & Kozak, 1986), all of which negatively reinforces and maintains worry (Borkovec et al., 1991).

GAD patients, who are intolerant of both uncertainty and emotional arousal, thus switch from one coping mode to the other in a futile attempt to deal with the perceived threat. Constant shifting from partial problem solving to avoidance of mental images and vice versa prevents GAD patients from adequately dealing with the threat and contributes to the establishment of a downward spiral in which worry and levels of anxiety and depression are maintained or increased.

Treatment Outcome Studies

Before presenting a detailed description of our assessment and treatment program, a brief review of treatment outcome studies will be carried out. The review will be restricted in three ways. First, treatment outcome studies that were carried out before DSM-III-R or that do not use DSM-III-R criteria to diagnose subjects will not be described (e.g., Barlow, Cohen, Waddell, Vermilyea, Klosko, Blanchard & Di Nardo1984; Butler, Cullington, Hibbert, Klimes & Gelder, 1987; Durham & Turvey, 1987; Jannoun, Oppenheimer & Gelder, 1982). Prior to DSM-III-R, GAD was characterized by a number of somatic symptoms that did not adequately discriminate it from other anxiety disorders. Therefore, to include these studies would add very little to our knowledge of treatment outcome for GAD, as described in DSM-III-R and DSM-IV. The only exception to this first restriction will be the stimulus control treatment study by Borkovec, Wilkinson, Folensbee and Lerman (1983b) because of its pioneering nature as well as its important theoretical and clinical implications for the treatment of excessive worry.

Second, because this chapter specifically concerns GAD worry, outcome studies of treatments that do not directly target GAD worry will not be described (e.g., Barlow, Rapee & Brown, 1992; Borkovec& Costello, 1993; Butler et al., 1991; Sanderson & Beck, 1991; White, Keenan & Brooks, 1992). Although these treatments indirectly target worry *via* various forms of cognitive restructuring, they will not be discussed because of the non-specific nature of their cognitive interventions. Finally, outcome studies that include pharmacological treatments (e.g., Lindsay, Gamsu, McLaughlin, Hood & Espie, 1987; Hoehn-Saric, McLeod & Zimmerli, 1988) are not described because they exceed the scope of this chapter.

Borkovec et al. (1983b) were among the first researchers to apply a treatment that specifically targets worry. In two distinct studies, they demonstrated the effect of a stimulus control treatment for university students who reported worrying for more than 50% of the day. After having identified their main worry themes, students were asked to delay worrying until a predetermined 30 min period of the day, always in the same place. In both studies, results showed a larger decrease in time spent worrying for experimental groups than for waiting list control groups. Considering that worries are related to the avoidance of mental imagery (Borkovec & Inz, 1990; Borkovec & Lyonfields, 1993; Freeston et al., 1994a) and somatic activation (Borkovec & Hu, 1990; Borkovec et al., 1993), a stimulus control treatment which resembles cognitive exposure may be an effective treatment component for GAD worry. However, Borkovec and colleagues did not instruct their subjects to specifically expose themselves to mental images, which may prove to be more efficient for the reduction of worry. Further, the generalizability of these results is limited because the researchers used non-clinical subjects and did not assess treatment maintenance.

O'Leary, Brown & Barlow (1992) applied a form of cognitive exposure (worry control) to three GAD patients in a multiple baseline design across subjects. In worry control, subjects are asked to expose themselves to their worries by conjuring up all possible consequences, including the worst potential outcomes. For two out three subjects, the treatment lead to a significant decrease in the tendency to worry, as measured by the Penn State Worry Questionnaire. Upon inquiry, all subjects reported a decrease in time spent worrying and in worry-related distress as well as an increase in their degree of daily pleasantness. The results reported by O'Leary and colleagues are particularly interesting considering that they applied only one treatment component, which suggests that cognitive exposure is indeed an active treatment component. Further, they used specific measures that assess key GAD dimensions such as tendency to worry and distress associated with worry (DSM-IV, APA, 1994). Although these results are encouraging, the comparative efficacy of this treatment awaits further study.

Recently, Brown et al. (1993) described a multidimensional treatment package for GAD. The treatment involves five components: (1) cognitive restructuring, (2) progressive muscular relaxation, (3) cognitive exposure (worry control), (4) response prevention, and (5) dealing with problems. Although many case histories suggest that this treatment package is effective, empirical comparative studies have yet to be carried out. Considering that cognitive exposure to the worst image related to worry leads to increased somatic activation (Borkovec & Hu, 1990; Borkovec et al., 1993) and to emotional processing of threatening material (Foa & Kozak, 1986), the inclusion of worry control in this treatment package seems to be a judicious choice. However, two aspects of this multidimensional intervention remain questionable. First, considering that worry is associated with poor problem orientation and not with a lack of knowledge about how to solve problems (Blais et al., 1993; Dugas et al., 1995d), why do the authors suggest applying all sub-components of problem-solving training? It may prove more effective (and less time consuming) to target problem orientation and briefly review problem-solving skills with GAD patients. Second, which worries should be targeted by the different treatment components? Should worry control and problem solving be applied indiscriminately to all worries? If not, how should the therapist decide which worries are amenable to the different treatment components? In order to facilitate treatment application and increase its effectiveness, we believe that these questions must be addressed.

Types of Worries

At Laval University, we have been fascinated by the different types of worries reported by our GAD patients. We believe that GAD worries can be divided into three distinct categories, each requiring a different treatment strategy. Our GAD patients have described worries that concern: (1) immediate problems which are grounded in reality and modifiable, (2) immediate problems which are grounded in reality but non-modifiable, and (3) highly remote events which are not grounded in reality and therefore non-modifiable. Each one of these types of worries will now be depicted. In addition, we will recommend specific treatment strategies for each type of worry which will be further described in the Process of Treatment section.

The first type of worry concerns immediate problems which are grounded in reality and modifiable. Examples include worries about interpersonal conflicts, dressing properly for specific situations, and daily hassles such as being on time for an appointment, getting the car fixed or making minor house repairs. Recall that GAD patients, when faced with problem situations, report initial cognitive, affective and behavioral reactions (problem orientation) which are ineffective or counter-productive (Blais et al., 1993). Although problem-solving training has been used in the treatment of excessive worry and GAD, it has either been added as a peripheral element to a pre-existing stimulus control treatment (Borkovec et al., 1983b) or included as a minor and unspecific component in a general treatment package (Brown et al., 1993). Considering that worry is associated with poor problem solving, we believe problem-solving training (PST) should be a major component in the treatment of GAD.

We further propose that two important considerations guide the use of PST. First, the therapist should adapt PST by focusing on the patient's initial reaction when faced with a problem, taking into account the cognitive, affective and behavioral dimensions of this reaction. Because GAD patients do not report a lack of problem-solving skills (Blais et al., 1993), extensive training in all phases of problem solving is inappropriate and may in fact decrease patient motivation. Second, PST with problem-focused goals should only be applied to worries about immediate problems which are grounded in reality and modifiable.

The second type of worry reported by our GAD patients involves immediate problems which are grounded in reality but non-modifiable. Examples include worries about the illness of a loved one or the state of the world such as poverty, war, increasing violence and injustice. Because these problem situations are non-modifiable, PST with problem-focused goals will not lead to desired outcomes. However, as Nezu and D'Zurilla (1989) have pointed out, PST with emotion-focused goals may help patients adapt to a non-modifiable problem situation. Therefore, this type of worry may be dealt with by using PST with emotion-focused goals. The following clinical example illustrates a worry involving an immediate problem which is grounded in reality but non-modifiable. A middle-aged man, who had been working for a well-known and established company over the past 25 years, worried about the direction the company had recently taken. Although he held an important position in the company and did not agree with its new direction, he could not modify the decisions taken at company headquarters. Although the patient's worries about his work originally seemed to concern a modifiable situation, further investigation clearly showed that the situation was in fact beyond his range of influence and thus non-modifiable.

GAD patients also report worrying about highly remote events that are not grounded in reality and consequently non-modifiable. Worries about the possibility of someday going bankrupt or becoming seriously ill (in the absence of immediate financial or health problems) are examples of this type of worry. These worries are not within the reach of PST with either problem-focused or emotion-focused goals because no problem situation actually exists. Recall that the verbal content of worry represents avoidance of fear provoking imagery and that worry is negatively reinforced by a decrease in aversive somatic activation (Borkovec & Lyonfields, 1993; Roemer & Borkovec, 1993). Thus, current accounts of the role of worry as avoidance of fearful images and the existence of a group of worries about problems which do not actually exist (and are not amenable to PST) both point toward the use of functional cognitive exposure to fearful images.

Although the Albany group suggests directing exposure at the fearful imagery component of worry (cf. Brown et al., 1993; Craske, Barlow & O'Leary, 1992; O'Leary, Brown & Barlow, 1992), they seem to apply cognitive exposure indiscriminately to all worries. In contrast to this view, we believe that exposure to the worst images should only be used with worries concerning highly remote events. Further, Craske and colleagues (1992) recommend using applied relaxation and cognitive restructuring during cognitive exposure while Brown et al. (1993) prescribe the generation of alternatives to the worst image in the final phase of exposure practice. Theoretical accounts of the processes involved in successful exposure (Foa & Kozak, 1986) as well as our own experience using exposure with obsessive ruminators (cf. Ladouceur, Freeston, Gagnon, Thibodeau & Dumont, 1993c; Ladouceur, Freeston, Gagnon, Thibodeau & Dumont, 1994) strongly suggest that exposure to the fearful imagery should be carried out independently of other treatment strategies. Other strategies, whether they be relaxation, cognitive restructuring or the generation alternative scenarios, may be used by the patient in order to neutralize the feared image and thus decrease the beneficial effects of exposure. Now that the different types of worries have been presented, let us turn to a detailed description of our assessment and treatment program.

Assessment

Considering the major changes in GAD diagnostic criteria since DSM-III (APA, 1980), it is not surprising that GAD assessment has also undergone significant change. Originally considered a non-specific disorder often referred to as "free-floating" or "pervasive" anxiety, GAD was assessed with general measures of anxiety. Although these general measures remain important, specific measures of key symptoms should be the mainstay of GAD assessment. We recommend that the complete assessment of treatment outcome for GAD include four levels of measures: (1) structured interviews for the diagnosis and evaluation of treatment outcome, (2) measures of GAD symptoms, (3) measures of key variables associated with GAD, and (4) general measures of anxiety and depression. Considering that GAD assessment has been neglected in the past and that poor assessment has contributed to a lack of specificity and effectiveness of treatment interventions, this section will describe in detail each level of measure which is essential to effective treatment planning for GAD.

Structured Interviews

Because of the poor diagnostic reliability of GAD as compared to other anxiety disorders (cf. Di Nardo et al., 1993; Williams et al., 1992), the use of a well established diagnostic structured interview is of the utmost importance. Ideally, the GAD diagnosis should be confirmed by a second independent diagnostic interview (i.e., a different clinician who administers the same structured interview). In order to properly assess treatment outcome and maintenance, the diagnostic structured interview should also be administered at post-test and at all follow-up assessments. We believe the Anxiety Disorders Interview Schedule for DSM-IV (ADIS-IV, Brown, Di Nardo & Barlow, 1994) represents the most practical and informative structured interview presently available for anxiety disorders. Although the ADIS-IV was designed for the anxiety disorders, it also contains items which screen for mood disorders, somatoform disorders, psychoactive substance use disorders, psychotic disorders, and medical problems. The section on GAD includes items which cover DSM-IV diagnostic criteria as well as other items about worry themes, percentage of the day spent worrying, alcohol and drug consumption, physical condition, duration of the disorder, etc. Administration of the ADIS-IV typically takes 1–2 h and yields information on the presence of Axis I disorders with severity ratings.

Measures of GAD Symptoms

The first measure of GAD symptoms is the *Worry and Anxiety Questionnaire* (WAQ, Dugas, Freeston, Lachance, Provencher & Ladouceur, 1995a). The WAQ contains 16 items and is derived from the Generalized Anxiety Disorder Questionnaire (GADQ, Roemer, Posa & Borkovec, 1991b) which was updated to include all DSM-IV diagnostic criteria for GAD as well as current research questions about worry. GADQ dichotomous items were changed to continuous scale items (rated on a nine-point Likert-type scale) given earlier problems with high and unstable endorsement rates for some items (cf. Freeston et al., 1994a). The WAQ initially asks for a list of up to six worry themes which are then each rated for their excessive and realistic nature. Next, there are eight items about worry and anxiety which include three items from the GADQ (minor worries, percentage of thoughts and images, and percentage of the day spent worrying) and five items for DSM-IV GAD criteria. The WAQ also contains four items which are highly representative of related constructs, namely intolerance of uncertainty, thought suppression, problem orientation and perfectionism. Each one of these items was drawn from existing measures and had the highest corrected item-total correlation. The final item asks about physical health. Although DSM-IV states that worry should not be about another Axis I disorder such as Hypochondriasis, the relationship between worry about health and actual physical illness remains important when assessing GAD.

We also recommend using the *Penn State Worry Questionnaire* (PSWQ, Meyer, Miller, Metzger & Borkovec, 1990) which consists of 16 items that measure a trait-like tendency to worry. Meyer et al. (1990) have shown that the

PSWQ is unifactorial, has high internal consistency and test-retest reliability, as well as adequate convergent and discriminant validity. Further, scores on the PSWQ distinguish GAD patients from other anxiety disorder patients (Brown, Antony & Barlow, 1992). Because the PSWQ and the WAQ are brief questionnaires which are very informative, we recommend they be administered at regular intervals during treatment in order to assess patient progress. Patients should also complete these measures at pre-test, post-test and at all follow-up evaluations.

Measures of Key Variables Associated with GAD

The first measure of associated variables which should be administered is the *Intolerance of Uncertainty* scale (IU, Freeston et al., 1994c) which consists of 28 items about uncertainty, emotional and behavioral reactions to ambiguous situations, implications of being uncertain, and attempts to control the future. The sum of these items distinguishes worriers meeting GAD criteria by questionnaire from those who do not and the relationship between measures of worry and the IU are not accounted for by shared variance with negative affect (Freeston et al., 1994c). Factor analyses revealed five factors corresponding to the ideas that uncertainty: (1) is unacceptable and should be avoided, (2) reflects badly on a person, (3) provokes frustration, (4) induces stress, and (5) inhibits action. The internal consistency of the IU is excellent and the scale shows good temporal stability over a five-week period ($r = 0.78$) (Dugas, Ladouceur & Freeston, 1995c). Although the IU does not assess GAD symptoms, it does provide valuable information about important cognitive variables. Therefore, we suggest that it be administered before and after treatment, and at follow-up assessments.

The second measure is the *Social Problem-Solving Inventory* (SPSI, D'Zurilla & Nezu, 1990). The SPSI is a multidimensional self-report measure of social problem solving which consists of 70 items (rated on a five-point Likert-type scale) that are divided into two major scales and seven subscales. The two major scales are the Problem Orientation Scale and the Problem-Solving Skills Scale. The Problem Orientation Scale, which refers to general motivational factors, contains three subscales: Cognition, Emotion, and Behavior. The Problem-Solving Skills Scale is divided into four subscales: Problem Definition and Formulation, Generation of Alternative Solutions, Decision Making, and Solution Implementation and Verification. The SPSI has sound psychometric properties and is a good multicomponent measure of social problem solving.

As many researchers have pointed out, GAD patients and high worriers believe that worrying has substantial benefits (cf. Brown et al., 1993; Dugas, Ladouceur, Boisvert & Freeston, 1996; Roemer & Borkovec, 1993). The *Why*

Worry? questionnaire (WW; Freeston et al., 1994c) was developed by our research team in order to assess appraisal of worries. The WW consists of 20 items giving reasons why people say they worry. Based on our clinical experience with GAD patients, a pool of items was developed and empirical criteria were used to select items. Factor analyses identified two types of beliefs: (1) worrying has positive effects such as finding a better way of doing things, increasing control, and finding solutions, and (2) worrying can prevent negative outcomes from happening or provide distraction from fearful images or from thinking about worse things.

Although some WW items deal with avoidance of images or emotional material, the questionnaire was not exclusively designed to assess thought suppression. We recommend using the *White Bear Suppression Inventory* (WBSI; Wegner & Zanakos, 1992) to complement the WW in assessing thought suppression. The WBSI, which shows good metric properties, measures individual differences in the tendency to suppress unwanted thoughts. Though the WBSI has mainly been used for research purposes, it has proven quite helpful in assessing thought suppression in our GAD patients.

General Measures of Anxiety and Depression

Although general measures of psychopathology are no longer the mainstay of GAD assessment, the Beck Anxiety Inventory (BAI, Beck, Epstein, Brown & Steer, 1988a) and Beck Depression Inventory (BDI, Beck, Rush, Shaw & Emery, 1979) remain valuable because of their proven psychometric qualities and their wide-spread use. The BAI is a 21-item state anxiety scale measuring the intensity of cognitive, affective, and somatic anxious symptoms experienced during the last 7 days. Our research team has confirmed the sound psychometric properties of the BAI on non-clinical, outpatient, and psychiatric samples (Freeston, Ladouceur, Thibodeau, Gagnon & Rhéaume, 1994b).

The BDI consists of 21 items covering the principal depressive symptoms and has been in use for over 25 years. Its psychometric properties have also been extensively studied (cf. Beck, Steer & Garbin, 1988b; Bourque & Beaudette, 1982) and proven to be excellent. Like the WAQ and the PSWQ, these brief inventories should be administered regularly during therapy, at pre-test, post-test and at all follow-up assessments.

Overview of Treatment

The treatment's main objectives are to help the patient recognize his worries as approach-avoidance behavior, discriminate between different types of worries, and apply the correct strategy to each type. Our intervention progresses over approximately 18 1-h sessions and involves four components: (1) presentation of treatment rationale, (2) behavioral analysis and awareness training, (3) specific worry interventions, and (4) reevaluation of worry appraisal. Although it always involves these four components, the treatment program is tailored to the individual needs of each patient. For instance, for patients who report worrying mostly about problems which are grounded in reality, adapted PST with emphasis on problem orientation would be the principal specific worry intervention. For patients who worry mostly about highly remote events, functional cognitive exposure would be the main specific worry intervention.

Treatment typically lasts 4 months with follow-up sessions over a one-year period. Ideally, the first eight sessions are conducted on a biweekly basis in order to closely monitor the patient's initial progress. Then, eight weekly sessions are followed by two fade-out sessions (usually two to four weeks apart). We also recommend three follow-up sessions over a one-year period, at three, six and 12 months. Although sessions typically last 1 h, those that involve exposure practice may last up to 1.5 h.

Process of Treatment

Presentation of Treatment Rationale

During the first two sessions, the therapist presents the treatment rationale. First, our clinical model of GAD worry is described and all patient questions about the model are dealt with. Right from the first session, the therapist stresses that the patient's perception of uncertainty is an important source of worry and anxiety. Considering that uncertainty is pervasive in everyday life for all individuals, the treatment's goal is not to help the patient attempt to eliminate uncertainty, but rather to recognize, accept and develop coping strategies when faced with uncertain situations. The clinical model, which is an abbreviated version of our model described above (cf. Clinical Conception of GAD Worry), is presented in Figure 7.1.

Although this general model is highly simplified, we believe that it is important initially to present a model which patients can easily grasp and identify with. We have found this model quite adequate for this purpose. The therapist then presents the three following components, namely behavioral analysis and awareness training, specific worry interventions, and reevaluation of worry appraisal. At this point, the different types of worries are introduced and briefly discussed. The therapist also presents the worry interventions and briefly explains why they are used. A highly structured format has proven helpful in presenting the treatment rationale.

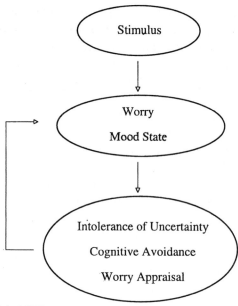

Figure 7.1. Clinical model of GAD worry.

Behavioral Analysis and Awareness Training

Following the presentation of treatment rationale, the therapist and patient proceed to the behavioral analysis and awareness training of situations related to worries. This treatment component is used to increase patient awareness and allow them to clearly discriminate between the three types of worries. Recall that we have identified worries that concern: (1) immediate problems which are grounded in reality and modifiable (e.g., a current interpersonal conflict with a work colleague), (2) immediate problems which are grounded in reality but non-modifiable (e.g., the illness of a loved one), and (3) highly remote events which are not grounded in reality and therefore non-modifiable (e.g., the possibility of someday going bankrupt). Because most worries relate to situations that may fit into more than one of these categories, a detailed behavioral analysis (cf. Ladouceur, Fontaine & Cottraux, 1993a) of each situation is required. Further, we have developed a series of therapist questions which help patients classify their worries on both critical dimensions.

To help determine if a worry concerns a problem which is grounded in reality, the therapist can investigate the following: (1) Does the patient have any real proof that the worry is about an immediate problem?, (2) Does he have any proof that the problem he is worried about will appear in the near future?, and (3) Does the worry reflect the patient's tendency to worry even when no real problem exists?. The patient may then be asked if, based on his previous answers, he thinks his worry concerns a problem which is grounded in reality. Because patients are often reluctant to answer this question in dichotomous terms, we recommend it be answered on a continuous scale. We have found that a nine-point Likert-type scale (0 = Not at all; 8 = Completely) is adequate for this purpose.

Next, the therapist and patient determine if the worry concerns a modifiable problem. The following questions may then be helpful : (1) Has the patient ever solved a problem similar to this one? (2) If he reacted better to the problem, could he solve it? and (3) Does he know someone who could solve this problem (because he reacts better or has better skills)? Finally, based on his answers to these questions, does the patient believe that his worry concerns a modifiable problem? Again, we recommend this final question be answered on a continuous scale.

Although this procedure helps patients to be more objective when assessing their worries on both critical dimensions, the choice of treatment strategy applied to the worry must be agreed upon by both patient and therapist. If the therapist does not agree with the patient's assessment, he should discuss this openly with him in order to come to a mutual agreement. In the course of treating GAD patients, we have noticed that they tend to overestimate the extent to which they can modify problem situations. Although this clinical observation was not originally expected, further reflection upon the consequences of intolerance of uncertainty has led us to the following conclusion. Problem situations which cannot be solved by instrumental problem solving (with problem-focused goals) may involve more uncertainty than those which can be modified by direct action. For instance, if other individuals must be counted on to solve a problem, their actions cannot always be predicted in advance, thereby adding to the uncertainty of the desired outcome. Further, when random effects such as natural phenomena are involved in solving a problem, the outcome becomes all the more uncertain. Therefore, problem situations which are non-modifiable by instrumental problem solving involve a greater degree of uncertainty and are more threatening to GAD patients who are intolerant of uncertainty. Their biased assessment of problem situations as being more modifiable than they actually are may be a consequence of their desire to subjectively decrease levels of uncertainty in non-modifiable situations. It is extremely important that therapists help patients reevaluate the extent to which problems that are grounded in reality are modifiable. For instance, patients can be asked to assess the impact of other individuals and random effects on solving a particular problem before evaluating their own impact. Not only is evaluating the extent to which a problem is modifiable the first step in applying the correct treatment strategy, it is therapeutic in itself as patients begin to clearly perceive and possibly accept the uncertainty involved in problem situations.

The behavioral analysis and awareness training component of our treatment typically lasts two to four sessions. All major worries are assessed on both critical dimensions before initiating the worry interventions. Though the following interventions may be applied in any order, we recommend that adapted PST with problem-focused goals (for worries about problems which are grounded in reality and modifiable) or adapted PST with emotion-focused goals (for worries about problems which are grounded in reality and non-modifiable) be employed first to increase patient motivation and compliance. We strongly suggest that worries about highly remote events which are not grounded in reality be dealt with last as functional cognitive exposure can be frightening for some patients and should be applied once they have already dealt with other worries successfully.

One final point should be stressed by therapists before moving on to the specific worry interventions. When a target worry has been agreed upon and a specific intervention has begun to be applied, the intervention should be carried out to its logical conclusion before targeting another worry. Because GAD patients typically worry about many topics, therapists should expect their patients to want to deal with a different worry when the target worry begins to decrease in intensity. Therefore, therapists should "warn" their patients that when an intervention is applied to a particular worry, it will be carried through to its conclusion even if other worries may eventually seem more important than the one originally agreed upon.

Specific Worry Interventions

Adapted problem-solving training. Adapted problem-solving training (PST) is applied to worries about problems which are grounded in reality. As described above, adapted PST with problem-focused goals is used for modifiable problems whereas adapted PST with emotion-focused goals is applied to non-modifiable problems. Although each type of adapted PST involves a different set of problem-solving goals, both types involve the same problem-solving process. Therefore in both cases, the treatment strategy involves two major components:

Problem orientation. The patient's problem orientation includes his cognitive, affective, and behavioral reactions to problems. Poor problem orientation is highly related to excessive worry and on a more specific level, perception of lack of personal control, which is a constituent of problem orientation, is associated with excessive worry. Because problem-orientation deficits seriously hinder the application of problem-solving skills, it is clearly the focal point of adapted PST. The therapist must stress the importance of recognizing counterproductive reactions to problems and correcting them by using cognitive reevaluation techniques (cf. Beck & Emery, 1985) and behavioral homework assignments (e.g., daily record keeping of reactions to problems). The patient should be made aware that his counter-productive reactions to problem situations are often expressions of intolerance of uncertainty (Dugas, Ladouceur & Freeston, 1995c). For example, when faced with an ambiguous situation, he may tend to interpret it as threatening (Butler & Mathews, 1983).

Problem-solving skills. This component includes all problem-solving behaviors and involves the following four steps: (1) defining the problem, (2) generating alternative solutions, (3) making a decision, and (4) applying and assessing the solution. Because poor problem orientation affects all problem-solving phases (Nezu & D'Zurilla, 1989), the behavioral steps are reviewed with emphasis on the patient's reaction to the problem situation. For instance, perceiving a problem as a threat rather than a challenge may impede the patient's attempts at defining it in an operational way, discourage him from generating possible solutions, prevent him from making a decision, and keep him from applying a solution.

The therapist should briefly present the key elements of each behavioral step. The first step, *defining the problem*, includes the description of problems and personal goals with objectivity, specificity, and clarity. Problem definition must provide information that will maximize performance in the following stages of problem solving but exclude information that is related to intolerance of uncertainty or arousal. Next, the *generation of alternative solutions* involves the following brainstorming rules: criticism is ruled out, "free-wheeling" is welcomed, quantity is wanted, and combination and improvement are sought. Expressions of intolerance of uncertainty or arousal must not restrict the generation of alternative solutions. The third behavioral step, *decision making*, consists of realistically rating likely consequences of each generated solution in order to determine the best strategy for the particular situation. The final decision must not simply reflect the patient's desire to avoid emotional arousal or situations related to uncertainty. Finally, *applying and assessing the solution* involves verifying to what extent the outcome prediction was accurate. Assessment primarily involves observing and recording consequences of actions. If the outcome is unsatisfactory, the patient begins again and attempts to find a better solution. If the outcome is satisfactory, the problem-solving process is terminated. The assessment of the solution must be made against criteria defining optimal outcome and not against criteria reflecting a decrease in uncertainty or emotional arousal.

Functional Cognitive Exposure. Functional cognitive exposure is used for worries concerning highly remote events which are not grounded in reality and therefore non-modifiable. For the purposes of this chapter, we will discuss the exposure component which is specific to our treatment program for GAD worry, namely the downward arrow technique, and briefly review the notion of covert response prevention.

The first step in cognitive exposure for GAD worry is identifying the worst image related to the worry by using the downward arrow or catastrophizing technique (cf. Beck & Emery, 1985; Burns, 1980; Vasey & Borkovec, 1992). Considering that worry serves to avoid threatening images, the identification of the worst image is a crucial step in worry exposure. Essentially, catastrophizing is accomplished by asking the patient a series of questions analogous to "If ...... were true, what would that lead to?" or "What would that mean to you?". The process is repeated until the patient is unable to generate another response or repeats the same response three consecutive times. Once the final image for each relevant worry has been described, the therapist helps the patient arrange them in hierarchical order, from the least threatening to the most threatening image. Because functional exposure is often difficult to achieve initially, we recommend starting with the least threatening image until the patient masters the exposure technique.

Once the first target has been identified, the therapist helps the patient develop the image until there is sufficient detail. Next, the threatening image is described by the patient and recorded on a looped tape for repeated exposure with a Walkman tape recorder. The patient is then exposed to the anxiety provoking image with covert response prevention. As we have described in detail elsewhere (Ladouceur et al., 1994), covert response prevention involves the identification and proscription of all effortful or voluntary activity used by the patient to control the image, including normal coping strategies. Because subjects expose themselves to mental images which provoke anxiety, cognitive exposure primarily addresses cognitive and emotional avoidance.

Reevaluation of Worry Appraisal

Because GAD patients tend to overestimate the advantages and underestimate the disadvantages of worrying (Brown et al., 1993; Ladouceur et al., 1993b; Roemer & Borkovec, 1993), their appraisal of the usefulness of worrying is examined and reevaluated for all types of worries. Although this suggestion is not a new one, specific therapy guidelines for identifying and correcting inappropriate appraisal of worries have yet to be outlined. First, therapists should carefully examine their patients' responses to items on the *Why Worry?* questionnaire to identify beliefs which may contribute to specific worries. GAD patients may believe that worrying can (1) prevent negative outcomes, (2) decrease guilt, (3) avoid disappointment, (4) distract them from thinking about worse things, (5) help them find a solution or a better way of doing things, and (6) help them increase control over their lives (cf. Ladouceur et al., 1993b). Beliefs such as these may be negatively reinforced, for instance by the non-occurrence of a feared event. Therefore, the appraisal of worry as a useful cognitive activity may make a significant contribution to maintaining worry. Clinicians should begin with items which are scored highest on the *Why Worry?* questionnaire. Next, they should help patients determine which one of the beliefs identified on the questionnaire apply to each specific worry. Therapists may also wish to ask patients about other beliefs about the usefulness of each worry.

Once beliefs about the usefulness of each specific worry are identified, reevaluation of beliefs may begin. Cognitive techniques should then be used to correct faulty beliefs about the advantages and disadvantages of each specific worry. Socratic questioning and behavioral hypothesis testing are particularly useful in helping GAD patients reevaluate the usefulness of worrying. Because a different set of faulty beliefs may contribute to each worry, therapists should help patients examine and correct worry appraisal independently for each worry. Since beliefs about the usefulness of each worry may overlap to some extent, generalization of more appropriate worry appraisal is not uncommon. However, it remains important to examine beliefs about the usefulness of each specific worry as various combinations of beliefs may require different cognitive interventions.

For instance, one of our GAD patients reported that his two most uncontrollable and distressing worries were the following: (1) becoming seriously ill (e.g., stroke, cancer, etc.), and (2) a family member becoming seriously ill (e.g., multiple sclerosis, cancer, etc.). He believed his worries about his own health were useful because they would help him detect the first signs of illness. If he were to worry less about his health, he may miss the first symptoms of a serious disease and by then it would be too late to treat the illness. In order to effectively treat these worries, the therapist used various cognitive techniques to help the patient reevaluate the usefulness of being constantly worried about his health as way of preventing illness. As for the patient's concerns that a family member may become seriously ill, these were also appraised as very useful but not for the same reasons. He believed that if a family member were to become ill, he would feel extremely guilty if he had not worried about this turn of events ahead of time. Hence, the patient believed these worries would help him decrease future feelings of guilt and shame. He also claimed that not worrying about this eventuality meant that he did not care enough about his family members. Therefore, although the patient's two main specific worries were both related to illness, his beliefs about the usefulness of each worry were quite different. As opposed to worrying about his own health, the patient did not believe that worrying about the health of family members would prevent them from becoming seriously ill by early detection of symptoms. He did believe however that worrying about their health proved that he cared for his family and would also help him decrease eventual feelings of guilt.

In conclusion, reevaluating the advantages and disadvantages of each specific worry is an important treatment component. Although the reevaluation of the beliefs contributing to one worry may generalize in some cases to other worries, therapists should not take this for granted and should examine specific beliefs related to each worry in order to maximize treatment effectiveness. As common sense dictates, if GAD patients believe that a specific worry is useful, they will be more reluctant to let it go.

Treatment Efficacy

Treatment packages for GAD have generally produced variable and limited gains (Dugas et al., 1996). Patients do improve, but worry often remains excessive and somatic symptoms are not entirely eliminated. We believe that treatment packages that directly target GAD worry may offer important advantages. Further, recent theoretical and clinical developments point to two central treatment strategies. First, adapted problem-solving training seems essential to address the approach component of worry, resulting from intolerance of uncertainty. Second, functional cognitive exposure would allow clinicians to decrease intolerance of emotional arousal by targeting the avoidance component of worry. Initial evaluation of our treatment package is presently underway and results will be available shortly.

References

APA (1980). *Diagnostic and statistical manual of mental disorders*, 3rd edition (DSM-III). Washington, DC: American Psychiatric Association.

APA (1994). *Diagnostic and statistical manual of mental disorders*, 4th edition (DSM-IV). Washington, DC: American Psychiatric Association.

Barlow, D. H. (1988). *Anxiety and its disorders: The nature and treatment of anxiety and panic*. New York: Guilford Press.

Barlow, D. H., Cohen, A. S., Waddell, M., Vermilyea, B. B., Klosko, J. S., Blanchard, E. B., & Di Nardo, P. A. (1984). Panic and generalized anxiety disorders: Nature and treatment. *Behavior Therapy, 15*, 431–449.

Barlow, D. H., Blanchard, E. B., Vermilyea B. B., & Di Nardo, P. A. (1986). Generalized anxiety and generalized anxiety disorder: Description and reconceptualization. *American Journal of Psychiatry, 143*, 40–44.

Barlow, D. H., Rapee, R. M., & Brown, T. A. (1992). Behavioral treatment of generalized anxiety disorder. *Behavior Therapy, 23*, 551–570.

Beck, A. T., & Emery, G. (1985). *Anxiety disorders and phobias: A cognitive perspective*. New York: Basic Books.

Beck, A. T., Rush, A. J., Shaw, B. F., & Emery, G. (1979). *Cognitive therapy of depression*. New York: Guilford Press.

Beck, A. T., Epstein, N., Brown, G., & Steer, R. A. (1988a). An inventory for measuring clinical anxiety: Psychometric properties. *Journal of Consulting and Clinical Psychology, 56*, 893–897.

Beck, A. T., Steer, R. A., & Garbin, M. G. (1988b). Psychometric properties of the Beck Depression Inventory: Twenty-five years of evaluation. *Clinical Psychology Review, 8*, 77–100.

Blais, F., Ladouceur, R., Dugas, M. J., & Freeston, M. H. (1993). *Résolution de problèmes et inquiétudes: Distinction clinique* (Problem solving and worry: Clinical distinction). Paper presented at the annual meeting of the Société Québécoise pour la Recherche en Psychologie, Québec.

Borkovec, T. D. (1985). Worry: A potentially valuable concept. *Behaviour Research and Therapy, 23,* 481–482.

Borkovec, T. D., & Hu, S. (1990). The effect of worry on cardiovascular response to phobic imagery. *Behaviour Research and Therapy, 28,* 69–73.

Borkovec, T. D., & Inz, J. (1990). The nature of worry in generalized anxiety disorder: A predominance of thought activity. *Behaviour Research and Therapy, 28,* 153–158.

Borkovec, T. D., & Costello, J. (1993). Efficacy of applied relaxation and cognitive behavioral therapy in the treatment of generalized anxiety disorder. *Journal of Consulting and Clinical Psychology, 61,* 611–619.

Borkovec, T. D., & Lyonfields, J. D. (1993). Worry: Thought suppression of emotional processing. In H. W. Krohne (Ed.), *Attention and avoidance.* Seattle, WA: Hogrefe and Huber.

Borkovec, T. D., Robinson, E., Pruzinsky, T., & DePree, J. A. (1983a). Preliminary exploration of worry: Some characteristics and processes. *Behaviour Research and Therapy, 21,* 9–16.

Borkovec, T. D., Wilkinson, L., Folensbee, R., & Lerman, C. (1983b). Stimulus control applications to the treatment of worry. *Behaviour Research and Therapy, 21,* 247–251.

Borkovec, T. D., Shadick, R. N., & Hopkins, M. (1991). The nature of normal and pathological worry. In R. M. Rapee & D. H. Barlow (Eds.), *Chronic anxiety: Generalized anxiety disorder and mixed anxiety-depression.* New York: Guilford Press.

Borkovec, T. D., Lyonfields, J. D., Wiser, S. L., & Deihl, L. (1993). The role of worrisome thinking in the suppression of cardiovascular response to phobic imagery. *Behaviour Research and Therapy, 31,* 321–324.

Bourque, P., & Beaudette, D. (1982). Étude psychométrique du questionnaire de dépression de Beck auprès d'un échantillon d'étudiants universitaires francophones. [Psychometric study of the Beck Depression Inventory with French-Canadian university students]. *Revue Canadienne des Sciences de Comportement, 14,* 211–218.

Bradwejn, J., Berner, M., & Shaw, B. (1992). *Malade d'inquiétude: Guide du médecin pour le traitement et le counseling* [Sick of worrying: Doctor's guide for treatment and counselling]. Montréal, Québec: Grosvenor.

Breslau, N., & Davis, G. C. (1985). DSM-III generalized anxiety disorder: An empirical investigation of more stringent criteria. *Psychiatry Research, 14,* 231–238.

Brown, T. A., & Barlow, D. H. (1992). Comorbidity among anxiety disorders: implications for treatment and DSM-IV. *Journal of Consulting and Clinical Psychology, 60,* 835–844.

Brown, T. A., Antony, M. M., & Barlow, D. H. (1992). Psychometric properties of the Penn State Worry Questionnaire in a clinical anxiety disorders sample. *Behaviour Research and Therapy, 30,* 33–37.

Brown, T. A., O'Leary, T. A., & Barlow, D. H. (1993). Generalized anxiety disorder. In D. H. Barlow (Ed.), *Clinical handbook of psychological disorders.* New York: Guilford Press.

Brown, T. A., Di Nardo, P. A., & Barlow, D. H. (1994). *Anxiety Disorders Interview Schedule for DSM-IV.* Albany, NY: Graywind Publications.

Burns, D. D. (1980). *Feeling good: The new mood therapy.* New York: New American Library.

Butler, G., & Mathews, A. (1983). Cognitive processes in anxiety. *Advances in Behaviour Research and Therapy, 5,* 51–62.

Butler, G., & Mathews, A. (1987). Anticipatory anxiety and risk perception. *Cognitive Therapy and Research, 11,* 551–565.

Butler, G., Cullington, A., Hibbert, G., Klimes, I., & Gelder, M. (1987). Anxiety management for persistent generalized anxiety. *British Journal of Psychiatry, 151,* 535–542.

Butler, G., Fennell, M., Robson, P., & Gelder, M. (1991). A comparison of behavior therapy and cognitive behavior therapy in the treatment of generalized anxiety disorder. *Journal of Consulting and Clinical Psychology, 59,* 167–175.

Butler, G., Wells, A., & Dewick, H. (1992). *Differential effects of worry and imagery after exposure to a stressful stimulus.* Paper presented at the World Congress of Cognitive Therapy, Toronto.

Craske, M. G., Rapee, R. M., Jackel, L., & Barlow, D. H. (1989). Qualitative dimensions of worry in DSM III-R generalised anxiety disorder subjects and nonanxious controls. *Behaviour Research and Therapy, 27,* 397–402.

Craske, M. G., Barlow, D. H., & O'Leary, T. (1992). *Mastery of your anxiety and worry.* Albany, NY: Graywind Publications.

D'Zurilla, T. J., & Nezu, A. M. (1990). Development and preliminary evaluation of the Social Problem-Solving Inventory. *Psychological Assessment, 2,* 156–163.

Davey, G. C. L. (1994). Worrying, social problem solving abilities, and problem-solving confidence. *Behaviour Research and Therapy, 32,* 327–330.

de Ruiter, C., Ruken, H., Garssen, B., van Schaik, A., & Kraaimaat, F. (1989). Comorbidity among the anxiety disorders. *Journal of Anxiety Disorders, 3,* 57–68.

Di Nardo, P. A., Moras, K., Barlow, D. A., Rapee, R. M., & Brown, T. A. (1993). Reliability of DSM-III-R anxiety disorder categories. *Archives of General Psychiatry, 50,* 251–256.

Dugas, M. J., Freeston, M. H., Blais, F., & Ladouceur, R. (1994a). *Anxiety and depression in GAD patients, high and moderate worriers.* Paper presented at the annual convention of the Association for Advancement of Behavior Therapy, San Diego, CA.

Dugas, M. J., Freeston, M. H., & Ladouceur, R. (1994b). *The nature of worry.* Paper presented at the annual convention of the Association for Advancement of Behavior Therapy, San Diego, CA.

Dugas, M. J., Freeston, M. H., Lachance, S., Provencher, M., & Ladouceur, R. (1995a). *The Worry and Anxiety Questionnaire: Initial validation in non-clinical and clinical samples.* Paper presented at the World Congress of Behavioural and Cognitive Therapies, Copenhagen.

Dugas, M. J., Freeston, M. H., Doucet, C., Provencher, M., & Ladouceur, R. (1995b). *Intolerance of uncertainty and thought suppression in worry.* Paper presented at the annual convention of the Association for Advancement of Behavior Therapy, Washington, DC.

Dugas, M. J., Ladouceur, R., & Freeston, M. H. (1995c). *Worry: The contribution of intolerance of uncertainty, problem solving and worry appraisal.* Paper presented at the World Congress of Behavioural and Cognitive Therapies, Copenhagen.

Dugas, M. J., Letarte, H., Rhéaume, J., Freeston, M. H., & Ladouceur, R. (1995d). Worry and problem solving: Evidence of a specific relationship. *Cognitive Therapy and Research, 19,* 109–120.

Dugas, M. J., Ladouceur, R., Boisvert, J.-M., & Freeston, M. H. (1996). Le trouble d'anxiété généralisée: Éléments fondamentaux et interventions psychologiques (Generalized Anxiety Disorder: Fundamental elements and psychological interventions). *Psychologie Canadienne, 37,* 40–53.

Durham, R. C., & Turvey, A. A. (1987). Cognitive therapy vs behavior therapy in the treatment of chronic generalized anxiety. *Behaviour Research and Therapy, 25,* 229–234.

Eysenck, M. W., Macleod, C., & Mathews, A. (1987). Cognitive functioning and anxiety. *Psychological Research, 49,* 189–195.

Eysenck, M. W., & van Berkum, J. (1992). Trait anxiety, defensiveness, and the structure of worry. *Personality and Individual Differences, 13*, 1285–1290.

Eysenck, M. W., Mogg, K., May, J., Richards, A., & Mathews, A. (1991). Bias in interpretation of ambiguous sentences related to threat in anxiety. *Journal of Abnormal Psychology, 100*, 144–150.

Foa, E. B., & Kozak, M. J. (1986). Emotional processing of fear: Exposure to corrective information. *Psychological Bulletin, 99*, 20–35.

Freeston, M. H., Dugas, M. J., & Ladouceur, R. (1994a). *Thoughts, images, worry, and anxiety*. Paper presented at the annual convention of the Association for Advancement of Behavior Therapy, San Diego, CA.

Freeston, M. H., Ladouceur, R., Thibodeau, N., Gagnon, F., & Rhéaume, J. (1994b). L'inventaire d'anxiété de Beck: Propriétés psychométriques d'une traduction française (The Beck Anxiety Inventory: Psychometric properties of a french translation). *L'Encéphale, XX*, 47–55.

Freeston, M. H., Rhéaume, J., Letarte, H., Dugas, M. J., & Ladouceur, R. (1994c). Why do people worry? *Personality and Individual Differences, 17*, 791–802.

Freeston, M. H., Dugas, M. J., Ladouceur, R. (1995). *The social basis of worry*. Paper presented at the World Congress of Behavioural and Cognitive Therapies, Copenhagen.

Hoehn-Saric, R., McLeod, D. R., & Zimmerli, W. D. (1988). Differential effects of alprazolam and imipramine in generalized anxiety. *Journal of Clinical Psychiatry, 49*, 293–301.

Jannoun, L., Oppenheimer, C., & Gelder, M. (1982). A self-help treatment for anxiety state patients. *Behavior Therapy, 13*, 103–111.

Kessler, R. C., McGonagle, K. A., Zhao, S., Nelson, C. B., Hughes, M., Eshleman, S., Wittchen, H.-U., & Kendler, K. S. (1994). Lifetime and 12-month prevalence of DSM-III-R psychiatric disorders in the United States. *Archives of General Psychiatry, 51*, 8–19.

Krohne, H. W. (1989). The concept of coping modes: Relating cognitive person variables to actual coping behavior. *Advances in Behaviour Research and Therapy, 11*, 235–247.

Krohne, H. W. (1993). Vigilance and cognitive avoidance as concepts in coping research. In H. W. Krohne (Ed.), *Attention and avoidance*. Seattle, WA: Hogrefe and Huber.

Ladouceur, R., Fontaine, O., & Cottraux, J. (1993a). *Thérapie comportementale et cognitive* (Behavioral and cognitive therapy). Paris: Masson.

Ladouceur, R., Freeston, M. H., & Dugas, M. J. (1993b). *L'intolérance à l'incertitude et les raisons pour s'inquiéter dans le Trouble d'anxiété généralisée* (Intolerance of uncertainty and reasons for worrying in Generalized Anxiety Disorder). Paper presented at the annual meeting of the Société Québecoise pour la Recherche en Psychologie, Québec.

Ladouceur, R., Freeston, M. H., Gagnon, F., Thibodeau, N., & Dumont, J. (1993c). Idiographic considerations in the behavioral treatment of obsessional thoughts. *Journal of Behavior Therapy and Experimental Psychiatry, 24*, 301–310.

Ladouceur, R., Freeston, M. H., Gagnon, F., Thibodeau, N., & Dumont, J. (1994). Cognitive-behavioral treatment of obsessions. *Behavior Modification, 19*, 247–257.

Letarte, H., Freeston, M. H., Rhéaume, J., & Ladouceur, R. (1998). Dispositional worry, beliefs, and self-focused attention. Manuscript in preparation.

Lindsay, W. R., Gamsu, C. V., McLaughlin, E., Hood, E. M., & Espie, C. A. (1987). A controlled trial of treatments for generalized anxiety. *British Journal of Clinical Psychology, 26*, 3–15.

Lovibond, P. F., & Rapee, R. M. (1993). The representation of feared outcomes. *Behaviour Research and Therapy, 31*, 595–608.

Macleod, C., & Mathews, A. (1988). Anxiety and the allocation of attention to threat. *Quarterly Journal of Experimental Psychology, 4*, 653–670.

Macleod, A. K., Williams, M. G., & Bekerian, D. A. (1991). Worry is reasonable: The role in pessimism about future personal events. *Journal of Abnormal Psychology, 100*, 478–486.

Mathews, A. (1990). Why worry? The cognitive function of anxiety. *Behaviour Research and Therapy, 28*, 455–468.

Mathews, A., Mogg, K., May, J., & Eysenck, M. (1989). Implicit and explicit memory bias in anxiety. *Journal of Abnormal Psychology, 98*, 236–240.

Metzger, R. L., Miller, M. L., Cohen, M., Sofka, M., & Borkovec, T. D. (1990). Worry changes decision making: The effect of negative thoughts on cognitive processing. *Journal of Clinical Psychology, 46*, 78–88.

Meyer, T. J. , Miller, M. L., Metzger, R. L., & Borkovec, T. D. (1990). Development and validation of the Penn State Worry Questionnaire. *Behaviour Research and Therapy, 28*, 487–496.

Nezu, A. M., & D'Zurilla, T. J. (1989). Social problem solving and negative affective conditions. In P. C. Kendall & D. Watson (Eds.), *Anxiety and depression.* San Diego, CA: Academic Press.

Noyes, R., Woodman, C., Garvey, M. J., Cook, B., Suelzer, M., Clancy, J., & Anderson, D. J. (1992). Generalized anxiety disorder versus Panic disorder. *The Journal of Nervous and Mental Disease, 180*, 369–379.

O'Leary, T. A., Brown, T. A., & Barlow, D. H. (1992). *The efficacy of worry control treatment in generalized anxiety disorder: A multiple baseline analysis.* Paper presented at the annual convention of the Association for Advancement of Behavior Therapy, Boston, MA.

Rapee, R. M. (1991). Generalized anxiety disorder: A review of clinical features and theoretical concepts. *Clinical Psychology Review, 11*, 419–440.

Roemer, L., & Borkovec, T. D. (1993). Worry: Unwanted cognitive activity that controls unwanted somatic experience. In D. M. Wegner & J. W. Pennebaker (Eds.), *Handbook of mental control.* Englewood Cliffs, NJ: Prentice Hall.

Roemer, L., Borkovec, M., Posa, S., & Lyonfields, J. (1991a). *Generalized anxiety disorder in an analogue population: The role of past trauma.* Paper presented at the annual convention of the Association for Advancement of Behavior Therapy, New York.

Roemer, L., Posa, S., & Borkovec, T. D. (1991b). *A self-report measure of generalized anxiety disorder.* Paper presented at the annual convention of the Association for Advancement of Behavior Therapy, New York.

Sanderson, W. C., & Barlow, D. H. (1990). A description of patients diagnosed with DSM-III-R generalised anxiety disorder. *The Journal of Nervous and Mental Disease, 178*, 588–591.

Sanderson, W. C., & Beck, A. T. (1991). *Cognitive therapy of generalized anxiety disorder: A naturalistic study.* Paper presented at the annual convention of the Association for Advancement of Behavior Therapy, New York.

Sanderson, W. C., Beck, A. T., & Beck, J. (1990a). Syndrome comorbidity in patients with major depression or dysthimia: Prevalence and temporal relationships. *American Journal of Psychiatry, 147*, 1025–1028.

Sanderson, W. C., Di Nardo, P. A., Rapee, R. M., & Barlow, D. H. (1990b). Syndrome co-morbidity in patients diagnosed with a DSM-III-Revised anxiety disorder. *Journal of Abnormal Psychology, 99*, 308–312.

Shadick, R. N., Roemer, L., Hopkins, M. B., & Borkovec, T. D. (1991). *The nature of worrisome thoughts.* Paper presented at the annual convention of the Association for Advancement of Behavior Therapy, New York.

Tallis, F. (1989). *Worry: A cognitive analysis.* Unpublished dissertation. University of London.

Tallis, F., Eysenck, M., & Mathews, A. (1991). Elevated evidence requirements and worry. *Personality and Individual Differences, 12*, 21–27.

Vasey, M. W., & Borkovec, T. D. (1992). A catastrophizing assessment of worrisome thoughts. *Cognitive Therapy and Research, 16,* 505–520.

Wegner D., & Zanakos, S. (1992). Individual differences in thought suppression and obsessional thinking. In R.J. McNally (chair), *Cognitive aspects of obsessive-compulsive disorder.* Symposium presented at the annual convention of the Association for Advancement of Behavior Therapy, Boston, MA.

Wells, A. (1994). Attention and the control of worry. In G. C. L. Davey & F. Tallis (Eds.), *Worrying: perspectives on theory, assessment and treatment.* Chichester, UK: Wiley.

White, J., Keenan, M., & Brooks, N. (1992). Stress control: A controlled comparative investigation of large group therapy for generalized anxiety disorder. *Behavioural Psychotherapy, 20,* 97–113.

Williams, J. B. W., Gibbon, M., First, M. B., Spitzer, R. L., Davies, M., Borus, J., Howes, M. J., Kane, J., Pope, H. G., Rounsaville, B., & Wittchen, H. (1992). The structured clinical interview for DSM-III-R (SCID), II: Multisite test-retest reliability. *Archives of General Psychiatry, 49,* 630–636.

Further Reading

Barlow, D. H. (1988). *Anxiety and its disorders: The nature and treatment of anxiety and panic.* New York: Guilford Press.

Borkovec, T. D., Shadick, R. N., & Hopkins, M. (1991). The nature of normal and pathological worry. In R. M. Rapee & D. H. Barlow (Eds.), *Chronic anxiety: Generalized anxiety disorder and mixed anxiety-depression.* New York: Guilford Press.

Brown, T. A., O'Leary, T. A., & Barlow, D. H. (1993). Generalized anxiety disorder. In D. H. Barlow (Ed.), *Clinical handbook of psychological disorders,* 2nd edition. New York: Guilford Press.

Craske, M. G., Barlow, D. H., & O'Leary, T. (1992). *Mastery of your anxiety and worry.* Albany, NY: Graywind Publications.

Rapee, R. M. (1995). Trastorno por ansiedad generalizada. In V. E. Caballo, G. Buela-Casal & J. A. Carrobles (Eds.), *Manual de psicopatología y trastornos psiquiátricos,* Vol. 1. Madrid: Siglo XXI.

8

Generalized Anxiety and Anxiety Management Training

JERRY L. DEFFENBACHER

Colorado State University, USA

Introduction

This chapter focuses on the application of anxiety management training (AMT) for both general and specific anxiety reduction, with a particular reference to generalized anxiety. It begins with a description of generalized anxiety disorder (GAD) which, in turn, is linked to the history and rationale of AMT. The empirical literature supporting AMT with anxiety and other psychophysiological and emotional disorders is then reviewed, concluding that AMT has solid empirical support. The bulk of the chapter describes the procedures of AMT with an individual client so that the clinician may apply AMT with his/her clients. The outline of individual AMT is followed with sections on adaptations to a group format of delivery for AMT and how AMT may be integrated with other interventions.

Characteristics of the Generalized Anxiety Disorder (GAD)

Individuals with GAD are characterized by a chronic, unrealistic worry and anxiety, often experiencing a kind of generalized sense of threat, apprehension, dread, tension and uneasiness. According to the diagnostic criteria of the *Diagnostic and statistical manual of mental disorders* (APA, 1994), an individual must experience, for at least 6 months or more, excessive anxiety and worry about a number of events or activities, to find difficult to control the worry, and experience three or more of six symptoms, such as restlessness, fatigue, difficulty concentrating, irritability, muscle tension and sleep disturbance.

Sometimes the individual with GAD experiences diffuse, vague, negative expectations and fears. For others, the worries are much more focused and defined, often around themes of interpersonal failure, inability in key life areas, financial or health concerns, and the like. The individual tends to turn these over and over in his or her mind, failing to reach resolution, make decisions, take decisive action, and live relatively comfortably with the consequences. To the contrary, they tend to ruminate and fret about negative possibilities, potential errors and mistakes, real and imagined embarrassments and failures. It is as if they are frozen in the early stages of problem solving (Deffenbacher & Suinn, 1987). However, unlike effective problem solving, the individual does not identify potential solutions, weigh and balance probabilities of positive and negative outcomes, and exit with solutions they are willing to try or enact. They tend to be locked into intractable identification of and preoccupation with the negative potentialities only. The result is a chronic apprehension about future negative events and recycling of past fears, mistakes and failures, a kind of tumbling cognitive torment. The individual cannot rest comfortably because there is always another negative "what if" type of thought to consider.

Other cognitive functions are often involved as well. The individual appears mentally to be "keyed up" or "on edge" as if his/her attentional processes are on alert and ready to intercept incoming negative messages. The cognitive radar is ready and scanning, often leading to problems in concentration and decision as well. The individual has difficulty focusing on the relevant parameters and making decisions and instead worries constantly about possible mistakes and negative outcomes. There is often no relief in sleep. The individual may experience sleep onset insomnia wherein he/she perseverates on past errors and mistakes or anticipates all kinds of future negative events. After a fitful time to fall asleep, he/she may then experience anxiety dreams in which the anxiety themes of the day are replayed, sometimes in more vivid and extreme form. The quality of sleep is also disrupted, and the person awakens with a sense of apprehension and fatigue.

The chronic worry and mental negativity continually readies the individual for action; however, there is no place to avoid as the aversive events, real or imagined, are in the individual's mind. Nonetheless, the body's physiology is readied for action. Excessive motor arousal is commonly experienced in shaky or trembly feelings, in tension and sore muscles, particularly in the neck, back and shoulder regions, in a kind of diffuse restlessness, and in a tendency to become easily fatigued and tired.

There are also many signs of sympathetic nervous system arousal as well. Some individuals show cardiovascular arousal such as an elevated heart rates, palpitations, and a sense of heart pounding. Others may experience a tightness across the chest and difficulty breathing, typically experiencing a shortness of breath and/or a sense of choking or smothering. Sweaty and clammy extremities may also be punctuated by hot flashes and chills. Periods of dry mouth where the individual needs to lick his/her lips frequently and/or experiences difficulty swallowing may also be present. Gastrointestinal problems are also common such as frequent bouts of nausea, chronic gastritis, and diarrhea which may lead to a medical workup for things such as ulcers and colitis. Frequent urges to urinate may also be present, and the individual may experience anxiety symptoms that are more parasympathetic in nature such as dizziness, lightheadedness, and a sense of physical instability or weakness.

In summary, individuals with GAD experience chronic, unrealistic worries and a host of cognitive, emotional and physiological indices of arousal. Individuals with GAD often experience other problems as well with mild to moderate depression, occasional panics, and abuse/misuse of tranquilizing drugs and alcohol being the most common (Barlow, 1988; APA, 1987). Although GAD is rarely incapacitating, much of the quality of the individual's life is drained by the anxiety and the comorbid problems.

Anxiety Management Training (AMT), the clinical focus of this chapter, was developed to deal with these kinds of individuals, although the problems were not labeled GAD at the time.

Anxiety Management Training: History and Rationale

In the 1960s, systematic desensitization, the primary behavioral treatment for anxiety disorders, had been shown to work well with phobias. However, theoretically and practically, desensitization was not appropriate for general, diffuse anxiety disorders. Unless anxiety arousing stimuli could be specified and organized hierarchically, desensitization could not proceed. But what was to be done with the patient who was suffering with generalized anxiety or free-floating anxiety, those persons who would now most likely be diagnosed with GAD? There was not a behavioral intervention for such individuals.

AMT (Suinn & Richardson, 1971) was developed to address this gap in intervention for such individuals. AMT originally was anchored in drive theory of anxiety in which anxiety was conceptualized both as a response to internal and external stimuli and as having stimulus properties which influenced subsequent responses. Specifically, in a chain of unfolding behavior, anxiety was both a response to preceding stimuli and a stimulus for subsequent behavior, and an individual learned responses which lowered anxiety's aversive stimulus properties. It was reasoned that individuals could be trained to discriminate the stimulus properties of anxiety and apply new coping skills with which to reduce anxiety. AMT, therefore, trains individuals to identify the internal cognitive, emotional, and physiological sensations and cues of anxiety, especially the early signs of arousal, and then to react to these cues with new behavior which is designed to lower the aversiveness of the anxiety response. In the early work (Suinn & Richardson, 1971), AMT involved the use of both relaxation and competence responses as anxiety incompatible coping responses. Subsequently, the use of competence responses was dropped because of the difficulty in locating them in anxious patients and in using them across anxiety-arousing circumstances and because of the ease of using relaxation across situations and individuals. Moreover, AMT was also recast in self-control or self-management terms in the mid-1970's (Suinn, 1990) such that the rationale and procedures are framed as training the client how to recognize the onset of anxiety and how to self-manage its reduction through the application of relaxation skills, thereby freeing the use of other coping skills.

Anxiety Management Training: Empirical Basis

A theoretically sound but empirically unsupported treatment has little to recommend it. This portion of the chapter will review some of the published outcome studies supporting the use of AMT. First, the effects with specific fears and anxiety conditions will be reviewed and followed by the applications with generalized anxiety and GAD-like conditions. The section will conclude with a brief summary of research involving other stress and emotional issues.

AMT has proven effective with a variety of situational anxieties. For example, in the original study of AMT (Suinn & Richardson, 1971), when AMT was compared to a control condition, it was shown to effectively reduce both math and test anxieties in math-anxious college students and was as effective as systematic desensitization. A subsequent study with math-anxious university students (Richardson & Suinn, 1973) replicated these effects with math-anxious students and suggested that AMT improved some indices of math performance. Test anxiety, too, has been successfully reduced with AMT. For example, Deffenbacher & Shelton (1978) showed that AMT was as effective as systematic desensitization in reducing test anxiety levels of students who had come to a college counseling center for test anxiety reduction. Moreover, AMT led to greater trait anxiety reduction than did desensitization, suggesting greater generalized anxiety reduction for AMT. Another study (Deffenbacher, Michaels, Michaels & Daley, 1980b) demonstrated that AMT effectively reduced both test and general anxiety levels in test anxious college students in comparison to a control. AMT was also as effective as self-control desensitization, another self-management relaxation procedure. This same research group (Deffenbacher, Michaels, Daley & Michaels, 1980a) worked with both test and speech anxious college students. Some were treated in homogeneous (i.e., only test or speech anxious subjects in a group) groups, whereas others were treated in heterogeneous groups (i.e., mixed group composition of both test and speech anxious subjects in the same group). AMT in both formats reduced not only test or speech anxiety but general anxiety as well. Mixed groups were as effective, if not more effective, than homogeneous groups, suggesting that clients could be effectively treated in groups with individuals who did not share the same anxiety. Moreover, 12–15 month follow-ups (Deffenbacher & Michaels, 1981a,b) showed that both the focal test or speech anxiety and generalized anxiety reductions were maintained over the long term. Finally, AMT has also effectively reduced both social anxiety (Hill, 1977) and anxiety surrounding vocational indecision (Mendonca & Siess, 1976).

General anxiety conditions have also been successfully treated with AMT. For example, in a study with generally anxious college students (Hutchings, Denney, Basgall & Houston, 1980) showed that when compared to an un-treated control condition, AMT led to reports of general anxiety reduction, physiological symptoms of anxiety, neuroticism, and state anxiety reduction in a stressful analog. General anxiety effects for AMT were equal to or superior to those of relaxation and placebo conditions. Moreover, the reduction of general anxiety for AMT was maintained at year follow-up. Daley, Bloom, Deffenbacher & Stewart (1983) also found significant general anxiety and neuroticism reduction for generally anxious college students. Cragan & Deffenbacher (1984) extended these findings to generally anxious medical outpatients. Once again, AMT lowered several indices of general anxiety and led to anger and depression reduction as well, compared to controls. It was also as effective as another self-management relaxation procedure. A study with generalized anxiety and panic disordered, psychiatric outpatients (Jannoun, Oppenheimer & Gelder, 1982) found that, compared to controls, AMT lowered general anxiety and anxiety medication. Depression, however, was not altered for this group. Finally, although not specifically related to GAD, AMT lowered general anxiety and therapist ratings of anxiety and anger in schizophrenic outpatients (Van Hassell, Bloom & Gonzalez, 1982). Additionally, their overall psychiatric status and ability to use general psychotherapy was rated as improved. Thus, AMT appears to be effective with a variety of general anxiety patients with varying degrees of psychiatric involvement.

AMT has also been successfully employed with a variety of other stress-related conditions. For example, AMT reduced Type A behavior (Kelly & Stone, 1987; Suinn & Bloom, 1978; Suinn, Brock & Edie, 1975). Trait anxiety reduction in Type A individuals was also evidenced as well (Suinn & Bloom, 1978). The effects of AMT in lowering blood pressure levels in hypertensive outpatients has also been demonstrated (Drazen, Nevid, Pace & O'Brien, 1982; Jorgensen, Houston & Zurawski, 1981). Reductions in gynecological symptoms and general anxiety have also been found for AMT with women with dysmenorrhea (Quillen & Denney, 1982) and with stressed gynecological outpatients (Deffenbacher & Craun, 1985). Moreover, these effects were maintained in 2-year follow-ups in both studies. Finally, a series of studies (Deffenbacher, Demm & Brandon, 1986; Deffenbacher & Stark, 1992; Hazaleus & Deffenbacher, 1986) have shown that AMT can be successfully adapted to anger and reduced anger and general anxiety in high anger college students. Moreover, AMT was as effective as cognitive and cognitive-relaxation conditions, and effects were maintained in 12–15 month follow-ups (Deffenbacher et al., 1986; Deffenbacher & Stark, 1992; Hazaleus & Deffenbacher, 1986).

Finally, recent studies of relaxation coping procedures, which are similar but not identical to AMT, have been effective with GAD patients. For example, Borkovec's (Borkovec & Costello, 1993; Borkovec, Mathews, Chambers, Ebrahimi, Lytle & Nelson, 1987) applied relaxation and self-control desensitization programs have significantly lowered anxiety in GAD individuals and generally have been as effective as other cognitive-behavioral interventions and more effective than nondirective therapy. Butler and colleagues (Butler, Cullington, Hibbert, Klimes & Gelder, 1987; Butler, Fennell, Robson & Gelder, 1991) have also achieved similar results although one study favored a cognitive intervention. Barlow, Rapee & Brown (1992) compared an applied relaxation program to a cognitive intervention and the combination of the two. All groups reduced anxiety, anxiety medication, and depression in GAD patients. However, there were no differences between the three active treatment groups. Such studies indirectly support the value of AMT because they are based on similar relaxation coping skills methodologies.

In summary, AMT is a fairly robust and well-established intervention. There is considerable literature showing the reduction of specific anxieties, and in several of these studies, generalization effects were found for other nontargeted anxieties. General anxiety conditions have also been effectively alleviated with AMT, and there has been generalization to other emotions such as anger and depression in some studies. AMT has also been effective with a number of other anxiety or stress-related conditions. In general, AMT is as effective as or more effective than other interventions and, where follow-up has been done, long-term effects have been demonstrated. In all, there appears to be a solid empirical literature supporting the efficacy of AMT. The remainder of this chapter will be devoted to outlining more clinical procedures of AMT.

Anxiety Management Training: Procedures for Individual AMT

Thomas Borkovec, one of the premier researchers on the treatment of GAD, recently reviewed GAD research (Borkovec & Costello, 1993) and suggested that cognitive-behavioral interventions for GAD should include the following characteristics:
1. emphasize the importance of self-observation in detecting anxiety processes;

2. pay particular attention to worrisome thinking as one of the crucial early cues for the initiation of coping skills;
3. provide thorough training in applied relaxation skills;
4. use of multiple relaxation methods;
5. expose the patient to anxiety laden imagery;
6. employ frequent in-session practice of coping skills; and
7. use cognitive therapy for catastrophic, worrisome thinking.

As will be outlined below, AMT provides a consistent, sequential methodology for the development of relaxation coping skills and meets the first six of these conditions, only failing to provide cognitive therapy.

AMT (for additional details see Suinn, 1990; Suinn & Deffenbacher, 1988) is generally introduced in the treatment of GAD or other anxiety or stress disorders when assessment has suggested significant emotional and physiological involvement in the disorder. AMT is built on a model of increasing client self-control over anxiety arousal. This is done through training the client to recognize the cognitive, emotional and physiological response-produced cues of anxiety arousal and then to employ relaxation coping skills when these cues are present. This increases a sense of calmness and mental clarity, freeing other cognitive and behavioral coping skills with which to cope with the external situation or internal concerns. To achieve this, AMT involves six overlapping, intermixed goals. AMT seeks to develop:
1. a cogent self-management rationale;
2. a basic relaxation response pattern from which to develop relaxation coping skills;
3. specific relaxation coping skills which can be deployed quickly and easily in vivo;
4. an increased awareness of the internal cues of anxiety arousal so that the perception of these cues can serve as a prompt for the initiation of relaxation coping skills;
5. competence and confidence within sessions in becoming aware of anxiety arousal and employing relaxation coping skills to reduce anxiety; and
6. ensuring application of the relaxation coping skills in day-to-day living for anxiety control and to other negative emotional states such as anger and depression.

Clinical procedures to achieve these goals are usually developed within six to ten weekly sessions which are devoted to primarily to AMT. Movement to new session content is based on individual progress. With this caveat in mind, a general session by session outline is provided. After the first session, each session typically begins with a brief interview to review the homework and progress between sessions and ends with a brief interview to assess the experiences and progress within that session. Based on progress within and between sessions, homework for the coming week's period of time is developed.

Session 1

The first session is devoted to giving the rationale, beginning the development of the relaxation response, and to continuing development of self-awareness of anxiety cues, as prior assessment probably has begun to enhance such awareness already.

The rationale should be brief and collaborative, linking AMT to the presenting concerns, anxiety experiences, and client metaphors. It should describe AMT in nontechnical terms to enhance client understanding and involvement. Basically, it should outline AMT as a procedure through which the client will develop the capacity to recognize increasing anxiety and then to use relaxation to lower it. The client should be told that first relaxation skills will be trained and then, within the sessions, this relaxation will be used to reduce anxiety that is induced by having clients imagine situations which have elicited anxiety in the past. They are also told that the anxiety level will start at a low to moderate level in the beginning and that the therapist will help them a great deal in retrieving the relaxation in early sessions. With time and success, the anxiety level will increase and the therapist assistance will decrease. Also, they should be told that as they gain success, they will apply the skills more and more in day-to-day living to reduce anxiety and other negative emotions. A sample rationale with a GAD client is given below.

> In the last couple of sessions, you have been describing those periods where you get really worried and anxious, where you get all "wound up" and really anxious, feel tense all over, especially in the stomach, the back and shoulders, sometimes triggering off those bouts of diarrhea and headaches and sometimes getting into that kind of depressed hopeless space. You also indicated that you do better when you are able to relax, but that you do not have a good way to relax and that you wanted some tools to better do this with. As I thought about it this last week, I think that there is a way that we can do that, developing the relaxation skills, I mean. I would like to describe that and see what you think.
>
> The first step will be to develop a pattern of relaxation, and I will start doing later in the session if we agree. Initially, this will take about twenty minutes or so to do, but as you practice it, we will build a variety of quick ways for you to relax. The second step will be for you to increase your sense of anxiety, especially when anxiety is starting to come on, so that you know later when to use the relaxation skills. We have already done some of this and you are more aware of anxiety already, but we will focus on this even more as we go. The third step will really be putting the first two steps together. Within the sessions, I will have you apply the relaxation to anxiety that we will generate by having you imagine situations where you have been really worried and anxious in the past, like the

other day when you were all anxious about the upcoming job interview. That is, we will have you imagine the situation, become anxious for a few seconds so you can pay attention to it, and then initiate the relaxation to bring the anxiety down. We will do this over and over until you get really good at it. Then, we will increase the anxiety level so that you can cope with even greater levels of anxiety. As you get better and better at this, I will help you less and less because you will not need me, and you can then begin to use it whenever you start to worry or get anxious. It will take a lot of practice and work on both our parts, but I anticipate that in six to ten sessions, you will be able to relax whenever you start to feel that worry and anxiety creep in. What do you think of this idea?

Although different forms of relaxation development might be used (e.g., autogenic training or biofeedback), AMT uses progressive relaxation training. Progressive relaxation involves systematically tensing and then releasing the various muscle groups in the body by way of one of procedures available in the literature (e.g., Bernstein & Borkovec, 1973; Wolpe, 1973). However, prior to actually beginning progressive relaxation training, the clinician should develop a relaxation image as it will be used following progressive relaxation exercises. This image will become one of the relaxation coping skills. The relaxation image should be a specific, concrete moment in the person's life that was calming and relaxing. Fantasy events, situations that the individual thinks might be relaxing but have not actually been experienced, or situations that were both relaxing but arousing should be avoided as they tend to create problems in getting into and maintaining focus on the scene. The scene should be like a snapshot or very brief moment in the person's life. The clinician should first inquire about such a scene and then elucidate all the situational and experiential details that crystallize that experience and help it become emotionally real. That is, the description of the scene should include as many of the emotional elements and all of the sense detail such as visual cues, sounds present, senses of motion, temperature and the like that instill a sense of calmness, relaxation and perhaps peacefulness. A sample relaxation scene is given below.

It is the time two years ago when you were on vacation at the beach in San Diego. It is about ten o'clock in the morning, and you have gone for a long walk by yourself and have just sat down on the sand dune, that wonderful white sand dune. You are there alone with no one else close around, although you can see others walking in the distance and some buildings down to your left. You are about twenty meters from the water's edge and are looking out at the sea. The waves are breaking in front of you and that brilliant blue sky is overhead with a few puffy white clouds drifting by. There are four or five gulls drifting in the gentle breeze over the waves, and you can hear them squawk every now and then as they seem to hover in the breeze. (Provision of external setting, some visual, and auditory detail). You are laying there in the sand, feeling all peaceful and relaxed, having that sense of "everything is O.K. with the world" feeling. You are very relaxed, kind of melting into the warm white sand. (Provision of emotional and temperature details). The sand is warm but not hot. You are feeling very pleasant and warm, yet there is a coolness over your face as you can feel the moisture in the air coming off the ocean. You also can smell the sea, that sense of salt and seaweed in the air, and can hear the waves gently breaking in front of you. (Provision of more temperature, auditory, and olfactory details). You are laying there in the sand, warm but not hot, just very peaceful and relaxed. You are feeling calm, that feeling of being one with nature, not having a care in the world. (Provision of more affective detail).

After developing the relaxation image, which should take about 5–10 min, the client should be given a brief description of progressive relaxation procedures and a demonstration of the exact tension-release processes through which he/she will be going. Clients should be told that they will tense each muscle group for approximately 10 s and that they should pay attention to the feelings of tension in those muscles as they are tensed. Then, they will be told to relax or release the muscles quickly and to focus on the contrast between the tense feelings and the relaxation feelings. This helps increase the client's awareness of his/her feelings and areas of tension in the body and how those are different from relaxed feelings. Then, the client is told that he/she will focus on the contrast and relaxation feelings for about 30 s. Then the tension-release process in that muscle group is either repeated or moved to the next muscle group. Overall, progressive relaxation training is described simply as a means of developing a relaxation response from which specific relaxation coping skills can be developed.

Following the tension-release exercise of progressive relaxation, the clinician will want to do a muscle review in which the muscles are focused on and relaxed further without actually tensing them. This might be done by some instruction such as the following.

Let us now review those muscles that we have been going through and increase that sense of relaxation even more, but this time without actually tensing the muscles up. As I describe each muscle group, I want you to focus your attention there and let it relax a little more. It may be like a kind of flow or wave of relaxation washing through that area. So now, focus on both of your hands...just letting them become more loose and relaxed...just letting the hands become more and more comfortably relaxed...letting that sense of relaxation increase...and now move up into the forearms…(continuing this kind of instruction through the various muscle groups).

When the muscle review is complete, then the relaxation scene is introduced. It might be introduced in a manner such as the following.

> In a moment, I am going to have you relax in a different way, this time by switching on your relaxation scene, the one involving being on the beach at San Diego (a brief reference to client scene to orient him/her). When I ask you to do that, I want you to put yourself right into that scene experiencing it like it is happening to you right now. When the scene is vivid and clear, then please signal me by raising your right index finger. So, right now, switch on that relaxation scene, put yourself right into it right now. So…(the clinician begins describing the relaxation scene).

After the signal of scene clarity is given by the client and acknowledged by the therapist, the client continues to visualize the scene for another 20–30 s with the therapist providing occasional prompts of emotional and situational detail. Then, the scene is terminated with an instruction such as: "O.K., now just erase that scene from your mind and refocus your attention on the feelings in your body." As time allows, the relaxation scene is repeated another time or two interspersed with three or four deep breaths between scenes or another muscle review.

With approximately 10 min to go in the session, the therapist arouses the client from progressive relaxation procedures and interviews him/her about the experiences during progressive relaxation training. At the end of this time, the therapist gives the homework for the week. The client is instructed to practice progressive relaxation on a daily basis and record experiences in a relaxation log. The log typically includes the date and time of practice, areas that were easy or difficult to relax, and a rating of tension before and after the relaxation period. The ratings would be typically on a 0–100 scale of tension. The second homework assignment is self-monitoring of worry and anxiety with the client paying attention to and recording not only external situational detail, but also internal cognitive, emotional, and physiological cues of anxiety arousal. This, too, would be recorded in an anxiety log in which the situational and experiential details are recorded along with a tension rating on the same 0–100 scale.

Session 2

The second session extends Session 1 and provides training in four relaxation coping skills. In the first few minutes of the session, the therapist reviews both relaxation practice and the self-monitoring homework with an eye toward making minor adjustments in relaxation procedures later in the session and towards sharpening the client's understanding of the situational and experiential cues of anxiety arousal.

A moderate-level anxiety scene is then constructed. It will be employed in the next session to elicit anxiety for the initial training in the application of relaxation coping skills. The anxiety level for the scene is generally about a 50–60 level on a 0–100 scale of anxiety. A lower level of anxiety can be employed if the client either has low self-efficacy expectations for anxiety control or if the review of homework suggests that the client tends to underestimate the experience of anxiety. As with the construction of the relaxation scene, the anxiety scene should capture the situational and experiential detail of a real moment in the person's life. The scene should include as many details as possible regarding the external events and the internal (cognitive, emotional and physiological details) experience of the anxiety. Behavioral elements may be included as long as they do not include escape, avoidance or other defensive qualities. If these elements were included, they would lead to covert rehearsal of anxiety escape when the scene is used for coping in the next session. For example, a behavioral element such as "I was really worrying about the interview and wanted to leave but forced myself to stay there and think the situation through" would be acceptable whereas "I was really worrying about the interview and wanted to leave, so I got up, went to the refrigerator for a beer, and watched television for the next two hours" would not be acceptable because it involves escape and self-medication elements. A sample scene at the 70 level is described below.

> Last Wednesday afternoon, I was home alone, sitting at the kitchen table and making notes for the upcoming job interview. I was worrying about the interview, thinking about all the things that could go wrong such as they would call and cancel the interview, I would get so anxious that it would be noticeable and I would be embarrassed, I would be dressed inappropriately or come across ineffectively, they would find me boring and uninteresting, and how awful it would be not to get the job. I just could not stop worrying about it. I knew I would be fine. but that did not seem to help. My thoughts were just all sort of jumbled up and I could not organize my thoughts and notes. (Cognitive detail elements) I had been there for some time, just kind of frozen at the table. My stomach hurt and was in knots and I was somewhat nauseous. My neck and shoulders were very tight and I had that feeling like a headache was coming on, a kind of band of strain around my forehead. I was feeling kind of weak and shaky and was really pretty anxious. (Physiological and emotional elements of anxiety arousal). I really wanted to get up and leave but I just could not seem to get it together. (Behavioral detail not involving actual avoidance).

Following the anxiety scene construction, progressive relaxation procedures are repeated tensing each muscle group once. This is followed by therapist direction in four basic relaxation coping skills:

1. relaxation without tension, i.e., reviewing the muscles and letting them go without tensing them (see Session 1);
2. deep breathing cued relaxation, i.e. taking three or four slow deep breaths and relaxing more on each exhalation;
3. relaxation imagery, i.e., imagining the relaxation image created in Session 1; and
4. cue-controlled relaxation, i.e., slowly repeating the word "relax" (or some similar word or phrase such as "calm" or "calm control") having the client relax more on each repetition. These four skills are repeated as time allows.

The homework for this session includes: (1) continued self-monitoring of anxiety reactions in order to enhance self-awareness of the situational and internal cues of anxiety arousal; (2) practicing and recording of progressive relaxation and relaxation coping skills practice to strengthen relaxation responses; and (3) daily deployment of at least one relaxation coping skill in nonstressful situations (e.g., watching television or riding on a bus) to begin the transfer of coping skill practice to the external environment.

Session 3

The third session continues the development of relaxation and awareness enhancement from earlier sessions and introduces the initial trials of the application of relaxation coping skills for anxiety reduction. This is achieved by having the client imagine the anxiety scene, involve him/herself in it fully, pay attention to anxiety arousal, and then retrieve relaxation through the therapist's instruction in one or more of the relaxation coping skills.

Following the homework review at the beginning of the session, the therapist relaxes the client by way of relaxation without tension. When the client signals the presence of relaxation, the therapist then initiates the first cycle of anxiety arousal and relaxation coping. The client is instructed to imagine the anxiety scene constructed in the prior session and put him/herself fully into the scene experiencing and paying attention to anxiety arousal. The anxiety scene is left in imagination for about 10–20 s on the first exposure and 30 or more seconds on subsequent exposures. Then, the therapist terminates the anxiety scene and actively assists the client in retrieving a state of calmness through the use of one or more of the relaxation coping skills. It is generally a good idea to use the relaxation image as the first coping skill on the first trial or two as it tends to remove any residual anxiety imagery. After clients gain greater control over anxiety imagery, then coping skills can be interspersed randomly. When the client signals the presence of relaxation again, then the anxiety scene is presented again with another trial of relaxation coping. This process is repeated as time allows. Examples of instructions for initiating anxiety scenes and relaxation retrieval for this session are listed below.

> In a moment, I am going to have you practice coping with anxiety. I am going to instruct you to imagine the anxiety scene involving (a general phrase or referent to scene content). When I do this, put yourself right into that scene. Really be there and experience the anxiety. Pay close attention to the anxiety, worry, and how they feel. Signal me when you experience the anxiety and then stay with those feelings of anxiety, let them build and notice it. After a few seconds, I will have you switch the scene off and then I will help you use the relaxation skills to reduce the anxiety. Signal me when you are once again relaxed, and then we will repeat the process to give you more experience coping with anxiety. So right now, put yourself right into this scene. (therapist then describes the anxiety scene using voice inflection to increase attention and anxiety). ...O.K., I see your signal...stay with that anxiety, let it build. Notice it. Pay attention to the worries, your stomach (exposing the scene for 10 to 20 seconds on the first trial and approximately 30 seconds on later trials). ... Now switch that scene from your mind and once again switch back on your relaxation scene. ...(therapist describes the relaxation scene)... therapist follows with one of other relaxation coping skills such as relaxation without tension, cue controlled relaxation, or breathing cued relaxation). (The therapist acknowledges the relaxation signal by some statement such as, "I see your signal," or if the relaxation signal is not forthcoming, then the therapist may prompt for it by some kind of instruction such as, "And signaling me when you are once again relaxed.")...

Homework for this session involves: (1) continued self-monitoring of anxiety experiences; (2) continued practice of relaxation coping skills in a full sequence at least once a day; and (3) application of relaxation coping skills any time anxiety is experienced and the recording of these in the anxiety log. Clients should be told that success with the relaxation coping skills is not expected at this point in time, but that it is important for them to begin to get experience applying relaxation for tension reduction in day-to-day living.

Session 4

This session is an extension and replication of Session 3 with minor modifications. The first modification is in the initial relaxation development. The client is asked to self-initiate relaxation on his/her own by whatever relaxation procedure works best for him/her. This is an increased step toward client responsibility for self-management of relaxation. Usually, relaxation is signaled in approximately a minute or two, but if it is not signaled within this time frame, the therapist may wish to prompt to see if the client is ready by some instruction such as, "And signaling me when you're relaxed." The second modification is in the anxiety arousal and relaxation retrieval sequence. The client is instructed to switch on the anxiety scene and experience it signaling anxiety arousal, to stay with that for awhile, and then when he/she is ready to switch the scene off and retrieve relaxation by whatever relaxation coping skills work best for him/her. When relaxation is retrieved, the client signals the therapist. If the client had been having considerable difficulty in relaxation retrieval in the prior session, then the therapist may not want to make this modification in this session but repeat the procedures of the prior session. However, the modifications increase the client control over relaxation retrieval. When the relaxation is signaled, then the therapist initiates another trial of relaxation coping, and this process is repeated as time allows, usually three to six repetitions of relaxation coping with anxiety. The interview following the relaxation coping focuses on identifying which coping skills work best and on the identification of the early cognitive, emotional and physiological cues of anxiety arousal for application of coping skills in vivo. Homework involves continued practice of relaxation coping skills daily and of continued in vivo application whenever tension (i.e., to all distressing situations) is felt and recording this in the self-monitoring log.

Session 5

Session 5 is a prototype for the remaining sessions. There are three additional modifications in procedures to maximize self-control and transfer. First, the homework is changed to encourage application of relaxation coping skills not only to anxiety but also to other distressing emotions such as anger and depression. Application to anxiety and these other distressing emotions is recorded in the self-monitoring log. That is, the range of application is increased to all kinds of distressing emotions and issues. Depending on the client, scenes for some of these other negative emotions may also be constructed and used in the same training format. Second, the anxiety level of the scenes is increased. If a single new scene is going to be used, one is developed at the 90 level on a 0–100 scale. If several scenes are going to be used, then it is suggested that scene intensity increase in approximately 10–15 unit gaps on this scale (e.g., scenes at 70, 80 and 90 levels). Increased scene intensity level leads the client to be controlling increasing levels of anxiety across sessions. Third, the procedures are shifted to the client having full control over anxiety arousal while staying in the anxiety scene. That is, the client imagines the scene, experiences and pays attention to the arousal, and then initiates the relaxation coping while staying in the scene. The anxiety scene instructions and signaling systems are modified to accommodate these changes as in the example below.

> In a moment, I am going to have you switch on the anxiety scene involving (brief mention of the content). When I do that, I want you to put yourself right into the scene and really pay attention to the anxiety arousal. When you are experiencing that anxiety arousal, please signal me by raising your finger. However, keep your finger up while you are experiencing the anxiety. Then, when you are ready, initiate the relaxation. When you are once again relaxed while staying in the scene, then signal me by lowering your finger. Then, I will instruct you to switch the scene off and continue relaxing.

Trials of coping with anxiety in this format are alternated using the two most recently developed anxiety scenes. As in earlier sessions, the session ends with a brief interview going over the coping within the session and setting up the homework as described above.

Session 6 and on

Subsequent sessions are essentially a repeat and extension of the format in Session 5. New scenes are created as necessary and used until the client gains increasing confidence and efficacy in self-managed relaxation both within and between sessions. If the client has other significant emotional issues (e.g., anger, embarrassment, guilt, etc.), such scenes can be constructed and rehearsed in the above format. This practice not only helps reduce these negative emotions, but also increases transfer to other issues.

As the client gains more success, the therapist may wish to lengthen the time between sessions, say to every two to three weeks, in order to give the client increasing opportunities in vivo practice. Monthly booster sessions for 3 or 4 months prior to termination may also help consolidate and gain self-efficacy. If the GAD client has difficulty monitoring tension build-up, then the therapist may also wish to encourage the client to apply relaxation coping skills either on a time or activity basis. This is, the client could apply the relaxation coping skills at specific times during the day, say every 2 h, and/or anytime he/she is engaging in a specific activity such as talking on the phone, waiting for an elevator, or the like. These procedures increase the frequency of application of relaxation throughout the day and the coping with gradual increments of general tension. The therapist may also want to contract for specific in vivo applications or simulations of anxiety arousing experiences for specific anxiety themes or situations that the individual may experience. That is, the GAD client may be encouraged to worry about specific topics or to confront specific fears or anxieties and apply the relaxation coping skills in vivo. The suggestion is also relevant for phobics, obsessive-compulsives, and panic disordered individuals as well. That is, the therapist and client may contract specific in vivo experiences to promote applications and transfer of coping skills. As appropriate, the therapist may wish to accompany the client on initial trials to assist in relaxation retrieval and structuring of experiences. Finally, if relevant, the therapist may begin to integrate other interventions with relaxation coping skills at this point in therapy. Generally, it is suggested that AMT precede other interventions as relaxation is generally less threatening and builds the therapeutic relationship early. Moreover, it is an intervention which is consistent with the client's conceptualization of problems, which increases both client's acceptance and lowers reactance to other interventions. That is, the development of relaxation coping skills seems to facilitate not only anxiety reduction directly, but also other interventions which might be more threatening initially.

Anxiety Management Training: Group Procedures

Several of the studies reviewed earlier demonstrated that AMT could be applied effectively to small groups of six to eight clients. AMT was effective in groups of individuals sharing common anxieties (e.g., Deffenbacher & Shelton, 1978; Suinn & Richardson, 1971) and in groups of clients with somewhat differing sources of anxiety and stress (e.g., Cragan & Deffenbacher, 1984; Hutchings et al., 1980; Jannoun et al., 1982). One study (Deffenbacher, Michaels, Daley & Michaels, 1980a) showed that some clients appeared to benefit even more from being mixed with clients with other anxieties. Thus, it would appear that AMT can be delivered effectively and efficiently in small groups of clients with different sources of anxiety. The efficacy of group AMT, however, may not extend beyond the small group format, as one study (Daley et al., 1983) showed that a large group or workshop format involving approximately 25 clients in a group was not effective for generalized anxiety clients, whereas in a small group AMT was effective.

Because several clients are involved in group AMT, several modifications in individual AMT are recommended.

1. The therapist should consider increasing the session length by approximately 20–30 min, i.e., to approximately 75–90 min in length. This provides the additional time to provide attention all clients and their issues, to answer their questions, to tailor intervention procedures to the details of the individual's life, and to provide time for interviewing for the different anxiety and relaxation scenes. If it is not possible to lengthen the session time, then the therapist should be ready to extend the number of sessions. Generally, group AMT takes approximately two to four more sessions than individual AMT. Nonetheless, group AMT represents a considerable effi-

ciency or cost-benefit gain as it represents approximately two therapist hours per client.

2. The pace of group AMT should be linked to the progress of the slowest client. This is necessary in order to ensure that all clients have gained success in order to move to the next step. This may require repetition of all or portions of a session before moving on. If one client is consistently significantly slower or out of step with other group members, then it may be desirable to remove him/her from the group and treat him/her individually.

3. Great portions of both relaxation and anxiety scenes are developed in homework. That is, the client is asked to identify and outline scenes prior to the sessions in which they are to be used. During the sessions, the therapist interviews clients and helps outline the details of the situational and internal cue properties of scenes. Then, these scenes are written out on pieces of paper or index cards to which the client can refer.

4. In individual AMT, the therapist is able to provide considerable detail of the relaxation and anxiety scenes. However, in group AMT, this is not possible because different group members have scenes that vary in content. Therefore, the therapist uses more general instructions to trigger either relaxation or anxiety scenes. Specifically, the therapist refers to having the client trigger on his/her relaxation scene or anxiety scene which refers to the material that the person has put on the index card or piece of paper.

5. The therapist should be ready to use more requests for hand signals in order to gain assessment of various issues. For example, if clients have gone through a period of relaxation and not all clients have signaled, the therapist will not know whether the client has experienced relaxation but is not signaling or is not relaxed. Therefore, he/she may wish to use an instruction such as, "If you are now relaxed and comfortable, please signal me by raising your hand." If a signal is not forthcoming from all clients, then he/she may wish to ask the reverse question, "If you are now not experiencing calmness and relaxation, please signal me by raising your hand." In this manner, the therapist can gain considerable information about the progress of different clients during the session.

6. With a group of individuals, there is a greater probability for the need of applying relaxation to a variety of other emotional and distressing issues. These concerns should receive attention in latter group sessions and may be addressed by the development of "other distressing emotion scenes" which can be used in the Session 5 format.

Integration of AMT with Other Therapeutic Approaches

Cognitive therapy is highly appropriate for GAD, given the significant cognitive elements involved, and AMT can be easily integrated with it. AMT could be introduced early in therapy to reduce the emotional and physiological arousal elements. As the client gains emotional control, he/she is then likely to be more ready for the cognitive changes. At the very least, AMT builds the therapeutic relationship reasonably well which could provide the base for subsequent integration with cognitive therapy. Moreover, cognitive restructuring and the rehearsal of cognitive coping skills can be easily added in the latter portions of AMT. That is, clients can practice relaxation and cognitive coping skills to reduce the anxiety generated by the anxiety scenes. Such a blend of relaxation and cognitive approaches has been effective with GAD (Borkovec & Costello, 1993), with general anxiety and panic disordered individuals (Barlow, Cohen, Wadell, Vermilyea, Klosko, Blanchard & Di Nardo, 1984), social anxiety (Butler, Cullington, Munby, Amies & Gelder, 1984), Type A behavior (Kelly & Stone, 1987), and anger (Deffenbacher et al., 1987, 1988, 1990a, 1994; Deffenbacher & Stark, 1992).

AMT can also be integrated with skill-building approaches for both anxious and skill deficit individuals. For GAD individuals, skill deficits might include problem-solving, assertiveness, and the like. Again, it is suggested that AMT, precede the major elements of the skill building program. Having an effective set of relaxation coping skills can allow clients to more comfortably approach and benefit from rehearsal activities typical of most skill building approaches. This is possible because they are more able to lower their anxiety and involve themselves more fully. Moreover, as the client learns to manage his/her anxiety, he/she may show greater skills than previously thought because these skills were masked with interfering anxiety.

Obviously, AMT can be combined with both cognitive and behavioral skill building programs. This has been done effectively with social anxieties (Pipes, 1982), vocationally anxious and undecided individuals (Mendonca & Siess, 1976), and anger (Deffenbacher, McNamara, Stark & Demm, 1990b).

For many GAD and other anxiety disordered clients, AMT may also be effectively combined with anxiolytic medication. Here it is suggested that the medication be given early in therapy to reduce the high levels of arousal or panic. This gives the client quick relief. As he/she develops greater self-management skills for anxiety with the AMT, medications can be decreased and the anxiety control shifted to the client's relaxation as he/she develops proficiency and efficacy in applied relaxation coping skills.

AMT may also be used adjunctively with other nonbehavioral forms of therapy. The relaxation skills developed in AMT might allow an individual to be able to relax and better stay with anxiety-laden material and work it therapeutically within other frameworks. Additionally, it may allow them to not avoid anxiety topics through forms such as dropping out of therapy, being resistant, defensive, and the like. One study with anxious schizophrenics (Van Hassell et al., 1982) suggested that AMT led to greater progress in other nonbehavioral therapies.

Finally, AMT might be used as part of psychoeducational and prevention programs. That is, AMT could be used in small groups to develop general relaxation coping skills for a wide range of individuals. These might be helpful to the individual throughout his/her life span or be targeted toward specific upcoming stressors such as elective surgery and its aftermath or coping with stressors in the workplace.

Conclusions

AMT is an effective, time-limited intervention for specific and general anxiety conditions. It is designed to develop relaxation coping skills for the self-management of anxiety which gives the GAD or other anxious individual greater capacity to calm down and to address anxiety arousing concerns with greater cognitive and behavioral effectiveness. Hopefully, this chapter has provided therapists with sufficient detail so that they can employ AMT and help their clients in these ways.

Acknowledgements

Preparation of this paper was funded, in part, by the Tri-Ethnic Center for Study of Drug Abuse Prevention grant #P50DA0707.

References

APA (1994). *Diagnostic and statistical manual of mental disorders*, 4th edition (DSM-IV). Washington, DC: American Psychiatric Association.

Barlow, D. H. (1988). *Anxiety and its disorders: The nature and treatment of anxiety and panic*. New York: Guilford Press.

Barlow, D. H., Cohen, A. S., Wadell, M., Vermilyea, J. A., Klosko, J. S., Blanchard, E. B., & Di Nardo, P. A. (1984). Panic and generalized anxiety disorders: Nature and treatment. *Behavior Therapy*, 15, 431–449.

Barlow, D. H., Rapee, R. M., & Brown, T. A. (1992). Behavioral treatment of generalized anxiety disorder. *Behavior Therapy*, 23, 551–570.

Bernstein, D. A., & Borkovec, T. D. (1973). *Progressive relaxation training*. Champaign, IL: Research Press.

Borkovec, T. D., & Costello, E. (1993). Efficacy of applied relaxation and cognitive-behavioral therapy in the treatment of generalized anxiety disorder. *Journal of Consulting and Clinical Psychology*, 61, 611–619.

Borkovec, T. D., Mathews, A. M., Chambers, A., Ebrahimi, S., Lytle, R., & Nelson, R. (1987). The effects of relaxation training with cognitive therapy or nondirective therapy and the role of relaxation induced anxiety in the treatment of generalized anxiety. *Journal of Consulting and Clinical Psychology*, 55, 883–888.

Butler, G., Cullington, A., Mumby, M., Amies, P., & Gelder, M. (1984). Exposure and anxiety management in the treatment of social phobia. *Journal of Consulting and Clinical Psychology, 52,* 641–650.

Butler, G., Cullington, A., Hibbert, G., Klimes, I., & Gelder, M. (1987). Anxiety management for persistent generalized anxiety. *British Journal of Psychiatry, 151,* 535–542.

Butler, G., Fennell, M., Robson, P., & Gelder, M. (1991). Comparison of behavior therapy and cognitive behavior therapy in the treatment of generalized anxiety disorder. *Journal of Consulting and Clinical Psychology, 59,* 167–175.

Cragan, M. K., & Deffenbacher, J. L. (1984). Anxiety management training and relaxation as self-control in the treatment of generalized anxiety in medical outpatients. *Journal of Counseling Psychology, 31,* 123–131.

Daley, P. C., Bloom, L. J., Deffenbacher, J. L., & Steward, R. (1983). Treatment effectiveness of anxiety management training in small and large group formats. *Journal of Counseling Psychology, 30,* 104–107.

Deffenbacher, J. L., & Shelton, J. L. (1978). A comparison of anxiety management training and desensitization in reducing test and other anxieties. *Journal of Counseling Psychology, 25,* 227–282.

Deffenbacher, J. L., & Michaels, A. C. (1981a). Anxiety management training and self-control desensitization -- 15 months later. *Journal of Counseling Psychology, 28,* 459–462.

Deffenbacher, J. L., & Michaels, A. C. (1981b). A twelve-month follow-up homogeneous and heterogeneous anxiety management training. *Journal of Counseling Psychology, 28,* 463–466.

Deffenbacher, J. L., & Craun, A. M. (1985). Anxiety management training with stressed student gynecology patients: A collaborative approach. *Journal of College Student Personnel, 26,* 513–518.

Deffenbacher, J. L., & Suinn, R. M. (1987). Generalized anxiety syndrome. In L. Michelson & L. M. Ascher (Eds.), *Anxiety and stress disorders: Cognitive-behavioral assessment and treatment.* New York: Guilford Press.

Deffenbacher, J. L., & Stark, R. S. (1992). Relaxation and cognitive-relaxation treatments of general anger. *Journal of Counseling Psychology, 39,* 158–167.

Deffenbacher, J. L., Michaels, A. C., Daley, P. C., & Michaels, T. (1980a). A comparison of homogenous and heterogeneous anxiety management training. *Journal of Counseling Psychology, 27,* 630–634.

Deffenbacher, J. L., Michaels, A. C., Michaels, T., & Daley, P. C. (1980b). Comparison of anxiety management training and self-control desensitization. *Journal of Counseling Psychology, 27,* 232–239.

Deffenbacher, J. L., Demm, P. M., & Brandon, A. D. (1986). High general anger: Correlates and treatment. *Behaviour Research and Therapy, 24,* 481–489.

Deffenbacher, J. L., Story, D. A., Stark, R. S., Hogg, J. A., & Brandon, A. D. (1987). Cognitive-relaxation and social skills interventions in the treatment of general anger. *Journal of Counseling Psychology, 34,* 171–176.

Deffenbacher, J. L., Story, D. A., Brandon, A. D., Hogg, J. A., & Hazaleus, S. L. (1988). Cognitive and cognitive-relaxation treatments of anger. *Cognitive Therapy and Research, 12,* 167–184.

Deffenbacher, J. L., McNamara, K., Stark, R. S., & Sabadell, P. M. (1990a). A comparison of cognitive-behavioral and process oriented group counseling for general anger reduction. *Journal of Counseling and Development, 69,* 167–172.

Deffenbacher, J. L., McNamara, K., Stark, R. S., & Sabadell, P. M. (1990b). A combination of cognitive, relaxation, and behavioral coping skills in the reduction of general anger. *Journal of College Student Development, 31,* 351–358.

Deffenbacher, J. L., Thwaites, G. A., Wallace, T. L., & Oetting, E. R. (1995). Social skill and cognitive-relaxation approaches to general anger reduction. *Journal of Counseling Psychology, 41,* 386–396.

Drazen, M., Nevid, J., Pace, N., & O'Brien, R. (1982). Worksite-based behavioral treatment of mild hypertension. *Journal of Occupational Medicine, 24,* 511–514.

Hazaleus, S. L., & Deffenbacher, J. L. (1986). Relaxation and cognitive treatments of anger. *Journal of Consulting and Clinical Psychology, 54,* 222–226.

Hill, E. (1977). A comparison of anxiety management training and interpersonal skills training for socially anxious college students. *Dissertation Abstracts International, 37,* (8-A), 4985.

Hutchings, D., Denney, D., Basgall, J., & Houston, B. (1980). Anxiety management and applied relaxation in reducing general anxiety. *Behaviour Research and Therapy, 18,* 181–190.

Jannoun, L., Oppenheimer, C., & Gelder, M. (1982). A self-help treatment program for anxiety state patients. *Behavior Therapy, 13,* 103–111.

Jorgensen, R., Houston, B., & Zurawaki, R. (1981). Anxiety management training in the treatment of essential hypertension. *Behaviour Research and Therapy, 19,* 467–474.

Kelly, K., & Stone, G. (1987). Effects of three psychological treatments and self-monitoring on the reduction of Type A behavior. *Journal of Counseling Psychology, 34,* 46–54.

Mendonca, J., & Siess, T. (1976). Counseling for indecisiveness: Problem-solving and anxiety-management training. *Journal of Counseling Psychology, 23,* 339–347.

Pipes, R. (1982). Social anxiety and isolation in college students: A comparison of two treatments. *Journal of College Student Personnel, 23,* 502–508.

Quillen, M., & Denney, D. (1982). Self-control of dysmenorrheic symptoms through pain management training. *Journal of Behavioral Therapy and Experimental Psychiatry, 13,* 123–130.

Richardson, F., & Suinn, R. M. (1973). A comparison of traditional desensitization, accelerated massed desensitization, and anxiety management training in the treatment of mathematics anxiety. *Behavior Therapy, 4,* 212–218.

Suinn, R. M. (1990). *Anxiety management training.* New York: Plenum Press.

Suinn, R., & Richardson, F. (1971). Anxiety management training: A non-specific behavior therapy program for anxiety control. *Behavior Therapy, 2,* 498–510.

Suinn, R., & Bloom, L. (1978). Anxiety management training for Pattern A behavior. *Journal of Behavioral Medicine, 1,* 25–35.

Suinn, R. M., & Deffenbacher, J. L. (1988). Anxiety management training. *The Counseling Psychologist, 16,* 31–49.

Suinn, R., Brock, L., & Edie, C. (1975). Behavior therapy for Type A patients. *American Journal of Cardiology, 36,* 269.

Van Hassell, J., Bloom, L. J., & Gonzalez, A. C. (1982). Anxiety management training with schizophrenic outpatients. *Journal of Clinical Psychology, 38,* 280–285.

Wolpe, J. (1973). *The practice of behavior therapy,* 2nd edition. New York: Pergamon Press.

Further Reading

Bernstein, D. A., & Borkovec, T. D. (1983). *Entrenamiento en relajación progresiva* (Original, 1973). Desclée de Brouwer.

Deffenbacher, J. L., & Suinn, R. M. (1982). The self-control of anxiety. In P. Karoly & F.

Kanfer (Eds.), *Self-management and behavior change from theory to practice.* New York: Pergamon Press.

Lehrer, P. M., & Woolfolk, R. L. (1993). *Principles and practice of stress management,* 2th edition. New York: Guilford Press.

Lichstein, K. L. (1988). *Clinical relaxation strategies.* New York: Wiley.

Suinn, R. M. (1990). *Anxiety management training.* New York: Plenum Press.

9

Cognitive-Behavioral Treatment of Sexual Dysfunctions

MICHAEL P. CAREY

Syracuse University, USA

Historical Overview and Overview of Chapter

In many ways, treatment of the sexual dysfunctions served as an important proving ground for the cognitive-behavioral therapies. One of the leading founders of the cognitive-behavioral approach was Albert Ellis, who started his career in sexology and published such seminal works as *The Folklore of Sex* (1951), *The American Sexual Tragedy* (1954), and *Sex Without Guilt* (1958). Although initially trained in psychoanalysis as a psychotherapeutic approach, Ellis profited from additional training in sexology and research; indeed, these experiences eventually led him in 1955 to reject psychoanalysis and to develop rational emotive therapy, the first of the cognitive-behavioral therapies (Ellis, 1992).

Cognitive-behavioral treatment of the sexual dysfunctions remained a somewhat esoteric specialty during the 1950s and 1960s. However, the empirical underpinnings were laid by the research and writings of Kinsey and his colleagues (Kinsey, Pomeroy & Martin, 1948; Kinsey, Pomeroy, Martin & Gebhard, 1953) as well as Masters and Johnson (1966, 1970). With the publication of *Human Sexual Inadequacy* by Masters and Johnson in 1970, the field of sex therapy, took hold and has since flourished. Subsequent writings by LoPiccolo and his colleagues (LoPiccolo & LoPiccolo, 1978; LoPiccolo & Friedman, 1988), Leiblum and Rosen (1988, 1991), and others have enhanced cognitive-behavioral approaches, which many sex therapists would agree are the treatment of choice for the sexual dysfunctions.

In this chapter, the commonly recognized sexual dysfunctions are described, their prevalence and etiology are briefly reviewed, information about the cognitive-behavioral treatment of these problems is presented, the future of cognitive-behaviorally based sex therapy is forecast, and additional readings for interested therapist are suggested.

The Sexual Dysfunctions

Current conceptualization of the sexual dysfunctions is based on the sexual response cycle first described by Masters and Johnson (1966) and later modified by several theorists, including Kaplan (1974). Masters and Johnson completed laboratory research with healthy adult volunteers and provided a physiological model of sexual functioning that included four stages: excitement, plateau, orgasm, and resolution. Kaplan (1974), drawing upon her clinical experience, proposed that another "stage" was missing and should be added. This stage was labeled "desire" and refers to a person's cognitive and affective readiness for, and interest in, sexual activity. Today, most models of healthy sexual functioning focus on desire, arousal, and orgasm.

Definitions and classification of sexual dysfunction include impairments or disturbance in one of these three stages; in addition, the experience of pain at any time during sexual activity is classified as a sexual dysfunction. Specific diagnostic criteria for nine dysfunctions have been published in the *Diagnostic and Statistical Manual of Mental Disorders*, also known as the DSM-IV (APA, 1994). Each of the nine dysfunctions can be characterized as *lifelong* versus *acquired*, *generalized* (occurs in all situations with all partners) versus *specific*, and due to *psychological* factors versus due to *combined* psychological factors and a general medical condition. (When any of the sexual dysfunctions occurs exclusively as a result of a medical condition, e.g., erectile dysfunction caused by advanced diabetic neuropathy, then the dysfunction would *not* be considered a psychological or mental disorder.)

According to the DSM-IV, formal diagnosis requires that the dysfunction "does not occur during the course of another Axis I disorder," such as a Major Depressive Disorder, and is not Substance-Induced (e.g., through the use of cannabis). Moreover, the clinician/diagnostician must determine that the dysfunction "causes marked distress or interpersonal difficulty." This qualification, new to the fourth edition of the DSM, may have an effect on the diagnosis and prevalence of the sexual dysfunctions; that is, individuals who would have previously been classified as experiencing a dysfunction based solely on physical symptoms will not be diagnosed if the individual and/or couple copes reasonably well with the difficulty.

Hypoactive sexual desire disorder refers to a condition in which a person is distressed by perceived low levels of sexual activity and fantasies. Clinicians must make this judgment based on factors that may affect desire and activity levels, such as gender and the context of the person's life. This disorder can be challenging to diagnose because the construct of desire is not yet well understood or defined, and is subject to many interpretations. Due to a wide variability in what individuals perceive as "normal" sexual drive, it is usually a *change* in desire that leads to help-seeking.

The interplay of behavior, cognitions, and affect are important in diagnosing this disorder. Clinicians have the latitude to make this diagnosis in different scenarios – when a person lacks desire and fantasies about sex, but has intercourse regularly in response to a partner's advances; or when a person in their 20s has no regular partner, is distressed by what they perceive is a significant lack of interest in sex, has little interest in masturbation, but does experience infrequent fantasies of sexual activity. The trade-off for this diagnostic flexibility is a potential sacrifice in inter-clinician reliability.

Sexual aversion disorder, although diagnostically distinct from hypoactive sexual desire disorder, may be understood as an extreme form of low sexual desire. The two disorders have been categorized as distinct clinical diagnoses primarily due to differences in clinical presentation; those with sexual aversion disorder fear and avoid sexual contact. There has been little systematic research of sexual aversion disorder, so it remains to be seen whether common etiologies underlie the two desire disorders. According to the DSM-IV, an individual with this disorder experiences persistent or recurrent extreme aversion to, and avoidance of all, or almost all, genital sexual contact with a sexual partner.

Male erectile disorder, often referred to as "impotence" (which many consider unintentionally pejorative) by physicians and the lay public, should be diagnosed when a man is persistently or recurrently unable to attain or maintain an erection until completion of sexual activity. *Female sexual arousal disorder* refers to a lack of responsiveness to sexual stimulation; specifically, a persistent or recurrent inability to attain or maintain the lubrication-swelling response of sexual excitement until completion of sexual activity.

Female orgasmic disorder refers to the persistent or recurrent delay in, or absence of, orgasm following a normal sexual excitement phase. The criteria allow that women exhibit a wide variability in the type and intensity of stimulation for orgasm; the clinician must make a judgment regarding orgasmic capacity based upon the woman's age, sexual experience, and adequacy of stimulation. *Male orgasmic disorder* refers to the persistent or recurrent delay or absence of orgasm, during sexual stimulation that is judged to be adequate in focus, intensity and duration whereas *premature ejaculation* refers to ejaculation with minimal sexual stimulation, before, upon, or shortly after penetration, and "before the person wishes it." The latter can be challenging to diagnose because it is not clear what should be considered a "normal" length of sexual contact before orgasm? Some men and women may have unrealistic expectations regarding time until orgasm, and clinicians may disagree about the precise definition of "premature." However, more clear cut cases typically involve ejaculation before intromission (when intercourse is desired), or immediately after penetration.

The DSM-IV criteria for *dyspareunia* are persistent or recurrent genital pain associated with sexual intercourse (in either a male or female) that is not caused exclusively by the lack of lubrication or vaginismus, and is not due to a general medical condition. *Vaginismus* refers to recurrent or persistent involuntary spasms of the musculature of the outer third of the vagina that interfere with coitus. Lamont (1978) reports that when couples attempt intercourse, the sensation is that the penis "hits a 'brick wall' about one inch inside the vagina" (p. 633). The repercussions of this difficulty can be significant; due to the importance that many couples place upon intercourse, the man may feel that the woman is resisting his intimacy. The woman, despite the involuntary nature of the spasms, may blame herself for the problem – anticipation of future occurrences can cause the spasms to occur prior to intercourse attempts (see Wincze & Carey, 1991).

Although familiarity with the formal diagnostic categories and criteria is recommended, so is a healthy skepticism of such classificatory systems. After all, although sexual dysfunctions in the DSM are defined as either present or not, sexual health is more accurately placed along a continuum. In addition, although the dysfunctions provide useful heuristics for diagnosis and communication, in clinical practice the treatment plan must often account for the biopsychosocial complexities of sexual functioning. For example, difficulties at one stage can impinge upon the functioning of a later stage (and vice versa). In a study of 374 men with sexual disorders, Segraves & Segraves (1990) found that 20% of the men with erectile disorder had an additional desire disorder. Undiagnosed biological disease and unrecognized interpersonal/dyadic factors can also play important roles in the development and maintenance of a sexual dysfunction. Therefore, although the DSM-IV represents a marked improvement over earlier editions, it should not be considered the last word on sexual function or dysfunction.

Empirical and Theoretical Foundations

Clinical experience, empirical research, and theoretical formulations have played an important role in our understanding of the sexual dysfunctions. In this section, a brief overview of research findings and theoretical approaches that have influenced the cognitive-behavioral treatment of the sexual dysfunctions is provided.

Empirical Foundations

Two important research traditions warrant review, namely, those that have focused on the (a) prevalence and (b) etiology of the sexual dysfunctions. The former is important because it establishes that sexual dysfunctions occur frequently and warrant the attention of health care professionals. The latter is important because it establishes the appropriateness of cognitive-behavioral treatment approaches.

Prevalence. Since the clinical observations of Freud, therapists have recognized the frequency with which sexual complaints emerge as significant clinical concerns. Not until recently, however, have empirically based estimates of the prevalence of the sexual dysfunctions been available. As pointed out by Spector & Carey (1990), however, much of the extant data must be interpreted with caution due to methodological limitations such as inadequate sampling, imprecise diagnostic categories, and measurement problems. Nevertheless, this literature does offer some information regarding the prevalence of the sexual dysfunctions.

Frequency estimates of *hypoactive sexual desire disorder* from community studies, which attempt to determine prevalence data for the general population, suggest that low desire occurred in about 34% of females and 16% of males (Frank, Anderson & Kupfer, 1978). However, these were not clinicians' diagnoses; rather, small samples of respondents endorsed items such as being currently "disinterested in sex." Additional information about the frequency of desire disorders comes from clinic-based studies. Recent research indicates that desire disorders are the reason for about one-half to two-thirds of persons presenting at sex therapy clinics (Segraves & Segraves, 1991). The recent introduction of *sexual aversion disorder* into the diagnostic nomenclature makes differentiation between rates of sexual aversion disorder and hypoactive desire disorder difficult. However, one recent report (Katz, Frazer & Wilson, 1993) indicates that 6% of college students experience severe sexual anxiety, which may be a proxy for sexual aversion.

Male erectile disorder accounts for 36–53% of men presenting at specialty clinics (Spector & Carey, 1990). In a recent study, Feldman, Goldstein, Hatzichristou, Krane & McKinlay (1994) used a cross sectional, random sample of non institutionalized, healthy men (aged 40–70 years) to determine the prevalence of erectile disorder in the general population. Of the 1290 men surveyed, 52% reported minimal, moderate, or complete "impotence" (defined as erectile difficulty during intercourse, lower rates of sexual activity and erection, and lower satisfaction with sex life); the prevalence of complete "impotence" was 9.6%, and tripled from 5 to 15% between the ages of 40 and 70 years. Based on this and other community-based studies (e.g., Kinsey et al., 1948), it is clear that erection problems are very common. Evidence for the prevalence of *female sexual arousal disorder* is scant. Frank et al. (1976)

reported that 57% of females seeking therapy experienced arousal disorders. Estimates from community studies yield prevalence rates of 11% (Levine & Yost, 1976) to 48% (Frank et al., 1978). In all cases, though, female arousal disorder has been poorly defined.

The frequency of *female orgasmic disorder* has ranged from 5% (Levine & Yost, 1976) to 20% (Ard, 1977; Hunt, 1974) in community samples. Clinicians report that between 18 and 76% of women at sex therapy clinics report lack of orgasm as their primary complaint. In clinical practice, *male orgasmic disorder* is infrequently observed. Spector & Carey (1990) identified this as the least common of disorders, occurring among 4–10% of men. These could even be overestimates because the "delay" in orgasm and the length of time considered normal before ejaculation have not been well-defined. In contrast, many sex therapists agree that *premature ejaculation* is prevalent. Spector & Carey (1990) concluded that 36–38% of men in the general population may experience this difficulty, and two studies found it to be the primary problem for about 20% of men at their clinics (Hawton, 1982; Renshaw, 1988).

Although community surveys suggest that as many as 33% of women experience pain during sexual activity (Glatt, Zinner & McCormack, 1990), only about 3–5% of clients in sex therapy clinics complain of *dyspareunia* (Hawton, 1982; Renshaw, 1988). Bachman, Leiblum & Grill (1989) used a questionnaire and direct inquiry to screen for sexual complaints among 887 consecutive gynecological outpatients. Only 3% offered sexual complaints on the survey; however, during inquiry, 9% described dyspareunia. Prevalence of dyspareunia in men is unknown. *Vaginismus* may be the least talked about of the dysfunctions, due to the embarrassment that is experienced. No prevalence estimates from the general population are available but vaginismus has been documented in 5–42% of women presenting for sex therapy (Spector & Carey, 1990).

Etiology. The focus on this chapter, and book, is on cognitive-behavioral approaches. Given the demonstrated value of such interventions for many problems, including sexual dysfunctions, this emphasis is warranted. However, it is particularly important when discussing the sexual dysfunctions to acknowledge the important role played by physiology. Leading scientist-practitioners explicitly adopt a biopsychosocial framework that recognizes the importance of the biological level of analysis. Thus, even though space constraints in this chapter require that we focus on the psychological and social levels of analysis, it is important to remember the hormonal, neurological, and vascular risk factors in the predisposition, triggering, and maintaining of many dysfunctions.

Clinicians have suggested an assortment of psychosocial causes for low sexual desire. Regarding individual factors, LoPiccolo & Friedman (1988) cite aging-related concerns, fear of loss of control over sexual urges, gender identity conflict, poor psychological adjustment, and fear of pregnancy or sexually transmitted disease. Hypothesized relationship causes have included a lack of attraction to partner, dyadic differences regarding optimal closeness, and marital conflict. (Pituitary and gonadal hormone levels and several pharmacological agents may also influence desire.)

Researchers have only recently begun to study these potential causes of hypoactive sexual desire. Schreiner-Engel & Schiavi (1986) reported that clients with desire disorder were twice as likely as control subjects to have *previously* experienced an affective disturbance. Donahey & Carrol (1993) compared the case presentations of 47 men and 22 women they had treated for low desire and reported that women were likely to report greater stress and distress levels, and more relationship dissatisfaction than were men. Stuart, Hammond & Pett (1987) studied women with desire disorder and control subjects and concluded that the poor quality of the marital relationship was most important in the development of the disorder.

Although *sexual aversion disorder* is understudied, victims of sexual traumas such as rape may be more vulnerable to the development of this extreme fear and avoidance of sex. Several studies provide preliminary support for this hypothesis. Chapman (1989) determined the frequency of sexual dysfunction in women who had experienced sexual or physical assault (30 rape victims and 35 abuse victims). Two to four years after their victimization, over 60% of these women experienced some sexual dysfunction. Katz, Gipson & Turner (1992) developed the Sexual Aversion Scale (SAS) to assess thoughts, feelings, and behaviors consistent with the diagnostic criteria (i.e., "I have avoided sexual relations recently because of my sexual fears"); responses from high school and college students as well as sexual assault victims suggest a positive relationship among a history of sexual victimization, generalized anxiety, and an elevated aversion score.

Male erectile disorder has been the most studied of the sexual dysfunctions. Because adequate blood flow and enervation are necessary for erections, vascular and neurological compromise are prominent physical causes of erectile disorder. In the psychological domain, negative affect, particularly anxiety, has often been proffered as a causal factor. Barlow (1986) conducted a series of studies delineating two main components apparent in men with erectile dysfunction. First, they tend to experience more cognitive interference during sexual activity, primarily negative thoughts which create performance anxiety, and are more likely to focus on their erectile response, usually underestimating the degree of erection. Second, men with erectile problems often experience a cycle of negative affect related to their erectile dysfunction.

Relatively little research has explored the etiology of *arousal disorders* in women. However, like male arousal, we know that the female lubrication-swelling response also relies on intact vascular and neurological functioning. Relationship factors are believed to be important in the development of female arousal disorder. Partners may not provide adequate stimulation; because of poor communication, the problem may be unresolved. A woman may experience a lack of attraction towards a partner despite a wish or desire to engage in sexual activity.

Derogatis and his colleagues (Derogatis & Meyer, 1979; Derogatis, Fagan, Schmidt, Wise & Gilden, 1986) have suggested that women with *orgasmic disorder* may have poorer psychological adjustment, including feelings of inferiority and negative body image. However, interpersonal and sexual technique factors may be more pivotal in the onset of this difficulty. Women with this disorder, compared to control subjects who experience orgasm consistently, are more often dissatisfied with their relationship and the type and range of sexual activity, and their partners were less informed of the woman's sexual preferences (Kilmann, Mills, Caid, Bella, Davidson & Wanlass, 1984).

We do not know much about *male orgasmic disorder*. Reports consist primarily of case studies with individual explanations ranging from fear of castration and previous sexual trauma to medication side effects (Munjack & Kanno, 1979). *Premature ejaculation* may be caused, at least in part, by penile hypersensitivity (Spiess, Geer & O'Donohue, 1984) whereby men ejaculate at a lower level of arousal. However, as a single cause for the problem, this explanation accounts for only a small percentage of cases. A conditioned response may also be involved; it may have been adaptive, in early sexual experiences, for sexual activity to end quickly (e.g., to avoid being discovered). Such sexual settings may also have been anxiety-provoking. Within a diathesis-stress framework, physical hypersensitivity, learned responses, and dyadic overreaction to a rapid ejaculation may each contribute to the development and maintenance of the difficulty.

Dyspareunia may be caused by post-operative tenderness from vaginal surgery, endometriosis, pelvic inflammation, vulvar vestibulitis, and other medical conditions (see Sandberg & Quevillion, 1987). When dyspareunia is not exclusively due to physiological effects, then psychosocial factors such as fear, depressed affect, low self-esteem, distrust, anger, and inadequate communication are often implicated. Several causes of *vaginismus* have been advanced. Painful hymenal tags, a rigid hymen, pelvic tumors, and obstruction from previous vaginal surgery should be evaluated as potential causes (Lamont, 1978). Silverstein (1989) reviewed the case histories of 22 women she had treated for psychogenic vaginismus; in these cases, nearly all of the women had domineering, aggressive fathers. In Silverstein's view, vaginismus was a symptom that served to protect the woman against intercourse which was perceived as a violation or invasion. Interestingly, in the Irish culture, where some of the highest rates of vaginismus have been reported, several authors have also found that women with vaginismus often come from a family where the father is a threatening figure (Barnes, 1986; O'Sullivan, 1979). Negative sexual conditioning involving religious themes was also more common. Based upon clinical observation, it has also been suggested that prior sexual trauma or assault may lead to vaginismus. This causal factor fits into a "learned response" (and "self-protective") model of the development of this disorder. Dyspareunia during assault or early intercourse attempts are thought to cause the involuntary tightening of vaginal muscles upon subsequent vaginal penetration.

As this rapid tour of the empirical foundations suggests, sexual dysfunction can result from a variety of biopsychosocial factors. Although research on etiology remains incomplete, it has influenced current theoretical formulations of the sexual dysfunctions.

Theoretical Foundations

In the space of a single chapter, it is impossible to review the large number of theoretical frameworks that have been proffered to explain the initiation, triggering, and maintenance of the sexual dysfunctions. Therefore, in this section we simply identify several key psychosocial factors that have been proposed by theoreticians to influence the course of sexual dysfunctions. This brief list of individual and dyadic factors is provided as a heuristic guide, which helps to explain why certain treatment strategies (presented in the next section) may be useful.

Theorists have identified several individual characteristics that may predispose or sustain sexual problems. *Lack of knowledge* about sexual anatomy and physiology can lead to difficulties; for example, ignorance about the need for extended foreplay or exogenous lubrication among older adults may lead to inadequate arousal or painful intercourse (Wincze & Carey, 1991). Such ignorance also proves to be a fertile breeding ground for numerous *myths or dysfunctional beliefs*. For example, Zilbergeld (1993), Heiman & LoPiccolo (1988) and others have reminded us over the years that, as a culture, we unwittingly subscribe to an unhealthy, performance-based model of sexuality. In this model, men and women measure themselves against an unwritten but widely accepted set of standards that are inappropriate for most or all of us.

Individuals may also have *skills deficits*; for example, people may not know how to provide pleasure and/or show affection to their partners, or how to maximize their own sexual pleasure. Some individuals report a very limited sexual repertoire that sets limits on what they can try. This can be especially difficult when chronic illness makes their traditional practices less satisfying. When sexual problems emerge, they are often temporary. However, as noted above, some individuals hold very high standards for their sexual "performance." They display *performance anxiety* that can inhibit normal sexual responses and psychological comfort (Masters & Johnson, 1970).

Individuals may also bring *other psychological problems* to the bedroom that impair their ability to participate fully in healthy sexual expression. Individuals who are clinically depressed or anxious, or who experience excessive levels of background stress, or who have alcohol or drug use problems may require individual therapy prior to sex therapy. Less severe psychological difficulties, such as *poor body image* or *mild dysphoria,* may be handled within the context of sex therapy. Individuals who have experienced *prior sexual trauma* may also require individual therapy to address the residual effects of such trauma.

Dyadic factors also play an important role in sexual function and satisfaction. *Global relationship conflict* presents major challenges, of course; because marital problems are the focus of an entire chapter in this book, this topic is not considered further except to say that such global discord must be resolved before mutually satisfying sexual encounters can be expected. Couples who have a solid relationship outside of the bedroom may experience difficulties due to *mismatched sexual scripts* (Rosen & Leiblum, 1988) and/or *inadequate communication.* These problems are commonly addressed in sex therapy.

Clearly other factors can be identified, but this serves as a short list of the most common theoretical foundations underlying the conduct of cognitive-behavioral sex therapy.

Cognitive-Behavioral Treatment

This section begins by noting the importance of a careful assessment and highlight a few preliminary considerations in the conduct of therapy. The majority of this section is devoted to a discussion of the major components in a cognitive-behavioral approach to treatment. (see Wincze & Carey, 1991, for further details.)

The Role of Assessment

The purpose of this chapter is to present information about cognitive-behavioral treatment approaches. However, it is critical to point out that a careful assessment must precede and accompany the therapeutic process. Assessment has several goals: diagnosis, case formulation and treatment planning, and treatment monitoring. In the context of the sexual dysfunctions, the initial goal of assessment is diagnosis, that is, to determine if psychosocial or lifestyle risk factors play a significant role in the maintenance of the disorder. As noted previously, if a "general medical condition" (i.e., endocrine, vascular, or neurologic pathology; cf. APA, 1994) alone can explain the disorder, then the dysfunction would not be considered a psychological or mental disorder. However, if the client functions satisfactorily under some circumstances, then the assessment process should lead toward the development of a comprehensive case formulation (i.e., a working hypothesis of the etiology of the erection problem). This case formulation should emerge from a careful assessment of the role of the previously identified psychosocial or lifestyle risk factors in the initiation and maintenance of the dysfunction, and lead to the development of a treatment plan (Carey, Flasher, Maisto & Turkat, 1984). An ongoing goal of assessment will be to measure the effectiveness of therapy. It is also critical to remind therapists that a careful, biopsychosocial assessment requires collaboration with a multidisciplinary team, typically including one or more medical specialists (e.g., urologist, neurologist). More information about collaborating with other health care providers can be found elsewhere (e.g., Ackerman & Carey, 1995; Carey, Lantinga & Krauss, 1994).

Preliminary Considerations

There are a few general considerations that might be made at the outset. First, my preference – when working with individuals who are currently in an intimate relationship – is to work with the couple, rather than just with the individual. There are certainly instances where this is not possible, but most sex therapists find that more efficient and lasting progress is possible when working with both partners. Second, the procedures discussed here are applicable to both men and women, and to straight and gay couples. Third, it is rarely effective to work on sexual problems when there is an ongoing alcohol or drug use problem. The substance use problem should be treated first before an effective program for sexual dysfunction can be established. Fourth, it is preferable to meet with clients on a weekly basis. Clients can be seen at a more accelerated pace during the initial assessment but weekly sessions allow for homework practice without losing continuity. The spacing of sessions should be reevaluated regularly to determine if a different schedule will better serve the couple, for whatever reason, without disrupting the flow of therapy. Once a couple or individual has demonstrated that they can follow therapy instructions, then spacing sessions every several weeks may be worthwhile, especially after progress has been established. When sessions are spaced out, instructions should be given which would allow frequent phone contact if appropriate. Fifth, for most couples, significant progress can be expected within 8– 16 sessions. Complicated cases (e.g., involving a partner with a history of sexual abuse or psychopathology, or severe marital difficulties) may require a longer commitment to therapy or preliminary individual therapy.

Components of Cognitive-Behavioral Sex Therapy

In this section several cognitive-behavioral components that tend to be useful for most sexual dysfunctions are reviewed. Treatment for each of the sexual dysfunctions incorporates one or more of these components, tailored to the specific context of the problem. For example, therapy for female orgasmic disorder may include education about the female sexual response, sensate focus, and communication skills training to help the couple become more comfortable expressing their sexual preferences.

Education: reducing ignorance and enhancing knowledge. Providing information to clients may be the most common component of sex therapy. Basic information about primary and secondary sexual characteristics, genital anatomy and physiology, the sexual response cycle, and gender differences in sexual preferences and experiences might be offered. Information on family planning and birth control may be appropriate. Education about the normal changes in male and female functioning due to aging, chronic illness, medication use, etc. can be used to support the important and "normal" role of foreplay in adult sexual activity. Normative data regarding common sexual practices and experiences, preferences and dislikes, can be shared with clients to help normalize their experience and reduce concerns that some clients harbor regarding their "normality."

Many clients are eager to learn more, and some request reading suggestions. There are many excellent books available. For men, consider Zilbergeld's (1993) book, *The New Male Sexuality: A Guide to Sexual Fulfillment*; for women, consider Heiman & LoPiccolo's (1988) *Becoming Orgasmic: A Sexual and Personal Growth Program for Women*. However, there are many fine books available (including many college-level human sexuality textbooks) and the therapist should develop a list of favorites. The therapist may want to purchase several copies of these favorites and have them available to loan. We advise that the therapist read any book before recommending it to a client. Also, be prepared to discuss its contents during the sessions.

Since the early 1980s, when the viral sexually transmitted diseases (STDs), including herpes and the human immunodeficiency virus (HIV) became increasingly prevalent, it has become increasingly common for clients to request information about STDs and safer sexual practices. Clients without adequate information sometimes avoid sexual encounters and the opportunities for intimate relationships, or engage unknowingly in high risk activities, two outcomes that cause concern. Thus, ethical practice of sex therapy requires that therapists be well-informed about HIV and other STDs, and educate clients about risk reduction (Carey, 1998).

Cognitive restructuring I: setting realistic goals for therapy. Often clients enter therapy with magical thoughts about miracle "cures" or fantasies about erotic pleasures described in the popular fiction. Clients who seek sex therapy have been influenced by misleading stories in the popular media of sexual prowess and new erotic experiences; many seek quick fixes to long-standing problems. In contrast, most empirically-oriented sex therapists do *not* believe that the primary goal of therapy should be to increase erections, choreograph simultaneous or multiple orgasms, or discover "g" spots. The therapist must not establish (or reinforce) goals that increase performance anxiety (discussed later). For example, goals such as "increasing erection firmness, "producing orgasm," or "controlling ejaculation" may actually exacerbate the problem, especially if performance anxiety already inhibits sexual satisfaction.

Therapists have the difficult job of helping clients to reframe their goals, and often to develop new ones. For example, clients are encouraged to create or restore mutual sexual comfort and satisfaction. We emphasize the importance of gaining a sense of comfort with one's sexuality, of taking more time for sexual expression and making it a priority, and eliminating performance pressures that can block the sexual response and impair enjoyment. We strive to help the couple to understand the psychological as well as the mechanical and technical factors that contribute to sexual satisfaction and enjoyment. These therapeutic goals must be developed *together with the clients* in such a way that the couple understands that, in order to reach advanced goals (e.g., heightened sexual pleasure), they must first work on preliminary goals (e.g., improved communication). Moreover, it is important for the couple to understand that achieving these preliminary goals may be slower than the "cure" they were expecting. We encourage clients to conceptualize these preliminary goals as "stepping stones" toward more advanced goals.

McCarthy (1993) points out that establishing realistic expectations also helps to prevent relapse following successful therapy. He reminds us that sex serves different purposes for each of us, and that these purposes may differ between partners on any given occasion. If partners expect sex to go perfectly on each occasion (as it does in the movies), then disappointment is likely. Rather, a couple can be encouraged to recognize the inherent variability in sexual experiences, and to understand this variability is usually not a sign of failure or incompatibility.

Cognitive restructuring II: reducing maladaptive beliefs. Sexual dysfunction is often associated with *general* negative thoughts and feelings toward sex (in general), oneself, or one's partner. With some clients, fears regarding fainting, losing control, or increased vulnerability have been encountered. Prior to the use specific sexual skills building procedures (e.g., masturbation training; discussed later), the therapist should first explore in detail whether these general negative cognitions are present. It would be a strategic blunder to outline masturbation training without first assessing the couple's beliefs about the nature of the problem, and the acceptability of masturbation. Cognitive restructuring strategies found helpful in the treatment of depression and anxiety may be useful.

Maladaptive cognitions often accompany specific dysfunctions; for example, a dysfunction may be misconstrued in such a way that the dysfunction creates larger problems. For example, a 35-year-old male client was troubled by "premature ejaculation" and sought professional assistance for this problem. His "problem" was that he ejaculated within 2 or 3 min of vaginal containment and thrusting. He had learned in his upbringing that such "premature ejaculation" was an indication that he was gay. Both his rapid ejaculation and the idea of being gay were very threatening to him, leading to mild clinical depression. Part of the intervention involved sharing information about latency to orgasm in young men, and debunking the previously acquired misinformation about premature ejaculation and sexual orientation. There were other, more complex aspects of this client that required additional attention, but these concerns could be resolved by providing normative, scientifically-based information.

Similarly, males who experience erectile disorder may become upset with themselves and fear ridicule from their partner. In heterosexual males, fears of homosexuality may emerge; that is, heterosexual men often interpret difficulty in obtaining or maintaining an erection as a sign that they are gay. Regardless of the precipitating factors, most cases of erectile disorder are maintained by interfering thoughts which may precede and occur during sexual relations. These interfering thoughts are not erotic thoughts and they decrease arousal. In non-dysfunctional men, thoughts preceding and occurring during sexual relations usually focus on their partner's or their own body parts, seductive behaviors, and anticipation of arousal and pleasure. In contrast, the dysfunctional male may be preoccupied with worries regarding the firmness of his erection; images of one's partner being disappointed or angry; and feelings of anxiety and depression (Ackerman & Carey, 1995).

The therapist must address interfering thoughts when they occur by helping the client to "restructure" her or his thoughts; that is, to focus on sexually facilitating thoughts rather than on sexually inhibiting ones. One way to help clients to refocus their thinking is to have clients recall their thought content during past *satisfying* sexual experiences. This usually sensitizes clients to the types of positive thoughts they should concentrate on. If they have difficulty remembering positive sexual thoughts, the therapist should suggest "typical" helpful thoughts. Once clients are able to readily identify the positive sexual thinking process, treatment may advance to sexual skills building exercises. During procedures such as sensate focus, the goal can be reframed to focus on positive sexual thinking (rather than achieving or maintaining an erection). Although the client may return to negative thinking, the therapist can help by encouraging him to return his focus onto erotic thoughts and images. Gradually, with practice, disruptive thoughts and images should become less intrusive.

When a partner is involved in treatment, it is important to also consider that partner's cognitions around the dysfunction. For example, in the case of a man with erectile disorder, the partner can be expected to have negative cognitions.

Partners may fear that they are no longer attractive, that the man does not love her anymore, that the partner is having an affair, etc. We usually ask the partner what she thinks is the cause of the erectile problem. It is very important to help to clear up possible misunderstandings before proceeding to an intervention, such as sensate focus exercises. If potential misunderstandings are not addressed, it is likely they will arise again and sabotage treatment progress.

As noted earlier, there are widespread *cultural myths* that can impair healthy sexual functioning and reduce sexual satisfaction. Zilbergeld (1993) argues that, although we think that we are sexually liberated and sophisticated, our behavior reveals the opposite. In connection with male sexuality, he identifies 12 myths that many men (and women) subscribe to:

1. We're liberated folks who are very comfortable with sex.
2. A real man isn't into sissy stuff like feelings and communicating.
3. All touching is sexual or should lead to sex.
4. A man is always interested in and always ready for sex.
5. A real man "performs" in sex.
6. Sex is centered on a hard penis and what's done with it.
7. Sex equals intercourse.
8. A man should be able to make the earth move for his partner, or at the very least knock her socks off.
9. Good sex requires orgasm.
10. Men don't have to listen to women in sex.
11. Good sex is spontaneous, with no planning and no talking.
12. Real men don't have sex problems.

Myths such as these, especially when they are shared by a couple, can impair sexual functioning and satisfaction.

Other beliefs and myths can be similarly harmful to clients. For example, among older clients there is sometimes the belief that foreplay is for "kids" or that intercourse is the only true form of sex. Such beliefs can be counterproductive for middle-aged or elderly couples. Similarly, the belief that an erection must appear before sexual activity in order to signal sexual interest can limit a person's sexual opportunities. The net effect of these beliefs is that a male who does not obtain an erection prior to intercourse (and without manual or oral stimulation) will not participate in sex.

Cognitive aspects of sex therapy can involve challenging some or all of these myths, sometimes by presenting new information, or by offering alternative views. Clients should always be encouraged to ask questions during therapy about things they "know" to be true about sex. This will not always be easy, though. For example, one middle-aged client – who was woefully ignorant about human sexuality – recently boasted during a session that he knew it all because he had spent 4 years in the military and during his tour he had "seen it all." His arrogance was really just a cover for his embarrassment about how little he truly knew.

Behavioral skills training I: enhancing client's sexual repertoire. The cognitive components of therapy can be supplemented with behavioral components that have proven helpful. Approaches have been developed to assist clients to broaden a narrow repertoire, and to overcome previously traumatic experiences. In this section, we focus on the former.

Use of erotic audiovisual materials. Many clients have had limited exposure to positive sexual models. Often the media attends only to negative sexual events, including sensational sexual crimes, sexual exploitation, or miscellaneous instances of sexual extremes. When more common sexual experiences are depicted, they often focus on youth and the early stages of courtship. Thus, individuals have few opportunities to expand their repertoire over the lifespan in a way that keep sex fresh and new.

Erotica (defined as the artistic depiction of consensual sexual relations) can often be used to foster more tolerant attitudes, teach partners how to eroticize safer sexual practices, encourage sexual experimentation, and introduce partners to novel positions and behaviors. Erotica can also be used when a couples' sexual repertoire has become stale or rigid. Elsewhere, it has been suggested that low desire in an otherwise happy couple may reflect a kind of sexual habituation (Wincze & Carey, 1991); that is, couples who are in stable, long-term relationships but who always approach sex in the same fashion may become bored. In such instances, erotica may be used (often in conjunction with other behavioral changes) to stimulate the couple's sexual appetite. If the use of erotica is approached as a sexual experience, attention should be paid to mood, setting, and other important ingredients.

However, erotic materials should be used only after a thorough discussion between the therapist and client. Objections to pornography, particularly the objectification and degradation of women, should be addressed so there are no barriers to accepting and experiencing non-degrading but erotic materials. When the therapist is confident that the client can use erotic stimuli without negative objections, then the nature of and details of use should be worked out.

Because tastes differ, therapists should develop their own library of materials that they have previewed so that they can make knowledgeable recommendations to clients. Clients can be encouraged to browse in video rental stores, or to subscribe to catalogs produced by reputable sexual supply vendors. The need for safer sex materials has increased the social acceptance of such vendors, which may allow these often marginal companies to survive in a competitive market place.

Masturbation training. Another harmless way to enhance a client's sexual repertoire involves masturbation, now increasingly used in sex therapy. The two most common applications are with women who are anorgasmic, and with men who experience premature ejaculation. The book *Becoming Orgasmic* by Heiman & LoPiccolo (1988) provides the rationale for masturbation training in women. Specifically, it is argued that, for most women, the easiest, most intense, and most reliable orgasms occur during masturbation. For those women who have not yet experienced orgasm, masturbation provides a reliable way to allow them this pleasure. Heiman and LoPiccolo outline a program for helping women to use masturbation as a vehicle for self-exploration and liberation. Over time, women include their partners, who are taught how to touch and pleasure the woman.

With men who are concerned about premature ejaculation, masturbation can also be used to raise the men's awareness of arousal and orgasm stimulation. Masturbation is often used in conjunction with the penile squeeze method (Masters & Johnson, 1970) or the stop-start technique (Semans, 1956); that latter is discussed below.

Masturbation training must also be approached in a similar fashion to the use of erotica. Negative cognitions must be explored first and then detailed attention must be paid to maximizing a positive sexual experience. The therapist must also not assume that the client knows how to masturbate. For example, one client reported to us a lack of success in attempting to masturbate. When he was asked how he masturbated he reported that he masturbated with his hand open so that his palm rubbed against the underside of his penis. In addition, he reported putting "honey" on his penis as a "lubricant." He thought he read somewhere that honey was a good lubricant. Specific instructions with pictures helped this client to learn how to masturbate successfully.

Masturbation training helps some clients to become more sensitive to the necessary conditions for a positive sexual experience. In clients who lack desire and sexual confidence, masturbation training can lead to positive experiences that build both desire and confidence.

Behavioral skills training II: overcoming maladaptive experiences. In addition to limited positive experiences, some clients have had negative sexual experiences whose residual effect is negative. Several behavioral strategies have been developed to help such clients to overcome this prior negative learning.

Progressive dilation for vaginismus and dyspareunia. The most common psychological etiologic explanation of vaginismus and dyspareunia is founded in prior sexual trauma and negative sexual messages. Overcoming these problems often involves the complex task of reviewing and processing negative sexual experiences and associated cognitions. In contrast, clients who have not had extreme sexual trauma often profit from an in vivo desensitization procedure involving gradual insertion of a finger or dilator into the vaginal opening. Some clinicians advise the use of a graduated set of dilators to desensitize a woman to vaginal insertion. The dilators may be obtained from a medical supply house and come in graduated thickness. The woman should be instructed to practice in privacy using the dilators starting with the thinnest dilator. Penetration depth can be varied and practiced and only when a woman is comfortable with inserting a dilator for a period of 5 min should she move on to the next size. A vaginal lubricant can be advised.

A recent report from Hong Kong describes a case in which a 30-year-old woman did not benefit from the usual type of dilating objects (Ng, 1992). This woman had been unable to consummate her marriage of 3 years, and did not profit from prior sex therapy. Interestingly, desensitization therapy with a string of plastic balls of graduated size was successful, and allowed the woman to have intercourse after 12 weeks. This example reminds us of the need to be creative and flexible.

However, it is probably more convenient and easier for most women to practice insertion using their own fingers. Again, the strategy should be thoroughly discussed and reviewed with the client before actually suggesting it. It may be helpful to approach the topic by saying "some women who have difficulty with penetration have found by practicing insertion very gradually they can overcome the problem. How would you feel about the technique of practicing insertion while you are alone and in complete privacy of your home?" Once a woman has agreed to try, the therapist should explain that she (the client) is in complete control of the procedures. It should be emphasized that the depth of penetration and length of time of penetration can be controlled and varied by the client. The client should approach this while bathing or while relaxed on their bed and should start with inserting her little finger. Over a number of sessions she should work up to inserting two fingers for a few minutes. Because many women will have strong objections to touching their genitals or masturbating, this exercise has to be put into perspective and distinguished from masturbation.

As a woman becomes more comfortable with insertion, her partner can be included in the procedure. Again, it should be emphasized that the woman must be in complete control of the procedure and that she can stop the procedure at any time. Moreover, the insertion process should be approached gradually with partial penetration and withdrawal. This process is usually started with digital penetration; over a number of sessions, the couple moves toward penile insertion. Again, the use of vaginal lubricants may be a useful addition to the insertion procedures.

Squeeze technique for premature ejaculation. The squeeze technique involves instructing the male to masturbate to a point that he feels would result in ejaculation if he continued. He should pause in the masturbation at this point and squeeze the head of his penis along the coronal ridge by placing his forefinger and middle finger on one side of his penis and his thumb opposite on the other side. The squeeze is recommended to be firm and lasting about 10 s. By repeating this process several times before allowing ejaculation to occur, and by practicing this procedure over a number of sessions, the man will learn to control his ejaculation.

Although the squeeze technique can be an effective procedure for overcoming premature ejaculation, therapists should be cautioned not to endorse this "solution" if there are other relationship problems. Complaints of premature ejaculation may mask difficult relationship problems. Therefore, in many cases of premature ejaculation, it is useful to direct our initial discussion to the question: "Why do you have sex?" After some thought, a number of reasons are suggested by clients. "To have pleasure, or because it feels good" may be common responses. We point out that couples have sex for a variety of reasons including pleasure, to express love and affection, to make up after an argument, to have children, to make oneself feel better, to please a partner, etc. Moreover, the reason will change from occasion to occasion. The goal of this general discussion is to impress upon our clients that pleasure, or pleasuring, and all of the other reasons we have sex, are *not* dependent upon on the length of time between intromission and orgasm. Furthermore, the length of time a man "lasts" should be looked upon as but one small part of the whole sexual exchange. Indeed, the goal of this discussion is to encourage the couple to focus on general pleasuring rather than orgasm. It can be helpful to encourage them to continue intercourse even after ejaculation. This takes the pressure off of the timing of ejaculation, and properly puts the emphasis on the total sexual relationship. This approach usually results in a couple reporting a more satisfying relationship. Interestingly, even though we do not focus on the length of time between intromission and ejaculation, this time interval usually increases.

A second question to ask clients and their partners is: "What do you believe is causing the problem?" In some cases of premature ejaculation, the female partner might express anger because her sexual needs are going unmet. Similarly, some women may believe that their men are able to control ejaculation more than is truly the case; they might interpret their partners haste as the man's way of being thoughtless, or inconsiderate. While there are insensitive lovers out there, it is rare for that a client can control his ejaculation in order to hurt his partner's feelings. To the contrary, most men who seek treatment for premature ejaculation want desperately to please their partners. They tend to be embarrassed and confused about their difficulty.

Sensate focus: reducing performance anxiety. Once a sexual dysfunction has emerged, it is common for men and women to worry about this problem during sexual activity. Worrying leads to self-depreciating cognitions and distracts attention away from pleasurable and arousing cognitions, creating a vicious cycle of dysfunction – worry – self-depreciating thoughts – increasing dysfunction – etc.

To address this vicious cycle, Masters and Johnson (1970) developed "sensate focus," a set of procedures designed to help a couple to develop a heightened awareness of, and *focusing* on, *sensations* rather than performance. One goal of this approach is to reduce client anxiety by seeking something that is immediately achievable (i.e., pleasurable touching) rather than striving toward a goal. Working for a larger erection or simultaneous orgasm that may not be achievable increases the risk of "failure" and embarrassment.

Optimally, sensate focus is structured but flexible. Sensate focus is structured in that clients are given explicit instructions for intimacy; if these instructions are followed, the couple will gradually regain confidence in themselves and in their relationship. Sensate focus is flexible in that it can be accommodated to any couple's unique circumstances. In general, sensate focus is designed to bring about change gradually. It is anticipated that change will take time, and there is no effort to rush ahead. One example is that clients are often advised to discontinue intercourse early in therapy so that they can relearn the basics of being affectionate, receiving pleasure, etc. The gradual approach can be disappointing to some clients because it can seem slow, so special care in needed in explaining the importance of this approach to clients.

Home-based sensate focus exercises need to be conducted in a shared and non threatening environment. The therapist should encourage the couple to "practice" in a physically and psychologically comfortable and private space. Awkward circumstances are not conducive to relaxed enjoyable sexual relations. Couples sometimes need to be told to minimize interfering circumstances. Even simple suggestions such as arranging for a baby-sitter, cleaning up the bedroom, or putting on relaxing music can be helpful. Many partners, once ensconced in a relationship, do not attend to courtship or romantic rituals. Sometimes they need to be reminded of the efforts they made during courtship to "set the mood." We often encourage clients to schedule a time for sex, and to plan for it with as much effort as they might for any other special event in their lives. We remind them that anticipation fuels desire.

As intimated above, the *procedures* of sensate focus involve encouraging intimacy through gradual, non-threatening "sexercises." The general operating procedure involves homework, which encourages the couple to engage in sexually-related exercises, and ongoing therapy sessions, which are used to discuss the exercises, emotions triggered by these exercises, problems, etc.

Homework involves explicit instructions that the therapist has provided to the client; these instructions require practice of some exercise outside of the therapeutic sessions. Both therapist and client understand that the homework will be reviewed and modified (as necessary) at each session. The homework exercises can be broken down into four "steps"; these steps are typically followed in a sequential fashion, but there are? o absolutes here. Whether each step should be included, and the amount of time devoted to each are clinical judgments.

The first step of sensate focus typically included *non-genital touching* (i.e., pleasuring) while both partners are dressed in comfortable clothing. Variations in the amount of clothing worn, the length of sessions, who initiates, the types of behaviors participated in, and the frequency of sessions should all be discussed in the therapy sessions before a couple goes home to practice. The couple should begin their physical involvement at a level that is acceptable to both participants.

Because many couples will find this to be a somewhat slow and indirect method, the therapist must emphasize right from the start that (a) they are going through a necessary process in order to address their long-term goal, but that (b) the short-term goal is to focus on sensations and not performance. Discuss with the couple the mechanics of the approach including structured versus unstructured, frequency, potentially interfering factors and anticipation of any problems.

Even if the therapist gives a clear explanation of the non-performance aspects of sensate focus, some clients will misunderstand. So, I tell clients: "The next time you have a therapy session, I will *not* ask you about erections or orgasms; what I will ask you about is your ability to concentrate on receiving and giving pleasure, and on your ability to enjoy what you are doing." This message is repeated because most couples are performance-oriented (i.e., focus on erection and orgasm) and, unless the therapist challenges this notion, they will retain performance criteria during the sensate focus exercises.

At this point, the therapist might also discuss with the client or couple the concepts of performance anxiety, "all-or-none" thinking (e.g., sex equals intercourse), and other factors that interfere with enjoyable sex. Sensate focus cannot proceed unless the couple understands these ideas, acknowledges their importance, and appreciates the need for a new approach in thinking and behavior.

The second step, typically, will involve *genital pleasuring*. During this phase of therapy, partners are encouraged to extend gentle touching to the genital and breast regions. Partners are encouraged to caress each other, in turn, in a way that is pleasurable. As before, the couple should be discouraged from focusing on performance-related goals (i.e., erection, orgasm, etc.). As the therapist progresses through sensate focus, he or she should review factors that facilitate or inhibit goals. By discussing these factors in a non judgmental way, the couple can become more in control of their own progress and feel less like pupils in a classroom.

Once a couple becomes comfortable with genital touching and is ready to resume sexual intercourse, it is often necessary to emphasize that even sexual intercourse can be broken down into several behaviors. Thus, some couples may be encouraged to engage in *"containment without thrusting."* That is, the receptive partner (i.e., the woman in heterosexual couples) permits penetration and controls all aspects of this exercise. For example, the depth of penetration and the amount of time spent on penetration can be varied. Again, flexibility and variation is encouraged in order to remove pressure associated with a couple's tendency to think in "all-or-none" terms.

A common problem with this stage of sensate focus is that therapists rigidly adhere to the proscription on intercourse (Lipsius, 1987). If employed mechanically, proscription of intercourse can lead to loss of erotic feelings, loss of spontaneity, unnecessary frustration, and increase in resistance. An alternative approach is to discuss with the couple the potential benefits and liabilities of proscription and point out that the couple is working on a process that will build for the future.

However, a proscriptive approach may help a couple resume physical contact under certain circumstances. Three circumstances that come to mind are if: (a) a couple is very stressed by sexual performance, (b) there are a lot of interfering performance-oriented thoughts, and/or (c) the couple has avoided all physical contact. On the other hand, couples who have not approached sexual relations so rigidly or with such intense emotional reactions may benefit from a general understanding of the purpose of sensate focus but with a more relaxed attitude toward proscription.

The final step of sensate focus proper includes thrusting and *intercourse*. Again, it is usually a good idea to encourage the receptive partner to initiate the movement, and for movements to be slow and gradual. As always, the couple is encouraged to focus on the sensations association with intercourse, and not to be concerned about orgasm. The couple might try experimenting with different positions, and not only assume the same position(s) they have used prior to therapy.

These are the procedures that generally constitute what is commonly referred to as sensate focus. Others have elaborated the basics provided here (e.g., Masters & Johnson, 1970; Wincze & Carey, 1991); the therapist may want to consult these references after having worked comfortably with those above. At this point, however, some of the potential problems that a therapist may encounter need to be identified.

Sensate focus can be misapplied and misunderstood by both therapist and client. It is not unusual for couples to enter therapy and report that they had previously tried to "abstain from sex" and this did not work. For example, a new couple explained that they had participated in sex therapy before and had tried sensate focus. From their perspective, the approach used was "not to have sex." The couple had no understanding of the purpose of the procedure and, as a result, left their previous therapy dissatisfied.

McCarthy (1985) pointed out a number of therapists' common mistakes in the use of sensate focus. One common mistake that therapists make is not engaging the couple in the decision making process. This often results in noncompliance. A second common mistake is when a therapist demands performance as part of the procedure – "the next step in the procedure is to stimulate your partner in the genital area to the point of orgasm." This type of a statement may increase performance anxiety, especially in a person vulnerable to that response. It would be preferable to state "you have done well so far in concentrating on your sensations and feelings as you and your partner stimulate each other. Thus far you have included genital caressing. What do you feel the next step should be?" This approach allows a variety of responses without an anticipation of sexual failure or pressure. One additional mistake some therapists make involves premature termination of the sensate focus approach when a couple is non-compliant or encounters difficulties. Premature termination only serves to reinforce avoidance. Difficulties should be discussed at length and barriers to progress should be identified and removed.

Another difficulty can occur when therapy moves into the arena of "homework procedures." At this time, a conflict could occur between being natural and unstructured, and being mechanistic and structured. Most couples and individuals express a preference to approach homework assignments in a "natural, unstructured" manner. With this approach the therapist describes the procedures involved and the principles behind the procedures but leaves it up to the couple to schedule other details such as the frequency. Although this may intuitively be the preferred strategy, the therapist can expect couples to return to therapy without having carried out the assignment! The reason for this is that all-too-often there is such a strong history of avoidance; thus, the individual or couple cannot get started without raising anxiety levels unacceptably high.

To avert these outcomes, the therapist can explain the pros and cons of structured versus unstructured strategies before providing homework exercises. The client can then choose a strategy and, in so doing, be fully aware of the potential for noncompliance. At times, a client may try out a certain strategy and upon failure, adopt a different approach. In addition to exploring the issue of structured versus unstructured practice, the therapist should explore other potential obstacles in the face of carrying out therapy procedures; for example, relatives living in the house, work schedules, medical concerns, and travel plans. Once these potential obstacles are identified, and solutions generated, then the rationale and details of homework can begin.

There are many benefits that may result from the sensate focus procedure. New behaviors may be learned along with new approaches to sexual interactions. I have dealt with couples who have had very narrow approaches to sex. It is not unusual, for example, for a couple to report that they engage in no touching behavior at all. They may kiss once, then have intercourse! It is not uncommon to work with couples who view foreplay as "something that kids do." For such couples, sensate focus offers a structured opportunity to challenge established habits that may be restricting pleasure and causing sex problems.

Sensate focus can also be quite diagnostic. Difficulties that emerge often carry important information about other problems that a couple is having. These other problems often cannot be addressed through sensate focus itself. Sensate focus may also help to change a person's perception of their partner. A common problem among men is to approach sexual intimacy with intercourse as the only goal. In a heterosexual couple, the female partner may begin to see herself as an object of her partner's pleasure and not as a companion who is loved. The sensate focus procedure can help a couple to focus on each other with mutual affection rather than as objects of arousal.

Communication training: talking through common difficulties. Occasionally, partners disagree, fight, are inconsiderate of one another, and become preoccupied with work, child care, or finances during sex; in other words, they are human. Normal difficulties that accompany all aspects of a shared life are to be expected. When such difficulties occur during sex, however, there is a greater chance that they will not be discussed. Traditional sex roles or other cultural constraints may impede healthy discussion of sexual difficulties. To overcome such difficulties, a couple needs to learn to talk through these everyday moments of disagreement. Thus, communication training serves a critical role in sex therapy.

Communication training should pervade all aspects of the therapy. That is, it is not really a separate component. Throughout assessment and therapy, the therapist should serve as a model of good communication. This is achieved by active listening, display of empathy, asking clients to express themselves clearly, and other such social and communication skills. In addition, the therapist should continually look for improvement in communication skills and point these out to a couple when they occur. It is helpful to inform the couple that, throughout the therapy, communication skills are important and will be addressed routinely. By stating this at the outset, an individual will not feel targeted when a communication issue is raised.

In some couples, there are problems communicating outside of the bedroom involving all shared experiences. In such cases, there may be an enhanced need for specialized training. For further discussion of these aspects, the interested reader is referred to the chapter on marital problems in this book.

Sexual scripting: recognizing and negotiating sexual preferences. A *sexual script* refers to an individual's organized set of preferences regarding the various circumstances (when, where, what, why, with whom) that surround sexual activity. Two types of sexual scripts have been identified (Rosen, Leiblum & Spector, 1994): (a) the performative or overt script, which describes the behavioral practices of the couple, and (b) the ideal or fantasized script, which each partner holds separately.

Rosen, Leiblum, and their colleagues have described several ways in which scripts may influence sexual adjustment and satisfaction (Gagnon, Rosen & Leiblum, 1982; Leiblum & Rosen, 1991; Rosen & Leiblum, 1988; Rosen et al., 1994). For example, they have hypothesized that sexual dysfunction may follow a "lack of congruence of (sexual) script parameters between partners" (Rosen & Leiblum, 1988, p. 168). A common instance involves partners with different levels of desire. Initially this difference might be masked because one partner (usually the less desirous) accommodates to the other. Over time, however, some resentment develops and the problem surfaces. In such couples, it is common for the less desirous partner to be labeled as the "client." As it turns out, however, there is simply a discrepancy between a relatively low desire partner and a relatively high desire partner. In such couples, the therapist can expect communication and problem-solving skills to be poor; these will require attention before the couple can begin to negotiate a sexual pattern that is mutually acceptable and satisfying.

Individual's sexual preferences are not expected to align perfectly, just as we do not expect vacation, or eating, or interior decorating preferences to be perfectly compatible. In these other domains, however, it seems that couples have less difficulty asserting their preferences and negotiating a compromise that is acceptable to both partners. With sexual preferences, individuals may often not have thought through their needs, or perhaps they feel guilty about such erotic preferences or needs. It can be helpful to encourage each partner to generate a "wish" list of intimate activities, and then discuss these with their partner. For example, in one couple, one partner expressed a strong desire for a sensuous back rub during sex. Her partner was happy to provide this, but had never realized her preference. In another couple, the male found oral stimulation ticklish, which reduced his arousal; however, he was reluctant to voice his preference because he thought he "should" enjoy oral sex.

Encouraging partners to recognize their preferences and communicate them effectively (Purnine & Carey, 1997) often proves to be quite helpful in therapy. When there are points of disagreement, for example, about the frequency of sexual activity, these can be negotiated in a fair and open discussion.

A second type of difficulty involving scripts occurs when the shared performative script is dysfunctional. Rosen et al. (1994) encourage therapists to assess carefully both the performative and ideal scripts of the couple, and then to analyze the performative script regarding its complexity, rigidity, and conventionality, as well as noting the resultant couple satisfaction. They have found that when performative scripts are unduly restricted, repetitive, and inflexible, that satisfaction is low for both partners. They suggest the introduction of novel or more effective stimulation techniques. These stimulation techniques can include the use of audio-visual materials, or discussion of ideal script and fantasies. In one approach, Rosen et al. (1994) encourage partners to construct and later exchange a list of sexual fantasies. This exchange can be done through the therapist, who might prescribe homework script modifications in a fashion similar to sensate focus exercises. Careful experimentation and subsequent discussion can lead to revised scripts that offer more stimulation and lead to greater mutual satisfaction. This process may serve as a model for future revisions, in a relapse prevention style.

Relapse prevention: building toward the future. Initial gains made in therapy can atrophy over time as other demands take priority, or as partners change due to other life circumstances. This, too, is to be expected and is not unusual. Thus, it is wise to anticipate such relapses and build in warning signs and relapse prevention strategies. The ultimate goal of relapse prevention strategies is to maximize the likelihood that therapeutic improvements will be preserved over a long period, and to minimize the disruptive effects of new stressors as they occur.

McCarthy (1993) has proposed a cognitive-behavioral approach for applying relapse prevention strategies to the treatment of the sexual dysfunctions. He provides several specific guidelines for preventing relapse and encouraging generalization of treatment gains:

1. Encourage clients to re-allocate therapy session time (i.e., the time used during therapy for meeting with the therapist) for couple dates after therapy termination. This is an investment in the relationship, and a reminder that the partners are committed to the success of their relationship, long-term. Couples might also be encouraged to establish intimacy dates and weekends without children. Such times take the pressure off of one partner, who may feel pressured to always initiate or establish "dates."

2. Establish 6-month follow-up sessions for at least 1 year, and preferably 2 years after termination. This communicates the therapist's continuing commitment to the couple, encourages the couple to maintain and enhance the therapeutic gains, and provides a tangible reminder of future accounting sessions.

3. Schedule sensate focus session at least monthly. This commitment to non-demand pleasuring without the pressure of intercourse helps to prevent the couple from falling back into a performance orientation.

4. Teach the clients that, when a problem occurs, it is a lapse to learn from, not an inevitable decline into relapse. Even among the best adjusted couples with wonderful sexual rapport, it is not unusual to have sexual misadventures. However, this normal variation might be misconstrued by couples made vulnerable by a history of dysfunction. It is wise to anticipate this, and prepare couples for it as well. Couples can be taught coping techniques for the inevitable miscommunications, or for sexual encounters that are disappointingly mediocre.

5. Advise the couple how to establish intimate and erotic ways to connect and reconnect. Many couples rely upon tired and restrictive sex roles, which require the man to initiate sexual encounters and the women to initiate emotional expression. Encourage couples to diverge from this limiting role, and to help each to assert his or her needs for both emotional and sexual intimacy.

McCarthy argues that use of these and related strategies will help the couple to develop a sexual style that is resilient and mutually satisfying. Couples who receive such therapy are more likely to inoculate themselves against sexual dysfunction in the future.

Conclusions and Future Directions

Understanding of cognitive-behavioral treatment of the sexual dysfunctions has advanced considerably since the pioneering work of Albert Ellis. Drawing upon these advances in this chapter, information about the prevalence and etiology of these difficulties has been presented and a guide provided for their treatment with cognitive-behavioral approaches. Our progress should not deceive us, however, for there is still much that we need to know about the cognitive-behavioral treatment of the sexual dysfunctions.

Many areas warrant further investigation. First, we need to know more about all of the sexual dysfunctions that occur in women. Relatively few investigations have explored the etiology of sexual impairment in women. Additional research is needed on the treatment of dysfunctions in women. Second, we need to know more about co-morbidity, that is, how commonly do sexual dysfunctions occur in the context of other Axis I or Axis II disorders, and what special considerations are required in such cases? Although the treatment of sexual dysfunction is often referred to as "sex therapy," this label may belie the complexity of many clients' difficulties. That is, "sex therapy" may be an apt descriptor for clients whose problems are relatively straightforward and not complicated by intrapsychic problems, or dyadic problems extending beyond the sexual domain. However, many clients in the 1990s present with a variety of complex concerns which require therapeutic strategies from outside the traditional sex therapy domain. Sex therapists have been recognizing for over a decade now that the excellent success rate of sex therapy in the 1970s and early 1980s has been replaced with outcomes more common to the general practice of psychotherapy (Hawton, 1992). Third, we need to explore the efficacy of combining medical and psychological treatments. Unidimensional treatments focusing on only one part of the person are likely to be less effective than are multi-modal interventions. Fourth, we continue to need high quality treatment outcome research documenting the strengths and weaknesses of cognitive-behavioral sex therapy. Continued investment in clinical research will increase the value and efficacy of cognitive-behavioral sex therapy, and ensure the continuation of this specialty into the 21st century.

Acknowledgments

Preparation of this chapter was supported by a Scientist Development Award to Michael P. Carey from the National Institute of Mental Health.

References

Ackerman, M. D., & Carey, M. P. (1995). Psychology's role in the assessment of erectile dysfunction: Historical precedents, current knowledge, and methods. *Journal of Consulting and Clinical Psychology, 63,* 862–876.

APA (1994). *Diagnostic and statistical manual of mental disorders,* 4th edition (DSM-IV). Washington, DC: American Psychiatric Association.

Ard, B. N. (1977). Sex in lasting marriages: A longitudinal study. *Journal of Sex Research, 13,* 274–285.

Bachman, G. A., Leiblum, S. R., & Grill, J. (1989). Brief sexual inquiry in gynecological practice. *Obstetrics and Gynecology, 73,* 425–427.

Barlow, D. H. (1986). Causes of sexual dysfunction: The role of anxiety and cognitive interference. *Journal of Consulting and Clinical Psychology, 54,* 140–148.

Barnes, J. (1986). Primary vaginismus (Part 2): Aetiological factors. *Irish Medical Journal, 79,* 62–65.

Bond, J. B., & Tramer, R. R. (1983). Older adult perceptions of attitudes toward sex among the elderly. *Canadian Journal on Aging, 2,* 63–70.

Carey, M. P. (1998). Assessing and reducing risk of infection with the human immunodeficiency virus. In G. P. Koocher, J. C. Norcross & S. S. Hill (Eds.), *Psychologist's desk reference.* New York: Oxford University Press.

Carey, M. P., Flasher, L. V., Maisto, S. A., & Turkat, I. D. (1984). The a priori approach to psychological assessment. *Professional Psychology: Research and Practice, 15,* 515–527.

Carey, M. P., Lantinga, L. J., & Krauss, D. J. (1994). Male erectile disorder. In R. T. Ammerman & M. Hersen (Eds.), *Handbook of prescriptive treatments for adults.* New York: Plenum Press.

Chapman, J. D. (1989). A longitudinal study of sexuality and gynecological health in abused women. *Journal of the American Osteopathic Association, 89,* 619–624.

Derogatis, L. R., & Meyer, J. L. (1979). A psychological profile of the sexual dysfunctions. *Archives of Sexual Behavior, 8,* 201–223.

Derogatis, L. R., Fagan, P. J., Schmidt, C. W., Wise, T. N., & Gilden, K. S. (1986). Psychological subtypes of anorgasmia: A marker variable approach. *Journal of Sex and Marital Therapy, 12,* 197–210.

Donahey, K. M., & Carroll, R. A. (1993). Gender differences in factors associated with hypoactive sexual desire. *Journal of Sex and Marital Therapy, 19,* 25–40.

Ellis, A. (1951). *The folklore of sex.* New York: Charles Boni (revised edition, 1961).

Ellis, A. (1954). *The American sexual tragedy.* New York: Twayne (revised edition, 1961; New York: Lyle Stuart and Grove).

Ellis, A. (1958). *Sex without guilt.* New York: Lyle Stuart.

Ellis, A. (1992). My early experiences in developing the practice of psychology. *Professional Psychology: Research and Practice, 23,* 7–10.

Feldman, H. A., Goldstein, I., Hatzichristou, G. G., Krane, R. J., & McKinlay, J. B. (1994). Impotence and its medical and psychosocial correlates: Results of the Massachusetts Male Aging Study. *Journal of Urology, 151,* 54–61.

Frank, E., Anderson, C., & Kupfer, D. J. (1976). Profiles of couples seeking sex therapy and marital therapy. *American Journal of Psychiatry, 133,* 559–562.

Gagnon, J. H., Rosen, R. C., & Leiblum, S. R. (1982). Cognitive and social aspects of sexual dysfunction: Sexual scripts in sex therapy. *Journal of Sex and Marital Therapy, 8,* 44–56.

Glatt, A. E., Zinner, S. H., & McCormack, W. M. (1990). The prevalence of dyspareunia. *Obstetrics and Gynecology, 75,* 433–436.

Hawton, K. (1982). The behavioural treatment of sexual dysfunction. *British Journal of Psychiatry, 140,* 94–101.

Hawton, K. (1992). Sex therapy research: has it withered on the vine? *Annual Review of Sex Research, 3,* 49–72.

Heiman, J. R., & LoPiccolo, J. (1988). *Becoming orgasmic: A sexual and personal growth program for women,* revised edition. New York: Prentice-Hall.

Hunt, M. (1974). *Sexual behavior in the 1970's.* Chicago, IL: Playboy.

Kaplan, H. S. (1974). *The new sex therapy.* New York: Brunner/Mazel.

Katz, R. C., Gipson, M., & Turner, S. (1992). Brief report: Recent findings on the Sexual Aversion Scale. *Journal of Sex and Marital Therapy, 18,* 141–146.

Kilmann, P. R., Mills, K. H., Caid, C., Bella, B., Davidson, E., & Wanlass, R. (1984). the sexual interaction of women with secondary orgasmic dysfunction and therir partners. *Archives of Sexual Behavior, 13,* 41–49.

Kinsey, A. C., Pomeroy, W. B., & Martin, C. E. (1948). *Sexual behavior in the human male.* Philadelphia, PA: Saunders.

Kinsey, A. C., Pomeroy, W. B., Martin, C. E., & Gebhard, P. H. (1953). *Sexual behavior in the human female.* Philadelphia, PA: Saunders.

Lamont, J. A. (1978). Vaginismus. *American Journal of Obstetrics and Gynecology, 131,* 632–636.

Leiblum, S. R., & Rosen, R. C. (Eds.) (1988). *Sexual desire disorders.* New York: Guilford Press.

Leiblum, S. R., & Rosen, R. C. (1991). Couples therapy for erectile disorders: Conceptual and clinical considerations. *Journal of Sex and Marital Therapy, 17,* 147–159.

Levine, S. B., & Yost, M. A. (1976). Frequency of sexual dysfunction in a general gynecological clinic: An epidemiological approach. *Archives of Sexual Behavior, 5,* 229–238.

Lipsius, S. H. (1987). Precribing sensate focus therapy without proscribing intercourse. *Journal of Sex and Marital Therapy, 11,* 185–191.

LoPiccolo, J., & LoPiccolo, L. (Eds.) (1978). *Handbook of sex therapy.* New York: Plenum Press.

LoPiccolo, J., & Friedman, J. M. (1988). Broad-spectrum treatment of low sexual desire: Integration of cognitive, behavioral, and systemic therapy. In S. R. Leiblum & R. C. Rosen (Eds.), *Sexual desire disorders.* New York: Guilford Press.

Masters, W. H., & Johnson, V. E. (1966). *Human sexual response.* Boston, MA: Little, Brown & Co.

Masters, W. H., & Johnson, V. E. (1970). *Human sexual inadequacy.* Bosto, MA: Little, Brown & Co.

McCarthy, B. W. (1985). Uses and misuses of behavioral homework exercises in sex therapy. *Journal of Sex and Marital Therapy, 11,* 185–191.

McCarthy, B. W. (1993). Relapse prevention strategies and techniques in sex therapy. *Journal of Sex and Marital Therapy, 19,* 142–146.

Munjack, D. J., & Kanno, P. H. (1979). Retarded ejaculation: A review. *Archives of Sexual Behavior, 8,* 139–150.

Ng, M. L. (1992). Treatment of a case of resistant vaginismus using a modified Mien-Ling. *Sexual and Marital Therapy, 7,* 295–299.

O'Sullivan, K. (1979). Observations on vaginismus in Irish women. *Archives of General Psychiatry, 36,* 824–826.

Purnine, D. M., & Carey, M. P. (1997). Interpersonal communication and sexual adjustment: The roles of understanding and agreement. *Journal of Consulting and Clinical Psychology, 65,* 1017–1025.

Renshaw, D. C. (1988). Profile of 2376 patients treated at Loyola Sex Clinic between 1972 and 1987. *Sexual and Marital Therapy, 3,* 111–117.

Rosen, R. C., & Leiblum, S. R. (1988). A sexual scripting approach to problems of desire. In S. R. Leiblum & R. C. Rosen (Eds.), *Sexual desire disorders*. New York: Guilford Press.

Rosen, R. C., Leiblum, S. R., & Spector, I. P. (1994). Psychologically-based treatment for male erectile disorder: A cognitive-interpersonal model. *Journal of Sex and Marital Therapy, 20,* 67–85.

Sandberg, G., & Quevillon, R. P. (1987). Dyspareunia: An integrated approach to assessment and diagnosis. *Journal of Family Practice, 24,* 66–69.

Schreiner-Engel, P., & Schiavi, R. C. (1986). Life psychopathology in individuals with low sexual desire. *Journal of Nervous and Mental Disease, 174,* 646–651.

Segraves, R. T., & Segraves, K. B. (1990). Categorical and multi-axial diagnosis of male erectile disorder. *Journal of Sex and Marital Therapy, 16,* 208–213.

Segraves, R. T., & Segraves, K. B. (1991). Hypoactive sexual desire disorder: Prevalence and comorbidity in 906 subjects. *Journal of Sex and Marital Therapy, 17,* 55–58.

Semans, J. M. (1956). Premature ejaculation: A new approach. *Southern Medical Journal, 49,* 353–357.

Silverstein, J. L. (1989). Origins of psychogenic vaginismus. *Psychotherapy and Psychosomatics, 52,* 197–204.

Spector, I. P., & Carey, M. P. (1990). Incidence and prevalence of the sexual dysfunctions: A critical review of the literature. *Archives of Sexual Behavior, 19,* 389–408.

Speiss, W. F., Geer, J. H., & O'Donohue, W. T. (1984). Premature ejaculation: Investigacion of factors in ejaculatory latency. *Journal of Abnormal Psychology, 93,* 242–245.

Stuart, F. M., Hammond, D. C., & Pett, M. A. (1987). Inhibited sexual desire in women. *Archives of Sexual Behavior, 16,* 91–106.

Wincze, J. P., & Carey, M. P. (1991). *Sexual dysfunction: Guide for assessment and treatment.* New York: Guilford Press.

Zilbergeld, B. (1993). *The new male sexuality.* New York: Bantam Books.

Further Reading

Leiblum, S., & Rosen, R. (Eds.) (1989). *Principles and practice of sex therapy: Update for the 1990's.* New York: Guilford Press.

Schover, L. R., & Jensen, S. B. (1988). *Sexuality and chronic illness: A comprehensive approach.* New York: Guilford Press.

Wincze, J. P., & Carey, M. P. (1991). *Sexual dysfunction: Guide for assessment and treatment.* New York: Guilford Press.

Zilbergeld, B. (1993). *The new male sexuality.* New York: Bantam Books.

10

Cognitive-Behavioral Approaches to the Treatment of the Paraphilias: Sexual Offenders

WILLIAM L. MARSHALL and YOLANDA M. FERNANDEZ

Queen's University, Canada

Introduction

According to DSM-IV (APA, 1994) the paraphilias "cause clinically significant distress or impairments in social, occupational, or other important areas of functioning" (p. 493). Their essential features, so the diagnostic manual declares, "are recurrent, intense sexually arousing fantasies, sexual urges, or behaviors generally involving: (1) nonhuman objects, (2) the suffering or humiliation of oneself or one's partner, or (3) children or other nonconsenting persons" (pp. 522–523). However, it is important to note that the diagnosis of paraphilia is applied only when the urges, fantasies, or behaviors "lead to clinically significant distress or impairment (e.g., are obligatory, result in sexual dysfunction, require participation of nonconsenting individuals, lead to legal complications, interfere with social relationships)" (p. 525). Thus, a person may enjoy what otherwise might be considered paraphilic fantasies or behaviors so long as neither they nor anyone else is significantly distressed as a result. Eight specific paraphilias are listed in DSM-IV: exhibitionism, fetishism, frotteurism, pedophilia, sexual masochism, sexual sadism, transvestic fetishism, and voyeurism. A nonspecific category "paraphilia not otherwise specified" is also included.

The diagnostic criteria for the paraphilias in DSM-IV reflects an improvement over DSM-III-R criteria. For example, in DSM-III-R the necessary condition of "recurrent sexual urges and sexually arousing fantasies" meant that, for example, a male who repeatedly exposed his genitals to an unsuspecting female and yet reported no fantasies associated with such behavior, was not to be diagnosed as suffering from a paraphilia. Yet many exhibitionists, at least initially, deny such fantasizing. Although some give in to the therapist's insistence that they must have had such fantasies, it cannot be clearly determined that this reflects truthful or coerced reporting. DSM-IV has eliminated this problem by making the diagnosis of a paraphilia dependent upon the presence of either fantasies, urges, or behavior. However, there are still problems with the current diagnostic criteria. For example, only a limited proportion of men (less than 50% in our studies) who sexually molest children meet the diagnostic criteria for pedophilia and less than 20% of rapists meet the criteria for sexual sadism. These observations imply that many men who persistently molest children or who persistently rape women, do not have a psychiatric disorder which, at the very least, should cause concern for treatment providers if not for diagnosticians.

These problems are typically circumvented by those who work with sexual offenders or sexual deviates, either by avoiding use of the DSM nomenclature, or by simply using the DSM descriptors (e.g., exhibitionists, pedophiles, etc.) whether or not clients meet the diagnostic criteria. The latter tactic often results in confusion, particularly when attempts are made to replicate research that has identified a target population as having one or the other paraphilia. For example, in our attempt (Marshall, Barbaree & Eccles, 1991) to at least in some respects replicate Abel, Becker, Cunningham-Rathner, Mittelman & Rouleau's (1988) findings of extensive multiple paraphilias in sexual offenders, we immediately recognized a possible diagnostic problem. Abel et al. included rape as a paraphilia and yet it does not appear anywhere in DSM. Similarly, they included all their child molesters and yet it is very unlikely that their total sample were all pedophiles, particularly their incest offenders. Since they likewise did not make clear their criteria for identifying additional paraphilias, it is possible that they applied similarly lax rules and this may have resulted in the surprisingly high frequency of multiple paraphilias that they reported. When we applied rather stricter criteria, more in conformity with DSM edicts, we found very few multiple paraphiliacs among our population of sexual offenders.

In terms of actual clinical practice with sexual offenders or sexual deviants, whether or not a client meets DSM criteria appears to be irrelevant. Predictions of risk and acceptance into treatment seems not to be influenced by diagnostic status. If a man has molested a child or raped a woman, he is deemed to be at some degree of risk for future offending and in need of treatment, even if he flatly denies recurrent urges and sexually arousing fantasies, and even if he has only offended once or twice. One way that practitioners have attempted to get around this diagnostic problem is to phallometrically assess sexual preferences. If a child molester, for example, denies having sexual urges or fantasies about children, but has molested at least one child, he is assessed to determine what sexual partners he prefers. Unfortunately, we (Marshall, Barbaree & Butt, 1988; Marshall, Barbaree & Christophe, 1986) have found that as many as 50% of nonfamilial child molesters, and over 70% of incest offenders, display normal sexual preferences at phallometric assessments. Among our populations of rapists only 30% displayed a sexual attraction to nonconsenting sex (Barbaree & Marshall, 1993) and adding degrading and greater aggression to the scripts had no impact (Eccles, Marshall & Barbaree, 1994). These findings, of course, may be taken to question the validity of phallometric evaluations and we have certainly challenged the use of such measures (Marshall, 1994, 1998; Marshall & Eccles, 1991, 1993).

As they are presently defined, the DSM diagnostic criteria for the paraphilias seem to be largely irrelevant to the practice of most clinicians and a stumbling block to accurate comparisons between research reports. In our clinical practice, therefore, we have ignored DSM criteria and have simply classified our offenders and deviates in terms of their actual behavior. If a man has sexually abused a child we call him a child molester; if he has sexually assaulted a woman we call him a rapist; if he has exposed his genitals we call him an exhibitionist. In fact, the only instance where such common sense descriptors may cause problems concerns men who wear women's clothing. It is apparent that men dress as women for a variety of reasons, but we are here only concerned with those who do so for the purpose of making themselves sexually aroused. Transvestic fetishism then, is the only case where our clinical practice approximately corresponds to DSM diagnostic criteria. Observation of most other practitioners in this field suggests that they too have adopted this common sense policy. We strongly suggest that the authors of future diagnostic manuals reconsider the current restrictive criteria for the paraphilias. In this chapter we will use the behaviorally descriptive labels of our everyday clinical practice.

Treatment

A Brief History

Treatment of nonoffending sexual deviates (i.e., those whose deviant behaviors do not contravene the law) has a long history (for historical reviews see Bancroft, 1974; Kilman, Wanlass, Sabalis & Sullivan, 1981; Travin & Protter, 1993) and these treatments served as models for the treatment of sexual offenders. Much of these early treatment approaches were, unfortunately, characterized by prejudicial attitudes toward such people. For example, until the mid 1970s one of the main subject groups targeted for treatment were homosexual males, most of whom did not display ego-dystonic features. Similarly, aversion therapy (typically involving either the ingestion of an emetic or the application of an unpleasant electric shock) was frequently the preferred treatment method. These two aspects of treatment were particularly evident in the nascent behavior therapy movement of the late 1950s through to the early 1970s. Reports of electric aversion therapy aimed at reducing homosexual interests (e.g., Bancroft, 1971; Feldman & MacCulloch, 1971) were received with great enthusiasm. However, it was not long before criticisms arose within the behavioral movement regarding the ethical merits of treating homosexuals, whether they were ego-dystonic or not (Davison, 1977). Similarly, the ethics of electric aversion therapy have been challenged (Erwin, 1978) and its use certainly does not enhance the therapeutic relationship. Most therapists have now abandoned treating homosexuals and no longer use electric aversion therapy, but there are behaviorists who continue to do both (e.g., McConaghy, 1993).

The early application of behavior therapy to sexual deviates and to sexual offenders, was characterized by the use of single treatment methods (e.g. Abel, Levis & Clancy, 1970; Bond & Evans, 1967; Eysenck & Rachman, 1965; Marks & Gelder, 1967) derived from simple conditioning theories of the development and maintenance of sexually aberrant behavior (McGuire, Carlisle & Young, 1965). Conditioning theories have been criticized as too limited and lacking in empirical support (Marshall & Eccles, 1993; O'Donohue & Plaud, 1994), and have been replaced by more comprehensive theories (Finkelhor, 1984; Hall & Hirschman, 1991; Marshall & Barbaree, 1990a). Single-component treatment approaches were challenged quite early in the behavioral treatment of sexual deviants (Marshall, 1971) and have subsequently been replaced by multicomponent cognitive-behavioral programs. A detailed description of our own program, to be outlined later in this chapter, will serve as an illustration of current cognitive-behavioral approaches, but the interested reader should also consult other sources (e.g., Abel, Osborn, Anthony & Gardos, 1992; Maletzky, 1991; Pithers, 1990).

Eccentric Sexual Desires

These clients (fetishists, transvestites, and consenting sadists and masochists) are typically described as sexual deviates (when not labelled as paraphiliacs) and it is difficult to think of an appropriate nonpejorative descriptor. Our choice of "eccentric sexual desires" may not please everyone, and our difficulty in choosing a nonpejorative title, of course, is a reflection of the persistent and unwarranted bias we all have toward those who display sexual desires contrary to our own. The approach taken by most therapists today toward homosexuals is to counsel them about their negative attitudes toward their behavior, and the likely external pressures that create these negative views, rather than attempting to modify the sexual preferences of these clients. We think this approach is also appropriate for those clients whose sexual interests do not entail direct harm or distress to others. Fetishists (transvestite or otherwise) do not hurt anyone by their sexual behavior. Although their preferences may cause them interpersonal problems, is that sufficient reason to dampen their ardent enthusiasm for their particular fetish? We suggest that at the very least therapists should thoroughly explore the reasons why it is that a fetishist seeks treatment before proceeding to attempt to eliminate their eccentric interests. The absence of more than a few published reports of treatment of sexual eccentrics over the past 20 years, presumably reflects attitudes in most therapists that are consistent with our own. McConaghy (1993), for example, suggests to transvestites that they seek alternative options to treatment, such as joining a transvestite club where they can crossdress free from social disapproval.

Aversion therapy using apomorphine (Davies & Morgenstern, 1960; Morgenstern, Pearce & Rees, 1965) and electric shock (Marks, Gelder & Bancroft, 1970) has been reported to significantly reduce crossdressing behavior in transvestites. These or similar procedures were also shown to have eliminated the undesired behavior of fetishistic clients (McGuire & Vallance, 1964; Raymond, 1956). A cognitive variation of aversion therapy, called "covert sensitization", has also been reported to be effective in reducing the unwanted sexual interests of fetishists (Kolvin, 1967), transvestites (Gershman, 1970), and sadists (Davison, 1968). These are not only single component treatment approaches, they also neglect the various other aspects of the clients that may restrict them from meeting their needs in more acceptable ways.

Although both Barlow (1973) and Marshall (1971) pointed to the limitations of single component treatment approaches, and thereafter treatment for sex offenders became more expansive, there has been little in the way of reports of comprehensive treatment for the sexual eccentrics. As we noted, there has been a remarkable dearth of descriptions of treatment of any kind for these clients since the early 1970s, particularly for sadists or masochists. One exception to this is a report by Haydn-Smith, Marks, Buchaya & Repper (1987) of the successful behavioral treatment (covert sensitization and training in coping skills) of an asphyxiophiliac.

Most accounts of sadists have been restricted to those who commit rape (McConaghy, 1993) with a serious neglect of attention to sadists who engage in their preferred behavior with compliant partners. Mees (1966) described a very extensive electric aversion program with a sadist and Laws, Meyer & Holmen (1978) used olfactory aversion with a similar client. Masochists have also been treated using aversion therapy (Marks, Rachman & Gelder, 1965).

However, while programs for sexual offenders have over the past 15–20 years become more comprehensive and multicomponent in nature, there does not seem to have been similar developments with the sexual eccentrics. It seems obvious that many of these clients have more extensive problems than simply their sexual attraction to their eccentric acts and that comprehensive cognitive-behavioral programs should be suited to the complexity of their problems as is the case for sexual offenders. We await the description, application, and evaluation of such an approach with fetishists, transvestites, sadists, and masochists. To facilitate this application let us now review treatment approaches with sexual offenders.

Sexual Offenders

Once again the initial treatment efforts with sexual offenders, derived from a behavioral perspective, were limited in scope. Arising as they did from the approaches used with sexual eccentrics, the early treatments designed for sexual offenders considered the problem behaviors to be exclusively sexually motivated. Sexual offending was thought to result from learned sexual preferences that were deviant in nature so it was believed that simply altering these preferences would eliminate the offensive propensities. Indeed, Bond & Evans (1967) went so far as to declare that reductions in the evocative strength of deviant sexual images (in this case, exhibitionism) would be sufficient to eliminate deviant behavior. Aversion therapy aimed at reducing the attractiveness of the deviant image was, therefore, considered to be all that was needed to treat sexual offenders.

As a result of this simple conceptualization, numerous reports described the application of aversion therapy (usually electric aversion) or covert sensitization to various sexual offenders. Many of these early reports involved the treatment of exhibitionists (for a review see Cox & Daitzman, 1979, 1980) but there were some similar reports involving nonfamilial child molesters (e.g., Barlow, Leitenberg & Agras, 1969; Quinsey, Bergersen & Steinman, 1976; Wijesinghe, 1977), incest offenders (Brownell & Barlow, 1976; Harbert, Barlow, Hersen & Austin, 1974) and voyeurs (Gaupp, Stern & Ratlieff, 1971). In 1971 Marshall described his treatment of a child molester that involved not only aversion therapy to reduce deviant sexual interests, but also orgasmic reconditioning to increase appropriate sexual interests, as well as assertiveness training and social skills enhancement to provide the skills necessary to act on the changed preferences. Marshall (1971) suggested that this broadened approach was applicable to other sexual offenders. Over the subsequent years programs for sexual offenders involved progressively expanding treatment targets and increasingly complex treatment procedures. However, there are still those who either continue to provide evaluations of limited treatment (e.g.,

Rice, Quinsey & Harris, 1991) or who make explicit their objections to these multicomponent programs (McConaghy, 1993). McConaghy (1993) claimed that at the time of his writing there was no evidence that these comprehensive programs were effective, but in fact there was at least one report (Marshall & Barbaree, 1988a) of an outcome study that found significantly lower recidivism rates among child molesters treated in one of the comprehensive cognitive-behavioral programs, than among matched, untreated offenders. In any case, by far the majority of treat- ment providers have now adopted some variant of the program to be described below.

A Comprehensive Cognitive-Behavioral Program

We will describe here our own program, although it appears that similar programs represent the most popular approach to the treatment of sexual offenders. The main variation across programs has more to do with how long it takes clients to complete each component, than it does with the actual content of treatment. Our view is that since there are so many sexual offenders to treat, we have to make our programs as economical of time and resources as we can, while at the same time covering all of the features of the offenders that are necessary.

Our treatment programs have been developed over the past 25 years in prison settings (Marshall & Williams, 1975), psychiatric hospitals (Marshall & McKnight, 1975) and outpatient settings (Marshall & Barbaree, 1988a,b). Over this time our programs have evolved from limited component approaches (Marshall, 1971; 1973) to broader-based programs (Marshall, Earls, Segal & Darke, 1983), and, finally, to the present multicomponent programs (Hudson, Marshall, Johnston, Ward & Jones, 1995; Marshall, 1993, Marshall & Eccles, 1998; Marshall, Eccles & Barbaree, 1991). The following description provides a brief summary of our present program.

Treatment structure. Marshall, Eccles & Barbaree, 1993a) have described the overall structure of our program as a "three-tiered approach". Our program involves sexual offenders who are either presently incarcerated, were incarcerated, or have never been sent to prison. We, therefore, have programs in prisons and in the community.

When sexual offenders first enter Canadian penitentiaries in the Ontario Region they are assessed to determine their security risk as well as their treatment needs. If they are deemed to be a high security risk and to need intensive treatment, they are transferred to an institution where a Tier 1 program is located. If they are found to be low risk and have rather less treatment needs, they are transferred to an institution where a Tier 2 program is located. After successful treatment at Tier 1 level some of the offenders move on to Tier 2 as part of their pre-release program. Recently, additional within-prison programs have been developed as a final pre-release step with these programs focussing upon strengthening and refining the relapse prevention plans developed in the Tier 1 or Tier 2 programs. Most clients, however, having completed the Tier 1 program are due for immediate release and do not progress on to Tier 2 or to the pre-release relapse prevention programs, but rather go directly to a community program (i.e., a Tier 3 program).

Clients who enter Tier 1 programs participate in all of the offense-specific components (to be described in detail later) and most of the offense-related components. They are involved in five 3-hour sessions of group therapy per week over a 6-month period aimed at offense-specific targets, while at the same time participating in whatever additional offense-related programs are thought necessary. Pre- and post-treatment evaluations determine whether or not progress has been satisfactory. If it has, then they move on to the next stage (i.e., release, or transfer to a Tier 2 or a relapse prevention extension program). If progress is deemed to be insufficient then they are recycled through Tier 1 again.

Those offenders who go directly to Tier 2 are involved in a more limited program. Tier 2 group therapy involves two 3-hour sessions per week and covers an abbreviated version of the offense-specific components, although most offenders are also involved in one or more of the offense-related components. Tier 2 programs operate as open-ended groups with each offender remaining in treatment for an average of 3 months.

Once an offender is released into the community he is typically required to enter an outpatient program (Tier 3) which again covers the offense-specific targets as well as, where necessary, the offense-related issues. Community treatment for released sexual offenders involves one 3-hour group session each week and each offender typically remains in treatment for approximately 6 months. These released offenders are also supervised by parole officers trained in relapse prevention principles. These officers are provided with a detailed relapse prevention plan devised for each offender so that they can monitor appropriate behaviors.

The following description of our treatment components, then, applies to each of the three tiers.

Treatment components. In Marshall and Eccles' (1998) detailed description of their comprehensive cognitive-behavioral treatment program for sex offenders, the targets of treatment were separated into two areas: offense-specific and offense-related targets. Offense-specific targets include overcoming denial and minimization, enhancing victim empathy, changing distorted attitudes and beliefs, modifying inappropriate fantasies, and developing a sound relapse prevention plan. Recently we have added intimacy training to these offense-specific targets and have inserted it after the attitude change component.

Marshall and Eccles (1998) suggest that the topics be approached in this particular order because progress in a specific area may not be accomplished until the preceding issues have been fully addressed. For example, it would be very difficult to increase empathy for a victim if an offender is still in denial or is still minimizing the extent of his forcefulness or the sexual intrusiveness of his behavior. However, all of the components of treatment are interrelated so that issues to do with distorted beliefs, for example, arise, and are responded to, throughout all components. As treatment progresses, important areas for each offender are repeatedly addressed within each component and the interconnection of all these issues is emphasized. Offense-related targets concern issues that could be considered influencing factors or precursors to an offense such as deficient relationship skills, poor problem-solving, substance abuse, limited anger control, and inadequate life skills.

One overriding feature of our approach concerns our belief that in order for an offender to change in a prosocial way, his sense of self-worth has to be enhanced. This means that he has to view himself as a person capable of change (which is analogous to Bandura's (1977) notion of self-efficacy), and as a person worthy of the affection and rewards derived from prosocial adult relationships. To this end the therapist sets a positive tone to treatment and models, and encourages other group members to imitate, a supportive but firm style of challenging and addressing each offender. Striking a balance midway between being overly supportive and collusive with offenders, and being unnecessarily forceful and confrontative, is not easy to achieve but it is, we believe, the appropriate therapeutic stance. At every step of the program we remind each offender of his strengths and potential, as well as pointing to the self-destructive and victim-destructive features of his previous abusive behavior. Offenders who feel as though they are in a supportive environment (where they will not be rejected) are less likely to be afraid to admit activities about which they are embarrassed and ashamed. One way to facilitate this is for the therapist to clarify the difference between the client as a whole person and the particular behaviors that are harmful and inappropriate. It is important to make it clear that it is a particular behavior (i.e., the sexual offense) that is unacceptable and not the client as a person. When necessary we also provide specific self-esteem enhancing procedures (Marshall & Christie, 1982) for those offenders whose self-worth is particularly low.

(a) Denial and minimization. Denial can be described as a refusal to admit having committed an offense, or a claim that the act was consensual, or an insistence that the offender is not, in fact, a sexual offender. Any of these positions may result in a refusal to enter treatment. Minimization is characterized as a refusal to accept responsibility for the offense, a denial of victim harm or a description of the offense that limits the extent, frequency, forcefulness or degree of intrusiveness of the offenses. Although studies have shown that denial and minimization are quite prevalent among sexual offenders (Scully &

Marollay, 1984), there are few reports of treatment designed to overcome these obstacles. Targeting these issues should be considered a fundamental first step in treatment and yet many programs exclude deniers and minimizers as unmotivated. We believe this is inappropriate since an examination of our records reveals that were we to exclude these offenders we would not only have refused treatment for some 60% of our clients, we would have left untreated some of the most dangerous sexual offenders. It seems to us that we have a responsibility to attempt to treat these men and to convince them that they need treatment. In fact, we accept that it is our job to attempt to involve all sexual offenders in treatment. Accordingly we have no exclusionary criteria and we certainly include all deniers and minimizers.

More detailed descriptions of our approaches to dealing with denial and minimization are provided elsewhere (Barbaree, 1991; Marshall, 1994b; Marshall & Eccles, 1998) so the present description will necessarily be a brief outline of our approach.

After a brief description of the goals and overall content of the program, we begin by having each offender disclose to the group his version of the sexual assault(s). The offender is asked to describe not only what he actually did, but also his emotional state at the time of the offense, any relevant preceding circumstances, any substance abuse at the time of the offense, his interpretation of the victim's behaviors, and, finally, his thoughts and feelings leading up to and during the assault. Each client may have to repeat his disclosure over a number of occasions before he is able to recognize and discuss all of these features.

Other group members are encouraged to challenge any areas of the disclosure they feel are ambiguous or inaccurate. The therapist models supportive challenges and criticisms, and appraises the challenges of other members. An official account, or the victim's version of the offense, is always available to the therapist and provides her/him with a basis for challenging the offender's account. This information is essential to effective treatment. Any inconsistencies between the official version and the offender's version results in further challenges by the group members and the therapist.

Although offenders often engage in a variety of manipulations in order to gain access to and ensure the secrecy of their victims, many do not realize the self-serving purpose of their actions. It is the task of the therapist and other group members to illuminate what the offender's version betrays about his behaviors, thoughts and feelings. Similarly, comments and challenges by one group member to another often reveals the challenger's own minimization and this offers a further opportunity to explore these problems for each client. As most group members draw on their own experiences when challenging other clients, their remarks frequently provide the therapist with insight into their understanding of their own offenses. Those group members who refrain from challenging other offenders, or who offer collusive support in a way that is obviously self-serving, are challenged by the therapist or by other offenders.

Offenders who display denial and minimization are informed by the therapist that this is quite common at the beginning of therapy, but they will be expected to move beyond this stage. Other members of the group who have successfully completed their disclosures may describe the benefits of "coming clean" such as the feeling of relief that they no longer have to constantly lie. The therapist ensures that the offender understands the advantages of an honest disclosure (e.g., a sense of relief from having to lie, an opportunity to resolve a variety of problems in his life, and an earlier release from prison or from parole supervision) as well as the disadvantages of continuing to deny or to minimize (e.g., he may be required to withdraw from treatment, he may be made to stay in prison longer or remain on parole for longer, as well as an increased risk of reoffending). Other more realistic views of the offensive behavior are offered for the client to consider before he attempts a further disclosure.

The disclosure process is repeated and continuously challenged until the account is considered acceptable. While some clients offer a complete and quite accurate account of the offense during their first disclosure, most demonstrate at least various distortions meant to minimize the extent or nature of their offenses. In these cases repeated disclosures are necessary.

While the disclosure and challenges are directly aimed at reducing denial and minimization, other subsequent components of the treatment procedure (e.g., the victim empathy component) also help reduce minimization in offenders who are resistant to challenges. As with all issues addressed within our treatment, each component is not a discrete unit but is functionally related to all other components; we repeatedly remind our clients of this fact. As a result, it is not essential to eliminate all denial and minimization before moving on to the next treatment component, although most of these issues should be dealt with in this initial component.

Because most programs exclude these men, there are few studies that have directly assessed the results of targeting denial and minimization in treatment. However, what limited data there are encourage confidence. Barbaree (1991), for example, reported that of a group of 40 incarcerated rapists and child molesters, 54% of the rapists and 66% of the child molesters initially completely denied having committed an offense. An additional 42% of the rapists and 33% of the child molesters significantly minimized their offense in terms of their responsibility for the offense, the extent of their offending, or the harm done to the victim. Following treatment the number of deniers was reduced from 22 to 3, although 15 of those that eventually admitted to offending continued to minimize their offenses to some degree. Unfortunately, the results for the minimizers were less encouraging. Of the original 15 minimizers only 3 completely abandoned their minimizing after treatment. Barbaree (1991) did note, however, that the degree of minimization was considerably reduced and motivation for treatment had increased among these offenders. In a similar study, Marshall (1994b) assessed treatment effects on denial and minimization in 81 incarcerated sexual offenders. Of the 25 pre-treatment deniers only 2 offenders continued to categorically deny their offenses upon completion of treatment. Similarly, the number of minimizers was significantly reduced from 26 to 9 following treatment. Marshall (1994b) also noted that the degree of minimization of these latter offenders was reduced from an average of 3.7 (on a 6-point scale) to 0.5 at post-treatment.

(b) Victim empathy. Although there appears to be a consensus among many theorists that empathy deficits are a significant factor in sexual offending, there has been little in the way of research supporting this claim. Previous investigations have offered confusing and somewhat contradictory evidence of empathy deficits in sex offenders (for a review of this literature see Marshall, Hudson, Jones & Fernandez, 1998). For example, while Rice, Chaplin, Harris & Coutts (1990) found a clear difference between sexual offenders and nonoffenders in empathy, Seto (1992) found that rapists were less empathic than community males on the Hogan Empathy Scale (Hogan, 1969), but not on Meharabian & Epstein's (1972) Emotional Empathy Scale. In addition, when education was used as a covariate in the analyses, Seto's group differences on the Hogan Scale disappeared. Despite these inconsistencies in observed empathy deficits, empathy training routinely appears as a major component in most North American sexual offender treatment programs (Knopp, Freeman-Longo & Stevenson, 1992).

These contradictory findings may be due, in part, to the confusion over the nature and extent of empathy. Marshall et al. (1998) have suggested that empathy is a staged process involving recognizing another person's emotional state, perceiving the world from another's point of view, replicating the emotional state of the other person, and, finally, engaging in some behavioral change as a response to the perceived distress (e.g., stopping harmful behavior or offering sympathy). Partial support for this conceptualization comes from evidence that sex offenders are deficient in recognizing emotions in others (Hudson, Marshall, Wales, McDonald, Bakker & McLean, 1993), and that they differentiate between their identification of distress in an observed person and their own feelings of distress in response to this observation (Marshall, Fernandez, Lightbody & O'Sullivan, 1994). Sexual offenders appear to be particularly impaired at recognizing anger, surprise, and fear which are the emotions most likely to be expressed by victims of sexual assault (Marshall, Jones, Hudson & McDonald, 1993c).

An additional problem with previous research is that it has failed to identify whether sex offenders suffer from a general, nonspecific empathy deficit or if their deficits are contextually bound or person specific. For example, in a recent study we (Marshall et al., 1994) found that child molesters exhibit deficits in empathy toward children who have been the victims of other offenders as compared to a group of non-offending community males, and they show even greater deficits in empathy toward their own victims; on the other hand, they displayed no impairment of empathy toward children in general. If these latter findings are independently confirmed, then treatment should attempt to enhance empathy toward these two particular classes of people – that is, toward victims of sexual abuse in general (i.e., adult women victims for rapists, and child victims for child molesters) and the offenders' own specific victims – rather than attempting to enhance empathy toward all people. These are the goals of our empathy training component.

As many offenders have learned throughout their lives to suppress their feelings, they may find it very difficult to express emotions. It is often necessary as an initial step in treating empathy deficits, to train clients to be emotionally expressive. Clients are asked to describe an event in their life, other than being arrested, that they remember as being emotionally distressing. The client is asked to describe the experience as if he was reliving it and to not hold back any feelings or emotions. Many participants describe the death of a loved one, the breakup of an important relationship, the rejection they may have felt as a child from their parents, or their own experience as a victim of sexual abuse. This latter account typically has a notable effect on the other group members and often the speaker and the listeners become quite emotional.

When the target offender has described his emotionally distressing experience, each other participant is required to describe how he felt during the target member's account and how he thought the target offender felt. Discussion of the adequacy of the target member's emotional expression follows, as does an appraisal of each other participant's response. The therapist points out that by expressing emotions similar to those displayed by the target member, the other clients are actually showing empathy.

After each group member has given his emotionally distressing account and it has been fully discussed and appraised, the group therapist then either reads an account by an actual victim or shows a videotape of a victim describing his/her response to the assault and the ensuing consequences on his/her life. Each member is then asked to describe how he felt while listening to or watching the victim. If a client does not appear to express appropriate emotions, or appears not to be honest in his expressions, the group challenges him.

After the therapist defines empathy for the group, each participant is asked to discuss the degree to which he now feels empathy for his own victim and other victims of sexual abuse. If necessary, clients are asked how they would feel if someone important to them was sexually assaulted. The therapist asks each client to describe such an assault and to discuss how he would feel toward the offender and the victim. Other offenders are encouraged to provide feedback as to the adequacy of each member's responses. The exercise is repeated until the group is satisfied.

In the next exercise clients are taught to recognize emotions in victims of sexual abuse by taking the perspective of the victim and attempting to experience their distress. Each participant is asked to describe what he believes are the immediate (during the offense), post-assault, and long-term effects of sexual abuse. The therapist writes each of the suggestions on a flip chart and adds any known consequences of sexual abuse that the group may have missed. The list is used to stimulate general discussion followed by each client describing to what extent he believes his own victim experienced each consequence. It is repeatedly emphasized that the client may not have realized at the time of the offense how much his victim was suffering, but that does not mean that the victim did not suffer. The therapist explains that it is likely that either the victim was too frightened to show his/her feelings, or the offender was so absorbed in seeking his own satisfaction that he did not notice the victim's anguish. Each participant is then required to describe their offense from the victim's point of view. If an offender presents the story in a self-serving way he is challenged by other group members. Many clients find it difficult to look at their offense from the victim's perspective. The importance of this exercise is that clients are forced to regard many aspects of the offense from a very different viewpoint and at a depth that they may never have considered before.

As the final element in victim empathy training, participants are given a homework assignment in which they are required to write two letters, one supposedly from the victim, and the other as a response to the victim's letter (which they are clearly instructed not to send). The letter from the victim should include all of the anger, self-blame, loss of trust and various other emotional, cognitive and behavioral problems that by now the offender should understand are common effects of sexual abuse. This letter is read out loud to the group by the therapist. Other members of the group provide feedback and challenge the letter writer on any areas they feel have been missed or presented in a self-serving fashion. The client revises the letter according to the group feedback. This process is repeated until the content and style of the letter meets the satisfaction of the entire group.

Once the letter from the victim has been completed the offender is required to write a letter to the victim expressing an understanding of the consequences the victim has had to suffer. This provides the client with an opportunity to further communicate his acceptance of full responsibility for the offense and to show what he is doing to ensure that he will not reoffend in the future. Although the participants are expected to apologize for the offense, they are told that they cannot ask for forgiveness. This is considered an unfair request to make of the victim. This letter is also challenged and revised until it meets the satisfaction of the entire group.

Two recent studies have demonstrated the value of these types of procedures for enhancing empathy in sex offenders. Pithers (1994) has shown that a treatment approach similar to that described above, effectively increased the nonspecific empathy of a group of incarcerated sexual offenders. More recently, Marshall, O'Sullivan & Fernandez (1998) have shown that our procedures markedly improve the empathy that child molesters show for their own victims and for children who have been the sexual victims of other abusers.

(c) Attitude change. It is widely believed (Burt, 1980; Field, 1978; Malamuth, 1981; Rapaport & Burkhart, 1984; Tieger, 1981) that most sexual offenders hold attitudes and beliefs that are supportive of their offensive behavior. For example, rapists are understood to accept a variety of myths about women's sexuality, about women's desires, and about rape itself. It is also suggested that rapists believe that women should take a subservient role to men and that aggression toward women is acceptable. Although research to date has not consistently supported these views about rapists (Stermac, Segal & Gillis, 1990), this may be because the questionnaires used to appraise these attitudes are relatively transparent and, therefore, readily open to dissimulation. For example, Scully & Marolla (1983) found that convicted rapists who denied their offense were far more likely to endorse distorted beliefs about rape than were those who admitted having committed the offense. The authors took this to indicate that the deniers wanted to justify rape and thereby make themselves appear less culpable, so they accepted the myths. The admitters, on the other hand, may have wanted to show their prosocial understanding of sexual assault and, therefore, responded in a manner intended to please the researcher. Presently this problem of the transparency of tests is an obstacle which no currently available measure appears able to circumvent. Nevertheless most clinicians report that rapists express many pro-rape views in the early stages of treatment.

Child molesters are similarly thought to accept pro-offending views of children and of sexual molestation. Abel and his colleagues (Abel, Becker, Cunningham-Rathner, Rouleau, Kaplan & Reich, 1984) were among the first to propose that child molesters held distorted beliefs and they (Abel, Gore, Holland, Camp, Becker & Rathner, 1989) subsequently provided supportive evidence. Stermac and Segal (1989) also found that child molesters endorsed more permissive attitudes toward sexual relationships between adults and children, and Howells (1978) reported that child molesters viewed children as less threatening, less dominating, and easier to relate to than were adults. Again the evidence is not strong and the measures employed to date readily allow for deliberate misrepresentation of the beliefs of the respondents, but clinicians routinely observe pro-offending attitudes among child molesters.

In our program we challenge offense-supportive attitudes and beliefs whenever they arise, although we do also specifically target these distortions. In this component we have each offender describe his beliefs about women and children and their sexual nature. We also describe hypothetical offenses where the offender's responsibility may be likely to be seen (incorrectly) as reduced, and the victim's behavior may be seen (again incorrectly) as inviting a sexual assault. These hypothetical cases frequently reveal pro-offending attitudes that might otherwise not emerge, and this allows us the opportunity to challenge these attitudes, to spell-out their implications, and to offer more pro-social alternatives. Therapists, of course, need to very thoroughly examine their own views before engaging in this process.

Essentially the so-called "cognitive restructuring" approach embodied in this way of eliciting, challenging, and outlining the implications of these attitudes and then suggesting alternatives, is a rather simple approach. Its effectiveness, however, has not yet been demonstrated although it is a widely practiced procedure (Murphy, 1990).

(d) Intimacy training. We (Marshall, 1989, 1993b, 1994a) have suggested that sexual offenders may turn to assaultive behavior not simply to meet sexual, aggressive, or power needs, but also to meet, in part at least, needs for intimacy that are not otherwise met in their lives. We proposed that sexual offenders are typically unable to effectively meet their intimacy needs and that this inability arises as a result of poor attachments with their own parents (Marshall, Hudson & Hodkinson, 1993b) and results in poor quality adult attachments (Ward, Hudson, Marshall & Siegert, 1998). Subsequent research has supported these proposals (Bumby & Marshall, 1994; Garlick, 1991; Hudson, Ward & Marshall, 1994; Marshall & Hambley, 1994; Seidman, Marshall, Hudson & Robertson, 1994), and we have outlined a treatment component to address these difficulties (Marshall, 1994b) and provided tentative evidence in support of its value. For a more complete description of our intimacy training component, the reader is referred to Marshall (1994b).

The initial step in this component is to provide information regarding the nature of intimacy and loneliness, and the value of developing greater intimacy. We also assist the offenders in identifying their present ability, or lack thereof, to achieve intimacy, and the origins of their present inadequacies. Revelations of the origins of their problems often leads to a need to help them resolve difficulties relating to either their parents or some early attempts at intimate experiences.

Next we discuss sexual relations and the role they play in intimacy. All too often these offenders think of sex as the only route to intimacy. We point out that satisfaction in sexual relations is closely tied to satisfaction with all aspects of their relationship and that intimacy, and full sexual satisfaction, are maximally realized only in equitable relations. Thus, forced sexual relations and sex with children, cannot produce the satisfactions they seek.

Jealousy, and the way in which our clients respond to the real or imagined infidelity of their partner, is critical and is the next focus of this component. While acknowledging that jealousy is an expected and perhaps appropriate response to clear betrayal, the magnitude of the response, and the tendency to be inappropriately jealous, are the result of the cuckold's low self-esteem, the degree of his own unfaithfulness, and inappropriate inferences about the meaning of the infidelity. We challenge the inappropriate attitudes of the clients regarding these issues and help them examine why it is that their past partners were unfaithful. All too often unfaithfulness in their partner seems to have been a product of the offender's own behavior; for example, his philandering, his secretiveness, his poor communication, his emotional distance, or his excessive jealousy.

We teach our clients relationship skills including the skills necessary to initiate a relationship (e.g., choosing an appropriate partner, developing conversational skills, not rushing into committed relationships, etc.) as well as the skills necessary to maintain relationships (e.g., self-disclosure, conflict resolution, expression of feelings, communication, listening skills, etc.). Various detrimental attitudes about relationships (e.g., the belief in "love at first sight", that disagreements are necessarily destructive, that passionate love must be maintained at high energy levels, etc.) are identified and challenged. When useful we also use role-play as a means of both training skills and identifying inappropriate beliefs.

Finally in this component we address the issue of loneliness. We help clients identify their fear of being alone as well as the irrational and self-destructive consequences of such a fear. They are required to list all of the advantages of being alone and why being alone is not necessarily identical with feeling lonely.

(e) Sexual preferences. As previously mentioned, in earlier treatment programs deviant sexual preferences were frequently considered to be the primary, if not the only, targets of treatment. Recently we (Blader & Marshall, 1989; Marshall, 1998a; Marshall & Eccles, 1991) have suggested that the importance of this component of treatment has been overstated. For example, as we noted earlier, far from all sexual offenders display deviant sexual preferences at phallometric evaluation, even though they have obviously committed an offense. Most of the offenders who show normal preferences at assessment also deny having recurrent deviant fantasies, so it is clear that we have not been able to demonstrate that deviant sexual preferences characterize more than a limited number of these men.

The sexual preference hypothesis (for a detailed analyses of the various forms of this hypothesis see Barbaree, 1990; Barbaree & Marshall, 1991) suggests that all sexual offenders actually prefer deviant sexual acts to any other form of sexual behavior and that their sexual fantasies focus exclusively on deviant acts. In fact, consensual sexual acts with adults are often construed as a "cover up" or as substitute responses in place of the preferred deviant acts. In contrast, Marshall & Eccles (1998) suggest that the notion that preferences are fixed and unvarying is as unlikely for sexual behavior as it is for any other behavior. Food preferences, for example, appear to be extremely variable and often change according to availability and experiences so why should sexual preferences be any different? While a person might particularly enjoy one type of sexual act it is highly unlikely that they would engage in that behavior exclusively and there is nothing to suggest that sexual offenders do not find a variety of sexual acts to be enjoyable. Certainly males have been show to be strongly attracted to variety in terms of sexual partners and sexual activities (Symons, 1979).

Consistent with this latter observation, Marshall & Eccles (1998) suggest that deviant sexual behavior may, to some extent, reflect a search for novelty or may simply reveal that the person took advantage of an opportunity that would otherwise be lower on the offender's hierarchy of preferences. As a number of contextual circumstances, such as emotional distress and substance abuse, appear to affect the likelihood of offending (Pithers, Beal, Armstrong & Petty, 1989a), it seems reasonable to infer that situational factors account for at least some of the behavior, and these factors are, of course, constantly changing.

Marshall & Eccles (1991) have suggested that the fantasies of sexual offenders may meet a variety of needs. In addition to specifically sexual features, deviant fantasies often deal with issues of power and control, aggression and the need to humiliate, as well as the need for admiration and respect. Therefore, in our program, all sexual offenders are taught procedures to reduce the frequency and potency of deviant fantasies, whether or not they display deviant sexual arousal during testing.

Of course, another alternative, perhaps more in keeping with the failure of research to clearly demonstrate the presence of deviant sexual preferences in many offenders, would be to ignore the issue in treatment. Even Quinsey & Earls (1990), who are strong proponents of the sexual preference hypothesis, suggested that other treatment procedures (e.g., empathy training, attitude change, anger control, etc.) may produce appropriate changes in sexual preferences, thereby avoiding the need to specifically target them in treatment. We believe this to be a distinct possibility and are presently pursuing research that should provide an answer to this question.

The two primary procedures that we employ in this component are covert sensitization and masturbatory reconditioning.

The main aim of covert sensitization is to make the unpleasant consequences of sexual offending foremost in an offender's thinking, especially in the early stages of his offense chain (e.g., at the point where a rapist is feeling angry and is thinking about going to a bar to look for a victim). Although some sexual offenders may catastrophize immediately following an offense, these concerns quickly fade when tangible negative consequences are not forthcoming. Unfortunately, disagreeable feelings do little to reduce the risk of reoffense when their impact is so fleeting. Through covert sensitization it is hoped that by having the offender repeatedly associate negative consequences with imagining engaging in the deviant behavior, the inappropriate activities will lose their appeal and the intensity and frequency of inciteful deviant thoughts will be reduced.

The exercise begins by having each offender produce at least three deviant fantasies or action sequences. One of the fantasies must describe an actual offense or portray the offender's characteristic offense cycle (i.e., from the first thoughts that lead to offending through the various steps that finally culminate in an offense). These fantasies are written on one side of a set of pocket-sized cards. The client then produces a list of all the negative consequences he believes could possibly happen to him as a result of offending. These are written on the reverse side of the cards. The offender is instructed to read the offense sequences at least three times a day, turning the cards over after each rehearsal to read the consequences. As the exercise progresses the offender is told to begin reading the consequences earlier in the fantasy sequence until he is reading them immediately after the first step of the offense chain. Once the client has completed reading the negative consequences he is asked to imagine a positive or prosocial response sequence such as turning from the deviant opportunity and engaging in an alternative, appropriate (perhaps nonsexual) activity. In order to ensure that offenders follow the exercise some clinicians have the client record on audiotape his practice of covert sensitization. This, however, can be burdensome and may make the procedure somewhat stilted. Another alternative is to enrol the help of others (e.g., other inmates or family members) to remind the client on a daily basis to maintain his practice. Unfortunately, the evidence supporting the use of covert sensitization, in whatever form, is rather limited, but it remains in wide-spread use. What is sorely needed is careful research with appropriate subjects to determine whether or not covert sensitization, as it is clinically applied, achieves its intended goals.

The process of masturbatory reconditioning combines what has been called "orgasmic reconditioning", with "satiation therapy". Thorpe, Schmidt & Castell (1963) were the first to describe a procedure involving masturbation to orgasm while the subject was shown or imagined appropriate sexual behavior with an appropriate partner. Variations on this procedure have been described (Davison, 1968; Marquis, 1970; Maletzky, 1991), but once again there is, at best, weak evidence in support of the efficacy of these procedures (for a review of the evidence see Laws & Marshall, 1991). Satiation therapy was first described by Marshall & Lippens (1977) and subsequently evaluated in two controlled single-case studies (Marshall, 1979). In this early form the client continued to masturbate beyond orgasm for up to one hour while fantasizing every variation he could generate on his deviant acts. Subsequently, Abel & Annon (1982) dropped the requirement of masturbating beyond orgasm and simply had the client generate deviant fantasies. Verbal satiation, as this variation came to be called, has the advantage of being more palatable to clients than is masturbatory satiation. While satiation appears to have somewhat stronger support than orgasmic reconditioning procedures (Alford, Morin, Atkins & Schoen, 1987; Johnston, Hudson & Marshall, 1992), overall the evidence for the efficacy of satiation is limited (Laws & Marshall, 1991) and more careful research is needed.

Laws & Marshall (1991) suggested that "directed masturbation" appeared to be the most effective approach to enhancing appropriate arousal and it is the procedure we routinely use. In this procedure the client generates (with the therapist's help) a set of fantasies involving an appropriate partner (male or female, depending on the client's gender orientation). The offender is then instructed to masturbate to orgasm while imagining these appropriate sexual activities with a consenting partner. If he finds it difficult to become aroused to appropriate fantasies, or if arousal diminishes during masturbation, the client is told to use deviant fantasies to reestablish arousal then immediately switch back to the appropriate fantasy. He is told that he may switch back-and-forth between appropriate and deviant fantasies , if necessary, until orgasm occurs. The goal of directed masturbation is to increase the appeal of appropriate fantasies by associating these fantasies with self-induced arousal.

Following orgasm the client begins the second component of masturbatory reconditioning; that is, "satiation therapy". Immediately after ejaculation, males are relatively unresponsive to sexual stimuli (they enter what Masters & Johnson (1966) call the "relative refractory period"). During this post-orgasmic period, then, the client is instructed to cease masturbating and re-hearse aloud, if possible, every variation of his deviant fantasies for a minimum of 10 min, but never more than 20 min. The aim of this procedure is to associate deviant fantasies with a sexually unresponsive state. Of course, simply repeating the deviant fantasies may, in itself, diminish their attractiveness and, in turn, their ability to produce sexual arousal.

We have found that for some clients, covert sensitization and masturbatory reconditioning appear to be ineffective. These clients complain that despite diligently using the procedures, they still frequently experience deviant thoughts that are so strong they cannot resist masturbating to them. Correspondingly, they feel that the associated urges to reoffend will overwhelm them. In these cases a variety of other techniques may be adopted.

Antiandrogens or hormonal treatments (cyproterone acetate or medroxy-progesterone acetate) appear to reduce overall arousal as well as the frequency and intensity of deviant thoughts (Bradford, 1990; Bradford & Pawlak, 1993). Recently Pearson, Marshall, Barbaree & Southmayd (1992) demonstrated that buspirone (a serotonergic drug) brought unwanted thoughts under control in a patient with very strong and seemingly uncontrollable deviant urges. One or the other of these medications should be used only as an adjunct to a compre-hensive cognitive-behavioral program, otherwise the client will not acquire self-directed behavioral controls. In this way the client should eventually develop adequate coping skills to warrant withdrawing the medication.

Other alternatives that we sometimes use include olfactory aversion and ammonia aversion. In olfactory aversion the client is presented a foul odor that he inhales while listening to, or watching, depictions of his deviant activities. We use rotting meat enclosed in a jar, as the aversive stimulus. Although we have found that olfactory aversion often produces reductions in deviant arousal after very few trials, the procedure is not user-friendly. Not only does this approach do little to strengthen the therapist/client relationship, foul odors spread throughout the treatment room and their tenacious molecules cling to clothing and are, accordingly, offensive to treatment staff.

Ammonia aversion, on the other hand, is self-administered and consequently less aversive to the therapist. The offender is required to carry a bottle of salts of ammonia which he is to open and nasally inhale rapidly whenever he feels an urge or has a persistent deviant thought. The aim is to interfere with and punish deviant thoughts as they occur in the natural context. Eventually many offenders become sensitive to lower intensity thoughts and urges which they are encouraged to control without the use of the ammonia.

We (Marshall, 1973) have, in the past, used electric aversion therapy to lower deviant arousal; we no longer employ this procedure. As we noted, there are serious ethical questions regarding its use with incarcerated offenders, not to mention that the therapist/client relationship and sense of trust may be seriously compromised.

(f) Relapse prevention. The final component of our offense-specific treatments concerns the need to develop sound relapse prevention plans. Relapse prevention strategies were originally developed by Marlatt and his colleagues (Marlatt, 1982; Marlatt & George, 1994; Marlatt & Gordon, 1985) for the treatment of addictive behaviors. Subsequently these principles were adapted for use with sexual offenders by Marques and Pithers and their colleagues (Marques, Day, Nelson & Miner, 1989; Pithers, Marques, Gibat & Marlatt, 1983; Pithers, Martin & Cumming, 1989b). The following is our adaptation of the processes suggested by these authors. The informed reader will note that our component is far less extensive than that advocated by most of the relapse prevention disciples (for a comprehensive account of this approach see Laws, 1989), and it will be obvious that we do not employ the language so characteristic of these treatment providers (e.g., we do not use labels or identify processes such as "Abstinence Violation Effect", "Seemingly Irrelevant Decisions", or the "Problem of Immediate Gratification"). Whether this component needs to be more extensive remains at present an unanswered empirical question.

Once offenders have acquired the behavioral and attitudinal changes targeted in the earlier components, the relapse prevention component integrates these skills into a self-management set of plans that is meant to maintain gains after discharge from formal treatment.

The first step in this process requires the offender to identify the emotions, cognitions and actions that constitute his typical offense chain. This chain includes background factors (e.g., childhood experiences, lifestyle, emotional distress, relationship difficulties, substance abuse, and sources of stress) that serve to disinhibit prosocial controls. Having clients complete an autobiography facilitates the identification of these background factors. Once in this disinhibited state the client's pro-offending attitudes, beliefs, cognitive distortions, and deviant thoughts and fantasies, initiate a process that leads the offender to set up the opportunity to offend. The offender may then begin a behavioral sequence that he typically pursues in search of a victim (e.g., driving his car aimlessly, loitering near school grounds, etc.), or he may begin to groom a victim and manipulate others so that he can have an opportunity to offend. The offense chain, then, includes background factors, thinking processes, and action sequences that culminate in offending. Each client details his offense chain and it is read to the group by the therapist and challenged, if necessary, by the other participants. Suggestions for improvement are offered and the client subsequently modifies his offense chain until it is deemed satisfactory.

From this offense chain, the client identifies all the factors that might put him at risk to reoffend and he creates a list of strategies for dealing with each of his risk factors. The client indicates how he will avoid high risk situations or how he will escape from them should they inadvertently arise. He describes several alternative strategies for avoiding or dealing with his relevant background factors and he identifies various ways in which he will respond to pro-offending attitudes or fantasies should these deviant cognitions return. This detailed list of avoidance and coping strategies is referred to as his "relapse prevention plans". Finally, each offender makes a list of the warning signs that might indicate he is moving toward a risk to reoffend. Two lists of warning signs are generated: one that tells the offender himself that his risk is increasing (e.g., fantasies, ruminations, urges, etc.); and one that might alert a support person or a supervisor that he is at risk.

Training the offenders to develop an offense chain, a set of relapse prevention plans, and a set of warning signs, constitute what Pithers (1990) has called the "internal management" aspect of relapse prevention training. Pithers also suggests that an "external management" component is necessary, whereby the client is supervised by persons having some understanding of relapse prevention procedures. We help the offender identify a support group who can assist him upon discharge from treatment (and during the process of treatment in the community). These support group members may include spouses, employers and friends, although we also insist on the inclusion of his community supervisors such as probation and parole officers. Each support person or supervisor receives a copy of the offender's relapse prevention plans (i.e., offense chain, prevention plans and warning signs) as well as recommendations regarding restrictions on behavior (e.g., not be alone with children, not drive aimlessly, avoid alcohol or drugs, etc.). Provision of these materials is meant to increase the efficiency of supervision, create a network that can aid overloaded probation and parole officers, and develop a cooperative relationship among the important members of the client's community (Pithers, Buel, Kashima, Cumming &

Beal, 1987). There is some evidence that including a relapse prevention component in a treatment program lowers recidivism (Marshall, Hudson & Ward, 1992), although much more research needs to be done, particularly on the need for the extensive and costly post-release supervision and monitoring that is employed by Marques and Pithers.

Treatment Effectiveness

The development of comprehensive cognitive-behavioral treatment programs for sexual offenders has been a relatively recent phenomenon, and, as we noted, there has not been a comparable development in the treatment of the sexual eccentrics. These issues, of course, present difficulties for determining the effectiveness of current programs. The proper evaluation of treatment programs for sexual offenders takes considerable time and effort and is beset by all manner of difficulties over-and-above those that present problems for the evaluation of any treatment. For example, perhaps the primary stumbling block to implementing an evaluation concerns the provision of an untreated comparison group. Ideally such a group results from the random allocation of volunteers to either treatment or a no-treatment control. This, however, is not so readily attained with sexual offenders as it is with other patient populations. If a sexual offender is randomly allocated to no-treatment, this will be extremely costly to him because parole boards will typically not release an untreated offender and his family and friends may refuse to accept him if he has not been treated. Consequently, sexual offenders are unlikely to volunteer for such a study. Even if they did, is it really only the sexual offenders' willingness to participate that is of concern? Marshall & Pithers, (1994) have suggested that since women and children are primarily the potential victims of untreated sexual offenders, it is they whose approval should be sought to run a random-designed treatment evaluation. Our guess is they would not approve. This ethical problem, of course, leaves evaluators with little choice but to seek elsewhere an estimate of the likely rate of reoffending of their treatment subjects and to use that as the yardstick to measure the effectiveness of their treatment. This, of course, will not satisfy methodological purists.

Other problems in evaluating sexual offender treatment programs arise from the fact that we must wait until sufficient numbers of offenders have been released, and been at risk for sufficient time, for an appraisal of effectiveness to be made. Base-rates are low enough that a large number of offenders must be at risk for at least 4–5 years before a satisfactory evaluation can be completed. Unfortunately, many programs meet their demise before these conditions can be met, resulting in very few, and perhaps somewhat selective, programs that have been appraised. However, what evidence is available appears to be encouraging.

We (Marshall & Barbaree, 1990b; Marshall, Jones, Ward, Johnston & Barbaree, 1991c; Marshall, Ward, Jones, Johnston & Barbaree, 1991d) have completed thorough reviews of the outcome literature, as well as having appraised our own programs (Marshall & Barbaree, 1988a,b; Marshall, Eccles & Barbaree, 1991). The literature certainly does not provide clear scientifically sound demonstrations of the efficacy of cognitive-behavioral programs for sexual offenders, but we are strongly persuaded that the evidence is encouraging and we (Marshall & Pithers, 1994) have offered rebuttals to the rather pessimistic conclusions of others (e.g., Furby, Weinrott & Blackshaw, 1989; Quinsey, Harris, Rice & Lalumiére, 1993).

Obviously we need more evaluations of treatment outcome, and future research needs to aim for as high a level of methodological sophistication as is possible, given the limitations inherent in dealing with sexual offenders. The primary way to achieve this is for governments to support, over an extended period of time, the implementation and evaluation of treatment programs.

Future Research

Although the literature reviewed in this chapter has been primarily concerned with the treatment of adult male sexual offenders, there has been a recent increase in attention to both juvenile offenders (Barbaree, Marshall & Hudson, 1993; Ryan & Lane, 1991) and female offenders (Knopp & Lackey, 1987; Mathews, Mathews & Speitz, 1989). While there are clear differences in the features of, and appropriate treatment response to, females and juveniles, most of the observations made in this chapter are also relevant to these offenders. No doubt the next few years will produce bodies of literature specific to these particular clients, and the same is likely to be true for other distinct subgroups of sexual offenders (e.g., ethnic minority populations and disabled offenders).

As noted above, far more careful research is needed to evaluate treatment efficacy with both sexual offenders and sexual eccentrics. However, we also need a clearer understanding of the factors that need to be addressed in treatment, whether or not our treatment procedures produce the changes they are intended to produce, whether or not these changes can be produced by other aspects of treatment than the components designed specifically to produce the intended changes, and, finally, whether or not the achieved changes are functionally related to reductions in recidivism.

We have only recently begun the systematic treatment of sexual offenders, but our efforts so far are, we believe, sufficiently encouraging to be optimistic about further developments. We do need, however, to begin the process of identifying features of offenders that tell us how extensive their treatment needs to be, and to begin stripping our treatment process down to a minimum necessary to reduce future risk to an acceptable level. We need to be economical of our limited staff and resources so that *all* sexual offenders can be treated. At present many programs accept only a limited few sexual offenders from the total available population, and these clients may be selected on factors that please therapists or meet their resource capacities, rather than on their risk to injure some future innocent woman or child.

References

Abel, G. G., & Annon, J. S. (1982). *Reducing deviant sexual arousal through satiation.* Workshop presented at the 1st National Conference on the Evaluation and Treatment of Sexual Aggressives, Denver, CO.

Abel, G. G., Levis, D., & Clancy, J. (1970). Aversion therapy applied to taped sequences of deviant behavior in exhibitionists and other sexual deviations: Preliminary report. *Journal of Behaviour Therapy and Experimental Psychiatry, 1,* 59–60.

Abel, G. G., Becker, J. V., Cunningham-Rathner, J., Rouleau, J. L., Kaplan, M., & Reich, J. (1984). *Treatment manual: The treatment of child molesters.* Atlanta, GA: Emory University School of Medicine.

Abel, G. G., Becker, J. V., Cunningham-Rathner, J., Mittleman, M. S., & Rouleau, J. L. (1988). Multiple paraphilic diagnoses among sex offenders. *Bulletin of the American Academy of Psychiatry and the Law, 16,* 153–168.

Abel, G. G., Gore, D. K., Holland, C. L., Camp, N., Becker, J. V., & Rathner, J. (1989). The measurement of cognitive distortions of child molesters. *Annals of Sex Research, 2,* 135–152.

Abel, G. G., Osborn, C., Anthony, D., & Gardos, P. (1992). Current treatments of paraphiliacs. *Annual Review of Sex Research, 3,* 255–290.

Alford, G. S., Morin, C., Atkins, M., & Schoen, L. (1987). Masturbatory extinction of deviant sexual arousal: A case study. *Behavior Therapy, 18,* 265–271.

APA (1994). *Diagnostic and statistical manual of mental disorders,* 4th edition (DSM-IV). Washington, DC: American Psychiatric Association.

Bancroft, J. (1971). The application of psychophysiological measures to the assessment and modification of sexual behaviour. *Behaviour Research and Therapy, 9,* 119–130.

Bancroft, J. (1974). *Deviant sexual behaviour: Modification and assessment.* Oxford: Clarendon Press.

Bandura, A. (1977). Self-efficacy: Toward a unifying theory of behavioral change. *Psychological Review, 84,* 191–215.

Barbaree, H. E. (1990). Stimulus control of sexual arousal: Its role in sexual assault. In W. L. Marshall, D. R. Laws & H. E. Barbaree (Eds.), *Handbook of sexual assault: Issues, theories, and treatment of the offender.* New York: Plenum Press.

Barbaree, H. E. (1991). Denial and minimization among sex offenders: Assessment and treatment. *Forum on Corrections Research, 3,* 30–33.

Barbaree, H. E., & Marshall, W. L. (1991). The role of male sexual arousal in rape: Six models. *Journal of Consulting and Clinical Psychology, 59,* 612–630.

Barbaree, H. E., & Marshall, W. L. (1993). *Sexual preferences of rapists: An analysis of different response patterns.* Queen's University, Kingston, Ontario. Unpublished manuscript.

Barbaree, H. E., Marshall, W. L., & Hudson, S. M. (Eds.) (1993). *The juvenile sex offender*. New York: Guilford Press.

Barlow, D. H. (1973). Increasing heterosexual responsiveness in the treatment of sexual deviation: A review of the clinical and experimental evidence. *Behavior Therapy, 4,* 655–671.

Barlow, D. H., Leitenberg, H., & Agras, W. S. (1969). The experimental control of sexual deviation through manipulation of the noxious scene in covert sensitization. *Journal of Abnormal Psychology, 74,* 596–601.

Blader, J. C., & Marshall, W. L. (1989). Is assessment of sexual arousal in rapists worthwhile? A critique of current methods and the development of a response compatibility approach. *Clinical Psychology Review, 9,* 569–587.

Bond, I., & Evans, D. (1967). Avoidance therapy: Its use in the cases of underwear fetishism. *Canadian Medical Association Journal, 96,* 1160–1162.

Bradford, J. M. W. (1990). The antiandrogen and hormonal treatment of sex offenders. In W. L. Marshall, D. R. Laws & H. E. Barbaree (Eds.), *Handbook of sexual assault: Issues, theories, and treatment of the offender*. New York: Plenum Press.

Bradford, J. M. W., & Pawlak, A. (1993). Double-blind placebo crossover study of cyproterone acetate in the treatment of the paraphilias. *Archives of Sexual Behavior, 22,* 383–402.

Brownell, K. D., & Barlow, D. H. (1976). Measurement and treatment of two sexual deviations in one person. *Journal of Behavior Therapy and Experimental Psychiatry, 7,* 349–354.

Bumby, K., & Marshall, W. L. (1994). *Loneliness and intimacy dysfunction among incarcerated rapists and child molesters*. Paper presented at the 13th Annual Research and Treatment Conference of the Association for the Treatment of Sexual Abusers, San Francisco, CA.

Burt, M. R. (1980). Cultural myths and supports for rape. *Journal of Personality and Social Psychology, 38,* 217–230.

Cox, D. J., & Daitzman, R. J. (1979). Behavioral theory, research, and treatment of male exhibitionism. In M. Hersen, R. M. Eisler & P. M. Miller (Eds.), *Progress in behavior modification*, Vol. 7. New York: Academic Press.

Cox, D. J., & Daitzman, R. J. (Eds) (1980). *Exhibitionism: Description, assessment, and treatment*. New York: Garland STPM.

Davies, B., & Morgenstern, F. (1960). A case of cystercosis, temporal lobe epilepsy, and transvestism. *Journal of Neurology, Neurosurgery, and Psychiatry, 23,* 247–249.

Davison, G. C. (1968). Elimination of a sadistic fantasy by a client-controlled counterconditioning technique. *Journal of Abnormal Psychology, 73,* 84–90.

Davison, G. C. (1977). Homosexuality and the ethics of behavioral intervention: paper 1. *Journal of Homosexuality, 2,* 195–204.

Eccles, A., Marshall, W. L., & Barbaree, H. E. (1994). Differentiating rapists and non-offenders using the rape index. *Behaviour Research and Therapy, 32,* 539–546.

Erwin, E. (1978). *Behavior therapy: Scientific, philosophical and moral foundations*. Cambridge: Cambridge University Press.

Eysenck, H. J., & Rachman, S. (1965). *The causes and cures of neurosis*. London: Routledge & Kegan Paul.

Field, H. S. (1978). Attitudes toward rape: A comparative analysis of police, rapists, crisis counsellors, and citizens. *Journal of Personality and Social Psychology, 36,* 156–179.

Feldman, M. P., & MacCulloch, M. J. (1971). *Homosexual behaviour: Therapy and assessment*. Oxford: Pergamon Press.

Finkelhor, D. (1984). *Child sexual abuse: New theory and research*. New York: Free Press.

Furby, L., Wienrott, M. R., & Blackshaw, L. (1989). Sex offender recidivism: A review. *Psychological Bulletin, 105,* 3–30.

Garlick, Y. (1991). *Intimacy failure, loneliness and the attribution of blame in sexual offending.* Unpublished Master's thesis, University of London.

Gaupp, L. A., Stern, R. M., & Ratlieff, R. G. (1971). The use of aversion-relief procedures in the treatment of a case of voyeurism. *Behavior Therapy, 2,* 585–588.

Gershman, L. (1970). Case conference: A transvestite fantasy treated by thought-stopping, covert sensitization, and aversive shock. *Journal of Behavior Therapy and Experimental Psychiatry, 1,* 153–161.

Hall, G. C. N., & Hirschman, R. (1991). Toward a theory of sexual aggression: A quadripartite model. *Journal of Consulting and Clinical Psychology, 59,* 622–699.

Harbert, T. L., Barlow, D. H., Hersen, M., & Austin, J. B. (1974). Measurement and modification of incestuous behavior: A case study. *Psychological Reports, 34,* 79–86.

Haydn-Smith, P., Marks, I., Buchaya, H., & Repper, D. (1987). Behavioural treatment of life-threatening masochistic asphyxiation: A case study. *British Journal of Psychiatry, 150,* 518–519.

Hogan, R. (1969). Development of an empathy scale. *Journal of Consulting and Clinical Psychology, 33,* 307–316.

Howells, K. (1978). Some meanings of children for pedophiles. In M. Cook & G. Wilson (Eds.), *Love and attraction.* London: Pergamon Press.

Hudson, S. M., Marshall, W. L., Wales, D., McDonald, E., Bakker, L. W., & McLean, A. (1993). Emotional recognition skills of sex offenders. *Annals of Sex Research, 6,* 199–211.

Hudson, S. M., Ward, T., & Marshall, W. L. (1994). *Attachment style in sex offenders: A preliminary study.* Submitted.

Hudson, S. M., Marshall, W. L., Johnston, P., Ward, T., & Jones, R. L. (1995). Kia Marama: A cognitive behavioural programme for incarcerated child molesters. *Behaviour Change, 12,* 69–80.

Johnston, P., Hudson, S. M., & Marshall, W. L. (1992). The effects of masturbatory reconditioning with nonfamilial child molesters. *Behaviour Research and Therapy, 30,* 559–561.

Kilmann, P. R., Wanlass, R. L., Sabalis, R. F., & Sullivan, B. (1981). Sex education: A review of its effects. *Archives of Sexual Behavior, 10,* 177–205.

Knopp, F. H., & Lackey, L. B. (1987). *Female sexual abusers: A summary of data from forty-four treatment providers.* Orwell, VT: Safer Society Press.

Knopp, F. H., Freeman-Longo, R. E., & Stevenson, W. (1992). *Nationwide survey of juvenile and adult sex-offender treatment programs.* Orwell, VT: Safer Society Press.

Kolvin, I. (1967). "Aversive imagery" treatment in adolescents. *Behaviour Research and Therapy, 5,* 245–248.

Laws, D. R. (Ed.) (1989). *Relapse prevention with sex offenders.* New York: Guilford Press.

Laws, D. R., & Marshall, W. L. (1991). Masturbatory reconditioning: An evaluative review. *Advances in Behaviour Research and Therapy, 13,* 13–25.

Laws, D. R., Meyer, J., & Holmen, M. L. (1978). Reduction of sadistic sexual arousal by olfactory aversion. *Behaviour Research and Therapy, 16,* 281–285.

Malamuth, N. M. (1981). Rape proclivity among males. *Journal of Social Issues, 37,* 138–157.

Maletzky, B. M. (1991). *Treating the sexual offender.* Newbury Park, CA: Sage.

Marks, I. M., & Gelder, M. G. (1967). Transvestism and fetishism: Clinical and psychological changes during faradic aversion. *British Journal of Psychiatry, 113,* 711–729.

Marks, I. M., Gelder, M. G., & Bancroft, J. (1970). Sexual deviants two years after electric aversion. *British Journal of Psychiatry, 171,* 173–185.

Marks, I. M., Rachman, S., & Gelder, M. G. (1965). Methods for assessment of aversion treatment in fetishism with masochism. *Behaviour Research and Therapy, 3,* 253–258.

Marlatt, G. A. (1982). Relapse prevention: A self-control program for the treatment of addictive behaviors. In R. B. Stuart (Ed.), *Adherence, compliance and generalization in behavioral medicine*. New York: Brunner/Mazel.

Marlatt, G. A., & George, W. H. (1984). Relapse prevention: Introduction and overview of the model. *British Journal of Addiction, 79*, 261–273.

Marlatt, G. A., & Gordon, J. R. (1985). *Relapse prevention: Maintenance strategies in the treatment of addictive behaviors*. New York: Guilford Press.

Marques, J. K., Day, D. M., Nelson, C., & Miner, M. H. (1989). The Sex Offender Treatment and Evaluation Project: California relapse prevention program. In D. R. Laws (Ed.), *Relapse prevention with sex offenders*. New York: Guilford Press.

Marquis, J. (1970). Orgasmic reconditioning: Changing sexual object choice through controlling masturbatory fantasies. *Journal of Behavior Therapy and Experimental Psychiatry, 1*, 263–271.

Marshall, W. L. (1971). A combined treatment method for certain sexual deviations. *Behaviour Research and Therapy, 9*, 292–294.

Marshall, W. L. (1973). The modification of sexual fantasies: A combined treatment approach to the reduction of deviant sexual behavior. *Behaviour Research and Therapy, 11*, 557–564.

Marshall, W. L. (1979). Satiation therapy: A procedure for reducing deviant sexual arousal. *Journal of Applied Behaviour Analysis, 12*, 10–22.

Marshall, W. L. (1989). Invited Essay: Intimacy, loneliness and sexual offenders. *Behaviour Research and Therapy, 27*, 491–503.

Marshall, W. L. (1993a). A revised approach to the treatment of men who sexually assault adult females. In G. C. N. Hall, R. Hirschman, J. R. Graham & M. S. Zaragoza (Eds.), *Sexual aggression : Issues in etiology, assessment and treatment*. Bristol, PA: Taylor & Francis.

Marshall, W. L. (1993b). The role of attachment, intimacy, and loneliness in the etiology and maintenance of sexual offending. *Sexual and Marital Therapy, 8*, 109–121.

Marshall, W. L. (1994a). The perpetrator of child sexual abuse. In J. W. W. Neeb & S. J. Harper (Eds.), *Civil action for childhood sexual abuse*. Toronto: Butterworths.

Marshall, W. L. (1994b). Treatment effects on denial and minimization in incarcerated sex offenders. *Behaviour Research and Therapy, 32*, 559–564.

Marshall, W. L. (1994c). Pauvreté de liens d'attachment et déficiences dans les rapports intimes chez les agresseurs sexuels. *Criminologie, XXVII*, 55–69.

Marshall, W. L. (1994d). *Treatment of intimacy deficits*. Paper presented at the 13th Annual Research and Treatment Conference of the Association for the Treatment of Sexual Abusers, San Francisco, CA.

Marshall, W. L. (1998a). Assessment, treatment, and theorizing about sex offenders: Developments over the past 20 years and future developments. *Criminal Justice and Behavior*, in press.

Marshall, W. L. (1998b). The treatment of sex offenders: Outcome data from a community clinic. In R. R. Ross, D. H. Antonowicz & G. K. Dhaliwal (Eds.), *Effective delinquency prevention and offender rehabilitation*. Ottawa: Centre for Cognitive Development, in press.

Marshall, W. L., & McKnight, R. D. (1975). An integrated treatment program for sexual offenders. *Canadian Psychiatric Association Journal, 20*, 133–138.

Marshall, W. L., & Williams, S. (1975). A behavioral approach to the modification of rape. *Quarterly Bulletin of the British Association for Behavioural Psychotherapy, 4*, 78.

Marshall, W. L., & Lippens, K. (1977). The clinical value of boredom: A procedure for reducing inappropriate sexual interests. *Journal of Nervous and Mental Diseases, 165,* 283–287.

Marshall, W. L., & Christie, M. M. (1982). The enhancement of social self-esteem. *Canadian Counsellor, 16,* 82–89.

Marshall, W. L., & Barbaree, H. E. (1988a). An outpatient treatment program for child molesters: Description and tentative outcome. *Annals of the New York Academy of Sciences, 528,* 205–214.

Marshall, W. L., & Barbaree, H. E. (1988b). The long-term evaluation of a behavioral treatment program for child molesters. *Behaviour Research and Therapy, 26,* 499–511.

Marshall, W. L., & Barbaree, H. E. (1990a). An integrated theory of sexual offending. In W. L. Marshall, D. R. Laws & H. E. Barbaree (Eds.), *Handbook of sexual assault: Issues, theories, and treatment of the offender.* New York: Plenum Press.

Marshall, W. L., & Barbaree, H. E. (1990b). Outcome of comprehensive cognitive-behavioral treatment programs. In W. L. Marshall, D. R. Laws & H. E. Barbaree (Eds.), *Handbook of sexual assault: Issues, theories, and treatment of the offender.* New York: Plenum Press.

Marshall, W. L., & Eccles, A. (1991). Issues in clinical practice with sex offenders. *Journal of Interpersonal Violence, 6,* 68–93.

Marshall, W. L., & Eccles, A. (1993). Pavlovian conditioning processes in adolescent sex offenders. In H. E. Barbaree, W. L. Marshall & S. M. Hudson (Eds.), *The juvenile sex offender.* New York: Guilford Press.

Marshall, W. L., & Hambley, L. S. (1994). *Intimacy and loneliness, and their relationship to rape myth acceptance and hostility toward women among rapists.* Submitted.

Marshall, W. L., & Pithers, W. D. (1994). A reconsideration of treatment outcome with sex offenders. *Criminal Justice and Behavior, 21,* 10–27.

Marshall, W. L., & Eccles, A. (1998). Sexual offenders: A treatment manual. In V. M. B. Van Hasselt & M. Hersen (Eds.), *Sourcebook of psychological treatment manuals for adult disorders.* New York: Plenum Press, in press.

Marshall, W. L., Earls, C. M., Segal, Z. V., & Darke, J. (1983). A behavioral program for the assessment and treatment of sexual aggressors. In K. Craig & R. McMahon (Eds.), *Advances in clinical behavior therapy.* New York: Brunner/Mazel.

Marshall, W. L., Barbaree, H. E., & Christophe, D. (1986). Sexual offenders against female children: Sexual preferences for age of victims and type of behavior. *Canadian Journal of Behavioral Science, 18,* 424–439.

Marshall, W. L., Barbaree, H. E., & Butt, J. (1988). Sexual offenders against male children: Sexual preferences. *Behaviour Research and Therapy, 26,* 383–391.

Marshall, W. L., Barbaree, H. E., & Eccles, A. (1991a). Early onset and deviant sexuality in child molesters. *Journal of Interpersonal Violence, 6,* 323–336.

Marshall, W. L., Eccles, A., & Barbaree, H. E. (1991b). Treatment of exhibitionists: A focus on sexual deviance versus cognitive and relationship features. *Behaviour Research and Therapy, 29,* 129–135.

Marshall, W. L., Jones, R., Ward, T., Johnston, P., & Barbaree, H. E. (1991c). Treatment outcome with sex offenders. *Clinical Psychology Review, 11,* 465–485.

Marshall, W. L., Ward, T., Jones, R., Johnston, P., & Barbaree, H. E. (1991d). An optimistic evaluation of treatment outcome with sex offenders. *Violence Update, March,* 1–8.

Marshall, W. L., Hudson, S. M., & Ward, T. (1992). Sexual deviance. In P. Wilson (Ed.), *Principles and practice of relapse prevention.* New York: Guilford Press.

Marshall, W. L., Eccles, A., & Barbaree, H. E. (1993a). A three-tiered approach to the rehabilitation of incarcerated sex offenders. *Behavioral Sciences and the Law, 11,* 441–455.

Marshall, W. L., Hudson, S. M., & Hodkinson, S. (1993b). The importance of attachment bonds in the development of juvenile sex offending. In H. E. Barbaree, W. L. Marshall & S. M. Hudson (Eds.), *The juvenile sex offender*. New York: Guilford Press.

Marshall, W. L., Jones, R., Hudson, S. M., & McDonald, E. (1993c). Generalized empathy in child molesters. *Journal of Child Sexual Abuse, 2*, 61–68.

Marshall, W. L., Fernández, Y. M., Lightbody, S., & O'Sullivan, C. (1994). *Victim specific empathy in child molesters*. Unpublished manuscript, Queen's University, Kingston, Ontario.

Marshall, W. L., Hudson, S. M., Jones, R., & Fernández, Y. M. (1995). Empathy in sex offenders. *Clinical Psychology Review, 15*, 99–113.

Marshall, W. L., O'Sullivan, C., & Fernandez, Y. M. (1998). The enhancement of victim empathy among incarcerated child molesters. *Legal and Criminological Psychology*, in press.

Masters, W. H., & Johnson, V. E. (1966). *Human sexual response*. Boston, MA: Little, Brown & Co.

Mathews, R., Matthews, J., & Speitz, K. (1989). *Female sexual offenders -- An exploratory study*. Orwell, VT: Safer Society Press.

McConaghy, N. (1993). *Sexual behavior: Problems and management*. New York: Plenum Press.

McGuire, R. J., & Vallance, M. (1964). Aversion therapy by electric shock: A simple technique. *British Medical Journal, 1*, 151–152.

McGuire, R. J., Carlisle, J. M., & Young, B. G. (1965). Sexual deviations as conditioned behaviour: A hypothesis. *Behaviour Research and Therapy, 2*, 185–190.

Mees, H. L. (1966). Sadistic fantasies modified by aversion conditioning and substitution: A case study. *Behaviour Research and Therapy, 4*, 317–320.

Mehrabian, A., & Epstein, N. (1972). A measure of emotional empathy. *Journal of Personality, 40*, 525–543.

Morgenstern, F. S., Pearce, J. P., & Rees, W. L. (1965). Predicting the outcome of behaviour therapy by psychological tests. *Behaviour Research and Therapy, 3*, 253–258.

Murphy, W. D. (1990). Assessment and modification of cognitive distortions in sex offenders. In W. L. Marshall, D. R. Laws & H. E. Barbaree (Eds.), *Handbook of sexual assault: Issues, theories, and treatment of the offender*. New York: Plenum Press.

O'Donohue, W., & Plaud, J. J. (1994). The conditioning of human sexual arousal. *Archives of Sexual Behavior, 23*, 321–344.

Pearson, H. J., Marshall, W. L., Barbaree, H. E., & Southmayd, S. (1992). Treatment of a compulsive paraphiliac with buspirone. *Annals of Sex Research, 5*, 239–246.

Pithers, W. D. (1990). Relapse prevention with sexual aggressors: A method for maintaining therapeutic gain and enhancing external supervision. In W. L. Marshall, D. R. Laws & H. E. Barbaree (Eds.), *Handbook of sexual assault: Issues, theories, and treatment of the offender*. New York: Plenum Press.

Pithers, W. D. (1994). Process evaluation of a group therapy component designed to enhance sex offenders' empathy for sexual abuse survivors. *Behaviour Research and Therapy, 32*, 565–570.

Pithers, W. D., Marques, J. K., Gibat, C. C., & Marlatt, G. A. (1983). Relapse prevention with sexual aggressives: A self-control model of treatment and maintenance of change. In J. G. Greer & I. R. Stuart (Eds.), *The sexual aggressor: Current perspectives on treatment*. New York: Van Nostrand Reinhold.

Pithers, W. D., Buell, M. M., Kashima, K., Cumming, G., & Beal, L. (1987). *Precursors to relapse of sexual offenders*. Paper presented at the 3rd Annual Research and Treatment Conference of the Association for the Behavioral Treatment of Sexual Abusers. Newport, OR.

Pithers, W. D., Beal, L. S., Armstrong, J., & Petty, J. (1989a). Identification of risk factors through clinical interviews and analysis of records. In D. R. Laws (Ed.), *Relapse prevention with sex offenders*. New York: Guilford Press.

Pithers, W. D., Martin, G. R., & Cumming, G. F. (1989b). Vermont Treatment Program for Sexual Aggressors. In D. R. Laws (Ed.), *Relapse prevention with sex offenders*. New York: Guilford Press.

Quinsey, V. L., Bergersen, S. G., & Steinman, C. M. (1976). Changes in physiological and verbal responses of child molesters during aversion therapy. *Canadian Journal of Behavioral Science, 8*, 202–212.

Quinsey, V. L., & Earls, C. M. (1990). The modification of sexual preferences. In W. L. Marshall, D. R. Laws & H. E. Barbaree (Eds.), *Handbook of sexual assault: Issues, theories, and treatment of the offender*. New York: Plenum Press.

Quinsey, V. L., Harris, G. T., Rice, M. E., & Lalumière, M. L. (1993). Assessing treatment efficacy in outcome studies of sex offenders. *Journal of Interpersonal Violence, 8*, 512–523.

Rapaport, K., & Burkhart, B. R. (1984). Personality and attitudinal characteristics of sexually coercive college males. *Journal of Abnormal Psychology, 93*, 216–221.

Raymond, M. (1956). Case of fetishism treated by aversion therapy. *British Medical Journal, 2*, 854–856.

Rice, M. E., Chaplin, T. E., Harris, G. T., & Coutts, J. (1990). *Empathy for the victim and sexual arousal among rapists*. Penetanguishene Mental Health Centre, Research Report No. 7.

Rice, M. E., Quinsey, V. L., & Harris, G. T. (1991). Sexual recidivism among child molesters released from a maximum security psychiatric institution. *Journal of Consulting and Clinical Psychology, 59*, 381–386.

Ryan, G. D., & Lane, S. L. (1991). *Juvenile sexual offending: Causes, consequences and correction*. Lexington, MA: Lexington Books.

Scully, D., & Marolla, J. (1983). *Incarcerated rapists: Exploring a sociological model*. Bethesda, MD: National Rape Center, National Institute of Mental Health.

Scully, D., & Marolla, J. (1984). Convicted rapists' vocabulary of motive. *Social Problems, 31*, 530–554.

Seidman, B. T., Marshall, W. L., Hudson, S. M., & Robertson, P. J. (1994). An examination of intimacy and loneliness in sex offenders. *Journal of Interpersonal Violence, 9*, 518–534.

Seto, M. C. (1992). *Victim blame, empathy, and disinhibition of sexual arousal to rape in community males and incarcerated rapists*. Unpublished Master's thesis, Queen's University, Kingston, Ontario.

Stermac, L. E., & Segal, Z. V. (1989). Adult sexual contact with children: An examination of cognitive factors. *Behavior Therapy, 20*, 573–584.

Stermac, L. E., Segal, Z. V., & Gillis, R. (1990). Social and cultural factors in sexual assault. In W. L. Marshall, D. R. Laws & H. E. Barbaree, (Eds.), *Handbook of sexual assault: Issues, theories, and treatment of the offender*. New York: Plenum Press.

Symons, D. (1979). *The evolution of human sexuality*. Oxford: Oxford University Press.

Tieger, T. (1981). Self-reported likelihood of raping and the social perception of rape. *Journal of Research in Personality, 15*, 147–158.

Thorpe, J. G., Schmidt, E., & Castell, D. A. (1963). A comparison of positive and negative (aversive) conditioning in the treatment of homosexuality. *Behaviour Research and Therapy, 1*, 357–362.

Travin, S., & Protter, B. (1993). *Sexual perversion: Integrative treatment approaches for the clinician*. New York: Plenum Press.

Ward, T., Hudson, S. M., Marshall, W. L., & Siegert, R. (1998). Attachment style and intimacy deficits in sex offenders: A theoretical framework. *Sexual Abuse: A Journal of Research and Treatment*, in press.

Wijesinghe, B. (1977). Massed aversion treatment of sexual deviance. *Journal of Behavior Therapy and Experimental Psychiatry, 8*, 135–137.

Further Reading

Barbaree, H. E., Marshall, W. L., & Hudson, S. M. (Eds.) (1993). *The juvenile sex offender.* New York: Guilford Press.

Hall, G. C. N., Hirschman, R., Graham, J. R., & Zaragoza, M. S. (Eds.) (1993). *Sexual aggression: Issues in etiology, assessment and treatment.* Bristol, PA: Taylor & Francis.

Knopp, F. H., & Lackey, L. B. (1987). *Female sexual abusers: A summary of data from forty-four treatment providers.* Orwell, VT: Safer Society Press.

Maletzky, B. M. (1991). *Treating the sexual offender.* Newbury Park, CA: Sage.

Laws, D. R. (Ed.) (1989). *Relapse prevention with sex offenders.* New York: Guilford Press.

Marshall, W. L., Laws, D. R., & Barbaree, H. E. (Eds.) (1990). *Handbook of sexual assault: Issues, theories, and treatment of the offender.* New York: Plenum Press.

11

Cognitive Behavioural Treatment for Hypochondriasis

CRISTINA BOTELLA and PILAR MARTÍNEZ NARVÁEZ

Universitat Jaume I, Castellón and Universidad de Granada, Spain

> *MISOMEDION.- So, this is "your Secret for the cure of this terrible Suffering"?*
>
> *PHILOPERIO.– I have several. I take the necessary time to listen and reflect upon my Patients' Suffering...and I take the trouble to get to know my Patients' way of life, not only to find out the Procathartic causes but also to better study the Circumstances, as well as (the) Idiosyncrasies of each particular Person*
>
> Mandeville (1711; cited in Baur, 1988; p. 133)

Introduction

One of the most deep-rooted themes when it comes to describing hypochondriasis is the implicit difficulty in treating it. The majority of clinics consider hypochondriasis to be a subject reluctant to change, with a very bad prognosis. Various reasons are put forward to justify this negative impression (Barsky, Geringer & Wool, 1988a). In the first place, hypochondriacs tend to respond to medical intervention by developing complications, exacerbating symptoms or presenting new complaints which replace old ones. In the second place, they show great resistance to psychiatric treatment since they believe their problem is exclusively physical. Finally, they are patients who appear, on the one hand, dependent on their doctors and, on the other, hostile and with a tendency to reject offers of help from them which inevitably hinders the establishment of an adequate therapeutic alliance. However, even recognizing that hypochondriasis is a difficult clinical problem to "cure", we should not forget that disinterest by some health professionals in this disorder is in part responsible for the belief that hypochondriacs are untreatable patients and as such, any method which attempt to improve their condition is doomed to failure.

Despite the "black legend" which for years has accompanied hypochondriasis treatment, luckily we are now showing an increased enthusiasm in the study of this disorder and all its aspects, especially therapeutic. This "new sap" is a product of cognitive-like theoretical models upon which promising therapeutic strategies have been designed. Beginning with these considerations and concentrating on such focuses in this present study we attempt to run through the most relevant contributions to conceptualization and treatment of hypochondriasis which have happened in recent years.

Concept and Diagnosis

The present-day notion of hypochondriasis as "excessive worry about one's health" is a result of a long historical-conceptual trajectory which goes back to the time of ancient medicine. Indeed hypochondriasis has been a recognizable term for more than two thousand years and has meant many things throughout its long existence. In fact, as Kellner (1986) rightly points out, "the history of hypochondriasis is more about the history of a term rather than that of a disorder or syndrome" (p. 7).

If we only pay attention to the concept of hypochondriasis in existence today it seems necessary to mention to comment upon the definitions formulated by the two most notable nosological systems in clinical circles: the fourth edition of the *Diagnostic and Statistical Manual of Mental Disorders* (APA, 1994) and the tenth revision of the *International Classification of Diseases* (WHO, 1992).

Classification by the American Psychiatric Association

The DSM-IV (APA, 1994) classifies hypochondriasis within the general category of somatoform disorders and states that the common trait which characterizes this group of disorders is "the presence of physical symptoms that suggest a general medical condition...and are not fully explained by a general medical condition, by the direct effects of a psychoactive substance or by any other mental disorder (e.g., panic disorder). The symptoms must cause clinically significant distress or impairment in social, occupational or other areas of functioning" (p. 445). According to the suggestions of Clark, Watson & Reynolds (1995), the definition given by the DSM-IV of somatoform disorders would not include disorders such as hypochondriasis or dismorphic body disorder since the main characteristic of them is not any physical symptomology. For this reason, Clark et al. (1995) suggest including the individual's erroneous perceptions about his/her somatic symptoms and his/her bodily characteristics in the conceptualization of somatoform disorders.

The main defining aspect of hypochondriasis, according to the DSM-IV, is fear of or believing that one is suffering from a serious illness stemming from incorrect interpretation of bodily symptoms. This fear or conviction does not have a delirious characteristic nor is it restricted to a physical aspect. It is persistent, it has a minimum duration of 6 months, not better accounted for by another mental disorder, it is maintained despite physical signs and medical explanations and causes a marked uneasiness and significant impairment in different aspects of the person's life.

The DSM-IV continues to invariably uphold the notion of hypochondriasis sustained by its predecessor DSM-III-R (APA, 1987), to the extent that some of the criticisms made of the third revised edition (Fallon, Klein & Liebowitz, 1993; Salkovskis & Clark, 1993; Schmidt, 1994; Starcevic, 1991; Warwick & Salkovskis, 1989) exist almost in their entirety in the fourth (Chorot & Martínez, 1995; Martínez, Belloch & Botella, 1995; Martínez & Botella, 1996).

Salkovskis & Clark (1993) have pointed out two problematic aspects of the definition of hypochondriasis put forth by the DSM-III-R. The first of them refers to the inclusion in the definition of patients convinced they are suffering from an illness as well as those who fear becoming ill. This same criticism can be made of the DSM-IV since, with the same lack of clarity, it conceptualizes this alteration as "fear" or "belief of" suffering from a serious illness. However, as far as the conceptual aspect of "fear" of illness is concerned, the DSM-IV has added some changes in order to clarify this question. It includes the phobia referred to illness within the general heading of anxiety disorders and, in particular, within the category of specific phobia (other type). Besides, it places the border between hypochondriasis and specific phobia (of illness) in the existence or not of conviction of illness: patients with hypochondriasis are worried about the fear of suffering from a physical disorder (which is already present); on the other hand patients with specific phobia (of illness) fear contracting or being exposed to an affection.

The second conflicting aspect pointed out by Salkovskis & Clark (1993) refers to criterion C of the DSM-III-R (that worrying about illness continues despite medical explanations). These authors have censured this defining element on the base of the following considerations: (1) Not all patients have access to comforting medical information; (2) Some patients refuse to go to the doctor; (3) Often hypochondriacs seek to assuage their fears through channels other than medical consultation (e.g., family, friends, medical books) and (4) This criterion does not specify the kind of comforting information which individuals find inaffective.

Following this same critical line Starcevic (1991) maintains that criterion C for the diagnosis of hypochondriasis in the DSM-III-R is ambiguous since it is subject to two interpretations. The first suggests that something co-exists with hypochondriasis which makes it such that explanations do not have the hoped-for curative effects. If this explanation were true, the validity of conceptualizing hypochondriasis as a nondelirious disorder might be put into doubt. The second interpretation implies the assumption that ordinary "common sense" explanations are of no help in this disorder. Although this interpretation is in line with clinical observations, the benefits drawn from medical attention for demands of explanations from the patient (Kellner, 1982, 1983) has lead Strarcevic to argue that depending upon the type and the way in which they are given, explanations could be useful for the treatment of hypochondriasis.

In relation to this point, the DSM-IV can be subject to the same criticisms as its predecessor. Although criterion B has incorporated a summary of the B and C criteria of the DSM-III-R, it does not specify which explanations do not eliminate the patient's worry. In our judgement, the definition of this diagnostic guideline is so vague and imprecise that in practice, using it becomes an impossible task or depends upon the interpretative subjectivity of each clinic.

Another debatable element in the definition of hypochondriasis in the DSM-III-R made by Fallon et al. (1993), refers to the requirement of the presence of somatic signals or sensations. This implies that cases lacking this type of symptomology would not be apt to receive the diagnosis of hypochondriasis. The DSM-IV continues to expound upon a restricted concept of this disorder excluding those patients who are physically asymptomatic who, however, are hypervigilant and nervous when faced with a possible body sign which indicates disease. Although for hypochondriacs their somatic symptoms represent the most convincing evidence that they are ill, it is not the only one, and so those other possible evidences (e.g., belief in personal vulnerability to illness) in and of themselves can justify diagnosis. In our opinion, the present-day conception of hypochondriasis tends to establish an unjustified predominance of physiological elements over cognitive or emotional ones.

Finally, as Schmidt (1994) has suggested the fourth conflictive question of the way in which the DSM-III-R defines hypochondriasis can be noted. It refers to the fact that it only contemplates worries about having a physical disorder, omitting those concerned with psychical illnesses associated with the erroneous interpretation of psychological manifestations. The DSM-IV continues without resolving this lack and does not pay any attention to the concept of "psychological hypochondriasis". Even if it is true that these cases are infrequent this fact should note determine its inclusion in the definition of hypochondriasis. We believe that not explicitly contemplating the worry about serious mental illness amongst the diagnostic criteria of the DSM-IV gives rise to a skewed conception which prevents consideration of the hypochondriacal disorder in all its phenomenological possibilities

Classification of the World Health Organization

The somatoform disorders of the DSM-IV are equivalent in the CIE-10 (WHO, 1992) to those grouped under *somatoform disorders* and *dissociative (conversion) disorders* which, in turn, are grouped under the category of *neurotic disorders secondary to stressful situations and somatoform disorders.*

The CIE-10 classifies hypochondriac disorder within the category of somatoform disorders. The main characteristic of these disorders is the "the repeated occurrence of somatic symptoms along with persistent demands for clinical exploration, despite repeated negative results from such clinical investigation and continual guarantees from doctors that the symptoms have no somatic justification" (p. 201).

According to the CIE-10, two requirements must be met to establish a diagnosis of hypochondriac disorder. Firstly, the persistent belief in the presence of, at least, one serious organic illness underlying symptoms despite repeated exams which have not identified them, or constant worry about a supposed physical deformity; and, secondly, the refusal to accept the doctor's explanation that rules out such an illness or abnormality.

The same critical observations can be made about the CIE-10 that were made about the recent editions of the DSM. The CIE-10 also does not clearly distinguish between the fear of conviction in an illness since the category of hypochondriasis defined as a "belief" also includes nosophobia.. However, and along the same lines as the DSM-IV, the CIE-10 places fear of suffering from a serious organic illness (nosophobia) within the category of hypochondriac disorder; on the other hand it classifies the fear of becoming ill derived from fear of contagion due to an infection, contamination, medical intervention or public conveniences as phobia disorder (specific phobia). The CIE-10, like the DSM-IV suggests the existence of ineffective medical explanations as a diagnostic criterion of hypochondriac disorder but does not specify the characteristics of those explanations which do not take the expected effects. We might even say that it adds another element of confusion as far as the number of doctors involved in the problem are concerned. With regards to the third and fourth inconvenience detected in the DSM-IV, the CIE-10 also requires the existence of somatic symptoms and does not contemplate the diagnosis of the "psychological" mode of hypochondriasis.

Cognitive Explanatory Modes

In the past few years various explanatory proposals for hypochondriasis have been suggested based on the conceptualization of this disease as a manifestation of an alteration at a cognitive level. In our opinion, the two most solid versions are, the one hand, that which suggests that hypochondriacs widen their normal bodily sensations and, on the other that which considers the possibility of patients incorrectly interpreting the symptoms they feel. Let's describe what each one states.

Somatosensorial Amplification

Barsky (1992) has suggested that the concept of amplification is useful in understanding the clinical conditions (psychological and physical) characterized by somatic complaints disproportionate to organic illness which exists. According to this author, amplification plays an etiopathogenic role in hypochondriasis, but, it also can adopt another series of functions: (1) being an unspecific characteristic associated with various psychological disorders which have physical symptomology (e.g., panic disorder); (2) playing an important role in processes of transitory and nonpathological somatization which are a result of vital stressful situations and (3) explaining differences in physical symptomology detected in individuals with the same medical condition (e.g., rheumatoid arthritis).

In line with Barsky's (1992) proposal, hypochondriac individuals amplify a wide variety of somatic and visceral symptoms such as normal physiological and anatomical sensations (e.g., peristaltic intestinal movements, postural hypotension, changes in heart rate) harmless dysfunctions and minor illnesses (e.g., occasional dizziness, twitching of the eyelids, dry skin) or the visceral or somatic concomitants of an emotional state (e.g., physiological stimulation which accompanies anxiety). In Table 11.1 some other sensations subject to amplification are brought together.

According to Barsky and collaborators (Barsky, 1979, 1992; Barsky & Klerman, 1983; Barsky, Goodson, Lane & Cleary, 1988b; Barsky & Wyshak, 1990),individuals with hypochondriasis increase their physical sensations and tend to experience them in a more intense, novel, threatening and perturbing way than individuals without this disorder. This "amplifying somatic style" of hypochondriasis is characterized by the following elements (Barsky et al., 1988b; Barsky, 1992): (1) A propensity to excessively watch the body state which is related to an increase in self-scrutiny and focalizing attention on uncomfortable bodily sensations; (2) a tendency to select and concentrate on certain infrequent or minor feelings; and (3) an inclination to consider such sensations as dangerous and indicators of illness.

The explanatory model of the development of hypochondriasis upheld by the authors referred to is that the tendency hypochondriac individuals have to experience bodily sensations with great intensity and disturbance leads them to interpret them, in an erroneous manner, as a manifestation of a serious physical illness, instead of attributing them to a benign cause (e.g., lack of physical exercise, too much work). The suspicion of any illness resulting from this misinterpretation makes them constantly vigilant of their body, examining the somatic sensations they notice, paying selective attention to the information which ratifies their hypothetical explanation of the symptoms and ignoring that which denies it. Likewise, the increase in anxiety which takes place causes new bodily sensations which individuals assess as proof of illness. Finally, all this intensifies the perception of danger causing a vicious circle (Barsky & Wyshak, 1990). Within this formulation, the rest of clinical characteristics of hypochondriasis are considered to be consequences derived from somatic amplification.

Amplification, as these authors conceptualize it, can be a stable trait or a transitory state. As a trait, amplification is considered a persistent perceptive style acquired during infancy by means of formative and educational experiences, or as a constitutional factor present in the nervous system since birth. As a state, amplification refers to the degree to which the individual amplifies a particular sensation in a specific moment (Barsky et al., 1988b). Amplification understood as a state can be influenced by various factors, such as cognitions (information and knowledge, opinion and beliefs and etiological attributions), the situational context (feedback from other people and future expectations) attention and emotions (anxiety and depression) (Barsky, 1992).

Catastrophic Interpretation of the Symptoms

According to the explanation proposal of Salkovskis (1989), Warwick (1989), Warwick & Salkovskis (1989, 1990) and Salkovskis and Clark (1993), the most important characteristic of hypochondriasis is the incorrect interpretation of nonpathological physical symptoms as a sign of serious illness. According to this formulation, the process through which hypochondriasis develops begins with previous experiences related to illnesses the individual has previously had. Amongst these experiences are illnesses the subject him/herself or family members have suffered and/or having been subject to a medical error. These negative occurrences lead to the formulation of dysfunctional beliefs or suppositions about symptoms, health and illness (e.g., "Bodily changes are habitually a sign of serious illness since every symptom has to have an identifiable physical cause"). These negative beliefs may remain relatively inactive until they are agitated by a critical event which may be of an internal nature (e.g., noticing a physical sensation) or external (e.g., the death of a family member or friend). Likewise, dysfunctional suppositions may cause a confirmatory bias by making the patient selectively direct his/her attention to the information which confirms the idea of illness and ignore that information which shows their good state of health. The activation of problematic beliefs provokes the appearance of disagreeable images and automatic negative thoughts whose content implies a cata-

Table 11.1. Sensations subject to amplification (Barsky, 1992)

Normal physiological and anatomical sensations
- Secondary tachycardia due to a change in posture (palpitations)
- Tissue anomaly of the chest (lump)
- Lack of breath due to exertion

Benign dysfunctions and common illnesses
- Dizziness
- Hiccups
- Diarrhoea
- Headache

Somatic concomitants of an intense affect
- Diaphoresis with anxiety
- Redness with embarrassment
- Cardiovascular arousal with anger

Symptoms of medical illness
- Serious organic pathology

strophic interpretation of feelings or bodily sensations (e.g., "My stomach aches mean that I have an undetected cancer".)

Finally , this chain of elements precipitates anxiety about health and its corresponding physiological manifestations (e.g., increase in physiological stimulation), cognitive manifestations (e.g., self-centred attention), affective manifestations (e.g., anxiety) and behavioural manifestations (e.g., the search for calming information). The illustrative scheme of this model of hypochondriasis development appears in Figure 11.1.

According to these authors, there are a series of factors which perpetuate the health worries. The maintenance model of hypochondriasis stems from the consideration of the existence of a trigger stimulus (e.g., receiving information about an illness) which, upon being perceived as threatening by the individual provokes fear or apprehension in him/her. This reaction triggers a series of physiological, behavioural and cognitive processes. In the first place, the increase in physiological stimulation carries with it an increase in somatic sensations measured by the autonomous nervous system (e.g., palpitations) which the individual may attribute to the existence of an organic disease. Second, the fact of permanently concentrating attention on the body may make the patient aware of normal changes in his/her body function (e.g., gastric distentions after eating) or aspects of his/her physical appearance (e.g., reddening of the skin) which, otherwise would have gone unnoticed, and s/he now interprets as abnormal. Besides, the individual also pays attention to the concordant facts with the idea of illness and with the confirmatory bias developed earlier. Finally, behaviours of bodily self-inspection and search for calm-

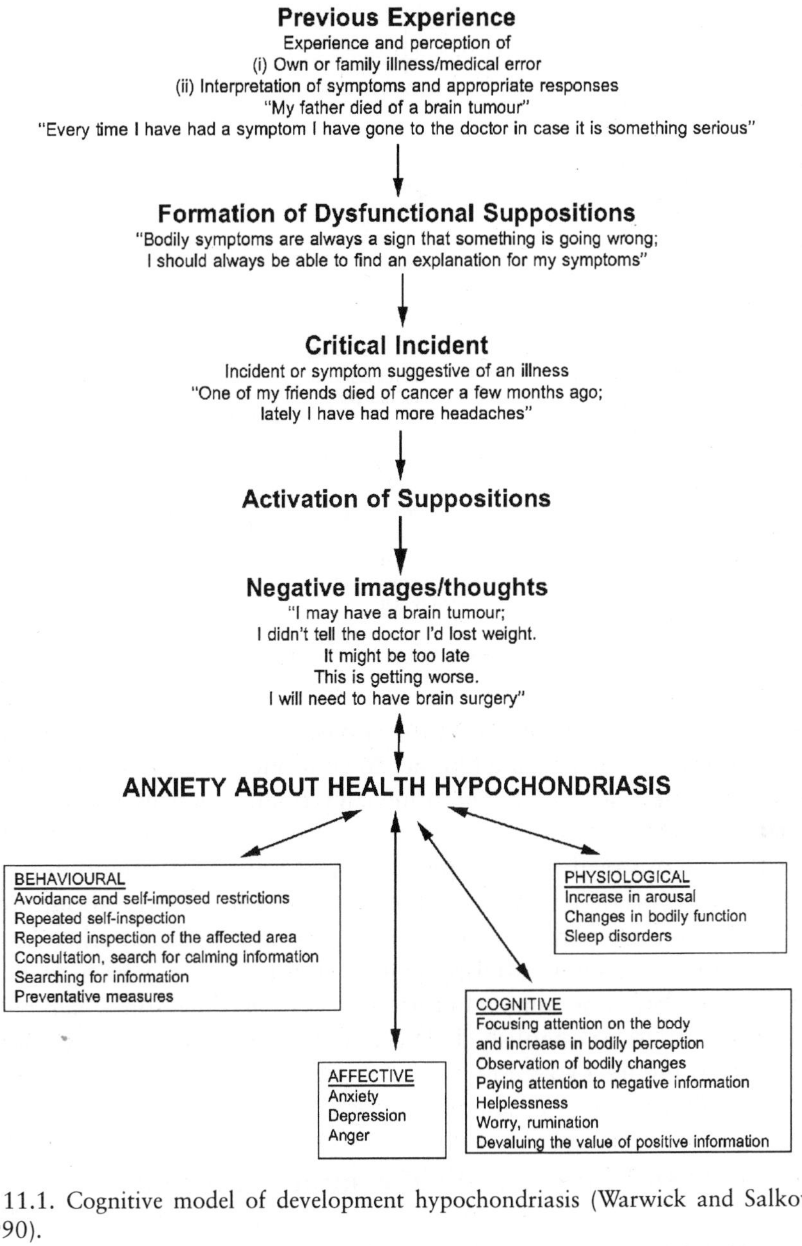

Previous Experience
Experience and perception of
(i) Own or family illness/medical error
(ii) Interpretation of symptoms and appropriate responses
"My father died of a brain tumour"
"Every time I have had a symptom I have gone to the doctor in case it is something serious"

Formation of Dysfunctional Suppositions
"Bodily symptoms are always a sign that something is going wrong;
I should always be able to find an explanation for my symptoms"

Critical Incident
Incident or symptom suggestive of an illness
"One of my friends died of cancer a few months ago;
lately I have had more headaches"

Activation of Suppositions

Negative images/thoughts
"I may have a brain tumour;
I didn't tell the doctor I'd lost weight.
It might be too late
This is getting worse.
I will need to have brain surgery"

ANXIETY ABOUT HEALTH HYPOCHONDRIASIS

BEHAVIOURAL
Avoidance and self-imposed restrictions
Repeated self-inspection
Repeated inspection of the affected area
Consultation, search for calming information
Searching for information
Preventative measures

PHYSIOLOGICAL
Increase in arousal
Changes in bodily function
Sleep disorders

AFFECTIVE
Anxiety
Depression
Anger

COGNITIVE
Focusing attention on the body
and increase in bodily perception
Observation of bodily changes
Paying attention to negative information
Helplessness
Worry, rumination
Devaluing the value of positive information

Figure 11.1. Cognitive model of development hypochondriasis (Warwick and Salkovskis, 1990).

ing information from medical or nonmedical sources also contribute to encouraging health worries. The way in which these behaviours work is similar to the compulsive rituals of obsessive-compulsive disorder since although they momentarily appease anxiety, they later increase it (Warwick & Salkovskis, 1989). This kind of behaviour sustains worry via the following methods

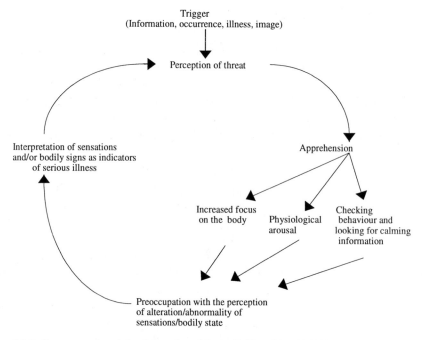

Figure 11.2. Factors maintaining hypochondriasis (Salkovskis, 1989).

(Warwick, 1989): (1) Not allowing the subject to learn that what s/he fear is not happening; (2) Encouraging him/her to continue paying attention to his/her negative thoughts; and (3) directly influencing bodily changes which produced the initial thoughts.

The three mechanisms described (physiological activation, attention focalization and inappropriate behaviour) make the individual worry about physical sensations which are perceived as pathological and make him/her interpret them as a sign that s/he is suffering from a serious illness, which, in turn increases the perception of danger. In this way, a circular relation which perpetuates hypochondriasis is established. This maintenance model of hypochondriasis is shown in Figure 11.2.

Behavioural and Cognitive-Behavioural Treatments

As we showed in the introduction to this chapter hypochondriasis has been considered an untreatable disease for some time. However, reports carried out (mostly in the last decade)on the therapeutic effectiveness of behavioural and cognitive-behavioural strategies on patients suffering from hypochondriasis, have made it possible to reject or, at least question this convincing argument.

Behavioural Techniques

As far as behavioural therapy intervention is concerned various techniques have been used to treat fear of illness, belief that one has an illness or hypochondriac behaviours present in other clinical manifestations. Amongst them, the following stick out: *systematic desensitization* (Floru, 1973; Rifkin, 1968), *thought detention and relaxation* (Kumar & Wilkinson, 1971), *implosive therapy and hypnosis* (O'Donnell, 1978), *applied relaxation* (Johansson & Öst, 1981), *positive reinforcement* (Mansdorf, 1981), *Premack principal* (Williamson, 1984) and *punishment* (Reinders, 1988).

One of the most useful intervention possibilities is that which has taken as a point of reference the similarities which exist between hypochondriasis and anxiety disorders (more specifically phobias and obsessive-compulsive disorder). Patients with hypochondriasis share high levels of anxiety and avoidance behaviour with phobic patients. Equally, behaviour similar to the compulsive rituals of obsessive-compulsive disorder is common, such as constant evaluation of the body state and the search for comforting information. Considering these appreciations and the fact that exposure is useful in the treatment of phobic disorders (Marks, 1987) and that response prevention is useful in treating obsessive-compulsive disorder (Emmelkamp, 1982) it has been suggested that these procedures might be beneficial for patients with hypochondriasis (Visser & Bouman, 1992).

In this regard, the results obtained in some of the studies which have used exposure therapy and/or response prevention (on occasion, in combination with other kinds of procedures) seem to show evidence in favour of its effectiveness for the treatment of this condition. Furst & Cooper (1970) used exposure to interoceptive and imagined stimulus to stop fear of having a heart attack. Tearnan, Goetsch & Adams (1985) successfully treated a heart attack phobia case using a multifaceted exposure programme, maintaining the improvement at 6 and 12 months of follow-up. Fiegenbaum (1986) used in vivo exposure to feared sensations in the natural environment with 33 patients with cardiophobia. He succeeded in bringing about an important improvement in many of them which was still evident after 3 years. Salkovskis & Warwick (1986) obtained positive results in the treatment of two patients with hypochondriasis using attention suppression of patients' complaints. Warwick & Marks (1988) obtained significant improvements in the majority of the 17 hypochondriasis or illness phobia cases which were treated with in vivo exposure to the feared stimulus, satiation, paradoxical intention and prohibition of asking for comforting information. Logsdail, Lovell, Warwick & Marks (1991) made use of exposure (in vivo and/or imaginary) to feared situations and other anxiety trigger signs and prevention of checking and cleaning behaviours in the treatment of 7 patients with a fear of AIDS, with improvements in almost all of them maintained 3 months after the end of therapy.

Structured Cognitive Behavioural Programmes

In the last few years various programmes of a cognitive-behavioural type for the treatment of hypochondriasis have been developed. Those which, in our judgement, are the most promising ones, are those proposed by Barsky, Geringer & Wool (1988a), Salkovskis (1989), Warwick (1989), Warwick & Salkovskis (1989, 1990), House (1989), Stern & Fernández (1991), Sharpe, Peveler & Mayou (1992), and Avia (1993). We are only going to describe the first two therapeutical proposals since they have the best empirical backing at this point in time.

Treatment of the "somatic amplification style". Barsky et al. (1988a) have developed a cognitive-educational therapeutic programme based on the conceptualization of hypochondriasis as a disorder characterized by a "somatic amplification style". According to this proposal, treatment is carried out in small groups of 6–8 patients who get together once a week for a month and a half. The therapy is presented as a "course" which will allow them to learn about the perception of physical symptoms. The therapist–patient relationship is explained as similar to that between student and teacher. The content of the course consists in analyzing factors involved in amplification or attenuation of somatic symptoms:

(1) *Role of attention and use of relaxation.* Beginning with the consideration that attention may have an amplifying effect on bodily sensations and that distraction may lessen them, didactic material illustrating this is given and patients are asked to exemplify these phenomena with personal experiences. Also, the extreme sensitivity of hypochondriacs to somatic sensations is used to teach them how to focalize their attention on feelings of relaxing and well-being and ignoring uncomfortable feelings. For this, visual imagination, progressive relaxation, muscular relaxation, breathing and simple yoga exercises are used. Finally, homework is assigned for the purpose of strengthening learning.

(2) *Cognition and reattribution of benign symptoms.* Two possible explanatory models of bodily sensations are introduced: the cognitive-perceptive model and the stress model. In relation to the former, the patients are suggested to consider their nervous system as a radio receptor which possesses such a high degree of sensitivity that any kind of signal it receives is highly increased and starts to become annoying. Then, the effects on the one hand which causal attributions made by the patient have on somatic sensations, and on the other hand the influence that illness cognitions have upon the perception of the symptoms, are analyzed and illustrated. As far as the second model is concerned, the concept of stress is introduced as well as techniques for controlling it. Patients are Informed about somatic concomitants of stress and their effects upon the immune system. Likewise, subjects are asked to assess the stressful

stimulus in their life and identify resources at their disposal for coping with them.

(3) *Situational context.*The role of the context which surrounds a person in the increase or decrease of their somatic symptoms, in the perception of them, in the significance given to them and in the generation of expectations as far as what one should feel, is explained. Subjects are asked to illustrate the effects of situational context from their own observations. This analysis allows individuals to realize that they can try to understand their bodily symptoms by placing them in a different "surrounding". So, instead of analyzing them from within a context of nondiagnosed serious illness, they can choose to accept them and cope with them.

(4) *Role of affect and dependency conflicts.* The repercussions of certain negative affective states (e.g., anxiety, depression) upon the perception of somatic sensations are explained and illustrated. However, this is introduced with the caution not to give the idea that physical symptoms are a result of emotional disturbance. Patients are also asked to analyze the emotional states which seem to make their symptoms worse. On many occasions this task allows dependency needs to flourish.

Avia, Ruiz, Olivares, Crespo, Guisado, Sánchez & Varela (1996) have carried out a controlled study to test the effectiveness of this treatment programme. The sample used was composed of 17 subjects who scored highly on certain measures of hypochondriasis (8 of them fulfilled the diagnostic criteria of the DSM-III-R). They were randomly assigned into three groups: two experimental groups (with 4–5 patients in each group) and a control group on a waiting list (of 8 patients). The experimental groups received structured group therapy in 6 weekly sessions of an hour and a half each. The first five sessions were dedicated to discussing the basic factors contributing to somatic discomfort: (1) selective and inadequate attention; (2) muscular tension/bad breathing habits; (3) environmental factors; (4) stress and disphoric mood; and (5) explanations of somatic signs. In the last session the themes dealt with during previous sessions were reviewed and some questionnaires were filled out. The individuals who remained on the waiting list were also given the same treatment once this had been finished in the experimental groups. After the treatment, the experimental groups showed improvements which were not seen in the control group. All in all the individuals who were treated (including those from the waiting list) showed improvements which were maintained in the follow-ups carried out a month and a half and a year after the end of treatment.

Treatment of catastrophic interpretations and dysfunctional suppositions. Warwick and Salkovskis (Salkovskis, 1989; Warwick, 1989; and Warwick & Salkovskis, 1989, 1990) have developed a treatment programme based upon their formulation of hypochondriasis as a disorder whose key component is the catastrophic interpretation of bodily signs and sensations. The intervention consists of helping the patient to detect and change automatic negative thoughts about their physical symptoms, maladaptive beliefs about health and illness and problematic behaviour. This treatment programme consists of the following elements:

(1) *Obtaining patient compromise.* In order to get this, the patient is given a new angle from which s/he can understand his/her problem. It is specifically proposed to him/her to consider the possibility for a long time (about 4 months) that their symptoms are not a sign of serious illness (old hypothesis) but an anxiety problem (new hypothesis). The latter is considered as a provisional hypothesis which the individual can put to the test through the accumulation of corresponding evidence.

(2) *Self-observation of anxiety episodes about health.* The patient is instructed to record the stimulus which act as detonators of an episode of excessive worry about health and to identify automatic negative thoughts and inappropriate behaviours.

(3) *Reattribution of symptoms.* The main core of intervention consists of modifying negative attributions about the origin of somatic symptoms. To do this identification of negative thoughts and the evidence which sustains them are needed, as well as elaboration and testing of more benign alternative explanations of the symptoms. The latter is carried out by using verbal techniques (e.g., drawing explanatory tables of the information in existence and adopting the point of view of another person) and behavioural experiments (e.g., paying attention to one's own body, manipulating behaviours which may provoke symptoms).

(4) *Changing maladaptive behaviours.* The aim is to show the influence of certain of the patient's behaviours upon the maintenance of his/her worries about health. Just for this, questions are asked, direct demonstrations and experiments with behaviours involved in the problem are made. Also, prevention of body checking and searching for comforting information behaviours is used and, on the other hand, the withdrawal of attention to the questions and commentaries about symptoms.

(5) *Modification of dysfunctional beliefs about health/illness.* To modify these beliefs similar procedures to the previous ones are used, centering upon reattribution and behaviour experiments.

The therapeutic programme of Warwick and Salkovskis also has evidence in its favour. Up until now, the description of several cases where it has been effective have been presented (Warwick & Salkovskis, 1989), and a study has been reported out in which the experimental group (who received treatment) was compared to a control group (waiting list) with the observation that treated patients got significant improvements (Warwick, Clark & Cobb, 1994; Warwick, 1995a).

Recently, we described the application of an adapted and modified version of the treatment programme developed by Salkovskis and Warwick, in a case of primary hypochondriasis (Martínez & Botella, 1995). With the therapy, which took place in 10 sessions of about an hour a week, the patient showed a notable improvement which was maintained in the follow-up carried out 2 and 6 months after treatment.

Intervention Protocol

This section is dedicated to describing in some detail the treatment programme we have structured from the directions suggested by Salkovskis and Warwick (Salkovskis, 1989, 1991; Salkovskis & Warwick, 1986; Warwick, 1989; Warwick & Salkovskis, 1989, 1990).[1]

The protocol we present consists of two phases; the first is concerned with the assessment of the problem and the second contains the core of the intervention itself.

Assessment Phase

The assessment process is carried out in three session, following in general terms the suggestions of Salkovskis (1989)[2] (Table 11.2).

The first two sessions are dedicated to deepening knowledge of the problem by using verbal information which is given by the patient. This information can be completed using a Clinical Anamnesis and a Biographical Questionnaire which allow for a more complete perspective of the patient's life situation.

Sessions I and II: Agenda
1. Discovering the patient's attitude towards psychological treatment.
2. Tactics for getting the patient's cooperation.
3. Brief description of the problem.
4. Onset and course of the problem.
5. Detailed description of the problem.
6. Modulating variables.
7. Avoidance.
8. Reaction of other significant people.
9. History of previous treatments.
10. Degree of handicap: social/work/spare time.

---

[1] Following Salkovskis' (1989) instructions, some of the techniques used in the treatment of panic disorders are incorporated (Clark, 1989).
[2] Along with Salkovskis' (1989) suggestions, the basic aspects of Kirk's (1989) cognitive-behavioural evaluation were also taken into account. In a recent work Warwick (1995b) described in great detail the evaluation process of hypochondriasiscal worries.

Table 11.2. Summary of the Main Assessment Areas (Salkovskis, 1989)

Interview

Patient's attitude towards having been referred to a psychologist and towards his/her problem

Details of the problem: cognitive, physiological, behavioural, affective; history of previous treatments

Which things make the problem better or worse

Degree of handicap: social/work/ free-time

Beliefs about the origin, cause and course of the illness

General beliefs about the nature and significance of the symptoms

Self-observation

Recording the problem, associated thoughts, emotional state, behaviour, use of medication, consequences of the problem

Questionnaires

Anxiety, depression, specific questionnaires

Physiological measures

Criteria measures specific to his/her case

Determination of the variations perceived in the bodily function implied

---

11. Beliefs about the origin, cause and course of the problem.
12. General beliefs about the nature and significance of the symptoms.
13. Psychosocial situation.

(1) *Discovering the patient's attitude towards psychological treatment.* Exploring the beliefs the patient may have with regards to therapy and to its possible consequences (e.g., when the doctor told him/her that s/he needed to be referred to a psychologist, what was his/her reaction? To what extent does s/he think that psychological help may be beneficial?)

(2) *Tactics for getting the patient's cooperation.* The aim is to get enough compliance from the patient to be able to facilitate the psychological evaluation of the problem. One way of achieving cooperation is to explain that the work of the psychologist also includes the treatment of problems which although they are organic (e.g., stomach ulcers, hypertension) may be influenced by various psychological factors. Another tactic involves explaining that the objective of the interview lies in gaining more insight into the problem and, therefore, the decision about whether psychological help is a good idea or not is not a good one to make at this moment, but should be postponed to a later date when all the information about the case has been obtained. If the patient continues to object to the evaluation despite these explanations, the following tactics may be used: the therapist may say that s/he understands the patient's negativity and the belief that his/her problem is definitely organic. However, the therapist may also ask if the patient has ever had at least a 1% doubt that

s/he may be wrong ("maybe you don't have such an illness"). Since the patient often responds positively, s/he is asked to consider the percentage of doubt as an exercise to make sure that s/he has tackled his/her problem in all possible ways.

(3) *Brief description of the problem.* Open questions are used, such as : "Can you explain your main problem to me in a few words?" To establish a good relationship it is useful for the therapist to show an understanding of the discomfort the patient suffers. Likewise, it is a good idea to summarize and paraphrase the patient's explanation of his/her problem to verify that s/he has been understood correctly.

(4) *Onset and course of the problem.* Identifying the factors which may have been responsible for the onset of the problem (e.g., When did you start to worry excessively about your health? Under what circumstances?) And its fluctuations (e.g., Has the problem been getting progressively worse? Have there been any moments in which the seriousness of the symptoms has oscillated?)

(5) *Detailed description of the problem.* In order to obtain more specific information about the state of the patient, s/he is asked to describe a recent occasion in which s/he has worried about his/her physical complaints (relative description of before, during and after the episode): situation (e.g., When did it occur? Where were you? What were you doing? Who was there?); physical symptoms (e.g., What kind of bodily sensations did you experience?); cognitions (e.g., When did you start to feel the symptoms? What thoughts went through your mind? What kind of mental images did you have? At the most serious moment of the symptoms, what did you think could be the worst thing to happen to you at that moment?, What did you think could happen with the passing of time?); behaviours (e.g., What did you do when the symptoms appeared? Did you do something to try to stop the problem?); and emotions (e.g., How did you feel when the problem began? Nervous, upset, sad, depressed, angry, etc.)

As far as the behavioural dimension of the problem is concerned, the presence of behaviours such as inactivity, sleeping, taking tablets has to be explored. There should also be a specific evaluation of body checking behaviours and search for comforting information from medical and nonmedical sources (e.g., telling friends/family about symptoms).

(6) *Modulating variables.* Determining which factors (situational, behavioural, cognitive, affective, interpersonal and/or physiological) make the problem worse and which ones make it better with questions such as the following: Have you noticed if there is anything which makes symptoms appear stronger or make them more likely to appear? Is there anything which helps you to control the problem or lessens the likelihood that it will appear? Have you noticed any norms of behaviour related to a day of the week, time of the month, or year? etc.

(7) *Avoidance.* Exploring those behaviours, activities, actions, etc., which the patient has stopped doing due to the problem (passive avoidance), as well as those which s/he now does because s/he thinks they control it or make it better (active avoidance). Also identifying thoughts associated with such behaviour. For this, questions such as the following may be used: Are there any situations you avoid because of the problem? Are there any things which your problem stops you from doing? Are there any things you usually did before the problem appeared that you no longer do?; when you notice your symptoms, is there any activity you wouldn't do? If you didn't avoid this activity, what do you think could happen? Is there something you do when you notice the problem to stop it from getting worse? ; When you notice the symptoms, what do you do to protect yourself?; If you didn't do it, what do you think could be the worst that would happen?, etc.

(8) *Reaction from other significant people.* What does X think (e.g., partner, parents, children, close friends) about your problem? What does X do when you tell him/her about your physical discomfort?

(9) *History of previous treatments.* This is explored by asking the following questions: Have you consulted a doctor about your problem? How many doctors have you seen? When? Did you trust them? What kind of clinical tests did they do? Do you think they were good? What were the results? What did they tell you that you have? Did it make you feel better? Do you take medication (prescribed or non -prescribed)?

(10) *Degree of handicap (work/social/spare time).* To evaluate to what extent the problem disturbs the patient's life in relation to his/her social relations, work, and free-time activities (e.g., To what extent does the problem affect your usual social life? Has your ability to work changed? Has your problem had an influence on the activities you usually do during your spare time? etc.)

(11) *Beliefs about the origin, cause and course of the problem.* For this, questions such as the following are useful: In your pinion, what is the cause of your problem? What do think produces your symptoms?, etc. When the patient explicitly states that s/he thinks the factor responsible is the presence of some organic problem, the therapist may intervene in the following way: Is there something about your symptoms which makes you think they are caused by a serious illness? What do your symptoms have to make you think that they may not be the result of another factor?

(12) *General beliefs about the nature and significance of the symptoms.* Determine dysfunctional beliefs about health and illness which may make the patient think s/he is suffering from a serious illness (e.g., "Bodily symptoms are always a sign of illness").

(13) *Psychosocial situation.* Exploration of the aspects relating to professional activities, family, social relations, sexuality, interests etc.

It is also necessary to obtain information about the family history of illness and attitudes towards illness. With this in mind, questions such as the following are asked: Which important illnesses have you suffered from? At what point in your life? What did it mean for you? Is there or has there ever been a case of illness in your family which deserves mention or which has particularly affected you? Which illness? Who had it? Has this influenced you? Has anyone close to you ever died? Who passed away? When? What was the cause of death? To what extent did this affect you? What was the family attitude (family, partner etc.) towards the illness? (e.g., protective, indifferent about health) etc.

At the end of the second evaluation session the patient is shown how to fill out the Diary of Hypochondriasis (Simple Form)[3] emphasizing the importance of filling it out to be able to record additional information about their condition. This tool allows the patient to register his/her own unpleasant bodily sensations and to estimate their seriousness according to a scale which goes from 0 (absence) to 5 ("intense, incapacitating- they don't allow me to do anything"); the time of day and situation before the episode in which they are experienced (what s/he was doing or thinking); the causal attributions of the symptoms and the estimate of the amount s/he believes in such attributions according to a scale from 0 ("I don't believe it at all") to 100 ("I'm completely convinced it's true"); the emotions generated and their intensity graded using a scale from 0 ("absence") to 100 ("extremely intense"); and finally, the behaviours they produce (what s/he do or stop doing). In Appendix 1 there is a sample of this journal.

Session III. This session is dedicated to gathering complementary data via self-report questionnaires which evaluate general clinical variables and more specific variables for hypochondriasis. So, for the anxiety estimation the *State-Trait Anxiety Inventory, STAI*, (Spielberger, Gorsuch & Lushene, 1970) may be used; to determine the amount of depression the *Beck Depression Inventory, BDI* (Beck, Rush, Shaw & Emery, 1979) can be used; to explore somatic symptoms the *Hypochondriasis Scale -Hs- Minnesota Multiphasic Personality Inventory, MMPI (*Hathaway & McKinley, 1967) can be used; and to determine the amount of disturbance the problem causes the *Escala de Adaptación* (Adaptation Scale) is useful (Echeburúa & Corral, 1987; in Borda & Echeburúa, 1991).

As tools which allow to explore the variables involved in the psychopathology of hypochondriasis more directly, the *Illness Attitude Scales, IAS* (Kellner, 1987); the *Illness Behaviour Questionnaire, IBQ (*Pilowsky & Spence, 1983), and the *Somatosensory Amplification Scale, SSAS;* Barsky, Wyshak & Klerman, 1990) can be used.

For weekly assessment of the patient's manifestations of hypochondriasis, the *Cuestionario de Evaluación del Estado Actual (Evaluation of Present*

---

[3] Developed by C. Botella and P. Martínez based on Clark (1989) and Salkovskis (1989).

Conditions Questionnaire) (CEEA)[4] can be used. It explores the present condition of the problem using 9 items that the patient has to answer according to a scale from 0 ("nothing") to 100 ("a lot"). In Appendix 2 there is a sample of this tool.

Treatment Phase

The treatment attempts to accomplish the following objectives (Warwick, 1989; Warwick & Salkovskis, 1990): (1) Detecting dysfunctional suppositions about somatic symptomology, illness and health behaviour, and replacing them with more adaptive behaviours; (2) Managing to reattribute nonpathological bodily symptoms to benign causes with a greater probability of occurrence; and (3) Suppressing problematic behaviours involved in maintaining exaggerated preoccupation about health.

The treatment programme is designed to be applied throughout 10 sessions, each lasting about an hour long (except the first which tends to be a little longer) for a week-long period. The sessions are structured into three different phases: 1st phase) development of the model and obtaining compromise (sessions 1 and 2); 2nd phase) intervention strategies (sessions 3, 4, 5, 6, 7 and 8); and 3rd phase) relapse prevention (sessions 9 and 10).

It is recommended to apply the various intervention strategies which the programme is made up of guided by the general principals presented in Table 11.3.

Formulation of the model and obtaining compromise: 1st Session Agenda
1. Introducing the hypothesis that the patient believes explains the problem ("organic disorder").
2. Proposing a new alternative hypothesis ("anxiety problem"). Explaining to the patient:
   (a) what anxiety is.
   (b) Adaptive value of anxiety.
   (c) Ways of showing anxiety.
   (d) Relation between thoughts, emotions and behaviours.
   (e) Presentation of Warwick and Salkovskis' cognitive-behavioural model of hypochondriasis by using a "cardiac phobia" example.
   (f) Explanation of a similar model for the patient's case.
3. Homework.

   (1) *Introducing the hypothesis that the patient believes explains his/ her problem ("organic disorder").* The session begins with a synthesis of the information the patient gave in previous encounters (e.g., symptoms s/he

---

[4] Developed by C. Botella and P. Martínez.

Table 11.3. General Principals of Cognitive-Behavioural Treatment of Somatic Problems Related to Anxiety (Salkovskis, 1989)

1.	The objective is to help the patient identify what his/her problem is and is not about
2.	Recognizing that the symptoms really exist and that treatment attempts to offer satisfactory explanation of them
3.	Distinguishing between giving relevant information and reassuring the patient with irrelevant or reseated information
4.	Treatment sessions should never be combative; asking and collaborating with the patient is the appropriate style, as in all cognitive therapies in general
5.	The patient's beliefs are always based on evidence which seems convincing to them; instead of disapproving of the belief, take note of the observation which the patient is using as evidence and work on it together with him/her
6.	Establish a contract for a limited period of time which meets the demands of the therapist whilst taking into account the fears of the patient
7.	The selective attention and easily-influenced minds of many patients should be used to illustrate the way in which anxiety can create symptoms and "information" from harmless facts
8.	What patients have understood from what has been talked about in the treatment session *should always* be verified, asking patients to make a summary of it and of the way in which it has affected them

experienced, what s/he think about them, the way in which s/he are affected) stressing the facts s/he put forward as evidence for the existence of a serious physical illness.

(2) *Proposing a new alternative hypothesis ("anxiety problem")*. A new alternative explanatory hypothesis may be introduced, making the patient see that there are facts which do not "fit" with the idea of illness that s/he claim to have. In order to do this, the fact that doctor has not found any illness, and that the medical tests and examinations have not shown the existence of any physical problem is highlighted. Then, faced with the initial explanatory hypothesis which the patient maintained (s/he is seriously ill) the therapist suggests the possibility of tackling the problem from a different perspective, considering it an anxiety problem.

To help the patient understand this new suggestion general introductory concepts are presented, discussed and illustrated with various examples which can be abstract or obtained from his/her own daily experience. The educative part of this session is aimed at commenting upon the following points:

(a) *What anxiety is*. Anxiety is described as an emotion all people experience and which works as an alarm mechanism which is activated when we perceive a situation to be threatening.

(b) *Adaptive value of anxiety*. It is stressed that this reaction has an adaptive value since it allows people to put into function the necessary means to face danger or escape from it. However, anxiety may become problematic in certain circumstances, such as, for example, when it is activated in safe situations.

(c) *Ways in which anxiety is shown.* Anxiety is expressed at three levels: physiological, cognitive and behavioural. With regards to the first, it is explained that when a person experiences high levels of anxiety a series of changes happen in the body. This is due to the increase in physiological stimulation of the autonomic nervous system which is the part of the nervous system which controls the functioning of many of our internal organs (e.g., cardiovascular and gastrointestinal systems). That is why when a person feels anxious s/he experiences a series of symptoms such as increase in heart rate, breathing difficulties, feelings of dizziness and vertigo, muscle tension, increased sweating, etc. All these feelings associated with physiological stimulation are bothersome but not dangerous to the person's health.

As far as the cognitive level is concerned, it is explained that the way in which we react to a certain situation depends, for the most part, upon the way in which we interpret it, that is, what we think about it. To illustrate the influence of thoughts the following example is given: we do not react in the same way to an insulting comment from someone we know if we interpret it as intentional display of hostility than if we consider it the consequence of our interlocutor's bad day.

Finally, it is pointed out that anxiety can also be shown on a behavioural level, making us avoid situations which have previously caused us anxiety or we anticipate may cause this emotional state (avoidance behaviour) or we abandon a situation in which we start to feel anxious (escape behaviour).;

(d) *Relation between thought, emotion and behaviour.* This relation can be illustrated using an example along the same lines as Beck et al. (1979, pp. 138–139). In this example the patient is invited to imagine him/herself home alone at midnight when s/he hears a crash in another room. Using a series of questions (e.g., How would you feel if you had thought...? What would you have done?), s/he is made to see that if s/he had had a thought along the lines of "there's a burglar in the house", s/he would have become anxious and would have started to act in a way that would minimize danger (hiding or calling the police). However, if s/he had thought "the window is open and the wind made a noise", s/he would have felt calm and behaved differently: s/he simply would have gone to close the window.

To illustrate the relation between thoughts, emotions and behaviour it may be useful to make use of some of the health worry episodes recorded by the patient in the simple diary.

Likewise, in relation to physical symptomology, information is given about the way in which certain factors influence the appearance and exacerbation of bodily signs and sensations. To illustrate this question examples such as noticing an increase in heart rate or suffering from diarrhoea when we feel nervous are given, or the worsening of the healing process of a wound if we touch it constantly.

(e) *Presentation of Warwick and Slakonskis' Cognitive-Behavioural model of hypochondria.* (development and mechanisms which maintain the problem) using an example of "cardiac phobia". The following description may be used as an example of a typical case of "cardiac phobia" (modified from Warwick & Salkovskis, 1989):

> "Since the death of his father from a brain tumor 15 years earlier a man started to believe that "bodily symptoms always indicate the presence of an illness because if it weren't so, they would not exist". Recently and since the sudden and unexpected death of a close friend due to a heart attack, he started to concentrate on his bodily sensations, such as an increase in palpitations, which until that moment had passed unnoticed. This fact activated his belief and a series of ideas related to his symptoms appeared. So, he started to have negative feelings such as: "I may have a heart disease", "I may be having a heart attack", "there's no solution", "I'm going to die", etc.; and also disagreeable images such as seeing himself in a coffin with his family surrounding him crying. All this caused great anxiety and worries about his health: he constantly noticed symptoms in his chest, took his pulse frequently, noticed pins and needles in his left arm when putting pressure on his muscles, asked his wife to calm him down, avoided physical exercise and went to the doctor almost every week, despite the fact that he had been assured on many occasions that his heart was absolutely fine."

From the story which is told and the questions the patient is asked so that s/he can generate information (e.g., What do you think about this case? How important do you think the death of his/her friend was? What influence does the patient's behaviour have upon his/her worries about his/her symptoms?[5] What do you think is the cause of the problem?), an explanatory scheme of the sequence of development and the maintaining factors of the cardiac neurosis is made.

(f) *Elaboration of a similar model for the patient's case.* The outlined illustrations put the patient in a good disposition to accept analysis of his/her case in similar terms to those given. To do this, explanatory diagrams are made including relevant information gathered during the evaluation , always trying to actively engage the patient.

In cases where the patient gives no credibility to the alternative suggested, the therapist intervenes by asking if s/he has ever thought, even for an instance, that the symptoms may be explained in another way than a serious organic illness; if s/he has ever had even 1% doubt that his/her belief in suffering from a certain illness may be wrong.

(3) *Homework.* The patient is given the figures drawn up during the session

---

[5] So that the patient understands how behaviour can influence symptoms, ask him/her to press hard on his/her forearm; after a while s/he will feel parasthesia.

and, for homework, is asked to think about them and make a list of ideas about which s/he is in agreement, another one with the ideas with which s/he disagrees as well as any other additional doubt or commentary s/he would like to discuss.

A crucial aspect to keep in mind throughout the treatment process is the hypochondriac patient's tendency to selectively pay attention to information which matches up to his/her belief in illness. Because of this and in order to maintain a constant feedback, it is advisable to ask the patient to summarize the main questions dealt with in the session as well as the ideas s/he thinks s/he has learned in it.

2nd Session Agenda
1. Clearing up doubts about the cognitive-behavioural model of hypochon-driasis.
2. Comparison of the two explanatory hypothesis for the problem.
3. Establishment of the therapeutic contract.
4. The logic of the treatment.
5. Homework.

(1) *Clearing up doubts about the cognitive-behavioural model of hypochon-driasis.* This point is dedicated to going over important questions introduced in the previous session and solutions to possible problems which may have come up. It is important to stress again and again throughout the sessions the suggested model, since this forms the base which justifies the use of the various treatment strategies.

(2) *Comparison of the two explanatory hypothesis for the problem.* The logic, utility, advantages and disadvantages of each one of the explanatory hypothesis for the problem are assessed (physical illness vs. anxiety). This can be discussed using the following questions: How many times have you tried to solve your problem as if it were an organic illness? How long have you been trying to resolve your problem and free yourself of the symptoms through medical means exclusively?(such as going to the doctor, carrying out test and examinations etc.) How effective has the patient's strategy been so far? Have you ever tried the suggested alternative psychological approach? Have you ever tried to treat the problem as if it were anxiety? Which of the hypotheses seems to make most sense given the facts in existence until now?

(3) *Establishing the therapeutic contract.* The patient is offered a consistent suggestion to tackle his/her problem according to the explanatory scheme discussed during a limited time (8 weeks). This alternative is offered as a working hypothesis which must be put to the test by gathering the appropriate evidence. The patient is made to see that accepting the suggestion is of no disadvantage to him/her since if psychological treatment fails s/he will at least have the certainty of knowing s/he has considered all possible ways of dealing with his/her problem and can revert to his/her initial somatic explanation.

In the hypothetical case of a patient showing him/herself reluctant to begin psychological treatment unless s/he is given a last "final test" (medical examination) we may act in the following way:

1. A doctor gives him/her a medical exam once again to calm him/her.
2. Evaluating anxiety about health, the conviction of having an illness and the need for comforting facts before, immediately after and after a longer period of time after medical intervention.

This kind of action will show the patient the role played by calming information in maintaining worries about health and will facilitate one of the facets of treatment: the prevention of response. In this case the technique is aimed at suppressing calming information, medical as well as nonmedical. This activity can be proposed as a behaviour experiment throughout treatment.

(4) *The logic of the treatment.* Starting with this new point of view which considers the patient's problem as an anxiety problem, the treatment is directed towards breaking the vicious circle which contributes to the worries about health. Of course, this focus does not doubt the truthfulness of the symptoms; it only attempts to explore alternative explanations and to look for evidence which allows the patient to see if this new conceptualization can be useful.

(5) *Homework.* The patient is asked to reflect upon how s/he thinks treatment will be and asked to answer the following questions: How could the vicious circle of health worries be broken? Which things should you do and not do to help yourself?

Treatment Strategies

3rd Session Agenda

1. Clearing up doubts about treatment.
2. Discussion of the behavioural factor in maintaining the problem.
3. List of "self-prohibitions".
4. Action guidelines for family.
5. Homework.

(1) *Clearing up doubts about treatment.* The subject's responses to questions given as homework in the previous session are commented upon. The components of treatment are explained stressing that the aim of treatment is to analyze factors involved in his/her excessive health worries and to teach him/her ways of thinking more realistically and adaptively about his/her symptoms.

(2) *Discussion of the behavioural factor in maintaining the problem.* The purpose of this discussion is to show the patient pernicious repercussions of some of his/her behaviour related to his/her somatic symptoms and worries about them. Such behaviour includes avoidance of certain activities (e.g., physical exercise, sexual relations), self-imposed restrictions, self-inspection and repeated manipulation of the affected area, the search for calming information (e.g., asking for medical attention, repeated clinical tests and analysis,

asking family and friends about symptoms, reading about serious physical disorders). More specifically, the analysis of the behaviour factor has a double purpose: firstly it tests the patient's belief that his/her behaviour "keeps him/her going despite serious physical illness" and secondly, it tests if the behaviour, which the patient believes relieve symptoms, actually does.

One useful behaviour experiment for the patient to understand the effects of his/her behaviour patterns of avoidance is to ask him/her to carry out the activities s/he avoids (e.g., sport if in fear of having a heart attack) and to test if this causes the fatal incident s/he is expecting.

To show the repercussions of bodily self-inspection on the symptoms the patient can be asked to touch and press hard on the part of the body which worries him/her so that s/he appreciates the increase in pain and discomfort this causes.

Discussion of the role of searching for medical advice in maintaining the problem can be carried out using the results of the "final test" exercise described in the previous session. This makes the patient see that although this kind of behaviour may initially have a calming effect, in the long run it increases anxiety and worries about health. This same logic can be used to demonstrate the influence of talking to others about symptoms in order to feel more at ease.

Likewise, it can be useful to point out the consequences of frequently reading about illness by asking the patient to read an article about a serious organic illness during the session (e.g., breast cancer, brain tumour, multiple sclerosis) exploring thoughts (immediate and later) that such reading provokes.

(3) *List of "self-prohibitions"*. After the discussion about previous problems the patient (along with the therapist) tends to feel ready to make a list of activities s/he will not be able to do. Self-imposed "prohibitions" are often the following: (1) to make unnecessary visits to the doctor and repeat clinical tests; (2) to speak to friends, family and work colleagues about symptoms; (3) to get informed (read books or watch TV, listen to the radio) or talk to other people about topics related to illness; and (4) to check or touch areas of the body which worry him/her.

(4) *Action guidelines for family*. Family members and other people important to the patient are also involved in treatment. They are specifically told about the negative effects that their attempts to calm the patient have and they are given the following guidelines: "When X speaks to you about his/her physical problems and topics related to illness, you should say in a neutral tone (not too aggressive or soft): "I can't make any comment". If s/he continues to insist, say this again and try to talk about something else. Repeat the sentence as often as needed.

(5) *Homework*. From the third session onwards and until the end of treatment, making a list of what has been learned in the session is given as a weekly exercise.

Likewise, if the patient has a strong phobia component, coping tasks can be given in order to make him/her learn to control stimulus (internal as well as external) related to illness and death.

4th Session Agenda
1. Clearing up problems with "self-prohibitions".
2. Verbal questioning of negative interpretation of symptoms (I)
    (a) Hypothesis testing.
    (b) Might there be other interpretations for what is happening to me?
    (c) Does it help me to think of the possibility that what I am worried about is going to happen or does it make me feel more anxious?
    (d) Have I set unrealistic and unattainable goals for myself?
    (e) Am I forgetting relevant facts or concentrating too much on irrelevant facts?
    (f) What would someone else think of my situation?

(1) *Clearing up problems with "self-prohibitions."* It is quite common for patients to say that they have not respected some of the suggested "prohibitions". The therapist can respond to this kind of situation using the suggestions of Avia (1993): to reinforce the patient for self-prohibitions s/he has been able to do, to explain that, since this behaviour is very ingrained, that it will take time to practice modifying it and learning a more appropriate way of behaving, to bring to the patient's memory the reasons for which it would not be a good idea to go back to the original behaviour pattern and encourage him/her to keep working along the proposed line.

(2) *Verbal questioning of negative interpretation of symptoms (I).* For the patient to learn to question his/her own ideas about illness, a series of procedures are used to allow him/her to analyze and assess in a logical and realistic way the degree of truth of falsehood contained in each one of the two explanatory hypothesis for his/her problem.

(a) *Hypothesis testing.* It consists of examining the evidence for and against negative interpretation of symptoms and alternative explanations for them. The steps to follow are:
1. Clearly introducing the patient's negative thinking, that is, erroneous interpretation of symptoms as indicators of the presence of a serious physical illness (e.g., I have multiple sclerosis).
2. Patient's estimation of how strongly s/he believes the negative thought on a scale of 1 to 100, where 0 means "I don't believe it at all" and 100 "I am completely convinced it is true".
3. Searching for, identifying and noting evidence in favour of negative thinking.
4. Searching for, identifying and noting evidence againts negative thinking.
5. Summing evidence (patient and therapist must agree upon the result).
6. Coming up with an alternative explanation for the symptoms by using questions and observations consistent with the alternative.

7. Searching for, identifying and noting evidence in favour of the alternative explanation.
8. Searching for, identifying and noting evidence against the alternative explanation.
9. Summing the evidence (patient and therapist must agree upon the result).
10. Estimating again the degree of belief in negative thinking at two moments: now when s/he is calm and in the therapist's office; when s/he notices the symptoms.
11. Estimating the amount of belief in the alternative explanation at two moments: when s/he is calm in the therapist's office and when s/he notices the symptoms.

The process of helping the patient to question his/her own negative thoughts can be done using another kind of reflection, as follows:

(b) *Might there be other interpretations for what is happening to me?* It is stressed that the symptoms are not necessarily the result of a serious illness only and exclusively, but there may be more likely and benign explanations which should be taken into account.

(c) *Does it help me to think of the possibility that what I am worried about is going to happen or does it make me feel more anxious?* This question concentrates on the usefulness/uselessness and possible benefits/detriments of being excessively worried about health.

(d) *Have I set unrealistic and unattainable goals for myself?* This question may help the patient to realize that it is impossible to be completely sure, without any doubt, that we are not ill.

(e) *Am I forgetting relevant facts or concentrating too much on irrelevant facts?* This makes the patient learn to consider other sources of information which are not exclusively physical problems.

(f) *What would someone else think of my situation?* This point is an attempt to make the patient adopt another person's point of view to try to see his/her problem with a greater degree of objectivity.

So that the patient will be able to put into practice the kind of techniques which make logical analysis of his/her symptoms easier, they are asked to fill out the Hypochondriasis Diary (Detailed Form).[6] This tool is a more detailed version of the simple diary previously described. It includes rational responses (alternative and more adaptive explanations of the origin of the bodily symptoms experienced) and evaluation of the degree to which they are believed on a scale of 0 ("I don't believe it at all") to 100 ("I am completely convinced it is true") as well as reevaluation (using an identical scale) of the extent to which s/he believes in the initial negative interpretation (Appendix 3).

(3) *Homework.* Planning a "behaviour experiment" which gives more in-

---

[6] Developed by C. Botella and P. Martinez from Clark (1989) and Salkovskis (1989).

formation to support one or another hypothesis. Filling out the detailed diary (this task will be included from this session on) .

From the fourth session on, if the patient's problem requires it, slow breathing training and/or muscle relaxation will take place. These strategies are used as a way of making it easier to attribute the symptoms to a benign cause (e.g., muscular tension or inappropriate breathing pattern).

5th Session Agenda

1. Clearing up problems via questioning negative interpretation of symptoms (I).
2. Verbal questioning of negative interpretation of symptoms (II).
3. Homework.

(1) *Clearing up problems via questioning negative interpretation of symptoms (I).* In general, it is not easy for the hypochondriac patient to undertake the response to his/her negative thoughts. So, it is a good idea to dedicate this first part of the session to discussing and suggesting rational responses to symptoms using episodes which have been recorded in the detailed diary.

(2) *Verbal questioning of negative interpretation of symptoms (II).* In this session there is a discussion of catastrophic interpretation of symptoms by analyzing that the patient may be over-estimating the possibility of being ill. In order to do this, pie charts and inverted pyramids are used to show him/her that the likelihood of him/her having an illness s/he fear or believe s/he have is very low. This question is worked on using a task called "Time to worry"[7] (Appendix 4). The task is structured like a notebook composed of a series of exercises which attempt to involve the patient in a continued job of saturation and imagined exposure to the possibility of suffering from the illness they believe they have, and also continues to analyze negative thoughts about illness.

With these objectives in mind, in one of the exercises the patient is given the instruction that it is very important for him/her to dedicate an hour each day to thinking and writing about what worries him/her about his/her physical symptoms and all their implications (the progress of the illness and its implications, his/her death, family grief and sadness). The remainder of the exercises are directed towards the patient reconsidering his/her negative thoughts about illness by searching for alternative explanations for his/her symptoms (a pie chart is used) and analyzing if s/he is overestimating the probability of suffering from an illness (an inverted pyramid is used).

(3) *Homework.* Completing the notebook "Time to Worry" (this task will be included until the end of treatment) and the detailed diary.

6th Session Agenda

1. Clearing up problems by means of questioning negative symptoms (II).
2. Role of self-monitoring in the perception of bodily sensations.

---

[7] Developed by C. Botella and P. Martínez.

3. Palliative effects of distraction.
4. Training in Distraction Techniques
5. Homework

(1) *Clearing up problems by means of questioning negative symptoms (II).* The same procedure from step one of the previous session is used.

(2) *Role of self-monitoring in the perception of bodily sensations.* The purpose is to show the patient how concentrating on the body and excessively checking it may make him/her notice symptoms which would pass unnoticed for other people.

Besides showing (with examples) the influence of paying attention to the detection of bodily symptoms (amongst others, those described by Barsky et al., 1988b) there are other ways of showing this process to the patient:

(a) Controlling the patient's attention throughout the session. S/he is asked to close his/her eyes and concentrate on his/her heart for 5 min. The patient will realize that, simply by paying attention to his/her heart, s/he can detect a pulse in various parts of the body without even touching them. However, when s/he opens his/her eyes and is asked to describe the room, s/he stops noticing his/her heart beat.

(b) Concentrating on observations "within the session". Often patients start to experience a concrete bodily sensation after having been speaking about it for a few minutes. The therapist should take advantage of this situation in order to help the patient to understand that concentrating on a sensation may make one more aware of it.

(3) *Palliative effects of distraction.* The patient is shown how concentrating on sources exterior to the body helps to reduce perceiving symptoms. For this purpose, using teaching material may be useful (for examples see Barsky et al., 1988a).

(4) *Training in distraction techniques.* Once the importance of paying attention to the body in intensifying bodily symptoms and the palliative effects of distraction have been explained, the patient is trained in certain distraction techniques:

(a) *Concentrating on an object.* The patient visually focalizes his/her attention on an external object and describes in the greatest detail possible, for example, in terms of its physical characteristics, use, position, etc. This procedure is a variation of the following technique.

(b) *Sensory consciousness.* The patient should try to pay attention to all the information s/he can detect from his/her sensory organs (sight, hearing, smell, taste and touch). It is important for the therapist to carefully determine the utility of this technique in each particular case given the hypochondriac's tendency to detect bodily sensations.

(c) *Mental exercises.* It consists of carrying out mental exercises with a moderate degree of difficulty (e.g., counting from 1000 to 0 in intervals of 6, saying women's names which begin with A, naming mammals).

(d) *Absorbing activities*. The patient carries out activities which require his/her attention. Many hobbies work well as absorbing activities (e.g., crosswords, painting, sports, chess).

(e) *Pleasant thoughts and fantasies*. It consists of the patient thinking about and generating mental images about a certain positive situation or event (real or fantasized).

(5) *Homework*. Filling out the "Time to worry" notebook, the Detailed Diary and practicing distraction techniques.

7th and 8th Sessions Agenda
1. Restructuring of spontaneous disagreeable images.
2. Deepening on the concept of dysfunctional belief.
3. Identification and discussion of dysfunctional beliefs.
4. Homework.

Many cognitive and behavioural techniques explained before, for the questioning of catastrophic interpretation of symptoms, can be used to modify underlying beliefs.

Besides automatic negative thoughts there may also be images containing unpleasant images related to the illness which must be restructured and substituted for more positive ones.

The content of sessions 7 and 8 is not as systematic as that of the previous ones since, depending on the patient's development throughout therapy, one question or another will be stressed.

Relapse Prevention

9th Session Agenda
1. Review of previous sessions
2. Review of the patient's development throughout therapy
3. Patient's assessment of this development
4. Assessment of the patient's residual beliefs
5. Patient's future expectations about his/her health worries
6. Convenience of generalizing therapy to other bodily sensations
7. Convenience of continuing to practice learned techniques
8. Homework

(1) *Review of previous sessions*. The educational material and the cognitive procedures used are briefly reviewed (e.g., anxiety and its manifestations, factors which maintain the worries about health, testing the hypothesis), emphasizing those which were most beneficial to the patient.

(2) *Review of the patient's development throughout therapy*. The evolution of the problem throughout the therapeutic process is reviewed by using the Evaluation Questionnaire of Present State or any other tool with similar characteristics.

(3) *Patient's assessment of this development.* The patient is asked to describe his/her opinion about the changes s/he have experienced since the beginning of treatment. Likewise, his/her assessment of the factors responsible for the positive changes in his/her condition is examined.

(4) *Assessment of the patient's residual beliefs.* The amount the patient believes in the two explanatory hypothesis of the problem is evaluated (physical illness vs. anxiety) asking him/her to assess on a scale of 0 to 100 the probability that his/her symptoms indicate the presence of a serious organic illness (or if they are the result of anxiety). Also, the evidence accumulated in favour of the alternative explanation is reviewed, evaluated and commented upon.

(5) *Patient's future expectations about his/her health worries.* Possible future worries about the reappearance of symptoms are identified, exploring the possibility that the patient believes his/her improvement is transitory and similar to previous experiences at the beginning of psychological treatment. Analysing differences between these two possible modes of improvement: present improvement due to treatment and previous improvements. Stressing that now the patient has a different perspective from which s/he can understand his/her condition and can make use of effective strategies to cope with it.

(6) *Convenience of generalizing therapy to other bodily sensations.* It is emphasized that it may be possible to apply strategies learned during therapy to worries which may occur in the future related to other types of symptoms.

(7) *Convenience of continuing to practice learned techniques.* The need to continue using strategies learned during therapy as a way of consolidating achievements is pointed out.

(8) *Homework.* The patient is asked to give written responses to the following questions:

    (a) What is anxiety? Which factors sustain health worries?
    (b) What negative thoughts did I have or do I have about my symptoms? Evidence in favour and against.
    (c) What dysfunctional beliefs did I have or do I have about health? Evidence in favour and against.
    (d) Which aspects of therapy have helped me most?
    (e) How can I cope with my health worries?

10th Session Agenda
1. Commentary on the patients' response to formulated questions.
2. Resolution of final doubts about treatment.
3. Final assessment of the therapy.
4. Insistence on the convenience to continue practicing strategies learned in order to maintain and generalise improvements.
5. Programming of post-treatment evaluations and follow-up.

Conclusions and Future Directions

Behavioural or cognitive-behavioural treatment of hypochondriasis is presently in a period of development characterized by a prudent optimism (from our point of view). This optimism is justified by the good results reported in scientific literature about the effectiveness of these kinds of strategies. It can be stated that use of exposure and/or response prevention techniques, as well as programmes which concentrate on modifying the tendency to amplify bodily sensations and to interpret them in a dramatic way are adequate alternative treatments. Prudence is necessary because there are still numerous questions to be resolved before affirming, with a reasonable margin of confidence, that these therapeutic directions are the most adequate for patients with excessive health worries.

Amongst the questions which are derived from a cautious attitude about the adequacy of this treatment are those referring to the following ambits:

(a) *Degree of effectiveness*: What are the success rates? How much abandonment is produced? Are the benefits maintained in a stable way in the medium and long term? Can results be generalized to other questions not directly dealt with in therapy? Which components contribute more than others to success in treatment?, etc.

(b) *Differential effectiveness*: Does this kind of treatment have greater benefits than those of a pharmacological nature? Is it more effective than other psychological treatments from different theoretical perspectives? Does it offer possibilities of change than other kinds of cognitive-behavioural strategies?, etc

(c) *Typology of patients*: Do different kinds of hypochondriasis require different treatment strategies? Are exposure and response prevention the strategies of choice for the treatment of fear of illness? Can belief in illness be changed through verbal denial and reattribution techniques?, etc.

(d) *Conceptualization of hypochondriasis*: At the moment there is no unanimous agreement about where this disorder should be located in diagnostic classifications (Chorot & Martínez, 1995) and, obviously, this needs adequate understanding of the problem. So, it is necessary to ask, from a psychopathological point of view, in reference to hypochondriasis: is there a change in perception, in attention, in memory or in thought? Or, what combination of processes are altered and how? The therapeutic tools to be used in each case would be quite different.

The responses to these questions will allow us to fill in the gaps which still remain in our knowledge of the hypochondriac phenomenon and will provide us with strategies to overcome it.

References

APA (1987). *Diagnostic and statistical manual of mental disorders*, 3rd edition revised. Washington, DC: American Psychiatric Association.

APA (1994). *Diagnostic and statistical manual of mental disorders*, 4th edition. Washington, DC: American Psychiatric Association.

Avia, M. D. (1993). *Hipocondría*. Barcelona: Martínez Roca.

Avia, M. D., Ruiz, M. A., Olivares, M. E., Crespo, M., Guisado, A. B., Sánchez, A., & Varela, A. (1996). The meaning of psychological symptoms: effectiveness of a group intervention with hypochondriacal patients. *Behaviour Research and Therapy, 34,* 23–31.

Barsky, A. J. (1979). Patients who amplify bodily sensations. *Annuals of International Medicine, 91,* 63–70.

Barsky, A. J. (1992). Amplification, somatization, and the somatoform disorders. *Psychosomatics, 33,* 28–34.

Barsky, A. J., & Klerman, G. L. (1983). Overview: hypochondriasis, bodily complaints, and somatic styles. *American Journal of Psychiatry, 140,* 273–283.

Barsky, A. J., & Wyshak, G. (1990). Hypochondriasis and somatosensory amplification. *British Journal of Psychiatry, 157,* 404–409.

Barsky, A. J., Geringer, E., & Wool, C. A. (1988a). A cognitive-educational treatment for hypochondriasis. *General Hospital Psychiatry, 10,* 322–327.

Barsky, A. J., Goodson, J. D., Lane, R. S., & Cleary, P. D. (1988b). The amplification of somatic symptoms. *Psychosomatic Medicine, 50,* 510–519.

Barsky, A. J., Wyshak, G., & Klerman, G. L. (1990). The somatosensory amplification scale and its relationship to hypochondriasis. *Journal of Psychiatric Research, 24,* 323–334.

Baur, S. (1988). *Hypochondria: Woeful imaginings*. Los Angeles, CA: University California Press (Barcelona: Gedisa, 1990).

Beck, A. T., Rush, A. J., Shaw, B. F., & Emery, G. (1979). *Cognitive therapy of depression*. New York: Guilford Press (Bilbao: Desclée de Brouwer, 1983).

Borda, M., & Echeburúa, E. (1991). La autoexposición como tratamiento psicológico en un caso de agorafobia. *Análisis y Modificación de Conducta, 17,* 993–1012.

Clark, D. M. (1989). Anxiety states. Panic and generalized anxiety. In K. Hawton., P. M. Salkovskis., J. Kirk & D. M. Clark (Eds.), *Cognitive-behaviour therapy for psychiatric problems: A practical guide*. Oxford: Oxford University Press.

Clark, L. A., Watson, D., & Reynolds, S. (1995). Diagnosis and classification of psychopathology: challenges to the current system and future directions. *Annual Review of Psychology, 46,* 121–153.

Chorot, P., & Martínez, M. P. (1995). Trastornos somatoformes. In A. Belloch, B. Sandín & F. Ramos (Eds.), *Manual de Psicopatología*, Vol. 2. Madrid: McGraw-Hill.

Emmelkamp, P. M. G. (1982). *Phobic and obsessive-compulsive disorders: Theory, research and practice*. New York: Plenum Press.

Fallon, B. A., Klein, B. W., & Liebowitz, M. R. (1993). Hypochondriasis: treatment strategies. *Psychiatric Annals, 23,* 374–381.

Fiegenbaum, W. (1986). Long-term eficacy of exposure in-vivo for cardiac phobia. In I. Hand & H. U. Wittchen (Eds.), *Panic and phobias*. Berlin: Springer-Verlag.

Floru, L. (1973). Attempts at behavior therapy by systematic desensitization. *Psychiatria Clinica, 6,* 300–318.

Furst, J. B., & Cooper, A. (1970). Combined use of imaginal and interoceptive stimuli in desensitizing fear of heart attacks. *Journal of Behaviour Therapy and Experimental Psychiatry, 1,* 57–61.

Hathaway, S. R., & Mckinley, J. C. (1967). *Minnesota Multiphasic Personality Inventory. Manual revised 1967*. New York: The Psychological Corporation.

House, A. (1989). Hypochondriasis and related disorders: assessment and management of patients referred for a psychiatric opinion. *General Hospital Psychiatry, 11*, 156–165.

Johansson, J., & Öst, L. G. (1981). Applied relaxation in treatment of "cardiac neurosis": a systematic case study. *Psychological Reports, 48*, 463–468.

Kellner, R. (1982). Psychotherapeutic strategies in hypochondriasis: a clinical study. *American Journal of Psychotherapy, 36*, 146–157.

Kellner, R. (1983). Prognosis of treated hypochondriasis: a clinical study. *Acta Psychiatrica Scandinavica, 67*, 69–79.

Kellner, R. (1986). *Somatization and hypochondriasis*. New York: Praeger.

Kellner, R. (1987). *Abridged manual of the Illness Attitude Scales*. University of New Mexico.

Kirk, J. (1989). Cognitive-behavioural assessment. In K. Hawton., P. M. Salkovskis., J. Kirk., & D. M. Clark (Eds.), *Cognitive-behaviour therapy for psychiatric problems: A practical guide*. Oxford: Oxford University Press.

Kumar, K., & Wilkinson, J. C. M. (1971). Thought stopping: an useful technique in phobias of internal stimuli. *British Journal of Psychiatry, 119*, 305–307.

Logsdail, S., Lovell, K., Warwick, H. M. C., & Marks, I. (1991). Behavioural treatment of AIDS-focused illness phobia. *British Journal of Psychiatry, 159*, 422–425.

Mandeville, B. (1730). *Treatise of the hypochondriac and hysteric diseases*. (1st edn., 1711). London: Tonson.

Mansdorf, I. J. (1981). Eliminating somatic complaints in separation anxiety through contingency management. *Journal of Behavior Therapy and Experimental Psychiatry, 12*, 73–75.

Marks, I. M. (1987). *Fears, phobias and rituals*. New York: Oxford University Press.

Martínez, M. P., & Botella, C. (1995). Aplicación de un tratamiento cognitivo-conductual a un caso de hipocondría primaria. *Análisis y Modificación de Conducta, 21*, 697–734.

Martínez, M. P., & Botella, C. (1996). Evaluación y tratamiento psicológico de la hipocondría: revisión y análisis crítico. *Psicología Conductual, 4*, 29–62.

Martínez, M. P., Belloch, A., & Botella, C. (1995). Hipocondría e información tranquilizadora. *Revista de la Asociación Española de Neuropsiquiatría, 15*, 411–430.

O'Donnell, J. M. (1978). Implosive therapy with hypnosis in the treatment of cancer phobia: a case report. *Psychotherapy: Theory, Research and Practice, 15*, 8–12.

Pilowsky, I., & Spence, N. D. (1983). *Manual for the Illness Behaviour Questionnaire*. Department of Psychiatry, University of Adelaide, Australia.

Reinders, M. (1988). Behavioural treatment of a patient with hypochondriacal complaints. *Gedragstherapie, 21*, 45–55.

Rifkin, B. G. (1968). The treatment of cardiac neurosis using systematic desensitization. *Behaviour Research and Therapy, 6*, 239–240.

Salkovskis, P. M. (1989). Somatic problems. In K. Hawton., P. M. Salkovskis., J. Kirk., & D. M. Clark (Eds.), *Cognitive-behaviour therapy for psychiatric problems: A practical guide*. Oxford: Oxford Medical Publications.

Salkovskis, P. M. (1991). Aspectos cognitivo-conductuales de problemas con presentación somática: ansiedad por la salud, hipocondría, fobia a la enfermedad y problemas psicosomáticos. *Cuadernos de Medicina Psicosomática, 18*, 42–55.

Salkovskis, P. M., & Clark, D. M. (1993). Panic disorder and hypochondriasis. *Advances in Behaviour Research and Therapy, 15*, 23–48.

Salkovskis, P. M., & Warwick, H. M. C. (1986). Morbid preoccupations, health anxiety and reassurance: a cognitive-behavioural approach to hypochondriasis. *Behaviour Research and Therapy, 24*, 597–602.

Schmidt, A. J. (1994). Bottlenecks in the diagnosis of hypochondriasis. *Comprehensive Psychiatry, 35,* 306–315.

Sharpe, M., Peveler, R., & Mayou, R. (1992). The psychological treatment of patients with functional symptoms: a practical guide. *Journal of Psychosomatic Research, 36,* 515–529.

Spielberger, C. D, Gorsuch, R. L., & Lushene, R. E. (1970). *STAI, Manual for the State-Trait Anxiety Inventory (Self Evaluation Questionnaire).* Palo Alto, CA: Consulting Psychologists Press.

Starcevic, V. (1991). Reassurance and treatment of hypochondriasis. *General Hospital Psychiatry, 13,* 122–127.

Stern, R., & Fernández, M. (1991). Group cognitive and behavioural treatment for hypochondriasis. *British Medical Journal, 303,* 1229–1231.

Tearnan, B. H., Goetsch, V., & Adams, H. E. (1985). Modification of disease phobia using a multifaceted exposure program. *Journal of Behavior Therapy and Experimental Psychiatry, 16,* 57–61.

Visser, S., & Bouman, T. K. (1992). Cognitive-behavioural approaches in the treatment of hypochondriasis: six single case cross-over studies. *Behaviour Research and Therapy, 30,* 301–306.

Warwick, H. M. C. (1989). A cognitive-behavioural approach to hypochondriasis and health anxiety. *Journal of Psychosomatic Research, 33,* 705–711.

Warwick, H. M. C. (1995a). Trastornos somatoformes y facticios. In V. E. Caballo, G. Buela-Casal & J. A. Carrobles (Eds.), *Manual de psicopatología y trastornos psiquiátricos,* Vol. 1. Madrid: Siglo XXI.

Warwick, H. M. C. (1995b). Assessment of hypochondriasis. *Behaviour Research and Therapy, 33,* 845–853.

Warwick, H. M. C., & Marks, I. M. (1988). Behavioural treatment of illness phobia and hypochondriasis: a pilot study of 17 cases. *British Journal of Psychiatry, 152,* 239–241.

Warwick, H. M. C., & Salkovskis, P. M. (1989). Hypochondriasis. In J. Scott., J. M. G. Williams & A. T. Beck (Eds.), *Cognitive therapy in clinical practice: An illustrative casebook.* London: Routledge.

Warwick, H. M. C., & Salkovskis, P. M. (1990). Hypochondriasis. *Behaviour Research and Therapy, 28,* 105–117.

Warwick, H. M. C., Clark, D. M., & Cobb, A. (1994). A controlled trial of cognitive-behavioural treatment for hypochondriasis. Submitted.

Williamson, P. N. (1984). An intervention for hypochondriacal complaints. *Clinical Gerontologist, 3,* 64–68.

WHO (1992). *Classification of mental and behavioural diseases: Clinical descriptions and diagnostic guidelines,* 10th edition. Geneva: World Health Organization.

Further Reading

Avia, M. D. (1993). *Hipocondría.* Barcelona: Martínez Roca.

Barsky, A. J., Geringer, E., & Wool, C. A. (1988). A cognitive-educational treatment for hypochondriasis. *General Hospital Psychiatry, 10,* 322–327.

Martínez, M. P., & Botella, C. (1996). Evaluación y tratamiento psicológico de la hipocondría: revisión y análisis crítico. *Psicología Conductual, 4,* 29–62.

Salkovskis, P. M. (1989). Somatic problems. In K. Hawton., P. M. Salkovskis, J. Kirk & D. M. Clark (Eds.), *Cognitive-behaviour therapy for psychiatric problems: A practical guide.* Oxford: Oxford University Press.

Warwick, H. M. C., & Salkovskis, P. M. (1989). Hypochondriasis. In J. Scott., J. M. G. Williams & A. T. Beck (Eds.), *Cognitive therapy in clinical practice: An illustrative casebook.* London: Routledge.

Appendix 1: Simple Diary

NAME: _____   WEEK: _____

	TIME OF DAY	SITUATION (What you are doing or thinking)	BODILY SENSATIONS (Estimate of seriousness 0–5) (a)	ASSOCIATED THOUGHTS (Estimate of belief 0–100) (b)	EMOTIONS (Estimate of intensity 0–100) (c)	ASSOCIATED BEHAVIOUR (What you do or stop doing)
MONDAY						
TUESDAY						
WEDNESDAY						
THURSDAY						
FRIDAY						
SATURDAY						
SUNDAY						

(Simple diary continued)

(a) Estimate the *bodily sensations* (discomfort or pain) which you experience according to the following scale:

    0 No sensation
    1 Very slight, I notice it sometimes
    2 Slight, I can ignore it now and again
    3 Quite annoying, but I can keep working
    4 Serious, it's difficult for me to carry out normal activities
    5 Intense, incapacitating (I can't do anything)

(b) Estimate your belief in the *thoughts associated* (explanation for it) to the bodily sensations experienced by using this scale.

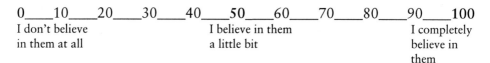

0   10   20   30   40   50   60   70   80   90   100
I don't believe   I believe in them   I completely
in them at all   a little bit   believe in
                                                        them

Remember that on this scale, as well as on the following one you can choose any number between 0 and 100, not only those illustrated.

(c) Estimate the intensity of *emotions* which you feel at that moment (anxiety, sadness, anger, etc.) by using the following scale:

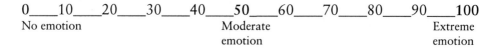

0   10   20   30   40   50   60   70   80   90   100
No emotion   Moderate   Extreme
                                         emotion   emotion

Appendix 2: Evaluation Questionnaire of Present State

NAME:_____ DATE:_____

   Following are a series of questions related to your problem. Please respond to each one using an X to indicate the number you believe best reflects your present state.

1. Are you worried about your health in general?

0____10____20____30____40____50____60____70____80____90____100
No   A little   Moderately   Quite   A lot

2. Are you worried about certain pains or bodily discomforts?

0____10____20____30____40____50____60____70____80____90____100
No   A little   Moderately   Quite   A lot

3. Does it frighten you that you may have a serious physical illness?

0____10____20____30____40____50____60____70____80____90____100
No   A little   Moderately   Quite   A lot

4. Do you think you are suffering from a serious physical illness?

0____10____20____30____40____50____60____70____80____90____100
No   A little   Moderately   Quite   A lot

5. Do you check yourself (sight, touch) to see what you notice or feel in your body?

0____10____20____30____40____50____60____70____80____90____100
No   A little   Moderately   Quite   A lot

6. Do you read, watch TV or listen to the radio about serious physical illnesses?

0____10____20____30____40____50____60____70____80____90____100
No   A little   Moderately   Quite   A lot

7. Do you talk to family or friends about your pains or physical disturbances?

```
0____10____20____30____40____50____60____70____80____90____100
No              A little        Moderately      Quite           A lot
```

8. Do you ever stay in bed, take your temperature, take your pulse, change your diet, take medicine, etc?

```
0____10____20____30____40____50____60____70____80____90____100
No              A little        Moderately      Quite           A lot
```

9. Do you avoid activities such as leaving the house, going to social gatherings, having fun, sporting activities, travelling, sexual relations?

```
0____10____20____30____40____50____60____70____80____90____100
No              A little        Moderately      Quite           A lot
```

Appendix 3: DETAILED DIARY

NAME:_____   WEEK:_____

	TIME OF DAY	SITUATION (What you are doing or think-ing)	BODILY SENSATIONS (estimate of seriousness 0–5) (a)	NEGATIVE INTERPRETATION (estimate of belief 0–100) (b)
MONDAY				
TUESDAY				
WEDNESDAY				
THURSDAY				
FRIDAY				
SATURDAY				
SUNDAY				

(Continuation Detailed Diary)

	EMOTIONS (intensity estimate 0–100) (c)	ASSOCIATED BEHAVIOURS (what you do or stop doing)	RATIONAL RESPONSE (estimate of belief from 0–100) (d)	REESTIMATION OF THE BELIEF IN THE NEGATIVE INTERPRETATION (0-100) (e)
MODAY				
TUESDAY				
WEDNESDAY				
THURSDAY				
FRIDAY				
SATURDAY				
SUNDAY				

(Detailed diary continued)

(a) Estimate the *bodily sensations* (discomfort or pain) which you experience according to the following scale:

    0 No sensation
    1 Very slight, I notice it sometimes
    2 Slight, I can ignore it now and again
    3 Quite annoying, but I can keep working
    4 Serious, it's difficult for me to carry out normal activities
    5 Intense, incapacitating (I can't do anything)

(b) Estimate your belief in *the negative interpretation* of bodily sensations experiences using this scale:

0____10____20____30____40____50____60____70____80____90____100
I don't believe   I believe in them   I completely
In them at all   a little bit   believe in
                                                 them

Remember that on this scale as well as on the following you can choose any number between 0 and 100, not only those illustrated.

(c) Estimate the intensity of *emotions* which you feel at that moment (anxiety, sadness, anger, etc.) Using the following scale:

0____10____20____30____40____50____60____70____80____90____100
No emotion   Moderate   Extreme
                              emotion   emotion

(d) Estimate your belief in *the rational response* to bodily sensations according to this scale:

0____10____20____30____40____50____60____70____80____90____100
I don't believe   I believe in it   I'm completely
in it at all   somewhat   convinced it
                                            is true

(e) Once again, estimate your belief in the *negative interpretation* of bodily sensations according to the following scale:

0____10____20____30____40____50____60____70____80____90____100
I don't believe   I believe in it   I'm completely
in it at all   somewhat   convinced it
                                            is true

Appendix 4: Time to Worry

NAME:_____ DATE:_____

This notebook contains a series of exercises. Please complete these exercises following the instructions for each one. Although this task requires considerable effort, remember the importance of daily work you do in improving your problem.

A. Following are a series of questions. Please, answer them all using an X to indicate the number which best reflects your present state.

1. Do you feel nervous?

0____10____20____30____40____50____60____70____80____90____100
No   A little   Moderately   Quite   A lot

2. Do you feel sad?

0____10____20____30____40____50____60____70____80____90____100
No   A little   Moderately   Quite   A lot

3. Are you worried about your health in general?

0____10____20____30____40____50____60____70____80____90____100
No   A little   Moderately   Quite   A lot

4. Are you worried about certain pains or physical discomforts?

0____10____20____30____40____50____60____70____80____90____100
No   A little   Moderately   Quite   A lot

5. Are you frightened you may have a serious physical illness?

0____10____20____30____40____50____60____70____80____90____100
No   A little   Moderately   Quite   A lot

6. Do you think you are suffering from a serious physical illness?

0____10____20____30____40____50____60____70____80____90____100
No   A littple   Moderately   Quite   A lot

B. Now it is time to worry. You will dedicate an hour to thinking about every-thing which worries you about your symptoms. In detail, write on this sheet what you think these symptoms mean , the consequences for yourself and your family because of suffering from the illness you fear, what your illness process would be like, your death, etc. Carrying out this exercise will probably bother you. If this is the case, do not give up, continue until you feel better.

C. Following are a series of questions. Please answer them all using an X to indicate the number which you feel best reflects your present state after having done the previous exercise:

1. Do you feel nervous?

0____10____20____30____40____50____60____70____80____90____100
No   A little   Moderately   Quite   A lot

2. Do you feel sad?

0____10____20____30____40____50____60____70____80____90____100
No   A little   Moderately   Quite   A lot

3. Are you worried about your health in general?

0____10____20____30____40____50____60____70____80____90____100
No   A little   Moderately   Quite   A lot

4. Are you worried about certain physical pain/physical discomforts?

0____10____20____30____40____50____60____70____80____90____100
No   A little   Moderately   Quite   A lot

5. Are you frightened you may have a serious physical illness?

0____10____20____30____40____50____60____70____80____90____100
No   A little   Moderately   Quite   A lot

6. Are you worried you may be suffering from a serious physical illness?

0____10____20____30____40____50____60____70____80____90____100
No   A little   Moderately   Quite   A lot

D. Following write down your negative thought about your symptoms. Make a list of all the possible alternative explanations for your symptoms. Considering that in the typical pie chart these alternative explanations are included (100%), dedicate a portion if the diagram to each one (a certain %).

Negative thought :_____

List of alternative explanations:

1) _____

2) _____

3) _____

4) _____

5) _____

6) _____

etc.

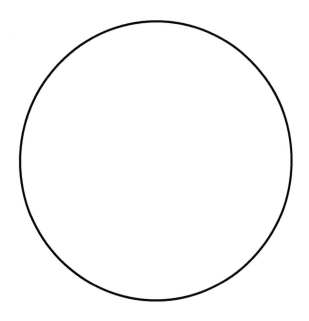

E. Write down the illness you fear having or think you have. Make a list with all the facts against this idea. Taking into account that the upper level of the inverted pyramid represents 100% probability of having the illness you fear, use each fact against to lessen the probability that you are really suffering from such an illness.

Illness you fear or think you have:_____

List of facts contradicting this:

1) _____

2) _____

3) _____

4) _____

5) _____

6) _____

etc.

100%

F. Finally, here is a list of questions again. Please, respond to them using an X to indicate the numbers which you believe best represents your *present state* after having carried out the previous exercises.

1. Do you feel nervous?

0____10____20____30____40____50____60____70____80____90____100
No   A little   Moderately   Quite   A lot

2. Do you feel sad?

0____10____20____30____40____50____60____70____80____90____100
No   A little   Moderately   Quite   A lot

3. Are you worried about your health in general?

0____10____20____30____40____50____60____70____80____90____100
No   A little   Moderately   Quite   A lot

4. Are you worried about certain physical pain/physical discomforts?

0____10____20____30____40____50____60____70____80____90____100
No   A little   Moderately   Quite   A lot

5. Are you frightened you may have a serious physical illness?

0____10____20____30____40____50____60____70____80____90____100
No   A little   Moderately   Quite   A lot

6. Are you worried you may be suffering from a serious physical illness?

0____10____20____30____40____50____60____70____80____90____100
No   A little   Moderately   Quite   A lot

12

Cognitive Behavior Therapy for Body Dysmorphic Disorder

JAMES C. ROSEN

University of Vermont, USA

Introduction

Perception and evaluation of one's physical appearance, or body image, is a psychological construct that is closely related to self-image as a whole, personality, and psychological well-being. Not only is it normal for people to be conscious of their appearance, but it is common to worry about and to be dissatisfied with appearance. According to studies of stress in middle-aged Americans, two of the ten most frequent routine hassles are concerns about weight and physical appearance (Kanner, Coyne, Schaefer & Lazarus, 1981). Most people would like to change something about their looks (Harris, 1987) and about one-third are dissatisfied overall (Cash, Winstead & Janda, 1986). Beauty and fitness fixation is conspicuous in the media and, indeed, people today worry more about their looks than in decades past.

Body dysmorphic disorder (BDD) is an intensification of normal concerns about physical appearance. Some symptoms of BDD, such as the subjective feeling of ugliness and worry about appearing unattractive or even repulsive to others, could be described as cognitive and perceptual features of body image, developed to a dysfunctional extreme. Because body image attitudes are strongly influenced by sociocultural factors and learning, body dysmorphic disorder should be amenable to psychological therapies that deal with these formative processes.

Diagnosable BDD takes many forms. Persons with body dysmorphic disorder frequently present with or have had social phobia, depression, obsessive-compulsive disorder, or eating disorders (Hollander, Cohen & Simeon, 1993; Phillips, McElroy, Keck, Hudson & Pope, 1994). Moreover, BDD has been conceptualized as being a variant of OCD (Hollander, Liebowitz, Winchel, Klumer & Klein, 1989; Phillips, McElroy, Keck, Pope & Hudson, 1993), social phobia (Marks, 1995; Takahashi, 1989), or hypochondriasis (Munro & Chmara, 1982). All these related disorders have been treated successfully with cognitive behavior therapy, indicating that persons with BDD could be helped with similar methods. In this chapter, I will review current knowledge about the effectiveness of psychological therapies as applied to the problem of BDD. In addition, I will provide an outline of BDD assessment and treatment that follows procedures similar to the cognitive behavioral treatment of phobias and obsessive compulsive disorder. Clinicians who work with BDD patients might encounter patients who do not meet the diagnostic criteria for BDD, but who are in need of treatment for other types of body image disturbances. Thus, as much as possible, we describe a treatment approach that can be used more broadly.

Clinical Features of Body Dysmorphic Disorder

The essential feature of BDD is: "Preoccupation with an imagined defect in appearance. If a slight physical anomaly is present, the person's concern is markedly excessive" (APA, 1994, p. 468). Unlike normal concerns about appearance, the preoccupation with appearance in BDD is excessively time consuming and causes significant distress or impairment in social situations.

Types of Appearance Complaints

The frequency of appearance complaints in five case series is presented in Table 12.1. This is a rough comparison, because the studies differed in the sex ratio, the number of complaints reported by each subject, and the categories or descriptions used by the authors. The results indicate that BDD patients can be distressed about virtually any aspect of their physical appearance. Some patients report vague complaints of being ugly, misshapen, or odd-looking and cannot locate or specify the nature of the defect. In contrast, others localize their concern exactly to small features or blemishes such as a big nose, crooked mouth, asymmetrical breasts, small penis, birthmark, hairline, acne, scar, and so on. On the other hand, whole body concern is not uncommon and dislike of body weight or shape in larger lower body areas is frequent.

Diagnostically, the location of the defect is not significant factor, though

Table 12.1. Type of Appearance Complaints in Patients with Body Dysmorphic Disorder (% of Ss With Each Complaint)

Location	Phillips et al., 1993 $N = 31$ 17 men 13 women	Hollander et al., 1993 $N = 50$ 31 men 19 women	Gomez-Perez et al., 1994 $N = 30$ 15 men 15 women	Rosen et al., 1995 $N = 54$ 0 men 54 women	Neziroglu et al., 1996 $N = 17$ 7 men 10 women
Body					
Thighs/legs	13	18	–	38	18
Abdomen	17	10	–	35	29
Breasts	10	8	–	20	–
Buttocks	7	–	–	15	24
Overall body	20	38	–	9	–
Height	–	–	–	6	–
Arms	7	14	–	3	–
Hips	3	–	–	5	–
Neck	3	–	–	–	–
Shoulders	3	–	–	–	–
Other	–	–	8	–	–
Facial features					
Nose	50	32	23	–	47
Eyes	27	16	7	–	35
Head shape	20	–	–	–	–
Lips	17	–	7	–	6
Chin	17	18	–	–	–
Facial features	–	–	–	12	–
Teeth	13	–	–	4	12
Face	13	34	–	–	–
Ears	7	–	–	–	–
Cheeks	7	–	–	–	–
Neck	3	–	–	–	–
					41
Other					–
Skin	50	26	7	25	29
Aging	–	–	–	7	12
Hair	63	34	10	7	–
Genitals	7	12	–	–	–
Symmetry	–	30	–	–	
Secretion/odor	–	6	30	–	

Note. Total is greater than 100% for most studies because Ss reported more than one defect.

there may be some exceptions to this claim. One is a question whether patients who complain exclusively of imagined body odor should receive the diagnosis of somatic delusional disorder instead of BDD. Gomez-Perez, Marks & Gutierrez-Fisac (1994) argued that their patients with body odor complaints were "dysmorphophobic" rather than delusional hypochondriacs, because they denied actually smelling their odor, i.e., were not delusional, and they shared the same type of social avoidance as classic BDD patients.

Another consideration is that weight and shape concerns that occur exclusively during the course of anorexia or bulimia nervosa are not diagnosed separately as BDD. Although, an eating disorder patient who believes she has a defective nose, for example, might meet the additional diagnosis of BDD. It happens that patients can shift from one diagnosis to the other, indicating that body dysmorphic and eating disorders are related (Hollander et al., 1993; Pantano & Santonastaso, 1989; Sturmey & Slade, 1986). The essence of anorexia and bulimia nervosa, in normal appearing persons, may be a body dysmorphic disorder plus eating pathology.

Cognitive and Affective Features

Unlike normal self-consciousness about physical appearance, BDD involves a preoccupation that is time consuming, distressing, and interfering. Although it can occur throughout the day, appearance preoccupation is even more intense in social situations in which the person feels self-conscious and expects to be scrutinized by other people. This attention makes the patient feel anxious, embarrassed, and ashamed because he or she believes the defect reveals some personal inadequacy. Although a striking feature of BDD is the person's conviction in the existence (or severity) of the physical defect, this distorted perception is only the first step in a sequence of BDD beliefs. Typically, the thought pattern would be: I look defective, other people notice and are interested in my defect, they view me as unattractive (ugly, deformed, deviant, etc.) and evaluate me negatively as a person, and consequently my appearance proves something negative about my character and worth to other people. The exaggeration of a flaw in appearance is only consequential in BDD because it leads to other maladaptive beliefs.

BDD beliefs have been described inconsistently as either obsessions, overvalued ideas, or delusions (de Leon, Bott & Simpson, 1989). Indeed, there appears to be no single type of thought process that accounts for all BDD patients. According to the DSM-IV system, BDD patients with delusional thinking can receive the additional diagnosis of delusional disorder, somatic type. However, Phillips and her colleagues (Phillips et al., 1994) found no substantial clinical differences between BDD patients with and without delusional thinking and because they also found that BDD thought processes vary on a continuum from fair insight to delusion, they concluded that the existence and importance of delusional and nondelusional variants are doubtful.

Obsessional thinking in body image disorders refers to repetitive, intrusive thoughts about appearance. BDD patients can recognize obsessions and admit that their preoccupation is excessive even if they are entirely convinced their appearance is abnormal. A patient might complain: "I *know* I look hideous, but I just wish I could stop thinking about it all the time; I can't concentrate when I am with other people; I know they don't care about it as much as me." Some patients have more insight and can acknowledge that entrenched, sensible beliefs might not be true. For example, a normal appearing woman complained that people at work did not respect her because she was short and had fat cheeks. She said: "I look like an awkward teenager, not someone who knows what she is doing; I realize looks aren't everything to people, but it's how I feel about myself that really matters."

Clearly, not all negative body image attitudes are symptomatic of body dysmorphic disorder. What seems like excessive concern about appearance can be appropriate in someone who is engaged in occupations such as dance, modelling, or athletics that have strict physical standards. In general, physical beauty is a status symbol of success and other virtues. Moreover, it is common for people to use appearance as an excuse to explain some negative everyday occurrence. Thus, reduced to their basic form, BDD beliefs are not completely incomprehensible given our appearance conscious culture (McKenna, 1984). The difference is that BDD beliefs are unreasonable exaggerations of normal ideas and disrupt normal functioning.

Behavioral Features

An estimate of the prevalence of behavioral symptoms of BDD in five patient samples is shown in Table 12.2. The most consistent feature is avoidance of social situations, usually because the patient expects that negative attention will be drawn to his or her appearance. Avoidance can become so extreme as to make the patient housebound (Phillips et al., 1993). However, most patients are capable of at least limited social and vocational functioning, using ways to avoid full exposure of their appearance in public by wearing clothes, grooming, or contorting body posture and movements in such a way as to hide the defect. Various kinds of body checking behaviors are common such as inspecting the defect in the mirror, grooming rituals, comparing one's appearance to other people, and asking others for reassurance. In some extreme cases, body checking is difficult to resist and can consume hours in a day. On the other hand, it is common also for patients to avoid looking at their appearance. Finally, body dysmorphic disorder patients are convinced the only way to improve their self-esteem is to improve they way they look. Thus, most BDD patients undertake beauty remedies such as skin or hair treatments, cosmetic surgery, weight reduction, and other measures to eliminate the defect that usually are unnecessary and ineffective for BDD symptoms.

Table 12.2. Behavioral Symptoms in Patients with Body Dysmorphic Disorder (% of Ss With Each Behavior)

Behavior	Phillips et al., 1993	Hollander et al., 1993	Gomez–Perez et al., 1994	Rosen et al., 1995	Neziroglu et al., 1996
	N = 31	N = 50	N = 30	N = 54	N = 17
Body checking	73	32[a]	–	78	88
Body camouflaging	63	–	–	78	–
Checking and/or Camouflaging			66		
Comparing self to others	–	–	–	72	–
Avoidance of social activities	97	52	100	63	82
Avoidance of other people seeing body unclothed	–	–	–	51	–
Contorted movements or posture to hide defect	–	–	–	42	–
Avoidance of looking at own Appearance	40	–	77	37	29
Reassurance seeking	33	–	–	21	–
Avoidance of sex	30	–	–	17	–
Hair combing/cutting	–	25	–	–	65
Make–up rituals	–	–	–	–	–
Excessive MD visits	–	25	–	–	–
Face picking	–	–	–	–	18

[a]Mirror checking only.

Psychotherapy Research on Body Dysmorphic Disorder

Evidence supporting psychological therapies for BDD is growing, however, with one exception, the psychotherapy research is limited to uncontrolled case studies.

Case studies of Non-Behavioral Psychotherapy

Bloch & Glue (1988) reported psychodynamic therapy with a young woman who was preoccupied with her eyebrows, which she viewed as repulsive. The preoccupation was interpreted as providing her with an excuse to avoid hetero-sexual relationships and as a defensive projection of her own negative self-image. They reported the preoccupation stopped after a year and a half of weekly therapy. Philippopoulos (1979) conducted psychoanalysis two to three times per week for about a year with an adolescent girl who was disturbed with irrational thoughts of being ugly and fat. The preoccupation was inter-preted as disguising unconscious sexual wishes. Reportedly, therapy helped rid the patient of her preoccupation. Finally, Braddock (1992) encouraged more effective social skills in a shy adolescent girl. The patient became more assertive with other people, but her belief in an abnormal forehead did not diminish.

Case studies of Behavioral Therapies

A young man preoccupied with red complexion was trained in relaxation and then exposed in-imagination to a hierarchy of distressing comments and scrutiny toward his redness (Munjack, 1978). For example, the patient imagined a person at work teasing him that his face matched his red shirt. After eleven sessions of this systematic desensitization, the patient no longer was bothered by facial redness.

Marks & Mishan (1988) were the first to report the use of in-vivo exposure and response prevention procedures. Exposure included having the patient gradually venture into more challenging public situations without trying to hide his or her body part. If coupled with response prevention, the patient would practice refraining from checking his or her appearance when exposed to ritual evoking cues. All five patients were significantly improved after treatment. As social avoidance decreased, the patients' conviction in their belief of appearing defective also decreased, even though no direct challenge of their thinking (i.e., cognitive therapy) was employed. Only two of their cases were treated purely with behavior therapy, without concurrent medication trials. In a later case series treated in the same clinical center, Gomez-Perez et al. (1994) reported that about one-quarter of patients dropped out of treatment and about one-half were improved at follow-up.

In comparison to the reports by Marks and his colleagues, Neziroglu and colleagues (Neziroglu, McKay, Todaro & Yaryura-Tobias, 1996; Neziroglu & Yaryura-Tobias, 1993) examined exposure and response prevention without medication. Also they added cognitive therapy designed to help the patient to refute irrational thoughts (need for approval and to be perfect) that triggered the patients' grooming rituals or desires to hide their appearance. About 12 out of 17 cases were improved.

Other successful case studies of cognitive-behavioral therapy are available by Cromarty & Marks (1995), Newell & Shrubb (1994), Schmidt & Harrington (1995) and Watts (1990).

Controlled Studies

The only controlled treatment study for body dysmorphic disorder to date was conducted by Rosen, Reiter & Orosan (1995b) using the cognitive behavioral treatment that will be described in the next section. Fifty-four female patients with body dysmorphic disorder were randomly assigned to cognitive behavior therapy or no-treatment. None of the patients started medication during the study. The appearance complaints and behavioral features are shown in Tables 12.1 and 12.2. Patients were treated in small groups for 8 2-h sessions and provided homework and audiotapes on body image change. BDD symptoms were significantly decreased in therapy subjects and the disorder was eliminated in 82% of cases at posttreatment and 77% at 4-month follow-up. Overall psychological symptoms and self-esteem also improved in therapy subjects.

Conclusion

The following observations are offered regarding the status of treatment outcome. There is not enough information on non-behavioral psychotherapy approaches to conclude on their effectiveness. Though two out of three reported cases were improved, the duration of therapy was excessive.

A much stronger recommendation can be made for cognitive-behavior therapy. Not only did most of the case studies improve, but in the controlled trial, three-quarters of treated cases eliminated their disorder, whereas control subjects did not improve. Despite the long duration of body dysmorphic symptoms in these patients, cognitive behavior therapy appears to be effective in as little time as 2 months, though some patients require massed exposure therapy sessions before their anxiety is extinguished. This rate of improvement should be encouraging to clinicians who encounter BDD patients. Although many present with a history of failed psychotherapy (Phillips et al., 1993), proper cognitive behavior therapy is worth attempting. Nonetheless, it is important to recognize that CBT is not uniformly effective, as the disorder is not eliminated in about one-quarter of patients who complete treatment. Hopefully, more research into BDD treatment will lead to an improvement in this figure.

The most important ingredients in cognitive behavior therapy cannot be identified at the present time. Marks and his colleagues stressed exposure. They and Munjack also helped patients to tolerate thoughts of looking imperfect, but therapy was more behavioral than cognitive. Whereas Rosen at al. and the authors of other case studies provided more extensive cognitive therapy to challenge faulty assumptions about appearance. It is difficult to compare these different mixtures of cognitive and behavioral procedures, especially because treatment in Marks and Mishan's study was combined with medication. The most likely case is that the two types of procedures can interact with each other to facilitate change.

All the patients in the case studies were treated individually, but Rosen et al. conducted their treatment with groups of patients. There probably are advantages and disadvantages for both formats, but the published results do not favor one over the other. Assessment of treatment outcome is undeveloped.

Most reports of changes in social avoidance and beliefs are based on clinical impressions. A simple numerical scale of percent belief in the defect was used in several cases. Neziroglu and Yaryura-Tobias used a modified version of the Yale-Brown Obsessive Compulsive Scale (Phillips, 1993) to measure time occupied by thoughts and activities related to appearance. The only psychometrically validated measure of body dysmorphic disorder, the Body Dysmorphic Disorder Examination (Rosen & Reiter, 1996) used by Rosen et al., showed that treatment results in objectively defined clinical improvement.

Guidelines for the Assessment and Treatment of Body Dysmorphic Disorder

The purpose of this section is to provide an overview of cognitive behavior therapy procedures. We have conducted this therapy in various formats including group and individual therapy, mixed gender groups, groups that also involved patients with non-BDD body image problems (e.g., more substantial appearance defects), therapists of the same or different gender as the patient(s), and as an adjunct to other concurrent psychotherapy. Each of these circumstances presents unique challenges and opportunities and requires some adjustment in the therapy.

A clinician who accepts referrals for treatment of BDD is likely to encounter other types of body image problems. In addition to BDD patients, we have found this basic program to be effective with negative body image in obese persons (Rosen, Orosan & Reiter, 1995a) and body dissatisfied college women (Rosen, Cado, Silberg, Srebnik & Wendt, 1990; Rosen, Saltzberg & Srebnik, 1989). In patients with eating disorder symptoms, body image therapy by itself can lead to reduced problems with negative eating attitudes, unnecessary dietary restraint, and binge-eating, even though eating is not targeted in treatment. Although we would not recommend body image therapy as a sole treatment for anorexia or bulimia nervosa, we have routinely used this program as an adjunct to eating disorder treatment. It appears standard cognitive behavioral programs for eating disorders produce only modest body image change and under-emphasize therapy for this problem (Rosen, 1996). More systematic body image work would be useful for eating disorder patients.

Our standard program is weekly sessions for 2 months. Most other case studies of behavior therapy found good results with short term treatment. However, longer therapy or more frequent sessions might be necessary with some patients. Neziroglu et al. (1996) scheduled their treatment over four weeks of daily sessions lasting 90 min, 60 min devoted to exposure plus response prevention and 30 min devoted to cognitive restructuring.

Besides the work in therapy sessions, we assign the patient to follow with a self-help book on body image therapy (Cash, 1995). These materials provide a great deal of basic information on body image, inspiring clinical case vignettes, and cognitive and behavioral change exercises. Although using the self-help book frees time in therapy sessions and is convenient, it is essential to provide the patient with hands-on assistance. BDD patients usually are too stuck in their distorted body image beliefs to attempt the homework without persuasion, guidance, and troubleshooting from the therapist. We do not recommend using bibliotherapy alone with BDD patients.

Initial Phase of Treatment

Assessment. Prior to beginning therapy, a thorough examination of BDD symptoms and appearance complaints is important. We developed the Body Dysmorphic Disorder Examination (BDDE; Rosen & Reiter, 1996) for this purpose. The BDDE has good reliability and validity, including agreement with independent diagnosis of BDD, and is sensitive to change following treatment of body dysmorphic disorder. To date, it is the only measure that has been evaluated psychometrically with BDD patients. Although many other body image measures were available at the time we developed the BDDE, they all were biased toward one sex or toward body weight and shape complaints or did not tap into clinically serious symptoms of BDD. The Yale-Brown Obsessive Compulsive Scale (Y-BOCS) was modified by Phillips (1993) to measure obsessions and compulsions in BDD. No formal psychometric study of the Y-BOCS in BDD patients is available. It is limited to OCD type symptoms.

In addition to providing standard probing questions, the BDDE was designed to supplement the diagnostic criteria in the DSM, which are vague and subjective. To develop the BDDE, an extensive list of BDD symptoms from the literature was presented to a panel of expert clinicians. Items were selected that best corresponded to the diagnostic criteria and clinical descriptions. A subset of BDDE questions and cutoff scores were identified that could used for diagnosis. A brief description of the BDDE items (without the exact probe questions or ratings scales) is presented in Table 12.3. The BDDE is available in a clinician interview and self-administration versions (a copy can be obtained from the author). Because it covers most BDD symptoms, the BDDE can help the therapist to select treatment targets. More detailed behavioral assessment of triggering situations and responses will be needed during treatment. Suggestions will be provided in the following sections.

Attitudes toward therapy. In our appearance conscious society, we are taught that if we want to feel better about our appearance, we should lose weight, exercise, have cosmetic surgery, and so forth. In other words, we should eliminate or correct the defect. Consequently, it is difficult for most patients at first

Table 12.3. Brief description of items on the Body Dysmorphic Disorder Examination

1. Subject's description of the defect(s) in physical appearance
2. Interviewer's rating of subject's physical appearance
3. Presence of other types of somatic complaints other than appearance
4. Perceived abnormality of the defect (extent to which subject believes the defect is common or rare)
5. Frequency of body checking
6. Dissatisfaction with appearance defect
7. Dissatisfaction with general appearance
8. Frequency of seeking reassurance about appearance from other people
9. How often subject experiences *upsetting* preoccupation with appearance
10. Self-consciousness and embarrassment about appearance in *public* situations (e.g. city streets, restaurants)
11. Self-consciousness and embarrassment about appearance in *social* situations (e.g. at work)
12. How often subject thought other people were scrutinizing his/her defect
13. Distress when other people pay attention to the defect
14. How often subject received comment(s) from others about his/her appearance
15. Distress when other people comment about his/her appearance
16. How often subject felt treated differently due to his or her appearance
17. Distress when other people treat him or her differently due to appearance
18. How important is physical appearance in self-evaluation
19. Extent of negative self-evaluation in a non-physical sense due to the appearance defect
20. Extent of negative evaluation in non-physical sense by others due to the appearance defect
21. Perceived physical attractiveness
22. Degree of conviction in physical defect
23. Avoidance of public situations due to appearance (e.g., restaurants, restrooms, city streets)
24. Avoidance of social situations due to appearance (e.g., parties, speaking to authority figures)
25. Avoidance of close physical contact due to appearance (e.g., hugging, kissing, dancing close, sex)
26. Avoidance of physical activities (e.g., exercise or outdoor recreation) due to appearance
27. How often subject camouflages or hides his or her appearance defect with clothes, make-up and so forth
28. How often subject contorts body posture in order to hide the defect (e.g., keeping hands in pocket)
29. Inhibiting physical contact with others (changes body movements or posture during contact in order to hide defect, e.g., doesn't let partner touch certain body area)
30. Avoidance of looking at own body
31. Avoidance of others looking at body unclothed
32. How often subject compares his or her appearance to that of other people
33. Remedies that the person has attempted to alter the appearance defect

to imagine how they could view themselves differently at the end of a psychological therapy if the offending appearance feature still will be present. Nothing, they might argue, could convince them that they look good, when they know, or the rest of society tells them, that they look bad. Also they might be concerned that learning to accept themselves would cause them to abandon self-control and develop a worse problem, as if disliking oneself is necessary to remain motivated to improve ones appearance.

To deal with skepticism about therapy and gain the patient's cooperation, it is important to be clear about the goal of therapy. Be prepared to reiterate that although the patient is free to pursue beauty remedies on his or her own, this therapy is designed to change body image, not his or her appearance. Explain that body image is a psychological construct and that because it is subjective it can be surprisingly independent of actual appearance (Cash & Pruzinsky 1990; Feingold 1992). Use examples, preferably from his or her own experience, that correcting a defect or using beauty remedies has not always led to a changed self-image, that it is possible to feel better about ones appearance without actually changing appearance, and that other people can perceive your looks very differently than you. Point out that aside from any physical "problem" that exists, he or she has developed habits that interfere with functioning. The goal of therapy will not be to like his or her appearance, but at least to tolerate it and to eliminate self-defeating behavioral tendencies. It is not necessary to convince the patient that the defect is imagined in order for him or her to participate in therapy. In fact, it is better to avoid a confrontation about this belief and to focus on the interference that the preoccupation has caused. It might help to reassure the patient that according to research, most participants in this type of cognitive behavior therapy, in fact, are able to change regardless of the severity of their defect and they do not give-up healthy beauty or fitness routines. For example, in a trial of cognitive behavioral body image therapy for obese persons, our patients overcame negative body image without losing weight, but at the same time, their self-acceptance did not cause them to gain weight or to give-up dietary restraint (Rosen et al., 1995a).

Developmental history of body image. It is helpful to have the patient write a brief developmental history of his or her appearance concerns. The patient should consider separately, early childhood (up to age 7), later childhood (before puberty), early adolescence, later adolescence (later teenage years), early adulthood, and the present. For each period, ask the patient to describe his or her physical appearance and the important events or experiences that influenced his or her body image.

The BDD patient's preoccupation with physical appearance is likely to begin during adolescence (Andreasen & Bardach, 1977; Munro & Stewart, 1991; Phillips, 1991; Thomas, 1984) when concerns regarding physical and social development peak (Pliner, Chaiken & Flett, 1990). Self-consciousness about appearance can be more intense for adolescents who are distinctive physically such as being unusually tall or unusually short, maturing early or late, having a large nose, having severe acne, being big breasted or small breasted, being overweight, and so forth. Indeed, many body dysmorphic disorder patients possess some real, albeit minor, physical anomalies that triggered more attention from people (Hay, 1970; Thomas & Goldberg, 1995).

The risk for developing a body dysmorphic disorder is even greater if the appearance feature is coupled with more traumatic incidents. The most common is being teased about appearance (e.g., case examples by Braddock, 1982; Hay, 1970; Munjack, 1978; Philippopoulos, 1979). Some BDD patients are subjected to repeated criticism of their appearance, generally by family members. Others trace the beginning of their preoccupation to a single instance, a passing remark that perhaps was not meant to be critical. Other incidents include being left out or rejected because of appearance, being physically or sexually abused or assaulted, failing in athletics, and having an injury or illness (Orosan, Rosen & Tang, 1996). Later, body-image distress can be triggered by events or situations that resemble these earlier ones. Also, it is natural for people to try to make sense of experiences that cause them deep feelings of humiliation. Unfortunately, BDD patients come to believe that a "defect" in their appearance means they are defective people.

To examine the history of BDD might help patients recognize that their symptoms are rational to some extent given their personal experiences. Nonetheless, the patient must understand that although cultural messages about appearance and personal historical events (e.g., being teased as a child) might be important in his or her BDD development, therapy will have to focus on overcoming the current attitudes and behaviors that maintain the disorder. These typically are negative body-talk, faulty assumptions about appearance, and avoidance and checking behavior.

Cognitive Restructuring

Therapy requires a detailed behavioral assessment in order to pinpoint the dysfunctional attitudes and the situations in which they occur. A self-monitoring diary, such as used with depression (Beck, Rush, Shaw & Emery, 1979) can greatly facilitate cognitive restructuring. The patient should record any situations that provoke self-consciousness about appearance - positive or negative, the body image thoughts or beliefs, and the effect of these on mood and behavior. Use a diary form in which the patient analyses the experience in an A-B-C sequence: (1) Activating events (the situation and trigger of physical self-consciousness or body dissatisfaction), (2) Beliefs (thoughts about the situation or self), and (3) Consequences (outcome of the situation or emotional and behavioral reactions.

Negative body talk. Much time can be spent dwelling on repetitive, intrusive thoughts of body dissatisfaction. "My face is really disgusting; it's so big and shapeless, like a melon with two dots on it; it makes me look repulsive". In therapy, we call this "negative body talk". These statements are just negative comments on the aesthetics of appearance, without referring to specific implications of that appearance. High rates of negative body talk during the day perpetuate self-consciousness and negative emotions. To begin changing body image, it is necessary to change the way one talks to oneself about ones own body. Help the patient to construct more objective, neutral, or sensory self-descriptions that are reasonably believable and not emotionally loaded self-criticisms. For example, the patient might practice calling his face "round" and "white" rather than "disgusting" and "repulsive". Ask the patient to practice neutral self-talk during the day when reminded by the sight of his face or by intrusive negative body talk. The new description should be rehearsed while carrying-out the mirror exposure at home which we prescribe at the beginning of therapy (see below). Positive self-descriptions are unnecessary at first and generally are rejected by the patient. The therapist should avoid arguing with the patient about the reality of the defect, and instead try to eliminate the negative body talk that causes distress (e.g., T: "No matter how large your face may be, another problem seems to be the way you talk about it to yourself."). A slip back to self-criticism should be a cue to the patient to follow it with a corrective self-statement. The point is to distract oneself from repeating the self-criticism over and over, rather than to stop the thought from occurring in the first instance. If the patient complains that he still doesn't like what he sees, reassure him that some body dissatisfaction is normal and may be appropriate so long as he can overcome needless self-denigration.

Self-defeating thoughts and assumptions. The cognitive assessment should go past negative body talk by asking the patient to elaborate on his or her appraisal of situations in which the dissatisfaction occurred. Using the diary, help the patient to follow the negative body talk to other thoughts about the situation or assumptions about the importance of his or her appearance. For example, ask: "What was upsetting about your "big" face in that situation? What did you imagine people were thinking when they saw you?" A frequent thought pattern is: "I look bad, people notice and care about my appearance, they judge me negatively as a person. Therefore, my appearance proves something negative about me (e.g., I'm unlovable, foolish, lazy, weak, unfeminine or unmasculine, undisciplined, alien, freakish, offensive, too aggressive, immoral, and so forth)." Other common assumptions (see Cash, 1995) are: "If I could look just as I wish, my life would be much happier. If people knew how I really look, they would like me less. My appearance is responsible for much of what has happened to me in my life. The only way I could ever like my looks would be to change how I look." These are the types of beliefs that account for the deep feelings of shame and embarrassment in body dysmorphic disorder patients. Finally, the therapist should consider other qualities of the cognitions such as: unreasonableness, preoccupation (frequency of the thought), distress (when dwelling on the thought), conviction (how strongly held is the belief), and perceived controllability and effort to resist the thought (Lowe & Chadwick, 1990; Kozak & Foa, 1994).

Cognitive restructuring of the more unreasonable and distressing convictions about appearance can be accomplished with the standard techniques used in the treatment of depression and anxiety disorders (Barlow, 1988; Beck et al., 1979). Accordingly, encourage the patient to evaluate the evidence for and against the belief, questioning the evidence, rather than the belief itself, at least in the beginning. For instance, a woman worried that people think she is unattractive, slovenly, and has a dirty complexion; even though she dressed meticulously, looked elegant, and had normal skin. The discussion could center on comments about her appearance that people actually make, rather than what people might think. If she cannot recall any or seems biased, she should record in her body image diary any new feedback. Then ask her if these instances or anything else that happened in-between therapy sessions altered her belief. Perhaps she will discover that people are complimentary or not that interested in her appearance. Ask questions that will encourage her to examine her assumptions: "How important are your looks compared to other characteristics? What would happen if you looked different? Is there anything other than looking different you would have to do in order to make that happen or would looking different be all that is necessary? If you didn't hide your looks, what do you imagine would happen? Have you ever tested that prediction? Are there other explanations for events that have happened besides your appearance? Has changing your looks always led to feeling better about your appearance? Are you really capable of changing your appearance the way you wish? Is the problem your body or your body image?"

The patient should develop alternative self-statements that reflect the body image situation more accurately (e.g., "People really do think I look nice. I am a neat and orderly person."). Change the body image diary from A-B-C to an A-B-C-D-E format. The **D** section will be the place for her to write the alternative, Disputing thoughts to correct the beliefs which she identifies as being self-defeating, erroneous, or unreasonable. Disputing thoughts should be rehearsed during and in anticipation of body image situations. Settle on thoughts that are reasonable and encourage her to practice them until they become familiar and believable. Gradual changes in attitudes might be assessed by asking the patient to rate believability on a 0 - 100 scale next to the written disputing thought in the diary. Then, in the diary at **E**, she should write the positive Effects of corrective thinking. For patients who have difficulty recognizing irrational beliefs or constructing alternatives, Cash (1995) lays out a model of the process in a self-assessment of typical cognitive errors and self-defeating assumptions.

At first concentrate on beliefs that are somewhat less convincing (they will be easier to modify) and then progress to her firm convictions. For example, she may be willing to question whether strangers or co-workers care a great deal about her appearance, but she is convinced her husband wants to leave her because she looks unattractive. The latter *seems* more justified because a husband should be more invested in his wife's appearance than strangers. Delve into these stronger convictions after the patient has made some progress with the others.

Like other somatoform disorder patients, persons with body dysmorphic disorders attribute most of their troubles to their perceived physical defect. Recovery from the disorder will be facilitated if the patient can identify explanations for distress other than his or her appearance. For instance, the patient who worries that people are repulsed by her weight should be asked how else she might discourage interest from other people. Maybe she doesn't know how to maintain conversations or feels uncomfortable being intimate. She should be asked to compare the importance of social skills versus appearance for developing relationships. Arriving at other explanations is a juncture where the patient can abandon the idea that she must change her appearance in order to be more happy and successful. Although it might be distressing to admit to another dysfunction, at least it may be one that is more modifiable than physical appearance.

Distorted perceptions of appearance. A discrepancy between actual appearance and the patient's mental picture of himself suggests a perceptual disturbance. Misperception of sensory information about the body (visual, kinesthetic, tactile, olfactory) has been hypothesized to be responsible for these experiences (Lacey & Birtchnell, 1986). The only controlled study of body size perception in body dysmorphic patients, interestingly, showed they were *more*, not less, accurate in judging the size of their facial features than rhinoplasty patients and normal controls (Thomas & Goldberg, 1995), suggesting that the patient's complaint might represent a distorted attitude rather than a distorted perception.

Little information is available on how to alter perceptions or beliefs about the existence of the appearance defect or when this core feature should be confronted. Schmidt & Harrington (1995) asked a male BDD patient with obsessions about small hands to search for statistics on hand size in men and to compare himself with a normal size. Eventually, the patient's belief in abnormally small hands subsided. Similar techniques of corrective body size feedback have been reported in body image therapy with eating disorder patients and weight dissatisfied women who were instructed to compare their weight to norms or to compare their estimated body dimensions with actual measurements (Rosen et al., 1990). One could concoct many experiences or behavioral experiments to give the patient more objective feedback about his or her appearance that might enable the patient to dispute his or her distorted images.

In reports of non-BDD patients, corrective exercises, indeed, produce less distortion of appearance (Goldsmith & Thompson, 1989; Norris, 1984; Rosen, Saltzberg & Srebnik, 1989), but not necessarily more satisfaction with appearance (Biggs, Rosen & Summerfield, 1980; Fernandez & Vandereyken, 1994). Moreover, perceptual training does not add to the overall benefit of the basic cognitive behavioral program (Rosen et al., 1990). The main advantage of corrective feedback might be to facilitate insight into the disorder, rather than to alter body image per se (Garner & Bemis, 1982). Vandereyken, for example, shows his anorexia nervosa patients a video-tape of how they looked in a bikini upon admission in order to help break through their denial (Vandereycken, Probst & Van Bellinghen, 1992).

Marks (Cromarty & Marks, 1995; Marks, 1995) and Newell & Shrubb (1994) recommended confronting the belief in the defect head-on with a role play debate in which the patient must find evidence to refute the perceived defect. For example, a man who complained his head was too big, role played a defendant in a mock trial (Cromarty & Marks, 1995):

T: "The prosecution notes to the Court that your head is so big it did not fit through the door properly when you came in!"
P: "My head may be big but that is not true, it did not even touch the sides."
T: "...the prosecution alleges that your head is so big you could never wear a hat."
P: "That is not true! I have worn hats in the past and have photographs to prove it!"
T: "But you had them specially tailor-made for outsize heads."
P: "No, I bought them in normal department stores like everyone else."

Newell and Shrubb (1994) used this type of challenge in order to break through the resistance of their patients to exposure therapy.

Although confrontation about the defect has the potential to be therapeutic, the timing is important. To present the patient with objective feedback brings with it an implied demand that he accept the clinician's reality over his own. It often is more effective to begin cognitive restructuring with beliefs that are less strongly held. In this case, be careful to not argue about whether the supposed defect really exists. As much as possible, validate, rather than discount, the patient's perception ("I see what you're pointing to. Your stomach isn't flat like you want, it's curved and rounded."). Build the patient's tolerance to admitting physical imperfections, but more importantly, challenge the perceived implications of the defect. Our experience has been that the belief in the defect begins to fade by itself and is more amenable to challenging by the therapist as the patient gives up secondary convictions of being scrutinized or evaluated negatively by other people.

Type of appearance complaint. One of the most fascinating features of BDD is the type of appearance complaint. The location of the defect and the meaning the patient gives it can be a window to other dysfunctions or self-images and consequently can be helpful in diagnosis or treatment. For instance, Birtchnell, Whitfield & Lacey (1990) reported that discomfort with sexuality is common among women who request breast reduction. In such cases, sexual connotations or thoughts should be identified and modified through the self-monitoring diary. Supplemental therapy might be necessary to address sexual dysfunction. Schmidt & Harrington's (1995) patient with "abnormally small hands" felt like a weakling and unmasculine. Beware, however, of applying stereotypic interpretations to body parts. We have had patients who felt their facial features made them appear promiscuous, and patients with breast obsessions who had no sexual concerns. The interpretation must be supported by other evidence.

Another dimension of appearance is the visibility of the defect. Many BDD patients possess perceptible anomalies (Thomas & Goldberg, 1995) whereas others complain of completely imperceptible flaws. The hallmark of BDD is the fact that the physical complaint is in excess of the objective evidence. Both types of complaints, imagined or exaggerated, can be diagnosed as body dysmorphic disorder. It is tempting to think that the patient who has some real flaw, though still normal appearing, is more justified in being distressed and is less disturbed, because he is not "distorting" his appearance. But perceptual distortion of appearance is only one facet of a disturbed body image. BDD also consists of cognitive and behavioral features. Not all patients exhibit all three types of dysfunctions. Consider this non-BDD example. A man with an amputated arm feels worthless, avoids being in public, and acts hostile if someone comments on his missing limb. This man's shame is distressing and interfering and warrants treatment, even though he has a real deformity and is subjected to real rejection. Similarly, in BDD, the therapist must address the patient's interpretation of his or her appearance and adjustments in behavior, regardless of actual appearance.

At present there is no study of BDD patients that has examined differences in severity of symptoms, psychopathology, or response to treatment when grouped according to body parts or appearance features. Like other somatoform disorders, the problem in BDD may not be how minimal the defect is or where in the body the patient sees it, but the very fact the patient is preoccupied.

Coping with stereotypes and prejudice. Negative body image symptoms are very common in overweight persons because of the social discrimination they experience. Although they may not meet the criteria for BDD due to their "real" defect, cognitive restructuring of appearance preoccupation is still appropriate. Realistic thoughts about discrimination encounters should not be discounted. However, help the patient to learn more self-enhancing ways to respond to them and to cope with the stigma of obesity. First, patients should be discouraged from always looking for defects within themselves to explain negative attitudes from other people. Rather than accepting criticism as being personally relevant, the patient should recognize it as prejudice and unfair and ignorant treatment of an entire segment of society. Moreover, because most obese persons buy-into obesity stereotypes and blame themselves to excess for their overweight, it is important to bolster their resistance by providing information on the nonbehavioral, genetic and physiological causes of obesity. The person might also be encouraged to find examples from his or her own experience to counter stereotypes (e.g., the person cannot be weak and undisciplined, because she is strong-willed and competent in many other areas of life).

Second, participants will have to learn to reduce the importance of the characteristics on which they are judged, i.e., their overweight appearance. Although overweight persons are judged by peers as less attractive, peer ratings do not show obese-nonobese differences in the amount liked or perceived social competence (Jarvie, Lahey, Graziano & Farmer, 1983; Miller, Rothblum, Felicio & Brand, 1998).

Third, participants should be discouraged from only comparing themselves to people who are thinner than they. Lopsided comparisons perpetuate feelings of alienation. Instead, the participants should compare themselves to a more diverse and representative range of body types. So long as it is does not become excessive, social comparisons should be made to other overweight persons. We have succeeded in reducing body image symptoms from clinically severe levels in obese men and women to normal levels using strictly this body image therapy, without any instruction or assistance in controlling weight (Rosen et al., 1995a).

Behavioral Procedures

Strong emotions of anxiety and accompanying avoidance behavior, body checking and grooming rituals make body dysmorphic disorder suitable for exposure and response prevention techniques.

Exposure to avoided situations. We recommend that before facing anxiety provoking situations in public, the patient should begin with exposure to the sight of the body, unsupervised in the privacy of his or her own home. A hierarchy of body parts from satisfying to most distressing can be created by interviewing the patient or using a simple body satisfaction scale such as the Body Cathexis Scale (Secord & Jourard, 1953). The patient should practice viewing each step in the hierarchy for up to a minute or two until he or she is able to do so without significant distress and negative body talk. The exposure should be carried out clothed and then unclothed in front of a full-length mirror. Cash (1995) recommended that the subject first learn relaxation and progress through the hierarchy using a systematic desensitization. Giles (1988) reported a similar desensitization therapy in a woman with bulimia nervosa who imagined viewing a hierarchy of distressing body areas in a mirror.

The patient should be sure to view the satisfying and mildly dissatisfying areas in order to take-in the whole picture of him or herself, rather than focus immediately on the offensive locations. Many BDD patients avoid looking at their defect and will find this assignment to be extremely challenging. The exposure may need to be conducted over several weeks. Practice several days a week will facilitate habituation. Other BDD patients already scrutinize themselves in the mirror. In those cases, the exposure assignment should be conducted anyway, however, the patient should be instructed to practice neutral, objective body talk while viewing him or herself. The goal is not to convince the patient that his or her appearance is attractive, but simply to tolerate the sight of his or her image.

After the mirror work at home, we often expand the exposure to include viewing oneself in more public situations such as in store window reflections, changing room mirrors, public restroom mirrors, and so forth. Seeing ones own image in a public context, seems to be more challenging, perhaps because the patient is also thinking about their appearance being exposed to other people.

Some BDD patients avoid public outings altogether and are quite disabled. Others function socially, but avoid full participation or full exposure of the defect. Because avoidance techniques can be subtle, a thorough assessment is needed. The more avoidance habits that can be identified, the more opportunities the therapist can concoct for the patient to unlearn self-consciousness. Avoidance only perpetuates the disorder because the patient never has the opportunity to extinguish anxiety responses to triggering stimuli.

The body image self-monitoring diary can reveal avoidance habits. The Body Dysmorphic Disorder Examination asks about general categories of avoidance (e.g., social and public places, clothing, nudity, physical activities, touching the body). Detailed examples of these types of avoidance should be obtained. Observation of the patient might reveal disguising types of nonverbal behaviors or dress (e.g., keeping hands over the mouth) that the patient is unaware of or does not volunteer. Contextual cues that influence the difficulty such as familiarity of people, physical proximity to others, and type of social interaction (e.g., speaking to a group v. speaking to an individual) should be taken into account when finally arriving at a hierarchy of distressing situations. An example of a hierarchy was presented by Munjack (1978) in his desensitization of a man concerned about attention to redness in his face.

Some BDD patients have successfully avoided unwanted attention to their appearance for so long, they are unaware of situations that will be difficult to manage. In these circumstances, it might be useful to begin with a series of behavioral avoidance tests to probe for distress. Thompson, Heinberg & Marshall (1994) gave an example of such an assessment that involved having the subject rate distress at increasing proximity to a mirror and measuring the distance she was able to approach.

Examples of exposure assignments we have used are: wearing a form fitting outfit instead of baggy clothes, undressing in front of spouse, not hiding facial features with hands or combed-down hair, dressing to reveal scars, exercising in public wearing work-out clothes, showering at the health club rather than home, drawing attention to appearance with more trendy clothes, accentuating a distressing feature (e.g., eyebrows) with make-up or not wearing make-up at all, standing closer to people, allowing eye contact with strangers, and trying-on clothes or make-up in stores and then asking sales clerks for feedback on their looks.

An example of graded exposure with a patient who was overly self-conscious about his hands was: keep hands out of pockets while in the presence of others, allow a stranger to greet him by shaking his hand, wearing a wrist watch and rings to attract more attention to hands, signing a check in front of the bank teller, trying on rings in a jewelry store in front of the salesperson, and finally, allowing dirty finger nails to be seen by a supervisor at work.

One of Marks and Mishan's cases (Marks & Mishan, 1988) had concerns about her red lips and complexion. She gradually re-entered avoided social situations from riding on buses to sitting close to others to eventually leaving bits of toothpaste on her lips to call more attention to them. Neziroglu & Yaryura-Tobias (1993) described several patients with hair concerns who were required to go in public with their hair messed up, while thoughts of needing to be perfect and approved were challenged by the therapist.

A self-defeating aspect of avoidance in BDD is that efforts to camouflage or hide the defect can actually worsen appearance by locking the patient into a rigid lifestyle of inhibited dressing, grooming, nonverbal behavior, physical activities, etc. Many of our patients who fear being viewed as unattractive, uninteresting, ugly, odd, and so, create their own reality by avoiding the very behaviors that might make them more attractive. In the course of exposure therapy, patients typically discover that not only can they tolerate the anxiety but they experience a sense of liberation when they incorporate new styles of dress and physical activity into their repertoire.

Response prevention of checking and grooming. Most body dysmorphic disorder patients engage in some form of body checking that involves deliberate efforts to inspect, scrutinize, measure, or correct their appearance. Typical behaviors are inspecting oneself in the mirror, weighing, and measuring body parts with measuring tapes. Excessive grooming behavior coupled with check-ing is common. Examples are checking oneself in several outfits before finish-ing dressing in the morning, straightening hair repeatedly, applying make-up many times in one day, trimming nails excessively, and plucking hairs or picking at skin. Like compulsions, in some instances the BDD patient will engage in body checking as a ritual to undo a distressing thought about the defect. For example, a patient might run to the mirror and scrutinize himself upon having the thought he looked hideous to someone with whom he just spoke. In other instances the behavior lacks compulsive features, nonetheless the checking perpetuates a negative preoccupation with appearance. For example, a patient berates herself while she takes her weight three times a day.

Checking behavior in BDD can be assessed briefly with the Body Dysmor-phic Disorder Examination or the modified Y-BOCS, which also assesses the degree of interference caused by the behavior. No case reports of BDD have used extensive behavioral measures of the frequency and time spent engaged in grooming and checking rituals, though such an assessment might be useful during the course of treatment. Behavioral avoidance tests also could be used to measure the patient's ability to resist the behavior. For example, one could measure the time a patient could view herself in the mirror while refraining from adjusting her hair. These behavioral assessments could help the therapist devise a planned reduction in the behaviors and provide an objective measure of treatment gains.

Checking and grooming behaviors generally can be decreased using simple self-management techniques. Examples are: reduce the frequency of weighing, cover mirrors, leave home without the make-up kit, set a fixed time for dress-ing, allow oneself only two changes of clothes, refrain from inspecting skin blemishes, etc. A situational assessment of these behaviors, recorded in the body image self-monitoring diary, is helpful to identify the cues that trigger checking behavior and to incorporate these into the behavior change plan. For example, a patient might report weighing herself after every meal in addition to morning and evening weighings. Based on degree of urge to engage in the behavior, the patient might start by eliminating weighings at night and morn-ing and later practice eating without weighing. Generally these interventions can be conducted without supervision by the therapist. Afterwards, the thera-pist should debrief the assignment by asking the patient about the actual effect of not-checking as compared with the prediction they feared. For instance, a patient might be relieved to discover that her weight remained stable even though she did not monitor it closely. Or a patient might find that people treated her no differently even though she ventured out without make-up. Cash (1995) provided a monitoring form on which the patient could identify the behavior, her plan to manage without it, and the effect of not engaging in the behavior. A worksheet such as this doubles as a cue for change in the patient and an assessment of progress for the therapist.

In cases when the frequency is high or the urge to engage in the behavior is strong, a supervised exposure plus response prevention procedure will be necessary. Marks & Mishan (1988) described a woman who worried that her sweat smelled terribly. They accompanied her at first to help her go on public outings without bathing or applying deodorant. To strengthen resistance to the behavior, it might be useful to first accentuate the desire to correct the defect and then prevent the behavior. For example, Neziroglu & Yaryura-Tobias (1993) had a woman exaggerate the vascular markings around her nose with a red pen and then refrain from applying make-up while she viewed herself in the mirror. Messing hair and then refraining from grooming in front of the mirror was used in several cases (Neziroglu & Yaryura-Tobias, 1993). One of our patients was obsessed with unevenness of his fingernails and constantly was biting nails and chewing skin. In therapy sessions, one nail would be shortened and he had to refrain from biting the others.

Elimination of reassurance seeking. Another form of checking behavior is seeking reassurance from other people, usually by asking if the defect is noticeable or worse than before. Reassurance seeking can reach high frequencies, to the point a patient might ask her spouse dozens of times if she looked okay before leaving home. This behavior is another example of negative body talk, only verbalized aloud to others. Reassurance seeking is self-defeating because it does not eliminate the preoccupation (the patient does not believe the reassurance), it inadvertently trains other people to take even more interest in the patient's appearance, and it can strain relationships with partners and family members. Generally it is possible and desirable to eliminate this behavior completely. The patient might need to be convinced to cooperate with the intervention by emphasizing the negative consequences of reassurance seeking on his or her relationships. Also, it helps to explain how therapy is designed to make them feel more self-confident and that to do so, they must learn to not depend on the opinions of others. In most cases, the patient can simply be instructed to stop asking for feedback. Indirect attempts to elicit reassurance need to be eliminated as well. For example, a patient should refrain from saying aloud, "Honey, my hair looks so uneven today." Exposure plus response prevention might be required as well. For example, the patient might practice walking in front of his spouse, dressed imperfectly, and refrain from asking her opinion. Medical reassurance seeking, such as repeated dermatology consultations, should be eliminated as one might do in the cognitive behavioral treatment of hypochondriasis (Warwick & Salkovskis, 1989).

Accepting compliments. Related to reassurance seeking is the problem of BDD patients discounting positive feedback they receive on a spontaneous basis. Unfortunately, due to distorted cognitive processes, the patient typically overlooks or refuses any feedback that is discrepant from his or her negative body image. Because other people can be more objective, and usually more positive, about the patient's appearance, it would be desirable for the patient to attend to such information and incorporate it into his or her self-image. To attack this problem on a behavioral level, we train patients using role-played conversations to refrain from discounting statements (e.g., "Oh, you can't mean that. I really look terrible today."). Instead, the patient practices accepting the compliment (e.g., "Thank you very much. It *is* a new hair style.) and rehearsing it subvocally to allow it to be absorbed.

Coping with social stigma. Some non-BDD patients with real flaws in appearance such as severe obesity or deformities, need help with behavioral coping responses in situations involving teasing, ridicule, or staring from other people. In addition to the cognitive restructuring that was presented earlier, we encourage patients to identify and alter maladaptive behaviors. Typical problems we find are: retaliating at the stranger by yelling insults or starting a fight, making a threatening face or gesture, avoiding public outings, crying and so forth. For example, a severely obese woman complained about children in public saying, "Mommy, look at that fat woman!" She would act angry toward the child or avoid going out altogether. We taught her to move nearer to children in stores and smile. She stopped feeling upset and discovered that negative remarks from strangers decreased as she acted more friendly.

Eliminating excessive comparing. A final type of checking behavior is comparing ones defect with the same body part in other people. The patient might be looking for confirmation of their negative self-perception or comfort in the knowledge that they are not alone. Regardless, it is easy to become preoccupied with these comparisons and the frequency can reach high levels, to the point that the patient is unable to look at other people without focusing on their appearance. Looking at pictures in fashion and fitness magazines is another common cue for comparing. Comparisons are usually flawed. Either they are biased toward people who are more perfect looking, rather than a normal range of people, or the patient perceives everyone as better looking regardless of the comparison in objective terms. Because it is so self-defeating an effort should be made to control this form of checking. Behavioral self-control strategies can be devised to suit the patient's habit. The patient might be asked to not buy fashion magazines, to stand at the front of the aerobics class where she will not be able to watch the other participants, and to not verbalize aloud comparison statements to other people (e.g., "You look so great, I wish I had your complexion."). A difficulty in reducing comparing is that it typically is manifested more cognitively than behaviorally. Cognitive strategies might include: focusing on an aspect of the person's appearance other than the one related to the patient's defect (looking at her smile rather than the size of her nose), interrupting negative comparisons ("I wish I had his build") with self-accepting statements, appreciating the beauty in others ("What a lovely figure she has") instead of dwelling on hostile, jealous thoughts ("I can't stand these skinny women"), and focusing on nonappearance features in other people ("How friendly she seems").

Conclusion

Although body dysmorphic disorder has been described in the psychiatric literature for many years, psychological approaches to its treatment have a very short history. Knowledge about effective treatment is extremely limited at the present time, mainly because almost none of the reports are based on experimental methodology and rigorous assessment. The one controlled study provided solid evidence in support of cognitive behavior therapy. However, this study needs to be replicated by other researchers. Many questions about treatment effectiveness remain unanswered. Some of these concern maintenance of improvement at long-term follow-up, effectiveness of treatment with men, group versus individual treatment, comparison of different psychological therapies, and treatment outcome according to clinical features such as type of appearance complaint and presence of delusional thinking. The success of behavioral approaches suggests that body dysmorphic disorder symptoms are habits subject to extinction through self-control and conditioning. Although this finding shows that learning is important in the maintenance of symptoms, the earlier antecedents of body dysmorphic disorder are uncertain. Theories of causation have lagged behind treatment models.

Body dysmorphic disorder is a challenge to clinicians because the disorder needs to be distinguished from other types of body image concerns, most persons with the disorder are initially resistant to psychological intervention, and the symptoms are diverse and sometimes profound. Some features of body dysmorphic disorder, such as compulsions, are familiar to clinicians who work with other, similar disorders. Nonetheless, how to change the mental picture or attitude the patient has about his or her appearance can be puzzling. Fortunately, people have within them the capability of changing their body image without changing their physical appearance if given systematic and concrete guidance from the therapist.

References

APA (1994). *Diagnostic and statistical manual of mental disorders*, 4th edition. Washington, DC: American Psychiatric Association.

Andreasen, N. C., & Bardach, J. (1977). Dysmorphophobia: Symptom or disease? *American Journal of Psychiatry, 134*, 673–676.

Barlow, D. H. (1988). *Anxiety and its disorders: The nature and treatment of anxiety and panic.* New York: Guilford Press.

Beck, A. T., Rush, A. J., Shaw, B. F., & Emery, G. (1979). *Cognitive therapy of depression.* New York: Guilford Press.

Biggs, S. J., Rosen, B., & Summerfield, A. B. (1980). Video-feedback and personal attribution in anorexic, depressed, and normal viewers. *British Journal of Medical Psychology, 53,* 249–254.

Bloch, S., & Glue, P. (1988). Psychotherapy and dysmorphophobia: A case report. *British Journal of Psychiatry, 152,* 271–274.

Birtchnell, S., Whitfield, P., & Lacey, J. (1990). Motivational factors in women requesting augmentation and reduction mammaplasty. *Journal of Psychosomatic Research, 34,* 509–514.

Braddock, L. E. (1982). Dysmorphophobia in adolescence: A case report. *British Journal of Psychiatry, 140,* 199–201.

Cash, T. F. (1995). *What do you see when you look in the mirror?: Helping yourself to a positive body image.* New York: Bantam Books.

Cash, T. F., & Pruzinsky, T. (Eds.) (1990). *Body images: Development, deviance and change.* New York: Guilford Press.

Cash, T. F., Winstead, B. A., & Janda, L. H. (1986). Body image survey: The great American shape-up. *Psychology Today, 20,* 30–44.

Cromarty, P., & Marks, I. (1995). Does rational roleplay enhance the outcome of exposure therapy in dysmorphophobia? A case study. *British Journal of Psychiatry.*

de Leon, J., Bott, A., & Simpson, G. M. (1989). Dysmorphophobia: Body dysmorphic disorder of delusional disorder, somatic subtype? *Comprehensive Psychiatry, 30,* 457–472.

Feingold, A. (1992). Good-looking people are not what we think. *Psychological Bulletin, 111,* 304–341.

Fernandez, F., & Vandereycken, W. (1994). Influence of video confrontation on the self-evaluation of anorexia nervosa patients: A controlled study. *Eating Disorders, 2,* 135–140.

Garner, D. M., & Bemis, K. M. (1982). A cognitive-behavioral approach to anorexia nervosa. *Cognitive Therapy and Research, 6,* 123–150.

Giles, T. R. (1988). Distortion of body image as an effect of conditioned fear. *Journal of Behaviour Therapy and Experimental Psychiatry, 19,* 143–146.

Goldsmith, D., & Thompson, J. K. (1989). The effect of mirror confrontation and size estimation feedback on perceptual inaccuracy in normal females who overestimate body size. *International Journal of Eating Disorders, 8,* 437–444.

Gomez-Perez, J. C., Marks, I. M., & Gutierrez-Fisac, J. L. (1994). Dysmorphophobia: Clinical features and outcome with behavior therapy. *European Psychiatry, 9,* 229–235.

Harris, L. (1987). *Inside America.* New York: Vintage Books.

Hay, G. G. (1970). Dysmorphophobia. *British Journal of Psychiatry, 116,* 399–406.

Hollander, E., Cohen, L. J., & Simeon, D. (1993). Body dysmorphic disorder. *Psychiatric Annals, 23,* 359–364.

Hollander, E., Liebowitz, M. R., Winchel, R., Klumer, A., & Klein, D. F. (1989). Treatment of body-dysmorphic disorder with serotonin reuptake blockers. *American Journal of Psychiatry, 146,* 768–770.

Jarvie, G. J., Lahey, B., Graziano, W., & Farmer, E. (1983). Childhood obesity and social stigma: What we know and what we don't know. *Developmental Review, 3,* 237–273.

Kanner, A. D., Coyne, J. C., Schaefer, C., & Lazarus, R. S. (1981). Comparison of two modes of stress measurement: Daily hassles and uplifts versus major life events. *Journal of Behavioral Medicine, 4,* 1–39.

Kozak, M. J., & Foa, E. B. (1994). Obsessions, overvalued ideas, and delusions in obsessive-compulsive disorder. *Behaviour Research and Therapy, 32,* 343–353.

Lacey, J. H., & Birtchnell, S. A. (1986). Body image and its disturbances. *Journal of Psychosomatic Research, 30,* 623–631.

Lowe, C. F., & Chadwick, P. D. J. (1990). Verbal control of delusions. *Behavior Therapy, 21,* 461–479.

Marks, I. (1995). Advances in behavioral-cognitive therapy of social phobia. *Journal of Clinical Psychiatry, 56,* 25–31.

Marks, I., & Mishan, J. (1988). Dysmorphophobic avoidance with disturbed bodily perception: A pilot study of exposure therapy. *British Journal of Psychiatry, 152,* 674–678.

McKenna, P. J. (1984). Disorders with overvalued ideas. *British Journal of Psychiatry, 145,* 579–585.

Miller, C. T., Rothblum, E. D., Felicio, D., & Brand, P. (1998). Compensating for stigma: Obese and nonobese women's reactions to being visible. *Personality and Social Psychology Bulletin,* in press.

Munjack, D. J. (1978). The behavioral treatment of dysmorphophobia. *Journal Behavior Therapy and Experimental Psychiatry, 9,* 53–56.

Munro, A., & Chmara, J. (1982). Monosymptomatic hypochondriacal psychosis: A diagnostic checklist based on 50 cases of the disorder. *Canadian Journal of Psychiatry, 27,* 374–376.

Munro, A., & Stewart, M. (1991). Body dysmorphic disorder and the DSM IV: The demise of dysmorphophobia. *Canadian Journal of Psychiatry, 36,* 91–96.

Newell, R., & Shrubb, S. (1994). Attitude change and behaviour therapy in body dysmorphic disorder: Two case reports. *Behavioural and Cognitive Psychotherapy, 22,* 163–169.

Neziroglu, F. A., & Yaryura-Tobias, J. A. (1993). Body dysmorphic disorder: Phenomenology and case descriptions. *Behavioural Psychotherapy, 21,* 27–36.

Neziroglu, F. A., McKay, D., Todaro, J., & Yaryura-Tobias, J. A. (1996). Effect of cognitive behavior therapy on persons with body dysmorphic disorder and comorbid Axis II diagnoses. *Behavior Therapy, 27,* 67–77.

Norris, D. L. (1984). The effects of mirror confrontation on self-estimation in anorexia nervosa, bulimia and two control groups. *Psychological Medicine, 14,* 835–842.

Orosan, P., Rosen, J. C., & Tang, T. (1996). *Critical incidents in the development of body image.* Presentation in symposium on body image, 7th International Conference on Eating Disorders, New York.

Pantano, M., & Santonastaso, P. (1989). A case of dysmorphophobia following recovery from anorexia nervosa. *International Journal of Eating Disorders, 8,* 701–704.

Philippopoulos, G. S. (1979). The analysis of a case of dysmorfophobia. *Canadian Journal of Psychiatry, 24,* 397–401.

Phillips, K. A. (1991). Body dysmorphic disorders: The distress of imagined ugliness. *American Journal of Psychiatry, 148,* 1138–1149.

Phillips, K. A. (1993). *Body dysmorphic disorder modification of the YBOCS, McLean version.* Belmont, MA: McLean Hospital.

Phillips, K. A., McElroy, S. L., Keck, P. E., Pope, H. G., & Hudson, J. I. (1993). Body dysmorphic disorder: 30 cases of imagined ugliness. *American Journal of Psychiatry, 150,* 302–308.

Phillips, K. A., McElroy, S. L., Keck, P. E., Hudson, J. I., & Pope, H. G. (1994). A comparison of delusional and nondelusional body dysmorphic disorder in 100 cases. *Psychopharmacology Bulletin, 30,* 179–186.

Pliner, P., Chaiken, S., & Flett, G. L. (1990). Gender differences in concern with body weight and physical appearance over the life span. *Personality and Social Psychology Bulletin, 16,* 263–273.

Rosen, J. C. (1996). Body image assessment and treatment in controlled studies of eating disorders. *International Journal of Eating Disorders, 19.*

Rosen, J. C., & Reiter, J. (1996). Development of the Body Dysmorphic Disorder Examination. *Behaviour Research and Therapy, 34,* 755–766.

Rosen, J. C., Saltzberg, E., & Srebnik, D. (1989). Cognitive behavior therapy for negative body image. *Behavior Therapy, 20,* 393–404.

Rosen, J. C., Cado, S., Silberg, S., Srebnik, D., & Wendt, S. (1990). Cognitive behavior therapy with and without size perception training for women with body image disturbance. *Behavior Therapy, 21,* 481–498.

Rosen, J. C., Orosan, P., & Reiter, J. (1995a). Cognitive behavior therapy for negative body image in obese women. *Behavior Therapy, 26,* 25–42.

Rosen, J. C., Reiter, J., & Orosan, P. (1995b). Cognitive behavioral body image therapy for body dysmorphic disorder. *Journal of Consulting and Clinical Psychology, 63,* 263–269.

Secord, P. F., & Jourard, S. M. (1953). The appraisal of body-cathexis: Body- cathexis and the self. *Journal of Consulting Psychology, 17,* 343–347.

Schmidt, N. B., & Harrington, P. (1995). Cognitive-behavioral treatment of body dysmorphic disorder: A case report. *Journal of behaviour therapy and experimental psychiatry, 26,* 161–167.

Sturmey, P., & Slade, P. D. (1986). Anorexia nervosa and dysmorphophobia. *British Journal of Psychiatry, 149,* 780–782.

Takahashi, T. (1989). Social phobia syndrome in Japan. *Comprehensive Psychiatry, 30,* 45–52.

Thomas, C. S. (1984). Dysmorphophobia: A question of definition. *British Journal of Psychiatry, 144,* 513–516.

Thomas, C. S., & Goldberg, D. P. (1995). Appearance, body image and distress in facial dysmorphophobia. *Acta Psychiatria Scandinavica, 92,* 231–236.

Thompson, J. K, Heinberg, L. J., & Marshall, K. (1994). The Physical Appearance Behavioral Avoidance Test (PABAT): Preliminary findings. *Behavior Therapist, January,* 9–10.

Vandereycken, W., Probst, M., & Van Bellinghen, M. (1992). Treating the distorted body experience of anorexia nervosa patients. *Journal of Adolescent Health, 13,* 403–405.

Warwick, H. M. C., & Salkovskis, P. M. (1989). Hypochondriasis. In J. Scott, J. M. G. Williams & A. T. Beck (Eds.), *Cognitive therapy: A clinical casebook.* London: Routledge, pp. 78–102.

Watts, F. N. (1990). Aversion to personal body hair: A case study in the integration of behavioural and interpretative methods. *British Journal of Medical Psychology, 63,* 335–340.

Further reading

Beck, A. T., Rush, A. J., Shaw, B. F., & Emery, G. (1979). *Cognitive therapy of depression.* New York: Guildford Press.

Cash, T. F. (1995). *What do you see in the mirror?: Helping yourself to a positive body image.* New York: Bantam Books.

Cash, T. F. & Pruzinsky, T. (eds.) (1990). *Body images: Development, deviance and change.* New York: Guildford Press.

Rosen, J. C., Reiter, J. & Orosan, P. (1995). Cognitive behavioral body image therapy for body dysmorphic disorder. *Journal of Consulting and Clinical Psychology, 63,* 263–269.

Rosen J. C., Saltzberg, E. & Srebnik, D. (1989). Cognitive behavior therapy for negative body image. *Behavior Therapy, 20,* 393–404.

Appendix 1: Protocol for the Cognitive-Behavioral Treatment of Body Dysmorphic Disorder

Session 1:	Education about body image and body image therapy
	Define body image
	Provide basic information about the psychology of physical appearance
	Define BDD and body image disorder and information about factors that cause and maintain the disorder
	Discuss the patient's attitudes toward therapy
Session 2:	Construct a developmental history of body image disorder
	Train patient in self-recording of body image situations, thoughts, and behaviors
Session 3:	Teach techniques to control negative body talk
	Construct hierarchy of distressing body areas or appearance features
	Provide instruction in relaxation
	Begin unsupervised exposure to sight of appearance in mirror at home
Session 4:	Identify and begin to evaluate maladaptive assumptions about appearance
	Continue exposure to appearance in mirror at home
Session 5:	Continue cognitive restructuring of maladaptive assumptions about appearance
	Practice exposure to appearance in mirrors or reflective surfaces in public
Session 6:	Begin exposure to more challenging body image situations
	Continue cognitive restructuring
Session 7:	Continue exposure to challenging body image situations
	Begin response prevention of excessive body image behavior
Session 8 to 10:	Continue exposure to challenging body image situations
	Continue response prevention of excessive body image behavior
	Preparation for termination and events that might trigger relapse

13

Cognitive-Behavioural Treatment of Problem Gambling

LOUISE SHARPE

West Middlesex University Hospital, UK

Introduction

The literature has described problematic levels of gambling behaviour utilising various different terminology. The terminology which has been used to describe problem gambling has generally been theoretically laden. Notably, such terms include descriptions of gambling as addictive (e.g., Brown, 1987); compulsive (e.g., Dickerson, 1990) and pathological (e.g., Dickerson & Hinchey, 1988). Each of these terms makes implicit assumptions about the nature of problematic gambling behaviour. For example, both DSM-III-R and DSM-IV (APA, 1987, 1994) refer to Pathological Gambling and place it in the category of Disorders of Impulse Control. At present there is simply insufficient evidence to categorically determine the nature of problem gambling behaviour as either impulsive, addictive or compulsive. To some degree the terminology which is used in referring to excessive levels of gambling is arbitrary. However, problem gambling will be favoured in the present chapter to avoid the theoretical arguments about the nature of problem gambling which are beyond the scope of the present chapter (for discussion see Dickerson, 1989; Walker 1989). Problem gambling will be defined in the present chapter by the criterion put forward in the DSM-IV (APA, 1994) for Pathological Gambling.

According to DSM-IV (APA, 1994) pathological gambling can be diagnosed when patients have "persistent or recurrent maladaptive gambling behaviour" characterised by five out of ten possible criteria: (1) a preoccupation with gambling. This can include dwelling on past gambling experiences, preoccupation with finding funds to gamble or planning the next bout of gambling; (2) a need to continually increase the amount of money gambled in order to achieve the same level of excitement; (3) failed efforts to reduce or stop gambling; (4) restlessness or irritability if unable to gamble; (5) gambles as a method of escaping life stresses; (6) behaviour known as chasing losses, where the gambler returns to gambling to try and recoup previous money which has been lost; (7) lying to significant people including family members, therapists or others with the intent of hiding the extent of involvement in gambling behaviour; (8) has committed some form of criminal or illegal activity in order to finance the gambling problem; (9) has jeopardised or lost significant parts of their lifestyle (such as family, relationships, employment) as a direct result of gambling; (10) has relied on others to provide finances to salvage a desperate financial situation which arose as a result of gambling. The criteria in DSM-IV (APA, 1987) specifically exclude episodes of gambling which are associated with a manic episode. However, a diagnosis of Pathological Gambling according to DSM-IV does not preclude another DSM-IV diagnosis.

Empirical Background of Treatment

The prevalence of problem gambling which has generally been estimated across studies as between 1 and 3% of the population (Lesieur & Rosenthal, 1991), but despite this there has been relatively little research on the treatment of problem gambling. Indeed, there is only one published treatment trial to date. The majority of early treatment literature focused on either psychodynamic approaches to the treatment of problem gamblers (e.g., Bergler, 1958) or treatment from specialised in-patient units (e.g., Russo, Taber, McCormick & Ramirez, 1984). Clearly, in-patient treatment is not an alternative which is available for most clinicians. Moreover, studies in this vein have generally utilised a multifaceted approach and no control group, which makes any results difficult to interpret.

More recently, behavioural approaches have become popular. Seager (1970) used aversion training with fourteen problem gamblers and found five of these gamblers to be abstinent at 3 years. Later, Greenberg & Marks (1982) treated a case series of seven patients with imaginal desensitisation and found reductions in gambling in three of these patients after 6 months. However, this represents less than 50% of their small sample. In a larger uncontrolled trial of twenty-six problem gamblers, Greenberg & Rankin (1982) used a number of behavioural techniques and found similar results. That is, at follow-up (9 months to 4.5 years) five had their gambling under control, seven were improved with occasional lapses and for the other fourteen their gambling remained problematic. Whilst this indicates that useful strategies may be derived from a behavioural approach to treatment, these results are far from impressive as less than half the subjects in these trials were markedly improved.

In keeping with the focus of these behavioural studies, McConaghy, Armstrong, Blaszczynski & Allcock (1983) conducted a controlled trial comparing aversion training with imaginal desensitisation with a group of problem gamblers. Their results indicated that imaginal desensitisation was superior to aversion training. One year following imaginal desensitisation, two of ten patients were abstinent and another five were gambling in a controlled manner compared with eight subjects still gambling problematically in the aversion training group. Furthermore, in an uncontrolled longer term follow-up (2–9 years) of patients seen in their in-patient programme, ten out of 33 treated with systematic desensitisation were abstinent and a further sixteen were able to control their gambling (McConaghy, Blaszczynski & Frankova, 1991). While these data provide strong support for the use of systematic desensitisation in the treatment of problem gambling, there is still much scope for the improvement of these results. McConaghy and his colleagues have been criticised for their limited focus on single mechanistic treatments (Dickerson, 1990). One may expect that if other important factors were included in treatment, such as cognitive skills, that the treatment efficacy may be enhanced.

However, there is a paucity of studies which utilise and apply a cognitive or cognitive behavioural approach to the treatment of problem gambling. Without exception the available literature is uncontrolled and limited to case studies which document the success of a cognitive approach. To the author's knowledge only three papers are available which document the use of a cognitive or cognitive-behavioural approach to problem gambling. Perhaps this is due, at least partly, to the limited theoretical understanding of problem gambling from a cognitive-behavioural viewpoint. Ladouceur, Sylvain, Duvall & Gabourey (1989) published an interesting study where they asked gamblers to talk aloud during play and had them challenge their irrational verbalisations at the time of play. This approach is based on the mounting evidence that poker machine gamblers make more irrational verbalisations during play than rational statements (Gabourey & Ladouceur, 1988; Walker, 1992). They taught four poker machine players to identify and challenge their thoughts while playing. Clearly, this is an interesting approach which is worthy of further research. However, it is unclear whether the intensive nature of this approach which requires the therapist to conduct sessions in vivo is necessary to achieve the desired result. More traditional clinic based versions of cognitive therapy may equally produce changes in the gambler's cognitions.

Indeed, two case studies have utilised a cognitive element in clinic based sessions and asked patients to apply these skills in between sessions. In both these cases, the gamblers were abstinent at follow-up (Tonneatto & Sobell, 1990; Sharpe & Tarrier, 1992). Such approaches can be administered in the clinical setting more readily. The other major difference between these approaches and that of Ladouceur et al. (1989) is that these studies used a more comprehensive cognitive-behavioural approach. While both these papers report the treatment of a single case and clearly can not be generalised to indicate that these approaches will be efficacious with all gamblers, both were successful in eliminating gambling behaviour. More recently, the strategic approach developed by Sharpe & Tarrier (1992) was examined to investigate its efficacy when used with small groups of problem gamblers. The trial compared an eight session cognitive behavioural approach with a waiting list control group. Unfortunately longer term results are not yet available. However, out of the ten patients in the treatment group, only three were still gambling at post-treatment and all were improved. Indeed, two out of the three had reduced their gambling by more than two thirds. Interestingly, all gamblers except one, in the waiting list group reported that their gambling became worse over the treatment period. Only three gamblers have been followed-up to 6 months at this stage, however, all three had remained abstinent from the beginning of treatment (Sharpe, Livermore, McGregor & Tarrier, 1994a). Clearly, more controlled outcome research on cognitive-behavioural approaches is required, however, these results are encouraging and suggest that cognitive-behavioural approaches may have much to offer in the treatment of problem gambling. The aim of the present chapter is to provide information about the types of interventions useful in a cognitive-behavioural treatment for problem gambling and how these might be applied to individual cases.

Assessment of Problem Gambling

In assessing problem gamblers for a cognitive behavioural approach to treatment it is necessary to conduct a cognitive-behavioural analysis of the behaviour just as one would with any other disorder. However, there are specific issues which also need to be borne in mind in this population. Specifically these have to do with (1) the functions of gambling; (2) the adaptive and maladaptive coping skills which the patient has; (3) the presence and nature of urges to gamble; (4) any irrational beliefs which the gambler holds in relation to the probability of winning; (5) the presence of other difficulties; 6) their level of motivation and (7) the patient's treatment goal.

Functional Analysis

Firstly, gambling tends to serve a number of functions for individuals. Indeed, some preliminary evidence suggests that these functions tend to vary depending upon the type of gambling which is involved. For example, Cocco, Sharpe & Blaszczynski (1994) found preliminary evidence to suggest that horse race gamblers appear to gamble in order to increase their level of arousal; whereas poker machine players are more likely to gamble to escape from stressors. Thus, it is important to assess the precise nature of the function of gambling for each individual. To do this it is most important to identify not only the negative aspects of gambling on the person's lifestyle, but also the positive aspects. Most gamblers have been told by others of the negative consequences but the positives are rarely acknowledged. Only by identifying the positive functions and finding alternative methods of achieving these, is long-term abstinence likely. Treatment will vary depending upon whether the patient gambles to avoid stress, reduce boredom, achieve a 'high' or for some other reason. It is necessary to ascertain from the patient what other ways they have to fulfil these same functions.

Coping Skills

Sharpe & Tarrier (1993) in their recent cognitive-behavioural formulation of gambling have argued that effective coping skills are important in mediating problematic levels of gambling. Specifically, it is necessary to assess (a) a patient's ability to monitor and control their levels of arousal, (b) their ability to delay gratification, (c) their ability to challenge their thinking and (d) their ability to solve problems. Often patients will have some adaptive coping skills which can be enhanced in therapy. However, equally it is important to check for maladaptive coping strategies, such as using alcohol, which need to be reduced and replaced by more adaptive alternatives. Low levels of skills, such as social skills or assertiveness, are also not uncommon in problem gamblers. Clearly weaknesses in these areas will make it more difficult for gamblers to form social networks. Since socialising can be a function of gambling for many gamblers, it is necessary to identify problems in this area. Targetting social skills can be necessary with some patients as an adjunct to work with their gambling behaviour.

Urges to Gamble

Most problem gamblers also report frequent urges to gamble which often lead them to engage in gambling behaviour. However, the nature of the urges differ markedly between different individuals. For some gamblers their urges are primarily cognitive and associated with a thoughts, such as "I feel lucky today". For other gamblers, the urges appear to be described more in terms of physical sensations like an increased heart rate, sweaty palms, a knot in the stomach or nausea. Some gamblers initially deny the presence of any form of urge to gamble. There seems to be a small minority of gamblers for whom their gambling is so automatic that it is not associated with identifiable urges. However, the majority of these patients who can not identify urges initially become more aware of their urges over the course of treatment. Therefore, it may be necessary to focus on urges even when the gambler initially denies the presence of any. The conclusion that a patient does not have identifiable urges may lead to a less than optimal treatment if that person is simply unaware of the urge.

Irrational Beliefs

Awareness is also an important issue in relation to the beliefs which gamblers have held about the probability of winning or losing with their form of gambling. Although the probabilities vary for different types of gambling, in all forms of gambling the chances of winning are poorer than the chances of losing. It is again imperative not to accept gambler's claims that "They know they can't win" as they often become more aware of cognitive distortions as treatment progresses. We know from research by Gabourey & Ladouceur (1989) and Walker (1989) that irrational verbalisations are more frequent than rational statements during play on a poker machine. Indeed, Coulombe, Ladouceur, Deshairnais & Jobin (1992) have documented the relationship between irrational thinking and arousal as measured by heart rate. That is, a gambler's heart rate was positively correlated with the number of irrational verbalisations during play. In addition, there are other studies which have documented the importance of the type of attribution in determining betting strategy on a race course even amongst a non-gambling population (Atlas & Peterson, 1991). Thus, there is accumulating evidence about the importance of cognitions in gambling and in mediating gambling related arousal, but it may be necessary for some patients to actively monitor their thinking in real life situations before they will become aware of distortions which they hold.

Concurrent Diagnoses

Assessing gamblers for the presence of a diagnosis of pathological gambling can be done by utilising DSM-IV's (APA, 1994) criteria. It is important to note, however, that a diagnosis of Pathological Gambling does not preclude other concurrent diagnoses. Indeed, evidence suggests that the reverse is true. It has been well documented in the literature that problem gamblers experience much higher levels of both depression (e.g., Blaszczynski, McConaghy & Frankova, 1990) and anxiety (e.g., Blaszczynski & McConaghy, 1989) than control groups. Indeed, research studies indicate that the prevalence of other problems amongst problem gamblers is very high indeed. McCormick, Russo, Ramirez

& Taber (1984) investigated the prevalence of other disorders and found that over one third of patients concurrently met criteria for a major depressive episode. Even more alarmingly, Linden, Pope & Jonas (1986) in a lifetime prevalence study of Gambler's Anonymous (GA) member found that nearly three quarters of their sample (72%) had experienced a major depressive episode in their life. Linden et. al. (1986) also found a high rate of panic disorder (20%) and over half of their sample had a cross-addiction with alcohol (52%). These results are consistent with the findings that one in three problem gamblers have attempted suicide in their lifetime (Moran, 1969). Thus, the need to screen for affective disorders, suicidality, anxiety disorders and other addictions is imperative with this population. It may be appropriate in some cases to treat the concurrent disorder before tackling the gambling problem. However, there is some evidence to suggest that both anxiety and depression also reduce with behavioural and/or cognitive-behavioural interventions which are successful in ameliorating the gambling problem (McConaghy et. al., 1983; Sharpe al., 1994a). Therefore, it is important to recognise that in the majority of cases improving or eliminating the gambling problem is likely to produce significant improvements in mood.

Motivation

Finally, it is necessary to assess the patient's level of motivation and the goal which they have for treatment. Gamblers often enter treatment either at someone else's insistence (e.g., a spouse), as a result of involvement with the criminal services or due to some other problem. Miller's (1983) approach to motivational interviewing can be quite helpful in engaging and motivating patients for treatment. The four key principles which Miller outlines to help foster motivation are (1) a de-emphasis on labelling. That is, the label of "addiction" or "compulsion" is not a prerequisite for treatment. The client should be encouraged to see that the need for treatment comes about because of the effect of the behaviour on their lifestyle and not because they have some "disease" that needs to be "cured"; (2) consistent with this, the patient needs to view themselves as having personal responsibility for their gambling behaviour; (3) the patient needs to make internal attributions which allow them to view the problem as potentially controllable and not an integral or unchangeable part of them; and (4) the therapist needs to encourage cognitive dissonance. That is, the patient needs to identify the that there is an inconsistency between their rational thought and their behaviour of continued gambling. The combined use of these principles can be helpful in engaging and motivating the patient.

There is a tendency, however, to assume that once a patient has been adequately motivated that they will continue to be motivated to stop gambling. This assumption is simply not correct. Motivation is thought to be phasic rather than constant and this is certainly the case with gamblers. It rests on a cost-benefit analysis by the patient which invariably changes over time. Thus, it can be necessary to continue to use these techniques throughout treatment to maintain a high level of motivation. Without frequently attending to issues of motivation, it is likely that high levels of treatment refusals and drop-outs will occur. Indeed, a recent study suggested that treatment refusers for a group cognitive behavioural programme when recontacted later indicated that lowered motivation was the major reason for non-attendance (Sharpe et. al., 1994a). Another major reason endorsed by many gamblers was the delay of the group (which was not greater than 8 weeks for any individual). Thus, it is important clinically to see gamblers at a time when their motivation is high and to facilitate this throughout treatment. In the early stages frequently spaced sessions may be particularly useful to achieve this end and ensure that motivation is likely to be enduring and stable.

It is also important to collaborate with the client on their goal of either abstinence or controlled gambling. In my experience, most gamblers will initially choose a goal of abstinence but some will change their mind over a longer period. Indeed, regardless of a goal of abstinence or controlled gambling, some period of abstinence is advisable to allow the patterns which have developed to be broken while skills are attained and consolidated (Sharpe & Tarrier, 1992).

Treatment

Stabilisation

The first step in treating problem gambling is to stabilise the gambling behaviour. Clearly, if patients were able to stop or reduce their gambling easily, they would not need to seek treatment. Initially, this must be done by using very practical methods which make it difficult or impossible for the gambler to have access to either (a) funds for gambling; or (b) gambling venues. Ideally, someone in the family may be used in order to take over responsibility for the patient's finances. This can be problematic either when the person has little social support and therefore there is nobody who can play this role for them or when there are significant marital difficulties which are not uncommon in this population. However, a sensible problem solving approach with the patient can generally find adequate solutions to any difficulties in this regard. People can frequently change their banking policies, for example, so that they limit the availability of ready cash through machines. They can change their method of payment through work so that the money is placed straight into a bank account and bills are paid through the banking system before they can be tempted to use the money for gambling purposes. Clearly, the harder one is able to make access to moneys for gambling, the more likely the person will be to eliminate their gambling in the first instance.

When choosing a family member to take over financial responsibility for the patient's finances, it must be made clear to both the patient and the family member that this is a short-term solution and not intended to be a long term intervention. Spouses, in particular, can have difficulty later in treatment allowing their partner's to resume some financial control for fear that they will return to gambling. Resuming financial independence in the longer term, however, is essential to the long term maintenance of gains. Avoidance results unless the individual gradually starts carrying money on their person and then when confronted with that situation by chance, this will act as a trigger which will increase the chance of returns to gambling. It can be necessary to bring the spouse into treatment initially to explain this or once the patient is ready to begin to resume financial control.

Not only should the gambler be instructed to reduce or eliminate access to funds over the short term, but also access to gambling venues. This can necessitate changing the route to or from work, or finding competing activities which are incompatible with gambling at danger periods. If steps can be taken to reduce access to both funds and gambling venues, the majority of gamblers will not have significant difficulties in sizeably reducing or eliminating their gambling in the short term. However, this is clearly only the first step.

Constructing an Alternative Behavioural Repertoire

For all problem gamblers, the activity of gambling has constituted a large proportion of their time prior to initiating treatment. Clearly, successfully reaching the goal of abstinence will thus create a bulk of time which previously did not exist for the gambler. It is therefore very important to plan for this eventuality early in treatment by constructing a behavioural repertoire of alternative activities. If this step is not taken the gambler can frequently resume gambling after long periods of abstinence due to boredom or lack of social interaction, particularly if these were some of the original functions that gambling served for the patient. Alternative behaviours, of course, serve the dual purpose of an active coping strategy to gain control over the urge to gamble.

Indeed, it can be useful to get patients early in treatment to make a list of positive and negative consequences of their gambling. Not only does this serve to strengthen the gamblers motivation, but it also serves to give guidelines as to the functions of gambling. These functions then provide a good direction for choosing appropriate alternative activities which fulfil the same functions for gamblers. For example, if the functions that gambling serves for one individual is (a) to escape boredom; (b) to cope with stress and (c) to get a physical high, an activity like reading would only be minimally helpful since is may serve only one of these functions (the relief of boredom). However, an activity like physical exercise of some sort may actually produce a physical rush of adrenaline, may relieve boredom and may also help in reducing stress. The nature of an appropriate activity will rest upon the functions which gambling plays for each individual. The more activities which serve some, if not all, of the functions of gambling, the less need the patient will have to return to gambling to achieve those positives.

Awareness

The next step which is important is awareness. Patient's differ in the extent to which they are aware of both thoughts and physical sensations associated with gambling behaviour. The majority will be able to become aware of these by standard monitoring of urges to gamble between sessions. Typically, one might monitor the presence or absence of an urge; the duration and intensity of the urge; what the individual was doing when the urge began; the first sign of the urge; the associated thoughts; physical symptoms; feelings; any coping skills used; whether or not the gambler has gambled; and the level of control which they had over gambling. This information will allow a comprehensive pattern of gambling behaviour to be established in collaboration between the patient and therapist (see Figure 13.1).

Occasionally, monitoring is not sufficient to elicit the thoughts and feelings associated with gambling, particularly when the person is successful in eliminating the gambling behaviour during the early stages of treatment. In such cases, it can be necessary to use imagery to evoke cognitions. Alternately, some patients start to become aware of these automatically while monitoring their urges later in treatment when they place themselves in gambling venues as exposure tasks.

Applied Relaxation Training

One of the coping skills deficits hypothesised to be important in the development of problematic levels of gambling is the inability to control high levels of arousal (Sharpe & Tarrier, 1992). Indeed, this is particularly thought to be the case with problem poker machine players (Cocco et. al., 1994). Thus, it can be important to learn ways in which to control subjective feelings of arousal. This is particularly important given that there are many studies which document that arousal is associated with gambling behaviour (Anderson & Brown, 1984; Leary & Dickerson, 1985; Blaszczynski, Winter & McConaghy, 1987; Coulombe et. al., 1992). Indeed, it has recently been empirically demonstrated that gambling cues are associated with increases in autonomic arousal in the

Fill out at midday	Fill out at approx. 6.00 p.m.	Fill out at bed time
Gambling urge present	Gambling urge present	Gambling urge present
yes/no	yes/no	yes/no
If yes, rate :	If yes, rate :	If yes, rate :
0 1 2 3 4 5 6 7 8 9 10 duration (in hours)	0 1 2 3 4 5 6 7 8 9 10 duration (in hours)	0 1 2 3 4 5 6 7 8 9 10 duration (in hours)
Intensity :	Intensity :	Intensity :
0 1 2 3 4 5 6 7 8 9 10 no worst urge urge	0 1 2 3 4 5 6 7 8 9 10 no worst urge urge	0 1 2 3 4 5 6 7 8 9 10 no worst urge urge
Ability to resist urge :	Ability to resist urge :	Ability to resist urge :
0 1 2 3 4 5 6 7 8 9 10 easy impossible	0 1 2 3 4 5 6 7 8 9 10 easy impossible	0 1 2 3 4 5 6 7 8 9 10 easy impossible
What were you doing ?	What were you doing ?	What were you doing ?
What was the first sign ?	What was the first sign ?	What was the first sign ?
What were you thinking ?	What were you thinking ?	What were you thinking?
Physical symptoms ?	Physical symptoms ?	Physical symptoms ?
How did you feel ?	How did you feel ?	How did you feel ?
How did you cope ?	How did you cope ?	How did you cope ?
Have you gambled ? yes/no	Have you gambled ? yes/no	Have you gambled ? yes/no
Rate control over gambling :	Rate control over gambling :	Rate control over gambling
0 1 2 3 4 5 6 7 8 9 10 no complete control control	0 1 2 3 4 5 6 7 8 9 10 no complete control control	0 1 2 3 4 5 6 7 8 9 10 no complete control control

Figure 13.1 Gambling diary.

absence of gambling behaviour (Sharpe, Tarrier, Schotte & Spence, 1994b). Learning to cope with these levels of arousal is likely to be important in learning to cope with urges to gamble.

The importance of relaxation skills is to be able to use relaxation in an applied setting. Therefore, it is important to ensure that not only are prolonged relaxation instructions given initially to help patients learn the skill, but that these are replaced with briefer skills to help them to learn to actually use the skills at the time that they need to.

Problem Solving

Problem gamblers frequently give the impression that they are unable to take account of the long-term consequences of actions and rather respond to immediate gratification. This difficulty which we have noted clinically can be conceptualised within a problem solving framework. Teaching gamblers basic problem solving skills, such as those exemplified by D'Zurilla & Goldfried (1980), can be very important to help gamblers consider the alternatives before impulsively engaging in gambling behaviour which they later regret. Problem solving techniques are also amenable to use in high risk situations. Problem solving can provide a useful coping strategy to help problem gamblers talk themselves through difficult situations and thus can be incorporated into the more cognitively oriented elements of treatment.

Exposure

Imaginal exposure. The results of McConaghy et. al. (1983, 1991) provide strong support for the use of imaginal exposure in the treatment of problem gambling. Indeed, the theoretical reasons for utilising imaginal exposure are also clear. Studies investigating the role of autonomic arousal in problem gambling have without exception found that all forms of gambling are associated with autonomic arousal (Anderson & Brown, 1984; Blaszczynski et. al., 1987; Coulombe et. al., 1992; Eves & Moore, 1991a,b; Sharpe, Tarrier et. al., 1994b). Therefore, one might expect that when exposed to an imaginal scene which is associated with arousal, the resulting arousal will habituate with subsequent presentations. Consistent with this hypothesis, McConaghy (1988) found that the lower the level of anxiety following treatment, the better the long term prognosis.

In order to provide an adequate imaginal exposure, one must elicit an example of a scene from the patient related to their gambling behaviour. It is important in getting a scene which includes not only the physical locality in which the scene takes place, but also the internal changes associated with the situation. This should include both thoughts and physical sensations. The imaginal scene can be taped during the session and then it can be played during the following week as homework. It can be expedient to use the imaginal exposure as a rehearsal for in vivo exposure which will follow and consolidate the patient's skills. Suggesting in the imagery the use of various skills which the patient may use to gain control over the physical sensations, thoughts or other aspects of the scene will generally facilitate these adaptive coping responses in the real life situation.

In vivo exposure. Sharpe & Tarrier (1992) have also included a role for in vivo exposure tasks. Their rationale is that in vivo tasks provide a number of opportunities for the patient, namely (1) habituation; (2) practice of coping learnt strategies; and (3) increasing a feeling of control, mastery and self-efficacy in difficult situations. As with other disorders it is necessary to construct a hierarchy of gambling related situations in which the client could practise. In constructing a hierarchy it is necessary to elicit from the patient an estimate of their ability to enter this situation *without gambling*. Tasks can be set for homework once the patient has learnt the necessary skills. Tasks can generally be recommended as long as patients are at least 75% confident that they can enter the proposed situation without gambling. Clearly, it is sensible to ensure that patients do not have sizeable amounts of money available during early practices. However, once some low grade tasks have been successfully completed is a good time to gradually begin to give gamblers back some control over their own finances. This is particularly useful in that it serves the dual purpose of providing a 24 h exposure task and providing a normalising experience which is likely to reduce the chance of relapse.

Cognitive Strategies

There is increasing evidence that cognitions play an important role in problem gambling (Gabourey & Ladouceur, 1989; Walker, 1992). Clearly where irrational beliefs about the probability of winning exist, it is necessary to examine the basis for these thoughts. Moreover, it is important to attempt to change any styles of thinking which increase the likelihood of patients continuing to gamble. Sharpe & Tarrier (1992) recommend using principles based upon Beck, Rush, Shaw & Emery's (1978) text which delineates the use of cognitive therapy with emotional disorders.

With these techniques as a basis for the style of cognitive therapy, it may be helpful to offer a few examples of typical cognitive distortions which are common to this population.

The gambler's fallacy. This term was initially coined by Leopard (1978) who

The winning glow. This distortion refers to the situation where gamblers will attend to the positive outcomes, but "forget" the negative ones. Gamblers frequently come home from the races, the club or the casino and boast about their "big win". At the same time they rarely mention the amount that they lost, even if that amount were greater than their winnings. This is often interpreted as the gambler lying to their spouse or friends, which is one of the DSM-IV (APA, 1994) criteria for problem gambling. However, many gamblers actually fail to register the losses even to themselves. Even those that acknowledge that they lose more heavily than they win will often grossly underestimate the extent of their losses. It frequently comes as a surprise to them the amount of money which they have lost, when they are asked to monitor it closely. Gamblers need to be taught to concentrate on both wins and losses in order to more accurately assess the level of their own gambling. Monitoring can often provide a ready made facility for testing out this particular type of thinking. Indeed, this discrepancy is often dealt with early in treatment with the introduction of self monitoring.

Emotional reasoning. Beck et. al. (1978) identify emotional reasoning as being one of their cognitive distortions which is often found in depressed patients. This form of thinking is also present in problem gamblers, however, in reverse. With depressed patients it is the negative emotions on which they focus and they assume that negative emotions represent facts. That is, "I feel bad, therefore, I am bad." Gamblers on the other hand, use positive moods as evidence for the probability of winning if they gamble. For example, "I feel lucky today, therefore, I am more likely to win". This is simply wrong. The following dialogue proved useful in testing this out with one gambler for whom this was a particular problem.

Therapist: "When you walk on the earth, does it feel round or flat ?"
Gambler: "Well, flat."
Therapist: "And do you believe that that is true, that the world is flat?"
Gambler: "Of course not, it's round."
Therapist: "What does that tell you about whether you can always trust you feelings to be correct?"
Gambler: "Well obviously you can't."

Relapse Prevention

By the end of treatment, most gamblers will have experienced a prolonged abstinence from gambling. However, the importance of effective maintenance can not be underestimated. Marlatt & Gordon's (1985) approach to relapse prevention with alcoholics provides a very useful framework within which to prevent relapse with gamblers (for a full discussion see Marlatt & Gordon,

1985). The most important aspect of this is to have gamblers understand that a lapse is not equivalent to a relapse. This realisation reduces the abstinence violation effect and ensures that patients no longer adhere to the "one drink, one drunk" mentality which leaves them at risk for relapse.

It is also important to identify high risk situations which may be associated with returns to gambling. Identifying these and having gamblers plan for how they might be able to manage these situations with their new skills is a very useful exercise. This not only allows the gambler to develop a plan for coping with difficult situations, but also allows the therapist to determine how well the gambler has been able to learn and consolidate the skills.

In addition to this, booster sessions over at least a 12 month period are advisable to ensure that a safety net is available since gamblers are renown for not recontacting sufficiently hastily when difficulties arise. Recontact contracts can also be useful where it is agreed in advance what the criterion will be for a time where a gambler should recontact the therapist. The guiding strategy here is to ensure that gamblers learn to cope with minor setbacks on their own but are able to recognise more major setbacks before they become fully blown relapses. A verbal or written contract will increase the chance that gamblers will recontact at an appropriate stage and therefore minimise the likelihood of a full blown relapse.

Table 13.1. shows a session by session cognitive-behavioural program for the treatment of pathological gamblers.

Adjunctive Treatments

The treatment which has been described previously, aims to provide a comprehensive programme specifically targeting problem gambling behaviour. However, as has been mentioned in the assessment section, many gamblers have concurrent difficulties which can warrant independent intervention. While treatments do appear to concurrently address some of the symptoms of depression or anxiety, other problems are unlikely to be reduced by focusing solely on the gambling behaviour itself. Clearly, the nature of adjunctive treatments would largely depend upon the nature of the problem and the decision to treat independently must rest with a cognitive-behavioural analysis of the interactions between the gambling and the other difficulties. However, there are some sufficiently common comorbid difficulties which arise when treating problem gamblers, which warrant discussion.

The role of the gambler's partner. It is not uncommon to find that there are significant difficulties in the marriages of problem gamblers (Lesieur & Rosenthal, 1991). Regardless of whether these difficulties precede the gambling or are a consequence of the gambling, they are likely to interfere with successful

Table 13.1. A session by session guide for the cognitive-behavioral treatment of pathological gamblers

Session 1:	Introduction	Session 5:	In vivo practice
	Ground rules		Goal setting
	Aims of the programme		Role of thoughts
	Session by session guide		Common styles of thinking
	How does gambling become a		
	problem	Session 6:	In vivo practice
	What is an urge?		Changing your unhelpful
	Consequences of gambling		thoughts
	The vicious cycle of gambling		Challenging thoughts
	What can be done?		Coping with difficult
	Where do we start?		situations
Session 2:	Awareness training		Setting of difficult
	Pros and cons of gambling		situations
	Goal setting	Session 7:	In vivo practice
	Relaxation training		Changing your unhelpful
	What is relaxation		thoughts
	training?		Assertion training
	Breathing control		Types of assertion
	Relaxation exercises		When to use assertive
			behavior
Session 3:	Awareness training:		
	1st sign of an urge	Session 8:	Maintaining your new skills
	Goal setting		Why it is important to main-
	Relaxation training		tain my skills?
	Problem solving		Setback vs. relapse
			Summary of programme
Session 4:	Problem solving		
	Goal setting		
	Brief relaxation		
	Applying your skills:		
	In vivo practice		

treatment. The two most common reasons for this is that either gambling has been used as a coping mechanism for stressors within the marriage; or because well meaning spouses who fear returns to gambling sabotage efforts of gamblers to learn to cope in gambling situations and regain financial independence.

Clearly, where marital problems are contributing to the gambling, these can need to be assessed and treated prior to any skills training for the gambling problem itself. During this phase the aim of treatment with regard to the gambling behaviour would be to contain any losses, rather than to change the behaviour. However, it is important to ensure that the partner's inclusion in marital therapy does not imply that the partner shares responsibility for the gambling problem. Thus, unless there are significant marital issues, it can be useful to encourage individual treatment so that individual responsibility rests on the shoulders of the gamblers themselves.

It can be useful to use treatment to allow the partner an opportunity to express their anger toward the patient and their behaviour, to learn about how problems in gambling develop and to learn about effective ways of reinforcing their partner's non-gambling behaviour. Although there is no empirical evidence relating to the inclusion of the partner or the timing of partner sessions, our practice has been to see the partner separately. This allows the partner to vent their anger without overtly "blaming" the gambler. Particularly where gamblers themselves feel guilty about the effects of gambling on the family's lifestyle, blaming is unproductive and can be counter therapeutic. However, it can be important for gambler's partners to vent this anger or it may continue to be an issue within the relationship.

Educational components should be the same as those which would be provided to the gamblers themselves. It is important to emphasise the role of reinforcement schedules in the initial acquisition of gambling behaviour. The role of arousal and thoughts in gambling should also be highlighted. This can then provide a rationale for the treatment which is being offered to the patient. One of the most important aspects is to help the partner understand the need for the gambler to place themselves in the gambling situation again in order to learn to cope with this situation without gambling. This can be difficult since the partner understandably will fear returns to gambling, particularly when they see that avoidance has worked in the short term. However, it is most difficult for gamblers to complete these tasks if their partners are opposed to them as they will often find ways to actively discourage the completion of the tasks. Usually, however, partners respond favourably to a session which makes the treatment goals clear to them and they can often find the support useful.

Social skills or assertiveness training. One of the most common reasons which gamblers report for initial gambling is for social interaction. Many gamblers are quite socially unskilled and therefore it can be problematic for them to find alternative ways in which to socialise effectively. For others, it may be that their peer group are actually involved in gambling at a social level and frequently try to draw the gambler back into the gambling scene without realising that they have a problem with gambling. For patients for whom this is a problem it can clearly be helpful to use social skills or assertiveness training in order to supplement the other coping skills and make the availability of alternative activities easier.

Other problems. A sizeable minority of problem gamblers appear to have more generalised difficulties which underpin not only their gambling behaviour but also other problems in their life. Where these patterns exist, it is rarely useful to address an isolated behaviour such as gambling.

For example, Blaszczynski, McConaghy & Frankova (1989) investigated the incidence of Antisocial Personality Disorder (APD) in a group of pathological gamblers. Their results indicated that nearly 15% of their sample fulfilled DSM-III (APA, 1980) criteria for APD. Although their study failed to use a control group, this statistic is high and worthy of consideration. Their study found that the group with APD were more likely to have committed *both* crimes associated with gambling and crimes independent of gambling. There was a lower incidence of APD in gamblers who either committed gambling related offences only or those that committed other offences only. For those who committed gambling only offences and had evidence of APD, the emergence of APD features occurred only following adolescence. The authors argued that this indicated the secondary nature of APD in this group. In contrast, the group having committed crimes both related and unrelated to gambling appeared to have had antisocial features prior to adolescence, indicating that these features may have been primary.

This distinction, while requiring replication and extension, may be helpful particularly for those working in social service settings. It would seem intuitive to suggest that for those with a preceding personality structure consistent with APD, treating the gambling would be insufficient to produce long-term gains and addressing the primary difficulty would be necessary. However, even where the personality features developed as a consequence of gambling, these may also require specific targeting once the gambling behaviour is under control. Unfortunately, there can be few guidelines for therapists with our present level of understanding about the treatment of complicating factors in problem gambling. Decisions in this regard will need to be made at the discretion of the clinician.

Conclusion

Problem gambling has frequently been considered a recalcitrant problem which is resistant to treatment. This is evidenced by the early case studies which documented success in less than half of the samples treated (e.g., Greenberg & Marks, 1982). However, recently there have been new developments in the treatment of problematic levels of gambling which give cause for optimism. Firstly, the work of McConaghy and his colleagues (1983, 1991) demonstrated the potential importance of imaginal desensitisation in the treatment of gambling difficulties. Indeed, the long term results of the more recent study, while uncontrolled and in need of replication, are definitely encouraging.

The advent of research into the role of cognitions in the development and maintenance of problem gambling, has increased the awareness of the need for more comprehensive programmes to facilitate the response to these early approaches. Indeed, case reports are only now emerging which document the efficacy of a cognitive behavioural approach. However, a pilot study investigating the efficacy of a strategic cognitive-behavioural approach has suggested that this programme has great potential in increasing the efficacy of less comprehensive treatments (Sharpe et. al., 1994a).

The present chapter has attempted to delineate the treatment strategies which were utilised and found to be effective in that trial. However, with our current level of empirical knowledge much of the information contained in this chapter comes from the clinical experiences of the author, rather than controlled research. Although there is some preliminary evidence regarding the short-term efficacy of this approach, the long-term efficacy awaits confirmation. Indeed, it remains unclear at this time, which of the many strategies which form the basis of cognitive-behavioural treatment for problem gamblers are active components.

Studies need to investigate further the efficacy, not only of comprehensive programmes, but also of individual techniques to determine what are the effective elements in treatment. It is also important for future research to consider the potential differences between sub-types of gamblers, highlighted by recent research (e.g., Cocco et. al., 1994), which may generalise to differential response to treatment. However, until studies provide further information about the nature of problem gambling and the treatments which help to ameliorate the problem, these will remain speculative. The aim of the present chapter has been to indicate that while the literature remains in its infancy, there is emerging evidence to suggest that cognitive-behavioural approaches to the treatment of problem gambling may be beneficial. Short term results demonstrate that significant reductions in gambling can invariably be achieved and that for the majority of cases an elimination in their gambling behaviour is possible. While far from conclusive, these results do provide cause for optimism.

References

APA (1980). *The diagnostic and statistical manual for mental disorders*, 3rd edition. Washington, DC: American Psychiatric Association.

APA (1987). *The diagnostic and statistical manual for mental disorders*, 3rd edition revised. Washington, DC: American Psychiatric Association.

APA (1994). *The diagnostic and statistical manual for mental disorders*, 4th edition. Washington, DC: American Psychiatric Association.

Anderson, G., & Brown, R. I. F. (1984). Real and laboratory gambling, sensation seeking and arousal. *British Journal of Clinical Psychology, 75*, 401–410.

Atlas, G. D., & Petersen, C. (1990). Explanatory style and gambling: How pessimists respond to losing wagers. *Behaviour, Research and Therapy, 28*, 523–530.

Bergler, E. (1958). *The Psychology of Gambling*. New York: International Universities Press.

Beck, A. T., Rush, A. J., Shaw, B. F., & Emery, G. (1979). *Cognitive therapy for depression*. New York: Guilford Press.

Marlatt, G. A., & Gordon, J. (1985). *Relapse prevention: maintenance strategies in the treatment of addictive behaviours.* New York: Guilford Press.

Miller, W. R. (1983). Motivational interviewing with problem drinkers. *Behavioural Psychotherapy, 11,* 147–172.

Sharpe, L., & Tarrier, N. (1993). Towards a cognitive behavioural model for problem gambling. *British Journal of Psychiatry, 162,* 193–203.

14

Cognitive-Behavioral Treatment of Impulse Control Disorders

DAN OPDYKE and BARBARA OLASOV ROTHBAUM

Georgia State University and Emory University School of Medicine, USA

Introduction

The DSM-IV (APA, 1994) has retained a chapter on Impulse Control Disorders Not Elsewhere Classified. The five specific categories of this disorder have been retained from the DSM-III-R with some modifications. Intermittent Explosive Disorder, Kleptomania, Pyromania, and Trichotillomania are discussed here. See Chapter 14 for a discussion of Pathological Gambling. Disorders that do not fit established criteria but share characteristics of the Impulse Control Disorders such as compulsive buying (Faber, 1992) and sexual impulsivity (Barth & Kinder, 1987) have been categorized as Impulse Control Disorder – Not otherwise Specified (NOS).

The Impulse Control Disorders are characterized by the patient's failure to resist an impulse that results in harmful behavior. Generally the impulse is experienced as increased arousal or tension culminating in the act which is felt as relief or gratification, i.e., is negatively reinforcing. There may be guilt or remorse following the behavior. Impulsive behaviors occur in the context of numerous Axis I and Axis II disorders, and the Impulse Control Disorders must be distinguished from these by close attention to differential diagnoses. Indeed, a high rate of mood disorders and anxiety disorders may appear comorbid to the Impulse Control Disorders (McElroy, Hudson, Pope, Keck & Aizley, 1992).

This chapter discusses the treatment of the Impulse Control Disorders from an empirical, cognitive-behavioral perspective. A detailed treatment protocol for Trichotillomania will be proposed as a model for the treatment of these little-studied disorders.

Intermittent Explosive Disorder

Description

Aggressive outbursts have long been the concern of clinicians. The Intermittent Explosive Disorder diagnosis is given only after a number of other diagnoses have been ruled out. Medical conditions and substance intoxication can result in aggressive behavior. Psychotic disorders, conduct disorders, and some of the personality disorders may feature aggressive outbursts. A culture-specific condition called Amok is characterized by aggressive outbursts with amnesia (APA, 1994). Simon (1987) described the Berserker/Blind Rage Syndrome as a subset of Intermittent Explosive Disorder deserving of study. Symptoms of "blind rage" have captured the imagination of the public for centuries.

Concerns have been voiced about the legitimacy of Intermittent Explosive Disorder as a separate disorder, especially because of the number of studies indicating abnormalities in serotonergic function, complex-partial seizures, and family histories of alcoholism (McElroy et al., 1992). Anger attacks have been posited as a variant of Panic Disorder (Fava, Anderson & Rosenbaum, 1990) and related to depression (Lion, 1992). Should such concerns seem moot, the legal defense of "irresistible impulse" highlights the importance of the nosology of this disorder.

Pure cases of Intermittent Explosive Disorder are found to be quite rare (APA, 1987) although reliable information is scarce. Onset is usually in the second or third decade of life and it is more common in males (APA, 1994). Patients with temper outbursts were previously considered to have limbic system dysfunction. The symptoms of Intermittent Explosive Disorder are found in so many of the disorders that it can be considered a diagnosis of exclusion (Lion, 1992). The category is retained in the DSM-IV with the elimination of the criterion indicating the lack of generalized impulsiveness or regression between episodes (APA, 1994). "Soft" neurological signs are acceptable in the new classification, and certain personality traits (e.g., narcissistic, paranoid, obsessive, schizoid) are listed as predisposing factors (APA, 1994).

Studies on Intermittent Explosive Disorder are few and far between, with most focusing on pharmacological interventions and neurological speculations as to etiology. A large study several years ago by Bach-y-Rita, Lion, Climent & Ervin (1971) examined 130 patients in a large metropolitan psychiatric emergency room. Conventional neuropsychological examinations proved negative, although histories of coma-producing conditions such as meningitis, febrile convulsions, and head injuries were often found. High incidence of family violence and alcoholism were found, and twenty five patients had idiosyncratic alcohol effects with violent eruptions after a few drinks. Pyromania was present in 21 cases. The average age was 28.

Bach-y-Rita's (1971) patients were mostly dependent males with hyper masculine sex role identifications who were chronically anxious and insecure. Poor coping skills and inadequate ego defenses were noted. Childhood deprivation and cultural impoverishment were factors. Usually there was a very short prodromal period of increased anxiety and fear of losing control. Small stimulations could then precipitate full-blown rages.

Twenty five years later, Bitler, Linnoila & George (1994) discussed their sample of Intermittent Explosive Disorder patients who "lose control" and are physically violent toward spouse or significant others. Their four cases each reported feeling trapped, criticized, rejected, and insecure before losing control. Somatic changes accompanied the aggressive outburst. Verbal aggression usually preceded the outburst as well. These patients reported a heightened sense of arousal before the incident, with a sense of release and fatigue immediately following. Guilt feelings often ensued. Bitler and colleagues (1994) proposed that preexposure to violence in childhood could have led to PTSD phenomena triggered by feeling "trapped." In each case, the reaction was out of proportion to any environmental stimulus or stressor. The autonomic symptoms suggest panic disorder, e.g., palpitations, feeling out of control, etc. These cases shed light on the topography of this peculiar disorder.

The nature of the Impulse Control Disorders is such that the impulsive behaviors are to varying degrees intermittent. The eliciting events and contingencies associated with the behaviors are often undetected by direct observation. Assessment may prove difficult, especially in cases where the behavior itself is a reinforcing event. In the case of Intermittent Explosive Disorder, there may not appear to be precipitants, but there are often noxious internal states preceding the outbursts. Negative reinforcement occurs with the escape from these aversive internal states. The behavior (outburst) itself is the reinforcer.

Feeling cornered, criticized, and rejected may be "setting events" (Wahler & Graves, 1983) for explosive behavior. Setting events are similar to what Michael (1982) described as "establishing operations." Depriving a pigeon of food will increase responding if the reinforcement is food. Likewise, the probability of an aggressive outburst may be increased with the number of perceived rejections and criticisms. These aversive stimulations are the establishing operations or "setting events" for escape and avoidance behavior. In the case of Intermittent Explosive Disorder, the aversive stimulation is mostly internal and noxious (feeling trapped). The escape , in the absence of a learning history for modulating ones' own mood states, is a violent outburst. Had there been demands put on the individual or even perceived slights, these stimuli will rapidly disperse once he explodes. A secondary function of the outburst may be to keep people at bay.

Treatment

Bach-y-Rita's patients were treated with medication and referred for psychotherapy to deal with anxiety and anger control (Bach-y-Rita et al., 1971). Medications have long been used for these sorts of behaviors. They likely have a palliative effect because they reduce the internal stimuli. While medicines may work for a short while, the intermittent nature of Intermittent Explosive Disorder might indicate the use of constant medication. The medication remedy may prove costly and ineffective, however, because no learning has occurred. The escape behavior, i.e., violence, must be blocked in the presence of the aversive stimulation for extinction to occur. Nonpharmacological treatment is characterized by identifying the psychosocial stressors and affective cues. Precipitating events, both external and internal, are explored in detail with the client so that the rage "triggers" can be defused (Lion, 1992).

The protocol for Intermittent Explosive Disorder, if one existed, might then include the presentation of escape-provoking stimuli while at the same time blocking the violent sequelae. In many cases this might involve the use of physical restraint in an inpatient setting. This form of treatment has a precedent in its application to mentally retarded individuals. Studies with retarded children indicate that aggressive outbursts are often maintained by negative reinforcement, in that the child escapes demand situations by acting aggressively. Preventing the escape behavior will extinguish the aggressive behavior. Alternatively, reducing the demands on the child contingent on nonaggressive behavior is equally effective (Carr, Newsom & Binkoff, 1980).

In cases where extinction is applied without attention to the setting events, however, there remains the task of reducing the internal stimulation via some other means. The differential reinforcement of other (DRO) behaviors approach has been successful in treating self-injurious behavior (Steege et al., 1990). DRO is generally more effective when combined with extinction of the target behavior. Thus, alternative methods of emotional modulation need to be modeled and reinforced for Intermittent Explosive Disorder clients. Of course all this must be done with the endorsement and collaboration of the client. Despite the above speculations for the treatment of Intermittent Explosive Disorder, the authors could find no such application in the literature.

Kleptomania

Description

Kleptomania is characterized by the recurrent failure to resist impulses to steal objects that are not needed or valued monetarily. There is a sense of tension before and pleasure or relief during the theft, often followed by guilt

(APA, 1994). Kleptomania is rare, representing only 5% of all shoplifters. Aside from ordinary theft, Kleptomania should be distinguished from stealing that occurs during manic episodes or as a result of dementia (APA, 1994).

Kleptomania is often concomitant with mood disorders (McElroy, Pope, Hudson, Keck & White, 1991b), with many patients reporting fluctuations in mood before and after the impulsive theft. Some report a "rush" that alleviates a chronic sense of despair and dysphoria (McElroy et al., 1992). This "rush" may be the result of risk-taking behavior (Fishbain, 1987). A study of 20 patients with Kleptomania found that 80% met the criteria for anxiety disorder, 60% had eating disorders, and half had substance use disorders. Among the first degree relatives of these subjects, 20% had mood disorders, and 21% substance use disorders (McElroy et al., 1991b). A recent study surveyed 1649 shoplifting cases to find only 29 (3.2%) with mental illness. Of these, only 4 were considered kleptomaniacs (Lamontagne, Carpentier, Hetu & Lacerte-Lamontagne, 1994).

Kleptomania may be established in adolescence and remain undetected for years. Traditional clinical wisdom suggests that depressive mood predisposes stealing in an effort to obtain symbolic compensation for a perceived loss. Most patients express guilt following the act and do not exhibit other antisocial behavior (Goldman, 1991). Some authors relate the development of Kleptomania to child abuse and other factors in the first few years of life (Goldman, 1991).

Treatment

There are few treatment reports available for Kleptomania, and these are case studies. Schwartz & Hoellen (1991) reported the use of cognitive behavior therapy over 39 sessions. Their patient, a 42-year-old female, was challenged repeatedly to dispute her irrational self-statements. Thoughts of unbearable wrong-doing, e.g., "I must not steal. It is damnable.", were replaced with "I do not want to." The therapist also worked with the patient's assertiveness with respect to her marital relations (Schwartz & Hoellen, 1991). Another case history by Marzagao (1972) details the use of systematic desensitization in the treatment of Kleptomania. In this case the high anxiety situations were desensitized in 16 sessions, and resulted in remission of stealing at follow-up. Gauthier & Pellerin (1982) had moderate success with covert sensitization training. Their client, a middle-aged female, imagined stealing incidents followed by arrest, prosecution, incarceration, and other aversive consequences. She was to practice imagining these scenarios 10 times a day, and to use the technique whenever the urge arose. The frequency of urges was 14 at baseline and 0 at treatment end. Gains were maintained at follow-up, although she reported stealing on one occasion while on a vacation (Gauthier & Pellerin, 1982).

Similar cases of the successful use of covert sensitization for kleptomania were reported by Glover (1985) and Guidry (1975).

Imaginal desensitization has also been used to treat kleptomania. A case report by McConaghy & Blaszczynski (1988) detailed the successful treatment of two female kleptomaniacs. Both were instructed in simple relaxation and asked to imagine scenes where they approach items to be stolen, but stop themselves at the last minute. Five daily sessions of this simple treatment resulted in a remission that was maintained at 3 week follow-up.

A caution is in order in light of the fact that so little research exists on this rare disorder. Kleptomaniacs rarely seek treatment unless they have been caught (Murray, 1992). In two of the cases above, the patients were facing charges. The high comorbidity reported for Mood Disorder (McElroy et al., 1992) suggests that treating only the compulsive stealing might not be sufficient. It should be noted that thymoleptic medications have been used successfully with diagnosed kleptomania. McElroy, Hudson, Pope & Keck (1991a) studied responses to medication and found that over 50% of clients treated had a complete remission of stealing while on the medication. More research is certainly needed, perhaps combining or contrasting behavioral methods with medications for those dually diagnosed with mood disorder and kleptomania. At present, covert sensitization has the most empirical support as a psychological approach. The adventurous clinician may wish to explore in vivo treatment of the urges to steal, perhaps joining the patient on shopping trips.

Pyromania

Description

Potentially devastating, pyromania is defined as the repeated deliberate setting of fires. As with other Impulse Control Disorders, there is arousal before and relief during and after the event. There may be a fascination with fire and related stimuli. Individuals with Pyromania do not set fires for profit or in order to damage property. True Pyromania is not the result of Mental Retardation or dementia. The diagnosis is not given if the behavior is a symptom of another disorder such as Conduct Disorder or Antisocial Personality Disorder (APA, 1994).

Onset of Pyromania is usually in childhood. Kolko & Kazdin (1988) found up to 20% of an outpatient sample of children had set fires. Child firesetters often had adult role models, experienced family stress, and had poor social skills. Bach-y-Rita et al. (1971) found a high rate of firesetting in their sample of adults with episodic dyscontrol.

Firesetting is the result of a myriad of causes. It is poorly understood, seldom identified in adults, and rarely treated. Most case reports pertain to children. Kolko & Kazdin (1994) asked 95 children to describe their firesetting incidents. Often the fires were set in and around the house with incendiary materials easily accessible. Peers were involved in many instances outside the home. Most children exhibited little remorse and few reported anger. Those who repeatedly set additional fires at 2-year follow-up were found more likely to have planned their fires. Firesetting children are indistinguishable from others in treatment, and may represent a subset of delinquents (Hanson, MacKay-Soroka, Staley & Poulton, 1994). Showers & Pickrell (1987) in a study of 186 juvenile firesetters found that more than 60% of them had primary diagnoses of Conduct Disorder. Another 20% were diagnosed with Attention Deficit Disorder. The family characteristics of these youngsters were distinguished by father absence and parental drug and alcohol abuse. Twenty-eight percent of the firesetters had histories of foster care placement. Physical abuse and neglect were contributing factors. The authors concluded that the firesetters were virtually indistinguishable from the Conduct Disorders except that they also lit fires. Early intervention with abused and neglected children was urged (Showers & Pickrell, 1987).

Leong (1992) studied 29 court-referred arsonists and found a high rate of psychosis (52%). He rarely found a diagnosis of Pyromania. Geller (1987) suggested that firesetting by adult psychiatric patients is more likely associated with schizophrenia, OCD, and personality disorders. Alcohol abuse and mental retardation may be contributing factors in firesetting. According to Geller (1987) firesetters often have social skill deficits and use firesetting as a vehicle of communication. Interventions based on social learning models are appropriate in such cases. This approach is supported by Rice & Harris (1991) whose results indicate that social incompetence and social isolation were important antecedents. Interventions targeting social skills and social support might prevent further firesetting in some cases (Rice & Harris, 1991).

Treatment

Treatment reports in the literature are predominantly case studies focused on children. Some form of parent training and overcorrection procedure is usually applied. Parents then spend time with the child setting 'safe' fires. alternative methods of problem solving are coached by the parent. Behavior contracts are often imposed. Fire safety may be taught directly. Firemen may be enlisted as positive role models. Family therapy addresses the broader context in which the firesetting occurs (Soltys, 1992).

An approach detailed by Bumpass, Fagelman & Brix (1983) had therapists recapitulate the firesetting behavior in session by having the child go over the event, detailing feelings and thoughts that arose while setting the fire. These thoughts and feelings were graphed out for the child and family in an effort to raise awareness of the moods and behaviors leading to the setting of fires. Exploring the antecedent conditions and suggesting alternatives was all that was necessary apparently, as 27 of 29 clients had set no fires in the 2 years following treatment (Bumpass et al., 1983).

There is evidence that cognitive-behavioral interventions for firesetting helps in some cases. Socials skills training combined with satiation, covert sensitization, relaxation, and response cost were combined in one treatment package and found effective (Koles & Jensen, 1985). Satiation and the positive reinforcement of alternative behaviors met with success in stopping recurrent firesetting (Kolko, 1983).

The literature on firesetting is very limited. The prevalence of this disorder is still an open question. Most reported work has been limited to clinical case studies, with the exception of the work of Kolko & Kazdin (1994). More such work is needed.

Trichotillomania

Description

Trichotillomania (Greek for "hair-pulling madness") is a term coined by Hallopeau over a century ago (Hallopeau, 1889) and has retained its classification as an Impulse Control Disorder (APA, 1994). Diagnostic criteria for trichotillomania require the recurrent pulling out of one's hair with noticeable hair loss, a sense of tension before pulling the hair or while trying to resist the impulse, and relief or pleasure when pulling out the hair (APA, 1994). The behavior must not be caused by another disorder or dermatological condition, and it causes significant distress in social or occupational functioning (APA, 1994). Little data is available on prevalence, as most sufferers conceal the behavior. A recent study of college freshman reveals a prevalence rate from 1% to 2% for trichotillomania (Rothbaum, Shaw, Morris & Ninan, 1993). In a study of sixty chronic hair-pullers, Christenson, Mackenzie & Mitchell (1991) found that 17% did not meet the tension reduction criteria (DSM-III-R criteria B and C). These criteria have not changed significantly in the DSM-IV (APA, 1994).

Trichotillomania can be quite disabling because it strikes during sensitive developmental years. The age of onset is often in childhood with peaks between 5–8 years and again at 13 years (APA, 1994). The course of the disorder is often chronic, with a mean duration of 21 years in one study (Christenson et al., 1991). Comorbidity is very common. Reeve, Bernstein, G. A. & Christenson (1992) attempted to delineate all Axis I conditions in a group of childhood hair-pullers. Children who did not report mounting tension and relief when hair-pulling were included in the study. Ten children underwent 3–

4 h of psychometric testing. Seven of the ten had at least one diagnosis on Axis I. Six had Overanxious Disorder, two had Dysthymia, one had Separation Anxiety Disorder with Simple Phobia and Overanxious Disorder. Criteria for OCD were not met by any. Only one child actually met the urge/gratification criteria. Stress was considered to be a major precipitating factor (Reeve et al., 1992).

Some clinical researchers have suggested that Trichotillomania may be a form of Obsessive-Compulsive Disorder (OCD) because of its response to serotonin reuptake inhibitors (Jenike, 1989). However, a large proportion of Trichotillomania sufferers pull their hair with 'incomplete awareness' (Christenson et al., 1991; Christenson, Ristvedt & MacKenzie, 1993) rather than to reduce anxiety or respond to an obsession. Further, OCD is driven by negative reinforcement whereas Trichotillomania appears to be an appetitive drive modulated by satiation. In one study, subjects with Trichotillomania were compared to those with Obsessive-Compulsive Disorder (OCD) and another group of nonclinical hair-pullers (Stanley, Swann, Bowers, Davis & Taylor, 1992). Both the clinical and nonclinical hair-pullers differed from the OCD group on scales measuring depression, extraversion, and OCD symptoms. The OCD group presented as more disturbed on these measures. A high level of generalized anxiety may be common to all three groups. (Stanley, Borden, Mouton & Breckenridge, 1995).

Treatment

As with most of the other Impulse Control Disorders, a variety of pharmacological treatments have been reported to be effective in the short term treatment of Trichotillomania (Ratner, 1989). Many of these medication studies are poorly controlled and without adequate follow-up (Rothbaum & Ninan, 1994). A recent comparison of cognitive-behavior therapy (CBT) to clomipramine in a double-blind placebo controlled study in fact suggests that CBT was significantly more effective than clomipramine or placebo (Ninan, Rothbaum, Marsteller, Knight & Eccard, 1995).

Behavioral treatments for Trichotillomania have been promising. Habit reversal was developed by Azrin & Nunn (1973, 1978) as a method to control tics and other habits such as nail-biting and hair-pulling. It involves increasing the patient's awareness of each occurrence of the habit and interrupting it by means of a competing response. In an uncontrolled investigation, they reported habits were "virtually eliminated" after one treatment session. However, only one of their subjects had trichotillomania (Azrin & Nunn, 1973). Habit reversal reportedly eliminated Trichotillomania in four subjects very quickly in another uncontrolled study (Rosenbaum & Ayllon, 1981). Various components or modifications of habit reversal have been successfully applied in the treatment of Trichotillomania (Miltenberger & Fuqua, 1985; Rodolfa, 1986; Rothbaum, 1990, 1992; Tarnowski, Rosen, McGrath & Drabman, 1987).

Taylor (1963) was the first to report a behavioral treatment for Trichotillomania. He instructed his patient to monitor the behavior and to tell her hands to stop. This simple intervention was successful, with only two brief relapses at 3 month follow-up. Many of the case studies since Taylor (1963) have reported good results with self-monitoring and self-imposed contingencies (Friman, Finney & Christopherson 1984).

Some recent studies with young patients do not rely as much on the motivation and self management aspects of treatment often required for successful treatment. Blum, Barone & Friman (1993) proposed physical nurturing by a parent combined with time-out and response prevention (wearing socks on the hands) to decrease hair-pulling. Lengthy or multiple component programs may not be necessary for younger children with uncomplicated Trichotillomania (Blum et al., 1993). Brief interventions may not always work with young children, however. Vitulano, King, Scahill & Cohen (1992) treated young hair-pullers with a six session program of self monitoring, relaxation, habit interruption (fist clenching), overcorrection (brushing the hair), annoyance review (Azrin, Nunn & Frantz, 1980), and reinforcement. Compliance with treatment was an issue, and conflicts between the parents and child arose often. The authors suggested removing the hair-pulling from its role in parent-child conflicts and being ever mindful of developmental and family system issues (Vitulano et al., 1992). Some children who are unresponsive to brief family interventions may require a complete and intensive CBT treatment such as that suggested by Hamdan-Allen (1991). The child can be taught to monitor the behavior closely while recognizing the maladaptive effects and cues. Incompatible overt and covert responses are then taught, such as positive self-talk, imagery, fist-clenching, and relaxation (Hamdan-Allen, 1991).

Yung (1993) reports a case study in China of a child hair-puller. Chinese parents traditionally view behavior problems as disciplinary issues. An aversive procedure was applied in this case due to the parents' rejection of a token economy approach. A bitter herbal solution was applied to the child's thumb, as thumb-sucking occurred concomitantly with hair-pulling. Both behaviors were eliminated within 6 days. This culture-relevant approach succeeded in part by modifying a covarying behavior. A study by Altman, Grahs & Friman (1982) treated a 3-year-old's Trichotillomania in such a manner by focusing on the covarying thumbsucking. An aversive substance was applied to the girl's right (sucking) thumb three times a day, resulting in clinically significant decreases in both behaviors (Altman, Grahs & Friman 1982). Token economies, time-outs, contingent parental attention, overcorrection by hairbrushing, and similar behavioral strategies for the treatment of child hair-pullers in the home have had mixed results due most often to parental noncompliance with the procedures (Friman, Finney & Christopherson, 1984). Treatment acceptability is an important factor in any intervention. The habit reversal procedure (Azrin & Nunn, 1973) seems most acceptable to children and their families (Tarnowski et al., 1987).

Negative practice, based upon the principles of satiation and increased awareness, has been applied to nervous habits including trichotillomania. For Negative Practice, the patient is instructed to go through the motions of pulling the hair for 30 s every hour without actually pulling. Azrin, Nunn & Frantz (1980) compared Negative Practice to habit reversal and found habit reversal to be about twice as effective. Habit reversal appears to have the best track record for the treatment of Trichotillomania (Friman, Finney & Christopherson, 1984; Rosenbaum & Ayllon, 1981).

A Trichotillomania Treatment Program has been developed by Rothbaum (1990) and is presented below. The stress management component is based on a treatment package developed by Kilpatrick and Veronen and their colleagues and adapted by Foa and Rothbaum and their colleagues (Foa, Rothbaum, Riggs & Murdock, 1991).

Cognitive-Behavioral Treatment of Trichotillomania

This program requires 9 weekly 45-min treatment sessions in which the patient is taught habit reversal (based on Azrin & Nunn, 1978), stimulus control, and stress management techniques (see Table 14.1 for summary treatment outline). The abbreviated treatment manual follows (Rothbaum, 1992).

Session 1
Information gathering. Any clinical intervention begins with a thorough assessment. In addition to the primary goal of assessment, i.e., learning the extent of hair-pulling, careful evaluation can provide other valuable information. Assessment should explore not only the number of hairs pulled, but also the pattern of pulling, the time of day pulling is most likely, the situations most associated with pulling, thoughts surrounding pulling, and whether pulling occurs in response to a strong urge or without awareness.

Self-monitoring. Self-monitoring involves having the client record each occurrence of hair-pulling, the number of hairs pulled as well as other relevant information, including the date and time, situation, thoughts, urge, and number of hairs pulled. Saving all hairs pulled is a powerful form of self-monitoring. It involves having the client save every hair pulled, putting it in an envelope or container, and bringing them in to the therapist for inspection. This also serves as a measure of treatment compliance, since collecting hairs is considered aversive by many clients.

Interview. A sensitive clinical interview will involve all aspects of hair-pulling as well as motivational concerns and general adjustment. A general

Table 14.1. Summary Treatment Outline

Session 1:	Information Gathering
	includes response description, response detection
	(awareness training), identifying response precursors (early warning),
	identifying habit prone situations, and self-monitoring
Session 2:	Habit Reversal Training
	includes rationale for treatment, habit inconvenience review, competing
	response practice, prevention training, and symbolic rehearsal
	Stimulus Control
	self-monitoring continues throughout treatment
	continue information gathering for general assessment
Session 3:	Deep Muscle Relaxation
Session 4:	Differential Relaxation plus Breathing Retraining
Session 5:	Thought-Stopping
Session 6:	Beck/Ellis Cognitive Restructuring
Session 7:	Guided Self-Dialogue (e.g., preparing for a stressor)
Session 8:	Covert Modeling and Role Play
Session 9:	Continuation of No. 8
	Relapse Prevention
	Termination

psychosocial assessment will include a history of hair-pulling, results of previous treatments, other problems, family history, etc. More specifically, information should be gathered as to what exactly the client does. "I pull out my hair," is insufficient. It is necessary to know when (e.g., only when alone, usually in the evening), where (e.g., at desk, at home, in bed), how (e.g., with index finger and thumb, right hand only), what (e.g., examines after pulls, puts in mouth, chews on root), etc.

Response detection. Is the client always aware when she is pulling? If not, the therapist can train her in session by pointing out when her hand goes towards her head. The client will need to be aware of every pull to prevent it. Help the client identify each step involved in the act of pulling a single hair, beginning with the earliest indicator (e.g., a twitch in the fingers of right hand, a thought). Sometimes it is easier to work backwards. Also list every situation in which pulling occurs. The therapist will teach the client to be prepared when entering these situations.

Trichophagia. Some clients with trichotillomania mouth or chew the hair. This can even result in trichobezoars (hairballs) besides actually interfering in the assessment of number of hairs pulled. Clients should be assessed for this behavior.

Observational rating. The therapist will often visually inspect the bald patches and make a rating. This is the basis for the Clinician's Global Improvement scale (CGI; Guy, 1976) and the Trichotillomania Impairment Scale

(Swedo, Leonard, Rapoport, Lenane, Goldberger & Cheslow, 1989), among other rating scales. Photographs of the bald spots are also useful, and can be compared pre-treatment to post-treatment as an objective indicator of treatment success (Friman, 1987; Rosenbaum & Ayllon, 1981). Privacy prohibits observation of all pulling sites, for example if a clients pulls pubic hair, so observational ratings may be limited.

Significant others' report. Significant others' reports of hair-pulling become important when the client is unreliable for any reason. Some clients are less than reliable reporters. Included here are children, mentally retarded or deficient persons, and clients who are not motivated for treatment. When clients' hair starts regrowing, it is often nice when others notice their improvement, and this praise can be elicited from significant others.

Standardized measures. Currently, there is no single standardized measure of trichotillomania. Clinicians use the methods described above, most typically client self-monitoring and interview. There are no standard objective criteria for rating bald patches. Probably the most used or adapted measure for trichotillomania is the Yale-Brown Obsessive Compulsive Scale (Y-BOCs) (Stanley et al., 1992), a 10-item scale that rates severity of obsessions and compulsions in obsessive-compulsive disorder (OCD). Derived from the Y-BOCS, the NIMH-Trichotillomania Severity and Impairment Scales (NIMH-TSS, NIMH-TIS; Swedo et al., 1989) has been used in studies of trichotillomania. It yields a severity score (NIMH-TSS) and an impairment score (NIMH-TIS).

Problems in assessment. Clients often conceal the effects of their hair-pulling with hair styles and make-up. Reactivity may be a problem, rendering self-monitoring inaccurate as a baseline measure. However, this can be used therapeutically. As with any disorder, there may be factors maintaining the behavior that are not readily noticeable. Many trichotillomania sufferers are quite distressed, embarrassed, and ashamed of their behavior and appearance. Then for some, especially children and adolescents, secondary gain may be involved. For example, hair-pulling may be used as a punishment against parents, to gain attention within the family, or as an excuse to avoid participation in undesired activities (e.g., swim practice). Sometimes it may be necessary to assess the family's response to the hair-pulling, as there may be patterns of interaction maintaining the disorder. Even for distressed adults, other factors may be operating, such as avoidance of relationships, intimacy, or certain activities (e.g., social events).

Target behavior. It is also sometimes difficult to determine the target behavior. While hair-pulling is the bottom line, assessment might focus on the number of hairs pulled, the duration of hair-pulling episodes, the resulting alopecia, the urge to pull, or precipitating behaviors. In addition, the primary areas pulled will affect how severe the hair-pulling appears. For example, there may be a ceiling effect if the client primarily pulls eyelashes or eyebrows. Clients may have completely pulled out all lashes and/or brows, yet appear less severe than someone who pulls out scalp hair with an absolute greater number to pull.

Session 2: habit reversal training

Assessment of self-monitoring. The therapist should always inspect the client's self-monitoring and respond accordingly. The self-monitoring component is a means to gather data and to increase awareness of the behavior. If the client has ceased pulling, lavish her with praise and inquire as to how she accomplished this. If the client did pull, look for patterns. For example, did she pull more during the week or on the weekend? More or less at any particular time of day? More or less in certain situations? You want to be able to identify her high-risk situations from the self-monitoring.

Rationale for treatment. Therapist explains habit reversal according to Azrin and Nunn's (1973) rationale:

> "nervous habit originally starts as a normal reaction...become(s) a strongly established habit that further escapes personal awareness because of its automatic nature...[To treat] the client should learn to be aware of every occurrence of the habit. Each habit movement should be interrupted so that it no longer is part of a chain of normal movements. A physically competing response should be established to interfere with the habit (p. 620)."

Therefore, the client will be taught habit reversal to help control the urge to pull. We also want to change situations to make them less likely that the client will pull. To accomplish this, we will explore stimulus control techniques. Since most hair-pulling occurs, increases, or reappears in conjunction with stress, the client must learn effective ways to handle stress. Therefore, in addition to the habit reversal and stimulus control, the client will be taught stress management techniques. Finally, to help maintain treatment gains relapse prevention procedures will be included before the client is discharged.

Habit inconvenience review. This is intended to increase motivation. The client generates a list of inconveniences, embarrassment, and suffering that result from hair-pulling. Common ones will include social embarrassment, restriction of activities (e.g., swimming, going to hairdresser), avoidance of intimate relationships, decrease in self-esteem, etc. The therapist records and reviews the items with the client. The client is encouraged to seek sources of positive reinforcement associated with controlling their behavior.

Competing response practice. The competing response is one that is incompatible with hair-pulling. It must be able to be maintained for at least 2 min, be inconspicuous and easy to implement. It should produce heightened awareness of the habit and use the same muscles as hair-pulling. Making tight fists and holding for 2 min is a common competing response. The therapist practices the competing response with the client in session for a full 2 min.

Prevention training. The client is instructed to use the competing response at the very first sign of the habit. She is instructed to use it if nervous, has an urge to pull, or enters a high-risk situation.

Symbolic rehearsal. The client is instructed to close her eyes and imagine using habit reversal successfully in common habit-prone situations. The client might be asked to talk out loud about common high risk situations. During such a discussion, the therapist can ask that the client be vigilant about urges, catching them at their first appearance. Minimal prompting might be needed. The client should be symbolically rehearsing the competing response while carrying on a conversation with the therapist. The client is instructed to practice the competing response during the therapy hour as well as out of the office.

Stimulus control. Stimulus control is used to decrease opportunities to pull. Typical techniques are listed in Table 14.2.

Social support. Social support is addressed as an important adjunct to the therapy. Once the client has demonstrate some control over the impulse, family and friends can be enlisted as agents of change. Simply by commenting on the absence of episodes, significant others can prevent relapses. Family members can encourage the client to practice the exercises, do homework, etc. Knowledge of the family system is imperative, however, lest these attempts backfire.

Sessions 3 and 4

Relaxation. All sessions begin with a review of self-monitoring, habit reversal, stimulus control, the previous session's activity, and the client's homework assignments. Clients are instructed to practice skills at least twice daily between sessions.

Table 14.2. Stimulus Control Suggestions

– No touching hair, except while grooming
– Stay out of the mirror; no looking at hair
– Wear bandages on pulling fingers
– Wear rubber fingertips on pulling fingers
– Eat sunflower seeds inshells in high-risk situations
– Cover hair in high-risk situations
– Put something on hair (e.g., conditioner, dippity doo)
– Do something with finger nails (paint, cut, grow)
– Be around people
– Get up and move, go for a walk, get something to drink
– Change the situation
– Exercise regularly
– Go to the library and study (especially for students)
– Wash hair more frequently
– Wear gloves
– Keep hands busy: can use koosh ball, squish ball, worry stone, needlework, Nintendo, etc.

The therapist teaches deep muscle relaxation beginning in Session 3. During the fourth session, relaxation training is repeated using the "focusing" and "letting go" procedures, adding the *breathing retraining* at the end. Instructions for the breathing retraining are as follows:

"Please try to take in a *normal* breath rather than a deep breath. Inhale normally through your nose. Unless we are exercising vigorously, we ought to always try to breath through our noses. After inhaling normally, I'll ask you to concentrate on the exhalation and drag it out. While slowly exhaling, we will also have you say the word CALM silently to yourself while you are exhaling, and I will say it aloud when you practice in here [May also use RELAX if client prefers]. CALM is a good word to use because in our culture it is already associated with nice things. If we are upset and someone tells us to 'calm down', usually it is associated with comfort and support. It also sounds nice and can be dragged out to match the long, slow exhalation: c-a-a-a-a-a-l-m."

"In addition to concentrating on slow exhalation while saying CALM to yourself, I want you to slow down your breathing. Very often, when people become frightened or upset, they feel like they need more air and may therefore hyperventilate. Hyperventilation, however does not have a calming effect. In fact it generates anxious feeling. Unless we are preparing for one of the three F's (i.e., fight, freeze, flee) in the face of a real danger, we often don't need as much air as we are taking in. When we hyperventilate and take in more air, it signals our bodies to prepare for one of the three F's and to keep it fueled with oxygen. This is similar to a runner, taking deep breaths to fuel her body with oxygen before a race and continuing to breath deeply and quickly throughout the race. Usually, when we hyperventilate, though, we are tricking our bodies. And what we really need to do is to slow down our breathing and take in *less* air. We do this by pausing between breaths to space them out more. After your slowed exhalation, literally hold your breath for a count of four [may be adjusted if necessary] before you inhale the next breath."

The therapist should instruct the client to take a normal breath and exhale very slowly as he or she says the word CALM or RELAX to herself. Train him or her to pause and count to 4 before taking a second breath. Repeat the entire sequence 10–15 times, for 10–15 breaths. Try to watch the client's chest or abdomen to follow his or her own natural breathing rhythms. Towards the end of the exercise, the therapist should start fading away his or her instructions while the client continues to practice.

Differential relaxation is taught following deep muscle relaxation. This involves teaching the client to recognize which muscles are necessary for specified activities and to use the minimal amount of tension in these muscles to complete that activity. She is to allow muscles not required for the activity to relax. Examples to use in session include sitting, standing, and walking. Emphasize practice in client's daily activities (e.g., driving, writing).

Session 5

Thought stopping. Thought stopping originally described by Wolpe (1958), is utilized to counter ruminative or obsessive thinking. Self-monitoring may reveal thoughts that set the occasion for hair-pulling. Such thoughts may occur very early in the response chain. Clients will often report particular thoughts that they notice just prior to hair-pulling. The client with trichotillomania can be trained to inhibit such thoughts. If a client reports such thoughts in their weekly review, these can be used to teach the thought-stopping method. Simply ask the client to close her eyes and to think the usual troublesome thoughts that typically occur prior to an episode. After about 30–40 s, the therapist slams the desk with a book or fist, shouting "STOP!" loudly. The thoughts invariably stop at this point, and the client should be made aware of this fact. Repeat this whole process a few times before having the client try it on her own. The command "STOP!" should be internalized at this point and will remain subvocal and covert. Many clients profit from using imagery by picturing a big red stop sign when shouting "STOP" silently. The key is to replace the unpleasant thought with a distracting one, in the meantime disrupting the chain of behavior leading to hair-pulling. Simple distraction may serve the same function as long as it is not anxiety-producing. Any thought will do as long as it doesn't cause the client distress and it actively engages her thinking. Help the client decide what his/her distracting thought will be before leaving the therapist's office.

Sessions 6

Cognitive restructuring. The therapist introduces cognitive restructuring (Beck, Rush, Shaw & Emery, 1979; Ellis & Harper, 1961) focusing on how our thoughts affect our reactions. Examples are generated and the therapist assists the client in assessing the rationality of the beliefs, consequently challenging them, and replacing them with positive (rational) self-statements.

Because negative thinking looms large in the disorders of anxiety and impulse control, cognitive restructuring is useful as an antidote. Much therapy is talking, and it is in the moments when the client utters an absurdity that the therapist must offer a healthy challenge. As the client has been introduced to the idea that thoughts affect behavior, it is no leap of faith to purport that through changing what we think we can change what we do.

Clients are taught to recognize the automaticity of their thoughts, and how they might lead to specific feelings and behaviors. Such thoughts are very often irrational and maladaptative. The therapist challenges the thoughts immediately in session with such questions as: "What's the evidence for that? Is there any other way to look at it? How could we test that? What's the worst that could happen? What could you then do?" Repeated assaults on dysfunctional thoughts will often unearth core beliefs about the self. These core beliefs or "schemata" are usually unconscious overgeneralizations and distortions which can be very self-defeating. Often included are such beliefs as "feelings are dangerous, I must be in control at all times, I'm worthless." The therapist challenges these thoughts while affirming the positive traits in the client. The most important component is teaching the client to change his or her own pattern of thinking.

Reframing is a technique to encourage clients to take a different view of things. Instead of "I didn't get the job. I'm a failure", the client is presented with "I didn't have the qualifications required for that job, so it's good that it didn't work out. I can look at it as a practice interview for the job I really want!" Another example often used with anxious clients is to regard anxiety as a friendly, creative energy source. "Use your anxious feelings to inspire your presentation. Feel the energy well up inside you. Make sweeping gestures, slam the podium, that anxiety is the energy you need to succeed. Don't fight it, celebrate it!" In short, negative thoughts almost always have an equally valid counterpart.

Session 7
Guided self-dialogue. During guided self-dialogue, the therapist teaches the client to focus on her self-talk. Irrational, faulty, or negative internal dialogue is replaced with rational, positive, task-enhancing cognitions. The client is instructed to ask and answer a series of questions or respond to a series of statements. The framework for the guided self-dialogue is taken from Meichenbaum (1974). The four dialogue categories include statements for (1) preparation, (2) confrontation and management, (3) coping with feelings of being overwhelmed, and (4) reinforcement.

First, when preparing for a stressor the client must focus on the behavioral requirements, i.e., "What is it I have to do?" Negative thinking is addressed, "What is the likelihood of anything bad happening? How bad is it?" Direct the thoughts to positive self-statements such as "I can handle this. I've done this before. I have the support of a loving spouse. I will prevail!".

Secondly, explain to your client that when confronting a stressor it is important to keep the stress reaction at bay. "The stress might signal you to use the reframing technique we practiced. Focus on all you rehearsed. You can do this. Don't make more of it than there is. Proceed one step at a time. Breathe.

The therapist instructs the client when feelings of being overwhelmed arise, to take a breath and exhale slowly as s/he focuses on the present. Fear may rise, but it can be managed. Think to yourself "this will be over soon". You may feel you need to pull your hair, but you don't have to pull your hair. Relax and slow things down a bit. Take your time responding.

Finally, the therapist explains, "As you look back over your stressful experience, you can make self-reinforcing statements such as, 'It was easier than I thought. I'm making progress. I handled that rather well. I'm getting quite good at this'" Rehearse the dialogue with your client until she internalizes it. Practice in session and use her daily stressors as opportunities to teach mastery over the internal dialogue.

Sessions 8 and 9: covert modeling, role play, and relapse prevention

Role-playing. During role-playing, the client and therapist act out scenes in which the client confronts a difficult situation. Usually, the therapist plays the client's role first and gets feedback, then roles are reversed. Role-plays are followed by feedback and are repeated until the client performs satisfactorily. The guided self-dialogue can serve as ideas for these role-plays.

Covert modeling. Covert modeling is analogous to role-playing in the imagination. The client is instructed to practice this technique by picturing someone else (e.g., a competent friend) successfully completing the activity, then substituting herself in the scene. Often it is difficult for the client to imagine him or herself successfully completing a feared activity, but s/he could imagine someone doing it well. So once they picture someone else completing it, it becomes easier to pull the other out and put themselves in the picture.

Relapse prevention. Discussion centers on how to control setbacks, which are highly likely. Between-session relapses are processed in detail. Teach the view that it is not a catastrophe, but an opportunity to further practice one's newly learned skills. Reviewing the skills that worked in the past will help. Often a quick run-through of stimulus control techniques is all that is necessary. Support and encouragement are always helpful. Remind the client that her goal is to go one day at a time without pulling.

It may be necessary to explore beliefs about relapse, especially if they are self-condemning. Dichotomous thinking might point to a failure experience, whereas a relapse could be an opportunity to strengthen the learning that has occurred. Slip-ups can be predicted and prepared for. They might even be "planned" as a paradoxical strategy to keep client awareness high. When a relapse occurs it should be gone over in session in explicit detail from start to finish. Relapse situations provide an excellent opportunity to review the entire treatment program.

Conclusion and Future Directions

Many patients have completed the above program successfully. In a controlled study, this program decreased hair-pulling more than clomipramine or pill placebo (Ninan et al., 1995). This appears to be a promising comprehensive treatment for trichotillomania. Since there are so few cognitive-behavioral treatment packages for the impulse-control disorders, adapting this program for kleptomania, pyromania, and others may be a worthwhile endeavor. This treatment program was developed for the treatment of trichotillomania but can be applied easily to other impulse control disorders. The essential ingredients include: (1) assessment, including self monitoring and determining high risk factors for the behavior; (2) teaching the client ways to control the behavior, even when they get the urge; (3) stimulus control techniques, designed to decrease the likelihood of the behavior; (4) stress management techniques to help the client handle stress more adaptively; and (5) relapse prevention to help maintain the treatment gains.

The Impulse Control Disorders Not Elsewhere Classified represent perhaps the least researched category of disorders in the DSM-IV. It remains unclear what relationship these disorders have to the mood and anxiety disorders with which they seem so often comorbid. Since some of these disorders have serious consequences for individuals and society (e.g., pyromania, intermittent explosive disorder) it is imperative that current treatments be evaluated for effectiveness. Since the Impulse Control Disorders are intermittent, concealed, denied, and rare, this is a difficult endeavor.

References

Altman, K., Grahs, C., & Friman, P. (1982). Treatment of unobserved trichotillomania by attention-reflection and punishment of an apparent covariant. *Journal of Behavior Therapy and Experimental Psychiatry, 13*, 337–340.

APA (1987). *Diagnostic and statistical manual of mental disorders*, 3th edition revised (DSM-III-R). Washington, DC: American Psychiatric Association.

APA (1994). *Diagnostic and statistical manual of mental disorders*, 4th edition (DSM-IV). Washington, DC: American Psychiatric Association.

Azrin, N. H., & Nunn, R. G. (1973). Habit-reversal: A method of eliminating nervous habits and tics. *Behavior Research and Therapy, 11*, 619–628.

Azrin, N. H., & Nunn, R. G. (1978). *Habit control in a day*. New York: Simon & Schuster..

Azrin, N. H., Nunn, R. G., & Frantz, S. E. (1980). Treatment of hairpulling (Trichotillomania): A comparative study of habit reversal and negative practice training. *Behavior Therapy and Experimental Psychiatry, 11*, 13–20.

Bach-y-Rita, G., Lion, J. R., Climent, C. E., & Ervin, F. R. (1971). Episodic dyscontrol: A study of 130 violent patients. *American Journal of Psychiatry, 127*, 1473–1478.

Barth, R. J., & Kinder, B. N. (1987). The mislabeling of sexual impulsivity. *Journal of Sex and Marital Therapy, 13*, 15–23.

Beck, A. T., Rush, A. J., Shaw, B. F., & Emery, G. (1979). *Cognitive Therapy ofDepression:A Treatment Manual*. New York: Guilford Press.

Bitler, D. A., Linnoila, M., & George, D. T. (1994). Psychological and diagnostic characteristics of individuals initiating domestic violence. *The Journal of Nervous and Mental Disease, 182*, 583–585.

Blum, N. J., Barone, V. J., & Friman, P. C. (1993). A simplified behavioral treatment of trichotillomania: Report of two cases. *Pediatrics, 91*, 993–995.

Bumpass, E. R., Fagelman, F. D., & Brix, R. J. (1983). Intervention with children who set fires. *American Journal of Psychotherapy, 37*, 328–345.

Carr, E. G., Newsom, C., & Binkoff, J. (1980). Escape as a factor in the aggressive behavior of two retarded children. *Journal of Applied Behavior Analysis, 13*, 101–117.

Christenson, G. A., Mackenzie, T. B., & Mitchell, J. B. (1991). Characteristics of 60 adult chronic hair pullers. *American Journal of Psychiatry, l48*, 365–370.

Christenson, G. A., Ristvedt, S. L., & Mackenzie, T. B. (1993). Identification of trichotillomania cue profiles. *Behaviour Research and Therapy, 31*, 315–320.

Ellis, A., & Harper, R. A. (1961). *A Guide to Rational Living.* Englewood Cliffs, NJ: Prentice-Hall.

Faber, R. J. (1992). Money changes everything: Compulsive buying from a biopsychosocial perspective. *The American Behavioral Scientist, 35*, 809–818.

Fava, M., Anderson, K., & Rosenbaum, J. F. (1990). "Anger attacks": Possible variants of panic and major depressive disorders. *American Journal of Psychiatry, 147*, 867–870.

Fishbain, D. A. (1987). Kleptomania as risk-taking behavior in response to depression. *American Journal of Psychotherapy, 41*, 598–603.

Foa, E. B., Rothbaum, B. O., Riggs, D., & Murdock, T. (1991). Treatment of Posttraumatic Stress Disorder in rape victims: A comparison between cognitive-behavioral procedures and counseling. *Journal of Consulting and Clinical Psychology, 59*, 715–723.

Friman, P. C., Finney, J. W., Christophersen, E. R. (1984). Behavioral treatment of Trichotillomania: An evaluative review. *Behavior Therapy, 15*, 249–265.

Friman, P. C., & Rostain, A. (1990). Trichotillomania. *New England Journal of Medicine, 322*, 471.

Gauthier, J., & Pellerin, D. (1982). Management of compulsive shoplifting through covert sensitization. *Journal of Behaviour Therapy and Experimental Psychiatry, 13*, 73–75.

Geller, J. L. (1987). Firesetting in the adult psychiatric population. *Hospital and Community Psychiatry, 38*, 501–506.

Glover, J. (1985). A case of kleptomania treated by covert sensitization. *British Journal of Clinical Psychology, 24*, 213–214.

Goldman, M. J. (1992). Kleptomania: An overview. *Psychiatric Annals, 22*, 68–71.

Guidry, L. S. (1969). Use of a covert punishing contingency in compulsive stealing. *Journal of Behaviour Therapy and Experimental Psychiatry, 6*, 169.

Guy, W. (1976). *ECDEU assessment manual for psychopharmacology Revised.* 217–222. NIMH Publ. DHEW Publ No (Adm) 76–338.

Hallopeau, M. (1889). Alopecie par grattage (Trichomanie ou trichotillomanie). *Annual of Dermatology and Venereology, 10*, 440–441.

Hamdan-Allen, G. (1991). Trichotillomania in childhood. *Acta PsychiatricaScandinavica, 83*, 241–243.

Hanson, M., MacKay-Soroka, S., Staley, S., & Poulton, L. (1994). Delinquent firesetters: A comparative study of delinquency and firesetting histories. *Canadian Journal of Psychiatry, 39*, 230–232.

Jenike, M. A. (1989). Obsessive-compulsive and related disorders: A hidden epidemic. *New England Journal of Medicine, 321*, 539–54l.

Kolko, D. J. (1983) Multicomponent parental treatment of firesetting in a six-year-old boy. *Journal of Behavior Therapy and Experimental Psychiatry, 14*, 349–353.

Kolko, D. (1990). Matchplay and firesetting in children: Relationship to parent, marital, and family dysfunction. *Journal of Clinical Child Psychology, 19*, 229–238.

Kolko, D. J., & Kazdin, A. E. (1988). Prevalence of firesetting and related behaviors among child psychiatric patients. *Journal of Consulting and Clinical Psychology, 4*, 628–630.

Kolko, D., & Kazdin, A. (1994). Children's descriptions of their firesetting incidents: Characteristics and relationship to recidivism. *Journal of American Academy of Child and Adolescent Psychiatry, 33,* 114–122.

Lamontagne, Y., Carpentier, N., Hetu, C., & Lacerte-Lamontagne, C. (1994). Shoplifting and mental illness. *Canadian Journal of Psychiatry, 39,* 300–302.

Leong, G. B. (1992). A psychiatric study of persons charged with arson. *Journal of Forensic Sciences, 37,* 1319–1326.

Lion, J. R. (1992). The intermittent explosive disorder. *Psychiatric Annals, 22,* 64–66.

Marzagao, L. R. (1972). Systematic desensitization treatment of kleptomania. *Journal of Behaviour Therapy and Experimental Psychiatry, 3,* 327–328.

McConaghy, N., & Blaszczynski, A. (1988). Imaginal desensitization: A cost-effective treatment in two shop-lifters and a binge-eater resistant to previous therapy. *Australian and New Zealand Journal of Psychiatry, 22,* 78–82.

McElroy, S. L., Hudson, J. I., Pope, H. G., & Keck, P. E. (1991a). Kleptomania: Clinical characteristics and associated psychopathology. *Psychological Medicine, 21,* 93–108.

McElroy, S. L., Pope, H. G., Hudson, J. I., Keck, P. E., & White, K. L. (1991b). Kleptomania: A report of 20 cases. *American Journal of Psychiatry, 148,* 652–657.

McElroy, S. L., Hudson, J. I., Pope, H. G., Keck, P. E., & Aizley, H. G. (1992). The DSM-III-R impulse control disorders not elsewhere classified: Clinical characteristics and relationships to other psychiatric disorders. *American Journal of Psychiatry, 149,* 318–327.

Meichenbaum, D. (1974). Self-instructional methods. In F. H. Kanfer & A. P. Goldstein (Eds.), *Helping people change.* New York: Pergamon Press.

Michael, J. L. (1982). Distinguishing between discriminative and motivational functions of stimuli. *Journal of the Experimental Analysis of Behavior, 37,* 149–155.

Miltenberger, R. G., & Fuqua, R. W. (1985). A comparison of contingent vs. non-contingent competing response practice in the treatment of nervous habits. *Journal of Behavior Therapy and Experimental Psychiatry, 16,* 195–200.

Murray, J. B. (1992). Kleptomania: A review of the research. *The Journal of Psychology, 126,* 131–138.

Ninan, P. T., Rothbaum, B. O., Marsteller, F., Knight, B., & Eccard, M. (1995). A placebo controlled trial of cognitive behavior therapy and clomipramine in trichotillomania. Manuscript in preparation.

Ratner, R. A. (1989). Trichotillomania. In T. B. Karasu (Ed.), *Treatments of psychiatric disorders,* Vol. III. Washington, DC: American Psychiatric Association.

Reeve, E. A., Bernstein, G. A., & Christenson, G. A. (1992). Clinical characteristics and psychiatric comorbidity in children with trichotillomania. *Journal of American Academy of Child and Adolescent Psychiatry, 31,* 132–138.

Rice, M. E., & Harris, G. T. (1991). Firesetters admitted to a maximum security psychiatric institution: Offenders and offenses. *Journal of Interpersonal Violence, 6,* 461–475.

Rodolfa, E. R. (1986). The use of hypnosis in the multimodal treatment of Trichotillomania: A case report. *Psychotherapy in Private Practice, 4,* 51–58.

Rosenbaum, M. S., & Ayllon, T. (1981). The habit-reversal technique in treating Trichotillomania. *Behavior Therapy, 12,* 473–481.

Rothbaum, B. O. (1990). *Trichotillomania Treatment Program.* Presentación en la reunión anual de la Association for the Advancement of Behavior Therapy, SIG Section, San Francisco, CA.

Rothbaum, B. O. (1992). The behavioral treatment of trichotillomania. *Behavioral Psychotherapy, 20,* 85–90.

Rothbaum, B. O., & Ninan, P. T. (1994). The assessment of trichotillomania. *Behaviour Research and Therapy, 32,* 651–662.

Rothbaum, B. O., Shaw, L., Morris, R., & Ninan, P. T. (1993). Prevalence of trichotillomania in a college freshman population (letter). *Journal of Clinical Psychiatry, 54*, 72.

Schwartz, D., & Hoellen, B. (1991). "Forbidden fruit tastes especially sweet." Cognitive-behavior therapy with a kleptomaniac woman – a case report. *Psychotherapy in Private Practice, 8*, 19–25.

Showers, J., & Pickrell, E. (1987). Child firesetters: A study of three populations. *Hospital and Community Psychiatry, 38*, 495–501.

Simon, A. (1987). The berserker/blind rage syndrome as a potentially new diagnostic category for the DSM-III. *Psychological Reports, 60*, 131–135.

Soltys, S. M. (1992). Pyromania and firesetting behaviors. *Psychiatric Annals, 22*, 79–83.

Stanley, M. A., Swann, A. C., Bowers, T. C., Davis, M. L., & Taylor, D. J. (1992). A comparison of clinical features in trichotillomania and obsessive-compulsive disorder. *Behaviour Research and Therapy, 30*, 39–44.

Stanley, M. A., Borden, J. W., Mouton, S. G., & Breckenridge, J. K. (1995). Nonclinical hair-pulling: Affective correlates and comparison with clinical samples. *Behaviour Research and Therapy, 33*, 179–186.

Swedo, S. E., Leonard, H. L., Rapoport, J. L., Lenane, M. C., Goldberger, B. A., & Cheslow, B. A. (1989). A double-blind comparison of clomipramine and desipramine in the treatment of trichotillomania (hair pulling). *New England Journal of Medicine, 321*, 497–501.

Tarnowski, K. J., Rosen, L. A., McGrath, M. L., & Drabman, R. S. (1987). A Modified habit reversal procedure in a recalcitrant case of trichotillomania. *Journal of Behavior Therapy and Experimental Psychiatry, 18*, 157–163.

Taylor, J. G. (1963). A behavioral interpretation of obsessive compulsive neurosis. *Behaviour Research and Therapy, 1*, 237–244.

Vitulano, L. A., King, R. A., Scahill, L., & Cohen, D. J. (1992). Behavioral treatment of children and adolescents with trichotillomania. *Journal of American Academy of Child and Adolescent Psychiatry, 31*, 139–146.

Wahler, R. G., & Graves, M. G. (1983). Setting events in social networks: ally or enemy in child behavior therapy? *Behavior Therapy, 14*, 19–36.

Wolpe, J. (1958). *Psychotherapy by reciprocal inhibition*. Stanford, CA: Stanford University Press.

Yung, P. (1993). Treatment for trichotillomania. (letter) *Journal of American Academy of Child and Adolescent Psychiatry, 32*, 878.

Further Reading

Azrin, N. H., & Nunn, R. G. (1987). *Tratamiento de hábitos nerviosos*. Barcelona: Martínez Roca. (Original: 1978).

Carrasco, I. (1995). Trastornos del control de los impulsos: Trastorno explosivo intermitente, cleptomanía, piromanía y tricotilomanía. In V. E. Caballo, G. Buela-Casal & J. A. Carrobles (Eds.), *Manual de psicopatología y trastornos psiquiátricos*, Vol. 1. Madrid: Siglo XXI.

Davis, M., McKay, M., & Eshelman, E. R. (1985). *Técnicas de autontrol emocional*. Barcelona: Martínez Roca. (Original: 1982).

Rothbaum, B. O. (1992). The behavioral treatment of trichotillomania. *Behavioral Psychotherapy, 20*, 85–90.

Rothbaum, B. O., & Ninan, P. T. (1994). The assessment of trichotillomania. *Behaviour Research and Therapy, 32*, 651–662.

15

Behavioral Treatment of Unipolar Depression

PETER M. LEWINSOHN[a], IAN H. GOTLIB[b] and MARTIN
HAUTZINGER[c]

[a]Oregon Research Institute, USA; [b]Stanford University, USA; [c]Universität Konstanz,
Germany

Introduction

We have four goals in writing this chapter. First, in order to place current
behavioral approaches to the conceptualization and treatment of depression
in an appropriate context, we shall briefly describe the history and development of early behavioral theories of depression. We then outline more recent
behavioral formulations of depression. Second, we present behavioral approaches to the assessment of various aspects of unipolar depression, and
describe several behavioral treatments for depression. In this section, we focus
particularly on two treatment packages for unipolar depression developed at
the Depression Research Unit of the University of Oregon: an individual
therapy approach and a psychoeducational group intervention. Third, we
discuss recent extensions of this intervention to different settings and to different populations, such as depressed adolescents and the elderly. Finally, we
outline what we believe are important directions for future investigations in
this field.

Behavioral Theories of Depression

Almost four decades ago, Skinner (1953) postulated that depression was the
result of a weakening of behavior due to the interruption of established se-

quences of behavior that had been positively reinforced by the social environment. This conceptualization of depression as an extinction phenomenon and as a reduction in the frequency of emission of behavior has been central to all behavioral positions. Ferster (1966) provided more detail by suggesting that such diverse factors as sudden environmental changes, punishment and aversive control, and shifts in reinforcement contingencies can give rise to depression, i.e., to a reduced rate of behavior. He suggested that the depressive's failure to produce adaptive behaviors may be due to a number of factors, including (a) sudden environmental changes that require the establishment of new sources of reinforcement; (b) engaging in aversive or punishable behavior that preempts the opportunity for positive reinforcement; and (c) inaccurate observation of the environment, resulting in socially inappropriate behavior and a low frequency of positive reinforcement. Ferster invoked the concept of chaining to explain the generalizability of the response to what is often a circumscribed loss of reinforcement (e.g., loss of a job). Ferster argued that the loss of a central source of reinforcement led to a reduction in all behaviors "chained to," or organized around the lost reinforcer. For example, retirement might lead to a reduction in all of the behaviors that were chained to working. Thus an individual who has retired might have difficulty getting up in the morning, grooming, and seeing friends or colleagues, if all of these behaviors were organized around work which in turn was a central source of reinforcement.

In a variant of this position, Costello (1972) distinguished between a reduction in the number of reinforcers available to the individual and a reduction in the effectiveness of available reinforcers. Costello proposed that depression was due to a disruption in a chain of behavior, likely caused by the loss of one of the reinforcers in the chain. Costello argued that the reinforcer effectiveness of all the components of the chain of behavior is contingent upon the completion of the chain. Thus, when a behavior chain is disrupted, there is a loss of reinforcer effectiveness associated with all of the components in the chain. Costello contends that the depressive's general loss of interest in the environment is a manifestation of this reduction of reinforcer effectiveness.

Lewinsohn and his colleagues (e.g., Lewinsohn, 1974; Lewinsohn & Shaw, 1969; Lewinsohn, Youngren & Grosscup, 1979) refined and elaborated these positions. Lewinsohn maintained that a low rate of response-contingent positive reinforcement constituted a sufficient explanation for aspects of the depressive syndrome, especially the low rate of behavior. Lewinsohn and his colleagues amplified the behavioral position through three additional hypotheses:

1. There is a causal relation between the low rate of response-contingent positive reinforcement and the feeling of dysphoria.
2. Depressive behaviors are maintained by the social environment through the provision of contingencies in the form of sympathy, interest, and concern.

3. Deficiencies in social skill function as an important antecedent to the low rate of positive reinforcement.

Lewinsohn hypothesized that a low rate of "response-contingent positive reinforcement" in major life areas, *and/or* a high rate of aversive experiences, leads to a reduction in behavior and to the experience of dysphoria. Lewinsohn suggested that there are three major factors that might lead to a low rate of reinforcement. The first involves deficits in the behavioral repertoire or skills of the individual that prevent the attainment of reinforcers or diminish the individual's ability to cope with aversive experiences. The second factor that might lead to a low rate of reinforcement is a lack of potential reinforcers in the individual's environment due to impoverishment or loss, or a surplus of aversive experiences. For example, a person who is confined to home while recuperating from a long illness may engage in few activities that are followed by reinforcement. Or the death or social exit of an individual who had provided social reinforcement might result in a loss of reinforcement. Finally, depression may result from a decrease in the person's capacity to enjoy positive experiences, or an increase in the individual's sensitivity to negative events (Lewinsohn, Lobitz & Wilson, 1973).

Lewinsohn's formulation thus focused on the reduction of social reinforcement obtained by the depressed individual from significant others in his or her environment. Lewinsohn posited that depressed individuals may lack adequate social skills and may therefore find it difficult to obtain reinforcement from their social environment, leading them to experience a reduced rate of positive reinforcement. Libet and Lewinsohn (1973, p. 304) defined social skill as, "...the complex ability both to emit behaviors which are positively or negatively reinforced, and not to emit behaviors which are punished or extinguished by others." Thus, an individual is considered to be socially skillful to the extent that he elicits positive (and avoids negative) consequences from the social environment. Because of insufficient positive reinforcement, depressed persons find it difficult to initiate or maintain instrumental behavior. The formulation also focused on the *maintenance* of depressive behavior (e.g., suicidal thoughts) by suggesting that the social environment often reinforces such behaviors through the provision of sympathy, interest and concern.

Complementing this formulation, Coyne (1976) contended that depression is a response to disruptions in the social field of the individual. Specifically, Coyne suggested that depression is maintained by the negative responses of significant others to the depressive's symptomatic behavior. Coyne maintained that depressed individuals create a negative social environment by engaging others in such a manner that support is lost, or at best, ambiguous. Both supportive and hostile reactions are elicited. Coyne postulated a sequence of behavior that begins with the depressed person's initial demonstration of depressive symptoms, typically in response to stress. Individuals in the depressed person's social environment respond immediately to these depressive symptoms with genuine concern and support. The depressive's behavior gradually becomes more demanding, i.e., symptomatic behaviors are expressed with increasing frequency. Consequently, the depressive's behavior becomes aversive to others and elicits feelings of resentment and anger. At the same time the depressed person's obvious distress also elicits feelings of guilt that serve to inhibit the open expression of this hostility. In an attempt to reduce both their guilt and anger, family members respond to the depressed person with veiled hostility and with false reassurance and support. Being aware of, and feeling rejected by, these discrepant or incongruous messages, the depressed person becomes more symptomatic in an attempt to gain support, thus making it even more aversive for others to interact with him or her. This "deviation-amplifying" process continues to the point where people either withdraw from interactions with the depressive, or have the person withdrawn through hospitalization.

Rehm (1977) proposed a self-control model of depression that attempts to integrate behavioral and cognitive aspects of the disorder. Rehm suggested that Kanfer's (1977) model of self-regulation may serve as an heuristic model for the study of depressive etiology, symptomatology, and treatment. According to this model, specific deficits in self-monitoring, self-evaluation, and self-reinforcement may explain the various symptoms of depression. Specifically, Rehm postulated that the behavior of depressed persons could be characterized by one or more deficits in self-control behavior. First, with respect to self-monitoring, depressed individuals selectively attend to negative events that follow their behavior to the relative exclusion of positive events, a cognitive style that might account for the pessimism and gloomy outlook of depressed individuals. Second, depressed persons selectively attend to immediate consequences of their behavior to the relative exclusion of delayed outcomes, and therefore cannot look beyond present demands when making behavioral choices.

The third deficit in the self-control behavior of depressed persons involves self-evaluation, essentially a comparison between an estimate of performance (which derives from self-monitoring) and an internal criterion or standard. Rehm posited that depressed individuals set unrealistic, perfectionistic, global standards for themselves, making attainment improbable. As a consequence, they often do not succeed in reaching their goals and, therefore, evaluate themselves negatively and in a global, overgeneralized manner. Depressed persons may also manifest a self-evaluation deficit with respect to their style of attribution. Rehm hypothesized that depressed persons may distort their perception of causality in order to denigrate themselves. If their performance is successful, for example, depressed persons may attribute their success to external factors such as luck and the simplicity of the task, thereby refusing to take credit for their success. Similarly, depressed persons may attribute the cause of an unsuccessful performance to internal factors such as lack of skill and effort, taking excessive responsibility for failure.

Finally, Rehm (1977) postulated that depressed persons fail to administer sufficient contingent rewards to themselves to maintain their adaptive behaviors. This low rate of self-reward may account in part for the slowed rates of overt behavior, the lower general activity level, and the lack of persistence that typify depression. In addition, depressed persons are hypothesized to administer excessive self-punishment, which suppresses potentially productive behavior early in a response chain, resulting in excessive inhibition.

Recent approaches

Lewinsohn, Hoberman, Teri & Hautzinger (1985a) argued that both cognitive and reinforcement theories of depression have been too narrow and simplistic. They proposed an integrative, multifactorial model of the etiology and maintenance of depression that attempts to capture the complexity of this disorder. In this model, which is presented in Figure 15.1, the occurrence of depression is viewed as a product of both environmental and dispositional factors. More specifically, depression is conceptualized as the end result of environmentally initiated changes in behavior, affect, and cognitions. Whereas situational factors are important as "triggers" of the depressogenic process, cognitive factors are critical as "moderators" of the effects of the environment.

Briefly, in this model the chain of events leading to the occurrence of depression is postulated to begin with antecedent risk factors (A), which initiate the depressogenic process by disrupting important adaptive behavior patterns (B).

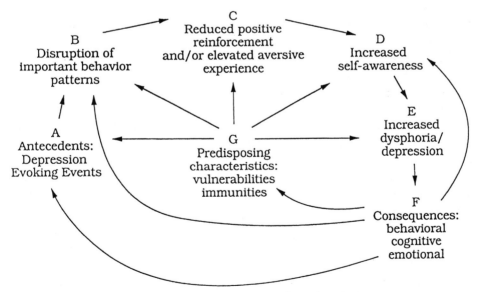

Figure 15.1. An integrated model of depression. From Lewinsohn et al. (1985a).

The general rubric of stressors at the macro (e.g., negative life events) and micro (e.g., daily hassles) levels are probably the best examples of such antecedents. These stressors disrupt behavior patterns that are necessary for the individual's day-to-day interactions with the environment. Thus, for example, stressful life events are postulated to lead to depression to the extent that they disrupt important personal relationships or job responsibilities (C). This disruption itself can result in a negative emotional reaction which, combined with an inability to reverse the impact of the stressors, leads to a heightened state of self-awareness (D). This increased self-awareness makes salient the individual's sense of failure to meet internal standards and leads, therefore, to increased dysphoria and to many of the other cognitive, behavioral, and emotional symptoms of depression (E). Finally, these increased symptoms of depression serve to maintain and exacerbate the depressive state (F), in part by making more accessible negative information about the self (cf. Gotlib & McCabe, 1992), and by reducing the depressed individual's confidence to cope with their environment (e.g., Jacobson & Anderson, 1982).

It is important to note that Lewinsohn et al.'s (1985a) model recognizes that stable individual differences, such as personality characteristics, may moderate the impact of the antecedent events both in initiating the cycle leading to depression, and in maintaining the depression once it begins. These person characteristics can be classified as *vulnerabilities*, which increase the probability of the occurrence of depression, and *immunities*, which decrease the probability of depression (G). Lewinsohn et al. suggest that vulnerability factors might include being female, having a history of prior depressions, and having low self-esteem. In contrast, examples of immunities include high self-perceived social competence, the availability of a confidant, and effective coping skills. Finally, it is important to note that Lewinsohn et al.'s model emphasizes the operation of "feedback loops" among the various factors. The feedback loops allow for either a "vicious cycle" or a "benign cycle." By reversing any of the components of the model, the depression will be progressively ameliorated.

It is apparent from this overview that behavioral theories of depression have evolved from relatively simple and constricted S-R formulations that emphasized response-contingent reinforcement and the behavioral dampening effects of punishment, to more complex conceptualizations that place greater emphasis on characteristics of the individual and the person's interactions with the environment. There is a greater awareness that depressed individuals often function in demanding and stressful environments. Moreover, some investigators contend that depressed persons themselves may be instrumental in engendering much of this stress (cf. Gotlib & Hammen, 1992). Given this changing perspective, it is clear that behavioral researchers and clinicians must assess depressed individuals in the context of their environment. As we shall see in the following section, behavioral assessment procedures are now characterized by a broader focus not only on depressed persons, but on their social environments as well.

Behavioral Assessment of Depression

Behavioral approaches to the assessment of depression typically focus on overt features of the disorder, such as psychomotor and verbal behavior. In addition, however, given the focus of behavioral theories of depression on environmental contingencies, behaviorally oriented clinicians and researchers also attempt to assess aspects of the environment, and of the person-environment interaction, that may be related to the onset or maintenance of the depression. Thus, behavioral assessment may include an examination of such factors as the social skills of the depressed individual, the behaviors of others with whom the depressed patient interacts, and the activities and reinforcers available to the depressed person. Moreover, as we shall see below, information may be gathered through interviews, self-report, and direct observations.

Interviews

In assessing the *social skills* of depressed persons, Becker & Heimberg (1985) recommend that a clinical interview be conducted in which the interviewer and the depressed patient role-play problematic target situations identified by the patient. During this role-playing, the interviewer should carefully observe the patient's performance, in terms of speech content, volume, tone, eye contact, posture, etc (see also Lewinsohn, Biglan & Zeiss, 1976). In addition, standardized role-play tests such as the Behavioral Assertiveness Test (Eisler, Hersen, Miller & Blanchard, 1975) can serve to augment the situations provided by the patient.

Self Reports

It is well known that there are a number of frequently used self-report measures of depressive symptomatology, such as the Beck Depression Inventory (BDI; Beck, Ward, Mendelson, Mock & Erbaugh, 1961), the Center for Epidemiologic Studies Depression Scale (CES-D; Radloff, 1977), and the Depression Adjective Check List (DACL; Lubin, 1967). Indeed, there have recently been several detailed reviews of these measures (e.g., Gotlib & Cane, 1989; Lewinsohn & Rohde, 1987). In addition to these measures of symptomatology, however, a number of self-report questionnaires have been developed to assess other aspects of the phenomena of depression. In particular, there are several self-report measures available to assess the social functioning of depressed persons. Youngren, Zeiss & Lewinsohn (1977), for example, developed the Interpersonal Events Schedule (IES), a self-report measure for assessing social interaction in depressed persons.

Another self-report measure of social interaction is the Social Interaction Self-Statement Test (SISST; Glass, Merluzzi, Bierer & Larsen, 1982). This measure consists of 30 statements comprising four subscales: self-depreciation, positive anticipation fear of negative evaluation, and coping. Glass et al. report acceptable psychometric properties for the SISST. Finally, Weissman, Prusoff & Thompson (1978) developed the Social Adjustment Scale - Self-Report (SAS-SR). This measure is a self-report version of the interviewer-rated Social Adjustment Scale (SAS; Weissman & Paykel, 1974). The SAS-SR contains 42 questions that measure affective and instrumental performance in occupational role, social and leisure activities, relationship with extended family, marital role, parental role, family unit, and economic independence.

Behavioral Logs

As a somewhat different perspective on self-report measurement, many behavioral therapists require depressed patients to maintain a daily event log. These logs or diaries can be useful in assessing the response consequences of the depressed patient's social behaviors and in providing information about the patient's social environment and the available social reinforcers. For example, MacPhillamy & Lewinsohn (1982) developed the Pleasant Events Schedule (PES) to facilitate behavioral programs designed to increase the amount of positive reinforcement received by depressed persons. The PES is an inventory designed for use in assessing, tracking, and modifying positive activity level in depressed persons.

Similarly, the Unpleasant Events Schedule (UES) was developed to assess the frequency and the subjective impact of a wide range of stressful life events (Lewinsohn, Mermelstein, Alexander & MacPhillamy, 1985b). The UES has been used to develop individualized unpleasant activities lists for patients for daily monitoring. The UES includes both relatively minor daily hassles and major life events. This measure consists of 320 items assessing the rate of occurrence and the experienced aversiveness of stressful life events.

Shortened versions of the PES have been developed for use with the elderly (Teri & Lewinsohn, 1982) and with adolescents (Carey, Kelley & Buss, 1986; Cole, Kelley & Carey, 1988; Lewinsohn & Clarke, 1986). The PES and UES can also be used to generate individualized activity schedules for monitoring daily pleasant activities and for identifying potential target pleasant activities for change (Lewinsohn, 1976). Finally, Teri, Logsdon, Wagner & Uomoto

(1994) recently modified the PES into a 53-item Pleasant Events Schedule-AD for use with Alzheimer's patients and family caregivers.

It is clear, therefore, that there are a number of self-report measures of behavioral aspects of depressive functioning. While these measures provide important information, it is likely that they are strongly influenced by the general negative response set characteristic of many depressed individuals. Consequently, some investigators have turned to observational measurement procedures, contending that measures based on objective data are more likely to represent "real" skill deficits, which can then become the targets for treatment intervention.

Observational Procedures

A number of investigators have observed the overt behavior of depressed persons. In an early study, Williams, Barlow & Agras (1972) developed an observer-rated scale to assess the behaviors of severely depressed inpatients on the hospital ward. Essentially, this scale assesses depressed patients' verbal behavior, social interactions, smiling, and motor activity, such as reading, sewing, grooming, etc. This measure yields a longitudinal record of the patients' depressed behaviors, and correlates highly with clinician ratings of depression severity.

Subsequent investigations have examined the behaviors of depressed persons in interactions with strangers. The results of these studies indicate that, compared with nondepressed controls, depressed individuals demonstrate a variety of deficits in their social skills. Specifically, depressed individuals have been observed to smile less frequently (Gotlib, 1982; Gotlib & Robinson, 1982), to make less eye contact with those with whom they are interacting (Gotlib, 1982), to speak more slowly and more monotonously (Gotlib & Robinson, 1982; Libet & Lewinsohn, 1973; Youngren & Lewinsohn, 1980), to take longer to respond to others in a conversation (Libet & Lewinsohn, 1973), and to make more self-focused and negatively toned comments (Blumberg & Hokanson, 1983; Gotlib & Robinson, 1982; Jacobson & Anderson, 1982). Given these differences in both conversation behavior and content, with few exceptions (e.g., Gotlib & Meltzer, 1987; Youngren & Lewinsohn, 1980), the interpersonal behaviors of depressed persons have been found to be rated by observers as less socially competent than are those of nondepressed individuals (e.g., Dykman, Horowitz, Abramson & Usher, 1991; Lewinsohn, Mischel, Chaplin & Barton, 1980; see Feldman & Gotlib, 1993, for a more detailed review of these studies).

It is clear, therefore, that depressed persons demonstrate deficits in their social skills in interactions with strangers. Gotlib & Hooley (1988) have argued, however, that the social skill difficulties of depressed individuals are even more pronounced in their marital and family interactions.

Other researchers results are consistent in reporting that the interactions of depressed persons and their spouses are associated with more negative verbal and nonverbal behaviors. For example, marital interactions of couples in which one partner is depressed have been found to be characterized by high levels of disruption, negative emotional outbursts, and incongruity between verbal messages and nonverbal behaviors (Hinchliffe, Hooper & Roberts, 1978), such that depressed individuals emit a greater number of behaviors in which the nonverbal communication is more negative than is the accompanying verbal message (Ruscher & Gotlib, 1988). When interacting with a spouse, depressed individuals have been found to emit a lower proportion of positive verbal behavior and a greater proportion of negative verbal behavior than do nondepressed individuals (Hautzinger, Linden & Hoffman, 1982; Ruscher & Gotlib, 1988). Moreover, Kowalik & Gotlib (1987) reported that this pattern of negative behavior on the part of depressed individuals may be deliberate; depressed persons in this study intentionally coded their communications to their spouses as more negative and less positive than did nondepressed couples. In addition, other findings suggest that depressed individuals are often openly aggressive when interacting with their spouses (Biglan, Hops, Sherman, Friedman, Arthur & Osteen, 1985; see Rehm, 1987).

Finally, there is evidence from observational assessment studies that depressed persons also experience problematic interactions with their children. A number of investigators have found that depressed women are withdrawn and/or overtly negative in interactions with their children.

Results indicating similarly negative behavioral interactions between depressed parents and their children have also been found in studies with older children as well (e.g., Goodman & Brumley, 1990; Gordon, Burge, Hammen, Adrian, Jaenicke & Hiroto, 1989; Mills, Puckering, Pound & Cox, 1985; see Gotlib & Lee, 1990, and Hammen, 1991, for more detailed reviews of this literature).

It is clear from the results of these studies, therefore, that the overt behaviors of depressed persons are problematic on hospital wards, and in interactions with strangers, spouses, and their children. A primary contribution of behavioral approaches to the assessment of the social functioning of depressed persons has been to identify and clarify the precise behaviors that appear to be particularly troublesome. We turn now to an examination of behavioral approaches to the treatment of depressed persons.

Behavioral Treatment of Depression

Given the focus of behavioral theories of depression on environmental contingencies and reinforcers, a major goal of behaviorally oriented therapies for depression involves increasing the positive reinforcement received by the depressed individual. In this context, a number of different behavioral treatment approaches have been described, all of which share this common goal (cf. Antonuccio, Ward & Tearnan, 1989). Moreover, as Hoberman & Lewinsohn (1985) note, there are a number of other commonalities associated with behavioral approaches to the treatment of depression. For example, patients are usually required to monitor activities, mood, and thoughts. Patients are encouraged to set achievable goals in order to ensure early success experiences, and to give themselves rewards for reaching their goals. Finally, most behavioral approaches involve training designed to remedy various performance and skill deficits of depressed patients (e.g., social skills training, assertiveness training) and are time-limited, typically designed to run from between 4 and 12 weeks.

Increasing Pleasant Activities and Decreasing Unpleasant Events

Lewinsohn and his colleagues (e.g., Lewinsohn, Sullivan & Grosscup, 1980b; Libet & Lewinsohn, 1973) have underscored the significant relation of depression with low rates of positive reinforcement and with high rates of aversive experience. As we noted earlier, these investigators posited that depression may be due, in part, to a low rate of response-contingent positive reinforcement. Based on this formulation, Lewinsohn et al. (1980b) developed a 12-session, highly structured behavioral program aimed at changing the quality and quantity of depressed patients' interactions with their environments. Specifically, through the use of overlapping behavioral and cognitive intervention tactics including training in assertiveness, relaxation, self-control, decision making, problem solving, communication, and time management, depressed patients are taught to manage and reduce the intensity and frequency of aversive events and to increase their rate of engagement in pleasant activities. A more detailed description of this treatment program with clinical illustrations is provided in Lewinsohn, Sullivan & Grosscup (1982).

The tactics, which are shown in Table 15.1, fall into three general categories: those that focus on changing environmental conditions; those that focus on teaching depressed individuals skills they can use to change problematic patterns of interaction with the environment, and those that focus on enhancing the pleasantness and decreasing the aversiveness of person-environment interactions.

Environmental interventions are especially useful when the patient's environment is highly impoverished and/or aversive, or when the individual has few personal resources. One kind of environmental intervention involves changing the physical and social setting of the patient by assisting the patient to move to a new environment. For example, in the treatment of an elderly

Table 15.1. Social Learning Tactics

Environmental interventions
    1.   Environmental shifts
    2.   Contingency management

Skills training
    1.   Self-change methods
        a.   Specifying the problem
        b.   Self-observing and "baselining"
        c.   Discovering antecedents
        d.   Discovering consequences
        e.   Setting a helpful goal
        f.   Self-reinforcement
        g.   Evaluating progress
        h.   Time planing
    2.   Social skills
        a.   Assertion
        b.   Interpersonal style of expressive behavior
        c.   Social activity
    3.   Relaxation
    4.   Stress management

Cognitive skills
    1.   Decreasing negative thinking by thought interruption, Premacking, worrying time, blow-up technique, self-talk, procedures, identification, and disputing of irrational thoughts.
    2.   Increasing positive thinking by priming, noticing of accomplishments, positive self-rewarding thoughts, time projections.

depressed woman with a history of paranoid schizophrenia, the diagnostic assessment suggested that social isolation was the major factor contributing to her depression. She accepted the recommendation that she move from a tiny studio apartment in an isolated house to a large retirement center with many ongoing recreational activities. Her depression improved substantially with the subsequent increase in social and recreational events in her life. Other examples of environmental shifts include moving to another city, separating from a spouse, and changing jobs.

Contingency management is another kind of environmental intervention. Contingency management involves changing the consequences of certain behaviors. With outpatients, the therapist may instruct family member to make attention, praise, and physical affection contingent on adapted behaviors and to ignore depressed behaviors (Liberman & Raskin, 1971).

Skills-training tactics focus on teaching depressed persons skills they can use to change problematic patterns of interaction with the environment, as well as skills they will need to maintain these changes after the termination of therapy. Specific skills-training interventions vary from case to case; they range from very structured and standardized programs to individually designed ad hoc procedures.

In our choice of self-management methods, we have made considerable use of procedures and techniques described by Goldfried & (1973), by Mahoney & Thoresen (1974), by Thoresen & Mahoney (1974), and by Watson & Tharp (1972). Lakein's (1973) "How to get control of your time and your life" is also useful because is presents a systematic format for organizing time and activities so as to be able to meet responsibilities and still have time for pleasant activities.

Tactics aimed at allowing the patient to change the quantity and the quality of his or her interpersonal relationships typically cover three aspects of interpersonal behavior: assertion, interpersonal style of expressive behavior, and social activity.

Cognitive skills are intended to facilitate changes in the way patients think about reality. The locus of control over thought can clearly be identified as being in the patient, since only the patient can observe his or her thoughts.

Stress-management skills include relaxation training (Benson, 1975; Rosen, 1977).

Each depressed person is unique, and hence treatment tactics must be flexible. Nevertheless, to assist therapists with the implementation of specific tactics, we have developed several therapist manuals. These manuals are called "Increase Pleasant Events and Decrease Unpleasant Events" and "Decrease Unpleasant Events and Increase Pleasant Events." (This manual can be obtained at cost by writing to Peter M. Lewinsohn, Ph.D., Oregon Research Institute 1715 Franklin Blvd., Eugene, OR 97403–1983, USA.)

As the title implies, the first part of treatment is devoted to assisting the patient in decreasing the frequency, and the subjective aversiveness, of unpleasant events in his or her life. The second phase concentrates on increasing pleasant ones.

The treatment is divided into 12 sessions. The first five sessions focus on decreasing the frequency and the aversiveness of unpleasant events. The second five sessions focus on increasing the frequency and enjoyment of pleasant activities. The goal of the final treatment session to facilitate the patient's ability to maintain their improvement mood level, and to prevent future depression. Each session outlines specific activities for the therapist and the patient to engage in to achieve these goals. Time limits for each activity are suggested. Any extra time should be spent with additional patient concerns.

Several approaches are used to obtain the treatment goals. They include daily monitoring, relaxation training, managing aversive events, time management, and increasing pleasant activities.

Step 1: Daily monitoring. We first teach patients to graph and to interpret their daily monitoring data. They seem to understand intuitively the relationship between unpleasant events and mood. But the covariation between pleasant events and mood is usually a revelation to patients. *Seeing* these relationships on a day-to-day basis impresses on patients in a powerful way the fact that the quantity and the quality of their daily interactions has an important impact on their depression. The depression is no longer a mysterious force, but a reasonable experience. The graphing and interpretation provide clients with a framework for understanding their depression and suggest ways of dealing with it. Monitoring specific events helps clients focus on coping with particular unpleasant aspects of their daily life and, of equal importance, makes them aware of the range of pleasant experience potentially accessible to them. Patients, in a very real sense, learn to diagnose their own depression.

Step 2: Relaxation training. The rationale for relaxation training is introduced at the end of the first session. Patients are told how tenseness can exacerbate the aversiveness of unpleasant situations and how it interferes with the enjoyment of pleasant activities. At the end of the first session, the patient is given the assignment of reading either a pamphlet (e.g., "Learning to Get Completely Relaxed") or a book (e..g, Benson, 1975; Rosen, 1977), and is instructed on how to become familiar with major muscle groups and how to tense and relax them. Much of the second session is used for progressive muscular relaxation intended to show patients how relaxed they can feel. The patient is then encouraged to practice relaxation two times per day and to keep a relaxation log. Later assignments involved patients' identifying specific situations in which they feel tense.

Step 3: Managing aversive events. The therapy then moves to teaching patients to manage aversive events. Patients often overreact to unpleasant events and allow them to interfere with their engagement in and enjoyment of pleasant activities. Relaxation training is, therefore, introduced early in treatment with the goal of teaching patients to be more relaxed generally, but especially in specific situations in which they feel tense.

The "decreasing unpleasant events" component then proceeds with pinpointing a small number of negative interactions or situations that trigger the patient's dysphoria. In order to reduce the aversiveness of these situations, the therapist has available a wide range of tactics, which might include teaching patients consciously to substitute more positive and constructive thoughts between the activating event and the feeling of dysphoria; to learn how not to take things personally; to prepare for aversive encounters; to learn how to use self-instructions; to prepare for failure; and to learn in other ways how to deal more adaptively with aversive situations. These tactics are described in greater detail by Beck, Rush, Shaw & Emery (1979), Ellis & Murphy (1975), Kranzler (1974), Mahoney (1974), Meichenbaum & Turk (1976), and Novaco (1977).

Step 4: Time management. Daily planning and time management training is another general tactic included in the module. In this phase, we have patients read and make considerable use of selected chapters from *How to Get Control of Your Time and Your Life* by Lakein (1973).

Depressed individuals typically make poor use of their time, do not plan ahead, and therefore have not made the preparations (e.g., getting a babysitter) needed in order to take advantage of opportunities for pleasant events. The training aims also to assist clients to achieve a better *balance* between activities that they want to do and activities that they feel they have to do. Using a daily time schedule, patients are asked to preplan each day and each week. Initially, this planning is done in the sessions with therapists' assistance; gradually, patients are expected to do the planning at home.

Step 5: Increasing pleasant activities. The daily planning is also useful in scheduling specific pleasant events, which becomes the focus of the next phase of the module. In helping patients to increase their rate of engagement in pleasant activities, the emphasis is on setting concrete goals for this increase and on developing specific plans for things the patients will do.

Patients begin rating their moods and monitoring the occurrence of the pleasant and unpleasant activities on their Activity Schedules on a daily basis. They continue this daily monitoring for the duration of treatment.

To monitor the occurrence of events, patients use a 3-point scale for each of the 80 pleasant events on their personalized schedule: 0 - did not occur to day; 1 - occurred but was neutral; and 2 - occurred and was pleasant.

Patients mark a similar scale for the unpleasant events on their schedule except that they indicate whether or not the event was neutral or unpleasant if it occurred. This easily provides scores for the pleasant and unpleasant events experienced that day. The mean pleasant-events score for daily monitoring in a normal population is 17.6 with a standard deviation of 10.4. The mean unpleasant-events score in a normal population is 5.1, with a standard deviation of 3.9. The daily frequency of various events provides immediate feedback on the impact of treatment in meeting the intermediate treatment goals of changing the overall rate of reinforcement and punishing events.

A person's activity schedule can be generated from him/her responses on the PES and on the UES. Each patient's schedule includes 80 events which he/she rated as most enjoyable and 80 activities which he/she rated as most aversive. Activity schedules can be created in one of two ways: (a) from the patient's responses on the PES and on the UES, listing unpleasant events rated by the patient as most aversive and pleasant events rated by the patient as most enjoyable; or (b) using the sample activity schedules shown in Figure 15.2. The events included in those lists are those which have been found to mood related for a substantial proportion of the population (Lewinsohn & Amenson, 1978).

The patient is instructed to track the daily occurrence and degree of pleasantness or unpleasantness of 160 activities as well as his/her daily mood. Based on these responses, the patient graphs his/her rate of engagement in pleasant

Part A

Name:_____Date:_____

Please check within the parentheses to correspond to the activities of this day.
Only activities that were at least a little pleasant should be checked.

Activity	Frequency (check)	Activity	Frequency (check)
1. Laughing	( )	32. Watching people	( )
2. Being relaxed	( )	33. Making a new friend	( )
3. Talking about other people	( )	34. Being complimented or told I	
4. Thinking about something		have done well	( )
good in the future	( )	35. Expressing my love to	
5. Having people show interest in		someone	( )
what I say	( )	36. Having sexual relations with a	
6. Being with friends	( )	partner of the opposite sex	( )
7. Eating good meals	( )	37. Having spare time	( )
8. Breathing clean air	( )	38. Helping someone	( )
9. Seeing beautiful scenery		39. Having friends come to visit	( )
10. Thinking about people I like	( )	40. Listening to the sounds of	
11. Having a frank and open		nature	( )
conversation	( )	41. Watching wild animals	( )
12. Wearing clean clothes	( )	42. Driving skillfully	( )
13. Having coffee, tea, a Coke,		43. Talking about sports	( )
etc., with friends	( )	44. Meeting someone new of the	( )
14. Wearing informal clothes	( )	same sex	( )
15. Being noticed as sexually		45. Planning trips or vacations	( )
attractive	( )	46. Having lunch with friends or	
16. Having peace and quiet	( )	associates	( )
17. Smiling at people	( )	47. Being with animals	( )
18. Sleeping soundly at night	( )	48. Going to a party	( )
19. Feeling the presence of the		49. Sitting in the sun	( )
Lord in my life	( )	50. Being praised by people I	
20. Kissing	( )	admire	( )
21. Doing a job well	( )	51. Doing a project in my own way	( )
22. Having a lively talk	( )	52. Being told I am needed	( )
23. Seeing good things happen to		53. Watching attractive women or	
family or friends	( )	men	( )
24. Being popular at a gathering	( )	54. Being told I am loved	( )
25. Saying something clearly	( )	55. Seeing old friends	( )
26. Reading stories, novels,		56. Staying up late	( )
poems, or plays	( )	57. Beachcombing	( )
27. Planning or organizing		58. Snowmobiling or dune buggy	
something	( )	riding	( )
28. Learning to do something new	( )	59. Petting; necking	( )
29. Complimenting or praising		60. Listening to music	( )
someone	( )	61. Visiting friends	( )
30. Amusing people		62. Being invited out	( )
31. Being with someone I love	( )	63. Going to a restaurant	( )

64. Talking about philosophy or religion ( )	73. Being in the country ( )
65. Singing to myself ( )	74. Seeing or smelling a flower or plant ( )
66. Thinking about myself or my problems ( )	75. Being asked for my help or advice ( )
67. Solving a problem, puzzle, crossword, etc. ( )	76. Doing housework or laundry; cleaning things ( )
68. Completing a difficult task ( )	77. Sleeping late ( )
69. Having an original idea ( )	78. Playing in sand, a stream, the grass, etc. ( )
70. Social drinking ( )	79. Being with happy people ( )
71. Getting massages or backrubs ( )	80. Looking at the stars or moon ( )
72. Meeting someone of the opposite sex ( )	

Part B

Name:_____Date:_____

Please check within the parentheses to correspond to the activities of this day.
Only activities that were at least a little unpleasant should be checked.

Activity	Frequency (check)	Activity	Frequency (check)
1. Being dissatisfied with my spouse (living partner, mate)	( ) ( )	15. Being rushed	( )
2. Working on something when I am tired	( ) ( )	16. Being near unpleasant people (drunk, bigoted, inconsiderate, etc.)	( ) ( ) ( )
3. Arguments with spouse (living partner, mate)	( ) ( )	17. Having someone disagree with me	( ) ( )
4. Being disabled (unable to work go to school, etc.)	( ) ( )	18. Being insulted	( )
5. Having a minor illness or injury (toothache, allergy attack, cold, flu, hangover, acne breakout, etc.)	( ) ( ) ( ) ( )	19. Having a project or assignment overdue	( ) ( )
6. Having my spouse (living partner, mate) dissatisfied with me	( ) ( ) ( )	20. Having something break or run poorly (car, appliances, etc.)	( ) ( ) ( )
7. Working on something I don't enjoy	( ) ( )	21. Living in a dirty or messy place	( )
8. Getting grades or being evaluated	( ) ( )	22. Bad weather	( )
9. Having too much to do	( )	23. Not having enough money for extras	( ) ( )
10. Realizing that I can't do what I had thought I could	( )	24. Failing at something (a test, a class, etc.)	( ) ( )
11. Taking an exam (test, license examination, etc.)	( )	25. Seeing animals misbehave (making a mess, chasing cars, etc.)	( ) ( ) ( )
12. Looking for a job	( )	26. Being without privacy	( )
13. Leaving a task uncompleted; procrastinating	( ) ( )	27. Eating a disliked food	( )
14. Working at something I don't care about	( )	28. Working under pressure	( )
		29. Performing poorly in athletics	( )
		30. Talking with an unpleasant person (stubborn, unreason- able, aggressive, conceited, etc.)	( ) ( ) ( ) ( )

31. Realizing that someone I love and I are growing apart ( )
32. Doing something I don't want to do in order to please someone else ( )
33. Doing a job poorly ( )
34. Learning that a friend or relative has just become ill, is injured, is hospitalized, or is in need of an operation ( )
35. Being told what to do ( )
36. Driving under adverse conditions (heavy traffic, poor weather, night, etc.) ( )
37. Having a major unexpected expense (hospital bill, home repairs, etc.) ( )
38. Having family members or friends do something I dis-approve (giving up religious training, dropping out of school, drinking, taking drugs, etc.) ( )
39. Learning that someone is angry with me or wants to hurt me ( )
40. Being misled, bluffed, or tricked ( )
41. Being nagged ( )
42. Being bothered with red tape, administrative hassles, paper-work, etc. ( )
43. Being away from someone I love ( )
44. Listening to people complain ( )
45. Having a relative or friend living in unsatisfactory sur-roundings ( )
46. Knowing a close friend or relative is working under adverse conditions ( )
47. Learning of local, national, or international news (cor-ruption, government decisions, crime, etc.) ( )
48. Being alone ( )
49. Disciplining a child ( )
50. Saying something unclearly ( )
51. Lying to someone ( )
52. Breathing foul air ( )
53. Being asked something I could not or did not want to answer ( )

54. Being in very hot weather ( )
55. Being awakened when I am trying to sleep ( )
56. Doing something embarrassing in the presence of others ( )
57. Being clumsy (dropping, spilling, knocking something over, etc.) ( )
58. Receiving contradictory information ( )
59. Having family members or friends do something that makes me ashamed of them ( )
60. Being excluded or left out ( )
61. Losing or misplacing something (wallet, keys, golf ball, fish on a line, etc.) ( )
62. Learning that someone would stop at nothing to get ahead ( )
63. Being in a dirty or dusty place ( )
64. Not having enough time to be with people I care about (spouse, close friend, living partner, etc.) ( )
65. Making a mistake (in sports, my job, etc.) ( )
66. Running out of money ( )
67. Having a relative or friend with a mental health problem ( )
68. Losing a friend ( )
69. Doing housework or laundry; cleaning things ( )
70. Listening to someone who doesn't stop talking, can't keep to the point, or talks only about one subject ( )
71. Living with a relative or room mate who is in poor physical or mental health ( )
72. Being with sad people ( )
73. Having people ignore what I have said ( )
74. Being physically uncomfortable (being dizzy, being consti-pated, having a headache, itchy, being cold, undergoing a rectal exam, having the hic-cups, etc. ( )
75. Having someone I care about fail at something (job, school,

etc.) that is important to him or her	( )	78. Having someone I know drink, smoke, or take drugs	( )
76. Being with people who don't share my interests	( )	79. Being misunderstood or misquoted	( )
77. Having someone owe me money or something else that belongs to me	( )	80. Being forced to do something	( )

Figure 15.2. Activity schedule. From Lewinsohn et al. (1982).

and unpleasant activities and mood in order to observe the relationship between his/her activities and daily mood. Mood is tracked by using a 9-point scale ranging from 1 = very happy to 9 = very depressed. A sample mood rating form is shown in Figure 15.3. Graphs for tracking activities and mood are included in the treatment manual.

Patients are provided with feedback about their rate of engagement and degree of enjoyment of pleasant and unpleasant activities and their relationship with their mood. Patients also are provided feedback about specific activities or events which correlate best with his/her mood. This provides additional information in pinpointing specific activities for the client to increase or decrease for optimal mood.

Treatment includes providing individuals with assistance and helping them to plan their daily life in such a way as to minimize rate of engagement in unpleasant events, maximize rate of engagement in pleasant activities and to achieve a better balance between the two.

At the end of treatment, the therapist and the patient develop a maintenance/prevention program for the patient to implement after the termination of treatment. This may include making an active effort to continue behaviors and skills learned during treatment as well as a periodic check (through daily monitoring) of pleasant and unpleasant activities and level of daily mood.

By the end of treatment the patient should have a good understanding of which activities he/she experiences as especially enjoyable and which correlate with feeling good; and those events which he/she is experiencing as especially aversive and which correlate with depressed mood. In addition, he/she should have developed skills which allow him/her to control his/her mood by increasing pleasant activities and decreasing the rate of occurrence of unpleasant events. He/she should also have developed a plan to maintain treatment gains beyond the treatment setting.

Lewinsohn et al. reported that this program of decreasing unpleasant activities and increasing engagement in pleasant activities was effective in reducing levels of depression (see also Hammen & Glass, 1975; Zeiss, Lewinsohn & Muñoz, 1979).

Daily Mood Rating Form

Please rate your mood for this day (how good or bad you felt), using the 9-point scale shown. If you felt really great (the best you have ever felt or can imagine yourself feeling), mark 9. If you felt really bad (the worst you have ever felt or can imagine yourself feeling), mark 1. If it was a "so-so" (or mixed) day, mark 5.

If you felt worse that "so-so", mark a number between 2 and 4. If you felt better than "so-so", mark a number between 6 and 9. Remember, a low number signifies that you felt bad and a high number means that you felt good.

Very
depressed _____ happy Very

         1   2   3   4   5   6   7   8   9

Enter the date on which you begin your mood ratings in Column 2 and your mood score in Column 3.

Monitoring day	Date	Mood score	Monitoring day	Date	Mood score
1			16		
2			17		
3			18		
4			19		
5			20		
6			21		
7			22		
8			23		
9			24		
10			25		
11			26		
12			27		
13			28		
14			29		
15			30		

Figure 15.3. A visual analogue depression scale. From Lewinsohn et al. (1982).

Social Skills Therapy

Given the consistent finding of poor social skills of depressed persons (e.g., Gotlib, 1982; Libet & Lewinsohn, 1973; Youngren & Lewinsohn, 1980), a number of investigators (e.g., Sanchez, Lewinsohn & Larsen, 1980) have described behaviorally oriented treatment programs for depression that focus explicitly on the training of social skills. One such treatment program for depression has been described by Becker, Heimberg, and Bellack (e.g., Becker

& Heimberg, 1985; Becker, Heimberg & Bellack, 1987; Bellack, Hersen & Himmelhoch, 1981). This program is based on the following assumptions:

1. Depression is a result of an inadequate schedule of positive reinforcement for the person's behavior.
2. A substantial portion of the most salient positive reinforcers in the adult world are interpersonal in nature.
3. A meaningful portion of the rewards in adult life may be received or denied, contingent on the person' interpersonal behavior.
4. Therefore, a treatment that helps the depressed patient to increase the quality of his or her interpersonal behavior should act to increase the amount of response-contingent positive reinforcement and thereby decrease depressive affect and increase the rate of "nondepressed behavior" (Becker & Heimberg, 1985, p. 205).

Becker and Heimberg suggest that inadequate interpersonal behavior may be due to a number of factors, such as insufficient exposure to interpersonally skilled models, learning of maladaptive interpersonal behaviors, insufficient opportunity to practice important interpersonal routines, decaying of specific behavioral skills due to disuse, and failure to recognize environmental cues for specific interpersonal behaviors.

The training program focuses primarily on three specific behavioral repertoires that appear to be particularly relevant to depressed individuals: negative assertion, positive assertion, and conversational skills. Negative assertion involves behaviors that allow persons to stand up for their rights and to act in their own best interest. Positive assertion refers to the expression of positive feelings about others, such as affection, approval, praise, and appreciation, as well as offering appropriate apologies. Training in conversational skills involves initiating conversations, asking questions, making appropriate self-disclosures, and ending conversations gracefully. In all of these areas depressed patients are given direct behavior training as well as training in social perception. Patients are encouraged to practice the skills and behaviors across different situations.

Treatment takes place over 12 weekly 1-h sessions, in which patients receive training in the four problem areas described above. These treatment sessions are followed by six to eight maintenance sessions over a 6-month period, in which the emphasis is on problem solving and review. Bellack and his colleagues (e.g., Bellack, Hersen & Himmelhoch, 1983; Hersen, Bellack, Himmelhoch & Thase, 1984) have demonstrated the efficacy of this approach in the treatment of depression. The results of these studies indicated that social skills training was more effective than psychotropic medication and insight-oriented psychotherapy in increasing level of social skill. Moreover, the gains made by patients in the social skills treatment groups were maintained at a 6-month follow-up assessment.

A similar approach to the treatment of depression that also focuses on the training of social skills has been described by McLean (1976, 1981). Because McLean views depression as resulting from individuals' perceived loss of control over their interpersonal environment, his treatment for depression is aimed at training in coping and social skills. McLean outlines a structured, time-limited treatment program aimed at improving social behaviors that are incompatible with depression. Graduated practice and modeling are used to effect improvements in the following six skills areas: communication, behavioral productivity, social interaction, assertiveness, decision-making and problem-solving, and cognitive self-control. Patients are required to engage in daily skill development activities and to use structured log sheets to monitor their achievements. Patients are also prepared for the experience of future depressive episodes, and contingency plans for coping are established and rehearsed with the patients.

McLean & Hakstian (1979) assessed the efficacy of this behavioral treatment with 178 unipolar depressed outpatients, randomly assigned to four treatment conditions: behavior therapy, "traditional" insight-oriented psychotherapy, relaxation training, and amitriptyline. Data from a two-year follow-up of these patients reported by McLean & Hakstian (1990) indicate that behavior therapy was superior to the other treatments and that this pattern of results is stable: Over a 27-month follow-up period, behavior therapy patients were found to be significantly improved in mood, more socially active, and more personally productive than were patients in the other treatment conditions, particularly in the relaxation therapy condition.

Self-Control Therapy

Self-control therapy, developed from Rehm's (1977) self-control model of depression, emphasizes progressive goal attainment, self-reinforcement and contingency management strategies, and behavioral productivity. As we noted earlier, the self-control model posits that depression is associated with deficits in self-monitoring, self-evaluation, and self-reinforcement. Consequently, these areas of functioning are the focus of self-control therapy. This therapy is a structured, time-limited, group-format treatment. It consists of six to twelve sessions divided into three parts, each focusing on one of the three deficit areas described above. With respect to self-monitoring, patients are required to maintain a daily record and graph of positive experiences and their associated mood. In the self-evaluation phase, patients are taught to develop specific, overt, and attainable goals in terms of positive activities and behavioral productivity. In addition, patients assign points to these goals and keep a tally of their points as they meet their goals. Finally, patients are taught to identify reinforcers and to administer these rewards to themselves as they accomplish their specific goals.

Rehm has demonstrated the efficacy of this self-control treatment for depression in a number of studies. In one of the first tests of this therapy, Fuchs & Rehm (1977) reported that self-control treatment was more effective than was nonspecific group therapy or a wait-list control condition in reducing depression in a sample of clinically depressed women. Moreover, improvement was maintained at a 6-week follow-up assessment. Rehm, Fuchs, Roth, Kornblith & Romano (1979) subsequently reported that self-control therapy was more effective in the treatment of depressed patients than was assertion skills training (see also Roth, Bielski, Jones, Parker & Osborn, 1982). Interestingly, Rehm (1990) notes that the effectiveness of this treatment does not depend on the inclusion of all three components; outcomes do not seem to be affected by the omission of the self-evaluation or self-reinforcement portions of the program. Finally, Rehm also notes that this therapy appears to be equally effective in altering cognitive and behavioral aspects of depression, suggesting a nonspecificity of treatment effects (cf. Zeiss et al., 1979).

Problem-Solving Therapy

The problem-solving model of depression (Nezu, 1987; Nezu, Nezu & Perri, 1989) focuses on relations among major negative life events, current problems, problem-solving coping, and depressive symptomatology. Thus, the treatment strategies and procedures that have been developed from this model are designed to reduce depressive symptomatology through training in problem-solving skills. Nezu et al. outline four goals of problem-solving therapy for depressed individuals: (1) to help them identify previous and current life situations that may be antecedents of a depressive episode; (2) to minimize the negative impact of depressive symptoms on current and future coping attempts; (3) to increase the effectiveness of problem-solving efforts at coping with current life situations; and (4) to teach general skills to deal more effectively with future problems. Training in maintenance and generalization are also built into this program.

Nezu et al.'s (1989) problem-solving therapy is a structured 10-week intervention program in which such therapeutic techniques as instruction, prompting, modeling, behavioral rehearsal, homework assignments, shaping, reinforcement, and feedback are utilized to increase problem-solving ability and decrease depressive symptomatology. The results of several studies suggest that problem-solving therapy may be efficacious for the treatment of depression (Nezu, 1986; Nezu & Perri, 1989).

Cognitive-Behavior Therapy

The cognitive-behavioral approach to treatment is based on the more recent models of behavioral theories of depression (Lewinsohn et al., 1985b) and includes elements described earlier of increasing pleasant activities, of decreasing unpleasant events, and of social and interpersonal skills training, in combination with Beck's cognitive therapy (Beck, Rush, Shaw & Emery, 1979). A specific treatment manual is available (Hautzinger, Stark & Treiber, 1992). The rationale behind this extension is illustrated in Figure 15.4. Depression is seen as a result of several factors, including aversive experiences and chronic difficulties (antecedents), which result in dysphoria and depression if a subject shows predisposing vulnerabilities, negative cognitive processes, social and interpersonal skill deficits, a lack of positive experiences, and a reduction in positive reinforcement and activities. Consequently, the cognitive-behavioral approach focuses on activity scheduling to increase reinforcing activities, on role playing and social skill training, on cognitive restructuring, and on influencing automatic negative thinking and dysfunctional basic assumptions.

The efficacy of this approach was tested recently in two large-scale, multicenter studies of patients with a diagnosis of major depression, with and without fulfilling the DSM-III-R melancholia criteria (Hautzinger, 1993; Hautzinger, deJong-Meyer, Treiber & Rudolf, 1992; deJong-Meyer, Hautzinger, Rudolf & Strauss, 1992). The first study tested the efficacy of cognitive-behavior therapy in comparison to a standard pharmacological treatment

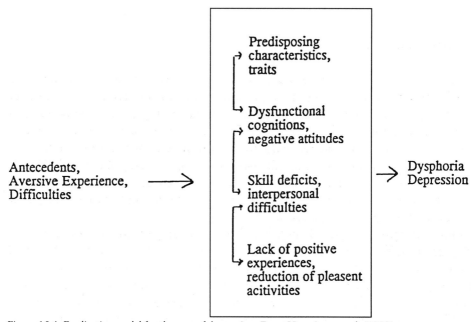

Figure 15.4. Explicative model for therapy of depression. From Hautzinger et al. (1992).

(Amitriptyline) and to the combination of drugs and cognitive-behavior therapy. Altogether, 191 unipolar depressed patients (Major Depression or Dysthymia) were treated either as outpatients or as inpatients over 8 weeks of active treatment, followed by a one-year follow-up assessment. All three treatments were equally effective in reducing depressive symptomatology. At one-year follow-up, the pharmacological group had relapsed more often and showed a higher level of depressive symptoms. This difference was most pronounced in the outpatient group. Interestingly, severity of symptomatology at pre-treatment did not have a differential influence on outcome. Finally, there was a much higher drop-out rate and a lower responder rate in the drug-only condition.

The second study included only unipolar depressed patients who met DSM-III-R criteria for melancholia (endogenous depression). The 155 in- and outpatients were randomly assigned either to a standard pharmacological treatment (Amitriptyline) plus supportive clinical management or to the combination of drug treatment and cognitive-behavior therapy. Unfortunately, according to ethical considerations, it was not possible to include a drug-free condition in this study. One of the goals of this investigation was to test the hypothesis that, relative to pharmacology alone, a combination treatment is more effective in reducing depressive symptoms and in maintaining a symptom-free level of functioning over a longer period of time. The results of this study indicated that both treatments were equally effective, with advantages for the combination treatment at one-year follow-up. Again, this effect at follow-up was not significant for the inpatient group.

Marital/Family Therapy

Given the consistent association described earlier between depression and difficulties in marital and family functioning, it is not surprising that a number of therapies have been developed aimed simultaneously at decreasing levels of depression and improving marital/family relationships. Because marital/family interventions for depression are the focus of other chapters in this volume and have also been reviewed in detail elsewhere (e.g., Gotlib, Wallace & Colby, 1990; Gotlib & Beach, 1995), we shall simply point out here that several recent studies have documented the efficacy of behaviorally oriented marital or family therapy for depression.

For example, O'Leary & Beach (1990) randomly assigned couples with a depressed wife to individual cognitive therapy (CT), conjoint behavioral marital therapy (BMT), or to a 15-week waiting list condition. At both post-therapy and one-year follow-up assessments, O'Leary and Beach found CT and BMT to be equally effective in reducing depressive symptomatology. Only BMT, however, was found to be effective in improving the marital relationship.

At post therapy, only 25% of persons receiving CT, compared with 83% of those receiving BMT, had at least 15-point increases in their scores on a measure of marital adjustment from pre-test to post-test. The same general pattern of results held at follow-up. The results of this study suggest that marital therapy can effectively reduce depressive symptomatology while simultaneously enhancing marital satisfaction, at least for those couples in which there is both depression and marital discord (cf. O'Leary, Risso & Beach, 1990).

Similar results for the treatment of depressed, maritally discordant couples were reported by Jacobson, Dobson, Fruzzetti, Schmaling & Salusky (1991). Again, while both individual cognitive therapy and behavioral marital therapy were equally effective in reducing depression in these couples, only marital therapy was found to be successful in enhancing marital satisfaction. At present, the advantage of using marital interventions for depression rather than individual approaches appears to lie primarily in their greater efficacy in patients with co-occurring marital discord and depression (cf. Gotlib & Colby, 1987).

The Coping with Depression (CWD) Course

The Coping With Depression Course for Adults (Lewinsohn, Antonuccio, Steinmetz & Teri, 1984) grew out of a series of early investigations (e.g., Lewinsohn & Atwood, 1969; Lewinsohn & Shaffer, 1971; Lewinsohn & Shaw, 1969; Lewinsohn, Weinstein & Alper, 1970; Lewinsohn, Weinstein & Shaw, 1969) in which a group behavioral treatment for depression was included. Most directly related to the development of the CWD Course, however, were results reported by Zeiss et al. (1979), who compared the efficacy of three treatments for depression (cognitive therapy, increasing pleasant activities, and social skill training). The results of this study indicated that while all three treatments were equally effective in reducing levels of depression, changes in the intervening dependent variables were not specific to the type of treatment received. For example, the cognitions of the patients who received social skills training changed as much as the cognitions of patients who were in the cognitive therapy group. Similarly, the pleasant activities of the patients in the Pleasant Activities treatment increased as much as those of the patients in the cognitive treatment. Thus, it appeared that none of the treatments was necessary for therapeutic change to occur, and that the effects of the treatments were nonspecific, affecting all of the assessed areas of psychosocial functioning that have been shown to be related to depression.

On the basis of these results, Zeiss et al. (1979, pp. 437–438) advanced the following hypotheses concerning what might be critical components for successful short-term, cognitive-behavioral therapy for depression:

1. Therapy should begin with an elaborated, well-planned rationale. This

rationale should provide the initial structure that guides the patient to the belief that s/he can control his/her own behavior and thereby change his/her depression.

2. Therapy should provide training and skills which the patient can use to feel more effective in handling his/her daily life. The skills must be of some significance to the patient, and must fit with the rationale that has been presented.

3. Therapy should emphasize the independent use of these skills by the patient outside of the therapy context, and must provide enough structure so that the attainment of independent skills is possible for the patient.

4. Therapy should encourage the patient's attribution that improvement in mood was caused by the patient's own increased skill from this, not by the therapist's skillfulness.

The CWD course was designed to incorporate these hypotheses. The course (and each of its subsequent modifications for special populations) was designed to be offered as an educational course or small seminar, teaching people techniques and strategies to cope with the problems that are assumed to be related to their depression. Specifically, the CWD course addresses several target behaviors (social skills, depressogenic thinking, pleasant activities, and relaxation), as well as more general components hypothesized to be critical to successful cognitive-behavioral therapy for depression (e.g., self-monitoring, baselining, self-change).

In its present configuration, the CWD course for adults consists of 12 2-h sessions conducted over 8 weeks. Sessions are held twice weekly for the first 4 weeks. Groups typically consist of six to ten adults (aged 18 and older), with a single group leader (although two therapists may be used). One- and 6-month follow-up sessions ("class reunions") are held to encourage maintenance of treatment gains and to collect information on improvement or relapse.

The first two CWD sessions are devoted to the presentation of the course rules, the rationale of the treatment and the social learning view of depression, and instruction in self-change skills. Participants are taught that being depressed does not mean that they are "crazy." Instead, their depression is conceptualized as due to their difficulty in dealing with stresses in their lives. The CWD course is presented as a way to learn new skills to allow the participants to deal more effectively with the stressors that contributed to their depression. Next, several self-change skills are taught, including monitoring specific behaviors targeted for change, establishing a baseline, setting realistic goals, and developing a plan and a contract to make changes in their behavior. The following eight sessions are devoted to teaching specific skills, including relaxation, increasing pleasant activities, control of negative or irrational thinking, and social skills. Two sessions are devoted to each skill area.

The relaxation sessions focus primarily on the Jacobson (1929) method, which requires participants to alternately tense and then relax major muscle groups throughout the body until fully relaxed. The rationale for teaching relaxation rests on the well demonstrated co-occurrence of depression and anxiety (e.g., Maser & Cloninger, 1990). The relaxation sessions take place early in the CWD course because, being a relatively easy skill to learn, it provides participants with an initial success experience. Using the Pleasant Events Schedule, described earlier, the pleasant activity sessions focus on identifying, baselining, and increasing pleasant activities. The cognitive therapy sessions incorporate elements of interventions developed by Beck, Rush, Shaw & Emery (1979) and Ellis & Harper (1961) for identifying and challenging negative and irrational thoughts. Finally, the social skills sessions focus on assertion, planning more social activities, and strategies for making more friends.

The final two sessions of the CWD course focus on integrating the skills learned, on maintaining therapy gains, and on preventing relapse. Participants identify those skills that they found to be most effective for overcoming their depressed mood. Aided by the group leader, each participant develops a written, personalized "emergency plan," detailing the steps they will take to counteract feelings of depression, should they ever experience them again.

All sessions are highly structured, and make use of a text, *Control Your Depression* (Lewinsohn, Muñoz, Youngren & Zeiss, 1986) and a Participant Workbook (Brown & Lewinsohn, 1984). In addition, an Instructor's Manual (Lewinsohn et al., 1984) provides scripts, exercises and guidelines. Each session involves lecturing, review of homework assignments, discussion, and role playing. A 10-min break in the middle of each session permits participants to socialize and to practice the new skills they have learned. An important feature of the CWD course is that it is nonstigmatizing. Because it is presented and conducted as a class rather than as therapy, it avoids the usual client reluctance and resistance that may prevent many depressed individuals from seeking help. The course also represents a cost-effective, community-oriented approach to reach the great majority of depressives who do not make use of the services of clinics and mental health professionals. For a more detailed description of the CWD course, the reader is referred to Lewinsohn et al. (1984).

The efficacy of the CWD course has been demonstrated in several outcome studies. For example, Brown & Lewinsohn (1984), Steinmetz, Lewinsohn & Antonuccio (1983), and Hoberman, Lewinsohn & Tilson (1988) all found that the CWD course was more effective in the treatment of depression than was a wait-list control condition, and was as effective as individual behavior therapy. Interestingly, Hoberman and colleagues found that positive perceptions of group cohesiveness was a significant predictor of treatment outcome, attesting to the efficacy of the group format of this approach.

Extensions of the CWD Course to Different Populations

Adolescents. Modeled after the adult CWD course, the Adolescent Coping With Depression course (CWD-A; Clarke, Lewinsohn & Hops, 1990) consists of 16 2-h sessions over 7 weeks. The content of the CWD-A groups, while similar to the content of the adult CWD course, has been substantially simplified, with a greater emphasis on experiential learning, and fewer homework assignments. Adolescents (Clarke, Lewinsohn & Hops, 1990b) and their parents (Lewinsohn, Rohde, Hops & Clarke, 1991b) are provided with comprehensive participant workbooks consisting of homework assignments, forms, short handouts, and readings. These participant workbooks are closely integrated with the group sessions. In addition to the skill areas included in the adult CWD course, the CWD-A was expanded to incorporate the teaching of basic communications, negotiation, and conflict-resolution skills. The addition of communication skills was based on the assumptions that adolescence is a period in which many parent-child conflicts arise as teenagers increasingly assert their independence from their families, and that unsuccessful resolution of the conflicts leads to reciprocally punishing parent-child transactions. The specific negotiation and communication techniques were adapted from materials developed by Robin (e.g., Robin, 1979; Robin, Kent, O'Leary, Foster & Prinz, 1977; Robin & Weiss, 1980), Gottman (e.g., Gottman, Notarius, Gonso & Markman, 1976), and Alexander (e.g., Alexander & Parsons, 1973; Alexander, Barton, Schiavo & Parsons, 1976).

The CWD-A course is based on the premise that teaching adolescents new coping skills and strategies will allow them to counteract the putative causal factors that contribute to their depressive episode and deal more effectively with the problems posed by their environment. Treatment is intended to help adolescents overcome their depression and to enable them to effectively deal with future occurrences of the putative risk factors.

The underlying theoretical model of depression is the multi-factorial model proposed by Lewinsohn et al. (1985a). This model assumes that there are several putative risk and/or etiological factors which can contribute to the final outcome of depression, none of which by themselves are necessary or sufficient preconditions. Depression is hypothesized to be the result of multiple causal elements acting either in concert or in combination; the exact mix or combination of contributory factors differs in individual cases. Depression is seen as occurring within the person-environment context, with person and environmental variables in reciprocal and continuous interaction. The model assumes the existence of vulnerabilities (person characteristics which increase the probability of becoming depressed, such as depressotypic cognitions, living in a stressful and conflictual environments) and immunities (person characteristics such as effective coping, social and other skills, engagement in pleasant activities, high self-esteem), which reduce the probability of becoming depressed.

The model hypothesizes that the depressogenic process begins with a disruption of important adaptive behavior patterns. Undesirable life events, at the macro (major life events) and micro (daily hassles) levels, are good examples of events which can cause serious disruptions of behavior patterns that are important for the individual's everyday interactions with the environment. If such disruptions lead to increased aversive experience, they results in a negative shift of the quality of the person's life. The inability to reverse such disruptions is hypothesized to lead to dysphoria and to other cognitive (e.g., pessimism) and behavioral (e.g., passivity) manifestations.

The CWD-A was adapted from the adult version of the CWD course (Lewinsohn et al., 1984). The relevance of the CWD course for depressed adolescents is suggested by research indicating that depressed adolescents show a pattern of psychosocial problems which is very similar to that manifested by depressed adults (Lewinsohn, Roberts, Seeley, Rohde, Gotlib & Hops, 1994). Unique and important aspects of the course as a form of therapy include (a) its psycho-educational, nonstigmatizing nature, (b) its emphasis on skill training to promote control over one's moods and to enhance one's ability to cope with problematic situations, (c) the use of group activities and role-playing, and (d) its cost-effectiveness. In modifying the course for use with adolescents, the material has been simplified with a greater emphasis on experiential learning. Homework assignments have been shortened and in contrast to the adult CWD course no between-session reading assignments are required.

The CWD-A course includes 16 2-h sessions conducted over an eight-week period for groups of up to ten adolescents. Each participant receives a workbook which provides brief readings, short quizzes, structured learning tasks, and forms for the homework assignments for each session. At the end of each session, adolescents are given homework assignments which are reviewed at the beginning of the subsequent session. The intent is for the skills to be practiced outside the treatment setting thereby increasing the likelihood of generalization to everyday situations. While evaluated in a group format, the CWD-A can be used in individual therapy.

A parallel course for the parents of depressed adolescents (Lewinsohn, Rohde, Hops & Clarke, 1991b) is derived from the concepts that parents are an integral part of an adolescent's social system, and that unresolved parent-adolescent conflicts contribute to the onset, and to the maintenance of depressive episodes. The goals of the parent course are to help parents accelerate the learning of the adolescents' new skills with support and positive reinforcement and assist in the use of these skills in everyday situations. Parents meet with their therapist weekly for 2 h during which the skills being taught in the adolescent course are described to them. The parents are also taught the communication and problem-solving skills being taught to the adolescent. Two joint sessions are held during which the adolescents and the parents practice these skills on issues that are salient to each family. Workbooks have been developed for the parents to guide them through the sessions.

Components of the adolescent course. In the first session the group guidelines, the rationale for treatment, and the "social learning" view of depression (Lewinsohn et al., 1985) are presented. From the very beginning, the adolescents are taught to monitor their mood to provide a baseline and a method for demonstrating changes in mood as a result of learning new skills and engaging in activities. The remaining sessions focus on teaching the various skills. As shown in Figure 15.5, while specific skills are introduced in specific sessions, discussion and practice continue throughout to facilitate the acquisition of the behavior.

Increasing social skills. Training in social skills, a basic deficiency in many depressed individuals (e.g., Libet & Lewinsohn, 1973), is spread throughout the course to provide a foundation upon which to build other essential skills (e.g., communication). Included in social skills training are conversation techniques, planning social activities, and strategies for making friends.

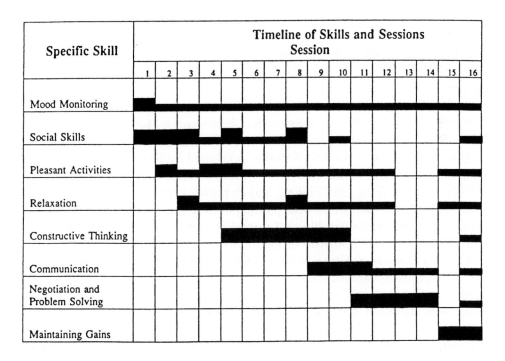

Figure 15.5. Timeline of skills and sessions. From Clarke et al. (1990).

Increasing pleasant activities. Sessions designed to increase pleasant activities are based on the assumption that relatively low rates of positive reinforcement (e.g., positive social interactions, participation in enjoyable activities) are critical antecedents of depressive episodes (see Lewinsohn, Biglan & Zeiss, 1976). Thus, depressed individuals are urged to increase pleasant activities. To accomplish this goal adolescents are taught basic self-change skills such as self-monitoring to establish a baseline, setting realistic goals, developing a plan and a contract for behavior change, and self-reinforcement for achieving the goals of the contract. The Pleasant Events Schedule (PES, MacPhillamy & Lewinsohn, 1982), a comprehensive list of potentially pleasant activities which has been adapted for use with adolescents, provides each participant with an individualized list of activities to be targeted for increase.

Decreasing anxiety. Relaxation training with the Jacobson (1929) procedure is provided. This technique requires participants to alternatively tense and relax major muscle groups throughout the body. A less conspicuous method is subsequently taught which does not require progressive tension and relaxation (Benson, 1975), for use in public settings such as classrooms. Relaxation training is provided because many depressed individuals are also anxious (e.g., Maser & Cloninger, 1990), which may reduce the potential enjoyability of many pleasant activities. Furthermore, tension and anxiety often interfere with performance in social situations. Relaxation skills are taught early in the course because they are easy to learn and thus provide participants with an early success experience.

Reducing depressogenic cognitions. Sessions focused on depressotypic cognitions are included on the assumption that depression is caused and maintained by negative or irrational cognitive schema. The course includes adapted and simplified elements of the interventions developed by Beck and his colleagues (e.g., Beck, Rush, Shaw & Emery, 1979), Ellis & Harper (1961), and Kranzler (1974) for identifying, challenging, and changing negative thoughts and irrational beliefs. Cartoon strips with popular characters which appeal to adolescents (e.g., Garfield the cat, Bloom County) are used to illustrate depressotypic negative thoughts and positive thoughts that may be used to counter them.

Conflict resolution. Six sessions involve teaching communication, negotiation, and conflict-resolution skills for use with parents and peers. Adolescent-parent conflict increases as adolescents assert their independence (Steinberg & Silverberg, 1986). Unsuccessful problem resolution paired with increased intrafamilial conflict may contribute to the occurrence of depression during this age group. The specific techniques used in the course were derived from techniques used in behavioral marital therapy (e.g., Gottman, 1979; Jacobson & Margolin, 1979; Weiss, Hops & Patterson, 1973) and their adaptations for use with parents and children (e.g., Forgatch, 1989; Robin & Foster, 1989). Communication training focuses on the acquisition of positive behaviors such as paraphrasing to verify the message, active responding, appropriate eye contact, and the deletion and correction of nonproductive behaviors such as accusations, interrupting, and put-downs. The adolescents are taught negotiation and problem-solving techniques such as defining the problem without criticism, brainstorming of alternative solutions, evaluating and mutually agreeing on a solution, and specifying the agreement with the inclusion of positive and negative consequences for compliance and noncompliance, respectively. All of these techniques are practiced during the two joint parent-adolescent sessions in which the adolescent and parent leaders participate as facilitators.

Planning for the future. The final two sessions focus on the integration of skills, anticipation of future problems, developing a life plan and goals, and the prevention of relapse. Aided by the group leader, each adolescent develops a written, personalized "emergency plan" detailing the steps they will take to counteract renewed feelings of depression in the future.

Three studies have examined the efficacy of the CWD-A course. The initial study (Clarke, 1985) was conducted with a sample of 21 adolescents. The results of this initial study were promising. In the second study, Lewinsohn, Clarke, Hops & Andrews (1990) randomly assigned 59 clinically depressed adolescents to one of three conditions: a) a cognitive-behavioral, psychoeducational group for adolescents only; b) an identical group for adolescents with their parents enrolled in a separate parent group; and c) a waitlist condition. Adolescents and their parents participated in extensive follow-up interviews at intake, post-treatment, and at 1, 6, 12 and 24 months post-treatment. The results of this study demonstrated that, compared to the waitlist subjects, treated subjects improved significantly on the depression measures. These gains were maintained at two years post-treatment.

A third test of the efficacy of the treatment program was conducted on 96 adolescents meeting DSM-III-R (APA, 1987) criteria for MDD or dysthymia (Lewinsohn, Clarke, Rohde, Hops & Seeley, 1996). For this trial, the course protocol was rewritten so that the components were laid out in a more systematic, hierarchical fashion, such that basic skill building occurred prior to more complex skills. For example, communication skills were established prior to conflict resolution skills because the former are basic prerequisites for successful negotiation that requires effective sending and receiving of messages and paraphrasing. The course was made more developmentally appropriate, adding components such as cartoons, etc. that would appeal to the adolescent. This study also examined the power of booster sessions to prevent relapse and maintain the adolescents' gains. The 96 adolescents were randomly assigned to similar treatment conditions as in the initial study.

The results were quite similar to that in the initial study. The two treatment groups showed significantly greater improvement than the waitlist control group, both in recovery rates and in decreases in BDI scores. Sixty-seven percent of the treated adolescents no longer met criteria at post-treatment compared to only 48% of the wait-list subjects. Further, there were no significant differences in recovery or relapse rates in the three follow-up conditions or by gender. By 12 months and 24 months post-treatment, 81.3% and 97.5% of the adolescents had recovered, respectively.

Components of the CWD for the elderly. Cognitive-behavioral interventions have been used in the treatment of older depressed adults for some time (e.g., Evans, Werkhoven & Fox, 1982; Hautzinger, 1992; Steuer & Hammen, 1983; Teri et al., 1991; Waller & Griffin, 1984; Yost, Beutler, Corbishley & Allender, 1986). In a recent review of this literature, Teri, Curtis, Gallagher-Thompson & Thompson (1994) concluded that all variants of cognitive-behavioral interventions (cognitive only, behavioral only, and combined) appear to be effective in decreasing depression, not only in physically healthy older adults, but in other less healthy subgroups, such as those with chronic disease and dementia. Moreover, treatment gains across all modalities appear to be maintained at follow-up.

The CWD Course has been modified for use with the elderly (Breckenridge, Zeiss, Breckenridge & Thompson, 1985; Hedlund & Thompson, 1980). Thompson, Gallagher, Nies & Epstein (1983) evaluated the modified course, the Life Satisfaction Course (LSC), in the treatment of depressed elderly persons. Six to eight participants per group met in 2-h weekly sessions over 6 weeks. Sessions focused on monitoring and rating mood, and on identifying pleasant activities and unpleasant events in their lives and learning how to record and monitor them on a daily basis. Participants were provided with exercises to help them experience the association between activity level and mood, and to gain some control over their mood through engagement in pleasant activities. In the fourth session self-reward techniques were taught, and each participant was instructed to identify one specific personal problem that appeared to be amenable to change. In the fifth session, a second reachable goal was identified. The sixth class focused on how to maintain and generalize progress attained in the course. The findings indicated that the approach was effective in reducing distress in elderly individuals. The participants who completed the course reported fewer symptoms of depression, less frequent negative thoughts and themselves and the future, and increased enjoyability and frequency of pleasant events in daily living. Studies on the application of cognitive-behavior therapy in depressed older adults have been reveiwed by Teri et al. (1994).

Components of the CWD for caregivers. Several researchers (Lovett, 1984; Lovett & Gallagher, 1988; Teri et al., 1994; Teri & Gallagher-Thompson, 1991) have developed variations of the CWD/LSC for use with caregivers of frail or demented elderly persons. This application is potentially important because such caregivers are at elevated risk of depression. The LSC for Caregivers includes 10 weekly 2-h sessions during which caregivers are taught to monitor their mood and pleasant activities, to identify pleasant activities in which they wish to engage more frequently, to set realistic, step-by-step goals for increasing their rate of these pleasant events, and to use the techniques of self-monitoring and self-reward to achieve these goals. Maximum enrolment in each group is limited to 10 caregivers, with two co-instructors. Preliminary results of this program indicate that the depression levels of both caregivers and nonclinically depressed elderly were reduced from pre-to post-treatment, while the waitlist control groups did not report any significant changes (Lovett & Gallagher, 1988).

Prevention of Depression

Finally, the CWD Course has also been adapted and examined as a means of preventing episodes of depression among individuals at elevated risk of developing such episodes. Muñoz, Ying, Armas, Chan & Gurza (1987) modified the CWD Course and employed it with a group known to be at high risk for future depressive disorders: low income, minority medical outpatients. Persons already experiencing an episode of depression were screened out of the study. Members of the experimental group were compared to two control groups: a no-intervention group and an information-only group who received a 40-min videotaped presentation of the ideas in the CWD Course. The results of this study indicated that participants receiving the CWD Course showed a significantly greater decrease in the level of depressive symptoms as measured by the BDI (Muñoz & Ying, 1993).

Manson and his colleagues (Manson, Mosely & Brenneman, 1988; Manson, 1988) have similarly modified the CWD for use as a prevention intervention with American Indians, age 45 and older. The course was modified to be culturally relevant to tribes from three Northwest reservations, and was simplified to accommodate the limitations imposed by the physical illnesses of the participants. Finally, Clarke et al. (1995) have modified the CWD Course to be offered to mildly depressed adolescents to help them avoid becoming more seriously depressed. The mildly depressed are an especially relevant target population for prevention because such individuals are known to be at elevated risk for developing a more serious episode of depression (Lewinsohn, Hoberman & Rosenbaum, 1988). Clarke et al. (1995) conducted a randomized trail of a school-based, group cognitive therapy prevention program to reduce the prospective incidence of unipolar affective disorders and symptomatology in a "targeted" sample of high-school adolescents with an elevated risk for future depression. The risk status for this study was based on a definition of demoralization, or sub-diagnostic levels of depressive symptoms, as proposed by Roberts (1987).

Ninth grade adolescents in three high schools were identified as potentially at-risk for depression through a two-stage procedure. The first screening stage consisted of a self-report depression scale, the Center for Epidemiological Studies-Depression Scale (CES-D), administered to an initial sampling frame of 1640 adolescents in high school health classes. Employing a CES-D cutoff score of 24 or greater as an operational definitions of demoralization (see Roberts, 1987; Roberts, Lewinsohn & Seeley, 1991), 222 adolescents in this sample were identified as potentially at-risk, and were subsequently interviewed in the second stage of the case-finding procedure; a confirmatory structured diagnostic interview, the Children's Schedule for Affective Disorders and Schizophrenia (K-SADS-E) along with the Longitudinal Interval Follow-up Evaluation (LIFE). This second case-finding stage determined which of the candidate adolescents were currently depressed (DSM-III-R major depression and/or dysthymia) and thus not candidates for prevention. Thirty-nine of the interviewed adolescents (17.6%) were found to meet criteria for current DSM-III-R unipolar affective disorder, and were referred for non-experimental treatment. The remaining sample of 183 adolescents wee not currently depressed but at risk for future depression due to their demoralized status. Eighty-two percent ($n = 150$) of these adolescents and parents accepted the invitation to enter the intervention phase of the study. While there were a few cases of anxiety or conduct disorder among these adolescents, the majority (>85%) had only subdiagnostic depressive symptoms with no current DSM-III-R diagnosis.

Across the three cohorts, the 150 demoralized adolescents were randomly assigned to either: (a) a 15-session, after-school, cognitive-behavioral group intervention ($n = 76$) or (b) a "usual care" control condition ($n = 74$). The active intervention was entitled the *"Coping With Stress"* Course, and consisted of fifteen 45-min sessions in which at-risk adolescents were taught cognitive therapy techniques to identify and challenge negative or irrational thoughts which might contribute to the development of future affective disorder. The prevention intervention was modified from cognitive therapy for depressed adults (Beck et al., 1979) and from the *Adolescent Coping with Depression Course* (Clarke, Lewinsohn & Hops, 1990a). Prevention groups were led by school psychologists and counselors with a minimum of a master's degree in either clinical, counseling, or school psychology.

In the "usual care" condition, adolescents were free to continue with any pre-existing intervention or to seek any new assistance during the study period. Adolescents enrolled in the active intervention were also permitted to continue any pre-existing treatment and/or to seek out any additional treatment, in order to equate extra-experimental intervention services across conditions.

Subject Retention. Starting with 150 subjects assigned to conditions, the study obtained retention rates of 125 at post-intervention, 120 at 6-month, and 109 at 12-month follow-up, for a total drop-out rate of 27.3% (41/150).

Lost and retained subjects were compared by experimental group on basic demographic and psychopathological variables, including intake CES-D depression scores; no main or interaction effects were detected for dropout.

The survival analysis method was used to compare the long-term outcome of the two groups, using LIFE interview weekly ratings to specify time to episode onset. The survival analysis method calculates successive interval-specific (conditional) probabilities of recovery, based on the number of subjects remaining at risk for the outcome event at successive points in time. Survival patterns for the two groups were compared at all points simultaneously using a summary Mantel-Cox chi-square test.

There were significantly fewer cases of either major depression (MDD) and/or dysthymia (Dy) in the experimental condition across the follow-up period (1-tailed Mantel-Cox $\chi^2 = 2.72$, $P < .05$). Total incidence rates of either MDD or Dy across the follow-up period were 25.7% (18/70) for the control group and 14.5% (8/55) for the experimental group.

Future Directions

In this chapter we have presented an overview of behavioral theories of depression, and have described a number of behavioral procedures for the assessment and treatment of this disorder. It is clear that there are a number of effective behavioral interventions for depression, virtually all of which attempt to alter the patient's interactions with the social environment in order to decrease level of depression. Interestingly, these programs are diverse, focusing variously on helping depressed patients to engage more frequently in pleasant activities, to sharpen their social skills, to become more accurate in self-monitoring, less stringent in self-evaluation, and more liberal in self-reinforcement, and to learn more effective coping and social problem-solving skills. Despite this diversity, it is apparent that a primary goal of these programs involves increasing the amount of positive reinforcement received by depressed patients; it is also evident that attainment of this goal typically leads to a significant reduction in depressive symptomatology.

We noted earlier that significant progress has been made in the evolution of behavioral theories of depression. Similar advances are also apparent with respect to both assessment of depression and behavioral interventions for this disorder. Nevertheless, there are a number of areas in which further work is clearly required. For example, while investigators have demonstrated the general efficacy of behavioral approaches to the treatment of depression, we know comparatively little about which components of these interventions are responsible for change in level of depression, or about what mechanisms are involved in the process of change.

As a related point, it is important to note that investigators have generally *not* found the outcomes of therapies for depression to be specific to the treatment under investigation. It appears, therefore, that regardless of the presumed specific target of intervention (e.g., cognitions, behavior, affect), they are all affected by treatment and, further, likely also affect each other in a reciprocal manner. With respect to behavioral interventions, this nonspecificity raises important questions about the role that changes in the target behaviors (e.g., increase in pleasant activities, improvement in social skills, increase in self-reinforcement) actually play in the amelioration of depression. It will be imperative to examine this issue more explicitly in future research. In this context, investigators should consider using causal modeling analyses in order to provide greater clarity concerning mechanisms of change in psychotherapy (cf. Hollon, DeRubeis & Evans, 1987).

Four final areas for future research warrant comment. First, although behavioral interventions have been demonstrated to be reasonably effective in alleviating depressive symptomatology by the end of treatment, it is now apparent that depression is a recurrent disorder (Belsher & Costello, 1988; Gonzales, Lewinsohn & Clarke, 1985). Indeed, Angst, Baastrup, Grof, Hippius, Poeldinger & Weiss, (1973) reported that the mean number of lifetime episodes in patients with unipolar depression is five to six. Given this high rate of relapse, it will be important for investigators to develop behavioral interventions that not only decrease levels of depression immediately following treatment, but that also prevent the recurrence of future episodes of depression. Preventing relapse through the use of booster sessions after the termination of treatment (e.g., Baker & Wilson, 1985) should become an area of active investigation. This additional focus on prevention (e.g., Muñoz et al., 1987, 1993) will be especially important in the treatment of depressed persons who are at increased risk for relapse: patients with a history of depressive episodes (Lewinsohn, Zeiss & Duncan, 1989), patients with secondary, as opposed to primary, depression (Keller, Shapiro, Lavori & Wolfe, 1982), and patients who live with hostile or critical relatives (Hooley & Teasdale, 1989).

Second, most investigators who have examined the efficacy of behavioral interventions with depression have selected patients with "pure depression" for inclusion in their studies. In particular, they have excluded depressed patients with other, comorbid, disorders. The results of recent studies indicate, however, that a substantial proportion of depressed individuals do present with comorbid psychiatric disorders, such as anxiety and substance abuse, and conduct disorder in children and adolescents (Maser & Cloninger, 1990; Lewinsohn, Rohde, Seeley & Hops, 1991; Rohde, Lewinsohn & Seeley, 1991). It is critical, therefore, that investigators examine the impact of comorbid disorders on the efficacy of behavioral interventions for depression.

Third, studies are needed to identify the distinguishing characteristics of those who benefit most and of those who benefit least from behavioral interventions. For example, five variables have consistently emerged as predictors of improvement for depressed participants in the Coping With Depression Course (Brown & Lewinsohn, 1979; Steinmetz et al., 1983; Teri & Lewinsohn, 1982): expected improvement, greater life satisfaction, lack of concurrent psychotherapy or antidepressive medication, high levels of perceived social support, and younger age. A number of writers have discussed the potential value of matching treatment components to patient characteristics in order to provide a problem-specific approach to the treatment of depression (e.g., Biglan & Dow, 1981; McLean, 1981). For example, McKnight, Nelson, Hayes & Jarrett (1984) compared the relative efficacy of treatments that were directly related to initial target areas, and found that depressed patients with social skill difficulties or irrational cognitions improved more after receiving specific interventions for those deficits than did patients who received interventions not related to their presenting problem areas. Some of the underlying theoretical issues in this area have been discussed recently by Rude and Rehm (1991), and we refer the interested reader to that article.

Finally, it is well documented in the depression literature that approximately twice as many women than men will experience this disorder (e.g., Nolen-Hoeksema, 1990; Weissman, Leaf, Holzer, Myers & Tischler, 1984). Despite the consistency of this finding, little attention has been given to the possibilities that depressed males and females may manifest different psychosocial problems, and that they may respond differentially to behavioral interventions. In one of the few studies to address this issue, Wilson (1982) reported that depressed male and female patients demonstrated comparable responses to behavioral treatments. Nevertheless, it is possible that the mechanisms responsible for change are different in males and females. For example, McGrath, Keita, Strickland & Russo (1990, p. 59) suggest that behavioral treatments may be effective with depressed women "because they teach women to confront and overcome the passive, dependent role they may have been taught since childhood and that may be feeding their depressions." It is not clear that this is, in fact, an active mechanism of behavioral interventions for depressed females, nor is it apparent that this process does not hold for males. Nevertheless, it is possible that behavioral treatment has a differential effect on depressed men and women. Certainly, this is an important area for further exploration. It is our hope that this chapter will serve as an impetus for such investigations.

References

Alexander, J. F., & Parsons, B. V. (1973). Short-term behavioral intervention with delinquent families: Impact on family process and recidivism. *Journal of Abnormal Psychology, 81,* 219–225.

Alexander, J. F., Barton, C., Schiavo, R. S., & Parsons, B. O. (1976). Systems-behavioral intervention with families of delinquents: Therapist characteristics, family behavior and outcome. *Journal of Consulting and Clinical Psychology, 44, 656–664.*

Angst, J., Baastrup, P. C., Grof, P., Hippius, H., Poeldinger, W., & Weiss, P. (1973). The course of monopolar depression and bipolar psychoses. *Psychiatrie, Neurologie et Neurochirurgie, 76, 246–254.*

Antonuccio, D. O., Ward, C. H., & Tearnan, B. H. (1989). The behavioral treatment of Unipolar depression in adult outpatients. In M. Hersen, R. M. Eisler & P. M. Miller (Eds.), *Progress in Behavior Modification*, Vol. 24. New York: Sage.

Baker, A. L., & Wilson, P. H. (1985). Cognitive-behavior therapy for depression: The effects of booster sessions on relapse. *Behavior Therapy, 16, 335–344.*

Beck, A. T., Rush, A. J., Shaw, B. F., & Emery, G. (1979). *Cognitive therapy of depression.* New York: Guilford Press.

Beck, A. T., Ward, C. H., Mendelson, M., Mock, J., & Erbaugh, J. (1961). An inventory for measuring depression. *Archives of General Psychiatry, 4, 561–571.*

Becker, R. E., & Heimberg, R. G. (1985). Social skills training approaches. In M. Hersen & A. S. Bellack (Eds.), *Handbook of clinical behavior therapy with adults.* New York: Plenum Press.

Becker, R. E., Heimberg, R. G., & Bellack, A. S. (1987). *Social skills training treatment for depression.* New York: Pergamon Press.

Bellack, A. S., Hersen, M., & Himmelhoch, J. (1981). Social skills training compared with pharmacotherapy and psychotherapy in the treatment of unipolar depression. *American Journal of Psychiatry, 138, 1562–1567.*

Bellack, A. S., Hersen, M., & Himmelhoch, J. (1983). A comparison of social skills training, pharmacotherapy, and psychotherapy for depression. *Behavior Research and Therapy, 21, 101–107.*

Belsher, G., & Costello, C. G. (1988). Relapse after recovery from unipolar depression: A critical review. *Psychological Bulletin, 104, 84–96.*

Benson, H. (1975). *The relaxation response.* New York: William Morrow.

Biglan, A., & Dow, M. G. (1981). Toward a "second generation" model of depression treatment: A problem specific approach. In L. P. Rehm (Ed.), *Behavior therapy for depression: Present status and future directions.* New York: Academic Press.

Biglan, A., Hops, H., Sherman, L., Friedman, L. S., Arthur, J., & Osteen, V. (1985). Problem-solving interactions of depressed women and their husbands. *Behavior Therapy, 16, 431–451.*

Blumberg, S. R., & Hokanson, J. E. (1983). The effects of another person's response style on interpersonal behavior in depression. *Journal of Abnormal Psychology, 92, 196–209.*

Breckenridge, J. S., Zeiss, A. M., Breckenridge, J., & Thompson, L. (1985). Behavioral group therapy with the elderly: A psychoeducational model. In D. Upper & S. Ross (Eds.), *Handbook of behavioral group therapy.* New York: Plenum Press.

Brown, R. A., & Lewinsohn, P. M. (1984a). *Participant workbook for the coping with depression course.* Eugene, OR: Castalia Press.

Brown, R. A., & Lewinsohn, P. M. (1984b). A psychoeducational approach to the treatment of depression: Comparison of group, individual, and minimal contact procedures. *Journal of Consulting and Clinical Psychology, 52, 774–783.*

Carey, M. P., Kelley, M. L., & Buss, R. R. (1986). Relationship of activity of depression in adolescents: Development of the Adolescent Activities Checklist. *Journal of Consulting and Clinical Psychology, 54, 320–322.*

Clarke, G. N. (1985). *A psychoeducational approach to the treatment of depressed adolescents.* University of Oregon, Unpublished manuscript.

Clarke, G. N., Lewinsohn, P. M., & Hops, H. (1990a). *Adolescent coping with depression course.* Eugene, OR: Castalia Press.

Clarke, G. N., Lewinsohn, P. M., & Hops, H. (1990b). *Student workbook: Adolescent coping with depression course.* Eugene, OR: Castalia Press.

Clarke, G. N., Hawkins, W., Murphy, M., Sheeber, L., Lewinsohn, P. M., & Seeley, J. R. (1995). Targeted prevention of unipolar depressive disorder in an at-risk sample of high school adolescents: A randomized trial of a group intervention. *Journal of the American Academy of Child and Adolescent Psychiatry, 34,* 312–321.

Cole, T. L., Kelley, M. L., & Carey, M. P. (1988). The adolescent activities checklist: Reliability, standardization data and factorial validity. *Journal of Abnormal Child Psychology, 16,* 475–484.

Costello, C. G. (1972). Depression: Loss of reinforcers or loss of reinforcer effectiveness? *Behavior Therapy, 3,* 240–247.

Coyne, J. C. (1976). Toward an interactional description of depression. *Psychiatry, 39,* 28–40.

Dykman, B. M., Horowitz, L. M., Abramson, L. &., & Usher, M. (1991). Schematic and situational determinants of depressed and nondepressed students' interpretation of feedback. *Journal of Abnormal Psychology, 100,* 45–55.

Eisler, R., Hersen, M., Miller, P., & Blanchard, E. (1975). Situational determinants of assertive behavior. *Journal of Consulting and Clinical Psychology, 43,* 330–340.

Ellis, A., Harper, R. A. (1961). *A guide to rational living.* Hollywood, CA: Wilshire Books.

Ellis, A., & Murphy, R. (1975). *A bibliography of articles and books on rational-emotive therapy and cognitive behavior therapy.* New York: Institute for Rational Living.

Evans, R. L., Werkhoven, W., & Fox, H. R. (1982). Treatment of social isolation and loneliness in a sample of visually impaired elderly persons. *Psychological Reports, 51,* 103–108.

Feldman, L., & Gotlib, I. H. (1993). Social dysfunction. In C. G. Costello (Ed.), *Symptoms of depression.* New York: Wiley.

Ferster, C. B. (1966). Animal behavior and mental illness. *Psychological Record, 16,* 345–356.

Forgatch, M. S. (1989). Patterns and outcome with family problem solving: The disrupting effect of negative emotions. *Journal of Marriage and the Family, 51,* 115–124.

Fuchs, C. Z., & Rehm, L. P. (1977). A self-control behavior therapy program for depression. *Journal of Consulting and Clinical Psychology, 45,* 206–215.

Glass, C. R., Merluzzi, T. V., Bierer, J. L., & Larsen, K. H. (1982). Cognitive assessment of social anxiety: Development and validation of a self-statement questionnaire. *Cognitive Therapy and Research, 6,* 37–55.

Goldfried, M. R., & Merbaum, M. (Eds.) (1973). *Behavior change through self-control.* New York: Holt, Rinehart & Winston.

Gonzales, L. R., Lewinsohn, P. M., & Clarke, G. N. (1985). Longitudinal follow-up of unipolar depressives: An investigation of predictors of relapse. *Journal of Consulting and Clinical Psychology, 33,* 461–469.

Goodman, S. H., & Brumley, H. E. (1990). Schizophrenic and depressed mothers: Relational deficits in parenting. *Developmental Psychology, 26,* 31–39.

Gordon, D., Burge, D., Hammen, C., Adrian, C., Jaenicke, C., & Hiroto, D. (1989). Observations of interactions of depressed women with their children. *American Journal of Psychiatry, 146,* 50–55.

Gotlib, I. H. (1982). Self-reinforcement and depression in interpersonal interaction: The role of performance level. *Journal of Abnormal Psychology, 91,* 3–13.

Gotlib, I. H., & Robinson, L. A. (1982). Responses to depressed individuals: Discrepancies between self-report and observer-rated behavior. *Journal of Abnormal Psychology, 91,* 231–240.

Gotlib, I. H., & Colby, C. A. (1987). *Treatment of depression: An interpersonal systems approach*. New York: Pergamon Press.

Gotlib, I. H., & Meltzer, S. J. (1987). Depression and the perception of social skill in dyadic interaction. *Cognitive Therapy and Research, 11*, 41–53.

Gotlib, I. H., & Hooley, J. M. (1988). Depression and marital distress: Current status and future directions. In S. Duck (Ed.), *Handbook of personal relationships*. Chichester: Wiley.

Gotlib, I. H., & Cane, D. B. (1989). Self-report assessment of depression and anxiety. In P. C. Kendall & D. Watson (Eds.), *Anxiety and depression: Distinctive and overlapping features*. Orlando, FL: Academic Press.

Gotlib, I. H., & Lee, C. M. (1990). Children of depressed mothers: A review and directions for future research. In C. D. McCann & N. S. Endler (Eds.), *Depression: New directions in theory, research, and practice*. Toronto: Wall & Thompson.

Gotlib, I. H., & Hammen, C. L. (1992). *Psychological aspects of depression: Toward a cognitive-interpersonal integration*. Chicester: Wiley.

Gotlib, I. H., & McCabe, S. B. (1992). An information-processing approach to the study of cognitive functioning in depression. In E. F. Walker, B. A. Cornblatt & R. H. Dworkin (Eds.), *Progress in experimental personality and psychopathology research*, Vol. 15. New York: Springer-Verlag.

Gotlib, I. H., & Beach, S. R. H. (1995). A marital/family discord model of depression: Implications for therapeutic intervention. In N. S. Jacobson & A. S. Gurman (Eds.), *Clinical handbook of marital therapy*. New York: Guilford Press.

Gotlib, I. H., Wallace, P. M., & Colby, C. A. (1990). Marital and family therapy for depression. In B. B. Wolman & G. Stricker (Eds.), *Depressive disorders: Facts, theories, and treatment methods*. New York: Wiley.

Gottman, J. M. (1979). *Marital interaction: Empirical investigations*. New York: Academic Press.

Gottman, J., Notarius, C., Gonso, J., & Markman, H. (1976). *A couple's guide to communication*. Champaign, IL: Research Press.

Hammen, C. (1991). *Depression runs in families: The social context of risk and resilience in children of depressed mothers*. New York: Springer-Verlag.

Hammen, C. L., & Glass, D. R. (1975). Depression, activity, and evaluation of reinforcement. *Journal of Abnormal Psychology, 84*, 718–721.

Hautzinger, M. (1992). Behavior therapy for depression in the elderly. *Verhaltenstherapie, 2*, 217–221.

Hautzinger, M., & deJong-Meyer, R. (1996). Depression. Zum Vergleich und zur Kombination psychologischer und medikament-ser Depressionsbehandlung. *Zeitschrift fur Klinische Psychologie (Themenheft), 25*, 76–160.

Hautzinger, M., Linden, M., & Hoffman, N. (1982). Distressed couples with and without a depressed partner: An analysis of their verbal interaction. *Journal of Behavior Therapy and Experimental Psychology, 13*, 307–314.

Hautzinger, M., Stark, W., & Treiber, R. (1992). *Kognitive Verhaltenstherapie bei Depressionen*, 2th edition. Weinheim, Germany: Psychologie Verlags Union.

Hedlund, B., & Thompson, L. W. (1980). *Teaching the elderly to control depression using an educational format*. Paper presented at the meeting of the American Psychological Association, Montreal, Canada.

Hersen, M., Bellack, A. S., Himmelhoch, J. M., & Thase, M. E. (1984). Effects of social skills training, amitriptyline, and psychotherapy in unipolar depressed women. *Behavior Therapy, 15*, 21–40.

Hinchliffe, M., Hooper, D., & Roberts, F. J. (1978). *The melancholy marriage*. New York: Wiley.

Hoberman, H. M., & Lewinsohn, P. M. (1985). The behavioral treatment of depression. In E. E.Beckham & W. R. Leber (Eds.), *Handbook of depression: Treatment, assessment, and research*. Homewood, IL: Dorsey.

Hoberman, H. M., Lewinsohn, P. M., & Tilson, M. (1988). Group treatment of depression: Individual predictors of outcome. *Journal of Consulting and Clinical Psychology, 56*, 393–398.

Hollon, S. D., DeRubeis, R. J., & Evans, M. D. (1987). Causal mediation of change in treatment for depression: Discriminating between nonspecificity and noncausality. *Psychological Bulletin, 102*, 139–149.

Hooley, J. M., & Teasdale, J. D. (1989). Predictors of relapse in unipolar depressives: Expressed emotion, marital distress, and perceived criticism. *Journal of Abnormal Psychology, 98*, 229–237.

Jacobson, E. (1929). *Progressive relaxation*. Chicago, IL: University of Chicago Press.

Jacobson, N. S., & Anderson, E. (1982). Interpersonal skills deficits and depression in college students: A sequential analysis of the timing of self-disclosures. *Behavior Therapy, 13*, 271–282.

Jacobson, N. S., Dobson, K., Fruzzetti, A. E., Schmaling, K. B., & Salusky, S. (1991). Marital therapy as a treatment for depression. *Journal of Consulting and Clinical Psychology, 59*, 547–557.

Jacobson, N. S., & Margolin, G. (1979). *Marital therapy: Strategies based on social learning and behavior exchange principals*. New York: Brunner/Mazel.

deJong-Meyer, R., Hautzinger, M., Rudolf, G. A. E., & Strauss, W. (1992). *Effectiveness of combined behavioral-cognitive and antidepressant treatment of inpatients and outpatients with endogenous depression*. Paper presented at the World Congress of Cognitive Therapy, Toronto.

Kanfer, F. H. (1977). The many faces of self-control, or behavior modification changes its focus. In R. B. Stuart (Ed.), *Behavioral self-management*. New York: Brunner/Mazel.

Keller, M. B., Shapiro, R. W., Lavori, P. W., & Wolfe, N. (1982). Recovery in major depressive disorder: Analysis with the life table and regression models. *Archives of General Psychiatry, 39*, 905–910.

Kowalik, D. L., & Gotlib, I. H. (1987). Depression and marital interaction: Concordance between intent and perception of communication. *Journal of Abnormal Psychology, 96*, 127–134.

Kranzler, G. (1974). *&ou can change how you feel*. Eugene, OR: RETC Press.

Lakein, A. (1973). *How to get control of your time and your life*. New York: New American Library.

Lewinsohn, P. M. (1974). A behavioral approach to depression. In R. J. Friedman & M. M. Katz (Eds.), *The psychology of depression: Contemporary theory and research*. New York: Wiley.

Lewinsohn, P. M., & Atwood, G. E. (1969). Depression: A clinical research approach. *Psychotherapy: Theory, Research, and Practice, 6*, 166–171.

Lewinsohn, P. M., & Amenson C. (1978). Some relations between pleasant and unpleasant mood-related events and depression. *Journal of Abnormal Psychology, 87*, 644–654.

Lewinsohn, P. M., & Clarke, G. N. (1986). *Pleasant events schedule for adolescents*. Unpublished manuscript.

Lewinsohn, P. M., & Rohde, P. (1987). Psychological measurement of depression: Overview and conclusions. In A. J. Marsella, R. M. A. Hirschfeld & M. M. Katz (Eds.), *The measurement of depression*. Chicester: Wiley.

Lewinsohn, P. M., & Shaw, D. A. (1969). Feedback about interpersonal behavior as an agent of behavior change: A case study in the treatment of depression. *Psychotherapy and Psychosomatics, 17,* 82–88.

Lewinsohn, P. M., & Schaffer, M. (1971). The use of home observations as an integral part of the treatment of depression: Preliminary report of case studies. *Journal of Consulting and Clinical Psychology, 37,* 87–94.

Lewinsohn, P. M., Weinstein, M., & Shaw, D. (1969). Depression: A clinical-research approach. In R. D. Rubin & C. M. Frank (Eds.), *Advances in behavior therapy.* New York: Academic Press.

Lewinsohn, P. M., Weinstein, M., & Alper, T. (1970). A behavioral approach to the group treatment of depressed persons: A methodological contribution. *Journal of Clinical Psychology, 26,* 525–532.

Lewinsohn, P. M., Lobitz, W. C., & Wilson, S. (1973). "Sensitivity" of depressed individuals to aversive stimuli. *Journal of Abnormal Psychology, 81,* 259–263.

Lewinsohn, P. M., Biglan, A., & Zeiss, A. M. (1976). Behavioral treatment of depression. In P. O. Davidson (Ed.), *The behavioral management of anxiety, depression and pain.* New York: Brunner/Mazel.

Lewinsohn, P. M., Youngren, M. A., & Grosscup, S. J. (1979). Reinforcement and depression. In R. A. Depue (Ed.), *The psychobiology of the depressive disorders: Implications for the effects of stress.* New York: Academic Press.

Lewinsohn, P. M., Mischel, W., Chaplin, C., & Barton, R. (1980a). Social competence and depression: The role of illusory self-perceptions. *Journal of Abnormal Psychology, 89,* 203–217.

Lewinsohn, P. M., Sullivan, J. M., & Grosscup, S. J. (1980b). Changing reinforcing events: An approach to the treatment of depression. *Psychotherapy: Theory, Research, and Practice, 47,* 322–334.

Lewinsohn, P. M., Sullivan, J. M., & Grosscup, S. J. (1982). Behavioral therapy: Clinical applications. In A. J. Rush (Ed.), *Short-term psychotherapies for the depressed patient.* New York: Guilford.

Lewinsohn, P. M., Antonuccio, D. O., Steinmetz, J. L., & Teri, L. (1984). *The Coping with Depression course: A psychoeducational intervention for unipolar depression.* Eugene, OR: Castalia.

Lewinsohn, P. M., Hoberman, H., Teri, L., & Hautzinger, M. (1985a). An integrative theory of depression. In S. Reiss & R. Bootzin (Eds.), *Theoretical issues in behavior therapy.* New York: Academic Press.

Lewinsohn, P. M., Mermelstein, R. M., Alexander, C., & MacPhillamy, D. J. (1985b). The unpleasant events schedule: A scale for the measurement of aversive events. *Journal of Clinical Psychology, 41,* 483–498.

Lewinsohn, P. M., Muñoz, R. F., Youngren, M. A., & Zeiss, A. M. (1986). *Control your depression* (2th edition). Englewood Cliffs, NJ: Prentice-Hall.

Lewinsohn, P. M., Hoberman, H., & Rosenbaum, M. (1988). A prospective study of risk factors for unipolar depression. *Journal of Abnormal Psychology, 97,* 251–264.

Lewinsohn, P. M., Zeiss, A. M., & Duncan, E. M. (1989). Probability of relapse after recovery from an episode of depression. *Journal of Abnormal Psychology, 98,* 107–115.

Lewinsohn, P. M., Clarke, G. N., Hops, H., & Andrews, J. (1990). Cognitive-behavioral treatment for depressed adolescents. *Behavior Therapy, 21,* 385–401.

Lewinsohn, P. M., Rohde, P., Hops H., & Clarke, G. N. (1991a). *Parent workbook: Adolescent coping with depression course.* Eugene, OR: Castalia Press.

Lewinsohn, P. M., Rohde, P., Hops H., & Clarke, G. N. (1991b). *Leader's manual for parent groups: Adolescent coping with depression course.* Eugene, OR: Castalia Press.

Lewinsohn, P. M., Rohde, P., Seeley, J. R., & Hops, H. (1991). Comorbidity of unipolar depression: I. Major depression with dysthymia. *Journal of Abnormal Psychology, 100,* 205–213.

Lewinsohn, P. M., Roberts, R. E., Seeley, J. R., Rohde, P., Gotlib, I. H., & Hops, H. (1994). Adolescent psychopathology: II. Psychosocial risk factors for depression. *Journal of Abnormal Psychology, 103,* 302–315.

Lewinsohn, P. M., Rohde, P., Hops H., & Seeley, J. R. (1996). A cognitive-behavioral approach to the treatment of adolescent depression. In E. Hibbs & P. Jensen (Eds.), *Psychosocial treatment research of child and adolescent disorders.* Washington, DC: American Psychological Association.

Liberman, R. P., & Raskin, D. E. (1971). Depression: A behavioral formulation. *Archives of General Psychiatry, 24,* 515–523.

Libet, J., & Lewinsohn, P. M. (1973). The concept of social skill with special reference to the behavior of depressed persons. *Journal of Consulting and Clinical Psychology, 40,* 304–312.

Lovett, S., & Gallagher, D. (1988). Psychoeducational interventions for family caregivers: Preliminary efficacy data. *Behavior Therapy, 19,* 321–330.

Lubin, B. (1967). *Manual for depression adjective check lists.* San Diego, CA: Educational and Industrial Testing Service.

MacPhillamy, D. J., & Lewinsohn, P. M. (1982). The Pleasant Events Schedule: Studies on reliability, validity, and scale intercorrelations. *Journal of Consulting and Clinical Psychology, 50,* 363–380.

Mahoney, M. J. (1974). *Cognition and behavior modification.* Cambridge, MA: Ballinger.

Mahoney, M. J., & Thoresen, C. E. (1974). *Self-control: Power to the person.* Monterey, CA: Brooks/Cole.

Manson, S. M. (1988). American Indian and Alaska Native mental health research. *The Journal of the National Center, 1,* 1–64.

Manson, S. M., Mosely, R. M., & Brenneman, D. L. (1988). *Physical illness, depression, and older American Indians: A preventive intervention trial.* Unpublished manuscript, Oregon Health Sciences University.

Maser, J. D., & Cloninger, C. R. (Eds.) (1990). *Comorbidity in anxiety and mood disorders.* Washington, DC: American Psychiatric Press.

McGrath, E., Keita, G. P., Strickland, B. R., & Russo, N. F. (Eds.) (1990). *Women and depression: Risk factors and treatment issues.* Washington, DC: American Psychological Association.

McKnight, D. L., Nelson, R. O., Hayes, S. C., & Jarrett, R. B. (1984). Importance of treating individually-assessed response classes in the amelioration of depression. *Behavior Therapy, 15,* 315–335.

McLean, P. (1976). Therapeutic decision-making in the behavioral treatment of depression. In P. O. Davidson (Ed.), *The behavioral management of anxiety, depression, and pain.* New York: Brunner/Mazel.

McLean, P. (1981). Remediation of skills and performance deficits in depression: Clinical steps and research findings. In J. Clarkin & H. Glazer (Eds.), *Behavioral and directive strategies.* New York: Garland.

McLean, P. D., & Hakstian, A. R. (1979). Clinical depression: Comparative efficacy of outpatient treatments. *Journal of Consulting and Clinical Psychology, 47,* 818–836.

McLean, P. D., & Hakstian, A. R. (1990). Relative endurance of unipolar depression treatment effects: Longitudinal follow-up. *Journal of Consulting and Clinical Psychology, 58,* 482–488.

Meichenbaum, D., & Turk, D. (1976). *The cognitive-behavioral management of anxiety, depression, and pain.* New York: Brunner/Mazel.

Mills, M., Puckering, C., Pound, A., & Cox, A. (1985). What is it about depressed mothers that influences their children's functioning? In J. E. Stevenson (Ed.), *Recent research in developmental psychopathology.* Oxford: Pergamon.

Muñoz, R. F., & Ying, Y. W. (Eds.) (1993). *The prevention of depression: Research and practice.* Baltimore, MD: The Johns Hopkins University Press.

Muñoz, R. F., Ying, Y. W., Armas, R., Chan, F., & Guzza, R. (1987). The San Francisco Depression Prevention Project: A randomized trial with medical outpatients. In R. F. Muñoz (Ed.), *Depression prevention: Research directions.* Washington DC: Hemisphere.

Nezu, A. M. (1986). Efficacy of a social problem-solving therapy approach for unipolar depression. *Journal of Consulting and Clinical Psychology, 54,* 196–202.

Nezu, A. M. (1987). A problem-solving formulation of depression: A literature review and proposal of a pluralistic model. *Clinical Psychology Review, 7,* 121–144.

Nezu, A. M., & Perri, M. G. (1989). Social problem-solving therapy for unipolar depression: An initial dismantling investigation. *Journal of Consulting and Clinical Psychology, 57,* 408–413.

Nezu, A. M., Nezu, C. M., & Perri, M. G. (1989). *Problem-solving therapy for depression: Theory, research, and clinical guidelines.* New York: Wiley.

Nolen-Hoeksema, S. (1990). *Sex differences in depression.* Stanford, CA: Stanford University Press.

Novaco, R. W. (1977). Stress inoculation: A cognitive therapy for anger and its application to a case of depression. *Journal of Consulting and Clinical Psychology, 45,* 600–608.

O'Leary, K. D., & Beach, S. R. H. (1990). Marital therapy: A viable treatment for depression. *American Journal of Psychiatry, 147,* 183–186.

O'Leary, K. D., Risso, L. P., & Beach, S. R. H. (1990). Attributions about the marital discord/depression link and therapy outcome. *Behavior Therapy, 21,* 413–422.

Radloff, L. S. (1977). The CES-D Scale: A new self-report depression scale for research in the general population. *Applied Psychological Measurement, 1,* 385–401.

Rehm, L. P. (1977). A self-control model of depression. *Behavior Therapy, 8,* 787–804.

Rehm, L. P. (1987). The measurement of behavioral aspects of depression. In A. J. Marsella, R. M. A. Hirschfeld & M. M. Katz (Eds.), *The measurement of depression.* Chichester: Wiley.

Rehm, L. P. (1990). Cognitive and behavioral theories. In B. B. Wolman & G. Stricker (Eds.), *Depressive disorders: Facts, theories, and treatment methods.* New York: Wiley.

Rehm, L. P., Fuchs, C. Z., Roth, D. M., Kornblith, S. J., & Romano, J. M. (1979). A comparison of self-control and assertion skills treatments of depression. *Behavior Therapy, 10,* 429–442.

Roberts, R. E. (1987). Epidemiologic issues in measuring preventive effects. In R. F. Muñoz (Ed.), *Depression prevention: Research directions.* Washington, DC: Hemisphere.

Roberts, R. E., Lewinsohn, P. M., & Seeley, J. R. (1991). Screening for adolescent depression: A comparison of depression scales. *Journal of the American Academy of Child and Adlescent Psychiatry, 30,* 58–66.

Robin, A. L. (1979). Problem-solving communication training: A behavioral approach to the treatment of parent-adolescent conflict. *American Journal of Family Therapy, 7,* 69–82.

Robin, A. L., & Weiss, J. G. (1980). Criterion-related validity of behavioural and self-report measures of problem-solving communication skills in distressed and nondistressed parent-adolescent dyads. *Behavioural Assessment, 2,* 339–352.

Robin, A. L., & Foster, S. L. (1989). *Negotiating parent-adolescent conflict: A behavioral family systems approach.* New York: Guilford.

Robin, A. L., Kent, R. N., O'Leary, K. D., Foster, S., & Prinz, R. J. (1977). An approach to teaching parents and adolescents problem solving skills: A preliminary reports. *Behavior Therapy, 8*, 639–643.

Rohde, P., Lewinsohn, P. M., & Seeley, J. R. (1991). Comorbidity of unipolar depression: Comorbidity with other mental disorders in adolescents and adults. *Journal of Abnormal Psychology, 100*, 214–222.

Rosen, G. M. (1977). *The relaxation response.* Englewood Cliffs, NJ: Prentice Hall.

Roth, D., Bielski, R., Jones, J., Parker, W., & Osborn, G. (1982). A comparison of self-control therapy and combined self-control therapy and antidepressant medication in the treatment of depression. *Behavior Therapy, 13*, 133–144.

Rude, S. S., & Rehm, L. P. (1991). Response to treatments for depression: The role of initial status on targeted cognitive and behavioral skills. *Clinical Psychology Review, 11*, 493–514.

Ruscher, S. M., & Gotlib, I. H. (1988). Marital interaction patterns of couples with and without a depressed partner. *Behavior Therapy, 19*, 455–470.

Sanchez, V. C., Lewinsohn, P. M., & Larson, D. W. (1980). Assertion training: Effectiveness in the treatment of depression. *Journal of Clinical Psychology, 36*, 526–529.

Skinner, B. F. (1953). *Science and human behavior.* New York: Free Press.

Steinberg, L., & Silverberg, S. (1986). The vicissitudes of autonomy in adolescence. *Child Development, 57*, 841–851.

Steinmetz, J. L., Lewinsohn, P. M., & Antonuccio, D. O. (1983). Prediction of individual outcome in a group intervention for depression. *Journal of Consulting and Clinical Psychology, 51*, 331–337.

Steuer, J. L., & Hammen, C. L. (1983). Cognitive-behavioral group therapy for the depressed elderly: Issues and adaptations. *Cognitive Therapy and Research, 7*, 285–296.

Teri, L., & Gallagher-Thompson, D. (1991). Cognitive-behavioral interventions for treatment of depression in Alzheimer's patients. *Gerontologist, 31*, 413–415.

Teri, L., & Lewinsohn, P. M. (1982). Modification of the pleasant and unpleasant events schedules for use with the elderly. *Journal of Consulting and Clinical Psychology, 50*, 444–445.

Teri, L., Logsdon, R. G., Wagner, A., & Uomoto, J. (1994a) The caregiver role in behavioral treatment of depression in dementia patients. In E. Light, B. Lebovitz & G. Niederehe (Eds.), *New directions in Alzheimer's disease and family stress.* New York: Springer.

Teri, L., Curtis, J., Gallagher-Thompson, D., & Thompson, L. (1994b). Cognitive-behavior therapy with depressed older adults. In L. S. Schneider, C. F. Reynolds, B. D. Lebovitz, & A. J. Friedhoff (Eds.), *Diagnosis and treatment of depression in late life.* Washington, DC: American Psychiatric Press.

Thompson, L. W., Gallagher, D., Nies, G., & Epstein, D. (1983). Evaluation of the effectiveness of professionals and non-professionals as instructors of "Coping with Depression" classes for elders. *The Gerontologist, 23(4)*, 390–396.

Thoresen, C. E., & Mahoney, M. J. (1974). *Behavioral self-control.* New York: Hold, Rinehart & Winston.

Waller, M., & Griffin, M. (1984). Group therapy for depressed elders. *Geriatric Nursing*, 309–311.

Watson, D. L., & Tharp, R. G. (1972). *Self-directed behavior: Self-modification for personal adjustment.* Belmont, CA: Wadsworth.

Weiss, R. L., Hops, H., & Patterson, G. R. (1973). A framework for conceptualizing marital conflict, a technology for altering it, some data for evaluating it. In L. A. Hamerlynck, L. C. Handy & E. J. Mash (Eds.), *Behavior change: Methodology, concepts, and practice.* Champaign, IL: Research Press.

Weissman, M. M., & Paykel, E. S. (1974). *The depressed woman: A study of social relationships.* Chicago, IL: University of Chicago Press.

Weissman, M. M., Prusoff, B. A., & Thompson, W. E. (1978). Social adjustment by self-report in a community sample and in psychiatric outpatients. *Journal of Nervous and Mental Disease, 166,* 317–326.

Weissman, M. M., Leaf, P. J., Holzer, C. E., Myers, J. K., & Tischler, G. L. (1984). The epidemiology of depression: An update on sex differences in rates. *Journal of Affective Disorders, 7,* 179–188.

Williams, J. G., Barlow, D. H., & Agras, W. S. (1972). Behavioral measurement of severe depression. *Archives of General Psychiatry, 27,* 330–333.

Wilson, P. H. (1982). Combined pharmacological and behavioral treatment of depression. *Behavior Research and Therapy, 20,* 173–184.

Yost, E., Beutler, L., Corbishley, M. A., & Allender, J. (1986). *Group cognitive therapy: A treatment approach for depressed older adults.* New York: Pergamon Press.

Youngren, M. A., & Lewinsohn, P. M. (1980). The functional relationship between depression and problematic behavior. *Journal of Abnormal Psychology, 89,* 333–341.

Youngren, M. A., Zeiss, A. M., & Lewinsohn, P. M. (1977). *Interpersonal Events Schedule.* Mimeograph, University of Oregon.

Zeiss, A. M., Lewinsohn, P. M., & Muñoz, R. F. (1979). Nonspecific improvement effects in depression using interpersonal, cognitive, and pleasant events focused treatments. *Journal of Consulting and Clinical Psychology, 47,* 427–439.

Further Reading

Gotlib, I. H., & Colby, C. A. (1987). *Treatment of depression: An interpersonal systems approach.* New York: Pergamon Press.

Hammen, C. (1997). *Depression.* East Sussex, UK: Psychology Press.

Hautzinger, M., Stark, W., Treiber, R. (1992). *Kognitive Verhaltenstherapie bei Depressionen,* 2th edition. Weinheim: Psychologie Verlags Union.

Lewinsohn, P. M., Antonuccio, D., Steinmetz, J., & Teri, L. (1984). *The coping with depression course.* Eugene, OR: Castalia.

Lewinsohn, P. M., Muñoz, R. F., Youngren, M. A., & Zeiss, A. M. (1986). *Control your depression.* Englewood Cliffs, NJ: Prentice Hall.

16

Cognitive Therapy and Depression

ARTHUR FREEMAN[a,b] and CAROL L. OSTER[b]

[a]Philadelphia College of Osteopathic Medicine, USA; [b]The Adler School of Professional Psychology, USA

Introduction

Depression is such a common human problem, across so many cultures, it has been called "the common cold of emotional disorders" The depressive response may be reactive to an external stressor (e.g. loss), or may be more characteristic of the person's pattern of responding to the world. It may occur as a single episode, or may be part of a recurrent series of episodes, and may occur in varying degrees of severity. However or whenever it occurs it can contribute to problems ranging from mild dysphoria or upset which impair an individual's functioning, to wishes and actions directed toward death by one's own hand. Giuven that depression appears to be a universal response it is nonetheless a response that can be limited in severity, decreased in frequency, and has less of a life-affecting or life-threatening impact.

Beck's cognitive therapy was developed specifically in response to the need to treat depression (Beck, 1967, 1976; Beck, Rush, Shaw & Emery, 1979), and thus the efficacy of cognitive therapy has been most studied in its application to depression.

Regardless of the variance in the manifestation of the symptoms and course of depression, the cognitive approach to the conceptualization and treatment of depression starts with the observation of common cognitive structures, processes, and products that appear to both mediate and moderate all instances of depression (Beck, 1991). This chapter describes the cognitive conceptualization of depression, and the treatment strategies that have evolved from this conceptualization.

The role of cognitions in depression, from the perspective of cognitive therapy, is often misinterpreted to be one of simple linear causality, i.e. negative cognitions (thoughts) cause depression. If this were so, the implications for treatment would be equally simple linear reasoning, i.e. positive thinking cures depression. Another common misunderstanding is that the cognitive perspective focuses exclusively on the internal processes in depression to the exclusion of contextual or external events. The implication of this misunderstanding would be that a person could be depression-resistant regardless of the severity of loss-related events in the person's life. The cognitive conceptualization of depression does not hold either of these simple causal models to be true. Rather, the cognitive perspective is a diathesis-stress model: that is, life events, thoughts, behaviors and moods are inextricably tied to each other in a reciprocal manner. Cognitions, behaviors, and moods all serve feedforward and feedback functions in a complex process of information processing, behavioral regulation, and motivation. Further, the cognitive perspective implicates early life events and learning in the creation of patterns of information processing called "schema." These schema may predispose persons to specific emotional vulnerabilities, and maintain emotional difficulties once behavioral, cognitive and mood patterns are initiated.

Cognition is likely to be related to mediation (vulnerability) and moderation (expression and maintenance) of depression. Two levels of cognition are viewed as influencing these processes. These two levels can be easily described as deep cognitions, and surface cognitions, respectively (Dobson & Shaw, 1986; Hollon & Bemis, 1981; Kwon & Oei, 1994).

Deep cognitions are seen as predisposing vulnerability factors that mediate the development of depression. Deep cognitions have been given a number of labels. These include schema, attitudes, basic assumptions, and core beliefs. Kwon and Oei (1994) describe this level of cognition as consisting of stable, cross-situational, and basic components of cognitive organization. These components develop in response to early life experiences, through both social and operant learning, and predate or accompany the first instance of depression. Schema may operate actively, determining a majority of the person's daily behavior, or may be latent, triggered by specific events. They may be compelling and hard to resist, or noncompelling and easily countered or resisted (Beck, Freeman et al., 1990; Freeman & Leaf, 1989).

The development of schema is a natural and necessary process. Schema are naive theories or hypotheses that guide the process by which a person organizes and structures information about the world. They guide the person's selection of information to attend to or seek, guide pattern search procedures, and provide "default values" when information is missing (Hollon & Garber, 1990). They affect not only information encoding, but also information retrieval processes. By directing the encoding and retrieval of information, they govern the person's interpretation of experience, or meaning-making. They are, in effect, a nexus for organizing information.

As the human brain works to process information, it compares, contrasts, creates categories, and arranges those categories in hierarchies or nested sets. These sets are not typically static and unchanging, nor are they unstable and fickle. If either of those were the case, learning could not occur. Instead, in the process of adaptation described by Piaget (1954) and Rosen (1985, 1989), incoming information is first compared with existing knowledge, categories and hierarchies. The person's first attempt to deal with internal or external stimuli is to ask, "What are you and where do you fit within my past experience/knowledge?" If enough similarities are found between the existing knowledge structures and the stimuli, the brain remains "equilibrated," with the information processing search procedures satisfied. The new event is assimilated into existing knowledge. However, if sufficient dissimilarities exist, knowledge structures and rules are altered to accommodate the contrasts that are detected. If the alterations are quite small, the individual may need to make only those minimal changes necessary for coping. If, on the other hand, the dissimilarities are broad, entirely new categories may be created based on what contexts are already in place, or new subsets of existing knowledge would be created.

Both the content of the knowledge base, and the learned and acquired rules that govern a person's information processing form the "apperceptive mass" that is, the assumptions that a person makes about the world that determine that individual's approach to new situations.

This process is not only normative, it is also efficient. A person cannot possibly attend to all of the available information that exists in even the simplest circumstance. Some information must be excluded. Other information must be arranged in order of priority and importance relative to decisions the person has to make in that situation. Under most circumstances, this efficient, global level of processing provides a "good enough" fit to guide the person's behavior, surface cognition, self-regulation, and mood. It is typically an adaptive process.

Cognitive Distortions

A number of things can, and do, go wrong, however. While all cognition is distorted by meaning-making processes and by the essential conservatism and efficiency of information processing, the cognition of depressed persons is distorted in ways that create distress and interfere with adaptive behavior. Schema that are resistant to change and accommodation make the person vulnerable to difficulties in adaptation. Schema are laid down early in life, in highly affectively charged situations, and reinforced often by credible and authoritative agents or agencies. They become potent in influencing the person's cognitions, behaviors and moods, when triggered by a life event that the person views as similar to the original event in some important way. Even if the similarity is inconsequential, the schema may be applied where it does not fit.

Because the schema directs the person's search strategies and meaning making (i.e., interpretive strategies), information inconsistent with the triggered schema may be ignored, or interpreted in a way that is not consistent with consensually validated interpretations. In addition, highly affectively charged schema may pre-empt more adaptive, possibly more logically derived schema, in what Beck terms a negative cognitive shift (Beck, 1991). The negative cognitive shift could be explained by primacy effects, and by state-dependent learning.

A schema may be erroneous to begin with. Even in the original situation, the meaning that a person attaches to an event may represent a misunderstanding, or an incomplete understanding, of cause and effect or of implications. Particularly when schema are acquired in early childhood (prior to age 7–8), the cognitive and experiential limitations of childhood would, even without any other problems occurring, ensure that some early schema that persist in adulthood would be immature and the basis for incorrect interpretations.

Adding to this is the impact of highly influential sources of interpretation, rule making, and meaning-making in childhood, the person's parents. The power of the parents, and the repeated exposure of the child to the parents' meaning-making, ensure that the parents' meaning making will strongly influence the child's. Even in seemingly benign situations, a parent's comment may have lasting impact on the person's view of self, world, and experience. The beliefs and attitudes that parents communicate to children are biased by the parent's life experience and learning. The schema may be part of a pattern of familial or cultural rules that may be nearly undetectable to the persons themselves. If the attitudes about world, self, and experience that the parents communicate to the person are extremely biased or very strongly affectively encoded, they may become what Young (1994) identifies as "early maladaptive schema".

Persons interpret their experiences in systematically biased ways. In order to sort experiences along one relevant dimension, other dimensional characteristics may be ignored for that moment. A number of processing errors that result (called cognitive distortions) have been identified (Beck et al., 1979; Burns, 1980; Freeman & Zaken-Greenburg, 1988). Five errors commonly made by depressed persons are arbitrary inference, personalization, selective abstraction, over-generalization, and magnification and minimization (Beck, 1976; Simon & Fleming, 1985). Each of these represents inappropriate application of existing schema, without the accommodation to unique aspects of experience that would bring about more adaptive emotional and behavioral responses. *Arbitrary inference* occurs when the person draws conclusions that are not consonant with objective evidence. A person who is depressed makes negative interpretations of events when neutral or positive ones would be more appropriate. For example, a 15 year old girl concluded that the persons who decorated her school locker were "targeting" her for punishment because they did not like her. However, decorating lockers was seen at that school as a sign of social favor. Two types of arbitrary inference are: (1) "mind reading", where the individual make the assumption that other people are looking down on her/him and is so convinced about this that s/he doesn't even bother to check it out ("S/he thinks I'm a bore"), and (2) the "fortune teller error", where the individual imagine that something bad is about to happen, and s/he takes this prediction as a fact even though it could be unrealistic ("I'll forget what to say. I'll become blank. I'll become embarrassed")

Personalization involves inappropriately attaching selfevaluative meanings to situations. A depressed person attributes failure and loss experiences to themselves, discounting factors attributable to the situation, or to others. The same 15 year old girl decided that a friend was getting harassing phone calls because a third person no longer liked her (the girl).

Selective abstraction occurs when a person overattends to schema-consistent information, and underattends to information inconsistent with those assumptions. It is an instance of confirmatory bias in information processing. In depression, the person seeks information consistent with their negative views of self, world, and future, and does not seek, perceive, or see as valid, information that contrasts with this view. A client viewed her son's difficulties in school as indicating that she was a failure as a mother. She did not spontaneously recall her son's competency in other matters, his compassion for others, and his confidence in himself despite his learning disability. When reminded of these, she did not see them as signs that she was a good mother, but rather as evidence of his resistance to her bad mothering.

Over-generalization involves applying conclusions appropriate to a specific instance to an entire class of experience based on perceived similarities. It is an instance of global reasoning. In depression, a person may state, "It's all ruined. My whole life is this way. Everyone has the same attitude." A client concluded that all people associated with a particular religion were child abusers, because of her experience with a few people.

Magnification and *minimization* occur when the person overattends to, and exaggerates the importance of, negative aspects of experience, and discounts or underestimates the relevance of positive experience. A client became depressed after every evaluation by students, attending more to the few critical comments than to the many appreciative comments students made.

Other cognitive distortions usually found in depressed people are:
a. *Dichotomous thinking* or "all-or-nothing" thinking, which refers to the tendency to place experiences in one of two opposite categories (i.e., "I'm a total success or otherwise I'm a total failure"). In describing him/herself, the patient selects the extreme negative categorization.

b. *Emotional reasoning,* where people take their emotions as evidence for the truth: "I feel like that, so it must be so" (i.e., I feel inadequate, so I am inadequate")

c. *Disqualifying the positive,* where some depressed individuals transform neutral or even positive experiences into negative ones (i.e., the compliment was undeserved"). In this manner, people can maintain a negative belief which is clearly unrealistic and inconsistent with their everyday experiences.

d. *Shoulds statements.* This refers to the individual who try to motivate her/himself with Shoulds and shouldn'ts, as if s/he had to be whipped and punished before s/he could be expected to do anything. "Oughts" and "musts" are also offenders. The emotional consequence is guilt.

e. *Externalization of self-worth* (i.e., "my worth depend on what others think of me")

f. *Perfectionism* (i.e., "I have to do everything perfectly or I will be criticized and become a failure")

g. The *control falacy* (i.e. "I must be able to control all the contingencies of my life")

h. The *comparison* (i.e., "I'm not so competent as my coworkers or supervisors")

Life Events and Schema

Schema determine which situations are judged to be relevant to the person, and which aspects of experience are important for decision-making. Persons are more likely to rely on past knowledge and behavior patterns (schema) in situations in which disconfirming information is not immediately present, when the situation is abstract rather than concrete, and when the situation is ambiguous (Beck et al., 1979; Beck, 1991; Kwon & Oei, 1994; Riskind, 1983). Depressed persons are more likely to negatively interpret situations with the above characteristics, particularly when the person sees the situation as relevant to their self-worth. In addition, negative events have greater impact on persons who have dysfunctional attitudes or schema (Stiles, 1990). Thus, when an event is most in need of critical analysis, the person may be less likely to accommodate, and more likely to attempt to assimilate the new situation into the existing repertoire of knowledge and responses. In the best of circumstances, this has adaptive purposes: a quick assessment of a strange situation, using old knowledge, may save one's life. It becomes problematic when the assessment discounts essential information that would call for a different response.

Assessing Schema

A person's rules for processing information, and the bias inherent in those rules, are not directly observable by others or reportable by the person. Although some measures of dysfunctional attitudes or basic assumptions exist, a limitation of many of them is that they rely on inventory- style self-report procedures. For example, the *Dysfunctional Attitudes Scale* (DAS; Weissman, 1979) has been criticized (Coyne & Gotlib, 1983; Segal, 1988) as potentially tapping surface cognitions rather than deep cognitions, and as being affected by social desirability. Hence, dysfunctional attitudes as measured by the DAS may be state dependent (Miranda & Persons, 1988). One reason that the DAS may access surface cognitions rather than core schema is that schema --at least dysfunctional schema --tend to be affectively encoded. In an emotionally neutral situation, more adaptive schema may predominate the person's report. Some measures correct for self-report bias by priming for affect by including vignettes describing life situations, about which subjects are asked to express or endorse attitudes (Barber & DeRubeis, 1992).

Regardless of the level of cognitions being tapped by existing instruments, research does support the connection between liability for depression and attitude, even as measured by the DAS (Thase, Simons, McGeary, Cahalane, Hughes, Harden & Friedman, 1992).

Surface Cognitions

Surface cognitions (or "automatic thoughts"), in contrast to deep cognitions, are relatively unstable, temporary, and situation-specific thoughts (Beck et al., 1979; Kwon & Oei, 1994). They arise quickly and automatically, and appear to be habitual or reflexive. They do not seem to be subject to conscious control by the person, and are uncritically accepted by the person, to whom they seem perfectly plausible. Most often the person is unaware of the fleeting thought, although they may be keenly aware of the emotion that precedes, accompanies, or follows it (Beck, 1991).

Unlike schema, which are relatively inaccessible to introspection, these automatic thoughts are accessible through introspection and self-report. They represent the conclusions drawn by the person on the basis of the information processing rules that they follow. That is, they are the products of the processes and structures that comprise the schema (Beck, 1963, 1967, 1976; Freeman, 1986). Because the rules about the way information is processed (schema) are biased by prior experience and learning, automatic thoughts tend to revolve around central themes; they tend to be repetitive in content and emotional tone.

A number of measures of automatic thoughts or surface cognitions exist, although not all of these instruments were designed with that construct in mind. These include the *Automatic Thoughts Questionnaire* (ATQ; Hollon & Kendall, 1980), the *Beck Depression Inventory* (BDI; Beck, Ward, Mendelson, Mock & Erbaugh, 1961), the *Beck Hopelessness Scale* (HS; Beck, Weissman, Lester & Trexler, 1974), the *Beck Anxiety Inventory* (BAI; Beck, Epstein, Brown & Steer, 1985), and others.

Automatic thoughts are most often assessed by directly asking the person about their thoughts. When the therapist or patient notes a change in affect, a simple probe, "What are you thinking right now?", interrupts the automatic processing and encourages the person to think about their thinking (metacognition) (Beck, 1991; Hollon & Garber, 1990).

Cognitive Triad

Not only do depressed persons process information in characteristically distorted ways, but the content of their thoughts is also characteristically negative and revolves around certain themes. These themes are thoughts about self, world or experience, and future. The affective tone is typically negative in both attribution (causal explanation after the fact) and expectancy (prediction). The attributions tend to be global ("It's just the way I am."), stable ("I've always been that way. It'll never change.", and internal ("There must be something wrong with me.") (Abramson, Seligman & Teasdale, 1978). The content in each area is evident in the person's overt and covert cognitions, and seen in the person's verbal and non-verbal behavior (Freeman, Pretzer, Fleming, & Simon, 1990). Although all persons have negative thoughts from time to time, in severely depressed persons, these thoughts are no longer peripheral, barely perceived, fleeting thoughts, but predominate their conscious awareness (Beck, 1991). In addition, the depressed individual does not believe that they have the right or ability to respond to these negative thoughts in a positive or adaptive manner. The negative thought stands "as stated", without response that may medicate or ameliorate the negative statement.

The three components of the cognitive triad (negative view of self, world/situation, future) are not assumed to equally contribute to a person's depression (Freeman et al., 1990). For example, negative views of the self and world were found in one study to be more common in depressed persons' thinking than were negative views of the future (Blackburn & Eunson, 1989). Negative views of the future are characteristic of the thinking of suicidal persons (Freeman & Reinecke, 1994; Salkovskis, Atha, & Storer, 1990). Negative views of the world are reported more often by persons who experience increased anger with depression (Blackburn & Eunson, 1989).

This variance in contribution of the components of the cognitive triad to the person's depression requires that the idiosyncratic combination of automatic thoughts that comprise the triad be collaboratively assessed. In this way, specific areas of concern to the person can be identified, and the therapy tailored to the person's idiographic needs.

The Integrative Model

Schema, automatic thoughts, and the distortions evident in them, combine to contribute both distally and proximally to the person's experience of depression. Schema, as distal structures and processes, result in a depressogenic style of global, internal, and stable negative attribution (Abramson et al., 1978). This style mediates the development of depression by creating a cognitive vulnerability that acts in concert with negative life events in a stress-diathesis model. In addition, schema contribute, with life events, to the development of negative cognitive content at the level of automatic thoughts.

Automatic thoughts in depressed persons are proximal events that cohere around negative attributions and expectations of self, world or experience, and future. At this level, cognitions operate in conjunction with negative life events, mood (distress) and behavior to maintain and moderate the expression of an existing depression.

Cognitive Therapy of Depression

The approach taken in cognitive therapy of depression is typically short-term. Clinical trials have generally included time periods of 12–20 weeks as a reasonable trial of cognitive therapy (Blackburn, Bishop, Glen, Whally, & Christie, 1981; Murphy, Simons, Wetzel & Lustman, 1984; Rush, Beck, Kovacs & Hollon, 1977; Thase, Simons, Cahalane, McGeary & Harden, 1991). In practice, the time period is adjusted to the particular circumstances of the person, including the co-occurrence of Axis I disorders (e.g. anxiety), Axis II disorders, or other psychological disorders, and the life events experienced or anticipated in the course of therapy. While most improvement is noted in the first weeks of therapy (for example, Berlin, Mann, & Grossman, 1991; Kavanagh & Wilson, 1989), relapse prevention may require sessions beyond sixteen or twenty (Shea, Elkin, Imber, Sotsky, Watkins, Collins, Pilkonis, Beckham, Glass, Dolan & Parloff, 1992; Thase et al., 1991, 1992).

Cognitive therapists are active and directive. The work is often of a psycho-educational nature. That is, the person may be actively taught skills, behaviors, or methods of altering cognitions. The therapist takes a proactive stance to setting agendas or determining the direction of the work. The therapist actively structures the therapy. However, there are limits to the directiveness of the therapist. Cognitive therapy is a collaborative model. Since a major goal is for the person to acquire the ability to address cognitions and behaviors on their own, the course of therapy must begin with, and see an increase in, the ability of the person to set the direction, focus, and pace of the therapy. The collaborative approach increases the person's sense of efficacy, and counters negative attributions about self, world and future.

Non-specific factors impact on the success of cognitive therapy, as they do on all other therapies (Frank, 1985). These include the development of a good working relationship, the empathy expressed by the therapist, the person's experience of universality, and the person's experience of hope within the therapy. Cognitive therapy of depression is a skill building or coping model, rather than a cure model. Schema are not eradicated, but modified. Automatic thoughts are not stopped, but managed and countered. The therapist helps the person to develop a range of cognitive and behavioral coping strategies for present and future exigencies of life, and thus to alter mood. The person's ability to control negative cognitions, and the person's perception of self-efficacy in regard to this at termination, predict a sustained response to cognitive therapy (Kavanagh & Wilson, 1989).

The primary targets of cognitive therapy for depression are both the negative automatic thoughts that maintain the depression, and the schema (assumptions and beliefs) that predispose the person to depression in the first place (Kwon & Oei, 1994). The major focus is to help persons to become aware of and to evaluate the ways in which they construct the meaning of their experiences, and to experiment with new ways of responding, both cognitively and behaviorally. Although cognition is a major focus of therapy, cognitive therapists also utilize a broad range of behavioral approaches, to meet both cognitive and behavioral ends (Freeman et al. 1990; Stravynski & Greenberg, 1992).

Altering dysfunctional cognitions, at both the deep and surface levels, appears to follow a typical pattern, whether client-led or therapist-led. A task analysis conducted by Berlin, Mann & Grossman (1991) identified three sequential requirements:

1. coming to view cognitive-emotional appraisals as hypothetical or subjective, and therefore worthy of testing, investigation or examination;
2. generating alternative appraisals, and using these as a basis for action and further thought, or as a basis for pattern-search or schema identification; and
3. generating more adaptive, useful, or accurate core assumptions, and using them as a basis for cognition and action.

Assessment and Socialization to the Cognitive Therapy Model

Both the course of therapy as a whole and a single session of cognitive therapy follow a specific sequence of events. The first tasks in cognitive therapy are assessment of the person and their circumstances, conceptualization of the problem according to the cognitive model, socializing the person to the cognitive model, and identifying goals and appropriate interventions consonant with the model. These tasks overlap and are intertwined with each other. Assessment is often, and should be, therapeutic. Socializing a person to the therapy model is an intervention that in itself may produce significant change, and that feeds back to assessment and conceptualization.

Preparation of the person for therapy must take into account the depressotypic information processing of the person, including the person's typical distortions. The low self-efficacy of the depressed person may lead them to expect that nothing that they can do will contribute to relief, and that any relief must come from others. At the same time, they may attribute any failure to themselves (internal), to the permanence of their mood (stable), and to their entire character (global). They may expect total, automatic, and immediate relief, and define anything less as failure (Abramson et al., 1978).

A structured, educational preparation for cognitive therapy can positively affect a person's ability to engage in cognitive therapy, and can improve the outcome of therapy. Preparation may be through the therapist's didactic explanations, through reading brochures or books (Burns, 1980; Freeman & DeWolf, 1989), or through video (Schotte, Maes, Benton, Vandenbossche & Cosyns, 1993). The severity of the person's depression, as measured by the *Beck Depression Inventory,* impacts negatively on the perceived helpfulness of preparatory procedures, as would be predicted by the model. Patients report that the most helpful aspects of preparation are explanations of the symptoms, causes and therapy of depression, and examples of the thoughts, actions and feelings common to depression (Schotte et al., 1993).

Cognitive assessment of the depressed person includes a number of measures in addition to the usual formal and informal assessment procedures. Specific attention is paid to the person's triadic view of self, world and future; the distortions evident in their attributional and expectancy style; and to the developmental history of the person's schema. It should be noted that the assessment is not intended to help therapist or patient label the person or their style, but to determine points of intervention with the potential for change, and methods of initiating the desired change.

Life events that may have triggered the current episode of depression are investigated. The presence of social supports is related to relapse and recurrence prevention. Marital conflict or support are strongly related to relapse or recovery for married persons. Mediators, moderators, precipitants and consequences of the thoughts, behaviors and moods that the person reports are all investigated.

From the assessment, a conceptualization of the person's depression is developed. The process of developing a conceptualization follows the steps in observation, hypothesis formation, and hypothesis testing that we ask the person to follow in the therapy itself.

1. What is the problem? How does it affect the person? The person and therapist develop an exhaustive problem list. It is assumed that the schema that create the vulnerability for depression will manifest in a number of cognitions, behaviors and emotions that affect the person's life in many ways. Examining the range of problems may point to the underlying schema.

2. How does the person explain the problem to him or herself? What is their causal model? What are their attributions and expectancies regarding their depression? These relate to the cognitive structures and processes that are assumed to create vulnerability to depression (schema), and that affect its expression (schema and automatic thoughts).

3. How does the interaction of the person's cognition, behavior, and life events result in depression? The sources of stress and support in the environment, and the person's response to or use of them are explored. What explanations other than the one the person holds might account for these connections?

4. What evidence is there for the person's model, and for any other models or hypotheses? How are the person's cognitions, behaviors and environment maintaining the depression?

5. How did the person come to think and behave the way they do? The therapist and person construct a hypothesis about how the person's cognitive biases and distortions developed -- typically by examining the person's childhood experiences related to schema. This is a search for antecedents and original stimulus-response connections and social learning episodes.

6. How would this hypothesis explain current and past events? What predictions could be made about the ways that the person's schema and automatic thoughts will be evident in, and will affect, the person's feelings and behavior within and outside of the therapy? What would be the evidence?

7. If the hypothesis is correct, what does that suggest, in terms of intervention? (Persons, 1989).

The therapist and the person may have different theories or models of the person's depression. The goal is not to convince the person of the correctness of the therapist's model, but to help them to be aware of their model as a theory or hypothesis about self, world, and future; that theories and models can be assessed for goodness of fit with information and experience; and that models can be revised when the fit is not good enough or useful. That is, the goal is to help them to distance themselves from their model in order to evaluate it. This is, in fact, the primary goal of the first stage of therapy.

Structure of a Typical Session

A typical session of cognitive therapy begins with agenda setting. A depressed person often has difficulty organizing themselves in order to problem solve. By collaboratively setting an agenda, the therapist models a problem-solving approach. A typical agenda might include:

1. Review of any weekly assessments the person fills out prior to the session, such as the BDI, the BAI, and other scales. This allows specific issues to be put on the day's agenda.
2. A brief overview of the weeks interactions and problems. The person can be asked to recount specifics of the week's events, including the reaction to the last session.
3. A review of homework, what worked, what was learned, what problems were encountered, and the emotions, behaviors and cognitions that attended the homework.
4. A specific problem focus for the session. Priorities are determined collaboratively, according to both client preference and consonance with the model. This might involve identifying and questioning automatic thoughts related to an event of the week, skill-building, hypothesis testing, and so forth. This points out the need for further information, or next steps in problem-solving, and thus directs attention to the next "homework" that needs to be done.
5. A wrap-up and review of the session, and feedback to the therapist. Time is always left before the close of the session for the person to be asked to review and outline what he or she has gotten from the session. Goals and accomplishments of the session re identified, and homework for the next session is reviewed and tied to goals. The person is asked for their response to the session. This gives the session closure and solidifies gains made.

Early Sessions

A number of factors affect the treatment plan early in therapy. The severity of the depression, as assessed by the BDI or the *Hamilton Rating Scale for Depression* (HSRD; Hamilton, 1960), and the *Hopelessness Scale,* may indicate the need for medication. A number of studies suggest that more severely depressed persons respond better and more rapidly to cognitive therapy with pharmacotherapy than to cognitive therapy alone (Bowers, 1990; Shea et al., 1992). In general, the more severely depressed the person is, the greater the need for pharmacological assessment, and the more behavioral and concrete the initial interventions need to be.

In general, initial interventions are aimed at helping the person to interrupt automatic information processing, which contains the dysfunctional, habitual and uncritically accepted negative thoughts and behaviors, and to increase deliberate information processing. The therapist teaches the person to notice, catch and interrupt automatic thoughts (Beck et al., 1979; Freeman et al., 1990). This is most often done through simple questioning, and through some form of the *Daily Thought Record* (DTR) (see Table 16.1). The use of the DTR is taught step by step, practiced in sessions, and then used as homework. The DTR helps to obtain examples of the person's automatic thoughts in vivo to use for assessment, encourage the person's independent metacognition (thinking about their thinking), increase the person's self-efficacy and hope, facilitate generalization and transfer of learning, and decrease attendant anxiety through distraction.

The DTR is not implemented completely in the first session(s) in which it is introduced, but as the person is able and develops the need. The DTR may be tailored to individual situation and person characteristics. We routinely "discover" the format of the DTR collaboratively with the person by using guided discovery, asking the person what would be worth knowing and what information might be useful next. Further, we alter the column headings for specific problems, or for children or adolescents. The basic goals and format (situation, thoughts, behaviors) are constant, however.

Other early interventions are similarly aimed at assessment and hypothesis formation, encouraging movement, distraction, and interrupting automatic processing. For example, more severely depressed persons are asked to complete an *activity schedule*. The person keeps track of their activities over the course of a week, several days, or one day. Their perception that, "I just can't seem to get anything done," is an example of low self-efficacy, negative expectations, minimizing the positive and maximizing the negative. Activity scheduling counters these by allowing the person and therapist to examine what the person has in fact done over the course of several days. Further, the activity schedule identifies the frequency of reinforcing or rewarding activities.

The activity schedule is also used to schedule tasks, to increase self-efficacy and counter hopelessness, to break down large tasks into small steps, and to counter all-or- nothing behavior and thought patterns. Pleasant activities can be scheduled, to increase reinforcement. Depressed individuals have difficulty identifying alternatives. Their recall is mood-congruent (Bradley & Matthews, 1988; Gotlib, 1981; Pace & Dixon, 1993). They often have difficulty identifying pleasant activities they have engaged in. It becomes important for the therapist to assess the person's potential for pleasure and range of activities, and to cue the person's recall or creation of pleasant alternatives that can be used as self-reinforcers.

Table 16.1. Self-monitoring to identifying dysfunctional thoughts

Daily Record of Dysfunctional Thoughts

Date	Situation	Emotion(s)	Automatic thought(s)	Cognitive distortion(s)	Rational response(s)	Outcome
	1. Briefly describe the actual event leading to unpleasant emotion, or 2. Stream of thoughts, memory, leading to the unpleasant emotion	1. Specify sad, angry, anxious, etc. 2. Rate intensity of emotion, 1 to 100	1. Write the automatic thought(s) that preceded the emotion(s) 2. Rate belief in the automatic thought(s), from 0 to 100%	1. Identify the distortion(s) present in each automatic thought 2. In what way I'm personalizing, selectively abstracting, minimizing, etc.?	1. Write rational response(s) to the automatic thought(s) 2. Rate belief in the rational response(s), from 0 to 100%	1. Rerate belief in the automatic thought(s), from 0 to 100% 2. Specify and rate subsequent emotion(s), 0–100

The activity schedule can later include pleasure and mastery ratings. Although this is often listed as a behavioral technique, the purpose of such ratings from the cognitive therapy perspective is to affect expectancies. The person is asked to make predictions about their ability to cope with and enjoy anticipated activities or events. This assesses the person's negative expectancies. Depressed persons typically overestimate the difficulty of the task, and underestimate both their ability to cope, and the potential for pleasure.

After the scheduled event takes place, the person is asked to re-rate their mastery of and pleasure in the task or event. The difference between expectancy and experience demonstrates the effect of cognition on behavior and mood. The activity being rated is often one that the person would have withdrawn from or avoided, due to negative predictions. Since most often the person's mastery and pleasure is greater than anticipated, the person is encouraged that "feelings are not reality", and the decision to act in a certain way is removed one step from affectively based automatic processing.

Through these records and examinations of the person's thinking and behaving between and within sessions, patterns in thought and behavior are sought, and brought to light, in accord with the integrative cognitive model.

Changes in affect within the session are cues to probe for automatic thoughts, asking, "What are you thinking right now?" The patterns in content, stimulus, and behavioral or emotional consequence (The ABC model or S-O-R model) are identified.

Case A. A 35 year old woman became tearful, depressed and anxious every time her mother called her. The mother had been critical and abusive when the client was a child. The client's mother would slap, pinch, and berate her grown daughter in public for any perceived deficiency. The mother's phone calls (antecedent) always resulted in the client's self-deprecating and suicidal thoughts. These represented both automatic thoughts ("I can't stand this. I'd be better off dead.") and core beliefs ("I'm no good. What's the use? It'll never be any better. It's my fault."). She responded with severe withdrawal and increased dependence on her husband (consequence).

Case B. A 10 year old boy identified any school performance less than perfection (antecedent) as failure and as evidence of his lack of worth (core belief about the basis of worth). He became despondent and angry, and withdrew into detailed fantasies revolving around themes of death and immortality (consequence).

Specific techniques such as the *downward arrow technique* (Burns, 1980), are used early in therapy to bring into awareness the person's meaning-making processes and underlying assumptions. The downward arrow technique involves asking the person a series of questions regarding the meaning and causal attributions of their thoughts or experiences: "And what would that mean?...."

And if that were so, what would that imply? And if that were the case, then what?"

Clarifying idiosyncratic meaning also involves making the reasoning and meaning-making of the person explicit. The therapist interrupts the client's use of global words and generalizations, and asks the person to make their terms specific and descriptive. The person is encouraged and helped to clarify words expressing absolutes, such as "always" and "never", or global categories of persons, such as "everyone" or "they", to break down global thinking.

Both techniques encourage the person to make explicit their associational chain and their causal reasoning. They expose the person's model or hypothesis, and encourage the person to be metacognitive: to think and wonder about their meaning-making process. Although it is likely possible to change schema purely through experiential or behavioral means, cognitive distancing from core assumptions and viewing them as subjective and hypothetical rather than veridical is assumed by cognitive therapy to make the change process easier (Meichenbaum & Turk, 1987).

Another intervention often used by cognitive therapists early in therapy is *labeling*, and helping the client to label, their cognitive distortions. Various lists of distortions, definitions, and examples exist (Burns, 1980; Freeman & Zaken-Greenburg, 1988). The purpose of labeling distortions is not to diagnose the person or their thinking, but to point out patterns or bias in the person's information seeking and interpretation, to interrupt automatic processing, and to give the person a tool for thinking about their thinking so that information processing becomes temporarily more deliberate. The triple-column technique (see Table 16.2) is used to identify the cognitive distortion and to propose a more rational response.

The first phase of therapy brings to light the person's explanatory model (schema, core beliefs, attributional style), the biases in their information search and sort habits, and the ways in which cognition, behavior, life events and mood are related for the person. Although a complicated stage, it is usually accomplished in relatively short order. Making the person's heuristic process apparent is itself a therapeutic experience for persons, and results in symptom relief and change. In fact, the biggest drop in self-reported symptoms of depression is routinely identified as occurring in the first 4 weeks of cognitive therapy (Berlin, Mann & Grossman, 1991).

Middle Phase of Therapy

The focus in the second phase of therapy is to generate, test, and practice alternative behaviors, attributions, expectancies, and hypotheses. That is, the goal is to modify maladaptive automatic thoughts and behavior patterns, and their underlying schema. This requires that the person become consciously

Table 16. 2. The Triple-Column Technique Used to Identify Cognitive Distortions and Substitute Automatic Negative Thoughts With More Objective Rational Thoughts

Negative automatic thoughts	Cognitive distortion	Rational response
Problems always arise when I'm in a hurry	Personalization	Problems can arise any moment
If I go to the party terrible consequences will follow	Catastrophization	Nothing terrible must happen. Simply I will try to enjoy it
I never do anything right	Overgeneralization	I do a lot of things right
People should be nice with me	Shoulds statements	I would like they to be nice with me, but they are free to behave
It was luck. It doesn't count	Disqualifying the positive	It was due to my effort. Good!

aware, on an ongoing basis, of their information processing and meaning-making activities (Hollon & Garber, 1990). Creating this level of awareness is akin to asking a person to alter the way they walk, to create a new way of carrying themselves physically. It is at best awkward, and usually uncomfortable. Self-reported symptoms of depression in the middle phase may fluctuate (Berlin, Mann & Grossman, 1991).

We often use *metaphor* to explain and predict this experience for persons. When a person first learns to drive a car, the person engages in frequent overt self-instruction. As driving is mastered, overt self-talk fades and becomes intermittent. Ultimately, driving is an automatic process that requires little thought or conscious decision-making. However, if the car acts up, there is an accident, or the weather turns foul, self-examination and self-talk reappears. Altering automatic thoughts and schema requires overt self-instruction and metacognition. Predicting this experience and the discomfort that accompanies it is a paradoxical technique aimed at normalizing the experience for the person, and at alleviating secondary distress.

Generating, testing, and practicing alternative attributions, expectancies, and behaviors is accomplished using a variety of interventions. Responses to automatic thoughts and schema fall into categories designed to interrupt automatic processing, increase metacognition, improve problem solving, and redistribute attribution.

In the middle stage of therapy, the patient is taught to identify, combat or countering automatic thoughts, first in retrospect, and then as they arise in vivo. When automatic thoughts are noticed, caught, and interrupted (first in sessions, then as homework) the person is taught to "argue the point". Automatic thoughts are countered by asking what the evidence is for and against their attribution or expectancy; by countering with an alternative hypothesis and examining the evidence for and against the alternative; or by stating the attribution as specific versus global, situational versus internal, and temporary versus stable.

However, a persistence in this line of guided discovery often results in the person's experience of some strong emotion. This can signify that the person has arrived at a statement of a core belief, usually relevant to their perception of self. This is an optimum moment for intervention: the affectively-coded, state-dependent learning and the *state* are both activated. With the activation of the state in which the original learning was encoded, the opportunity exists to create a new schema inconsistent with the original schema, or to significantly modify the original schema. Alternative explanations, attributions, expectancies that are discovered or provided at this moment have maximum impact. The original schema may be rendered conditional rather than absolute. Examining alternatives or generating options of thought, affect, and behavior involves considering the existence of, and then exploring, other possible views or explanations of the situations to which the person attends. Both Socratic questioning ("I wonder what other explanations you have considered?") and Stochastic questioning ("Could another explanation be that....") are used in helping the person to develop a list of alternatives. Listing alternatives breaks down the all-or-nothing thinking characteristic of depressed persons, initiates reattribution, and interrupts premature termination of data-search routines.

The person is asked to investigate and evaluate their thoughts regarding their attributions and expectancies. It is important to ask the person to consider both the evidence against and the evidence for their own hypotheses. In addition, questioning evidence for and against alternative models, even if they appear to the therapist to be clearly more adaptive, is important.

Demanding immediate or hasty abandonment of the person's causal model, or immediate allegiance to an alternative explanation, are likely to result in failure. The person needs to explore and consider the social, emotional, personal, and behavioral consequences of altering their causal model (Berlin, Mann & Grossman, 1993). Schema become defining characteristics of the person, and are held to firmly because they become the very basis on which the person predicates important as well as trivial decisions. Giving up long-held attributions can alter the person's very sense of identity. Further, one cannot give up a dysfunctional hypothesis or schema until an equal or better working model is proposed and accepted.

Decatastrophizing is used when the person predicts strongly negative consequences for events, and attributes little power to themselves for coping. It is a method of countering negative expectancies. The focus in decatastrophizing is on prediction of the future. The person is asked, "What would happen then? And then what would you do?" If the focus is kept on coping behavior, rather than on the meaning the person attributes to the event, the person will often arrive at a conclusion that they can ultimately cope.

Case C. A client became depressed when she and her husband experienced financial problems. Her automatic thoughts included, "We're going to lose the business. We're going to go bankrupt. How are we going to feed the children? Everyone will know we failed." Her mood was both depressed and anxious. She withdrew from friends and stopped eating "in order to save money". Two approaches were used to reduce her catastrophic reasoning. First, she was encouraged to gain information about the true state of their finances. This enabled her to use specific rather than global attributions and expectancies. Second, she was asked to imagine that what she feared would in fact happen, and to make contingency plans, answering the question, "And then what will you do?" The development of a plan of action, defocusing from the question about what this meant about her, her husband, their marriage, or the future, countered her personalization and global negative expectancies.

Scaling is used to break down dichotomous or exaggerated thinking. A person who is expressing an exaggerated point of view, or categorical thinking, is asked to anchor both ends of a relevant continuum (from 1 to 10, 1 to 3, or 1 to 100) with some life event representing one extreme of the characteristic, and then to place the current experience on that continuum. For example, the most and least anger the person has felt anchor the ends of the continuum, and today's anger is compared to those extremes. Repeated use of scaling over time can help the person to track and attend to improvement in symptoms.

Case D. A person continually described herself as "totally depressed", despite subjective report (improving weekly BDI scores), objective evidence (more work done around the house), and her spouse's report of improvement in activity level and mood. She was asked, "What was the day when you felt the most depressed?" and described the day her beloved sister was diagnosed with cancer. That day was assigned a value of 100. The day she was least depressed, the day of her wedding, was assigned a value of 1. Using those anchors, and keeping a record of events or days rated on this life- referenced scale, she was able to place her daily experience of depression in perspective.

Depressed persons engage in dichotomous thinking. That is, they tend to describe experience as belonging in one of two opposite and mutually exclusive categories, such as perfection or failure. Persons can be helped to see categorized variables as continuous. For example, the person in Case D concluded, "I can't trust my son at all." Scaling helped her to identify that although the son was not completely trustworthy, neither was he completely untrustworthy. This lead to a discussion of the specific (rather than global), external (rather than internal), situational (rather than permanent) factors that correlated with instances of honesty and dishonesty in the son.

Externalization of voices is a method of identifying automatic thoughts and schema in order to assess, examine or counter them. In addition, it can help to identify the origin of the schema that, in concert with life events, generates the thought. Externalization of voices makes overt the internal dialog that goes on between dysfunctional and more reasonable schema. It is used when the person reports, or demonstrates some awareness of alternate points of view, but is having trouble holding onto the more useful or adaptive point of view. The person is asked to report the automatic thought and the rational or more adaptive counter to that thought. These two "voices" are then made more explicit. Through highlighting the "argument" between the two points of view, the person is able to more deliberately process data or evidence on either side.

At times, the therapist takes the side of the weaker of the two voices, to enable the "argument" to be sustained long enough for deliberate examination of information. Later in therapy, externalization of voices may be used to help the person practice interrupting automatic processing, and engage in more deliberate information processing, and to role-play anticipated stressful events.

Hypothesis testing. The process of developing hypotheses teaches a step in problem solving, and enhances the person's sense of efficacy. Listing advantages and disadvantages can be done orally or in writing. Putting the process on paper makes the problem- solving more concrete. It enables more deliberation about alternatives and allows comparison of both sides of the situation. It creates a record of the process that the person can use as a model in future problem solving. Once again, it is important to list advantages of the person's dysfunctional attributions or behaviors as well as disadvantages of the more adaptive alternatives.

The examination of life experiences through both cognitive and behavioral experiments allows the person to test their attributions and expectancies about themselves and their situation. This can be accomplished within sessions through role play, imaginal procedures, and skill acquisition and practice. Tests of hypotheses most often include extra-therapy tasks (homework) that require persons to observe themselves and others, or to act in ways different from those consistent with schema, to gather information about the validity of expectancies or attributions. These tests must include "fail safe" mechanisms that allow for partial successes, predict problems, and give the person a way to respond to problems that occur.

The client in Case A was helped to develop an alternative hypothesis about her mother's cruel and abusive behavior, one that focused on attributing the behavior to the mother's need for absolute control, and countered the internal attribution of the client. During sessions, the client listed the various control tactics her mother used during phone calls, and the order in which she used them. She further hypothesized about the reasons for the various tactics and their order. She posted this list near the phone. During the next two phone calls from her mother, she checked her mother's tactics and their order against her written prediction, and against the hypothesis of "mother's dictatorial control". This in itself was helpful, as it helped the client to interrupt her automatic thoughts and to engage in deliberate information processing. The client practiced testing the mother's statements (i.e., "You're a terrible housekeeper.") against the evidence. The client then explored alternative ways to respond to the mother's behavior, given her reattribution. She settled on a firm but non-confrontational method of ending conversations as soon as mother's communication became abusive. This was later generalized to face-to-face interactions between the client and her mother, and to the mother's behavior and communication with the client's children.

In the course of testing alternate hypotheses and generating alternate solutions, clients often catastrophize about the consequences of changing existing patterns. Realistic reactions from others and realistic consequences need to be identified, and plans made to minimize negative effects for both clients and significant others. This is a practical concern: alternatives with negative consequences are not likely to be sustained, even if they are demonstrably more healthy or useful in other ways.

Where automatic thoughts and behavioral patterns or habits can be anticipated regarding changes, clients are helped to develop alternative behaviors, images, and thoughts. Imagining in detail the desired outcome or goal state, and developing coping self-statements to use in the pursuit of the goal, and in particular, to counter anticipated negative automatic thoughts, is critical to performing a behavioral and cognitive change outside of the therapy room. This process begins by asking the person to consider the toll, impact or price they pay for the negative thoughts or behaviors or to inquire as to the overall value of maintaining the present cognitions, affect, or behavior. The patient can then be helped to develop self-statements or behaviors that carry less of a price, or that are more useful.

Although cognitive therapy conceptualizes the change process by punctuating the interaction between cognition, mood, behavior and life events with an emphasis on cognition, behavioral techniques have always been utilized in cognitive therapy. The change process is not complete until the person's behavioral patterns are affected. *Activity scheduling, imagery techniques* and others already mentioned have both behavioral and cognitive aspects.

Techniques considered to be behavioral, but often used in the repertoire of the cognitive therapist, include *social skills training, assertiveness training, graded task assignments for successive approximation, behavioral rehearsal, in-vivo exposure,* and *relaxation training.* These are used to improve coping strategies through direct teaching and practice of specific skills related to interpersonal functioning, problem solving and self-regulation. In the hands of a cognitive therapist, the cognitive aspects of each of these methods are highlighted. That is, the attributional and expectancy self-statements that accompany the introduction and mastery of each technique or skill are attended to in the therapy along with behavioral performance.

The use of emotion in therapy. Emotion and mood are central aspects of cognitive therapy. The theory holds that affectively encoded schema are more potent than logically encoded learning. Further, affectively encoded schema are prepotent in directing the person's response to situations that have emotional meaning to the person. Therefore, schema are best modified when the affect that accompanied their encoding and that currently accompanies their expression is activated. Emotional activation occurs naturally in the person's telling of their life stories. If a person tells of difficulties in an affect-less fashion, emotion can be activated through use of the downward arrow technique, or by asking the person to describe an incident that best represents the problem they are describing (a critical incident).

New learning will remain subject to the negative cognitive shift if not affectively encoded. It is critical to anchor them by encoding them along with analogous affective states as the maladaptive schema. Encoding state- dependent learning that conflicts with the original schema weakens the association between the critical characteristic of the situation, and the thought and behavior patterns that follow. That is, the original stimulus-response connection is weakened by creating an equally viable alternative response. This makes it more likely that the person will have available in vivo at least an alternative to the problematic behavior and cognition pattern.

Case E. A client with a history of severe abuse at the hands of her father decided to sever relations with her family when her brother and mother decided to remain with the father following exposure of the abuse. This extremely difficult decision, and her family's lack of protest to her withdrawal, was experienced by her as abandonment, a global, stable attribution. She described herself as an orphan, and experienced this loss as a severe depression. She defined herself as a victim not only of the father's abuse, but also of her mother's and brother's abandonment. She described the latest experience of rejection, and her original experience when confronting her mother with the father's abuse, in a tearful, heart-rending session. After fully hearing and responding to her pain and loss, the therapist paused, and stated, "I'm a little confused. It seems to me that, rather than you being abandoned, being left, instead something quite different happened. It seems to me that you made a decision here to save yourself."

This intervention proved to be pivotal in the client's therapy. The new attribution was internal in locus of control, situational rather than stable, and specific to the circumstance rather than global. It was presented at a time when the person was actively, affectively recounting the original negative attribution. The new attribution successfully competed with the old schema when the client next thought of and had contact with the family.

Homework. Cognitive therapy can be distinguished by its approach to transfer and generalization through the use of intersession "homework". Systematic extension of the work of therapy to non-therapy hours results in faster, more comprehensive improvement (Burns & Auerbach, 1992; Meichenbaum, 1987; Neimeyer & Feixas, 1990). Skills, new cognitions, and new behaviors must be applied in vivo. Learning and changes relative to one situation must be actively generalized to similar situations. In this way, new learning's become natural and automatic aspects of the person's behavioral and cognitive repertoire.

Homework can be specifically cognitive or behavioral. Most often, it is both. Homework early in therapy focuses on helping the person to interrupt automatic routines, and to observe the connections between thought, behavior and mood. Thus, early homework tasks may include observing automatic thoughts through the use of the DTR, activity scheduling, collecting evidence for and against the person's attributions and expectancies, and mastery and pleasure ratings. In the middle of therapy, homework includes trying out new behaviors through graded task assignments; acting differently in order to gather information about alternative hypotheses; noticing, catching, interrupting and responding to negative thoughts and behaviors; and enacting a plan designed to lead to a specific goal.

"Homework" may be an unfortunate term to use in describing the things a person does between sessions to extend the therapy into their life. It carries connotations that, for some, may sound authoritarian, suggesting that homework is "assigned". In cognitive therapy, homework should arise naturally out of the content of the session, and relate both to the therapist's (and the client's) conceptualization of the person's depression, and to the clinical model. That is, the task should be something known to be likely to facilitate desired changes.

Clients' adherence to recommendations that they act between sessions to further their therapy is affected by the way the "homework" is conceived, the follow-up that occurs, and the complexity of the tasks themselves. A number of suggestions to increase adherence have been given by Meichenbaum and Turk (1987).

1. Homework should be collaboratively developed. The therapist can "lead" the discussion in such a way that clients themselves develop ideas for the work that is needed. The therapist lays the groundwork by asking questions, reflecting on what is already known or the skills the person has, and what is missing, and "going public" with his/her rationale or theories.
2. Tasks should be simple. For tasks that are beyond the person's skill level, the smaller the task, and the greater the likelihood of success, the better. For a more skilled client, more challenging tasks are better. Regardless, the task must be able to be performed with reasonable time and effort.
3. Provide the client with a choice. If more than one method exists to monitor behaviors or thoughts, using the one the person prefers increases the likeli-

hood of follow-through. Choice, or the perception of choice, enhances a person's sense of control and self-efficacy.

4. Specify what will be done, when, and how. Moderately specific plans result in better adherence than overly specific ones, particularly with longer- term goals. Moderately specific plans give the person choices and engage them in decision-making.

5. Engage significant others in the task, in reinforcing the person for completing or engaging in the task, and in determining the task whenever possible.

6. Directly, and in a stepwise fashion, teach monitoring skills, including recording, interpreting, and using the results.

7. Specify contingencies that follow adherence or non-adherence. Specify the results the person can expect from the task, or the purpose of the task. "Go public" with the rationale for the task. Better yet, have the person identify the rationale as part of collaboratively designing the task.

8. Offer mild counter-arguments about completion of the task. For example, anticipate difficulties, drawbacks, obstacles the person is likely to face in attempting the task. Help the person to plan cognitive and behavioral responses to obstacles, and to identify partial success or partial completion as useful.

9. Provide the person with feedback on adherence and on the accuracy of their performance of the task. Defocus from the product and focus on the attempt: effort and new information are more important than specific results.

10. Record positive behaviors rather than negative ones. Assign "do" tasks rather than "don't do" tasks. Particularly when the task involves interrupting an old routine, plan a substitute behavior or cognition. In the absence of a better plan, the person will fall back on old behaviors and cognitions.

11. Help the person to internally attribute success and improvements that result from adherence. Depressed persons tend to self-attribute blame, and to see good events or results as being due to uncontrollable, external forces. Internal attribution of success enhances self-efficacy. Shelton & Levy (1981) suggested a homework assignment should specify what the person is to do, how often or how many times, how they are to record their efforts, what they are to bring to the next appointment (e.g., the record), and consequences or contingencies attendant on either adherence or non adherence.

An example of homework was given in Case A above, when the client was asked to observe and record her mother's abusive verbal behavior in order to verify that her perception of her mother's behavior and its purpose was accurate. The client brought in the record, and a DTR of her automatic thoughts and feelings before and after phone calls with her mother. The connection between expectancy, cognition (attribution), and depression was clear in her records. Even more clear was that seeing mother's behavior as meaning something about the mother, but not about the client herself, significantly decreased her depressed thoughts and mood.

The second phase of therapy has helped the person to generate, test, and practice alternative behaviors, attributions, expectancies, and hypotheses. Maladaptive automatic thoughts and behavior patterns, and their underlying schema, have been modified. The person has been consciously aware, on an ongoing basis, of their information processing and meaning-making activities. New patterns of thought and behavior have been practiced in vivo, in a variety of situations, and are becoming automatic.

Ending Phase of Therapy

The last phase of therapy is devoted to further generalization and transfer of learning, self-attribution for gains made, and relapse prevention. Termination in cognitive therapy begins in the first session. Since the goal of CT is not cure, but more effective coping, the therapy is seen as time-limited. When formal assessments such as the BID, the patient's reported symptoms, observations of significant others, and the therapist's observation confirm decreased depression, greater activity, higher levels of adaptive functioning, and increased skills, the therapy can move toward termination.

Termination is accomplished in a planned, graded manner, with sessions tapered off from weekly to every other week, monthly, and then as follow-up sessions for outcome assessment or as part of a relapse prevention strategy. Contact between client and therapist between sessions may be scheduled or simply allowed as needed. Clients may call to get reinforcement of a particular behavior, to report success, to get information, and so on. The collaborative consulting role of the cognitive therapist allows this as appropriate and important.

It appears that even those persons who relapse within the current episode of depression continue for some time following termination to attempt to apply the skills and methods learned in the therapy. Thus, even those that eventually relapse take longer to do so than for other therapies, or for pharmacotherapy. Correlates of relapse include a history of prior depressive episodes, greater severity of symptoms at intake, slower response to therapy, unmarried status, and higher BID and DAs scores at termination (Beach & O'Leary, 1992; Clarke, Hops, Lewinsohn, Andrews & Williams, 1992; Evans, Hollon, DeRubeis, Piasecki, Grove, Garvery & Tuason, 1992).

Relapse prevention strategies address a number of key factors. Goals of therapy and initial symptoms are reviewed. Progress is measured both against initial symptoms and against goals. It is important for the person to identify how far they have come, and to develop a scale against which to measure current concerns and moods.

The person is asked to account for changes made: what changed? How did that come about? What did the person do to effect this change? The purpose is to self-attribute the successes experienced. Further, the person is asked to identify new learning, attitudes and skills, and to contrast these with old ones. We often have clients list the things that they will take away from the therapy, and plan where to keep this list for easy referral and reminder.

The person is asked to anticipate stressors. The therapist ensures that the list developed includes events similar to those that brought the person into therapy, events similar to those assumed to be the origin of the underlying depressogenic schema, and anticipated life events, such as developmental transitions the person or their family will encounter. The person is asked to imagine as vividly as possible that these events is occurring or has occurred, and to identify the skills, reattributions, and new patterns of behavior or cognition that can be called to bear on the stressor. This behavioral and imaginal rehearsal is conducted in as specific detail as possible, with an emphasis on coping thoughts and behaviors, self-attribution of efforts and success, and referral to the use of new resources. Both resourcefulness and utilizing therapy as a resource are promoted.

Finally, the meaning of the therapy to the person and to their life, and the meaning of the relationship with the therapist, is addressed. The goal is to integrate the experience of therapy into the personal narrative of the person so that it is seen as part of, rather than apart from, their life.

Conclusions

Beck's cognitive therapy was developed specifically in response to depression. The cognitive approach to the conceptualization and treatment of depression starts with the observation of common cognitive structures, processes, and products that appear to both mediate and moderate all instances of depression. The role of cognitions in depression is often misinterpreted to be one of simple linear causality: negative cognitions cause depression. If this were true, the implications for treatment would be further simple linear reasoning: positive thinking cures depression. Another misunderstanding of the CT model, is that the cognitive perspective implicates internal processes in depression to the exclusion of contextual events. The implication would be that a person could be depression-resistant regardless of events in the person's life. The cognitive conceptualization of depression does not hold either of these simple causal models to be true. The cognitive perspective is a diathesis-stress model where life events, thoughts, behaviors and moods are inextricably tied to each other in a reciprocal manner. Cognitions, behaviors, and moods all serve feed-forward and feedback functions in a complex process of information processing, behavioral regulation, and motivation. Further, the cognitive perspective implicates early life events and learning in the creation of patterns of information processing. These patterns may both predispose persons to specific emotional vulnerabilities, and maintain emotional difficulties once behavioral, cognitive and mood patterns are initiated.

Cognition is likely to be related to mediation (vulnerability) and moderation (expression and maintenance) of depression. Two levels of cognition are viewed as influencing these processes. These two levels can be easily described as deep cognitions, and surface cognitions, respectively.

Deep cognitions are seen as predisposing vulnerability factors that mediate the development of depression. Deep cognitions have been given a number of labels. These include schema, attitudes, basic assumptions, and core beliefs all of which of stable, cross-situational, and basic components of cognitive organization. These components develop in response to early life experiences, through both social and operant learning, Schema may operate actively, determining a majority of the person's daily behavior, or may be latent, triggered by specific events. They may be compelling and hard to resist, or non-compelling and easily countered or resisted. They guide the person's selection of information to attend to or seek, guide pattern search procedures, and provide "default values" when information is missing. By directing the encoding and retrieval of information, they govern the person's interpretation of experience,

While all cognition is distorted by meaning-making processes and by the essential conservatism and efficiency of information processing, the cognition of depressed persons is distorted in ways that create distress and interfere with adaptive behavior. Schema that are resistant to change and accommodation make the person vulnerable to difficulties in adaptation. Highly affectively charged schema may pre-empt more adaptive, possibly more logically derived schema, in what has been termed a negative cognitive shift.

Surface cognitions, in contrast to deep cognitions, are relatively unstable, temporary, and situation-specific thoughts. They do not seem to be subject to conscious control by the person, and are uncritically accepted by the person, to whom they seem perfectly plausible. These automatic thoughts are accessible through introspection and self-report and represent the conclusions drawn by the person on the basis of the information processing rules that they follow.

Not only do depressed persons process information in characteristically distorted ways, but the content of their thoughts is also characteristically negative and revolves around themes about self, world or experience, and future. The affective tone is typically negative in both attribution (causal explanation after the fact) and expectancy (prediction). The attributions tend to be global ("It's just the way I am."), stable ("I've always been that way. It'll never change.", and internal ("There must be something wrong with me.") The content in each area is evident in the person's overt and covert cognitions, and seen in the person's verbal and non-verbal behavior.

Schema, automatic thoughts, and the distortions evident in them, combine to contribute both distally and proximally to the person's experience of depression.

The cognitive model has matured significantly over the last two decades. From a peripheral model seen largely as a mechanistic and technique-focused outgrowth of behavior therapy, cognitive therapy has become a central and mainstream model of treatment of a broad range of emotional disorders. The cross-cultural interest in cognitive therapy is an expression of the nature of the model as process-oriented as opposed to models that are content-oriented and may not fit diverse cultures. It has become an expression of the therapy *zeitgeist* and serves as a meeting place for therapists from a range of theoretical positions.

References

Abramson, L. Y., Seligman, M. E. P., & Teasdale, J. D. (1978). Learned helplessness in humans: Critique and reformulation. *Journal of Abnormal Psychology, 87*, 49–74.

Barber, J. P., & DeRubeis, R. J. (1992). The ways of responding: A scale to assess compensatory skills taught in cognitive therapy. *Behavioral Assessment, 14*, 93–115.

Beach, S. R. H., & O'Leary, K. D. (1992). Treating depression in the context of marital discord: Outcome and predictors of response of marital therapy versus cognitive therapy. *Behavior Therapy, 23*, 507–528.

Beck, A. T. (1963). Thinking and depression: I. Idiosyncratic content and cognitive distortions. *Archives of General Psychiatry, 9*, 324–333.

Beck, A. T. (1967). *Depression: Causes and treatment.* Philadephia, PA: University of Pennsylvania.

Beck, A. T. (1976). *Cognitive therapy and the emotional disorders.* New York: International Universities Press.

Beck, A. T. (1991). Cognitive therapy: A 30-year retrospective. *American Psychologist, 46*, 368–375.

Beck, A. T., Ward, C. H., Mendelson, M., Mock, J. E., & Erbaugh, J. K. (1961). An inventory for measuring depression. *Archives of General Psychiatry, 4*, 561–571.

Beck, A. T., Weissman, S., Lester, D., & Trexler, L. (1974). The measurement of pessimism: The hopelessness scale. *Journal of Consulting and Clinical Psychology, 42*, 861–865.

Beck, A. T., Rush, A. J., Shaw, B. F., & Emery, G. (1979). *Cognitive therapy of depression.* New York: Guilford Press.

Beck, A. T., Epstein, N., Brown, G., & Steer, R. A. (1988). An inventory for measuring clinical anxiety: Psychometric properties. *Journal of Consulting and Clinical Psychology, 56*, 893–897.

Beck, A. T., Freeman, A., et al. (1990). *Cognitive therapy of personality disorders.* New York: Guilford Press.

Berlin, S. B., Mann, K. B., & Grossman, S. F. (1991). Task analysis of cognitive therapy for depression. *Social Work Research and Abstracts, 27*, 3–11.

Blackburn, I. M., & Eunson, K. M. (1989). A content analysis of thoughts and emotions elicited from depressed patients during cognitive therapy. *British Journal of Medical Psychology, 62,* 23–33.

Blackburn, I., Bishop, S., Glen, A. I. M., Walley, L. J., & Christie, J. E. (1981). The efficacy of cognitive therapy in depression: A treatment using cognitive therapy and pharmaco therapy, each alone and in combination. *British Journal of Psychiatry, 139,* 181–189.

Bowers, W. A. (1990). Treatment of depressed in-patients: Cognitive therapy plus medication, relaxation plus medication, and medication alone. *British Journal of Psychiatry, 156,* 73–78.

Bradley, B. P., & Matthews, A. (1988). Memory bias in recovered clinical depressives. *Cognition and Emotion, 2,* 235–245.

Burns, D. D. (1980). *Feeling good.* New York: William Morrow.

Burns, D. D., & Auerbach, A. H. (1992). Does homework compliance enhance recovery from depression. *Psychiatric Annals, 22,* 464–469.

Clarke, G., Hops, H., Lewinsohn, P. M., Andrews, J. R., & Williams, J. (1992). Cognitive-behavioral group treatment of adolescent depression: Prediction of outcome. *Behavior Therapy, 23,* 341–354.

Coyne, J. C., & Gotlib, I. H. (1983). The role of cognition in depression: A critical appraisal. *Psychological Bulletin, 94,* 472–505.

Dobson, K., & Shaw, B. F. (1986). Cognitive assessment with major depressive disorders. *Cognitive Therapy and Research, 10,* 13–29.

Evans, M. D., Hollon, S. D., DeRubeis, R. J., Piasecki, J. M., Grove, W. M., Garvery, M. J., & Tuason, V. B. (1992). Differential relapse following cognitive therapy and pharmacotherapy for depression. *Archives of General Psychiatry, 49,* 802–808.

Frank, J. (1985). Therapeutic components shared by all psychotherapies. In M. Mahoney & A. Freeman (Eds.), *Cognition and psychotherapy.* New York: Plenum Press.

Freeman, A. (1986). Understanding personal, cultural, and family schema in psychotherapy. In A. Freeman, N. Epstein & K. M. Simon (Eds.), *Depression in the family.* New York: Haworth.

Freeman, A., & DeWolf, D. (1989). *Woulda, coulda, shoulda.* New York: William Morrow.

Freeman, A., & Leaf, R. (1989). Cognitive therapy of personality disorders. In A. Freeman, K. M. Simon, L. Beutler & H. Arkowitz (Eds.), *Comprehensive handbook of cognitive therapy.* New York: Plenum Press.

Freeman, A., Pretzer, J., Fleming, B., & Simon, K. M. (1990). *Clinical applications of cognitive therapy.* New York: Plenum Press.

Freeman, A., & Reinecke, M. (1994). *Cognitive therapy of the suicidal patient.* New York: Springer-Verlag.

Freeman, A., & Zaken-Greenberg, F. (1989). Cognitive family therapy. In C. Figley (Ed.), *Treatment studies in families.* New York: Bruner/Mazel.

Gotlib, I. H. (1981). Self-reinforcement and recall: Differential deficits in depressed and non-depressed psychiatric inpatients. *Journal of Abnormal Psychology, 90,* 521–530.

Hamilton, M. (1960). A rating scale for depression. *Journal of Neurology, Neurosurgery, and Psychiatry, 23,* 56–62.

Hollon, S. D., & Bemis, K. M. (1981). Self-report and the assessment of of cognitive functions. In M. Hersen & A. S. Bellack (Eds.), *Behavioral assessment: A practical handbook.* New York: Pergamon Press.

Hollon, S. D., & Garber, J. (1990). Cognitive therapy for depression: A social cognitive perspective. *Personality and Social Psychology Bulletin, 16,* 58–73.

Hollon, S. D., & Kendall, P. (1980). Cognitive self-statements in depression: Development of an automatic thoughts questionnaire. *Cognitive Therapy and Research, 4,* 383–395.

Kavanagh, D. J., & Wilson, P. H. (1989). Prediction of outcome with group cognitive therapy for depression. *Behavior Research Therapy, 27,* 333–343.

Kwon, S., & Oei, T. P. S. (1994). The roles of two levels of cognitions in the development, maintenance and treatment of depression.

Meichenbaum, D. (1977). *Cognitive-behavior modification: An integrative approach.* Nueva York: Plenum Press.

Meichenbaum, D., & Turk, D. C. (1987). *Facilitating treatment adherence.* New York: Plenum Press.

Miranda, J., & Persons, J. B. (1988). Dysfunctional attitudes are mood-state dependent. *Journal of Abnormal Psychology, 97,* 76–79.

Murphy, G. E., Simons, A. D., Wetzel, R. D., & Lustman, P. J. (1984). Cognitive therapy versus tricyclic antidepressants in major depression. *Archives of General Psychiatry, 41,* 33–41.

Neimeyer, R. A., & Feixas, G. (1990). The role of homework and skill acquisition in the outcome of group cognitive therapy for depression. *Behavior Therapy, 21,* 281–292.

Pace, T. M., & Dixon, D. N. (1993). Changes in depressive self-schemata and depressive symptoms following cognitive therapy. *Journal of Counseling Psychology, 40,* 288–294.

Persons, J. B. (1989). *Cognitive therapy in practice: A case formulation approach.* New York: Norton.

Piaget, J. (1954). *The construction of reality in the child.* New York: Ballantine Books.

Riskind, J. (1983). Misconceptions of the cognitive model of depression. Comunicación presentada en la 91st Annual Convention of the American Psychological Association, Anaheim, CA.

Rosen, H. (1985). *Piagetian concepts of clinical relevance.* New York: Columbia University.

Rosen, H. (1989). Piagetian theory and cognitive therapy. In A. Freeman, K. M. Simon, L. Beutler, & H. Arkowitz (Eds.), *Comprehensive handbook of cognitive therapy.* New York: Plenum Press.

Rush, A. J., Beck, A. T., Kovacs, M., & Hollon, S. (1977). Comparative efficacy of cognitive therapy and imipramine in the treatment of depressed outpatients. *Cognitive Therapy and Research, 1,* 17–37.

Salkovskis, P. M., Atha, C., & Storer, D. (1990). Cognitive-behavioural problem solving in the treatment of patients who repeatedly attempt suicide: A controlled trial. *British Journal of Psychiatry, 157,* 871–876.

Schotte, C., Maes, M., Beuten, T., Vandenbossche, B., & Cosyns, P. (1993). A videotape as introduction for cognitive behavioral therapy with depressed inpatients. *Psychological Reports, 72,* 440–442.

Segal, Z. V. (1988). Appraisal of the self-schema construct in cognitive models of depression. *Psychological Bulletin, 103,* 147–162.

Shea, M. T., Elkin, I., Imber, S. D., Sotsky, S. M., Watkins, J. T., Collins, J. F., Pilkonis, P. A., Beckham, E., Glass, D. R., Dolan, R. T., & Parloff, M. B. (1992). Course of depressive symptoms over follow-up: Findings from the National Institute of Mental Health treatment of depression collaborative research program. *Archives of General Psychiatry, 49,* 782–787.

Shelton, J. L., & Levy, R. L. (1981). *Behavioral assignments and treatment compliance: A handbook of clinical strategies.* Champaign, Ill: Research Press.

Simon, K. M., & Fleming, B. M. (1985). Beck's cognitive therapy of depression: Treatment and outcome. In R. M. Turner & L. M. Ascher (Eds.), *Evaluating behavior therapy outcome.* New York: Springer-Verlag.

Stiles, T. (1990). Cognitive vulnerability factors in the development and maintenance of depression. Tesis doctoral. University of Trondheim, Trondheim, Norway.

Stravynski, A., & Greenberg, D. (1992). The psychological management of depression. *Acta Psychiatrica Scandinavica, 85,* 407–414.

Thase, M. E., Simons, A. D., Cahalane, J. F., McGeary, J., & Harden, T. (1991). Severity of depression and response to cognitive behavior therapy. *American Journal of Psychiatry, 148,* 784–789.

Thase, M. E., Simons, A. D., McGeary, J., Cahalane, J. F., Hughes, C., Harden, T., & Friedman, E. (1992). Relapse cognitive behavior therapy of depression: Potential implications for longer courses of treatment. *American Journal of Psychiatry, 149,* 1046–1052.

Weissman, M. M. (1979). *The Dysfunctional Attitudes Scale: a validation study.* Unpublished dissertation, University of Pennsylvania.

Young, J. E. (1994). *Cognitive therapy for personality disorders: A schema-focused approach* (revised edition). Sarasota, Fl: Professional Resource Exchange.

Further Reading

Bas Ramallo, F., & Andrés Navia, V. (1994). *Terapia cognitivo-conductual de la depresión: un manual de tratamiento.* Madrid: Fundación Universidad-Empresa.

Beck, A. T., Rush, A. J., Shaw, B. F., & Emery, G. (1979). *Cognitive therapy of depression.* New York: Guilford Press.

Fennell, M. (1989). Depression. In K. Hawton, P. M. Salkovskis, J. Kirk & D. M. Clark (Eds.), *Cognitive Behaviour therapy for psychiatric problems.* Oxford: Oxford University Press.

Freeman, A., & Davis, D. D. (1990). Cognitive therapy of depression. In A. S. Bellack, M. Hersen & A. E. Kazdin (Eds.), *International handbook of behavior modification and therapy,* 2nd edition. New York: Plenum Press.

Young, J. E., Beck, A. T., & Weinberger, A. (1993). Depression. In D. H. Barlow (Ed.). *Clinical handbook of psychological disorders,* 2nd edition. New York: Guilford Press.

17

Cognitive-Behavioral Treatment of Bipolar Disorder

MONICA RAMIREZ BASCO[a] and MICHAEL E. THASE[b]

[a]University of Texas, Southwestern Medical Center, USA; [b]University of Pittsburgh School of Medicine, USA

What is Bipolar Disorder?

Bipolar I disorder is a severe, recurrent, and disabling mental illness. It is characterized by episodes of depression and mania during which dramatic changes in mood, cognitions, and behavior occur. According to the *Diagnostic and Statistical Manual of Mental Disorders-IV* (APA, 1994), Bipolar I disorder is defined by the occurrence of at least one manic or mixed episode. Individuals suffering from Bipolar I disorder also typically experience episodes of major depression during the course of their illness. Tables 17.1–17.3 summarize the DSM-IV criteria for manic, major depressive, and mixed episodes, respectively.

While this chapter focuses on Cognitive Behavior Therapy (CBT) in the treatment of Bipolar I Disorder, there are other variations of bipolar disorder worth noting. In particular, bipolar II disorder, in which the individual experiences recurrent episodes of major depression and hypomania (see Table 17.4) and schizoaffective disorder, bipolar type, in which the individual has significant psychotic symptoms during episodes of depression or mania and which persist after the mood episodes remit. A diagnosis of Bipolar II disorder or recurrent major depressive disorder can change to Bipolar I disorder with the occurrence of at least one manic or mixed episode.

Bipolar I Disorder afflicts about 1% of the adult population in the US (Robins 1984). It is usually lifelong once it begins, with episodic recurrences

Table 17.1. DSM-IV Criteria for Manic Episode

A.	Abnormally and persistently elevated, expansive, or irritable mood lasting 1 week or requiring hospitalization.
B.	3 or more of the following symptoms (4 if mood is irritable):
	1. Inflated self esteem or grandiosity
	2. Decreased need for sleep
	3. More talkative or pressured speech
	4. Racing thoughts or flight or ideas
	5. Distractibility
	6. Increased activity or psychomotor agitation
	7. Excessive involvement in risky activities
C.	Not a mixed episode
D.	Impaired functioning or need for hospitalization
E.	Not due to a general medical condition, substance abuse, or antidepressant treatments

Adapted from Diagnostic and Statistical Manual of Mental Disorders – Fourth Edition (DSM-IV), American Psychiatric Association (1994).

that are a threat to life, family bonds, and economic stability. Recurrent episodes of depression and mania are the rule for over 95% of those who suffer from bipolar disorder (see reviews by Goodwin & Jamison, 1990; Zis & Goodwin, 1979). One-fourth of affected patients attempt suicide (Weissman et al., 1987). Not only is each episode of depression or mania itself potentially devastating, but there is also evidence that cycle length (the period of time between the onset of an index episode and the onset of the subsequent episode) decreases during the course of the illness (Angst, 1981; Kraepelin, 1921; Roy-Byrne, Post, Unde, Porcu & Davis, 1985; Zis, Grof, Webster & Goodwin,

Table 17.2. DSM-IV Criteria for Major Depressive Episode

A.	5 or more symptoms have been present during the same 2 week period (for the majority of the time) including depressed mood or loss of interest or pleasure. Symptoms are a change from previous levels of functioning and are not due to a general medical condition or psychotic symptoms.
	1. Depressed mood
	2. Markedly decreased interest or pleasure
	3. Significant change (increase or decrease) in appetite and/or weight
	4. Insomnia or hypersomnia
	5. Psychomotor agitation or retardation
	6. Loss of energy or fatigue
	7. Feelings of worthlessness or excessive guilt
	8. Impaired concentration or indecisiveness
	9. Suicidal ideation, actions or recurrent thoughts of death
B.	Not a mixed episode
C.	Symptoms cause clinically significant distress or impaired functioning
D.	Not due to a general medical condition or substance abuse
E.	Not bereavement

Adapted from Diagnostic and Statistical Manual of Mental Disorders – Fourth Edition (DSM-IV), American Psychiatric Association (1994).

Table 17.3. DSM-IV Criteria for Mixed Episode

A.	For 1 week period met criteria for manic episode *and* major depressive episode.
B.	Impaired functioning or need for hospitalization
C.	Not due to a general medical condition, substance abuse, or antidepressant therapy

Adapted from Diagnostic and Statistical Manual of Mental Disorders – Fourth Edition (DSM-IV), American Psychiatric Association (1994).

1980) and that the probability of recurrence increases with each new episode (Keller, Shapiro, Lavori & Wolfe, 1982). Post (1992) has described this process as a type of neurobiological sensitization or *kindling*. One practical implication of this phenomenon is an apparent uncoupling of episodes of illness from stressful life events as the illness progresses, resulting in apparently autonomous or unprovoked bouts of illness. Another potential consequence is development of rapid relapses following withdrawal of lithium, on occasion apparent within days or even hours of dosage discontinuation (Suppes, Baldessarini, Faedda & Tohen, 1991). Together, these changes in illness course may reinforce the demoralizing perception of being out of control and/or markedly vulnerable.

During episodes of major depression, mood can change from euthymic to neutral, blah, blue, empty, sad, hopeless, or irritable. When depressed, individuals with bipolar disorder describe themselves as impatient, intolerant, edgy, nervous, lost, misunderstood, disinterested, sensitive, angry, and/or "blunted". Depressed moods are usually very apparent to the person who is suffering, but may not be obvious to others if the individual's internal coping resources compensate for the depression. In contrast, the mood changes in mania are often quite noticeable to others, but may be less apparent to the patient. Mood changes in mania are described as uplifting, positive, elated, hopeful, excited,

Table 17.4. DSM-IV Criteria for Hypomanic Episode

A.	Abnormally and persistently elevated, expansive, or irritable mood lasting at least 4 days
B.	3 or more of the following symptoms (4 if mood is irritable):
	1. inflated self esteem or grandiosity
	2. decreased need for sleep
	3. more talkative or pressured speech
	4. racing thoughts or flight or ideas
	5. distractibility
	6. increased activity or psychomotor agitation
	7. excessive involvement in risky activities
C.	Symptoms are an unequivocal change from the person's normal level of functioning
D.	Mood and symptoms are observable by others
E.	No marked impairment in functioning, does not require hospitalization, not psychotic
F.	Not due to a general medical condition, substance abuse, or antidepressant therapy

Adapted from Diagnostic and Statistical Manual of Mental Disorders – Fourth Edition (DSM-IV), American Psychiatric Association (1994).

euphoric, "on top of the world," or optimistic. Although the stereotypic manic is happy and engaging, few patients have consistently pleasant manic episodes. Mania can also leave people feeling extremely irritable, agitated, anxious, tense, and fearful. For some patients, the pleasant or euphoric mood evolves into irritability as the mania progresses and worsens. For yet others, a distressing admixture of manic and depressive thoughts and feelings predominate.

Many of the cognitive changes associated with depression are apparent to others only when verbalized by the patient. In fact, depressed patients are often unaware of their own changes in views or beliefs because these cognitive shifts are subtle at first (e.g., less optimism and more pessimism) and often reinforced by negative life events. The cognitive changes in depression include negative distortions in perception of self, the world at large, and the future (Beck, Rush, Shaw & Emery, 1979). More observable cognitive changes include slowed speed of thought, word finding difficulties, and poor concentration. Some patients report a virtual paralysis of decision making and a loss or inhibition of volitional activity.

The cognitive changes observed in mania are qualitatively different from depression. Cognitive "symptoms" of mania may include changes in the content of thoughts and changes in the thinking process. The same distortions in perception of self, others, and the future are often exemplified by increased self-confidence, grandiosity, self-absorption, optimism, and fearlessness. Irritable manias can be accompanied by greater suspiciousness of others, ideas of reference, and paranoia. As the episode worsens, these cognitive shifts can evolve into grandiose and/or persecutory delusions.

Along with changes in the content of cognitions, the thinking process is often altered. This includes racing thoughts, distractibility, impaired judgment, and auditory and visual hallucinations. These changes in cognitive processing are usually unpleasant for the individual with bipolar disorder, and, may lead to behaviors that have a high potential for self-harm.

Observers, such as friends or family members, can usually identify the behavioral symptoms of depression and mania, particularly when these individuals have seen the patient in both symptomatic states. The depressed phase of bipolar illness is usually characterized by a reduction in psychomotor activity. Goal directed activities decrease, posture may "slump" and there may be a marked reduction in spontaneous motor movements, including diminished arm swing and slowed facial expressivity. Unless able to compensate, depressed persons may neglect their daily responsibilities (e.g., household chores), cease to engage in their usual social activities or hobbies, and withdraw from others. As noted above, they may move or talk more slowly than usual. Other symptoms that are manifested in behavioral changes in depression include sleep changes, altered eating habits, decreased sex drive, and low energy. Although both insomnia and hypersomnia are commonplace, oversleeping is particularly problematic for younger patients.

In striking contrast, is the increased activity associated with mania. Patients in the early stages of mania or hypomania often exhibit more ideas and interests than actual changes in activity. As mania progresses, their physical activity may increase. Restlessness or agitation may become evident in pacing, walking long distances, and seeking out activity. While in a manic episode, they may have a strong drive to be more socially or sexually active. They may start new tasks that they never complete. Every new opportunity seems like a good idea that is worth their time, energy, and money. The concomitant impairment in social judgment often fails to inhibit inappropriate actions.

The marked fluctuations in mood, personality, thinking, and behavior inherent in bipolar disorder often have profound effects on patients' interpersonal relationships. Affective lability financial extravagance, fluctuations in levels of sociability; sexual indiscretions and violent behaviors are all clearly a source of turmoil, conflict, and concern to patients and their significant others. (Goodwin & Jamison, 1990; Murphy & Biegal, 1974; Spalt, 1975; Winokur, Clayton & Reich, 1969).

Given the recurrent nature of bipolar disorder and its often devastating consequences, maintenance (i.e., prophylactic) treatment, after containment of acute episodes, is generally indicated, but often fails. Effective maintenance treatment can decrease patient suffering, hospitalization and cost, and improve psychosocial functioning. While maintenance pharmacotherapy may not altogether eliminate recurrences of mania or depression, it can decrease the frequency, duration, and severity of episodes of both depression and mania (Baastrup & Schou, 1967).

The most commonly used and best studied maintenance medication is lithium. Seven studies of patients with bipolar disorder (Baastrup, Poulsen, Schou, Thomsen & Amdisen, 1970; Coppen, Noguera, Bailey, Burns, Swani, Maggs & Gardner, 1971; Coppen, Peet, Bailey, Noguera, Burns, Swani, Maggs & Gardner,1973; Cundall, Brooks & Murray, 1972; Fieve, Kumbaraci & Dunner,, 1976; Prien, Caffey & Klett, 1973a; Prien, Klett & Caffey, 1973b; Stallone, Shelley, Mendlewizc & Fieve, 1973) have demonstrated superior prophylactic effects of lithium relative to placebo in reducing the frequency of relapse. These studies also illustrate, however, that lithium alone is not sufficient to achieve long term prophylaxis in many patients. Symptom breakthroughs are common, and without immediate intervention often lead to relapses or recurrences of depression or mania. Alternate medication strategies include the anticonvulsants carbamazapine (Luznat, Murphy & Nonn, 1988; Small, Klapper, Milstein, Kellams, Miller, Marhenke & Small, 1991) and sodium valproate (Bowden, Brugger, Swann, Calabrese, Janicek, Petty, Dilsaver, Davis, Rush, Small, Garza-Trevino, Risch, Goodnick & Morris, 1994; Calabrese & Delucchi, 1990), calcium channel blockers (Dubovsky, Franks, Allen & Murphy, 1986) and, for patients with persistent psychotic features, antipsychotic medications (Goodwin & Jamison, 1990). Despite this range of medications, approximately 10–20% of patients remain chronically ill for months or years at a time.

Why Does Maintenance Pharmacotherapy Fail?

Poor adherence compromises the effectiveness of maintenance pharmacotherapy in bipolar disorder (Goodwin & Jamison, 1990). Depending on the study design, 15–46% of patients with bipolar disorder have been found to have plasma lithium levels outside the therapeutic range, a common indicator of medication nonadherence (Connelly, 1984; Connelly, Davenport & Nurnberger, 1982; Danion, Neureuther, Krieger-Finance, Imbs & Singer, 1987; Kucera-Bozarth, Beck & Lyss,1982; Schwarcz & Silbergeld, 1983). Attrition from treatment is also common (Prien et al., 1973a,b, 1984; Stallone et al., 1973).

It is difficult to predict which patients with bipolar disorder will be more likely to adhere to treatment based on demographics or clinical features of bipolar disorder (Basco & Rush, 1995). However, studies on treatment adherence suggest that patients with comorbid personality disorders or substance abuse problems are less likely to adhere to treatment recommendations (Aagaard & Vestergaard, 1990; Danion et al., 1987).

Another common reason why traditional maintenance pharmacotherapy fails is that symptom exacerbations are not identified early enough and/or not appropriately treated. Thus, a portion of patients develop "breakthrough" episodes despite adequate or even exemplary compliance. Symptom breakthroughs can be precipitated by environmental, medical, seasonal, or unknown factors. Sleep disruption, for example, caused by events such as medical illness, "cramming" for an exam, travel or schedule changes, is one of the several pathways that may mediate breakthrough episodes. (Wehr, Sack & Rosenthal, 1987). Psychosocial stressors also may precipitate the onset of episodes of mania and depression (e.g., Aronson & Skula, 1987; Bidzinska, 1984; Dunner, Murphy, Stallone & Fieve, 1979; Glassner & Haldipur, 1983; Kennedy, Thompson, Stancer, Ray & Porsad, 1983; Kraeplin, 1921), particularly early in the course of the illness (Goodwin & Jamison, 1990; Post, 1992). Environmental and other factors may interact. For example, preoccupation with problems may cause patients to forget to take medication, cause sleep disruption due to worry, or be accompanied by severe and prolonged emotional distress that, in turn, help to provoke relapses/recurrences of depression or mania.

How can a Psychosocial Treatment Help to Modify a "Biological" Disorder?

Patients and families sometimes chafe at our notion of bipolar disorder as a biomedical illness, assuming that, simply put, "biology is destiny". From this distorted perspective, patients may see themselves as powerless victims of an uncaring God or cruel fate. Yet other patients may react with relief, as if they have been given permission to "let go" of trying to be responsible for something they cannot control. In either case, the patient's emotional reaction during the discussion may reveal his or her thoughts and feelings about the illness and/or its treatment, opening the way for a more frank discussion. Moreover, the onus of responsibility can now shift towards more controllable factors that influence outcome, including treatment adherence, maintaining a healthy lifestyle, symptom monitoring, and use of more active means to cope with and/or overcome problems. A psychotherapeutic intervention, such as cognitive behavior therapy, can augment medical management by:

a. improving adherence to pharmacotherapy;
b. helping patients to identify subsyndromal symptoms so that early intervention may prevent a full relapse or recurrence or perhaps limit the length of a new episode;
c. providing patients with techniques that may help contain subsyndromal symptoms from worsening; and
d. teaching patients strategies for coping with common social and interpersonal stressors which may be triggers or exacerbating factors in symptomatic manifestations.

There is some preliminary evidence that psychoeducational and psychotherapeutic interventions can augment the prophylactic effect of medication through improvement in treatment adherence and psychosocial functioning. (Cochran, 1984; Basco & Rush, 1995). Some of these studies included patients with unipolar depression (Jacob, Frank, Kupfer, Cornes & Carpenter, 1987), but they provide a model which may be applicable to bipolar disorder.

Enhancement of Psychosocial Functioning and Prevention of Recurrence

In a 12-month follow-up study where bipolar patients were assigned to post-acute treatment (Davenport, Ebert, Adland & Goodwin, 1977) couples psychotherapy group ($N = 12$), lithium maintenance group ($N = 11$), or community-based aftercare ($N = 42$), Davenport et al. (1977) found that patients with bipolar disorder assigned to the couples psychotherapy group had fewer instances of rehospitalization and fewer marital failures, as well as better social functioning and family interaction than did the comparison groups. Clarkin, Glick, Haas, Spencer, Lewis, Peyser, DeMane, GoodEllis, Harris & Listell (1990) found the same pattern of findings in female patients with affective disorders, although couples treatment did not enhance the outcome of male patients. These studies suggest that psychosocial treatments may enhance the outcome of bipolar patients.

Other reports describing long- and short-term group therapies, (when combined with pharmacotherapy), also suggest that psychosocial treatment may be helpful in reducing the frequency and length of relapse and/or need for hospitalization in bipolar patients (Benson, 1975; Powell, Othmer & Sinkhorn, 1977; Shakir, Volkmar & Bacon, 1979; Wulsin, Bachop & Hoffman, 1988). For example, although not a controlled clinical trial, Shakir et al. (1979) found that for the 2 years prior to the initiation of long-term group psychotherapy, 10 of their 15 bipolar disorder group members had been hospitalized for a total of 16.2 weeks and only 5 were continuously employed. For the 2 years following initiation of group therapy, only 3 patients were rehospitalized for a total of 3.2 weeks. Moreover, 10 patients had been continuously employed for at least 6 months. Powell et al. (1977) similarly found that providing group therapy for bipolar disorder patients limited relapse to only 15% of the 40 group participants over 12 months.

Improvement in Treatment Adherence

Altamura and Mauri (1985) ($N = 14$) and Youssel (1983) ($N = 36$) examined the effectiveness of patient education on treatment adherence in unipolar depressed outpatients. Both studies found, increased treatment adherence following the psychoeducational intervention, as measured by pill count (Youssel, 1983) or blood level to dose ratio (Altamura & Mauri, 1985).

There is some evidence that patient education can improve adherence by enhancing acceptance or adjustment to the illness. Peet & Harvey (1991) randomly assigned 60 lithium clinic patients to one of two conditions: (1) an education group that viewed either a 12-minute videotaped lecture on lithium treatment and received a written transcript or, (2) a treatment as usual condition that did not systematically address educational issues. Measurements of patients' attitudes toward lithium and understanding of treatment showed a significant improvement in patients' attitudes and knowledge about the illness and its treatment intervention.

Van Gent & Zwart (1991) provided educational sessions to 14 patients with bipolar disorder and their partners. After five educational sessions, the patients' partners demonstrated more understanding of the illness, of lithium treatment, and of social strategies for coping with their partners' symptoms. A 6 month follow-up indicated that these beneficial changes were maintained. Moreover, patients' serum lithium levels remained stable during the year following the education program from the levels achieved during the program. This suggests that the education program may have helped to prevent the deterioration in compliance over time often observed in lithium-treated patients. A 5-year follow-up of the educational group (Van Gent & Zwart, 1993) was conducted in a larger sample ($N = 26$) in order to assess rates of discontinuation of lithium prophylaxis and number of psychiatric hospitalizations. Using a "mirror image" design (i.e., comparing against the patients' own baseline) there was a 50% improvement in the number of patients remaining on lithium and a 60% decline in hospital admissions.

A more extensive patient education study was conducted by Seltzer, Roncari & Garfinkle (1980). Patients included three diagnostic groups (schizophrenic, $N = 44$; bipolar disorder, $N = 16$; and unipolar depressed, $N = 7$). Each group received 9 lectures addressing diagnosis, course of treatment, medication, side effects, relapse, and importance of support. At a 5-month follow-up, patients who attended lectures demonstrated greater treatment adherence (91 vs. 32%) and were less fearful of side effects and development of drug dependency than the patients who did not receive the intervention.

Myers & Calvert (1984) randomly assigned depressed outpatients ($N = 120$) to one of three groups. One group received written and verbal information about medication side effects. The second received written and verbal information on the beneficial effects of treatment. The third group received no systematic education. A comparison of the three groups at 3 week follow-up showed no significant differences between the 3 groups in level of adherence or side effects. However, at 6-week follow-up, the two groups receiving education, reported significantly fewer side effects and had better treatment adherence than the no-education control.

To evaluate the utility of cognitive therapy for enhancing adherence and improving outcome, Cochran (1984) randomly assigned lithium-maintained bipolar patients to either standard clinical care or a short-term (6 weeks), individual cognitive therapy intervention. Patients assigned to the 6-week cognitive therapy intervention were less likely than the standard care group to have significant adherence problems, including being less likely to terminate lithium against medical advice. Over a 3 and 6 month follow-up period, the cognitive therapy group had fewer nonadherence-precipitated episodes and fewer hospitalizations. Although this was a short-term intervention with limited follow-up, Cochran's (1984) finding provides some evidence for the utility of cognitive-behavior therapy as an adjunct to pharmacotherapy in the treatment of bipolar depression.

It seems clear that psychoeducational interventions have tangible value in the long-term management of recurrent mood disorders. As CBT is, among other things, inherently psychoeducational, it may be particularly well suited for this purpose.

Control of Symptom Breakthroughs

The occurrence of subsyndromal mood symptoms in a cohort of patients with bipolar disorder increases the risk of recurrent mood episodes fourfold

(Keller, Lavori, Kane, Gelenberg, Rosenbaum, Walzer & Baker, 1992). Hypomania was more commonly followed by a major affective recurrence, primarily mania, than was minor depression: 75% of patients who became hypomanic suffered a recurrent episode. These facts suggest that, early identification of subsyndromal mood "fluctuations" might allow preemptive interventions that lessen the risk of development of a "full blown" episode or permit quicker containment of symptoms. Patients receiving CBT learn to monitor their symptoms closely so that the reemergence of symptoms may be detected early in their development thus allowing for early intervention and avoidance of a recurrence of illness.

Cognitive Behavior Therapy for Bipolar Disorder

CBT appears effective in acute (e.g., Rush, Beck, Kovacs, Khatami, Fitzgibbons & Wolman, 1977; Murphy & Biegel, 1984) and possibly continuation (e.g., Blackburn, Evanson & Bishop, 1987) treatments of major depression. For severe depression, starting CBT in combination with pharmacotherapy while patients are still hospitalized and continuing treatment for 5 months post-discharge may improve outcomes (Miller, Norman & Keitner, 1989). The advantage of combined treatment with CBT and pharmacotherapy was most evident for patients with high DAS scores (Miller, Norman & Keitner, 1990) and on measures of hopelessness and cognitive distortion (Whisman, Miller, Norman & Keitner, 1991). Treatment of unipolar depression with CBT appears to convey some enduring prophylactic benefit (e.g., Hollon, Shelton & Loosen, 1991). Relapse following CBT has been associated with the level of residual symptoms (Thase, Simons, McGeary, 1992). Jarrett, Basco, Ramanan & Rush (1993) have found that survival time for CBT responders is significantly enhanced when acute therapy is supplemented by an extended course of continuation therapy is significantly longer. While never tested with prodromal symptoms of mania, CBT has proven to be successful in treating the physical, cognitive, and behavioral residual symptoms associated with depression (Fava, Grandi, Zielezny, Canestrari & Murphy, 1994).

CBT techniques have been standardized for depression in ambulatory and inpatient settings (Beck et al., 1979; Thase & Wright, 1991). Procedures have been objectively defined in sufficient detail to be followed by therapists, thus allowing for standardized treatments across trained therapists. This increases the feasibility both of testing efficacy and of implementing CBT augmentation as part of standard treatment if found to be effective. These advantages in quantifying the quality of the experimental treatment will, of course, extend to studies of bipolar disorder.

Cognitive-behavioral therapy (CBT) for the maintenance phase treatment of Bipolar Disorder augments rather than replaces pharmacological management of this illness. The primary goals of CBT for Bipolar Disorder are to:

1. educate patients and their significant others about the illness, its treatment, and common difficulties associated with the illness;
2. teach patients methods for monitoring the occurrence, severity, and course of manic and depressive symptoms to allow for early intervention should symptoms worsen;
3. facilitate compliance with prescribed medication regimens by removing the obstacles that interfere with compliance;
4. provide nonpharmacological strategies for coping with the cognitive and behavioral symptoms of mania and depression;
5. teach skills for coping with common psychosocial problems that are the precipitants or sequelae of depressive and manic episodes.

The following is a summary of procedures for addressing each of these goals. A more thorough discussion of these methods is available in Basco & Rush (1996).

Patient and Family Education

As the studies above have illustrated, patient education is an essential part of treatment. A well informed patient can be a more active participant in the treatment process. Patients can be self-advocates if they understand what to expect from treatment, from the health care provider, and from the illness itself. Studies involving family education attest to the value of family involvement in patients' care.

Patient education can take many forms. The health care provider can talk with the patient about bipolar disorder, answer questions and direct him or her to other educational resources. There are several national clearinghouses for information on bipolar disorder in the United States such as the National Depressive and Manic Depressive Association, the National Alliance for the Mentally Ill, the National Institute of Mental Health, and the Mental Health Association. Whatever the modality, patient education is essential, however, it is generally not sufficient to ensure compliance, control symptoms, or prevent relapse. Patient education should be an ongoing process, particularly as more is learned about this mental disorder.

Although most educational pamphlets on bipolar disorder document the symptoms and common treatments for mania and depression, these materials will not be tailored to the unique experiences of each person with the disorder. Health care providers can help patients to identify and label their symptoms, behaviors, emotions, and cognitions that occur during the active phases of depression, mania, hypomania, and mixed states. This personalization of patient education sets the stage for the next component of CBT, symptom monitoring.

Symptom Detection

Symptom breakthroughs are common among people with bipolar disorder, even when they take their medications consistently over time. Unfortunately, these moderate symptom exacerbations can and do evolve into full episodes of mania or depression often before efforts can be made to control them. An early warning system is needed to help patients and their family members detect symptoms and take action early in their course of their evolution. Early intervention can increase the chance of relapse prevention. There are three levels of symptom detection, each of which will be described briefly below. These are:

1. life charts, a historical time line documenting episodes of illness;
2. symptom summary, a list of physical, cognitive, emotional and behavioral symptoms that occur during episodes of depression, mania, and mixed episodes; and
3. mood graphs, daily ratings of mood or other symptoms that are likely to change early in the course of an episode of illness.

Life Charts

Post and his colleagues (Post, 1992; Altshuler, Post, Leverich, Mikalauskas, Rosoff & Ackerman, 1995) have demonstrated the usefulness of life charts for understanding the interactions among episodes of illness, treatment initiation and discontinuation and significant life events across patients. For each individual, a life chart shows graphically their course of illness from onset to present. Construction of a life chart requires, at minimum, the approximate date of the onset and offset of each depressive, manic, hypomanic, and mixed episode. It is useful to add the onset and offset dates of treatments, including hospitalizations, emergency room visits, pharmacotherapies, and psychotherapies. Significant life events such as life transitions (e.g., job changes, marriages, births of children) and major losses (e.g., deaths, divorce) are useful to document, particularly if they relate to relapses or recurrences of illness. With this information displayed on a time line, patterns between symptoms, stress, and treatment may emerge.

Figure 17.1 shows an example of a 40 year old man with a 15 year history of bipolar disorder. His first manic episode began at shortly after treatment of major depression with a tricyclic antidepressant. He began taking lithium at age 26. He stopped taking his medication twice, at age 27 and at age 30 when he believed he no longer had the illness. He suffered from a severe episode of major depression at age 35 when his mother died. Although he has continued to have mild symptoms breakthrough when under considerable stress, he had not had a recurrence of depression mania since age 36 when he began taking sodium valproate.

People with bipolar disorder can begin to live life as a daily struggle to contain symptoms, each day awaiting the next plunge into depression or spin into

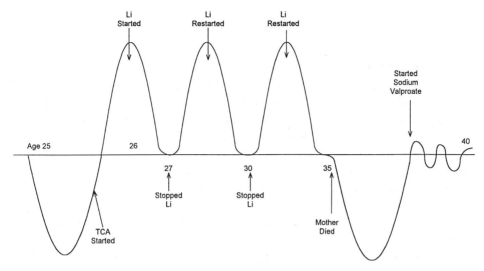

Figure 17.1. Sample life chart.

mania. They can begin to feel helpless, out of control, and fearful of things to come. Some stop planning for the future. The past blurs, as the memory of each episode of illness blends into the next. Construction of a life chart helps patients to gain a clearer perspective on their experiences with the illness. As they work with their therapist to construct the life chart, they begin to see patterns, times of euthymia, responses to treatment, and times of vulnerability. Patients report that this process is therapeutic. It helps them to make sense of a what feels like a lifetime of uninterrupted illness.

The life chart runs along a horizontal axis that represents time. This line, which is also the vertical midpoint of the graph, also represents normalcy of mood or euthymia. Elevations above the line represent elevations in mood toward euphoria or mania. Below the line are decreases in mood with the lowest points representing severe depression. Thus in the case represented in Figure 17.1, the first episode of illness was a major depression. It became more severe over time and then remitted with treatment, returning mood to a more euthymic level. Periods of substance abuse, anxiety, or general medical conditions can be added to the time line. Some patients prefer to omit the drawing of episodes, including only a list of events in chronological order on the time line.

In Figure 17.1, once the chart was completed, the patient could see how discontinuation of medication soon led to the onset of another episode. He was also able to make an association between times of increased stress and a destabilizing of his mood and symptoms. As new episodes of illness emerge, treatment changes or other major life events occur, the life chart can be appended. Clinicians and patients can use the chart to track more global changes in the course of the illness that occur with age, changes in treatment, or with more diligent symptom tracking.

Symptom Summary Sheet

The second step in symptom detection is to sensitize individuals with bipolar disorder to the changes they typically experience during episodes of depression, mania, hypomania and during mixed episodes. A symptom summary sheet as shown in Table 17.5, can facilitate this process. Patients list the physical, emotional, cognitive and behavioral symptoms that occur during manic and depressive episodes. A third column is provided to indicate what the individual experiences when asymptomatic. For example, in the Depressed column the patient indicates that he or she sleeps 10 h or more with occasional afternoon naps. The Manic column indicates that sleep is reduced to 4–5 h per night usually waking up earlier than usual and not needing more sleep. In the Normal column, the patient indicates usual sleep pattern when not symptomatic. In Table 17.5, this patient indicated that she usually sleeps no more than 8 h per night and does not nap during the day. For any symptom listed, compare and contrast to the other mood states and to periods of euthymia. Family members and friends may be able to contribute to the list by adding their observations of the patient during symptomatic times.

Mood Graphs

Mood graphs can be used to track daily changes in mood, cognitions, and behavior that might signal the onset of a new episode of mania and depression. The graph can be used to rate mood or other symptoms that are noticable to the patient and tend to appear early in the episode. Some people are most sensitive to changes in attitude (more optimistic or pessimistic). Others notice changes in sleep patterns (increased or interrupted) or activity (more active or more socially withdrawn). The Symptom Summary Sheet can help the clinician and patient decide which symptoms will be most useful to monitor.

The anchor row in the middle of the graph shown in Table 17.6 represents euthymia similar to the midline of the life chart. The points above the midline, from +1 to +5, represent levels of mania; with +5 indicating a severe manic episode. The points below the midline, from −1 to −5, represent levels of depression, with the lowest points indicating a severe major depressive episode. Mood will likely vary from −1 to +1 on most euthymic days. Ratings of +2 to −2 alert patients to begin to watch their symptoms a little more closely and take any protective measures necessary (e.g., normalize sleep, remember to take medications). A score of −3 or +3 indicates that it is time to intervene to keep the symptoms from worsening. This can mean calling the doctor and using the CBT techniques described below.

It is best to tailor a mood graph to the special needs of each patient. For example, those whose mood changes midway through the day (e.g., when the

Table 17.5. Symptom Summary Sheet for Manic and Depressive Episodes

Normal	Depression	Mania
6–8 h of sleep, no naps	Sleep 10 h and nap	Needs 5 h sleep
More introverted	Withdrawn and lonely	Outgoing, sociable
Life seems to have purpose	Suicidal thoughts	Life is grand
I think I'm alright	Worthless	I'm brilliant
Confident	Hopeless	Ambitious
Thinking is clear	Can't concentrate	Very creative
Visit with some close friends	No interest in people	Want to be with people
I feel comfortable	Mood is black	I'm excited about life

children come home from school), a graph can be designed for morning and evening ratings. The patient can make notes on the graph about any circumstances related to the change in mood. This information can help clinicians to design interventions that prevent worsening of moods. For example, patients may find that their mood shifts when they reach work, when they drive in traffic, when they see their spouses, or when they are hungry. These mood shifts do not necessarily require a pharmacological intervention, but may be addressed with CBT techniques.

Methods for Enhancement of Treatment Compliance

Another goal of CBT for bipolar disorder is to maximize compliance with

Table 17.6. Mood Graph

Name of patient: _____   For week of: _____
Completed by: _____   Relationship to patient: _____

Mood Graph

	Day 1	Day 2	Day 3	Day 4	Day 5	Day 6	Day 7
Date:							
Manic							
+5	:	:	:	:	:	:	:
+4	:	:	:	:	:	:	:
+3 Time to intervene	:	:	:	:	:	:	:
+2 Monitor closely	:	:	:	:	:	:	:
+1	:	:	:	:	:	:	:
0 Normal	:	:	:	:	:	:	:
−1	:	:	:	:	:	:	:
−2 Monitor closely	:	:	:	:	:	:	:
−3 Time to intervene	:	:	:	:	:	:	:
−4	:	:	:	:	:	:	:
−5	:	:	:	:	:	:	:
Depressed							

pharmacotherapy and other forms of treatment during the entire length of time that the patient is under treatment. The emphasis on maximization of compliance assumes that even under the best circumstances, most people will be unable to comply perfectly with treatment at all times, particularly if treatment is life long. If the goals and methods of treatment are acceptable to patients, the effort of CBT is to increase the probability that patients can follow treatment as it is prescribed by identification and removal of factors that interfere with compliance.

This approach begins with the structure of behavioral contracting, refined and augmented with the identification and resolution of obstacles to compliance. This critical element in the contract differs from standard behavioral contracting methods in that it helps patients to anticipate problems with compliance before they occur. This "trouble-shooting" process allows patients and clinicians to openly discuss compliance with treatment as a goal rather than as a mandate or misbehavior as is traditionally done. Clinicians introduce the notion that full compliance with treatment is a goal, providing a rationale for the need for consistent use of medications to maximize their effectiveness. Clinicians should probe for whether this rationale is understood and accepted by patients. If not, further discussion is necessary to clarify how psychotropic medications work and to determine if patients have any misconceptions about pharmacotherapy. It is not unusual for people with bipolar disorder to have had bad experiences with medications in the past, particularly if their symptoms had been severe enough to require emergency treatment or hospitalization or if their diagnoses had not been clear at the time that treatment was initiated. These types of experiences may leave patients somewhat suspicious about the intentions of their psychiatrists and about the usefulness of pharmacotherapy.

Another way in which the CBT approach to compliance differs from traditional behavioral contracting is that an external reward for compliance in not typically provided. The focus of the intervention is on patients assuming full responsibility for their compliance with treatment. Clinicians can help patients to understand why it is important to be consistent in taking medication and to work toward maximizing compliance, but taking medications regularly is ultimately the responsibility of the patient. The consequences for noncompliance are internal, personal. The rewards for compliance must be, as well. The metamessage in this intervention is that there should be an internal attribution for the degree to which people are compliant with treatment and for the results of their compliance (i.e., "I am taking this treatment consistently because I think it is helpful and is in my own best interest"). External rewards, which can be helpful in short term interventions such as weight loss, will not create and maintain the behavioral changes needed in the long term, prophylactic treatment of bipolar disorder.

As with other behavioral contracting interventions for improving compliance, CBT begins with a clear definition of treatment goals. These goals are

Table 17.7. Compliance Contract: Part I: Treatment Plan

I, [patient name], plan to follow the treatment plans listed below.
  1. Take 300 mg of lithium 3 times each day (morning, noon, and evening)
  2. Take 25 mg of Benedryl at bedtime to help me sleep.
  3. See my doctor once each month and my caseworker once each month.
  4. Call my doctor if I think I am beginning to have more symptoms or if I think a change in medication is needed. I agree to call before making changes to the regimen myself.

written down as specifically as dose schedules (e.g., take 300 mg of lithium in the morning, at noon, and at bedtime), appointment plans (e.g., attend appointment with doctor next Monday, attend AA meetings 3 times next week), and/or homework assignments (e.g., read pamphlet on bipolar disorder). To be successful, the patient and the health care provider must both understand and agree upon the goals of treatment. Once treatment goals have been defined, they should be documented in a form that provides a record for both the patient and the clinician. Table 17.7 provides an example of the first part of a behavioral contract where treatment plans are specified.

The second part of the behavioral contract is to identify factors that could

Table 17.8. Obstacles to Adherence

A. *Intrapersonal variables*
  1. Remission in symptoms and seeing no need for further treatment.
  2. Patient ran out of medication. Did not refill prescription.
  3. Denial that they have a chronic illness/stigma associated with bipolar illness.
  4. Forgetfulness.
B. *Treatment variables*
  1. Side effects of medication.
  2. Medication schedule does not conform to patient's personal schedule.
  3. Patient assigned a new doctor who changes treatment plans.
C. *Social system variables*
  1. Psychosocial stressors.
  2. Competing medical advice.
  3. Discouragement from family and friends.
  4. Publicized stories of others' bad experiences with medications.
D. *Interpersonal variables*
  1. Poor rapport with the therapist and/or psychiatrist.
  2. Busy, uncomfortable, or otherwise unpleasant clinic environment.
E. *Cognitive variables*
  1. Patient does not like the idea of having to depend on drugs.
  2. Patient thinks he or she should be able to handle mood swings on his own.
  3. Patient misattributes symptoms of bipolar illness to another source.
  4. Patient is suspicious of the intentions of the psychiatrist.

Adapted from Basco, M.R. and Rush, A.J. (1996). *Cognitive-behavioral therapy for bipolar disorder*. New York: Guilford.

Table 17.9. Compliance Contract: Part II. Compliance Obstacles

I anticipate these problems in following my treatment plan.

1. I might continue to gain weight with lithium.
2. One Benedryl might not be enough so I may have to take two.
3. I might not have a ride to my next appointment.
4. I might need more medicine before you return my phone call.

interfere with treatment. This would include things within the individual (e.g., mood, fears about medications, forgetfulness) and external influences (e.g., family members discouraging use of medications, conflicting medical advice). Table 17.8 lists some of the common obstacles to adherence with treatment.

The behavioral contract includes, in a second section, a list of factors that the patient has identified as potentially interfering with treatment compliance (see Table 17.9). The clinician helps the patient to anticipate problems with each of the treatment goals (e.g., "What could keep you from taking your medication? What could keep you from making it to your next appointment?)". Some patients who are eager to please their doctors will say that nothing will keep them from taking their medications. While this enthusiasm is usually genuine, the health care provider should not omit discussion of obstacles that while unplanned, could emerge. In these cases, it can be helpful to review past experiences where patients have had difficulty following through with treatment as it was prescribed (e.g., "Have there been times in the past when it was difficult to always take medication that was prescribed for you or when you changed the way you took your medications? What about adding medications on your own to help manage symptoms?")

The last section of the compliance contract consists of plans for avoiding or overcoming the obstacles listed in the previous section. For each obstacle, the patient and the health care provider work out a plan that reduces the probability that the problem will occur or for coping with the obstacle should it arise. Patients will likely have strategies that they have tried in the past with

Table 17.10. Compliance Contract: Part III. Plan for Reducing Obstacles to Adherence

To overcome these obstacles, I plan to do the following:

1. Get a list of high fat foods from my doctor. Limit my intake of high fat food at each meal. Eat sweets only twice each week.
2. Improve sleep by not drinking coffee after 4 p.m. or other caffeinated beverages.
3. Plan ahead. Ask family for a ride at least 1 week before my appointment. Set money aside to take a bus or cab if needed.
4. My doctor will have someone return my call if he is too busy. If it cannot wait, limit extra medicines to the ones my doctor and I have agreed are safe and helpful. Call my caseworker if I need help.

varying amounts of success. The plan for overcoming each obstacle to compliance is written in the third part of the compliance contract. An example is provided in Table 17.10.

The contract can be developed by any of the health care providers working with the patient who are knowledgeable of the medication treatment plan. It will take approximately 45 min to initially develop the contract. The contract is reviewed at each visit thereafter to modify the treatment goals if necessary, assess for any problems with compliance, and to modify the plan for addressing treatment obstacles if needed. Sometimes patients will be more comfortable in admitting noncompliance to clinicians other than their physicians. They wish to make a good impression or fear the consequences of disappointing their doctors. A nurse, caseworker, or therapist can review the contract at their regular visits with patients. The psychiatrist can review the contract more briefly, modifying the plan when needed.

Control of Subsyndromal Cognitive Symptoms

Symptoms of depression and mania include changes in the content of thoughts, the clarity of thoughts, and the number of thoughts. In both emotional states, cognitions appear to be both a product of the mood state and seem to affect mood. Views or attitudes about self, about the world, or about the future change, often unrealistically. Information processing can be dramatically slowed when concentration is impaired by depression or when racing thoughts and distractibility overload the system with too much data. Levels of creativity are altered with hypomania and mania often stimulating a plethora of new ideas and inspirations while in depression, the generation of new ideas can come to a grinding halt. In both depression and mania, reality testing can become impaired, particularly when episodes are at their most severe levels. The content of the delusions and hallucination are generally congruent with the mood state.

The CBT intervention for impaired concentration in depression and in mania is similar. The task is to reduce noise or overstimulation and focus thinking on one target at a time. In mania, this is not easily accomplished because internal control over racing thoughts is limited for many people. Some find that relaxation techniques and controlling environmental stimulation slows racing thoughts. Symptom monitoring will help patients to detect cognitive changes early in their evolution when they are easier to control.

Evaluation and Modification of Cognitive Distortions

Logical analysis of emotionally biased thoughts, whether they be negative automatic thoughts associated with depression, suspicious or angry thoughts accompanying irritability, or overly positive thoughts in mania, can be accomplished with traditional cognitive therapy techniques such as evaluating their validity by examining the supporting and refuting evidence or by generating alternative explanations. With angry, irritable, or paranoid thoughts, it can be particularly helpful to teach patients to gain emotional distance from the stimulus of the thought before attempting to evaluate its validity. This emotional distancing can be sufficiently powerful to help the individual to gain a less emotional and more accurate perspective on the situation.

Typically with positively biased thoughts, it will not be the patient, but those around him or her that complain about the overly optimistic and unrealistic thinking. The patient who is entering a hypomanic or manic episode may feel better than usual, have more self-confidence and creativity, and see nothing pathological about these positive changes. Therefore, the cue to evaluate the validity of these thoughts will likely be a therapist, a family member, or those in the patient's work environment. When challenged to evaluate positively biased thoughts, patients are often offended or irritated. The message in this suggestion is "you are not creative, you are sick". Those individuals who are fearful of having another episode of mania and are sensitized to the cognitive changes that can occur, will questions their own thinking when it becomes positively biased. Negative automatic thoughts that accompany depression or an irritable mania or hypomania are accompanied by an uncomfortable change in mood. This discomfort, that is not present in a euphoric mania or hypomania, will serve as the cue to monitor and evaluate negative automatic thoughts.

The following is a brief review some methods for evaluating positively and negatively distorted thoughts. Automatic thought diaries such as the *Daily Record of Dysfunctional Thoughts* (Beck et al., 1979; Wright, Thase, Beck & Ludgate, 1993) provide a structure for the evaluation. When a mood shift occurs, note the date and the circumstances under which the mood shift occurred. The stimulus can be an event in the person's environment or something internal, like a recollection of a past event. It will take some practice to be able to identify the specific stimulus for a shift in mood. Because episodes of illness in bipolar disorder are often biologically driven, there may be no identifiable stimulus for a shift in mood. Next, the patient describes the types of emotions that he or she is experiencing (e.g., sadness, anger, anxiety). If several emotions are present simultaneously (e.g., sadness mixed with anxiety), list each. Use a 0% to 100% scale to rate the approximate intensity of these emotions as they were initially felt, (i.e., at the time of the event). On this scale, 0% is the absence of that emotion, and 100% is the greatest intensity of that emotion ever experienced. Rerate the intensity of these same emotions as they are experienced at the time that the logical analysis exercise is attempted. The reason for making both of these ratings is that there is usually a change in the intensity of emotion from the time of the initial mood shift to the time this exercise is initiated. There can be an increase in intensity of the emotion caused by a compounding of the problems (e.g., the stressors become more complicated or difficult) or by rumination about the stimulus event. Likewise, there can be a decrease in the intensity with time and emotional distance from the stimulus or by thinking through the problem and attempting resolution. Changes in direction of emotional intensity and their causes will help therapists to better understand how patients cope internally with emotional shifts. Have the patient write out the thoughts that were associated with each emotion listed. Using the same 0–100% scale, the intensity with which the automatic thought was believed at the time of the event is rated. In this case 0% means a total lack of belief in the idea and 100% means absolute certainty. Have the patient rerate the intensity with which the automatic thought is believed at the time the logical analysis exercise is initiated.

To begin reducing the intensity of the emotional shift, select one of the automatic thoughts that is associated with the most intense emotional shift or one that the patient identifies as particularly troubling. The logical analysis task is to first generate evidence to support and refute the automatic thought and then to objectively review the evidence and draw a conclusion. In two respective columns, the patient lists evidence supporting and refuting the automatic thought under analysis. It is considerably more power for the patient to generate the evidence, rather than accept the word of the therapist. The therapist can ask questions to prompt the patient to consider other evidence and provide a few suggestions.

After the patient examines the evidence for and against the thought, he or she may conclude that the thought is invalid, that the evidence is inconclusive, or that the thought is indeed valid. If the thought is invalid, help the patient to revise the original automatic thought to make it more accurate. For example, "I'm a complete loser" could be modified to "I made a mistake". Again, it is most effective when the patient revises the thought. If the thought is valid (e.g., "My forgetfulness caused the company to lose the account"), the patient should evaluate the potential consequences that follow as well as the probability that these consequences will occur ("I could lose my job" - 50% chance). If the probability is high and the consequences are significant, take a problem-solving approach to generate a plan for decreasing the probability of negative consequences and/or for coping with their occurrence, (e.g., Talk with my boss about my error. Discuss my job security. Read the want ads for potential new job should I get fired. Find ways to compensate for my poor concentration and memory.).

If the evidence is inclusive, determine what type of evidence would be needed to confirm or disconfirm the thought (e.g., "I'm not certain that it was my fault. I will need to ask my boss to be certain."). Generate a plan for accumulating more evidence, (e.g., "I will first talk with a coworker that I trust. Then I will talk with my boss about the event."). Add this evidence to that already generated and reevaluate the validity of the thought. When the exercise has been completed, rerate the intensity of each emotion originally listed. Rerate the intensity of belief in each automatic thought. If the exercise was useful, the intensity of emotion should decrease. If the intensity of emotion remains high, explore the automatic thoughts now associated with the emotion and repeat the exercise.

In mania, a common concern among patients and their family members, friends, and business associates is the euphoric mood and the desire to make dramatic changes on the job changes or in relationships. The hypomanic or manic patient may have more self-confidence and believe that his or her ideas are guaranteed for success, while others find these plans risky or inappropriate. One strategy for slowing the process and reducing excessive risk taking is to evaluate the validity of that these new ideas are, in fact, guaranteed for success using the method described above. Perhaps a more useful method for evaluating new ideas is to examine the advantages and disadvantages of executing the new plan (e.g., changing jobs, making a financial investment, ending or beginning a romantic relationship) and the advantages and disadvantages of not executing the new plan (i.e., remaining at status quo). If the patient, the family, or the therapist is uncertain whether or not the new ideas are creative plans or a symptom of mania that is doomed to failure, monitor symptoms further using a mood graph before making any changes (e.g., "If it is a good idea today, it will be a good idea next week."). Remind the patient how the urgency to act can be a symptom of hypomania.

Control of Subsyndromal Behavioral Symptoms

The behavior activating interventions used in traditional cognitive therapy for depression, work to contain activity in hypomania or the early stages of mania. In depression, there is often self-criticism about inactivity that should be tracked while executing the behavioral interventions. Increased activity should ameliorate a negative view of self, and the feeling of being overwhelmed. In mania, the cognitions surrounding overactivity and accompanying disorganization are related to issues of self-control. Success with behavioral containment not only helps to reduce the stimulation that may interfere with sleep and escalate mania, but can also help to improve patients' sense of self-efficacy.

The behavioral interventions for both depression and mania involve setting goals and planning and executing a finite number of activities. The increased mental stimulation in mania can leave the patient with too many plans, most of which are poorly organized. In depression, the patient is usually too overwhelmed to organize and initiate activity, therefore responsibilities from work or home accumulate. Feeling overwhelmed with responsibilities only worsens inertia. Goal setting helps to organize the patient's thoughts and plans. There are many formats for setting goals. They generally begin with having the patient list all the activities or behaviors that he or she has to or wants to accomplish. This part of the intervention can be started during the therapy session and completed as homework. Both the manic patient and the depressed patient will create lists with more activities than they can accomplished immediately.

The second step is to order the proposed activities by priority. Higher priority items will be attempted first. In depression, the amount of activity assigned will depend on the patient's level of energy. Assign only enough activity that can realistically be accomplished before the next therapy session. This can be troublesome for some patients who feel guilty about their inertia and feel the need to catch-up as soon as possible.

In hypomania, limits must also be set on the amount of activity assigned as homework. Although the patient may feel that he or she can accomplish anything and everything, the continued emergence of new ideas coupled with distractibility, usually lead to many projects started, but few completed. Increased activity during the day means overstimulation and less sleep at night. This process fuels the hypomania, which, in turn, further fuels physical and mental activity, pushing the episode further into mania.

One way to satisfy the guilt ridden depressed patient and the enthusiastic hypomanic patient is to assign two sets of activity, an "A list" and a "B list". The "A list" includes activities that are higher in priority. If the patient completes the tasks or activities on the "A list", he or she may go on to those on the "B list". The clinician must use his or her judgment about how much can reasonably be accomplished between sessions without the patient losing sleep. Start the depressed patient out with a small number of items (1 or 2) on the "A list" that can be easily completed. With the person who is in a hypomanic state, the idea is to provide enough activity to be satisfying and to focus the extra energy, but to avoid overstimulation or "burning the midnight oil". The emphasis should be on completing one project before beginning another.

Reduction of Psychosocial Stressors

The last component of the CBT approach to the treatment of bipolar disorder is the reduction of psychosocial stressors. Episodes of depression and mania interfere with functioning at home, at work, and in relationships in part by compromising a person's ability to solve problems of daily living. Symptoms such as inactivity, irritability, risk taking, or impulsivity, compound stress on the patient and on his or her family members. The emotionality of the patient and the reactions of others disrupt relationships. Before family members or friends recognize the patient's behaviors as symptoms of an illness, they are more likely to take the remarks of the patient at face value. This may allow resentments to build that do not dissipate when the patient's episode of depression or mania ends. The residual problems can be hurtful to all and contribute to a stressful environment that can predispose some to another episode of illness. Therapy, therefore, must work at resolving existing psychosocial stressors, teaching skills to cope with new problems as they arise, and providing patients with corrective feedback on their interpersonal communication skills so that they can maintain health relationships.

Psychosocial Problem-Solving

For some patients, crisis intervention may be the reason that therapy was sought. Therapists are, therefore, challenged to address presenting problems while attempting to teach the CBT skills that have been outlined above. It is easy to be sidetracked by issues that feel pressing to the patient and his or her family. If the number of sessions is restricted by finances, there may not be sufficient time for thorough skills training. However, as the therapist helps the patient to resolve crises, he or she can demonstrate and teach problem-solving skills. This leaves the patient with a structure for addressing future problems when the therapist cannot be present.

Identification and definition of the problem is the first step its resolution, but can be colored or distorted by the patient's mood. The patient should be encouraged to be specific about the behavior, situation, timing, and/or circumstances that are problematic. If there is more than one participant in therapy, some discussion may be necessary until there is an agreed upon statement of the problem (e.g., "Bills are due tomorrow and I don't have enough money to pay them all"). The second step in the process is to generate potential solutions to the problem. It is most helpful to begin by listing all possible solutions without evaluating their quality or feasibility. After reviewing each and eliminating the less desirable or unreasonable solutions, the remaining solutions can be ranked in terms of their likelihood of success. If one solution does not stand out as the most appropriate, evaluate the remaining solutions in terms of their advantages and disadvantages. Specify how, when, and by whom the solution will be implemented and assign this as homework. Evaluate the outcome and, if not completely successful, revise the existing plan to better address the problem.

Interpersonal Communication

One of the most common obstacles to good communication is emotion. Emotion is a filter through which messages can get distorted. Bipolar disorder is marked by dramatic emotional changes that are accompanied by changes in view of self and of others. Both cognitive or attitudinal changes and emotional changes will effect how messages are sent and how they are received. This results in the listener hearing things differently than they were intended. Responses will, in turn, reflect what was heard rather than what was intended to be communicated. In these situations, it does not take long for tension or conflict to develop. The goal of therapy is to reduce the filters that distort communication so that the patient can effectively send messages to others and receive messages without misinterpretation. The following is a summary of communication rules that will aid this process.

- *Be calm.* Anger will dictate the choice of words and the solutions offered. It is better to wait until the emotion subsides than to risk making bad decisions in the heat of anger.
- *Be organized.* Take time to think through a problem and its possible solution before discussing it with others.
- *Be specific.* Global complaints (e.g., "I can't stand this anymore", "You don't support me") cannot be easily resolved and generally lead to more conflict as it forces the recipient of the complaint to defend him or herself, often by counterattacking. Specify the action, event or process that is problematic.
- *Be clear.* Trying to be gentle by staying vague leaves too much room for misinterpretation.
- *Be a good listener.* Attentive listening without interruption means trying to understand the speaker's perspective rather than using the other person's talking time as an opportunity to prepare a response (or defense).
- *Be flexible.* Consider others' ideas before selecting a solution.
- *Be creative.* In generating a solution to a specific problem, it is useful to look beyond strategies used in the past. Be imaginative. Try out new plans. If they do not work, another method can be used.
- *Keep it simple.* Resist the urge to bring into the discussion other problems or issues that come to mind. Monitor the conversation for digressions away from the main point. Solve one problem at a time.

While these rules seem fairly simple to follow, it takes practice to be a good communicator, particularly if the topic is conflictual or if the person is feeling depressed, irritable, or anxious. The key to successful communication training is to slow the process down so that strengths and weaknesses in communication skills can be pointed out to the patient. The patient, and sometimes his or her family members, need an objective evaluation of their communication behaviors. Self-observation, while useful, is biased by the speaker's view of him or herself and the appropriatness of their messages. The therapist's objective observations can be very valuable if the patient is ready to hear them.

Conclusions and Future Directions

A strong case can be made for the use of CBT as an adjunct to pharmacotherapy in patients with bipolar affective disorder. Hopefully, more empirical data will be forthcoming to establish the cost-effectiveness of this additive strategy. For bipolar disorder, an exclusive focus on pharmacotherapy may be penny-wise, but it is pound foolish. Failure to attend to the psychosocial issues that affect how patients cope with this chronic and devastating illness will result in repeated episodes of illness and the need for more expensive treatments such as emergency room visits and hospitalizations. Meanwhile, patients' ability to function continues to diminish and they become less able to contribute in terms of social and vocational roles. Research is also needed to determine what elements of the CBT intervention for bipolar disorder are most useful in helping patients to maximally control symptoms throughout their lives. The challenge to clinicians is to provide a comprehensive treatment such as this in a health care environment in which less is considered better (i.e., less expensive).

References

Aagaard, J., & Vestergaard, P. (1990). Predictors of outcome in prophylactic lithium treatment: A 2-year prospective study. *Journal of Affective Disorders, 18,* 259–266.

Altamura, A. C., & Mauri, M. (1985). Plasma concentration, information and therapy adherence during long-term treatment with antidepressants. *British Journal of Clinical Pharmacology, 20,* 714–716.

Altshuler, L. L., Post, R. M., Leverich, G. S., Mikalauskas, K., Rosoff, A., & Ackerman, L. (1995). Antidepressant-induced mania and cycle acceleration: A controversy revisited. *American Journal of Psychiatry, 152,* 1130–1138.

APA (1994). *Diagnostic and statistical manual of mental disorders,* 4th edition (DSM-IV). Washington, DC: American Psychiatric Association.

Angst, J. (1981). Clinical indications for a prophylactic treatment of depression. *Advances in Biological Psychiatry, 7,* 218–229.

Aronson, T. A., & Skukla, S. (1987). Life events and relapse in bipolar disorder: The impact of a catastrophic event. *Acta Psychiatrica Scandinavica, 75,* 571–576.

Baastrup, P. C., & Schou, M. (1967). Lithium as a prophylactic agent: Its effect against recurrent depression and manic-depressive psychosis. *Archives of General Psychiatry, 16,* 162–172.

Baastrup, P. C., Poulsen, J. C., Schou, M., Thomsen, K., & Amdisen, A. (1970). Prophylactic lithium: Double-blind discontinuation in manic-depressive and recurrent depressive disorders. *Lancet, 2,* 326–330.

Basco, M. R., & Rush, A. J. (1995). Compliance with pharmacotherapy in mood disorders. *Psychiatry Annals, 25,* 78–82.

Basco, M. R., & Rush, A. J. (1996). *Cognitive-behavior therapy for bipolar disorder.* New York: Guilford Press.

Beck, A. T., Rush, A. J., Shaw, B. F., & Emery, G. (1979). *Cognitive therapy of depression.* New York: Guilford Press.

Benson, R. (1975). The forgotten treatment modality in bipolar illness: Psychotherapy. *Disorders of the Nervous System, 35,* 634–638.

Bidzinska, E. J. (1984). Stress factors in affective diseases. *British Journal of Psychiatry, 144,* 161–166.

Blackburn, I. M., Evanson, K. M., & Bishop, S. (1987). A two year naturalistic follow-up of depressed patients treated with cognitive therapy, pharmacotherapy and a combination of both. *Journal of Affective Disorders, 10*, 67–75.

Bowden, C. L., Brugger, A. M., Swann, A. C., Calabrese, J. R., Janicak, P. G., Petty, F., Dilsaver, S. C., Davis, J. M., Rush, A. J., Small, J. G., Garza-Trevino, E. S., Risch, S. C., Goodnick, P. J., & Morris, D. D. (1994). Efficacy of divalproex sodium vs. lithium and placebo in the treatment of mania. *Journal of the American Medical Association, 271*, 918–924.

Calabrese, J. R., & Delucchi, G. A. (1990). Spectrum of efficacy of valproate in 55 patients with rapid-cycling bipolar disorder. *American Journal of Psychiatry, 147*, 431–434.

Clarkin, J. F., Glick, I. D., Haas, G. L., Spencer, J. H., Lewis, A. B., Peyser, J., DeMane, N., GoodEllis, M., Harris, E., & Listell, V. (1990). A randomized clinical trial of inpatient family intervention. V. Results for affective disorders. *Journal of Affective Disorders, 18*, 1728.

Cochran, S. D. (1984). Preventing medical noncompliance in the outpatient treatment of bipolar affective disorders. *Journal of Consulting and Clinical Psychology, 52*, 873–878.

Connelly, C. E. (1984). Compliance with outpatient lithium therapy. *Perspectives in Psychiatric Care, 22*, 44–50.

Connelly, C. E., Davenport, Y. B., & Nurnberger, J. I. (1982). Adherence to treatment regimen in a lithium carbonate clinic. *Archives of General Psychiatry, 39*, 585–588.

Coppen, A., Noguera, R., Bailey, J., Burns, B. H., Swani, M. S., Hare, E. H., Gardner, R., & Maggs, R. (1971). Prophylactic lithium in affective disorders: Controlled trial. *Lancet, 2*, 275–279.

Coppen, A., Peet, M., Bailey, J., Noguera, R., Burns, B., Swani, M., Maggs, R., & Gardner, R. (1973). Double-blind and open prospective studies of lithium prophylaxis in affective disorders. *Psychiatry, Neurology and Neurochirurgy, 75*, 500–510.

Cundall, R. L., Brooks, P. W., & Murray, L. G. (1972). A controlled evaluation of lithium prophylaxis in affective disorders. *Psychological Medicine, 2*, 308–311.

Danion, J. M., Neureuther, C., Krieger-Finance, F., Imbs, J. L., & Singer, L. (1987). Compliance with long-term lithium treatment in major affective disorders. *Pharmacopsychiatry, 20*, 230–231.

Davenport, Y. B., Ebert, M. H., Adland, M. L., & Goodwin, F. K. (1977). Couples group therapy as an adjunct to lithium maintenance of the manic patient. *American Journal of Orthopsychiatry, 47*, 495–502.

Dunner, D. L., Murphy, D., Stallone, R., & Fieve, R. R. (1979). Episode frequency prior to lithium treatment in bipolar manic-depressive patients. *Comprehensive Psychiatry, 20*, 511–515.

Dubobsky, S. I., Franks, R. D., Allen, S., & Murphy, J. (1986). Calcium antagonists in mania: A double blind study of verapamil. *Psychiatry Research, 18*, 309–320.

Fava, G. A., Grandi, S., Zielezny, M., Canestrari, R., & Morphy, M. A. (1994). *American Journal of Psychiatry, 151*, 1295–1299.

Fieve, R. R., Kumbaraci, T., & Dunner, D. L. (1976). Lithium prophylaxis of depression in bipolar I, bipolar II, and unipolar patients. *American Journal of Psychiatry, 133*, 925–930.

Gelenberg, A. J., Carroll, J. A., Baudhuin, M. G., Jefferson, J. W., & Greist, J. H. (1989). The meaning of serum lithium levels in maintenance therapy of mood disorders: A review of the literature. *Journal of Clinical Psychiatry, 50 (Suppl)*, 17–22.

Glassner, B., & Haldipur, C. V. (1983). Life events and early and late onset of Bipolar Disorder. *American Journal of Psychiatry, 140*, 215–217.

Goodwin, F. K., & Jamison, K. R. (1990). *Manic-depressive illness*. New York: Oxford University Press.

Hollon, S. D., Shetton, R. C., & Loosen, P. T. (1991). Cognitive therapy and pharmacotherapy for depression. *Journal of Consulting and Clinical Psychology, 59(1)*, 88–99.

Jacob, M., Frank, E., Kupfer, D. J., Cornes, C., & Carpenter, L. L. (1987). A psychoeducational workshop for depressed patients. *Hospital and Community Psychiatry, 38,* 968–972.

Jarrett, R. B., Basco, M. R., Ramanan, J., & Rush, A. J. (1993). Is there a role for continuation phase cognitive therapy for depressed outpatients? Unpublished manuscript.

Keller, M. B., Shapiro, R. W., Lavori, P. W., & Wolfe, N. (1982). Relapse in major depressive disorder: Analysis with the life table. *Archives of General Psychiatry, 39,* 911–915.

Keller, M. B., Lavori, P. W., Kane, J. M., Gelenberg, A. J., Rosenbaum, J. F., Walzer, E. A., & Baker, L. A. (1992). Subsyndromal symptoms in Bipolar Disorder: A comparison of standard and law serum levels of Lithium. *Archives of General Psychiatry, 49,* 371–376.

Kennedy, S., Thompson, R., Stancer, H., Roy, A., & Persad, E. (1983). Life events precipitating mania. *British Journal of Psychiatry, 142,* 398–403.

Kraepelin, E. (1921/1976). Manic depressive insanity and paranoia. In G. M. Robertson (Ed.), *Textbook of Psychiatry.* New York: Arno Press (translated by R. M. Barclay, original work published in 1921).

Kucera-Bozarth, K., Beck, N. C., & Lyss, L. (1982). Compliance with lithium regimens. *Journal of Psychosocial Nursing and Mental Health Services, 20,* 11–15.

Luznat, R., Murphy, D. P., & Nonn, C. M. H. (1988). Carbamazapine vs lithium in the treatment and prophylaxis of mania. *British Journal of Psychiatry, 153,* 198–204.

Miller, I. W., Norman, W. H., & Keitner, G. I. (1989). Cognitive-behavioral treatment of depressed inpatients: Six- and twelve-month follow-ups. *American Journal of Psychiatry, 146,* 1274–1279.

Miller, I.W., Norman, W. H., & Keitner, G. I. (1990). Treatment response of high cognitive dysfunction depressed inpatients. *Comprehensive Psychiatry, 30,* 62–71.

Murphy, D. L., & Beigel, A. (1974). Depression, elation, and lithium carbonate responses in manic patient subgroups. *Archives of General Psychiatry, 31,* 643–648.

Myers, E. D., & Calvert, E. J. (1984). Information, compliance and side-effects: A study of patients on antidepressant medication. *British Journal of Clinical Pharmacology, 17,* 21–25.

Post, R. M. (1992). Transduction of psychosocial stress into the neurobiology of recurrent affective disorder. *American Journal of Psychiatry, 149,* 999–1010.

Powell, B. J., Othmer, E., & Sinkhorn, C. (1977). Pharmacological aftercare for homogeneous groups of patients. *Hospital and Community Psychiatry, 28,* 125–127.

Prien, R. F., Caffey, E. M., Jr., & Klett, C. J. (1973a). Prophylactic efficacy of lithium carbonate in manic-depressive illness. *Archives of General Psychiatry, 26,* 146–153.

Prien, R. F., Klett, C. J., & Caffey, E. M., Jr. (1973b). Lithium carbonate and imipramine in prevention of affective episodes: A comparison in recurrent affective illness. *Archives of General Psychiatry, 29,* 420–425.

Robins, L. N., Helzer, J. E., Weissman, M. M., Orvaschel, H., Gruenberg, E., Burke, J. D., & Regier, D. A. (1984). Lifetime prevalence of specific psychiatric disorders in three sites. *Archives of General Psychiatry, 41,* 949–958.

Roy-Byrne, P., Post, R. M., Uhde, T. W., Porcu, T., & Davis, D. (1985). The longitudinal course of recurrent affective illness: Life chart data from research patients at the NIMH. *Acta Psychiatrica Scandinavica, 71 (Suppl. 317),* 1–34.

Rush, A. J., Beck, A. T., Kovacs, M., Khatami, M., Fitzgibbons, R., & Wolman, T. (1977). Comparative efficacy of cognitive therapy and imipramine in the treatment of depressed outpatients. *Cognitive Therapy & Research, 1,* 17–37.

Schwarcz, G., & Silbergeld, S. (1983). Serum lithium spot checks to evaluate medication compliance. *Journal of Clinical Psychopharmacolopy, 3,* 356–358.

Seltzer, A., Roncari, I., & Garfinkel, P. (1980). Effect of patient education on medication compliance. *Canadian Journal of Psychiatry, 25,* 638–645.

Shakir, S. A., Volkmar, F. R., & Bacon, S. (1979). Group psychotherapy as an adjunct to lithium maintenance. *American Journal of Psychiatry, 136,* 455–456.

Small, J. G., Klapper, M. H., Milstein, V., Kellams, J. J., Miller, M. J., Marhenke, J. D., & Small, I. F. (1991). Carbamazapine compared with lithium in the treatment of mania. *Archives of General Psychiatry, 48,* 915–921.

Spalt, L. (1975). Sexual behavior and affective disorders. *Disorders of the Nervous System, 36,* 974–977.

Stallone, F., Shelley, E., Mendlewicz, J., & Fieve, R.R. (1973). The use of lithium in affective disorders: Ill: A double blind study of prophylaxis in bipolar illness. *American Journal of Psychiatry, 130,* 1006–1010.

Suppes, T., Baldessarini, R. J., Faedda, G. L., & Tohen, M. (1991). Risk of recurrence following discontinuation of lithium treatment in bipolar disorder. *Archives of General Psychiatry, 48,* 1082–1088.

Thase, M. E., & Wright, J. H. (1991). Cognitive behavior therapy with depressed inpatients: An abridged treatment manual. Behavior Therapy, 22, 595.

Thase, M. E., Simons, A. D., McGeary, J., Cahalane, J. F., Hughes, C., Hrden, T., & Friedman, E. (1992). Relapse after cognitive behavior therapy of depression: Potential implications of longer-term courses of treatment. *American Journal of Psychiatry, 149,* 1046–1052.

Wehr, T. A., Sack, D. A., & Rosenthal, N. E. (1987). Sleep reduction as a final common pathway in the genesis of mania. *American Journal of Psychiatry, 144,* 201–204.

Weissman, M. M., Leaf, P. J., Livingston, B. M., et al. (1987). The epidemiology of dysthymia in the community: Rates, risks, comorbidity and treatment. Paper presented at the Convention of the American Psychiatric Association, Chicago, IL.

Whisman, M. A., Miller, I. W., Norman, W. H., & Keitner, G. A. (1991). Cognitive therapy with depressed inpatients: Side effects on dysfunctional cognitions. *Journal of Consulting and Clinical Psychology, 59,* 282–288.

Winokur, G., Clayton, P. J., & Reich, T. (1969). *Manic depressive Illness.* St. Louis, MO: C.V. Mosby.

Wright, J. H., Thase, M. E., Beck, A. T., & Ludgate, J. W. (1993). *Cognitive therapy with inpatients: Developing a cognitive milieu.* New York: Guilford Press.

Wulsin, L., Bachop, M., & Hoffman, D. (1988). Group therapy in manic-depressive illness. *American Journal of Psychotherapy, 2,* 263–271.

Youssel, F. A. (1983). Compliance with therapeutic regimens: A follow-up study for patients with affective disorders. *Journal of Advances in Nursing, 8,* 513–517.

Zis, A. P., & Goodwin, F. K. (1979). Major affective disorders as a recurrent illness: A critical review. *Archives of General Psychiatry, 36,* 835–839.

Zis, A. P., Grof, P., Webster, M., & Goodwin, F. K. (1980). Prediction of relapse in recurrent affective disorder. *Psychopharmacology Bulletin, 16,* 47–49.

Further Reading

Basco, M. R., & Rush, A. J. (1996). *Cognitive-behavior therapy for bipolar disorder.* New York: Guilford Press.

Beck, A. T., Shaw, B. F., Rush, A. J., & Emery, G. (1979). *Cognitive therapy of depression.* New York: Guilford Press.

Cochran, S. D. (1984). Preventing medical noncompliance in the outpatient treatment of bipolar affective disorders. *Journal of Consulting and Clinical Psychology, 52,* 873–878.

Goodwin, F. K., & Jamison, K. R. (1990). *Manic-depressive illness.* New York: Oxford University Press.

Palmer, A. G., Williams, H., & Adams, M. (1995). CBT in a group format for bi-polar affective disorder. *Behavioural and Cognitive Psychotherapy, 23,* 153–168.

Wright, J. H., Thase, M. E., Beck, A. T., & Ludgate, J. W. (1993). *Cognitive therapy with inpatients: Developing a cognitive milieu.* New York: Guilford Press.

Sources of Educational Materials

National Mental Health Information Center
National Mental Health Association
1021 Prince St.
Alexandria, Virginia
USA
(800) 969–6642
(703) 684–7722

National Institute of Mental Health and the D/ART Program
National Institute of Mental Health
Public Inquiries Branch, Room 15C-05
5600 Fishers Lane
Rockville, MD 20857
USA
800/2234427

National Depressive and Manic Depressive Association
53 West Jackson Boulevard, Room 618
Chicago, IL 60604
USA
312/642–0049
312/939–2442

National Alliance for the Mentally Ill
2101 Wilson Boulevard, Suite 302
Arlington, VA 22201
USA
800/950–6264

18

Cognitive Behavioral Treatment of Schizophrenia

KIM T. MUESER

Dartmouth Medical School, USA

Introduction

Schizophrenia is a severe psychiatric illness, afflicting approximately 1% of the population worldwide. Schizophrenia usually has an onset in late adolescence or early adulthood, and tends to have an episodic course punctuated by symptom exacerbations requiring brief hospitalizations throughout the lifetime. Although the prevalence of schizophrenia is similar across males and females, females experience a milder course of the illness, including a later onset of symptoms, less time in the hospital, and better social functioning. Despite the serious and long-term nature of schizophrenia, many patients gradually improve over time, and total symptom remissions occur in some patients in their later years.

Symptoms and Impairments of Schizophrenia

Schizophrenia is characterized by two broad classes of symptoms: Positive symptoms and negative symptoms. *Positive symptoms* refer to cognitions, sensory experiences, and behaviors that are present in patients, but are ordinarily absent in persons without the illness. Common examples of positive symptoms include hallucinations (e.g., hearing voices), delusions (e.g., believing that people are persecuting you), and bizarre behavior (e.g., maintaining a peculiar posture for no apparent reason). *Negative symptoms*, on the other hand, refer to the absence or diminution of cognitions, feelings, or behaviors which are ordinarily present in persons without the illness. Common negative symptoms include blunted or flattened affective expressiveness (e.g., diminished facial expressiveness), poverty of speech (i.e., diminished verbal communication), anhedonia (i.e., inability to experience pleasure), apathy, psychomotor retardation (e.g., slow rate of speech), and physical inertia.

The positive symptoms of schizophrenia tend to fluctuate over the course of the disorder and are often in remission between episodes of the illness. In addition, positive symptoms tend to be responsive to the effects of antipsychotic medication. In contrast, negative symptoms tend to be stable over time and are less responsive to antipsychotic medications.

In addition to positive and negative symptoms, many patients with schizophrenia experience negative emotions as a consequence of their illness. Depression and suicidal ideation are common symptoms of schizophrenia, and approximately 10% of the persons with this illness die from suicide. Difficulties with anxiety are common, which is often due to positive symptoms, such as hallucinations or paranoid delusions. Finally, anger and hostility may also be present, especially when the patient is paranoid.

Aside from the characteristic symptoms of schizophrenia, many patients have cognitive impairments that may limit their ability to participate in traditional cognitive behavioral treatments. Cognitive deficits in areas such as attention, memory, and abstract thinking are frequently present. These impairments require specially tailored clinical procedures designed to remediate or compensate for these basic deficits.

A final core characteristic of schizophrenia is impairments in social functioning. Common problem areas include difficulties establishing and maintaining interpersonal relationships, inability to work, and difficulties in self-care skills, such as grooming and hygiene. Indeed, impairments in social functioning are thought to be such a cardinal characteristic of schizophrenia that many diagnostic systems (such as DSM-IV: APA, 1994) require such impairments to establish a diagnosis of schizophrenia.

As is clear from a review of the characteristic symptoms and impairments of schizophrenia, this disorder is multiply handicapping, impacting on all spheres of life functioning. Cognitive behavioral treatment is aimed at improving the wide range of difficulties experienced by patients with schizophrenia.

The Stress-Vulnerability-Coping Skills Model

The stress-vulnerability-coping skills model of schizophrenia provides a valuable heuristic to clinicians in guiding their treatment efforts. This model posits that the severity, course, and outcome of schizophrenia are determined by three interacting factors: vulnerability, stress, and coping skills. *Biological vulnerability* is thought to be determined by a combination of genetic and early environmental influences (e.g., obstetric complications leading to subtle neonatal brain damage). Without the necessary biological vulnerability, symptoms of schizophrenia will never develop.

The second factor, which impacts on biological vulnerability, is *socio-environmental stress*. Stress can be defined as contingencies or events that require the individual to adapt in order to minimize negative effects. Common sources of stress include: life events (e.g., the death of a loved one) and exposure to high levels of criticism and intrusiveness from relatives. The greater the amount of stress to which a patient is exposed, the more vulnerable he or she will be to relapses and rehospitalizations.

The third factor which can influence the course and outcome of schizophrenia is *coping skills*. Coping skills can be defined as the ability to either minimize the noxious effects of stress on biological vulnerability, or the ability to remove or escape from stressors which impinge upon the patient. For example, a patient who experiences the death of a loved one might employ good coping skills by talking about the loss with significant others thereby gaining acceptance and support, and decreasing the negative effects of this life event. Similarly, a patient who is confronted by a relative for forgetting to purchase a requested item at the store could display good social skills by acknowledging the relatives complaint, thereby resolving the conflict and its accompanying stress. Thus, good coping skills mediate the noxious effects of stress on biological vulnerability.

The stress-vulnerability-coping skills model has several implications for cognitive-behavioral treatment of schizophrenia. With respect to vulnerability, antipsychotic medications can effectively reduce risk of relapse. However, efforts may need to be undertaken to enhance medication compliance, a significant problem in this population. Drug and alcohol abuse can worsen biological vulnerability, leading to relapses of symptoms. Therefore, cognitive behavioral strategies may be applied to decrease substance abuse behavior. The role of stress in precipitating relapses in schizophrenia points to the importance of reducing stress. Cognitive-behavioral interventions most frequently target familial stress for reduction, although other types of environmental stress may also be the focus of treatment. Last, a variety of different strategies can be employed to improve the coping skills of patients with schizophrenia, thereby decreasing their vulnerability to stress-induced relapses and enhancing their functional capacity.

Cognitive Behavioral Interventions

A wide range of cognitive-behavioral strategies can be applied to persons with schizophrenia. It is beyond the scope of this chapter to describe each possible intervention. The focus here will be on describing how to implement those interventions which are most commonly used, and for which there is support for their clinical efficacy (for reviews, see Penn & Mueser, 1996;

Mueser & Bellack, 1995). The following interventions will be described: social skills training, behavioral family therapy, training in coping skills for managing psychotic symptoms, and integrated treatment for substance use disorders.

Cognitive-behavioral intervention does not work in a vacuum. Thus, in order for any psychosocial treatment to be effective for schizophrenia, consideration must be given to the necessary ingredients of comprehensive treatment (Bellack & Mueser, 1986). Patients with schizophrenia require pharmacological treatment with antipsychotic medication, which needs to monitored on a routine basis throughout the course of the illness. Attention must also be paid to the basic living and medical needs of patients with schizophrenia. Schizophrenia frequently interferes with the ability of patients to recognize and seek help for medical conditions, or to advocate for adequate housing, nutritional, and other self-care needs. Finally, it is critical that patients receive case management to integrate the various facets of their treatment program, and ensure continuity of care over time. Without attending to these basic elements of comprehensive treatment, cognitive-behavioral interventions are unlikely to result in success.

Social Skills Training

Even with appropriate medication management, yearly relapse rates are often as high as 40%. Additionally, antipsychotics do not improve social skills which are necessary for community living. Social skills deficits reflect the combined influences of symptoms intruding on skills, inadequate learning history before the onset of the illness, lack of environmental stimulation, and the loss of skill due to prolonged disuse (Liberman, DeRisi & Mueser, 1989). Social skills training is a set of techniques, based on social learning theory, which are packaged together in order to systematically teach new interpersonal skills to persons. Patients with schizophrenia have been repeatedly found to have poor interpersonal competence. Social skills training is an effective strategy for rectifying these problems.

Assessment of social skills. Social skills are defined as the specific component behaviors which, in combination, are necessary for effective social interactions. Social skills can be divided into four broad categories: non-verbal skills, paralinguistic features, interactive balance, and verbal content. *Non-verbal features* refer to skills such as the appropriateness of facial expression, use of gestures, posture, and eye contact, which are involved in the communication of affect and interpersonal exchanges. *Paralinguistic features* refer to the qualities of the voice tone, including voice loudness, pitch, tone, rate of speech, and vocal inflection. Similar to non-verbal skills, paralinguistic features convey critical information about the person's affect and involvement in the interaction.

Verbal content refers to the choice of words and phrasing, irrespective of the manner in which the words were said. *Interactive balance* refers to the meshing or latency between responses during an interaction, as well as the amount of speech made by the patient compared to the interactive partner. Poor interactive balance, indicated by problems such as a slow response latency or minimal speech, conveys to the partner a lack of engagement, and is unrewarding.

A number of strategies are available to the clinician for assessing specific deficits in social skill. It is best to proceed from the general to the specific by first posing questions to patients, significant others, and treatment providers. Then, when specific problem areas have been identified, more detailed behavioral assessment can be conducted. Useful questions for assessing the presence of social impairments include:

- Is the patient lonely?
- Is the patient able to initiate conversations with others?
- Is the patient able to get others to respond to him or her positively?
- Is the patient able to resolve conflicts?
- Is the patient able to express his or her feelings?
- Does the patient desire friends/more intimate relationships?
- Is the patient often socially withdrawn?

These questions are not an exhaustive list of all the possible areas of social dysfunction that may need to be assessed. For example, the patient's ability to negotiate medication issues with his or her physician, job interviewing skills, or ability to resist offers to use drugs or alcohol are other possible topic areas that may require assessment.

Once specific problem areas have been identified, a more fine-grained assessment of social skill deficits can be conducted. There are a number of methods for assessing social skill. The most practical strategy is conducting role play assessments. *Role plays* are simulated social interactions in which the patient interacts with a confederate during a brief encounter designed to assess a specific social skill area. Role plays are generally brief, lasting three to ten exchanges, and are constructed so as to resemble actual situations the patients frequently face. The patient is instructed to show how he or she would handle that situation in real life. Patients participate in several role plays of each problem situation in order to evaluate consistent skill deficits. The most reliable assessment of social skill can be obtained when the role plays are videotaped or audiotaped, and later rated for dimensions of social skill.

Social perception skills must be also assessed. Social perception and/or receptive elements of social skill refer to skills implied in the perception of the meaning of interpersonal communications. The ability to adequately receive and process interpersonal stimuli is essential for effective social performance. To perform skillfully, the individual must be able to identify the emotions or intent expressed by the other person and make complex judgements about the form and timing of the appropriate response. Inaccurate conclusions about another person's intended meanings can be reached in a social interaction because a person fails to listen or look at the interaction partner, fails to integrate what is heard, does not know the meaning of what is heard, or looks for cues that are irrelevant to the moment. An important prerequisite is focusing attention. Given that attention impairment is frequent among patients with negative symptoms, many of them will need prolonged training in order to learn to attend to relevant interpersonal signals. It has also been found that schizophrenic patients suffer a greater impairment in facial expression perception skills, particularly in the area of discriminating and recognizing emotions. However, the relationship between the discrimination of emotions and other social skills measures have not been adequately considered.

Although a detailed assessment of social skill deficits may be conducted before engaging the patient in social skills training, it is also possible to engage patients immediately in treatment after identifying general areas of social impairment. As will be reviewed in the following section, social skills training involves ongoing assessment and training of new social skills. However, if the clinician wishes to more rigorously evaluate the effects of social skills training on the patient's interpersonal competence, conducting role play assessments before and after skills training provides the most reliable measure.

Social skills training formats. Social skills training can be conducted either in an individual or group format. There are several advantages to conducting the training in a group format. First, group-based skills training is more economical, because several patients can participate at the same time. Second, the group format provides multiple role models per patient, facilitating their acquisition of social skills. Third, conducting role plays in a group rather than individual setting is easier because there are more possible people to participate in the role plays. When skills training is conducted in groups, it is best if at least two or three sessions take place per week, as "massed practice" results in more rapid learning than practice spaced over longer periods of time.

Despite the advantages of group-based social skills training, social skills can be taught in the context of individual psychotherapy sessions. In these sessions, skills training is usually combined with psychoeducation, training and stress management, and teaching coping skills for management of residual symptoms. As most skills training takes place in groups, the clinical procedures for conducting such training are briefly described below.

Social skills training techniques. Social skills training follows a standardized set of procedures, summarized in Table 18.1. Social skills training sessions begin with establishing a rationale for the importance of learning the targeted skill. This rationale can be both elicited from group participants by asking leading questions ("Why do you think it might be important to learn how to express negative feelings constructively"?), as well as by providing additional

Table 18.1. Schedule of a session on social skills training

1. *Establish rationale for the skill*
   - Elicit reasons for learning the skill from group participants
   - Acknowledge all contributions
   - Provide additional reasons not mentioned by group members

2. *Discuss the steps of the skill*
   - Break the skill down into 3 or 4 steps
   - Write the steps on a board or poster
   - Discuss the reason for each step
   - Check for understanding of each step

3. *Model the skill in a role play*
   - Explain that you will demonstrate the skill in a role play
   - Plan out the role play in advance
   - Use two leaders to model the skill
   - Keep the role play simple

4. *Review the role play with the participants*
   - Discuss whether each step of the skill was used in the role play
   - Ask group members to evaluate the effectiveness of the role model
   - Keep the review brief and to the point

5. *Engage a patient in a role play of the same situation*
   - Request the patient to try the skill in a role play with one of the leaders
   - Ask the patient questions to make sure he or she understands their goal
   - Instruct members to observe the patient
   - Start with a patient who is more skilled or is likely to be compliant

6. *Provide positive feedback*
   - Elicit positive feedback from group members about the patient's skills
   - Encourage feedback that is specific
   - Cut off any negative feedback
   - Praise effort and provide hints to group members about good performance

7. *Provide corrective feedback*
   - Elicit suggestions for how patient could do the skill better next time
   - Limit the feedback to one or two suggestions
   - Strive to communicate the suggestions in a positive, upbeat manner

8. *Engage the patient in another role play of the same situation*
   - Request that the patient change one behavior in the role play
   - Check by asking questions to make sure the patient understands the suggestion
   - Try to work on behaviors that are salient and changeable

9. *Provide additional feedback*
   - Focus first on the behavior that the patient was requested to change
   - Engage patient in 2–4 role plays with feedback after each one
   - Use other behavior shaping strategies to improve skills, such as coaching, prompting, supplemental modeling
   - Be generous but specific when providing positive feedback

10. *Assign homework*
    - Give an assignment to practice the skill
    - Ask group members to identify situations in which they could use the skill
    - When possible, tailor the assignment to each patient's level of skill

Table 18.2. Components of specific social skills

Starting a conversation
1. Choose the right time and place.
2. Introduce yourself or greet the person you want to talk with.
3. Make small talk (for example, the weather or sports).
4. Decide if the other person is listening or wants to talk.

Expressing negative feelings
1. Look at the person and speak firmly.
2. Say exactly what the person did that upset you.
3. Tell the person how it made you feel.
4. Suggest how the person might prevent this from happening in the future.

Expressing positive feelings
1. Choose a time and place when you can talk with the other person in private
2. Judge if person appears interested
3. Express affection in warm, caring voice tone
4. Tell person why you feel this way

Compromising and negotiation
1. State your personal viewpoint
2. Listen to the other person's viewpoint
3. Repeat back what you heard
4. Suggest a compromise

reasons. Developing a rationale for the skill is critical to motivating patients to actively participate in the training.

After a rationale has been established, the different steps of the skill are presented and discussed. Skills are broken down into different component steps in order to facilitate the gradual learning of skills over repeated role plays. Table 18.2 provides examples of the components of four social skills. After reviewing the steps of the skill, the leaders model the skill in a role play. This demonstration of the skill is intended to help group participants understand how the different components of the skill are combined into an effective overall communication. After the skill has been modeled, there is a brief discussion regarding the specific steps of the skill, and the overall effectiveness of the leader in the role play is evaluated.

Immediately after the social skill has been modeled by the leaders in a role play, a patient is engaged in a role play of the skill. The purpose of this role play is to give patients an opportunity to practice the skill they have just observed. Patients are instructed to "do the best you can trying to use this skill". Following completion of the role play, the leader elicits positive feedback from group members and provides additional feedback for specific components of the skill which were performed well. Then, corrective feedback is provided in the form of suggestions for how the patient could do the skill more effectively next time. Effort is always reinforced, and the leader strives to ensure that all feedback is constructive and specific.

Following positive and corrective feedback, the leader engages the patient in another role play of the same situation, requesting that he or she make one or two minor changes in the skill based on the feedback provided. It is essential that participants engage in at least two role plays, because it is through the process of practice, feedback, and additional practice that improvements in social skill gradually occur over time. When the patient has completed the second role play, further positive and corrective feedback is provided, followed by an optional third role play, if the patient is willing and improvements can still be made. After one patient has had the opportunity to practice the skill in several role plays, the leader moves on and engages a second patient, and so forth until all patients have participated in role plays. At the end of the social skills training session, the leader gives a homework assignment to participants to practice the skill on their own. It is sometimes helpful to give the participants homework sheets or reminders to complete their homework. At the beginning of the next session homework is reviewed and role plays are set up based on actual experiences participants had using the skills, or for situations in which the participants might have used the skills. Usually between two and five sessions are spent learning a specific skill before moving on to the next skill.

Although the main strategy for teaching social skills include modeling, role play rehearsal, feedback, and additional role playing, other methods may be used as well. For example *coaching* (providing verbal prompts) and *prompting* (providing hand signals) during role plays can help patients improve their performance. Additional information on teaching techniques and the structure in the social skills training sessions can be obtained in Liberman et al. (1989) and Bellack, Mueser, Gingerich & Agresta (1997). A wide variety of areas of social dysfunction can be targeted in social skills training. Some of the most common topic areas are summarized in Table 18.3.

Table 18.3. Curriculum for social skills training

Assertiveness
Conversational skills
Medication management
Unemployment
Leisure and recreational skills
Friendship and dating skills
Family communication
Conflict resolution

Behavioral Family Therapy

As previously reviewed, stressful family relationships can have a negative impact on the course of schizophrenia. Furthermore, schizophrenia has a disruptive and burdensome effect on the lives of relatives. Therefore, the goals of behavioral family intervention are to reduce the stress on all family members and to improve the ability of the family to monitor the course of the illness. These goals are achieved in behavioral family therapy through a combination of education, and training in communication and problem-solving skills. A detailed explication of the behavioral family therapy model is provided in Mueser & Glynn (1995) and Falloon, Boyd & McGill (1984).

Format. Behavioral family therapy is provided to individual families over extended, but usually time-limited intervals. Sessions usually last 1 h, include both the patient and relatives, and take place on a declining contact basis over at least 6–9 months (e.g., weekly for 3 months, biweekly for 6 months, monthly for 3 months). It is advantageous to conduct at least some sessions at home. Home-based sessions provide valuable information about the natural environment in which patients and relatives live or interact, and they may reduce canceled appointments by making sessions easy for family members to attend. Relatives and patients can be engaged in behavioral family therapy at any stage of the illness. Early engagement, such as soon after the first or second break, may have the advantage of providing necessary information and skills to family members before they become frustrated and burned out from trying to manage the illness. One convenient time to begin family intervention is shortly following an acute exacerbation requiring hospitalization. Relatives and patients are frequently motivated after a relapse to participate in a program that has the goal of reducing further relapses and improving patient functioning and independence.

Structure of family sessions. Behavioral family therapy is divided into five sequential stages, although each stage is repeated a number of times throughout therapy: assessment, education, communication skills training, problem solving training, and special problems. The amount of time spent on each stage of treatment depends both on the specific needs of the family and the rate at which they acquire the targeted skills.

In the *assessment* stage, assessments are conducted of each individual family member as well as the family as a unit. In individual family interviews, it is helpful to ascertain information to questions such as: "What is your understanding of schizophrenia and what causes it?", "How is this illness treated?", "What personal goals do you have?", "Are other family members supportive of these goals?", and "What interferes with your ability to achieve these goals?" It is critical to assess both the knowledge and goals each individual family member in order to ensure that the intervention will improve the functioning of every family member. It is assumed in behavioral family therapy that in order to effectively reduce family stress, the well-being and self-efficacy of each family member needs to be enhanced. Usually, one to two interviews with each person before beginning behavioral family therapy is sufficient to complete the individual assessments.

In addition to individual assessments, the therapist observes the naturalistic interactions between family members to evaluate their communication skills. Special attention is paid to stressful communication styles, such as raising one's voice, "put-downs", frequent blaming statements, and lack of behavioral specificity. It is also useful for the family to participate in a problem-solving assessment, which the therapist uses to identify assets and deficits in family problem-solving skill. This assessment can be conducted by requesting that the family work on solving the problem for a 10–15 min period, while the clinician sits back and observes. When the problem-solving discussion is completed, the therapist discusses his or her observations with the family, and asks family members to describe other examples of problems they have recently tried to resolve. Routine problem-solving assessments can be conducted every 3–4 months to evaluate progress in learning the targeted problem-solving skills.

Education. Usually 3–4 educational sessions are conducted. These sessions generally cover information about the psychiatric illness, medications, and the stress-vulnerability model of schizophrenia. Educational sessions are most effective when they are taught in a highly interactive style, eliciting the experiences of the patient and his or her relatives, asking questions frequently to check on understanding, and avoiding confrontation or conflict whenever possible. Posters, handouts, and books (e.g., Mueser & Gingerich, 1994) can be used to facilitate communication of information to family members about the psychiatric illness.

Education about schizophrenia includes information about how a diagnosis is established, the characteristic symptoms, common myths, and the course and outcome. Sessions focusing on medication discuss the major effects of medication on decreasing symptoms and preventing relapses, common names, dosages, side effects of psychotropic medications, names and side effects of side effect medications, and strategies for dealing with common problems with these medications. Education regarding the stress-vulnerability model is focused on helping families understand how stress, medication, decreased substance abuse, and enhanced coping skills can improve the long term course of schizophrenia. At the conclusion of the educational sessions, family members develop a relapse prevention plan for responding to early warning signs of relapses.

Communication skills training. After basic educational material about the illness has been covered, sessions are devoted to training communication skills. Communication skills are taught which emphasize the use of "I" statements, clear verbal feeling statements, and reference to specific behaviors. Because of the cognitive impairments characteristic of schizophrenia, the importance of keeping communications brief and to-the-point is emphasized. Up to six different communication skills are typically taught over 4–8 sessions, including: Expressing positive feelings, expressing negative feelings, making positive requests, active listening, compromise and negotiation, and requesting a time-out. As in social skills training, each skill is broken down into component steps, which are the focus of the training.

Procedures for training communication skills follow those described previously in the section on social skills training. Family members rehearse the targeted skills in role plays followed by feedback and additional role playing. At the end of the session, members are given homework assignments to practice the skills on their own, which are reviewed in the following session.

The goal of communication skills training is to decrease tense and negative interactions between family members by replacing them with more behaviorally specific, constructive social skills. Until family members demonstrate some improved competence, therapists should not proceed to the next stage of training problem-solving skills. A basic assumption of behavioral family therapy is that families will not be able to participate in successful problem-solving if they are unable to discuss problems with a minimum of negative affect.

Problem-solving training. In most families, particularly when the patient lives at home, more sessions need to be devoted to the training of problem-solving skills than in any other stage of behavioral family therapy. Usually, 5–15 sessions are devoted to problem-solving training, but even more sessions can be spent if the duration of work with the family is long (e.g., over 2 years). The primary goal of problem-solving training is to teach the family the skills necessary to resolve problems and achieve goals without the assistance of the therapist. This is intended to decrease reliance on the therapist, and to prepare the family for the eventual end of therapy. Training problem-solving involves teaching family members to follow a basic sequence of behavioral steps, outlined in Table 18.4. Family members are taught to elect a chairperson, who leads the family through the different steps of problem-solving. A secretary may also be elected, whose responsibility is to record the decisions reached at each step of problem-solving. Family members are encouraged to establish a weekly meeting time, when problems can be discussed and dealt with, and progress on previous problems can be reviewed. Problem-solving records are stored in the family notebook, which is kept at a place accessible to all family members.

Problem-solving training begins with the therapist taking the role of the

Table 18.4. Steps of problem solving

1.	Define the problem to everyones' satisfaction
2.	Generate a list of possible solutions for the problem
3.	Evaluate the advantages and disadvantages of each solution
4.	Choose one "best" solution or combination of solutions
5.	Formulate a plan for implementing the selected solution
6.	Review progress towards solving the goal at a later time and do additional problem solving as necessary

chairperson, and leading the family through the steps of problem-solving, explaining the purpose of each step along the way. After family members have become acquainted with the problem-solving sequence, they assume the roles of chairperson and secretary, with the therapist stepping into the role of a trainer, rather than an active participant in the problem-solving. Initially, easy, affectively benign topics are selected for problem-solving training to build up the competence of the family at solving problems. Gradually, over a period of time, more difficult problems are addressed when the family's skills are sufficiently developed. Progress in problem-solving is routinely monitored by conducting problem-solving assessments, as previously described.

A wide variety of different problems and goals can be addressed in this stage of treatment. For example, household chores, dealing with problematic symptoms, looking for a job, and planning a vacation, are all problems or goals which have been resolved or achieved through problem-solving. Some families do not require further intervention when problem-solving has been completed. However, other families may face problems which have not yet responded to the problem-solving approach. For such families, the last stage of behavioral family therapy may be appropriate.

Special problems. In this final stage of treatment, the therapist may use a wide variety of strategies to help families cope with persistent difficulties. Cognitive-behavior therapists possess specific clinical skills for managing problems which families are incapable of resolving through problem-solving. The therapist applies his or her skills to addressing these problems, and whenever possible teaches family members how to implement and monitor the basic strategies. Examples of special problems which can be addressed in this stage include setting up a token economy at home to improve the patient's hygiene, teaching relaxation strategies to reduce tension, behavioral contracting for suicidal behavior, parent training for child rearing problems, and scheduling pleasant events for depression.

Coping Skills for Residual Psychotic Symptoms

Approximately 25–40% of patients with schizophrenia experience chronic residual psychotic symptoms between episodes of their illness. Despite optimal pharmacological treatment, psychotic symptoms are unavoidable for some patients. These symptoms are frequently associated with high levels of distress, including depression, suicidality, anger, and anxiety. Although it was once believed that little could be done to help these patients, recent advances in cognitive-behavioral treatment have found that patients can learn coping strategies for dealing more effectively with these problematic symptoms.

Naturalistic surveys of how patients respond to psychotic symptoms indicate that a substantial proportion report using different coping strategies. The use of different coping strategies, as well as the total number of strategies employed, is related to lower levels of distress from psychotic symptoms. The goal of teaching coping skills is to expand the repertoire of skills available to patients, thereby improving self-efficacy and decreasing distress. The primary criterion for patients to benefit from learning strategies for coping with their psychotic symptoms is a motivation and willingness to learn these strategies. Therefore, patients who experienced little distress from their psychotic symptoms, or who are unwilling to work on these symptoms, are poor candidates for this training.

The overall process of teaching coping skills involves conducting a careful behavioral analysis of the problematic symptom, followed by systematically teaching coping strategies through the use of instruction, practice, and homework assignments. Details on the training of coping skills can be found in Tarrier (1992). The principles of this procedure are briefly summarized below.

Describe and conduct a functional analysis of the psychotic symptom. First, a specific symptom to be addressed is described as specifically as possible, including its form, frequency of occurrence, duration, and intensity. Although the patient may experience several persistent psychotic symptoms, only one symptom is addressed at a time when teaching coping skills. It is best to begin working on a symptom that is frequently occurring and associated with a high level of distress.

After describing the problematic symptom, information considering the antecedents, patient reactions to, and consequences of the symptom are identified. The purpose of this analysis is to identify the situations in which the symptoms are most likely to occur, the level of distress associated with them, and possible consequences of the symptoms, including both positive and negative consequences. Information concerning the antecedents and consequences of persistent psychotic symptoms are generally obtained from the patient, although other informants (e.g., family members) may be helpful as well.

Evaluate current coping efforts. When a functional analysis of the psychotic symptom has been completed, specific coping strategies that the patient has used are identified. Most patients have tried a variety of different coping methods, some of which have met with greater success than others in reducing the stress associated with the symptom. For each coping strategy, the therapist obtains a detailed description of the specific strategy, the frequency with which it has been used, and its effectiveness in reducing distress associated with the symptom. Obstacles to the use of specific coping strategies are also explored. For example, it may be noted that a patient who finds initiating social interactions decreases the severity of auditory hallucinations is often socially isolated and lacks opportunities for initiating conversations with others.

Select and rehearse a coping strategy in the session. After reviewing the patient's coping efforts, one strategy is selected to begin work on. The chosen strategy can be one that the patient has previously used and reported success with, but currently uses infrequently. Alternatively, the selected strategy may be a new one which is anticipated to be helpful.

Coping strategies fall under three broad categories: cognitive methods, changing behavior, and altering sensory input. Examples of cognitive strategies include positive self-talk, shifting attention (e.g., doing a puzzle), ignoring, and focusing on the symptom. Examples of behavioral strategies include initiating conversations, taking a walk, and playing a game with someone. Examples of changes in sensory input include relaxation, listening to music, and humming or singing to oneself.

After a specific coping strategy has been selected, it is rehearsed in the session. Cognitive coping strategies can be practiced by first demonstrating the strategy to the patient by talking aloud, second having the patient practice the strategy by talking aloud, and third by having the patient practice the strategy covertly. After a coping strategy has been selected for rehearsal, plans are made for the patient to practice the skill in specific situations in which he or she is likely to experience the targeted symptom. A homework monitoring sheet is devised that includes information about the situation in which the symptom occurred, the patient's use of the targeted coping strategy, and the effectiveness of the strategy in reducing distress and symptom severity.

Follow-up homework assignment. During the following session the therapist reviews the patient's homework assignment, praises efforts, and problem-solves to overcome obstacles to implementing the coping strategy. The effectiveness of coping strategies usually increases with practice and familiarity. Therefore, patients need to be encouraged to continue practicing a specific coping strategy, even when early efforts have resulted in apparently minimal benefits. If, after several weeks of trying a coping strategy, little improvement is noted, the therapist may explore with the patient an alternative coping strategy. If repeated trials of different coping strategies are unsuccessful at either reducing distress or the severity of the symptom, despite concerted efforts to implement the coping strategies, consideration should be given to either attempting to narrow or redefine the targeted symptom, or to move on to a different problematic symptom. For example, if repeated attempts to cope with auditory hallucinations have been unsuccessful, the therapist might work with the patient on the goal of reducing distress associated with only those auditory hallucinations that are derogatory in nature.

Develop a second coping strategy for the symptom. A consistent finding in surveys of coping with chronic symptoms has been that the number of coping strategies employed is related to lower levels of distress associated with these symptoms. Therefore, after successfully teaching one coping strategy for a particular symptom, the therapist helps the patient develop at least one more coping strategy for that same symptom. It can be helpful to develop a second coping strategy that employs a different modality of coping from the first strategy. For example, if a cognitive coping strategy was first selected and trained, then another strategy may be selected from the behavioral or sensory modalities. This maximizes the variety of the coping strategies marshaled to deal with a persistent psychotic symptom. After at least two coping strategies have been developed to manage a symptom, an assessment is conducted to determine whether coping for a second symptom needs to be enhanced.

Treatment of Substance Abuse

Epidemiological surveys indicate that the prevalence of substance abuse in patients with schizophrenia is substantially greater than in the general population (Regier, Farmer, Rae, Locke, Keith, Judd & Goodwin, 1990; Mueser, Bennett & Kushner, 1995). Substance abuse can compromise the effects of antipsychotic medication and precipitate symptom relapses and rehospitalizations. Because of the high prevalence of substance use disorders in patients with schizophrenia, and the negative clinical effects of such abuse, it is imperative that therapists maintain a high index of suspicion of substance abuse when working with these patients, and to attempt to address these issues when they arise.

There is no one single method that is best for assessing the presence of a substance use disorder. Patients often deny substance abuse, either because of sanctions associated with such abuse, or denial of the negative effects of drug and alcohol use. In the absence of any "best" assessment strategy, therapists should attempt to pool information about substance abuse obtained from a variety of sources. Self-reports by patients, the reports of clinicians working with patients, and significant others are usually the most valuable sources of information. When urine and blood screens can be conducted to detect use of substances, this can further aid the therapist in identifying a substance use disorder.

When substance abuse has been detected, clinical intervention needs to be guided by an understanding that recovery from substance use disorders progresses through a series of stages (Drake, Bartels, Teague, Noordsy & Clark, 1993). Identifying a patient's stage of treatment is the first step towards selecting clinical interventions designed to help the patient progress to the next stage of recovery. The failure to match treatment to stage of recovery may result in ineffective interventions, which in some cases can worsen patients' substance abuse.

Specific stages of recovery from a substance abuse disorder are described below. At each stage of recovery, the primary treatment goal is to help the patient move on to the next stage.

Engagement. At this stage of recovery, the patient is actively using drugs or alcohol, and is not engaged in a helping relationship with a mental health professional. Before attempts can be made to change substance use behavior, a relationship must first be established with a therapist. Therefore, the goal of the engagement stage is to engage the patient in a relationship with a clinician. Naturally, the focus of this relationship is not on reducing the substance use behavior at this stage of treatment.

In order to establish a relationship with a patient, therapists must often do assertive outreach with patients in community settings such as their homes, restaurants, or parks. Helping clients stave off crises, or manage an acute crisis often serves as an initial basis for a therapeutic relationship. The therapist's primary aim is to show the patient that he or she can be useful, and through providing that help, the seeds of a therapeutic relationship are sown.

Persuasion. Once a therapeutic relationship has been established, the therapist's goal is to persuade the patient that his or her substance abuse is a problem, and to work on reducing substance use. Denial of the negative consequences of substance abuse is a common feature of substance use disorders. Therefore, the persuasion process is also an integral part of treatment.

A wide range of different educational and cognitive-behavioral techniques can be employed in the persuasion stage. Confrontation is avoided, but persistence is important. Education about the effects of substance use on the symptoms of schizophrenia is provided, such as the fact that substance abuse can precipitate relapses and rehospitalizations. In addition to education, motivational interviewing techniques (Miller & Rollnick, 1992) can be useful in persuading patients to address their substance use behavior.

Motivational interviewing refers to strategies for helping patients to understand the discrepancy between their personal goals and their use of drugs and alcohol. Empathic listening skills, trying to understand the patient's perceptions, "rolling with resistance", and exploring personal long-term goals play a role in helping patients consider the effects of their substance use behavior.

Although the primary goal at the persuasion stage is to encourage the patient to begin working on reducing substance use, it is also important to establish a working alliance with other members of the patient's social network. Relatives of patients with a substance use disorder and schizophrenia often do not recognize the negative effects of substance abuse. Establishing a working relationship with family members allows the clinician to begin to address substance abuse issues that may contribute to the patient's behavior.

Active treatment. Active treatment refers to the stage at which patients endorse the goal of reducing their substance use or obtaining abstinence altogether from drugs or alcohol. Many different cognitive-behavioral strategies can be used to help patients reduce their substance use. Some strategies are aimed at directly reducing substance use, while others target factors that may contribute to vulnerability to use drugs or alcohol.

Three motivating factors contribute to the vulnerability of patients with schizophrenia to substance abuse. First, patients may use substances in an effort to self-medicate troublesome symptoms. Second, substance abuse may take place in a social context, thus filling patients needs for social acceptance and contact. Third, substance use may be a convenient way of seeking pleasure. The role of different motivational factors can be identified through interviews with the patient and significant others. Identifying the motivating factors leads to specific interventions for reducing substance abuse.

Substance abuse that is secondary to self-medication of symptoms can be reduced if alternative coping strategies are developed for the management of problematic symptoms. For example, a patient who drinks excessively because of persistent auditory hallucinations could be taught strategies for coping more effectively with these hallucinations. The social motives for substance abuse can be addressed through social skills training, in which patients are taught the rudiments of establishing and deepening relationships with non-substance abusing peers. Finally, substance abuse that occurs as a form of pleasure seeking can be reduced by teaching patients alternative skills or engaging in leisure and recreational activities.

Relapse prevention. Relapse prevention training is that stage of recovery from a substance use disorder in which the individual has obtained abstinence from psychoactive substances and effort is directed at reducing vulnerability to relapses of substance use. Individuals with primary or comorbid substance use disorder frequently fluctuate between different stages of recovery over the course of their illness. Therefore, it is common for individuals to cut down on their use of substances and to achieve abstinence, but to remain vulnerable to relapse. The goal of the relapse prevention stage is to bolster the patient's skills for averting such relapses.

One of the most important components of relapse prevention is helping patients maintain a high level of awareness of their vulnerability to relapses of substance use. After a period of successful abstinence, many patients feel increasingly confident that they will now be able to handle moderate use of alcohol or drugs. However, abundant evidence indicates that patients with schizophrenia have extraordinary difficulty using moderate amounts of drugs or alcohol. Therefore, helping patients maintain an awareness that they are vulnerable to relapses of their substance use disorder is an important element of relapse prevention.

In addition to maintaining a high level of awareness of vulnerability, a range of other clinical strategies may be used to facilitate relapse prevention. It may be helpful to develop a relapse prevention plan to prepare patients for the possibility of a relapse. A relapse prevention plan should include information about those situations associated with relapses in the past, early signs of a relapse, and a specific plan for responding to these warning signals. This relapse prevention plan is similar to the plan for responding to relapses of psychotic symptoms, and serves the main purpose of anticipating stressful situations and formulating a plan for responding to these situations.

Aside from maintaining awareness and developing a relapse prevention plan, it is critical at this stage of treatment that efforts focus on achieving interpersonal goals and developing competencies that will improve the quality of patients' lives and lower their susceptibility to substance abuse. For example, improving interpersonal skills, the ability to manage stress, skills for recreation and leisure, and health and fitness may help patients feel better about themselves and less inclined to resort drug and alcohol use. Thus, the essence of effective relapse prevention involves addressing factors related to vulnerability to substance abuse, rather than substance use behavior itself.

Conclusions

Schizophrenia is a severe and debilitating disorder. Despite the multiple handicaps associated with this illness, cognitive-behavioral interventions can have a significant, beneficial impact on course of the disorder and the quality of patients' lives. A wide range of cognitive-behavioral strategies can be useful in the treatment of schizophrenia. Prominent among those strategies are social skills training, behavioral family therapy, training in coping with psychotic symptoms, and stage-wise treatment of substance use disorder. Through the collaborative efforts of therapists, patients, and relatives, there is good reason for being optimistic about the ability to successfully manage this chronic mental illness.

References

APA (1994). *Diagnostic and statistical manual of mental disorders*, 4th edition (DSM-IV). Washington, DC: American Psychiatric Association.

Bellack, A. S., & Mueser, K. T. (1986). A comprehensive treatment program for schizophrenia and chronic mental illness. *Community Mental Health Journal, 22,* 175–189.

Bellack, A. S., Mueser, K. T., Gingerich, S., & Agresta, J. (1997). *Social skills training for schizophrenia: A step-by-step guide.* New York: Guilford.

Drake, R. E., Bartels, S. B., Teague, G. B., Noordsy, D. L., & Clark, R. E. (1993). Treatment of substance abuse in severely mentally ill patients. *Journal of Nervous and Mental Disease, 181,* 606–611.

Falloon, I. R. H., Boyd, J. L., & McGill, C. W. (1984). *Family care of schizophrenia.* New York: Guilford.

Liberman, R. P., DeRisi, W. J., & Mueser, K. T. (1989). *Social skills training for psychiatric patients.* Needham Heights, MA: Allyn & Bacon.

Miller, W. R., & Rollnick, S. (1991). *Motivational interviewing: preparing people to change addictive behavior.* New York: Guilford Press.

Mueser, K. T., & Bellack, A. S. (1995). Psychotherapy for schizophrenia. In S. R. Hirsch & D. Weinberger (Eds.), *Schizophrenia.* Oxford: Blackwell.

Mueser, K. T., Bennett, M., & Kushner, M. G. (1995). Epidemiology of substance use disorders among persons with chronic mental illnesses. In A. F. Lehman & L. Dixon (Eds.), *Double jeopardy: chronic mental illness and substance abuse.* New York: Harwood.

Mueser, K. T., & Gingerich, S. L. (1994). *Coping with schizophrenia: A guide for families.* Oakland, CA: New Harbinger.

Mueser, K. T., & Glynn, S. M. (1995). *Behavioral family therapy for psychiatric disorders.* Needham Heights, MA: Allyn & Bacon.

Penn, D. L., & Mueser, K. T. (1996). Research update on the psychosocial treatment of schizophrenia. *American Journal of Psychiatry, 15,* 607–617.

Regier, D. A., Farmer, M. E., Rae, D. S., Locke, B. Z., Keith, S. J., Judd, L. L., & Goodwin, F. K. (1990). Comorbidity of mental disorders with alcohol and other drug abuse. *Journal of the American Medical Association, 264,* 2511–2518.

Tarrier, N. (1992). Management and modification of residual positive psychotic symptoms. In M. Birchwood & N. Tarrier (Eds.), *Innovations in the psychological management of schizophrenia.* London: Wiley.

Further Reading

Bellack, A. S. (Ed.) (1989). *A clinical guide for the treatment of schizophrenia.* New York: Plenum Press.

Birchwood, M., & Tarrier, N. (Eds.) (1994). *Psychological management of schizophrenia.* Chichester, UK: Wiley.

Drake, R. E., & Mueser, K. T. (Eds.) (1996). *Dual diagnosis of major mental illness and substance abuse disorder II. Recent research and clinical implications. New directions in Mental Health Services, Vol. 70.* San Francisco, CA: Jossey-Bass.

Fowler, D., Garet, P., Kuipers, E. (1995). *Cognitive behaviour therapy for psychosis: Theory and practice.* Chichester, UK: Wiley.

Mueser, K. T., Bond, G. R., Drake, R. E., & Resick, S. G. (1998). Models of community care for severe mental illness: A review of research on case management. *Schizophrenia Bulletin, 24,* 37–74.

Mueser, K. T., & Tarrier, N. (Eds.) (1998). *Handbook of social functioning in schizophrenia.* Boston, MA: Allyn & Bacon.

19

Psychoeducation for People Vulnerable to Schizophrenia

SERGIO REBOLLEDO[a] and MARÍA JOSÉ LOBATO[b]

[a]Private practice; [b]Hospital Psiquiátrico Cabaleiro Goas, Spain

Introduction

There has been a considerable development of psychoeducative approaches for family and friends of people who suffer from schizophrenia and even for those close to people with other somatic or mental disorders. However, in comparison there are very few psychoeducational programmes directed towards the very person who is affected.

This study attempts to demonstrate a model of psychoeducation for people affected by schizophrenia which we have been developing from other clinics' and researchers' ideas but also from our own professional experience in psychiatric hospitals as well as community rehabilitation centres. The psychoeducation programme we present is highly structured. As such, it can be easily taught to other professionals, *titulados medios* (these are people with 3-year diplomas, i.e. nurses, social workers) and superiors. It consists of two main lines of development: one for health education and the other to promote emotional and affective development. It has been designed to be applied throughout a course, from October to June, divided into three trimesters. 20 to 30 sessions are programmed for each trimester, with four each week, alternating the sessions dedicated to health education with those for emotional development. Each trimester is organized around a common global objective: the first is *body consciousness* and *self-care*; the second, *vulnerability consciousness* and *self-esteem*; and the third, *adherence to treatment* and *self-control*.

The Psychological Impact of Schizophrenic Experiences as a Foundation of Psychoeducative Intervention

The known distinction between positive and negative symptoms (Andreasen, 1982; Crow, 1982; Marneros, Andreasen & Tsuang, 1991) allows for a high degree of clarity when it comes to identifying the psychopathology of schizophrenic disorders. However, what now interests us is identifying the impact that the symptoms have upon the affected person, since it is imperative to preserve the concept of the person before the invasion of the symptoms and to educate him/her in identifying and coping with them.

The disconcerting and oftentimes terrible experience of having hallucinations, memory loss or giving explanations which others do not consider valid, diminishes the psyche of the affected person and can be a self-maintaining mechanism of the symptoms or a source of new symptomology. Fowler, Garety & Kuipers (1995) point out some of the consequence that the psychotic experience can have on the people affected:

a. Patients may believe themselves to be extremely vulnerable to injury. This belief is associated with delirious or hallucinatory experiences in which others are able to hurt or injure them.

b. The belief that at any moment they may lose control of themselves, torturing themselves with the idea that they are "going crazy". This comes from experiences of being controlled by external forces or feelings of not being in control of their own actions, or even sometimes the fear of going crazy or completely losing their self-control in the psychotic experience.

c. The belief they are condemned to social isolation. This can stem from real experiences of social rejection or people looking down upon them when they know they have been through psychiatric treatment.

d. The person affected may internalize the belief that their symptoms and disabilities are due to such fundamental defects that it is inevitable for them to be degraded in front of others. Sometimes a moral judgement is placed upon the problems of mental illness, as if it were due to a lack of moral fibre, of values or divine punishment. In extreme cases this experience can lead to delusions of identity.

e. The affected person may start to build a delusional self-image. These are the cases in which they are considered delusional gains (Scharfetter, 1979).

When considering psychopathology it is imperative to understand the impact of the consequences on the individual affected. We still have a lot to learn about how intelligent, skilled people manage to cope, often successfully, with the psychotic experience. Breir & Strauss (1983) noted three phases in the spontaneous process of self-regulation which some schizophrenics experienced: in the first phases, the person is conscious of the existence of psychotic behaviour and learns to point it out to him/herself. At the second step, they are able to identify this behaviour as a sign of maladaption or disorder, consisting of a phase of self-evaluation. In the third phase, individuals are capable of developing self-control strategies and some intervening self-instructions, whilst others reduce their activity level, get involved in another kind of behaviour or change their environment. In this process of three phases it is fundamental for the individual to discriminate between situations, effects and warning feelings which allow them to tie together the processes of self-observation, self-evaluation and self-control. Nowadays, research offers new cognitive-behavioural tools to help people affected by schizophrenia to cope with their symptoms. In this context, *coping* is understood as the use of cognitive and behavioural resources to control or dominate the symptoms, or, to reduce to a minimum the anxiety they cause (Birchwood & Tarrier, 1995). The authors propose four sensitive strategies to be taught to affected people:

1. Cognitive Strategies
   a. Attention diversion
   b. Attention restriction
   c. Assertiveness
2. Behavioural Strategies
   a. Increasing activity levels
   b. Increasing social activity
   c. Reducing social activity
   d. Reality-checks
3. Sensorial strategies
4. Physiological strategies

Fowler, Garety & Kuipers (1995) complement this list of techniques with an element we have been using in our psychoeducational programme for some time: the development of a new model of psychosis along with the affected person. The use of such a model can be divided into various elements:

a. Identification of abnormal experiences (hallucinations, cognition disorders and delusional thoughts).
b. Clarification of the personal beliefs about these experiences (which may or may not be delusional.)
c. Exploration of these particular beliefs in relation to a sickness model or in relation to what happens.
d. Evaluation of emotions, self-respect and aspects of cognitive functioning to start after the explanation of the sickness model.

In the psycho-educative programme described here, the model is based on the hypothesis of vulnerability (Birchwood, Hallet and Preston,1988; Ciompi, 1988; Kay, 1986; Liberman, 1986; Murray y Reveley, 1986; Neufeld, 1984; Sánchez & Ruiz Vargas, 1987; Straube & Hahlweg, 1990; Watt, 1982; Zubin, 1980; Zubin, Magaziner & Steinhauer, 1983; Zubin & Spring, 1977; Zubin & Steinhauer, 1981), with the objective of getting the affected person to come to terms with their vulnerability to schizophrenic crisis. The patient must avoid alternatives such as assuming the role of the useless, handicapped invalid, or complete rejection of the idea that they are suffering from a mental disorder and, as a result encouraging a high-risk lifestyle, with little adherence to treatment.

Concept of Psychoeducation

Psychoeducation is a learning experience about oneself, about the process or disorder one is suffering from and the best way of coping with the consequences of such a disorder. It seeks the participation of the user in what is scientifically known about their problem. It attempts for the knowledge to be applied to improve their life, their personal development and their family unit.

Some of the objectives of psychoeducation, which have already been commented upon in a previous publication (Rebolledo & López de Heredia, 1990), are characterized by:

–   Giving participants up-to-date and understandable information about schizophrenia, emphasising the relationship between the still-unknown biological and psychosocial vulnerability and the patient's susceptibility to stress and over-stimulation.
–   Teaching participants to discriminate between symptoms of the illness and warning symptoms, to value neuroleptic medication as a protection factor, to recognise the secondary effects of this medication and to know how to inform the psychiatrist about them.
–   Increasing participants' understanding and their ability to cope with environmental stress, considering it as a risk factor, along with alcohol consumption, the use of cannabis derivatives, of other hallucinogens and changes in the normal circumstances of daily life.
–   Creating an alliance between sufferers, family and friends and professionals directed towards the lessening of guilty feelings, to the accomplishment of short-term goals and establishing coping strategies in crises given the fluctuating character that the course of schizophrenic disorders often adopts.
–   Identifying and increasing resources in victims and their families for the development of day to day activities. Encouraging consciousness and control of positive and negative symptoms, as well as other dysfunctional behaviours.
–   Giving participants a continued learning environment and socioaffective support over time to favourise generalization of goals to the daily life of the patient and their family.
–   Encouraging affected people to overcome the isolation and stigmatization of schizophrenia.
–   Giving patients and friends/family realistic hopes based on successes in research about schizophrenia.

Barter (1984) defines psychoeducation as "the use of techniques, methods and educational focus whose objective is to overcome the incapacitating effects of mental illness or providing a complementary treatment for mental illness, normally without being included in continuous treatment or forming part of a research programme". Goldman (1988) defines it as "education or training of a person with a psychiatric disorder in various areas which helps to reach treatment and rehabilitation goals. For example, increasing the person's own acceptance of his/her illness, encouraging his/her active cooperation in the treatment and rehabilitation and increasing his/her coping skills in a way that compensates for the deficiencies caused by the psychiatric disorder".

Psychoeducation is a valid intervention procedure for application within a treatment or rehabilitation programme. More than anything else research has been carried out in to the benefits for families of people suffering from schizophrenic disorders. Amongst the most well-known we can mention the research of Anderson, Reiss & Hogarty (1986), Barrawclough & Tarrier (1992), Falloon, Boyd & McGill (1984), Goldstein (1986), Hatfield & Lefley (1987), Hatfield (1990), Kuipers & Bebbington (1990), Kuipers, Leff & Lam (1992), Leff & Vaughn (1985), and Thorthon & Seeman (1991) and, in our case Rebolledo and Lobato (1994). All these studies explain psychoeducative models to inform, direct and train friends and family to cope with the consequences of suffering a schizophrenic disorder with a chronic course.

However, our purpose at this moment is to explain a psychoeducative procedure geared, not towards the family, but to the affected person about which some studies have been published (e.g., Amdur & Cohen, 1981; Asher-Svanum & Krause, 1991; Barter, 1984; Carson, 1991; Goldman, 1988; Gordon & Gordon, 1985; Liberman, 1993; Pilsecker, 1981). This increasing interest reflects, perhaps, new problems facing clinics and health officials about new public attention to mental health in the community. The increased focus in psychoeducation is rooted in a new way of tackling the study of mental health problems which focuses on risk factors and protection given to a vulnerability condition when schizophrenic episodes happen (Liberman, 1986; Zubin, 1977, 1983), analysis of the role of important occurrences during the course of the mental illness (Brown & Harris, 1989; Day, 1989), the influence lifestyle has on the prognosis of an illness (Kickbush, 1986; Ozámiz, 1987) and the important role of the availability of a social support network when facing a long-term psychiatric disorder (Caplan, 1974; Hammer, 1981).

Progressive Learning Scale in Psychoeducation of People Affected by Schizophrenic Disorders

This learning ladder lasts three trimesters. There is one rung per trimester, composed of 20/30 sessions which take place four times a week and are divided into two topics (Figure 19.1).

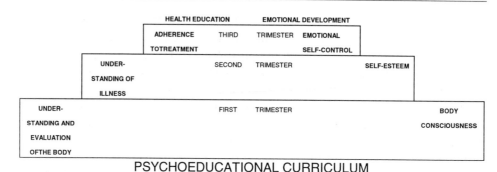

PSYCHOEDUCATIONAL CURRICULUM

Figure 19.1. Progressive learning scale in the psychoeducation of people affected by schizophrenic disorder..

The first trimester is dealt with by the group *Look After Yourself*, whose objective is to learn the parts of the body, their function and how to take care of them. The group gets together on alternate days, perhaps Monday and Wednesday, whilst on Tuesday and Thursday the *Body Consciousness* group gets together. Their objective is to develop activities which provoke positive and enjoyable sensations in the bodies of the participants by using a number of psychometric, relaxation, bodily expression and dance methods. It is very important to begin with these groups concerned with knowledge and bodily experiences since they promote understanding and feelings upon which concepts such as self-esteem and self-care are based. Unfortunately, people affected by schizophrenic disorders often experience huge debilitating bodily sensations, creating disorders in bodily consciousness. These groups must serve as a "security" rung which allows the patient to move on to the next step where s/he will to have to cope with his/her awareness of vulnerability and illness. If, on the first rung (with the *Look After Yourself* and *Body Consciousness* groups) the person manages to grasp a more real and living image of their body by understanding how to look after it and feeling that it belongs to them, that it is alive and can provide enjoyment, then they are ready to move on to the next rung.

The second trimester is the most difficult since the patient may feel torn apart as they begin to understand their vulnerability and illness. This is always painful because the individual starts to understand that his/her disorder is chronic, limiting, carries with it a social stigma and that s/he is going to have to continue with psychiatric consultation and neuroleptic medication for a long time. Basically, the concept which should be explained is their vulnerability and predisposition to experiencing crises and schizophrenic disorders, the concept that this vulnerability will be its defining trait and that the schizophrenic disorders will be in a fluctuating state. These concepts are dealt with in the *Know Yourself* group which can take place on Mondays and Wednesdays whilst *the Self-Esteem* group can meet on Tuesdays and Thursdays dedicated to coping with depressive and destructive situations which are going to be caused by an awareness of the illness. The objective of this last group is to give the patient a more positive evaluation of him/herself, an enjoyable learning experience, although s/he understands his/her vulnerability, and a positive way of coping with his/her illness and life. S/he will have to learn to value other aspects, to concentrate on immediate goals and value each moment, to be responsible for his/her own happiness and to behave for his/her own satisfaction. These achievements signal that it is time to move onto the third rung.

On this third rung the person is informed of means of protection s/he has at his/her disposal to combat the discomfort caused by his/her vulnerability to experience crisis. Many affected people refuse to take neuroleptic medication because they do not understand that the biochemical imbalance in their brain causes a maladjustment in their social behaviour and way of being. However, the difference is huge once they accept medication and are convinced that the drug is necessary to diminish the symptoms which cause their illness and that this is the most effective way of attenuating their vulnerability to experience crisis . We may call this rung *Your Help and Support or Your Medication*. This group, following the format of the previous ones can meet Monday and Wednesdays, whilst Tuesdays and Thursdays the prevention of anxiety and depression group takes place. Patients may call this group *Control Yourself*. Its basic objective is to help people to understand their emotions and develop skills for controlling them. The impact of this group is big when the person succeeds in integrating skills for the control of their emotions whilst following treatment, as well as self-care methods and ways of preserving their personal life.

Methodology of Activities

It is valuable to carry out these activities in small groups. Given that the objective is to draw out a personal concept of vulnerability and schizophrenia, the group is the first socialization of this concept. Likewise, the group dynamic helps to overcome motivation problems, comprehension problems and elaboration of concepts. Via social reinforcement and learning through imitation the group promotes the acquisition of skills and their maintenance. This requires that the person responsible for carrying out the activity should be especially sure to:

1. Create a gratifying group environment by using (in good measure) humour and social reinforcement. S/he should also try to channel the leadership towards the objective of the activity.
2. Encourage intense participation from everyone in the group. For this s/he should interpolate group members by frequent use of first names and by requiring their interaction. Encourage a safe and non-threatening environ-

ment by use of positive reinforcement, putting aside punishment and assuming a selective perception of the most advantageous or positive aspect of a situation

3. Make sure that the level of the task becomes progressively more difficult, use modelling or reinforcement as the primary therapeutic tool.

4. Begin each session by reviewing the objectives of the group. In each session time should be dedicated to the verbalization of goals by patients (according to their individualized rehabilitation plan).

5. Centre the assistant's attention on the theme or exercises related to the activity. Other problems should not be allowed to intrude for long periods of time. When other themes cause an interruption they should be directed to another person ("you would be better telling this idea of yours to your doctor").

6. Always start sessions on time. The total length of the session may vary with the atmosphere created and the theme to be developed.

7. Always try to introduce the same routine in the development of the sessions. Choose a greeting which is always used and always have the same order for the development of the session. Clear and explicit norms should exist about others' attitudes. With agitated patients, or patients whose behaviour harms the development of the session, "Time Out" should be used, asking them to leave the session for a few minutes.

Each activity demands structure so that it can be evaluated, perfected and used to create guided application of objectives. A psychoeducative activity is characterized by the following structure:

1. *Identification of the Activity.* Along with a technical identification of the activity, it can also be identified by more "catchy" names for the patients. For example, patients may call an activity for self-control of anxiety and depression as "control yourself".

2. *Objectives of the activity.* Consists of the goals the patients should reach if they meet the demands of the activity. These goals should be defined in operative and concrete terms, avoiding over-generalization. Colloquial language should also be used to define the objectives of the activity to patients to promote guidance and understanding of what they can and should obtain from their participation.

3. *Entry Repertoire.* Thisis the prerequisites the patient should be familiar with or the skills they should possess to be able to continue with the activity successfully. For example to be able to carry out *Self-administration* of their medication, the patient should first go through the "Knowledge", "Assessing Your Body" and "Understanding Illness" sessions.

4. *Exercise or session modules.* Consists of the central part of the activity where the concrete always takes precedence over the abstract, or practice and rehearsal over simple discussion. The activity can be structured in exercise modules, which can be applied in a sequential or alternative way ac-

cording to the requirements of the group or each patient. Or, the activity may also be structured in sessions, each with its own list of topics.

5. *Register and assessment.* The activity should make use of one or several measuring instruments which can be used to evaluate the patient before, during and at the end of the activity. They should always refer to the concrete objectives of the activity. This kind of register should be technical but in a format which allows the patient to recognise their own progress in carrying out the activity. The self-report is an important source of motivation and shows what the patient has learned.

6. *Definition of the material and economic resources* needed to carry out the activity.

7. *Coverage and frequency of the sessions, timetable and location.* Each activity lasts a trimester.

The group takes place in a "Classroom" with desks, chairs and a blackboard where coloured chalk, slides and videos are used, all of them resources intended to increase control of attention and understanding. When the class begins simply note the name of the group being worked on and the date since some participants may be confused about time. This way it is possible to help them organize space and time. Then, pass around the attendance list. It may seem a little childish, but it is an opportunity to get to know the names of each patient and greet them, making them feel that their presence in the group is recognized and important. This also gives them the opportunity to play the student once again and also to get to know their colleagues making progressive group integration easy. Each participant has their notebook where they write down day by day the themes they are dealing with. This daily discipline of taking notes keeps them attentive, makes them feel as though they are participating more in the class and makes it more likely that they will remember the content of the class. Once the course is over they can use their notebook as a help guide.

It is important for the class to meet regularly and at the same time since people affected find it important to have a routine. It is also easier for them to make it to class, thus preventing abandonment. All the topics and drawings should be written on the board since it easier to keep their attention if they see what they are listening to written down. Sketches should be simple, easy to understand and to remember.

To satisfy the requisites of a teaching curriculum which involves a psycheducative activity, the activities have been structured into various "subjects", each one with its own programme.

The First Goal: Self-Care and Bodily Experience

In this first trimester self-care, understanding vulnerability and adherence to treatment is established. The most important thing is to arrive at a basic understanding of anatomy, establishing a rational base for care of the body and shared affection, as well as attending to immediate worries about health that the participants have. Along with this, development of activities which encourage positive bodily experiences. This is achieved by procedures which are in line with the interests and characteristics of the participants. The general objectives are:

- Encouraging participants to understand their bodies and how they work, trying to bring about a *positive assessment* of the body and to promote care of it.
- To encourage valuing health as *a good which can be actively obtained and preserved. Promoting a healthy lifestyle* in terms of diet, hygiene, exercise and other aspects of interest to participants (for example, being overweight, skin or hair condition or the use of glasses, etc.).
- To help patents to understand their ability and their body and to contribute to *positive bodily awareness*.

To carry out these objectives a 20/30 session trimester meeting four times a week is needed, structured into two topics: (a) *Understanding and assessing the body*, as we have already mentioned; participants may call this group as "Look after Yourself". It consists of 10/15 sessions on Mondays and Wednesdays. It uses methodology typical of a "classroom". A blackboard is used and written texts which are handed out to "students" for studying. (b) *Body Consciousness*, which participants may call "*Enjoy it*". It consists of 10/15 sessions on Tuesdays and Thursdays. It uses a different methodology, taking place in a bigger space which allows for freedom of movement.

Description of the group "Look after Yourself"

Specific objectives

1. Evaluating the education level of participants and their specific understanding of anatomy as well as their belief system concerning health and illness.
2. Increasing their knowledge of health education, establishing rational foundations for the care of their own physical and emotional health.
3. Establishing habits for self-care of the body, including hygiene habits, diet and rest.
4. Giving help to lessen health risk behaviour: smoking, drinking, bad eating habits or others which are detected in participants.
5. Encouraging bodily self-satisfaction.

Methodology

(a) Text books are used as guides to explaining the main apparatus and bodily systems. In general, amongst young adults the education level is usually the last years of E.G.B. (this is from ages 6–14) and in older or institutionalized people may be more basic.

(b) For each system basic notions of anatomy are used.

(c) It is important to draw diagrams and charts illustrating concepts on the board and to make participants copy them down in their textbooks. Transparencies, slides and videos can also be used.

Session scheme

In each session you should convey the message that the body is a working system, that it is a marvel, a source of pleasure, that it is exciting to explore its sensual possibilities, its movements, that the body is a friend which needs to be looked after every day and that everyone is "boss" of their own body.

Study of the different anatomical and physiological systems is dealt with (respiratory system, digestive system, etc.) following a scheme which goes over its importance, its functioning and the care each system requires. This final point is always tried out with tasks and exercises carried out in class.

Evaluation of the "Look After Yourself" group

To evaluate the learning and understanding level different kinds of evaluation are used. A common characteristic is that evaluations are geared towards reinforcing achievements rather than highlighting failures. There is continuous evaluation class to class. Each session begins by asking the participants questions about topics dealt with in the previous session. When one of the "students" stammers or does not assert him/herself, s/he is corrected by stimulation control to provoke the correct response. That is, you start by giving successively greater clues and signals until you get the right response and reinforce them for this.

In accordance with the educational level of the "students" and following previous studies, test type true or false/multiple choice questions have been developed. Texts can be put together where the search for key words is deduced from previous concepts or sentences.

Description of the Group on Bodily Consciousness

Specific objectives

1. Helping the patients to gain better understanding of their bodies, helping them to direct themselves in space and in relation to their bodies.
2. Stimulating concern for care of the body and its well-being.
3. Training them in a relaxation procedure.
4. Promoting interest in physical activities.

Methodology

This must be in accordance with the interest and education of the participants. In general, activities which allow participants to use psychometric and movement skills should be used. The ideas of Feldenkrais (1972) are especially useful. Likewise, García Arroyo's (1995) manual gives us a series of ideas and exercises which can be adapted to this purpose. With young adults very good results have been seen with exercises based upon psychomotricity, bodily expression and Swedish gymnastics as well as popular games. In some groups they have been successful in learning volleyball, handball, table tennis, bowls and hopscotch. With adults, teaching ballroom dancing has proven to be very motivating. Jacobson's (1961) relaxation technique has also been particularly useful. In all these activities, the final objective is to create an understanding of movement and bodily sensations.

Structure of the exercises

In general the sequence already described for the Knowledge and Body Assessment should be followed although, depending on the chosen methodology, this can be varied. In general it's a good idea to begin with activities which gradually increase movement and bodily expression. There are people who may consider an open space in which they can actively move around threatening, making it necessary to scale the exercise in order to make them feel safe.

Evaluation of the bodily consciousness group

Many techniques are used. At the beginning of each session (depending on the kind of activity to be carried out) sensations which may be experienced are graphically described. At the end of the session each participant should explain their bodily symptoms, sometimes just after finishing the session or after having showered, describing what they feel in this relaxed state. Word games (Osgood, Succi & Tannenbaum, 1976) are particularly useful when they take into account the various aspects of bodily awareness and self-image. Word games can be developed about assessment of the body, about bodily sensations before and after an activity or about physical attractiveness. Psychometric tests of the outline of the body, rhythm and other tests (Zazzo, 1970) have been useful in evaluating programmes and activities. Drawing or other art forms are used to evaluate bodily consciousness and self-image.

Second Goal: Understanding Vulnerability and Self-Esteem

Being on this second rung is going to help patients to form a concept of what is happening to them and, at the same time, to keep a dignified and positive self-image. One has to consider the burden of stigmatization and social rejection that goes along with mental illness. The ideas of Fink & Tasman (1992), Goffman (1963) and Schaff (1973) are useful when it comes to classifying the social framework of mental illness. It is very important in these groups to make a distinction between the person and their disorder. It must be constantly emphasized that the person is much more than their predisposition towards experiencing schizophrenic crisis. And even if we do have to understand our own vulnerability because it helps us to organize our lifestyle, our value as people goes much further beyond this, making how I feel about myself, what I do to make me feel better about my abilities, my projects, my triumphs and failures all important. And this is the logic of combining in this trimester the work of building an awareness of vulnerability to crisis along with the work on self-image and self-esteem.

Description of the understanding vulnerability group

The name this group can be given is *Know Yourself*. The important thing is to help patients to grasp the idea that all human beings are vulnerable to some kind of disorder and that this vulnerability forms part of the person. The ideas of Fitzpatrik (1990) about illness as an experience gives us a wider perspective of this theme. For the study of risk and protection factors in the course of schizophrenic disorders as well as vulnerability or predisposition to experiencing schizophrenic crisis a number of authors have been studied particularly the ideas of Birchwood & Tarrier (1995), Ciompi (1988), Colodron (1983), Liberman (1993), Neufeld (1984), Perris (1989), Roder, Brenner, Hodel & Kienzle (1996), Ruiz Vargas (1987), Straube & Hahlweg (1990) and Strauss, Boker & Brenner (1987).

The experience of predisposition to illness or suffering certain disorders is common amongst all the patients. Examples of somatic disorders abound. Everyone knows someone with heart problems or another illness. With regard to this the need to know how to look after oneself is introduced. So, describing illnesses such as diabetes where sufferers must learn to cope with their vulnerability, risk and protection factors as well as sticking to a diet and taking medication and getting on with their life help them to grasp the idea of vulnerability and self-care in schizophrenic disorders. Beforehand the concept of vulnerability is explained as a personal *characteristic* which manifests itself as a predisposition to experience crisis and schizophrenic crisis as a state which fluctua*tes*. Once this idea has been understood a meticulous rundown of the risk and protection factors in the course of schizophrenic disorders should be made. Normally the topics it is best to talk about are the abandonment of neuroleptic medication and the use of drugs such as marijuana or stimulants. Is it common in groups with young adults to find people who require a double diagnosis since as well as their psychotic disorder they are dependent on drugs, often cannabis, but also alcohol or other substances. If this situation occurs, some time should be dedicated to the topic. It may even be useful to organize a group on the side where drug use as a precipitating factor in crisis is discussed. When these habits are serious you may have to resort to other strategies such as reinforcement for incompatible behaviour, increasing their involvement through participation in other kinds of groups and/or the explanation of the fact that drugs are a precipitating factor in the individual's case, seeking to increase their motivation to prevent crisis.

Finally, this vulnerability awareness group should work on the idea of preventing crisis via detection of warning systems and psychiatric treatment as protection factors.

Specific objectives
1. Encourage the idea that illness is a vulnerable condition which makes it important to understand risk and protection factors.
2. Promote the understanding of illness through knowledge of somatic, brain and mental illnesses.
3. Training in the recognition of positive and negative symptoms of schizophrenia.
4. Training in self-recognition of warning symptoms, concentrating on these in an emergency situation.

Methodology
It is important to be especially careful of concepts and their explanation to the group. At this stage, the group coordinator should completely know all participants. S/he was already with the group the previous trimester and should be able to introduce the group to ideas without provoking rejection or referential statements (a patient should not feel personally referred to). For this we strongly suggest beginning with the most common experiences of illness to be able to later move on to the idea of vulnerability rather than mental illness. This later concept should be dignified and patients made to see how, historically, society has marginalized numerous groups but how today we are moving towards a tolerant and open society where being different should not necessarily imply marginalization.

Due to the complexity of these concepts and particular sensitivity participants may have about it the rule is that the group draws the line. These general ideas are elaborated upon more or less in accordance with the questions, the education level and the attitudes of the participants. To make explanations easier pamphlets have been made with the contents of this group: "Mental Illness", and "Living With Schizophrenia", as guides for the group's development and extracts of the schemes which will be used in class. In some groups they are handed out as reading material.

Sequence of the sessions
1. General ideas about vulnerability such as predisposition to somatic, cerebral, emotional and mental disorders.
2. Emphasis on social organization as a way of coping with illness and its consequence. Explanation of social stigma associated with people in psychiatric treatment.
3. Study of some chronic somatic disorders characterized by a predisposition to developing crisis, taking medication as a protection factor and organization of a lifestyle which maintains personal development.
4. Introduction to the vulnerability of experiencing crisis founded on a predisposition to biochemical imbalances in the brain.

5. Study of risk and protection factors during the course of schizophrenic disorders.
6. Study of positive and negative symptoms. Study of the prodromic symptoms as alert methods in preventing crisis.
7. Collective explanation of attitudes and behaviour for a healthy lifestyle when faced with a predisposition to psychotic crisis.

Group evaluation of vulnerability awareness

As in previous groups continuous evaluation is important class by class where the main technique consists of provoking the correct response in the pupil to be able to reinforce success. Questions with two alternatives are used (true or false) to evaluate various concepts about somatic illnesses and caring for them and about classification of mental and emotional disorders, There are various scales for evaluating and self-evaluating symptoms of illness and warning symptoms.

Description of the self-esteem group

Self-esteem is the amount of confidence and respect one has. It reflects the implicit judgement each one makes about their ability to cope with life's ups and downs (to understand and overcome problems) and their right to be happy (respect and defend their interests and needs (Branden, 1987).

Participants know it as *Like Yourself*. It meets on alternate days to the last group. Basically it is about collectively discussing attitudes and feelings which dignify the value of a person about any kind of consideration regarding disorders or illnesses they suffer. It tries to encourage a realistic and worthy self-image. This latter point is emphasized as the relative ability of autonomy and the possibility people have of achieving it. To explain the topic and exercises the ideas of Branden (1988), Davis, McKay & Eshelman (1985), McKay, Davis & Fanning (1985), McKay & Fanning (1991), Palmer & Alberti (1992) and Ruiz (1992) are particularly useful.

Specific objectives

1. To develop in patients a realistic image of themselves, learning to positively value themselves.
2. To positively reinforce participants when faced with the impact of knowing more about the disorder from which they suffer.
3. To encourage greater confidence in participants and love for themselves.
4. To make them feel greater satisfaction about themselves so that they feel proud of their achievements.
5. To make them understand the value of being alive. To make them feel responsible for themselves and for other and to make them feel independent.
6. To make them appreciate the various concrete positive aspects of their life

(eating, music, sports, etc.) And for them to enjoy things which surround them (nature, their room, etc.).

7. To make them understand that they should not feel guilty or embarrassed about their illness.

Methodology

You should try to make the group very active with sessions that take place in various environments. A selection of the activities and exercises should be related to the interests of the group's participants. They should try to behave in a gratifying way for themselves and others. A clear example is of a self-esteem session which takes place in a kitchen. Some of the participants can show off their cooking abilities whilst others enjoy it compliment them. Another session could be a walk in the park where the group enjoys stimulating their senses. Listening to music or reading as a group are also examples of sessions. And, of course, more common formats such as those which centre on group dynamics where reinforcing oneself and others is learned.

Sequence of the sessions

1. To create a relaxed and optimistic environment. To use various teaching methods and experimentation, such as blackboard, notebook, mattresses, mirrors etc.
2. To work with structured exercises to highlight positive aspects of each one of the participants. Positive social reinforcement should be used to stimulate each group member.
3. The therapist will investigate the positive aspects of each participant and will create situations in which they can demonstrate them and be reinforced. S/he will also encourage putting into practice of this of each participant.
4. Reading of poems which assess life. Collective listening to music and other exercises to awaken the sense and understanding.

Group evaluation of self-esteem

Self-esteem slogans are encouraged and their verbalization by participants. Personal work such as sentences, poetry, photographs or favourite songs which illustrate aspects of self-esteem should also be considered progress. The use of word games, of drawing and other creative means of expression also help us to evaluate progress in self-esteem.

The Final Goal: Adherence to Treatment and Self-Control

This final rung in the third trimester consists of the operative goal of the entire psychoeducative programme. The basic objective is to achieve adherence to treatment, an adequate amount of self-administration of medication, a substantial improvement in communication with the psychiatrist and promoting a feeling of self-control and a corresponding behaviour over one's own emotions.

Description of the "keeping up with treatment" group

Participants may refer to this group as *Your Security, Your Medication, Help and Support*, etc. To explain this curriculum the "Medication Management" module of the Liberman programme (1982), *Social and Independent Living Skills* is particularly useful, as Well as works by Meichenbaum & Turk (1991), Rochon (1991) and Salleras (1985). As far as organizing concepts about neuroleptics and other psychiatric drug therapies the following texts are useful: Bradley & Hirsch (1986), Chinchilla (1989), Fernández and Más (1993), Flórez (1994), González (1993), Guza, Richeimer & Szuba (1993) and, in particular, Lickey & Gordon (1983).

The basic theme of this group is to justify neuroleptic therapy as the most scientifically fundamental treatment and prophylactic for schizophrenic disorders. For this, the group must be given a reasoned and accessible explanation of the way in which it possibly works, stopping to consider in depth the benefits effects and particularly side effects and to value its prophylactic action before a crisis. Along with modelling the habit of self-administration of medicine it is important to improve the patient's image of their psychiatrist and increase their ability to talk about their symptoms and problems as well as the disagreeable effects neuroleptic medication. Other medication should be discussed, such as tranquilizers, hypnotic and anti-Parkinsonians.

Specific objectives

1. To inform participants of the main medications they take, giving them a classificatory table of neurolepetics, hypnotics, tranquilizers and correctors.
2. Teaching them to value neuroleptic medication and regular contact with the psychiatrist as protection factors.
3. Helping them to recognize the effects of neuroleptic medication, to distinguish the benefits and side effects it has. Training them to be able to talk about these details with their psychiatrist.
4. Teaching them to recognize the risk factors involved in their condition, such as abandonment of medication, drug or alcohol use, exposure to stressful situations.

Methodology

The classroom situation is combined with skill training. Simple diagrams should be used to classify medication and help participants to draw up their own guideline sheets for self-administration of medication. Interaction skills with the psychiatrist should be taught using role-play. The use of the group as a model and social reinforcement is vital.

To facilitate group development written material has been prepared for the group coordinator although in certain groups this may be directly handed to the participants. The outline of the written material is the following:

1. Neuroleptics or the price of tranquility.
2. List of side-effects produced by neuroleptics.
3. Guide to the use of role-play during training.

Sequence of the sessions

This can vary according to the initial attitude of the group towards neuro-leptic medication. Normally, in the previous trimester participants have accepted the need for treatment and this makes them more interested in having more information about the characteristics of this medication. Normally we are inclined to follow the order proposed by Liberman (1985):

Module 1: "Information on medication". This is dedicated to teaching participants about various medications and the group in which they belong: neuroleptics, tranquilizers, hypnotics and correctors. Their main effects are explained and the need to keep up neuroleptic therapy. Each member of the group must finally know how to classify and identify their own medicine.

Module 2: "Training in the correct self-administration of medication and the assessment of its principal effects". This trains patients self-administrative behaviour: use of medication, registration card for medication and self-discipline with a ritual for taking medication (a certain time, etc.).

Module 3: "Identification of the side effects of medication". Is dedicated to helping each participant to identify the side-effects that this medication will cause. A list of the most common side-effects is used so patients can identify them in themselves. The role of correctors is also studied.

Module 4: "Skills for communicating problems about medication". Increases communication with the psychiatrist. The final sessions are dedicated to training participants in communication skills with the psychiatrist to express their needs and worries about medication. This includes skills for discriminating when they need psychiatric counselling using what they learned the previous semester about warning symptoms.

Group evaluation of adherence to treatment

Questions with two alternatives, true or false can be useful for testing knowledge about classification of medicine which they take, about the benefits and effects of neuroleptics . Also word games can be used to evaluate attitudes about medicine and psychiatrists. In training in communication skills with the patient and their family diagnostic role-playing is used for evaluation means.

Group description of anxiety and depression prevention

Participants may call this *Control Yourself*. In explaining the exercises involved in this group behavioural therapy manuals are very useful, such as: Caballo (1991), Cautela & Groden (1985), Carnwath & Miller (1989), Davis, McKay & Eshelman (1985), Dyer (1983), Ellis & Grieger (1990), Fowler, Garety & Kuipers (1995), Hawton, Salkovskis, Kirk & Clark (1989), Lazarus (1980), Magaro (1991), McKay, Davis & Fanning (1985), Meichenbaum (1987), Weisinger (1988) and Wolpe (1958), amongst many others.

The basic point of this group which is carried out on alternate days in relation to the last one is to help participants to identify their emotional state and
to promote self-controlling behaviours. Ideally, they should be resources people
normally use when they feel nervous or sad: having a cup of tea, a shower,
relaxing, phoning a friend, etc. It is not so much about developing a complete
self-control programme, than teaching patients the experience of recognizing
and modelling their emotions. The main goal is to increase knowledge of
emotions and empathy of the patient bearing in mind the deficits which people
suffering from schizophrenia face.

Specific objectives
1. Teaching participants to recognize their emotional states, especially happiness, sadness anxiety and anger.
2. Training them to self-register various depressive and anxious symptoms.
3. Using a series of resources to combat, disquiet, apathy and sadness, resources such as relaxation, teas, change of environment, anticipation of
   positive consequences, music, hobbies, etc..
4. Encouraging a philosophy of self-control in participants and the personal
   ability to restructure disagreeable situations.

Methodology
This should be more experience-based than didactic although when necessary resources such as the board and written explanations can be used to
facilitate learning. To approach emotional experience external, publicly observable expressive acts as well as related aspects for each group member. The
coordinator should highlight common aspects of human emotions. In the
second part when self-control skills are being explained it is vital to go over
participants' daily experiences of emotional recognition and of self-control for
social reinforcement for the use of these skills.

Sequence of the sessions
1. The first sessions are dedicated to describing the most common human
   emotions making reference to the expressive aspects which allow for their
   identification in others and the experience of each one. A more advanced
   step consists in establishing that the emotion depends upon the way in
   which we think about situations or rationalize them. For this a text has
   been written about "Rejection of Irrational Ideas and Development of
   Coping Techniques", based on the ideas of Ellis, even if in certain groups
   Dryer's (1983) novel "The Rules of Eykis" has been used.
2. The following sessions are dedicated to training participants to distinguish
   between their emotional states. For this Beck's Depression Inventory is
   used (Beck, Ward, Mendelson, Mock & Erbaugh, 1961) along with Hamilton's Anxiety Evaluation Scale (Hamilton, 1959) and the Inventory of
   Anxiety State-Traits (Spielberger, Gorsuch & Lushene, 1970), as well as
   self-report designs.

3. Finally, the majority of these sessions is dedicated to practicing relaxations, imagination techniques, detention of perturbing ideas, personal planning, preparation of teas and physical exercises, speaking or meditation, amongst other resources of self-control which are chosen in accordance with participants' previous experiences and their educational level.

Group evaluation of preventing anxiety and depression
We use brief and simplified scale formats for self-evaluation of depression and anxiety. Various ways of self-control are taught via diagnostic, training and evaluation role-playing. Social reinforcement is used for achievements carried out outside the group environment. Likert-type scales are also used to evaluate knowledge and the putting into practice self-control skills.

Conclusions

This psychoeducation programme was evaluated in a design with a control group and its results published (Otero & Rebolledo, 1992) within a wide psychiatric rehabilitation programme (Rebolledo & Pastor, 1991). The most obvious benefits with 1 year of follow-up was the decrease in the rate of admittance to critical wards, the ability to take medication in an independent way and better attendance to psychiatric consultations. The developing experience of these groups makes us think that the programme promotes better understanding of the illness, adoption of a safer lifestyle for people facing their vulnerability to experience schizophrenic episodes, preservation of self-esteem and acquisition of better motivation for rehabilitation and reinsertion programmes.

It is true that the evaluation carried out refers to a wide investigation that included the assessment of a rehabilitation and psychoeducation programme. Each component of this offered assistance now needs analyzing and evaluating in great detail to be able to weigh up the contribution of each activity. However, global evaluation allows us to affirm that psychoeducation, along with other rehabilitation activities id a valid focus in therapy and help for schizophrenic disorders.

In short, the most important aspects of the psychoeducative focus are the following:
1. Offering a new perspective on the difficult problem of living with schizophrenia. Whilst therapeutic techniques (strictly curative) do not yet reach a level of efficiency which guarantees full and total; recuperation from the schizophrenic process, psychoeducation provides a valid alternative for victims and their families.
2. Psychoeducation is a focus which recognizes the right of families and victims to know the reality of present scientific knowledge about the prob-

lem and to use this knowledge to their benefit with the purpose of evaluating their quality of life and coping better with the daily difficulties of family and social life.

3. The psychoeducative focus attempts to dignify the person affected by schizophrenia considering them as an independent person with rights and with the ability to manage their life. When faced with psychotic episodes a prosthetic rather than disabled judgement is made. That is, one should think about what the best way to help to affected person out so that they can play out their social roles despite their handicap.

4. Psychoeducative activities use several methods to overcome cognitive disabilities and behavioural dysfunctions which go along with suffering from schizophrenia. Failures should always be attributed to the method used not to psychopathology or deterioration. All affected people can learn to organize their behaviour to reach self-care goals if we know how to give them information via methods in line with their understanding and if we provide them with the ideal environment and modulated stimulation in line with their vulnerability.

5. Because of their group focus, psychoeducation activities appear to be an adequate resource for use in services concerned with mental health as well as out-patient clinics and hospitals because they can be developed by a multi professional team, because they are operative and can be adapted to different groups according to age, interests or education and because they can be evaluated and taught to mental health teams.

Our job as psychoeducators is to form an intelligent link with people suffering from schizophrenic disorder with the aim of increasing their possibilities of personal development..

References

Amdur, M., & Cohen, M. (1981). Medication groups for psychiatric patients. *American Journal of Nursing*, 343–345.

Anderson, C., Reiss, D., & Hogarty, G. (1988). *Esquizofrenia y familia. Guía práctica de psicoeducación*. Buenos Aires: Amorrortu.

Andreasen, N. (1982). Negative symptoms in schizophrenia definition and reliability. *Archives of General Psychiatry, 39*, 784–788.

Ascher-Svanum, H. (1989). A psychoeducational intervention for schizophrenic patients. *Patient Education and Counselling, 14*, 81–87.

Ayllon, T., & Azrin, N. (1979). *Economia de fichas. Un sistema motivacional para la terapia y la rehabilitación*. México: Trillas (Original: 1972).

Barter, J., Queirolo, J., & Ekstrom, S. (1984). A psychoeducational approach to educating chronic mental patients for community living. *Hospital and Community Psychology, 35*, 793–800.

Barter, J. (1984). Psychoeducation. In M. Talbott (Ed.), *The chronic mental patient. Five years later*. New York: Grune and Stratton.

Barrowcluogh, C., & Tarrier, N. (1992). *Families of schizophrenic patients. Cognitive behavioural intervention.* London: Chapman and Hall.

Beck, A. T., Ward, C. H., Mendelson, M., Mock, J., & Erbaugh, J. (1961). An inventory for measuring depression. *Archives of General Psychiatry, 4,* 561–571.

Birchwood, M., Hallet, S., & Preston, M. (1988). *Schizophrenia. An integrated aproach to research and treatment.* London: Longman.

Birchwood, M., & Tarrier, N. (1995). *El tratamiento psicológico de la esquizofrenia.* Barcelona: Ariel. (Original: 1994).

Bradley, P., & Hirsch, S. (1986). *The psychopharmacology and treatment of schizophrenia.* Oxford: Oxford Medical Publications.

Branden, N. (1987). *Como mejorar su autoestima.* Barcelona: Paidós.

Breier, A., & Strauss, J. (1983). Self-control in psychotic disorders. *Archives of General Psychiatry, 40,* 1141–1145.

Brown, G., & Harris, T. (1989). *Life events and illness.* New York: Guilford Press.

Caballo, V. E. (Ed.) (1991). *Manual de técnicas de terapia y modificación de conducta.* Madrid: Siglo XXI.

Caplan, G. (1974). Support systems and community mental health. New York: Behavioral Publications.

Carson Bisbee, C. (1991). *Educating patients and families about mental illness. A practical guide.* Gaithersburg, MD: Aspen Publications.

Cautela, J., & Groden, J. (1985). *Técnicas de relajación. Manual práctico para adultos y niños en educación especial.* Barcelona: Martínez Roca.

Carnwath, T., & Miller, D. (1989). *Psicoterapia conductual en asistencia primaria: Manual práctico.* Barcelona: Martínez Roca.

Chinchilla, A. (1989). *Tratamientos psicofarmacológicos en psiquiatría.* Barcelona: Sanofi-Winthrop.

Ciompi, L. (1988). *The psyche and schizophrenia. The bond between affect and logic.* Harvard, MA: Harvard University Press.

Colodrón, A. (1983). *Las Esquizofrenias.* Madrid: Siglo XXI.

Crow, T., Cross, A., Johnstone, E., & Owen, F. (1982). Two syndromes in schizophrenia and their pathogenesis. In F. Henn & H. Nasrallah (Eds.), *Schizophrenia as a brain disease.* New York: Oxford University Press.

Day, R. (1989). Schizophrenia. In G. Brown & T. Harris (Eds.), *Life events and illness.* New York: Guilford Press.

Davis, M., McKay, M., & Eshelman, E. R. (1985). *Técnicas de autocontrol emocional.* Barcelona: Martínez Roca. (Original: 1982).

Dyer, W. (1983). *Los regalos de Eykis. Hacia una vida sin límites.* Barcelona: Grijalbo.

Ellis, A., & Grieger, R. (1990). Manual de terapia racional emotiva. Bilbao: Desclée de Brouwer.

Falloon, I., Boyd, J., & McGill, C. (1984). *Family care of schizophrenia.* New York: Guilford Press.

Feldenkrais, M. (1972). *Autoconciencia por el movimiento.* Barcelona: Paidós.

Fernández, A., & Mas, J. (1993). *Guía para el uso de psicofármacos.* Madrid: Idepsa.

Fink, P., & Tasman, A. (1992). *Stigma and mental illness.* Washington: American Psychiatric Press.

Fitzpatrick, R. (1990). *La enfermedad como experiencia.* México: Fondo de Cultura Económica (Original: 1984).

Fowler, D., Garety, P., & Kuipers, E. (1995). *Cognitive behaviour therapy for psychosis.* New York: Wiley.

García, M. (1995). *Intrenamiento de habilidades psicorporales en la vejez.* Salamanca: Amaru Ediciones.

Goffman, E. (1986). *Estigma. La identidad deteriorada.* Buenos Aires: Amorrortu (Original: 1963).

Goldman, C. (1988). Toward a definition of psychoeducation. *Hospital and Community Psychology, 39,* 666–667.

Goldman, C., & Quinn, F. (1988). Effects of a patient education program in the treatment of schizophrenia. *Hospital and Community Psychology, 39,* 282–286.

Goldstein, M., Hand, I., & Hahlweg, K. (1986). *Treatment of schizophrenia, family assessment and intervention.* New York: Springer-Verlag.

González, E. (1993). *Psicofarmacología aplicada.* Barcelona: Organon Española.

Gordon, R., & Gordon, K. (1989). A program of modular psychoeducational skills training for chronic mental patients. In L. L. Abate & M. A. Milan (Eds.), *Handbook of social skills: training and research.* New York: Wiley.

Guze, B., Richeimer, S., & Szuba, M. (1992). *Guía farmacológica en psiquiatría.* New York: Mosby Year Book, Wolfe Publishing.

Lazarus, A. (1980). *Terapia conductista. Técnicas y perspectivas.* Barcelona: Paidós. (Original: 1971).

Hamilton, H. (1959). The assessment of anxiety states by rating. *British Journal of Medical Psychology, 32,* 50–55.

Hammer, E. (1969). *Test proyectivos gráficos.* Barcelona: Paidós.

Hammer, M. (1981). Social supports, social nerworks and schizophrenia. *Schizophrenia Bulletin, 7,* 1981.

Hatfield, A. (1990). *Family education in mental illness.* New York: Guilford Press.

Hatfield, A., & Lefley, H. (1987). *Families of the mentally ill. Coping and adaptation.* New York: Guilford Press.

Hawton, K., Salkovskis, P., Kirk, J., & Clark, D. (1989). *Cognitive behaviour therapy for psychiatric problems. A practical guide.* Oxford: Oxford Medical Publications.

Jacobson, E. (1961). *Aprenda a relajarse.* Buenos Aires: Compañia General Fabril Editora.

Kay, D. (1986). Assessment of familial risks in schizophrenia and their application in genetic counselling. In A. Kerr & P. Snaith (Eds.), *Contemporary issues in schizophrenia.* London: Gaskell.

Kickbush, I. (1986). Life styles and health. *Social Science and Medicine, 22,* 2.

Kuipers, L., & Bebbington, P. (1990). *Working in partnership.* Oxford: Heinemann Medical Books.

Kuipers, L., Leff, J., & Lam, D. (1992). *Family work for schizophrenia. A practical guide.* London: Gaskell.

Laffal, J., Brown, M., Pearlman, L. A., & Burns, G. L. (1983). Therapeutic education of psychiatric inpatients in a classroom setting. *Quarterly Review Bulletin,* 190–195.

Laing, R. (1982). *El yo y los otros.* México: Fondo de Cultura Económica.

Leff, J., & Vaughn, C. (1980). The interaction of life events and relative's expressed emotion in schizophrenia and depressive neurosis. *British Journal of Psychiatry, 136,* 146–153.

Leff, J., & Vaughn, C. (1985). *Expressed emotion in families.* New York: Guilford Press.

Liberman, R. P. (1986). Coping and competence as protective factors in the vulnerability-stress model of schizophrenia. In M. Lickey & B. Gordon (Eds.), *Medicamentos para las enfermedades mentales.* Barcelona: Labor.

Liberman, R. P. (1985). *Social and Independent Living Skills. Medication Management Module.* Los Angles, CA: Camarillo State Hospital.

Liberman, R. P. (1993). *Rehabilitación integral del enfermo mental crónico.* Barcelona: Martínez Roca. (Original: 1988).

Magaro, P. (1991). *Cognitive bases of mental disorders.* Beverly Hills, CA: Sage.

Marneros, A., Andreasen, N., & Tsuang, M. (1991). *Negative versus positive schizophrenia.* New York: Springer-Verlag.

McKay, M., Davis, M., & Fanning, P. (1985). *Técnicas cognitivas para el tratamiento del estrés.* Barcelona: Martínez Roca. (Original: 1981).

McKay, M., & Fanning, P. (1991). *Autoestima. Evaluación y mejora.* Barcelona: Martínez Roca.

Meichenbaum, D. (1987). *Manual de inoculación del estrés.* Barcelona: Martínez Roca. (Original: 1985).

Meichenbaum, D., & Turk, D. (1991). *Como facilitar el seguimiento de los tratamientos terapeuticos. Guía práctica para los profesionales de la salud.* Bilbao: Desclée de Brouwer.

Murray, T., & Reveley, A. (1986). Genetic aspects of schizophrenia: overview. In A. Kerr & P. Sanith (Eds.), *Contemporary issues in schizophrenia.* London: Gaskell.

Neufeld, R. (1984). *Psicopatología y estrés.* Barcelona: Toray.

Osgood, C. E., Succi, G., & Tannebaum, P. (1976). *La medida del significado.* Madrid: Gredos.

Otero, V., & Rebolledo, S. (1992). Evaluación de un programa de rehabilitación psiquiátrica. *Psiquis, 13,* 135–142.

Ozámiz, J. (1987). Estilos de vida y salud mental. In J. Ozámiz (Ed.), *Psicosociología de la salud mental.* San Sebastián: Tartalo.

Palmer, P., & Alberti, M. (1992). *Autoestima.* Valencia: Promolibro.

Perris, C. (1989). *Cognitive therapy with schizophrenic patients.* London: Cassell.

Pilsecker, C. (1981). On educating schizophrenics about schizophrenia. *Schizophrenia Bulletin, 7,* 379–382.

Rebolledo, S., & López de Heredia, N. (1990). Psicoeducación de pacientes esquizofrénicos y sus familias. *Revista de Psiquiatría de la Facultad de Medicina de Barcelona, 17,* 92–100.

Rebolledo, S., & Pastor, A. (1991). Programa y recursos de los dispositivos de rehabilitación psiquiátrica. *Psiquiatría Pública, 3,* 204–214.

Rebolledo, S., & Lobato, M. (1994). *Como afrontar la esquizofrenia. Guía para las familias.* Madrid: Fundación ONCE.

Rochon, A. (1991). *Educación para la salud. Guía práctica para realizar un proyecto.* Barcelona: Masson.

Roder, V., Brenner, H. D., Hodel, B., & Kienzle, N. (1996). *Terapia integrada de la esquizofrenia.* Barcelona: Ariel. (Original: 1994).

Ruiz Vargas, J. (1987). *Esquizofrenia, un enfoque cognitivo.* Madrid: Alianza University.

Ruiz, A. (1992). *Como ayudarse a uno mismo.* Ediciones Paulinas.

Sánchez, P., & Ruiz-Vargas, J. (1987). Vulnerabilidad a la esquizofrenia. In J. Ruiz Vargas, *Esquizofrenia, un enfoque cognitivo.* Madrid: Alianza University.

Salleras, L. (1985). *Educación sanitaria. Principios, métodos, aplicaciones.* Madrid: Díaz de Santos.

Scharfetter, C. (1979). *Introducción a la psicopatología general.* Madrid: Morata.

Schaff, T. (1973). *El rol de enfermo mental.* Buenos Aires: Amorrortu.

Spielberger, C. D., Gorsuch, R. L., & Lushene, R. E. (1970). *Manual for the State/Trait Anxiety Inventory.* Palo Alto, CA: Consulting Psychologists Press.

Straube, E., & Hahlweg, K. (1990). *Schizophrenia. Concepts, vulnerability and intervention.* New York: Springer-Verlag.

Strauss, J., Böker, W., & Brenner, H. (1987). *Psychosocial treatment of schizophrenia.* Berlin: Hans Huber.

Thorton, J., Plummer, E., & Seeman, M. (1982). The family's reaction to schizophrenic illness. *International Journal of Family Psychiatry, 3,* 33–44.

Watt, D. (1982). A search for generic linkage in schizophrenia. *British Journal of Psychiatry,* *142,* 532–537.

Weinsinger, H. (1988). *Técnicas para el control del comportamiento agresivo.* Barcelona: Martínez Roca.

Wolpe, J. (1978). *Psicoterapia por inhibición recíproca.* Bilbao: Desclée de Bouwer.

Zazzo, R. (1971). *Manual para el examen psicológico del niño.* Madrid: Fundamentos.

Zubin, J. (1980). Chronic schizophrenia from the standpoint of vulnerability. In C. Baxter & T. Melnechuk (Eds.), *Perspectives in schizophrenia research.* New York: Raven Press.

Zubin, J., & Spring, B. (1977). Vulnerability: a new view of schizophrenia. *Journal of Abnormal Psychology, 86,* 103–126.

Zubin, J., & Steinhauer, S. (1981). How to break the logjam in schizophrenia: a look beyond genetics. *Journal of Nervous and Mental Disease, 169,* 477–492.

Zubin, J., Magaziner, J., & Steinhauer, S. (1983). The metamorphosis of schizophrenia from chronicity to vulnerability. *Psychological Medicine, 13,* 551–571.

Further Reading

Birchwood, M. (1995). Esquizofrenia. In V. E. Caballo, G. Buela-Casal & J. A. Carrobles (Eds.), *Manual de psicopatología y trastornos psiquiátricos,* Vol. 1. Madrid: Siglo XXI.

Birchwood, M., & Tarrier, N. (1994). *Psychological management of schizophrenia.* Chichester: Wiley.

Rebolledo, S. (1993). *El programa de rehabilitación en los servicios de salud mental.* Monograph no. 5, SISO/SAUDE. Boletin da Asociación Galega de Saude Mental.

Rebolledo, S., & Lobato, M. (1994). *Como afrontar la esquizofrenia. Guía para las familias.* Madrid: Fundación ONCE.

Roder, V., Brenner, H. D., Hodel, B., & Kienzle, N. (1996). *Terapia integrada de la esquizofrenia.* Barcelona: Ariel. (Original: 1994).

20

Cognitive Therapy for Delusions and Hallucinations

CHRIS JACKSON[a] and PAUL CHADWICK[b]

[a]All Saints Hospital, UK; [b]University of Birmingham, UK

Introduction

In recent years there has been a growing dissatisfaction amongst clinicians and researchers about the use of broad diagnostic categories such as schizophrenia (Costello, 1993; Bentall, Jackson & Pilgrim, 1988). Mirrored by increases in our knowledge of ordinary cognitive processes (Brewin, 1988) and the application of cognitive psychotherapy to a wide range of clinical conditions (Hawton, Salkovskis, Kirk & Clark, 1989) there has been increased interest in the study and treatment of psychotic symptoms in their own right (Bentall, 1994; Chadwick & Lowe, 1990; Tarrier, 1992). In the present chapter we describe our own research and clinical practice establishing a cognitive approach to understanding and managing auditory hallucinations and delusions.

A Cognitive Approach to Voices

Although hallucinations may occur in a number of modalities, including visual, tactile and olfactory, in a review of 15 studies of people with a functional psychosis Slade & Bentall (1988) noted that on average auditory hallucinations were found to be present in 60% of patients. This compared with only 29% experiencing visual hallucinations which, in general, are considered to be more often associated with organic brain syndromes (Goodwin, 1971). It is for such reasons, and for the sake of space, that this review will concentrate on working with people with "voices"\f "a" (i.e. auditory hallucinations).

Auditory hallucinations are traditionally associated with a diagnosis of schizophrenia. In the World Health Organization's International Pilot Study of Schizophrenia (WHO, 1973) auditory hallucinations were reported by 73% of people diagnosed as having an acute episode of schizophrenia. Yet they can be reported by individuals who have been sexually abused, or suffered a bereavement, as well as by individuals diagnosed as having a manic depressive illness or an affective psychosis. Indeed, because they feature in many different disorders, the diagnostic importance of auditory hallucinations has been doubted (Asaad & Shapiro, 1986).

In addition, it appears that auditory hallucinations are not restricted to clinical groups. Auditory hallucinations can be reported by individuals who, whilst showing signs of a specific clinical disorder, display insufficient symptoms for a firm diagnosis to be made (Cochrane, 1983). Again, it appears that under laboratory conditions many ordinary people display a propensity to report hearing sounds which are not there, prompting researchers to speculate that proneness to hallucinate may be a predisposition spread across the general population (Slade & Bentall, 1988). Current opinion in psychology veers towards accepting the possibility that hallucinations lie on a continuum with normality (Strauss, 1969).

The auditory hallucination itself can be a noise, music, single words, a brief phrase, or a whole conversation. The present chapter is concerned only with voices, that is, hallucinations which are experienced as someone talking. The experience of hearing voices is a powerful one that demands a reaction. However, the experience is also very personal. Whilst it is known that a common first reaction to voices is puzzlement (Maher, 1988), individuals evolve different ways of interacting with their voices. Certain people, for example, experience voices as immensely distressing and frightening and will shout and swear at them. In contrast, other individuals might find their voices reassuring and amusing and actually seek contact. Again, in the case of imperative voices, many individuals desperately resist the commands, and comply only at times of great pressure, whilst others comply willingly and fully.

This diversity in the way individuals relate to their voices illustrates the point that voices are not necessarily a problem to the individual concerned – indeed, it is fairly common for individuals to believe their voices to be a solution to a problem. This in turn draws attention to the point that the serious disturbance associated with voices, like with so many other symptoms, tends to be located in the way an individual feels and behaves. People who hear voices are typically referred to our service because they are desperate, depressed, angry, suicidal, helpless, harming themselves, isolated, violent, etc. This point is implicit in traditional treatment approaches, which have usually been directed at easing distress and altering behaviour (e.g. methods of anxiety reduction, punishment procedures) as well as at eliminating the hallucinatory experience (medication, ear plugs, headphones). Such treatments were based on the premise that a particular individual's coping behaviour and affect followed necessarily from the nature of his or her hallucination (e.g. Benjamin, 1989).

However, this explanation may be too simple. Research has shown how voices with similar contents may evoke different coping behaviour (Tarrier, 1992). Also, an inventive study by Romme & Escher (1989) has revealed how voices frequently do not evoke a sufficiently strong reaction to bring the individual to the attention of services, even when the content is extremely serious. It would appear that the nature and strength of an individual's response to voices is mediated by psychological processes.

We speculated that the degree of fear, acceptance and compliance shown to voices might be mediated by *beliefs* about the voices' power and authority, the consequences of disobedience, and so on (Chadwick & Birchwood, 1994). For example, an individual who believes his voice to come from a powerful and vengeful spirit may be terrified of the voice and comply with its commands to harm others; however, if the same voice were believed to be self-generated, terror and compliance would be unlikely.

In other words, voices might be viewed from a cognitive perspective. The defining feature of the cognitive model within clinical psychology is the premise that people's feelings and behaviour are mediated by their beliefs, and therefore are not inevitable consequences of antecedent events, such as an auditory hallucination.

Applicability of the Cognitive Model to Voices

If the cognitive perspective is to be applicable to voices, two hypotheses must be supported. One is that the cognitive model will make sense of why individuals respond in such different ways to their voices; specifically, diverse affective and behavioural responses must be understandable by reference to differences in the *beliefs* individuals hold about their voices. Second, the cognitive model needs to *add* to our understanding of voices. That is to say, if differences in voice content accounted for people's diverse behaviour and feelings, then from an explanatory point of view the cognitive model would be superfluous (although it could still have important strategic implications for treatment).

In a recent experiment (Chadwick & Birchwood, 1994) we found support for both hypotheses. We interviewed twenty-six people who had heard voices for at least 2 years in order to assess their behavioural, cognitive and affective responses to persistent voices. All participants met DSM III R criteria for schizophrenia or schizoaffective disorder (APA, 1987). All save one were receiving depot neuroleptic medication at All Saints Hospital, Birmingham; one was in hospital and the remainder were out-patients. Participants volunteered for the study with no refusals.

Information was gathered using a semi-structured interview. This covered formal properties of the voices, including content; beliefs about the voices' identity, power and purpose, and about the consequences of compliance; collateral symptoms that were regarded as supporting the beliefs; other confirmatory evidence; and influence over the voice. Confirmatory evidence referred to actual occurrences that were perceived to support a belief; for example, the belief that voices give good advice would be strengthened if complying with a command led to a desired outcome. Influence concerned whether the individual could determine the onset and offset of the voice, and could direct what it said. Also, the behavioural and affective responses were elicited. It usually took more than one interview to collect all relevant information.

Beliefs About Voices: Omnipotence, Malevolence, and Benevolence

All voices were believed to be extraordinarily powerful, or omnipotent, and this belief seemed to be supported by four types of evidence. First, nineteen individuals (73%) reported collateral symptoms that contributed to the sense of omnipotence. One man, for example, was commanded by his voice to kill his daughter; he recalled one occasion when she was standing by an open window and he experienced his body being moved towards her. A second man heard a voice telling him that he was the son of Noah, and occasionally when he heard his voice he experienced concurrent visual hallucinations in which he was dressed in a white robe and walked on water. Second, 11 people (42%) gave examples of how they attributed events to their voices, and then cited the events as proof of the voices great power. Thus, although two individuals cut their wrists under their own volition, both subsequently deduced that the voices had somehow made them do it. Similarly, one man attributed responsibility for his having sworn out loud in church to his satanic voices. Third, 21 people (81%) were unable to influence either the onset and offset of their voices or what was said, once again suggestive of the voices' power.

Finally, all voices gave the impression of knowing all about people's past histories, their present thoughts, feelings and actions, and what the future held. Frequently voices would refer to behaviour and thoughts of a highly personal and emotive nature, such as a criminal act or personal weakness, which the individual feared others knowing. Perhaps because of this lack of privacy, individuals would often attribute more knowledge to the voice than the content actually displayed; for instance, general statements like "We know all about you", were thought to refer to specific actions. Understandably, this appearance of omniscience left many individuals feeling exposed and vulnerable.

However, because in our sample a belief in omnipotence was ubiquitous, it would not account for differences in behaviour and affect. On the basis of their beliefs about the voices identity and purpose, people saw individual voices as being either *malevolent* or *benevolent*. Thirteen people believed their voice or voices to be malevolent. Beliefs about malevolence took one of two forms; either that the voice was a punishment for a bad deed, or that it was an undeserved persecution. For example, one man believed he was being punished by the Devil for having committed a murder, and another man believed he was being persecuted without good reason by an ex-employer. Six people believed their voices to be benevolent. For example, one woman believed that she heard the voice of a prophet who was helping her become a better mother and wife, and one man believed that the voices were from God and were there to help develop a special power. Four people believed they heard a mixture of benevolent and malevolent voices; paradigmatic of this group was a man who was tormented by a group of evil space travellers on the one hand and yet protected and nurtured by a guardian angel on the other.

Three people were uncertain about their voices because of an inconsistency or incongruity in what was said. *Uncertainty* was defined as having a strong doubt about the voice's identity, meaning or power, where this doubt was the result of the person's deduction. For example, one man was certain that his voices wanted to help, but observed that they had got things wrong : they wanted him to kill himself and move on to the next and better life, yet his religion told him that suicide is a sin and those who commit it go to hell.

Connection Between Beliefs, Coping Behaviour, and Affect

The behavioural and emotional responses to voices were organized into three categories. *Engagement* comprised co-operative behaviour (e.g. elective listening, willing compliance, seeking contact with voices, trying to call them up) and positive affect (e.g. joy, reassurance, amusement). *Resistance* comprised resistant and combative behaviour (e.g. arguing, covert and overt shouting back and swearing, non-compliance or reluctant compliance when pressure is extreme, avoidance of cues that trigger voices, and distraction) and negative affect (e.g. fear, anxiety, anger, depression) *Indifference* was defined as not engaging with the voice. In an early study (Chadwick & Birchwood, 1994) we found that voices believed to be malevolent were resisted, and benevolent voices were engaged with.

In order to establish the reliability and validity of these concepts, we have developed a 30 item *Beliefs About Voices Questionnaire* (Appendix 1) to

Table 20.1. Connections Between Malevolence, Benevolence, Engagement and Resistance

	Resistance (%)	Engagement (%)	Neither (%)	Both (%)
Malevolent (*n* = 26)	17 (66%)	2 (8%)	3 (11%)	4 (15%)
Benevolent (*n* = 17)	0	13 (76%)	3 (18%)	1 (6%)
Neutral (*n* = 16)	3 (19%)	4 (25%)	8 (50%)	1 (6%)

measure malevolence (6 items), benevolence (6 items), resistance (9 items) and engagement (8 items) and power (1 item). A statistical analysis conducted on a preliminary sample of sixty completed Voices Questionnaires has shown the BAVQ to be both reliable and valid (for details see Chadwick & Birchwood, in press), and has established provisional scoring guidelines to define malevolence (a score of four or more), benevolence (3 or more), engagement (five or more) and resistance (six or more). Data from this study strongly supported our proposed connections between on the one hand malevolence and resistance, and on the other benevolence and engagement (see Table 20.1).

Connection Between Malevolence, Benevolence, and Voice Content

Having found that differences in coping behaviour and distress were rendered understandable by reference to beliefs about malevolence and benevolence, it remained to be shown that voice content could not account for these differences with equal clarity. In other words, the distinction between malevolence and benevolence needed to say something about the maintenance of voices which could not be said by inspecting voice content alone.

It is clear that there is a link between voice content and the person's associated feelings and behaviour, and therefore that in many cases resistance and engagement might have been predicted on the basis of content. However, the class of belief was not always understandable in light of voice content alone – that is, in 8 cases (31%) the beliefs appeared to be at odds with what the voice said. Two voices of benign content were believed to be malevolent; for instance, one of these voices simply urged the individual to "take care", "mind his step", and "watch how he went", yet he believed these words to have been spoken by evil witches intent on driving him mad. The reverse was also true; two voices commanded the hearers to commit suicide, yet both were believed to be benevolent. Three voices commanded the hearers to commit murder (in two instances, of immediate family members), and yet again were believed to be benevolent. Perhaps most strikingly, one woman's voice identified itself as God and yet she disregarded this and believed it to be an evil force.

In summary, we have found the meaning individuals attach to their voices renders their coping behaviour and affect understandable; when beliefs are not taken into account, many responses seem perplexing or incongruous (see also Strauss, 1991).

Cognitive Therapy for Voices

The cognitive approach within clinical psychology (e.g. Trower, Casey & Dryden, 1988) presupposes first, that extreme feelings and behaviour (e.g. depression and suicide) are consequences of particular beliefs (e.g. I am worthless) rather than events (e.g. divorce) and second, that if these beliefs are weakened using cognitive therapy, then the associated distress and disturbance will diminish. Although traditionally applied to non-psychotic disorders (Hawton et al., 1989), more recent evidence indicates that cognitive therapy has a role to play in the management both of schizophrenia (see Birchwood & Tarrier, 1992) and of delusions (see Chadwick & Lowe, 1990).

Traditional treatments for voices have been aimed at reducing either the hallucinatory experience (e.g. medication, ear plug therapy) or their consequences (e.g. anxiety reduction methods, punishment procedures). The purpose of using CT for voices is to ease distress and problem behaviour by weakening *beliefs* about omnipotence, malevolence or benevolence, and compliance. The possible importance of this new approach is considerable because even the most effective treatment for voices, neuroleptic medication, leaves many voices unchanged (Slade & Bentall, 1988).

The CT we use for people who hear voices draws very heavily from the work of Beck (Beck, Rush, Shaw & Emery, 1979; Hole, Rush & Beck, 1973) although we have found it necessary to adapt and develop traditional CT in order to work collaboratively and effectively with individuals who hear voices. We have found it can be difficult to engage people in CT for voices, because of their powerful beliefs and emotions about their voices. Therefore we have developed a number of strategies to promote engagement and trust. One such strategy is to use our understanding of the connections between malevolence, benevolence, resistance, and engagement to anticipate how an individual is likely to feel, think and behave in relation to the voice. This understanding seems to bring individuals a sense of relief. We always inform clients that they may withdraw from therapy at any point without penalty, and this may also reduce anxiety and facilitate engagement. Again, people can meet other hallucinators and watch a video of individuals who have completed therapy successfully discussing their experience; the discovery that others have similar problems – "universality" (Yalom, 1970) – is an important therapeutic process.

The central beliefs are defined early on, together with the evidence used to support them, and we discuss how any distress and disruption attributed to the voices is actually a consequence of the beliefs the individual holds. We emphasize that individuals are free to continue holding their beliefs, and may drop out of therapy at any time; the atmosphere is one of 'collaborative empiricism' (Beck et al., 1979) in which beliefs are considered as possibilities that may or may not be reasonable.

Disputing a belief's veracity involves the use of standard cognitive techniques (see Chadwick & Lowe, 1990). At first the evidence for each belief is challenged; this process begins with the piece of evidence the individual rates as least important and progresses to that rated most important. Next the therapist challenges the belief directly. This involves first pointing out examples of inconsistency and irrationality ,and second, offering an alternative explanation of events. This alternative is always that the beliefs are an understandable reaction to, and attempt to make sense of, the voices. However, in our experience this leaves the person searching to understand the meaning of the hallucinations. We conceptualize the voices as self-generated, and try to explore the possible connection, or personal significance, between the voice content and the individuals history.

We use two approaches to testing beliefs empirically. On the one hand, we have a set procedure for testing the universal belief "I cannot control my voices". First, it is reframed as "I cannot turn my voices on and off". The therapist then engineers situations to increase and then decrease the probability of hearing voices. An initial thorough cognitive assessment should identify the cues that provoke voices, and one technique with a high likelihood of eliminating voices for its duration is concurrent verbalisation (Birchwood, 1986). The person rouses and quells the voices several times to provide a complete test.

With all other beliefs the empirical test was negotiated by the client and therapist. It is essential to examine beforehand the implications of the test not bearing out the belief; if the belief will be modified or adapted, or whether the patient has a ready explanation for the outcome that leaves the belief untouched.

Case Example R.P. (C.T. for voices) . R.P. was a 43 year old unemployed laboratory technician with a long standing psychiatric history dating back to 1979. He admitted to having heard voices for the last 15 years and for the last few years that these had occurred on a daily basis. He described the hallucinations coming in 45–60 min bursts throughout the day. In addition to the voices R.P. experienced secondary delusions and depressed mood. He found it difficult to go out of his flat because of his ideas of reference and associated anxious affect. He had made three serious attempts to kill himself.

Content of voices. R.P. heard 2 sets of voices which he referred to as "good" and "evil". The "evil" voice tended to play on issues that R.P. felt guilty about such as the death of his grandfather (e.g. "you should have been there") and his limited support of his grandmother with her food shopping (e.g. "you don't help her").The "evil" voice was also derogatory , and would often shout insults at him ("you're useless", "you are a shithead" etc.) which R.P. often interpreted as coming from strangers in the street. In contrast, the "good" voices "rescued him", saying "don't listen to them" and "we're here to protect you".

Beliefs about voices. Identity: R.P. believed the "evil" voice was male, very powerful and responsible for all "evil in the world". In contrast, R.P. believed that the good voices (a mix of a few men and women) had been sent by God to protect him. In general the "evil" voices were described as the more dominant of the two.

Meaning: R.P. believed the evil voice had been sent to "underwhelm him, to try and break him down in order to undermine his sanity". The good voices were there to "encourage, help and support". He believed he had no *control* over any of the voices and was unable to influence their onset or offset. The voices had on occasions during the baseline period told him to kill himself ("why don't you end it?") but he had not attempted to comply. However, he did believe what the evil voices were telling him and as a result held a number of damaging negative self-evaluative thoughts ("I'm worthless", "I'm evil") with more or less absolute conviction.

Affect and behaviour. The omnipotent evil voices had a profound impact on R.P. making him feel threatened anxious and depressed when they spoke. The "good" voices were not always able to counteract this influence. He remained paranoid and hypervigilant when outside and on occasions experienced panic attacks. He therefore avoided going out unless absolutely necessary, rendering him socially isolated.

Cognitive therapy. R.P. was seen at home by the first author every 2 or 3 weeks. Sessions lasted on average approximately 1 h. Over the course of 5 months he was seen on 8 occasions.

Engagement. Overall an agenda of collaborative empiricism was encouraged. The first author (C.J.) was introduced to R.P. by his case manager/keyworker (Community Psychiatric Nurse – CPN). An assessment was carried out and the goals of the intervention were negotiated. Emphasis was put on the reduction of distress from the evil voice as opposed to elimination or removal of the hallucinations.

Disputing. The activating event (**A**) for R.P. was the presence of the auditory hallucination he called the "evil" voice. This was usually triggered by noises such as slamming doors, "stress" and/or talking about the voice (it was usually present during the sessions). The evil voice ultimately gave rise to the belief (**B**) that R.P. was "worthless" and a "failure" which in turn made him feel anxious and depressed (**C**). This is illustrated in Table 20.2. In order to challenge this belief and generate alternative beliefs (**aB**) it was put to R.P. that such beliefs were hypotheses and not truisms. It was also suggested that because someone

Table 20.2. Cognitive Model of R.P.'s Hallucinatory Experience

Antecedent (A)	Beliefs (B)	Consequences (C)
Door slams and triggers "evil" voice which tells R.P. that he is a "failure" and "worthless"	R.P. believes that the voice is external and is speaking the truth. As a result he becomes convinced that he is a worthless failure.	Depressed and anxious

said something it didn't make it true (a neutral example was provided). Possible alternatives to the idea that these voices were "real" were discussed by R.P. and the therapist. A medical model of illness was played down in favour of a discussion about the personal significance of the voices. R.P. recalled always having had a sense of failure because he believed that he had let others down, especially his father. All his siblings were professionals and in high status jobs. R.P. embraced this idea and admitted it may be a viable explanation for the evil voice.

Testing. During the assessment interview R.P. had mentioned that he had in the past been able to control the activity of the evil voice through the use of a personal cassette player ("Walkman") which had since broken. A replacement one was arranged and within 2 weeks R.P's belief that the "evil" voices were very powerful and in total control of him fell from 100% to only 40%; eventually this belief was rejected altogether and the voices lost their sense of omnipotence.

Outcome. R.P's conviction in his depressogenic beliefs of worthlessness and failure fell significantly. The consequence of this was an increase in self esteem and reduction in depressive symptoms and anxiety. He was more able and willing to venture outside (when the voices were most distressing) and at one point was able to go on holiday with his mother. As mentioned previously he was less convinced by the power of the evil voice and therefore felt less threatened and frightened by it.

R.P. still believed his voices were external and intent on destroying him (convinced by the reality of the voice) but unlike before he was more able to hold a neutral view of it. That is, he no longer took it for granted that it was real. It was only his theory or hypothesis. He acknowledged that there may be other explanations for the hallucinations.

Thus, it seemed that although cognitive therapy had a direct influence over R.P's belief in *control* its impact upon his beliefs about *identity* and *meaning* was not as great. Little change in these latter two types of belief may not be unusual and may not necessarily be a requisite for a reduction in levels of distress. This obviously needs further investigation but adequately illustrates the point that the goal of cognitive therapy is not to try and convince the client of their irrationality in their beliefs about whether the voice is real or not but to dispute the beliefs which are maintaining their distress.

Personal significance of voices. In our experience a critical component of CT for voices is often that of drawing out the personal significance of the voices – that is, tentatively making a connection between voice content and beliefs on the one hand, and the individual's history on the other. Indeed, in this chapter we have argued that voices are a powerful experience, one which individuals feel compelled to try and understand. Beliefs about voices are the result of this endeavour and they carry the psychological force of relieving a sense of puzzlement and unease. It has been our experience that whilst many individuals are able to recognize that all or some of their beliefs about voices are mistaken, this can leave them once again struggling to understand the fact that they experience hallucinations.

One possible response open to the therapist is to label the voice a sign of "illness". However, there are reasons for not doing this. First, concepts like schizophrenia are of uncertain scientific validity (Bentall, Jackson & Pilgrim, 1987). Second, and perhaps of most importance, attributing voices to illness is such an impersonal explanation that it rarely satisfies people. What individuals seem to value is tentatively connecting the content of the their own voices to their own histories. For example, in the case of RP, it was suggested that the voice might give a clue as to underlying depressive concerns. The speculation was that RP's childhood experience established a strong need to achieve and earn respect from his father and that as an adult he had experienced a growing sense of failure and inadequacy.

A Cognitive Model of Delusions

In effect, our CT for voices is a specific adaptation of a general CT approach to delusions (Chadwick & Lowe, 1994); that is, we work to reduce distress and disturbance associated with a class of secondary delusions (i.e. the beliefs about identity, meaning etc.) about a common event – an auditory hallucination.

Delusions have until recently been subject to relatively little research. This is surprising bearing in mind the wealth of studies looking at the formation and maintenance of ordinary beliefs and belief structures (Tesser & Shaffer, 1990) as well as the central role that delusions play in diagnostic systems, and more general definitions of madness (Winters & Neale, 1983). For example, delusion has always been present in the legal definition of mental illness (Sims, 1991).

Defining delusions is notoriously difficult. The traditional approach has been based on establishing qualitative differences between delusions and other beliefs. In this vein, the American Psychiatric Association offered the following definition in the 4th edition of the *Diagnostic and Statistical Manual of mental disorders* (APA, 1994):

> "A false personal belief based on incorrect inference about external reality and firmly sustained in spite of what everyone else believes and in spite of what constitutes incontrovertible and obvious proof or evidence to the contrary. The belief is not one ordinarily accepted by other members of the person's culture."

In keeping with others (Garety, 1985; Harper, 1992) we shall consider these criteria in turn. Defining a delusion as a "false belief" has been criticized on two grounds. First, taking the simplified view that truth and falsity are clear terms, delusions need not be false. An individual who (correctly) believes his partner to be unfaithful might be said to have a delusion of jealousy if he had no good grounds for making the accusation (Brockington, 1991). Second, defining truth and falsity is so troublesome that one thinker has concluded that "it is nearly hopeless for a lone clinician to try to judge whether a belief is a delusion by determining its truth value " (Heise, 1988, p. 266).

The criterion of being based on "incorrect inference" has also been strongly challenged; indeed, one of the most prominent theories of delusion formation argues that delusions are *reasonable* attempts to make sense of abnormal experience (Maher, 1988). The firmest evidence against Maher came with the discovery that people with delusions follow biased reasoning (see Bentall, Kinderman & Kaney, 1993). It has emerged that under certain experimental conditions people with delusions appear to show bias in their attributional style, in their judgement of covariance, and in their probabilistic reasoning (Garety, 1991).

However, this raises a number of considerations. First, it is sometimes difficult to interpret such findings vis-a-vis rationality. For example, Huq, Garety & Hemsley (1988), using a neutral task which required subjects to make inferences about the likely ratio of different coloured beads in a jar, investigated the probabilistic reasoning of a group of deluded people, a group of mixed psychiatric patients who were not deluded, and a group of matched controls. People with delusions were found to require the least beads to be drawn from the jars before forming their conclusions, and also to express most confidence in their decisions, and yet this 'jumping to conclusions' was nearer optimum reasoning than the caution displayed by other subjects. Also, it is not always clear how specific findings in analogue studies might apply to delusional thinking. For example, how might it be established if delusions are formed on the basis of less information than, say, religious beliefs or depressive beliefs? Second, the evidence is for bias, not deficit; it might reasonably be inferred that the observed bias is a consequence of delusional behaviour, rather than the delusion being a consequence of the bias.

The criterion of being "firmly sustained" shifts the focus from formation to maintenance. The implication is that all delusions are held with total (or near total) and unwavering conviction. Although this may be true of many delusions (Chadwick & Lowe, 1990) it is not true of all delusions; Brett-Jones, Garety & Hemsley (1987) showed that conviction can be less than total and can fluctuate quite dramatically. Again, Harrow, Rattenbury & Stoll (1988) found in a sample of 34 people diagnosed as schizophrenic, that even at the height of the disorder 6 individuals (18%) showed only partial conviction. Also, it would be odd if delusions were not firmly sustained, because this appears to be the *sine qua non* of core beliefs of any kind.

The criterion that delusions are unmodifiable, or utterly insensitive to reason, is perhaps the notion most associated with delusions. However, there are strong empirical grounds for rejecting this association. There have been a modest number of studies, including our own, reporting attempts to weaken delusions, with generally favourable results (Alford, 1986; Beck, 1952; Chadwick & Lowe, 1990; Chadwick, Lowe, Horne & Higson, 1994; Fowler & Morley, 1987; Hartman & Cashman, 1983; Hole, Rush & Beck, 1973; Johnson, Ross & Mastria, 1977; Lowe & Chadwick, 1990; Milton, Patwa & Hafner, 1978). It might be more reasonable to assert that delusions are difficult to modify, sometimes fiendishly so. This position would acknowledge that the class of beliefs called delusions varies considerably along a number of dimensions, and it would encourage examination of the multitude of factors which might be thought to influence therapeutic outcome. It would also encourage an exploration of whether delusions are more difficult to modify than political or religious beliefs, or the core beliefs associated with sexual abuse, and anorexia, for instance.

The final criterion, "in spite of what almost everyone else believes" relates to the unusual content, or bizarreness, of delusions. Delusions are beliefs which the vast majority of the individual's group do not hold. However, using this as a point of definition may be questioned on empirical grounds, for research has demonstrated how difficult it is to rate the 'bizarreness' of delusions (Kendler, Glazer & Morgenstern, 1983), and on conceptual grounds because of the shifting sands of what people in different cultures, groups, and periods of history will believe (Harper, 1992).

A further approach to identifying delusions, which retains the character of the traditional view, is to propose a disjunctive definition. Thus, Oltmanns (1988) lists eight defining characteristic of delusions, and suggests that none be viewed as either necessary or sufficient. Research could then begin to resolve which characteristics are most important. An advantage of this strategy is that it acknowledges individual differences, and recognizes the need for empirical investigation. Nonetheless, if the individual criteria do not distinguish delusions from other beliefs, then even a disjunctive definition would seem flawed.

Traditional criteria have also been challenged by a radical and exciting call to define delusions (and hallucinations) as points on a continuum with normality, position on this continuum being influenced by dimensions of thought and behaviour, such as degree of belief conviction and the extent of preoccupation with the belief (Strauss, 1969). Rather than playing down individual differences and similarity with other beliefs, Strauss' perspective embraces them and elevates them to the position of defining characteristics. This view has shaped our view of delusions and hallucinations enormously.

Therefore the last 20 years has seen a shift in emphasis away from discontinuity to continuity, and from qualitative to quantitative differences. Individuals with paranoid delusions, for example, are acknowledged to be thinking and behaving in ways which can be detected in ordinary people.

Cognitive Therapy for Delusions

Brett-Jones, Garety & Hemsley (1987), in 9 single case studies, attempted to measure variables that described the relationship between the believer and the belief. They found that it was possible to evaluate certainty, preoccupation with and behavioural interference of the delusional belief. Given, also, that there was little covariation between the different dimensions, it could be hypothesized that there are a multitude of factors which might be thought to influence therapeutic outcome.

Watts, Powell & Austin (1973) studied the delusional beliefs of 3 paranoid schizophrenic patients. Using a non-confrontational style, these authors first tackled those parts of the delusion which were most weakly held. Clients were then asked to consider an alternative view to the delusion as opposed to having one forced upon them. As much evidence as possible was used and the subjects were encouraged to acknowledge the arguments against the delusions. These were endorsed and discussed further by the therapist. After six sessions all three patients showed significant reductions in the strength of the delusional beliefs although none of the subjects completely abandoned them.

As pointed out above, Watts, Powell & Austin (1973) argue against the use of confrontation. Further evidence for such a stance comes from Milton, Patwa & Haffner (1978) who in an empirical test of this noted that belief modification (as adapted by Watts et al., 1973) had benefits over and above those of pure confrontation. These authors also found that confrontation was more likely to produce greater increases in disturbance than a non-confrontational approach.

Underpinned by Maher's anomalous experiences model and Beck's approach to cognitive therapy, Chadwick & Lowe (1990, 1994) developed a cognitive approach to measuring and modifying delusions which attempted to understand more about the relevant contributions of two defined interventions applied within an atmosphere of collaborative empiricism (Beck et al., 1979).

Thus, as for C.T. with voices, instead of being told that they were wrong, individuals were encouraged to see their delusions as being only one possible interpretation of events and they were asked to consider and evaluate an alternative view. Once again, and for the reasons given previously, labels such as schizophrenia or delusion were avoided.

Drawing on these developments Chadwick & Lowe (1990, 1994) began their verbal challenge phase disputing only the evidence for the belief, and in an order which was inversely related to its importance to the delusion. An integral part of this discussion involved the therapist making clear to individuals how beliefs which are strongly held can exert a profound influence over their behaviour and affect. The therapist then progressed to disputing the belief itself, in three stages: first, any inconsistency and irrationality was pointed out and discussed. Second, an alternative explanation was offered, namely that the delusion was formed in response to and as a way of making sense of certain experiences (see Maher, 1974); this often included the involvement of a primary symptom but for some clients it was hypothesized that the delusion was in part a response to important life events. Finally, in light of this new information, the individual's interpretation and therapist's alternative were re-evaluated.

After the verbal challenge, therapist and client collaborated to devise and execute an empirical test of the belief. It has been a long standing tradition of cognitive-behavioural therapies such as Rational Emotive Behavior Therapy (REBT) to encourage the use of behavioural techniques to back up and confirm initial cognitive disputing (Dryden, 1990). This point has been alluded to by Beck et al. (1979) who, when talking about cognitive therapy for depression, commented:

> "There is no easy way to "talk the patient out" of his conclusions that he is weak, inept or vacuous.....By helping the patient change certain behaviours, the therapist may demonstrate to the patient that his negative overgeneralized conclusions were incorrect" (p. 118)

The main feature of the reality testing intervention is the performing and planning of an activity which could invalidate the delusion, or some part of it (Hole et al., 1979). Beck et al. (1979) called such activities behavioural experiments, conveying that they were performed in order to test a hypothesis.

Case study. DD was a 46 year old man with a history of schizophrenia and multiple hospital admissions dating back to 1971. A devout Roman Catholic since childhood, DD believed with 100% conviction that he was the "Son of God" who had been given the task by God to "redeem the souls in hell and the devil and his angels". As a consequence of this, because he was the "Son of Man" he intermittently believed that staff at the hospital and strangers were human robots sent to persecute him and eventually kill him which naturally was quite distressing. Far from being pleased with the responsibility of being the "Son of Man" DD saw it as a burden, and talked about the relief he would feel if such responsibility was taken away from him. He had held this delusion since 1972. At the time of assessment there was no evidence that he was hallucinating and medication (Chlorpromazine, Modecate depot and procyclindine) remained stable throughout baseline and intervention periods.

Baseline assessments over a 4 week period indicated that conviction in his belief that he was the "Son of Man" remained absolute (i.e., 100%). He claimed to be preoccupied with it 2 or 3 times a day and denied that there was any evidence over the 4 week period that would make him want to alter his belief.

In an atmosphere of empirical collaboration, DD was asked for the evidence which supported the delusion. It fell into three main parts. Firstly, the onset of the delusion has followed a period of acute psychosis when he reported having "Jesus talking through him" saying 'love your enemies'. Confirmation that it was Jesus talking through him came from the fact that these words do actually appear in the Bible.

It was put to DD that "love your enemies" is a fairly common phrase used not infrequently by a great number of people. He agreed. He was also asked whether there could be another possible explanation for his experiences. He suggested that he "may have been unwell at the time". The outcome of this was that, although he maintained his 100% conviction in his belief, he began to doubt the reliability of this evidence.

The second piece of evidence cited in favour of his delusion was that the Bible contained a description of the "Son of Man" which DD thought was an accurate picture of himself. Investigation of this claim revealed an unmistakable confirmation bias, and DD acknowledged that he selected out those bits of the text which were consistent with his belief and ignored all others. At this stage his delusion was further undermined to the extent that he now had serious doubts about whether his belief was in fact true, and his conviction score fell to 55%.

His conviction score fell again after challenging inconsistencies in his evidence that he had been granted the power to cure people by God (because he was the "Son of Man"). Four years previously, whilst an in-patient, he had been convinced that he had stopped the "confusion" of another patient by simply touching that person. Asked for alternative explanations of these events he admitted that he could not recall with 100% accuracy whether in fact he had cured her or whether she had merely reported it. Again, the main feature here had been to challenge his beliefs in the reliability of the evidence which supported the delusion.

In between sessions, over a period of a week, DD reported that he no longer believed that he was the "Son of Man". His conviction score of 3% reflected perhaps the last remnants of doubt about the belief. As DD put it: "I am now convinced that it is false".

As a final test of the evidence that he had been granted special powers, a behavioural experiment was set up. Because it was felt that it would be unethical to attempt to "cure" another person, DD agreed to test the belief on himself, to "give Jesus the opportunity to improve his eye sight". DD suffered from a congenital eye condition which meant that he was extremely short-sighted and had to wear specially designed glasses. It was agreed that DD should have his eyes tested at his optician's (which he did on a routine basis anyway) in order to provide a baseline against which to measure any improvement. If at anytime, over an agreed testing period, he felt that he had been granted special powers to improve his own eye sight then he would go back to his optician's to obtain independent valuation. At the time of writing and drawing to the end of this agreed time period, no improvement had been reported. DD belief that he was the "Son of Man" fell to 0%.

Conclusion

We have offered an introduction to our work using a cognitive approach to voices and delusions. This perspective assumes that delusions and voices lie on a continuum with normality and that any distress and disturbance associated with them is the result of an active search for meaning. In addition to increasing our understanding of the maintenance of these phenomena, a cognitive approach allows clinicians to work collaboratively with their clients to reduce distress and disturbance associated with such positive psychotic symptoms.

References

Alford, B. A. (1986). Behavioral treatment of schizophrenic delusions: a single case experimental analysis. *Behavior Therapy, 17,* 637–644.

APA (1987). *Diagnostic and statistical manual of mental disorders,* 3th edition revised (DSM-IIII-R). Washington, DC: American Psychiatric Association.

APA (1994). *Diagnostic and statistical manual of mental disorders,* 4th edition (DSM-IV). Washington, DC: American Psychiatric Association.

Asaad, G., & Shapiro, M. D. (1986). Hallucinations: theoretical and clinical overview. *American Journal of Psychiatry, 143,* 1088–1097.

Beck, A. T. (1952). Successful outpatient psychotherapy of a chronic schizophrenic with a delusional based on borrowed guilt. *Psychiatry, 15,* 305–312.

Beck, A. T., Rush, A. J., Shaw, B. F., & Emery, G. (1979). *Cognitive therapy of depression.* New York: Guilford Press.

Benjamin, L. S. (1989). Is chronicity a function of the relationship between the person and the auditory hallucination? *Schizophrenia Bulletin, 15,* 291–230.

Bentall, R. P. (1994). Cognitive biases and abnormal beliefs: towards a model of persecutory delusions. In A. S. David & J. Cutting (Eds.), *The neuropsychology of schizophrenia*. London: Erlbaum .

Bentall, R. P., Jackson, H. F., & Pilgrim, D. (1988). Abandoning the concept of schizophrenia: Some implications of validity arguments for psychological research into psychotic phenomena. *British Journal of Clinical Psychology, 27*, 303–324.

Bentall, R. P., Kinderman, P., & Kaney, S. (1994). The self, attributional processes and abnormal beliefs: towards a model of persecutory delusions. *Behaviour research and Therapy, 32*, 331–341.

Birchwood, M. J. (1986). Control of auditory hallucinations through occlusion of monoaural auditory input. *British Journal of Psychiatry, 149*, 104–107.

Birchwood, M. J., & Tarrier, N. (1992). *Innovations in the psychological management of schizoprhenia*. Chichester: Wiley.

Brett-Jones, J., Garety, P. A., & Hemsley, D. R. (1987). Measuring delusional experiences: a method and its application. *British Journal of Clinical Psychology, 26*, 257–265.

Brewin, C. R. (1988). *Cognitive foundations of clinical psychology*. London: Erlbaum.

Brockington, I. F. (1991). Factors involved in delusion formation. *British Journal of Psychiatry, 159 (suppl)*, 42–46.

Chadwick, P. D. J., & Birchwood, M. J. (1994). Challenging the omnipotence of voices: A cognitive approach to auditory hallucinations. *British Journal of Psychiatry, 164*, 190–201.

Chadwick, P. D. J., Birchwood, M. J., & Trower, P. (1996). *Cognitive therapy with delusions and voices*. Chichester: Wiley.

Chadwick, P. D. J., & Lowe, C. F. (1990). Measurement and modification of delusional beliefs. *Journal of Consulting and Clinical Psychology, 58*, 225–232.

Chadwick, P. D. J., & Lowe, C. F. (1994). A cognitive approach to measuring and modifying delusions. *Behaviour Research and Therapy, 32*, 355–367.

Chadwick, P. D. J., Lowe, C. F., Horne, P. J., & Higson, P. J. (1994). Modifying delusions: the role of empirical testing. *Behavior Therapy, 25*, 35–49.

Cochrane, R. (1983). *The social creation of mental illness*. Essex: Longman.

Dryden, W. (1990). *Rational-emotive therapy in action*. London: Sage.

Fowler, D., & Morley, S. (1989). The cognitive behavioural treatment of hallucinations and delusions: a preliminary study. *Behavioural Psychotherapy, 17*, 267–282.

Garety, P. A. (1985). Delusions: Problems in definition and measurement. *British Journal of Medical Psychology, 58*, 25–34.

Garety, P. A. (1991). Reasoning and delusions. *British Journal of Psychiatry, 159 (suppl)*, 14–18.

Harrow, M., Rattenbury, F., & Stoll, F. (1988). Schizophrenic delusions: An analysis of their persistence, of related premorbid ideas, and of three major dimensions. In T. F. Oltmanns & B. A. Maher (Eds.), *Delusional beliefs*. New York: Wiley.

Hartman, L. M., & Cashman, F. E. (1983). Cognitive behavioural and psychopharmacological treatment of delusional symptoms: a preliminary report. *Behavioural Psychotherapy, 11*, 50–61.

Hawton, K., Salkovskis, P., Kirk, J., & Clark, D. M. (Eds.), *Cognitive behavioural therapy for psychiatric problems*. Oxford: Oxford University Press.

Hole, R. W., Rush, A. J. and Beck, A. T. (1973). A cognitive investigation of schizophrenic delusions. *Psychiatry, 42*, 312–319.

Huq, S. F., Garety, P. A., & Hemsley, D. R. (1988). Probabilistic judgments in deluded an non-deluded subjects. *Quarterly Journal of Experimental Psychology, 40A*, 801–812.

Johnson, W. G., Ross, J. M., & Mastria, M. A. (1977). Delusional behavior: an attributional analysis. *Journal of Abnormal Psychology, 86*, 421–426.

Kendler, K. S., Glazer, W. M., & Morgenstern, H. (1983). Dimensions of delusional experience. *American Journal of Psychiatry, 140,* 466–469.

Maher, B. A. (1974). Delusional thinking and perceptual disorder. *Journal of Individual Psychology, 30,* 98–113.

Maher, B. A. (1988). Anomalous experience and delusional thinking: The logic of explanation. In T. F. Oltmanns & B. A. Maher (Eds.), *Delusional beliefs.* New York: Wiley.

Milton, F., Patwa, K., & Haffner, R. J. (1978). Confrontation vs. belief modification in persistently delude patients. *British Journal of Medical Psychology, 51,* 127–130.

Oltmans, T. F. (1988). Approaches to the definition and study of delusions. In T. F. Oltmans & B. A. Maher (Eds.), *Delusional beliefs.* New York: Wiley-Interscience.

Romme, M. A., & Escher, S. (1989). Hearing voices. *Schizophrenia Bulletin, 15,* 209–216.

Slade, P. D., & Bentall, R. P. (1988). *Sensory deception: A scientific analysis of hallucination.* Baltimore, MD: The John Hopkins University.

Strauss, J. S. (1969). Hallucinations and delusions as points on continua functions. *Archives of General Psychiatry, 21,* 581–586.

Strauss, J. S. (1991). The person with delusions. *British Journal of Psychiatry, 159 (suppl),* 57–62.

Tarrier, N. (1992). Management and modification of residual positive pschotic symptoms. In M. Birchwood & N. Tarrier (Eds.), *Innovations in the psychological management of schizophrenia.* Chichester: Wiley.

Trower, P., Casey, A., & Dryden, W. (1988). *Cognitive behavioural counselling in action.* Bristol: Sage.

Watts, F. N., Powell, E. G., & Austin, S. V. (1973). The modification of abnormal beliefs. *British Journal of Medical Psychology, 46,* 359–363.

WHO (1973). *The internatinal pilot study of schizophrenia.* Geneva: World Health Organization.

Winters, K. C., & Neale, J. M. (1983). Delusions and delusional thinking in psychotics: A review of the literature. *Clinical Psychology Review, 3,* 227–253.

Yalom, I. (1970). *The theory and practice of group psychotherapy.* New York: Basic Books.

Further Reading

Beck, A. T., Rush, A. J., Shaw, B. F., & Emery, G. (1979). *Cognitive therapy of depression.* New York: Guilford Press.

Chadwick, P. D. J., & Lowe, C. F. (1990). Measurement and modification of delusional beliefs. *Journal of Consulting and Clinical Psychology, 58,* 225–232.

Chadwick, P. D. J., & Birchwood, M. J. (1994). Challenging the omnipotence of voices: a cognitive approach to auditory hallucinations. *British Journal of Psychiatry, 164,* 190–201.

Chadwick, P. D. J., & Lowe, C. F. (1994). A cognitive approach to measuring and modifying delusions. *Behaviour Research and Therapy, 32,* 355–367.

Chadwick, P. D. J., Birchwood, M. J., & Trower, P. (1996). *Cognitive therapy for hallucinations and delusions.* Chichester: Wiley.

Oltmanns, T. F., & Maher, B. A. (Eds.) (1988). *Delusional beliefs.* New York: Wiley.

Appendix 1. Beliefs About Voices Questionnaire items

There are many people who hear voices. It would help us to find out how you are feeling about your voices by completing the enclose questionnaire which simply asks you to circle "Yes" or "No" to the following questions.

If you hear more than one voice, please fill in the questionnaire for the dominant voice

1.	My voice is punishing me for something I have done	YES	NO
2.	My voice wants to help me	YES	NO
3.	My voice is persecuting me for no good reason	YES	NO
4.	My voice wants to protect me	YES	NO
5.	My voice is evil	YES	NO
6.	My voice is helping to keep me sane	YES	NO
7.	My voice wants to harm me	YES	NO
8.	My voice is helping me to develop my special powers or abilities	YES	NO
9.	My voice wants me to do bad things	YES	NO
10.	My voice is helping me to achieve my goal in life	YES	NO
11.	My voice is trying to corrupt or destroy me	YES	NO
12.	I am grateful for my voice	YES	NO
13.	My voice is very powerful	YES	NO
14.	My voice reassures me	YES	NO
15.	My voice frightens me	YES	NO
16.	My voice makes me happy	YES	NO
17.	My voice makes me feel down	YES	NO
18.	My voice makes me feel angry	YES	NO
19.	My voice makes me feel calm	YES	NO
20.	My voice makes me feel anxious	YES	NO
21.	My voice makes me feel confident	YES	NO

WHEN I HEAR MY VOICE, *USUALLY*...

22.	I tell it to leave me alone	YES	NO
23.	I try and take my mind off it	YES	NO
24.	I try and stop it	YES	NO
25.	I do things to prevent it talking	YES	NO
26.	I am reluctant to obey it	YES	NO
27.	I listen to it because I want to	YES	NO
28.	I willingly follow what my voice tells me to do	YES	NO
29.	I have done things to start to get in contact with my voice	YES	NO
30.	I seek the advice of my voice	YES	NO

21

Behavioral Management of Problem Behaviors Associated with Dementia

BARRY EDELSTEIN, LYNN NORTHROP and NATALIE STAATS

West Virginia University, USA

Introduction

The proportion of older adults in the population is rapidly rising. Though behavior therapists have appeared somewhat dilatory in their move to address the mental health problems of older adults, there is evidence of an increasing trend, beginning in the 1970s, to do so (cf. Carstensen, 1988). One of the more devastating disorders experienced by older adults is dementia, particularly dementia of the Alzheimer's type. While dementia is, by definition (see below) an organic disorder which cannot be directly addressed by behavior therapists, many of the problem behaviors associated with dementias (e.g., urinary incontinence, memory impairment, wandering/disorientation, aggressive/agitated behavior, and failure to perform activities of daily living), are amenable to behavioral interventions. In this chapter we will define dementia, describe physiological changes associated with aging that should be considered when assessing and developing treatment programs, describe behavioral approaches to problems commonly associated with dementias, and offer a case study to illustrate the application of behavioral principles.

The word *dementia* is used to describe a collection of cognitive and behavioral symptoms that are characteristic of a number of organic brain disorders including Dementia of the Alzheimer's Type (DAT), vascular dementia, Wernicke-Korsakoff's syndrome, and many others. Dementia is marked by "multiple cognitive deficits that include memory impairment and least one of the following cognitive disturbances: aphasia, apraxia, agnosia, or a disturbance in executive functioning. The cognitive deficits must be sufficiently severe to cause impairment in occupational or social functioning and must represent a decline from a previously higher level of functioning," (APA, 1994, p. 134).

In addition to identification of characteristic cognitive or behavioral features, diagnosis of dementia requires evidence from medical examination (e.g. MRI, CAT scan, etc.) of an organic basis for the observed cognitive and behavioral disturbances. An exception is made in the case of suspected DAT. A diagnosis of DAT can be made without solid evidence of organicity as long as other disorders that may cause dementia have been ruled out by history, physical examination and/or laboratory tests (APA, 1994). Each of the specific organic brain disorders falling under the rubric of dementia has its own characteristic etiology, course, and prognosis, some being reversible with treatment. Therefore, differential diagnosis of the specific disorder causing the dementia symptom is essential to appropriate treatment. A thorough understanding of the presentation and features of dementia will aid the practitioner in developing realistic and effective treatment goals and plans. The interested reader is referred to the *Diagnostics and statistics manual of mental disorders*, 4th edition (APA, 1994) for addtional diagnostic information.

Dementia is, for the most part, a disorder of older adults. Behavior therapists who desire to work with older adults should understand that changes in the physiology and behavior of adults are inevitable as they age. Consequently, there are many factors associated with aging that complicate at least the assessment, if not also the treatment, of older adults. Though this chapter focuses on dementia, we believe it behooves the behavior therapist to understand some of the more salient physiological features of older adults that should be considered when assessing and treating older adults with and without dementia.

Physiological Considerations

Sensory Systems

Most aging individuals experience declines in all of the sensory systems, although the extent of impairment varies across individuals. Changes in the visual system include decreased pupil size (miosis), slowed pupillary response to changes in illumination, pigmentation (opacification) and thickening of the lens, and decreased ability and speed of accommodation. The foregoing and other changes result in decreased visual acuity (usually presbyopia), increased susceptibility to glare, increased time required for dark adaptation, decreased color sensitivity, poorer depth perception, and an increased need for illumination. Moreover, various diseases and medications can hasten the development of such changes. For example, the rate of opacification can be accelerated by diabetes mellitus, hypoparathyroidism, myotonic dystrophy, Wilson's disease, and the use of chlorpromazine or corticosteroids (Hunt & Lindley, 1989).

Hearing is also impaired as one ages, beginning around the age of 25 (Zarit & Zarit, 1987). Pitch discrimination declines steadily until approximately age 55. More dramatic losses occur in the higher frequencies after this age. One in three individuals over the age of 60 suffers from significant hearing impairment (Zarit & Zarit, 1987). The foregoing impairments can result in speech perception difficulty in general and significant impairment in the ability to understand broken or rapid speech, and/or in the ability to accurately hear speech in the presence of background noise.

Olfactory sensitivity declines with age, which can affect both gustatory pleasures and preferences, and place an individual at risk of harm due to a diminished ability to detect olfactory cues or signals of danger (e.g., natural gas, smoke). Changes in food preferences and decreased pleasures in eating may have serious consequences for the nutritional status of an individual. Additionally, since preferred foods are frequently used as reinforcers, consideration of olfactory sensitivity is of particular importance. Reduced sensitivity to smells can also diminish the pleasures once experienced through the scents of flowers and perfumes. Even one's grooming habits can change as a function of being less sensitive to the smell of deodorants, perfumes, and body odors.

Gustatory or taste sensitivity also declines with age (e.g., deGraaf, Polet & van Staveren, 1994). There appears to be a decrease in sensitivity to salty, sweet, sour and bitter tastes over the lifespan (Whitbourne, 1985), with sensitivity also varying as a function of the particular food flavors. This variability in sensitivity can result in decreased gustatory pleasure. Schiffman & Warwick (1993) note that older adults consume more flavor-enhanced foods compared to nonflavor-enhanced foods. Reduction in taste sensitivity, coupled with diminished olfactory sensitivity, can lead to nutritional deficits. Such changes should be considered when selecting potential food related reinforcers and when faced with apparent appetite disturbances among older adults..

The somesthetic senses also do not escape the aging process, although the effects are less clear cut than those of other sensory modalities. These senses include information about touch, pressure, pain and ambient temperature. The sensation of touch in the smooth (non-hairy) areas of the skin is impaired with age. Aging also affects sensations of body orientation and movement (Laidlaw & Hamilton, 1937; Whitbourne, 1985), which must be taken into consideration when addressing problems and formulating treatment programs which involve movement and coordination. Sensitivity to heat and cold also decreases with age. Such changes can place older adults at risk for injury due to either very high or low temperatures. Finally, though one expects to hear more reports of aches and pains from older adults, the evidence regarding changes in pain thresholds is inconclusive (Whitbourne, 1985). It is difficult to sort out changes in absolute sensitivity to pain from changes in thresholds for reporting pain.

Musculo-Skeleto System

When considering movement of older adults, one must not only consider muscle strength and coordination, but also the strength and resiliency of the bones and the conditions of the joints involved in the movements (Whitbourne, 1985). There appears to be little reduction in muscle strength until at least age 40 or 50, and loss until age 60 or 70 appears to be minimal (10 to 20%) (Whitbourne, 1985). From the age of 70 on, greater loss in muscle strength occurs (30 to 40%), with greater loss occurring in the legs than in the hands and arms (Shephard, 1981, as cited in Whitbourne, 1985).

Cartilage and ligaments can become calcified with aging. Degeneration of joint cartilage can cause pain as individuals move about. Bones lose their mass with age, increasing the likelihood of fractures (Lindley, 1989).

Cardiovascular System

Changes occur in the heart chambers, heart valves and blood vessels with age. The amount of blood pumped per contraction of the heart decreases and heart rate slows with time. The heart also loses its ability to generate high rates in response to increased activity and stress demands (Leventhal, 1991; Lindley, 1989; Morley & Reese, 1989; Simpson & Wicks, 1988).

Limitations caused by an aging cardiovascular system have implications for one's ability to engage in what were once rewarding, physically demanding, activities. The two most significant effects of age on the cardiovascular system are the reduction in aerobic power (maximum oxygen consumption) and a reduction in maximal heart rate.

Respiratory System

The pulmonary system changes with age, resulting in decreased work capacity as chest wall muscles and smooth muscles in bronchi, diaphragm, and chest wall weaken (Lindley, 1989, p. 58). The amount of oxygen taken up from the blood during aerobic exercise diminishes with age. "The effect of aging in the respiratory system therefore compounds the limitations on the ability to perform muscular work caused by the changes in the cardiovascular and muscular systems" (Whitbourne, 1985, p. 51).

Excretory System

Significant changes occur in the bladder and kidneys with increasing age (Zarit & Zarit, 1987). Bladder capacity decreases with age and urinary tract infections increase in frequency. The bladder of a younger individual expands to hold urine between voiding opportunities and empties completely. Both of these functions are impaired with age. Therefore, older adults may need to void more often and are less likely to completely empty their bladders. The sensation of needing to void, which occurs when the bladder is half full in younger adults, may also be impaired in older adults. Older adults may not experience this sensation until the bladder is almost full, or there may be no sensation at all (Whitbourne, 1985).

As a consequence of the foregoing, clinicians are frequently called upon to develop behavior management programs for urinary incontinence. The physiological changes occurring with age, as well as the behavioral repertoire that develops to deal with concomitant changes, should be considered prior to the development of behavior management programs for problems associated with voiding.

Behavior Management

Urinary Incontinence

Urinary incontinence (UI) is a problem for over 10 million Americans, most of whom are older adults (Urinary Incontinence Guideline Panel, 1992). UI affects 15–30% of non-institutionalized adults over the age of 60 and at least 750 000 residents of nursing homes (Van Norstrand et al., 1979). The prevalence of UI among women is twice that of men. Incontinence can have significant consequences, including an increased likelihood of developing decubitus ulcers and urinary tract infections, and may contribute to depression, anxiety and social isolation (Burgio & Burgio, 1991).

There are several types of incontinence, which can be manifested individually or in combination. *Urge incontinence* is the "involuntary loss of urine associated with an abrupt and strong desire to void (urgency)" (Urinary Incontinence Guideline Panel, 1992, p. QR-3). Such incontinence can occur when one experiences the urge to urinate and cannot get to the bathroom in time to urinate. Urges often follow drinking a small amount of liquid, hearing running water, or touching water. *Stress incontinence* is the "involuntary loss of urine during coughing, sneezing, laughing, or other physical activity" (Urinary Incontinence Guideline Panel, 1992, p. QR-3). Activities causing increased abdominal pressure increase the likelihood of stress incontinence. *Overflow incontinence* refers to the "involuntary loss of urine associated with overdistension of the bladder (overflow)" (Urinary Incontinence Guideline Panel, 1992, p. QR-3). *Functional incontinence* refers to "urine loss resulting from inability or unwillingness to use the toilet appropriately," (Burgio & Burgio, 1991, p. 321). Burgio & Burgio (1991) have classified the factors that contribute to functional incontinence as deficits of mobility, mental status, motivation, and environmental barriers. *Mixed incontinence* is a combination of two or more types of incontinence (Urinary Incontinence Guideline Panel, 1992, p. QR-3). Frail elderly, for example, may have components of urge, stress, and functional incontinence.

Causes of incontinence. Some of the causes of urinary incontinence include, but are not limited to, weakness of muscles holding the bladder in place, weakness of the bladder, weakness of the urethral sphincter muscles, overactive bladder muscles, blocked urethra (possibly from prostate enlargement), hormone imbalance in women, neurologic disorders, infection (symptomatic urinary tract infection), sedative hypnotic medications, diuretic medications, anticholinergic agents, alpha-adrenergic agents, calcium-channel blockers, excessive urine production, stool impaction, restricted mobility, poor motivation, attention seeking, and avoidance behavior.

Assessment. A thorough medical evaluation is essential before proceeding with behavioral assessment since urinary incontinence can be influenced by numerous factors. The basic evaluation should include a medical and social history, physical examination with additional tests, and a urinalysis (Urinary Incontinence Guideline Panel, 1992). Additional information may be gathered via a voiding record, evaluation of environmental (e.g., access to toilets) and social factors (e.g., living arrangements, social contacts, caregiver involvement), blood tests, and urine cytology.

Further assessment will depend upon the variables thought to be controlling the voiding. A functional analysis is appropriate for determining antecedent and consequence control. Virtually any stimulus in an individual's environment can set the occasion for voiding. External stimuli can range from the bathroom and its fixtures to the sound of running water. Pressure resulting from a full bladder can also set the occasion for voiding, particularly if the individual is unable to resist the feelings of urgency. The consequences of voiding must also be considered. Individuals may find that inappropriate voiding brings desired attention. Inappropriate voiding may also be a function of weak stimulus control with individuals who are experiencing depression or confusion. In such cases the punishing value of inappropriate voiding may be absent (cf. Burgio & Burgio, 1991). One may also void inappropriately because it is more convenient than urinating in the appropriate receptacle (Hussian, 1981). Finally, inappropriate voiding may result from inappropriate stimulus control. Though the urination may be preceded by the appropriate precursor responses, such as the exposure of the genitals, it often occurs around objects which share some of the physical characteristics of a toilet. Unlike voiding for attention, such voiding may occur in areas not under direct observation. This inappropriate stimulus control is seen in progressive dementia and is frequently the referring problem (Hussian, 1981).

Intervention. The three major categories of intervention are behavior management, pharmacologic treatment, and surgical treatment. The least invasive and least dangerous treatment is typically the most appropriate, which is usually one or more behavior management procedures. We will focus exclusively on behavior management of voiding. Behavioral interventions include habit training for urge and functional incontinence, bladder training for urge and stress incontinence, contingency management for functional incontinence, prompted toileting for urge and neurogenic incontinence, and biofeedback for urge and stress incontinence.

Habit training. Habit training is useful when voiding is not under adequate stimulus control, whether it is an internal stimulus (e.g., full bladder) or an external stimulus (e.g., presence of bathroom). Habit training involves voiding on a schedule of approximately every 2–4 h, regardless of whether an urge to void is present (Clay, 1980). The goal of habit training is to avoid inappropriate voiding through frequent scheduling of voiding opportunities. The schedule can be altered depending upon the capabilities of the individual. For example, one might begin with a schedule that approximates the current frequency of inappropriate voiding and either increase or decrease the frequency of scheduled voiding depending upon the ability of the individual to achieve continence with the schedule. One may also combine contingency management with habit training, wherein appropriate voiding is reinforced (Burgio & Burgio, 1991). Success using habit retraining appears to have ranged from 50% (e.g., Spangler, Risley and Bilyet, 1984) to 85% (e.g., Sogbein and Awad, 1982), with success sometimes depending upon the levels of physical and psychological impairment. Staff compliance can be a limiting factor with the success of this procedure.

Bladder training. The purpose of bladder retraining is to increase bladder capacity through encouraging the individual to increase intervals between voiding by resisting or inhibiting the sensation of urgency and postponing voiding. Such training may also include procedures that induce bladder distention (e.g., adjustment in fluid loads and delayed voiding) (Keating, Schulte & Miller, 1988). Bladder training may include written, visual and verbal instructional materials that explain the physiology and pathophysiology of the lower urinary tract. Contingency management procedures may be included to reinforce extension of voiding intervals. Consequences of this procedure are longer intervals between voiding, improved ability to suppress bladder instability, diminished urgency (Burgio & Burgio, 1991) and reduced stress incontinence (Fantl, Wyman, Harkins & Hadley, 1990). Using bladder training, Fantl et al.

(1990) reduced incontinent episodes completely in 12% of their subjects and by at least 50% in 75% of their subjects. Frewen (1982) has demonstrated 97% success with outpatients using bladder training.

Contingency management. Contingency management involves the systematic manipulation of antecedents and consequences of inappropriate voiding to reduce the frequency of such behavior. Inappropriate voiding maintained by staff attention, for example, can be managed by instructing staff members to be as matter of fact as possible with incontinent individuals following incontinence episodes. Incontinence due to "convenience" may be conceptualized as behavior which is not controlled by the consequences which control the behavior of most individuals. The consequences of incontinence may not be as aversive as the behavior which is required to preclude an incontinent episode. A careful arrangement of positive contingencies for appropriate voiding may alter the balance of positive and negative consequences of "convenient" voiding.

Multiple contingency management procedures may be combined as well. Schnelle, Traughber, Morgan, Embry, Binion & Coleman (1983), for example, made hourly checks for incontinence coupled with reminders to void. Social approval was made contingent upon dry checks and patient requests for toileting assistance. Mild social disapproval was the consequence of incontinence. Correct toileting increased by 45% and incontinence was reduced by 49% among 11 geriatric patients, many of whom had diagnoses of senile dementia or organic brain syndrome.

The foregoing procedure is also termed *prompted voiding*. Prompted voiding involves monitoring of dryness by caregivers, prompting of individuals to use the toilet, and social reward for attempts to void appropriately and maintain appropriate toileting. Prompted voiding in nursing homes has been evaluated in at least two controlled (Hu, Igou, Kaltreider, Yu, Rohner, Dennis, Craighead, Hadley & Ory, 1989; Schnelle, 1990) and one uncontrolled (Engel, Burgio, McCormick, Hawkins, Scheve & Leahy, 1990) study. The authors of these studies reported an average reduction of 1.0 to 2.2 inappropriate voiding episodes per patient per day.

Biofeedback. Biofeedback is used to alter physiological responses of the bladder and pelvic floor muscles that mediate incontinence (Burgio & Burgio, 1991; Burgio & Engel, 1990). Operant conditioning procedures are used to teach individuals to control bladder and sphincter responses by observing the results of their efforts via auditory or visual displays. Response measures have included EMG and manometric measures of detrusor activity. Biofeedback has been found to be effective with urge incontinence (e.g., Burgio, Whitehead & Engel, 1985) and stress incontinence (e.g., Kegel, 1956; Shepherd, Montgomery & Anderson, 1983). Effectiveness of biofeedback has ranged from 54 to 95% improvement in incontinence across a variety of patient types (Urinary Incontinence Guideline Panel, 1992).

Memory

The short and long term memory impairment that characterizes dementia often interferes significantly with the daily functioning of dementia sufferers and presents concomitant problems for their care givers. With progressive dementias, a decline in memory functioning during the early to middle stages of the disorder is often accompanied by anxiety and fear associated with the cognitive losses. The memory impairment also makes everyday life a significant challenge for dementia sufferers when so much of what they were accustomed to doing relied upon memory. An increased frequency and complexity of behavior management problems can also accompany memory changes as the individual becomes increasingly cognitively impaired. In spite of the impairment in patient cognitive abilities, one can devise strategies that capitalize upon an individual's strengths and the use of external environmental supports, thereby minimizing limitations imposed by cognitive deficits. In this section we will briefly present a discussion of the types of memory loss encountered by older adults and dementia patients, followed by a discussion of behavioral strategies for addressing problems associated with memory deficits.

Memory deficits occur among many older adults, although the amount of deficit appears to vary according to the type of memory task (e.g., Craik, 1984; Poon, Gurland, Eisdorfer, Crook, Thompson, Kaszniak & Davis, 1986). For example, recognition of stimuli declines less with age than does free recall of material (e.g., Craik, 1984). Moreover, older adults perform more poorly on complex, as opposed to simple, memory tasks (e.g., Cerella, Poon & Williams, 1980; Craik, Morris & Gick, 1990; Salthouse, Babcock & Shaw, 1991). Older adults also perform more poorly on *working memory* tasks, that is, tasks that require holding information and using that information to solve problems (Craik & Jennings, 1992). Memory for specific events also declines with age.

Adding dementia to the normal changes in memory over time increases the severity of problems. Individuals with at least moderate DAT, for example, experience difficulties in concentration and memory. More specifically, these individuals have difficulty sustaining attention to complex tasks and those requiring cognitive flexibility (La Rue, 1992). DAT also affects primary memory, with individuals demonstrating difficulty retaining new information. Individuals with DAT also have difficulty with secondary memory, performing poorly on tasks requiring the recall of material that has been dropped from conscious awareness. Recognition memory is also not spared by DAT. In fact, individuals with DAT frequently behave as though they recognize stimuli even though they are incorrect (false-positive errors). Autobiographical memory is usually spared in the early stages of DAT. However, other forms of remote memory requiring the recall of public events or prominent people of the distant past, may be impaired. The most remote material appears to be recalled better than the more recent, although recall of the most remote events is impaired with moderate and severe DAT.

Assessment. A discussion of the various approaches to the assessment of memory is beyond the scope of this chapter. Readers interested in more standardized approaches to memory assessment are referred to the work of Crook and his colleagues (e.g., Crook & Youngjohn, 1993) for discussions of everyday memory assessment and treatment, and to Poon (1986) and Zarit & VandenBos (1990) for discussions of conceptual and practical issues of clinical memory assessment. In the following section we will focus on interventions for addressing memory impairment. In many cases, a thorough functional analysis of the conditions under which memory impairment affects the behavior an individual is the only assessment required.

Interventions. Individuals with progressive dementias do not appear to profit from the cognitive or self- management memory enhancement techniques that have been found to be effective with healthy older adults. Dementia patients are more likely to benefit from external memory aids that provide cues for the recall of information and/or serve as memory storage devices. A good memory aid is "one which is readily available at the right time, is specific to the task, is not much trouble to use, and is reinforcing to use" (Duke, Haley & Bergquist, 1991, p. 260).

Memory and skill problems can often be analyzed as problems in antecedent and consequence control. The stimuli which ordinarily set the occasion for recall of relevant material fail to exert their original stimulus control. Reasons for the loss of stimulus control can range from changes at the antecedent level (e.g., failure to attend to the stimulus) to changes in the consequences of emitting the behavior formerly associated with the stimulus (e.g., reduction or loss of reinforcement for responding).

Failure to recall the location of objects is a frequent problem of dementia patients. For example, individuals might forget or become confused about where they have placed specific articles of clothing. Stimulus control can be enhanced in the case of clothing loss by simply insuring constancy of the stimulus that is associated with the clothing. Storage of the clothing in the same location at all times can increase the likelihood that the clothing is found. Individuals may also forget or become confused about the location of their own room in an institution or at home. The stimulus for the bathroom can be made more distinctive and apparent by color coding the door (Harris, 1980), hanging a flag from the wall with "restroom" written on it or by drawing a colored line on the floor or wall leading to the bathroom. Stimuli could also be made more familiar to the individual or at least more compatible with prior knowledge (cf. Craik & Jennings, 1992). For example, a sign indicating the presence of a favorite red shirt in a drawer could have a sketch of that red shirt, colored the same shade of red as the favored shirt.

The provision of such external stimulus aids is sometimes insufficient to improve performance. Individuals may need to be trained to attend to the relevant stimulus, as noted above. Hanley (1986), for example, found that training residents to attend to signs posted for room location was more effective than merely posting the signs.

Recall of information can be enhanced by providing external memory aids and storage devices such as notebooks, calendars, signs, timers, cue cards tape recorders, memory wallets and maps (e.g., Bourgeois, 1992; Smith, 1988, as cited in Bourgeois, 1991; Wilson & Moffat, 1984). Bourgeois (1990), for example, successfully taught individuals with Alzheimer's disease to use a prosthetic memory aid (memory wallet) when conversing with familiar individuals. In conversation, the subjects made more statements of fact, made fewer ambiguous statements, and generated novel statements.

During the early stages of a progressive dementia an individual is likely to be particularly aware of his/her memory deficits, to the point of becoming distressed about cognitive impairment. This is a particularly good time to perform an analysis of the types of problems that the individual is experiencing and develop intervention programs to assist him/her. Such training may also alleviate some of the anxiety and fear that is associated with progressive cognitive loss. As the dementia progresses, the individual may become less aware of the severity and extent of the memory deficits (Bourgeois, 1991) and require prompting to use the external memory aids discussed above.

Wandering and Disorientation

Wandering behavior is highly correlated with dementias and other forms of organic impairment (Hussian, 1987). Prevalence estimates of wandering behavior among organically impaired individuals vary, depending upon the specific patient group (i.e., dementia of the Alzheimer's type, vascular dementia, head injury, etc), the severity of organic impairment, and the narrowness of the definition of wandering that is used. In spite of varying prevalence estimates, there is abundant literature to suggest that wandering behavior presents problems to patients and their caregivers, often warranting intervention. Wandering behavior has been shown to have serious consequences including patients becoming lost or physically injured (Carstensen & Fisher, 1993), increased use of chemical and physical restraints (Burton, German, Rovner & Brant, 1992; Lam, Sewell, Bell & Katona, 1989), increased caregiver burden and stress (Chiverton & Caine, 1989; Pinkston & Linsk, 1984), and increased probability of the patient becoming or remaining institutionalized (Moak, 1990).

Wandering behavior can be defined as ambulation that occurs independent of *usual* environmental cues and that may appear to the casual observer to be random or uncontrolled behavior (Hussian, 1987). Thorough observation and functional analysis of wandering behavior typically reveals environmental and intrapersonal stimuli that set the occasion for wandering, as well as consequences that reinforce or punish wandering behavior. Thus, interventions that are based upon functional analyses of the antecedents and consequences of wandering behavior are recommended (Carstensen & Fisher, 1991; Hussian, 1987, 1988).

In an effort to further define wandering and to facilitate functional analysis and intervention planning, categories of wandering have been developed based on the observed causes and/or functions of the behavior. For example, after conducting systematic observations of 13 geriatric inpatients in a psychiatric facility, Hussian and Davis (1985) identified four distinct types of wandering. The first type, *akathisia wandering*, was observed in patients receiving high doses of neuroleptics. *Akathisiacs* tended to exhibit relatively high frequency wandering and were unlikely to attempt to leave the ward or engage in self-stimulatory behavior (Hussian & Davis,1985). *Exit seeking* was sometimes accompanied by verbal requests to leave the ward. *Exit seekers* tended to approach exit doors more frequently than other doors (e.g., closets, offices), and they were unlikely to engage in self-stimulatory behavior. *Self-stimulation wandering* involved frequent rattling, touching, or turning of door knobs, with no preference for exit doors over other types of doors. *Self stimulators* engaged in other types of self-stimulatory behavior such as rubbing their hands along walls, clapping, or making repetitive noises. *Model-cued wandering* occurred only in the presence of another ambulator. Although *model-cued wanderers* engaged in some self-stimulatory behavior (e.g. rattling doorknobs, clapping hands), this generally occurred only as an imitative response in the presence of another self-stimulator.

Disorientation is another phenomenon that is often used to categorize some wandering responses. Disorientation is a term used to refer to a person's inability to (1) answer questions regarding his or her current location, place in time, or identity and/or (2) to physically locate areas in his/her environment (Hussian, 1987). *Disorientation wandering* is thought to occur because of memory or other cognitive impairments. An individual loses the ability to rely on cues in his or her environment to guide ambulation (Hussian, 1987).

Hope and Fairburn (1989) provided another wandering classification scheme following their observation of 29 community-dwelling dementia patients identified as wanderers by their family caregivers. Wanderers were categorized based upon the following: overall amount of walking, tendency to avoid being alone, impairment in navigational ability, faulty goal-directed behavior, and degree of diurnal rhythm disturbance. Readers may wish to use the typologies or classification schemes presented above to aid in identifying the factors causing or controlling wandering behavior. Please note that the above categories are neither exhaustive nor thoroughly validated and should not be used in lieu of an ideographic assessment of an individual's behavior.

Assessment. Medical examination is recommended prior to conducting behavioral assessment of wandering behavior. As previously noted, neuroleptic medications, sleep disturbances, and other medical and physical conditions can contribute to wandering behavior. Determining the influence of such variables and developing strategies for dealing with them is integral to the potential accuracy of behavioral assessment and to the effectiveness of behavioral intervention.

Behavioral assessment of wandering behavior is conducted with the goal of identifying the antecedent and consequent variables that control the behavior. *Functional analysis* is the process typically used to gather information that can be used to build effective behavioral intervention plans. A functional analysis of wandering behavior is complete when three main objectives have been met: (1) thorough, operational description of the wandering behavior, (2) identification of the times and situations in which the wandering behavior typically occurs (i.e., when, where, with whom, in what situations), and (3) definition of the function(s) of the wandering behavior (i.e., what reinforces or maintains the behavior).

A number of strategies can assist in collecting information for a functional analysis (O'Neill, Horner, Albin, Storey & Sprague, 1990). First, the wandering-behavior classifications schemes developed by Hussian (1987) and Hope and Fairburn (1989) can be used to generate hypotheses regarding variables that might control the wandering behavior of a given dementia sufferer. Caregivers or perhaps even the patient him or herself can be interviewed in an effort to narrow the range of variables that may be affecting or controlling the wandering behavior. In addition, the patient can be observed in his or her daily routine for an extended period of time. Direct observation must be conducted in a manner that does not disrupt or influence the patient's behavior. A final strategy is to manipulate or adjust the environmental situations that one thinks will and will not elicit, change, or eliminate wandering behavior. The purpose of the manipulation strategy is to test whether one understand the wandering behavior and its controlling variables well enough to predict and control it. This is the final step prior to developing an effective intervention.

Intervention. Several behavioral intervention procedures have been applied successfully in the management of wandering behavior in dementia patients. Successful interventions have typically involved antecedent and/or consequence manipulation. For example, Hussian (1988) paired verbal and physical prompts with a variety of environmental stimuli such as floor grids and signage to decrease wandering and increase orientation in 5 psychogeriatric patients.

Even after prompts were faded out, subjects maintained at least an 86% change in behavior in the desired direction.

Namazi, Rosner & Calkins (1989) placed canvas flaps over doorknobs to change the stimulus property of doors. Similarly, Mayer & Darby (1991) placed a mirror on an exit door to change its stimulus properties and successfully decreased successful "escapes" from the ward from 76.2 to 35.7%. By altering the appearance of doors and knobs, and thus removing discriminative stimuli for touching and/or opening doors, several types of wandering may be addressed. As a result of door/knob camouflage, individuals won't be cued to exit by sight of the door or knob, and "stimulation seekers" won't inadvertently exit by handling doorknobs.

Selection of appropriate interventions may be aided by observing an individual's wandering behavior and determining into which, if any, of the above described categories or types of wandering it best fits. For example, whereas a medication adjustment may be all that is required for *akathisia wandering*, *self-stimulation wandering* can be reduced by modifying the patient's physical environment such that stimulation is available in contained, safe areas and unavailable in more distant or dangerous areas. *Disorientation wandering* is often treated by increasing the availability and salience of relevant environmental stimuli (e.g., by placing the persons name on the outside of his bedroom door or painting arrows on the floor to guide patients to the dining room).

Wandering behavior need not always be considered a problem behavior or a target for intervention. It carries with it potential benefits such as providing exercise and increased stimulation. Wandering may also decrease isolation or even increase the opportunity for socialization. Kikuta (1991) went so far as to encourage wandering in an effort to decrease aggressive behavior. Kikuta (1991) presented a case study of a chemically and sometimes physically restrained dementia patient who had a history of yelling and physical aggression. When chemical and physical restraints were decreased and a safe wandering area was established, yelling was cut in half and physical aggression was eliminated. In addition, other indicators of well-being and quality of life increased, such as increased relaxation, increased alertness, increased tendency to sleep through night, and appropriate weight loss. Thus, in this patient's case, wandering behavior turned out to be a solution rather than a problem.

Readers are encouraged to be creative and use their understanding of basic behavioral principles and the knowledge they gain from functional analysis to develop behavioral interventions that are uniquely appropriate to each dementia patient.

Aggressive and Agitated Behavior

The aggressive and agitated behavior of dementia patients is highly stressful and problematic to caregivers. Such behavior is often described by staff and family members as the most difficult behavior problem to manage (Haley, Brown & Levine, 1987). In addition, aggressive behavior is frequently cited as the most common reason for admission to geriatric psychiatry units or nursing homes (Cohen-Mansfield, Werner, Culpepper, Wolfson & Bickel, 1998). Extreme agitation and physical aggression are among the most dangerous behaviors in inpatient settings (Fisher, Carstensen, Turk & Noll, 1993), and the consequences can include injury to the elderly person, other residents, and/or caregivers. Aggressive and agitated behavior often results in restraints, medication delivery, or other restrictive measures (Hussian, 1981).

Aggressive Behavior. In the absence of any widely accepted definition of aggressive behavior, we will employ Patel and Hope's (1993, p. 458) definition: "an overt act, involving the delivery of noxious stimuli to (but not necessarily aimed at) another object, organism or self, which is clearly not accidental." Aggressive behavior can be classified using the following dimensions: (a) topography of the behavior, such as verbal, physical, or sexual aggression (Ryden, 1988b), (b) the target of the behavior (self or others), and (c) the degree of disruption (disturbing vs. endangering) (Cohen-Mansfield, Werner, Culpepper, Wolfson & Bickel, 1998; Winger, Schirm & Stewart, 1987). These dimensions are neither clear-cut, nor mutually exclusive. For example, disturbing aggressive verbal behavior could consist of sexual statements directed toward a caregiver, or dangerous physically aggressive behavior could be directed toward oneself.

Estimates of the prevalence of aggressive behavior in dementia patients present a variable picture, perhaps due to discrepant definitions. However, in general, verbally aggressive behavior is most common, followed by physically aggressive, sexually aggressive and self-abusive aggressive behaviors. The most frequent physically aggressive behaviors of older adults with dementia appear to be biting, scratching, spitting, hitting and kicking (Patel & Hope, 1992b).

Again, because the definition of aggressive behavior varies, the literature exploring variables predictive of such behavior in demented older adults is equivocal. In general, the greater the degree of cognitive impairment experienced by older adults, the more frequent and severe are their aggressive behaviors (Cohen-Mansfield, Werner & Marx, 1990). Men, in both community dwellings and nursing homes, are more likely to be aggressive than women (Cohen-Mansfield et al., 1998). In addition, demented individuals who suffer from psychotic symptoms are more likely to be physically aggressive than those without psychotic symptoms (Hussian, 1981; Lopez, Becker, Brenner, Rosen, Bajulaiye & Reynolds, 1991). Finally, a higher frequency of premorbid aggressive behavior seems to be predictive of aggressive behavior in patients suffering from dementia (Hamel, Gold, Andres, Reis, Dastoor, Grauere & Bergman, 1990).

Agitated Behavior. The terms "agitation" or "agitated behavior" typically encompass various topographies of excessive behavior aversive to caregivers such as pacing, shouting, repeated plucking (Patel & Hope, 1993), name calling, emotional outbursts, and repetitive questioning. Agitated behaviors occur more frequently than physically aggressive behaviors (Cohen-Mansfield, 1986; Patel & Hope, 1992b). The variables predicting agitated behavior are increased cognitive impairment, poor social networks, and greater impairment in activities of daily living (Cohen-Mansfield et al., 1990). However, there is no clear relationship between sex or age of patients and frequency of agitated behavior (Donat, 1986); nor is there any clear relationship with frequency of agitated behavior and the degree of patient dependency on nursing staff (Patel & Hope, 1992b).

Assessment. Even though the topography and target of the agitated and aggressive behavior may be different, agitated and aggressive behavior can function similarly. As a result, we will treat both behaviors as members of the same class and their assessment and treatment concurrently.

Because the antecedents and consequences controlling aggressive/agitated behavior are likely to differ from individual to individual, a thorough idiographic functional analysis is imperative. Assessment should involve recording frequency, duration, antecedents and consequences of the behavior, as well as the individual's level of functioning, cognitive ability, and past incidences of aggressive or agitated behavior (Cohen-Mansfield et al., 1998). Assessment information can be obtained from direct observation and from responses of caregivers to various psychometric instruments. For example, instruments like the *Staff Observation Aggression Scale* (Palmstierna and Wistedt, 1987) or the *Agitation Behavior Mapping Instrument* (Cohen-Mansfield, Werner & Marx, 1989) can be used to facilitate direct observation data gathering. Ratings by caregivers can be obtained using instruments like the *Ryden Aggression Scale* (Ryden, 1988), the *Rating Scale for Aggressive Behavior in the Elderly* (Patel & Hope, 1992a,b)., and the *Cohen-Mansfield Agitation Inventory* (Cohen-Mansfield et al., 1989). These measures are only a sample of available measures. Therefore, the behavioral assessor must determine whether these measures are reliable, valid, and appropriate in his or her particular setting.

Virtually any stimulus in an individual's environment can set the occasion for aggressive and/or agitated behavior. Some antecedents are correlated with impairment stemming from the disease itself. For example, failure or inability to complete tasks, impaired ability to communicate (Leibovici & Tariot, 1988), and confusion (Rapp, Flint, Hermann & Proulx, 1992) can set the occasion for aggressive or agitated behavior. In addition, the neurological damage associated with severe dementia may also have a disinhibiting function, especially in individuals with a high frequency of premorbid aggressive behavior (Cohen-

Mansfield et al., 1998). Catastrophic (highly emotional) outbursts, delusions and/or hallucinations accompanying dementia can also set the occasion for aggressive and agitated behavior (Rapp, Flint, Herrmann & Proulx, 1992).

Misinterpretation or increased sensitivity to environmental stimuli is another common antecedent to aggressive or agitated behavior. Misperception of caregiver actions (Silliman, Sternberg & Fretwellet, 1988), frequent or confusing caregiver requests, or approach by another patient also tend to set the occasion for aggressive and agitated behavior (Meyer, Schalock & Genaidy, 1991). The frequency of aggressive and agitated behaviors tends to increase when caregiver activities are most frequent (i.e. in the morning, when preparing the older adult for the day) and intrusive to the patient (i.e. bathing, dressing) (Patel and Hope, 1992b).

The research describing other environmental antecedents of aggressive and agitated behavior is contradictory. For example, some authors report that overstimulation, excessive noise, inadequate lighting, and moving to an unfamiliar place (Silliman, Sternberg & Fretwellet, 1988) tend to set the occasion for aggressive and agitated behavior. On the other hand, Hussian (1986) indicated that repetitive agitated behaviors such as pacing or shouting are typically a response to a paucity of environmental stimulation, especially in patients with advanced dementia. Once again, a functional analysis should take into account how particular environmental variables affect a certain individual.

A variety of consequences can maintain the aggressive/ agitated behavior of dementia sufferers. The behavior may serve a particular function. For example, aggressive/agitated behavior is often reinforced with attention, favored items, or assistance with a task (Cohen-Mansfield et al., 1998; Hussian, 1981). In other instances, aggressive/agitated behavior may serve an escape or avoidance function. For example, frustrated staff members may decrease the number of required showers per week for a particular resident rather than endure multiple aggressive outbursts.

Physical and chemical restraints are frequent consequences of aggressive and/or agitated behavior. However, neither of these consequences are desirable. Older adults typically take multiple medications and run a high risk for developing adverse side effects from those drugs. Therefore, treating aggressive and agitated behavior pharmacologically can lead to iatrogenic effects. For example, medications may increase the likelihood of falls, exacerbate confusion, or actually lead to worsening of the behavior (Patel & Hope, 1993). Physical restraints may also lead to increased frequency, duration, or intensity of aggressive/ agitated behavior (Werner, Cohen-Mansfield, Braun & Marx, 1989). In addition, physical restraint usage is associated with muscle atrophy, osteoporosis, limb ischemia, and strangulation (Fisher, Carstensen, Turk & Noll, 1993).

Intervention. Behavior modification techniques provide caregivers with efficacious, humane, and ethical alternatives for managing aggressive and agitated behaviors. Behavioral interventions are frequently the least invasive treatment option, posing few or less severe side effects than pharmacological interventions.

Environmental manipulations have proven successful in modifying aggressive and agitated behaviors (Rabins, 1989). For example, Cleary, Clamon, Price & Shullaw (1988) set up a "reduced stimulation unit." Pictures and wall colors were neutral in design and color, and t.v.'s and radios were eliminated. Patients were allowed to ambulate anywhere, and to eat and rest anytime. Staff and visitor access to the unit was controlled, and activities were scheduled in small groups throughout the day. This environment reduced the frequency of agitated behaviors and decreased restraint use.

Agitated and aggressive behaviors have also been targeted by providing mildly demented individuals with a model to imitate (Rabins, 1989). Presenting the older adult with easy to follow instructions broken down into smaller steps, and requesting performance of only one task at a time is also effective (Rabins, 1989). Other successful techniques are: moving slowly into a client's visual field, interacting from the front of the client, ensuring adequate sleep at night, and decreasing prn medication and neuroleptic usage (Hussian, 1981). Similarly, one can reduce the likelihood of aggressive behavior by approaching an individual calmly, adopting a reassuring and gentle voice, and using touch and non-threatening postures (Teri and Logsdon, 1990). Leaving the room of an individual demonstrating agitated behavior can be effective if one's presence is reinforcing the patient's agitated behavior. Timeout is also often effective in decreasing the frequency of aggressive and agitated behaviors (Hussian, 1981; Vaccaro, 1988b).

Few empirical studies have systematically explored the efficacy of the behavioral approach to reducing aggressive and agitated behavior, perhaps because the traditional first step to modify this behavior has been pharmacologic (Vaccaro, 1988b). However, some studies have applied behavioral techniques to non-demented older adults emitting aggressive behavior. For example, Vaccaro (1988b), used operant procedures with a physically and verbally aggressive 69 year-old-male in a case study. After an initial baseline recording phase, non-aggressive behavior was reinforced (with juice, fruit, cookies or a granola bar) on a modified differential-reinforcement-of-other-behaviors schedule. After each aggressive response, the older adult was removed from the activity or setting and placed in a timeout room for 10 min. After a second baseline phase, the second experimental condition was instituted. This phase involved systematically fading the tangible reinforcers to verbal and social praise. Both experimental conditions resulted in significant decreases in physical and verbal aggressive behaviors that were maintained at follow-up. Since the older adult in this study was not affected by dementia, systematic replication with dementia sufferers is warranted. However, this procedure seems to hold promise, regardless of the cognitive functioning level of the individual. Other studies exploring the use of behavioral techniques in non-demented older adults emitting aggressive behavior that may be applicable to demented individuals include Vaccaro (1998a); Rosberger & McLean (1983); and Colenda & Hamer (1991), for example.

Self-Care Behaviors

As dementia progresses and individuals become more cognitively impaired, many individuals require increasing assistance with self-care skills, or activities of daily living (ADLs). Basic ADLs include dressing, bathing, toileting, grooming, tooth brushing, drinking, and eating. Inadequate self-care is problematic, and can contribute to the placement of individuals in nursing facilities (McEvoy & Patterson, 1986).

In the early stages of dementia, older adults may demonstrate mild impairment in self-care behaviors due to memory loss. For example, an individual might put on two different types of shoes or repeatedly forget to brush his/her teeth. The middle and severe stages of dementia may include problems like forgetting how to operate devices such as drinking fountains and eating utensils. Severely impaired individuals may be unable to communicate hunger or thirst, or forget how to meet these basic needs. For example, residents may fail to drink from a glass of water when dehydrated (Knapp & Shaid, 1991).

Negative consequences of failure to perform ADLs or ineffective self-care behaviors can include frustration, decreased autonomy and dignity, aggressive/agitated behavior, blaming other individuals for the older adults' difficulties (Knapp & Shaid, 1991), and increased dependence on caregivers.

Assessment. An initial thorough functional analysis of the self-care repertoire and controlling variables is required to determine the capabilities of the individual and potential sources of environmental influence. A proper analysis might determine, for example, whether the treatment approach should involve increasing environmental control so that existing skills are maximized, or focus on the elimination of situations requiring skills beyond the individual's capabilities (Carstensen & Fisher, 1991; Horgas, Wahl & Baltes, 1996). For example, serving finger foods to clients who are able to self-feed but cannot use utensils may set the occasion for eating behavior. Increasing the amount of "pull on" clothing (rather than clothes with multiple small fasteners) could maximize existing skills in the self-dressing repertoire.

Failure to maintain ADLs can also result from environmental variables. Caregivers, especially institutional staff, may reinforce dependent behaviors with attention and support (Baltes & Werner-Wahl, 1987; Carstensen & Fisher, 1991). In contrast, independent ADL behaviors may be ignored or discouraged.

Intervention. The effectiveness of the behavioral approach to maintaining or enhancing self-care behaviors in older adults with dementia has yet to be validated through empirical research. However, there are arguments in favor of adopting a behavioral strategy. The literature supports the notion that some previously well-learned, over-rehearsed self-care behaviors can sometimes be restored and/or maintained, even in older individuals with cognitive impairment (Carstensen & Fisher, 1991; McEvoy & Patterson, 1987; Patterson, Dupree, Eberly, Jackson, O'Sullivan, Penner & Dee-Kelly, 1982). The loss of independent self-care skills may be influenced by both physical disabilities and environmental conditions (Baltes & Werner-Wahl, 1987). In addition, several techniques involving manipulating consequences are commonly and successfully utilized to modify the ADL behaviors of developmentally disabled individuals (Lemke & Mitchell, 1972; Whitney & Barnard, 1966) could be utilized with older adults with dementia.

Much of the literature focusing on modifying ADL behaviors of physically disabled individuals involves manipulating consequences to either increase non-existent or low-frequency behavior, or decrease inappropriate behaviors. For example, to increase self-feeding behavior, the chain of eating behaviors can be broken into smaller components that are shaped and then chained together into more complex combinations of behaviors (e.g., Van Hasselt, Ammerman & Sisson, 1990). Both forward and backward chaining procedures have been used successfully to establish or maintain physically disabled clients' ability to dress and feed themselves (Whitney & Barnard, 1966; Lemke & Mitchell, 1972; Azrin, Schaffer & Weslowski, 1976; Risley & Edwards, 1978).

Building on the forward chaining technique by including gentle manual guidance and high density reinforcement, graduated guidance also has been used successfully to establish or maintain physically disabled clients' ability to dress and feed themselves (Azrin, Schaeffer & Weslowski, 1976; Stimbert, Minor & McCoy, 1977).

Shaping of multiple self-care behaviors has proven successful using tokens as reinforcers with multihandicapped individuals. Token delivery is first made contingent upon completion of a task (e.g., toileting, showering, dressing, toothbrushing, cleaning up living space, and removing bed linens). Eventually delivery of tokens occurs only when all target behaviors are completed (Jarman, Iwata & Lorentzson, 1983).

Finally, time-out (e.g., Baltes & Zerbe, 1976; Sisson & Dixon, 1986), restitution (i.e. client cleans up spills), and positive practice overcorrection are sometimes effectively utilized with physically disabled individuals (Azrin & Armstrong, 1973), and could be used successfully with demented older adults as well.

Because behavioral techniques to enhance ADL's have been empirically validated with other populations (i.e. physically disabled or cognitively intact older adults), researchers may have assumed that treatment efficacy extends unequivocally to individuals with dementia. This may partially account for the dearth of research in this area. However, an older adult's degree of cognitive impairment may interact with environmental variables and influence treatment outcome. For example, Carstensen & Fisher (1991) indicated that verbal instruction and prompting with simple step commands can be used to elicit self-care behaviors in *mildly* cognitively impaired individuals. Baltes & Zerbe (1976), used verbal prompting combined with stimulus control procedures, immediate reinforcement, and a time-out procedure for refusal to eat and for behaviors like throwing food on the floor, to increase eating behavior in a 67-year-old woman. Self-feeding increased dramatically from a baseline frequency of close to zero. However, the older woman did not suffer from cognitive impairment, so generalization of results to cognitively impaired individuals should be made cautiously. Likewise, Rinke, Williams, Lloyd & Smith-Scott (1978), used prompts and reinforcement in the form of praise, visual feedback, and food items to increase the frequency of self-bathing behavior in six older adults. Once again, this intervention would have to be replicated with older adults with dementia before making unconditional recommendations.

Though the literature discussing behavioral techniques for establishing and maintaining ADL's in demented older adults is sparse, it is encouraging. Carstensen & Fisher (1991) indicate that a timeout procedure can be effective for increasing ADLs in older adults with dementia. The technique can be used to decrease inappropriate behaviors, such as refusing to eat, taking others' food, and throwing food or utensils. Withdrawing a client's chair from the table, or removing food and social reinforcement provided by the caregiver are suggested timeout strategies. In addition, McEvoy & Patterson (1987), used a combination of highly structured group and individual training exercises including verbal instruction, modeling and practice of personal hygiene skills such as bathing, and toothbrushing to increase ADLs in older dementia patients. The authors utilized the least amount of prompts necessary to elicit behavior and faded prompts until ADL skills were performed independently. Social praise and tokens were effective reinforcers in this study. Both mildly and severely demented individuals demonstrated improvement on the treatment outcome measure (mean general appearance rating scale scores).

Because failure to maintain ADLs also can result from environmental variables, caregivers should be trained in behavioral principles as well. For example, educating a caregiver to rearrange the environment so that independent behaviors of older adults (rather than dependent behaviors) are verbally, socially and tangibly reinforced should set the occasion for future independent behavior.

The lack of research regarding older adults with dementia, and their failure to maintain self-care skills, is frustrating. Basing the selection of strategies on successful behavioral techniques with other populations is a useful heuristic, however, empirical studies should begin to explore whether these techniques are appropriate with a cognitively impaired older population. The choice of whether to build upon existing skills or remove obstacles requiring skills beyond the individual's capabilities is an important component of a functional analysis and, consequently, choice of treatment.

Conclusion

Dementia sufferers present a multitude of difficult but tractable problem behaviors. The physiological changes which often occur with aging, coupled with the learning and memory impairments accompanying dementia, yield difficult but exciting challenges for behavior therapists. Though behavior therapists have been slow to address the behavior problems associated with dementia, several promising approaches to the management of the most common behavior problems have been documented in the literature and reviewed herein. We have also attempted to apprise the reader of physiological aspects of aging that could influence the assessment and treatment processes. Finally, we have offered below a case study that illustrates the assessment and treatment process. We are convinced from our review of the literature and own experiences with the problems of dementia sufferers that virtually all of the problem behaviors associated with dementia are amenable to behavioral interventions. The key to successful interventions rests with careful functional analyses and continued hypothesis testing regarding controlling variables. We hope that more behavior therapists will experience the rewards and challenges of working with older adults in general and those suffering from dementia in particular.

Hypothetical Case Illustration

Albert is a 73-year-old, white male. He completed high school and 2 years of college and has been married for 53 years to his wife, Sophie, with whom he has four children and ten grandchildren. During his 43 years of work for a public utility company, Albert worked primarily in middle-management positions. He enjoyed his work and co-workers and was known as a dedicated and capable employee. Albert retired from the utility company at age 65. Although he told his family, friends, and colleagues that he was retiring because he "had earned the time off," he later admitted that his decision to retire was based largely upon increasing difficulty "keeping track of things" at work.

Albert's memory difficulties progressed, and at age 67 he was diagnosed with probable dementia of the Alzheimer's type (DAT). Unfortunately, at the time of diagnosis, little counseling was offered to Albert or his wife regarding what they could expect as his illness progressed or what they could do to manage the problems that arose as a result of the illness.

Albert is now in the moderate stages of DAT. Sophie recently went to her family physician experiencing stress-related physical symptoms (i.e., dysphoric mood, head-aches, acid stomach, difficulty sleeping, fatigue). Recognizing that she was overwhelmed with the task of caring for her husband, Sophie's doctor referred her to a geriatric therapist. Throughout the course of the intervention, the therapist taught Sophie basic stress-management techniques, educated her more fully about DAT, and arranged for Albert's children and adult grandchildren to provide respite. In addition the therapist taught Sophie several strategies for managing Albert's behaviors which were particularly troubling for her. These included Albert turning on all of the stove burners, removing items from kitchen and bathroom cabinets ("for no reason"), and "roaming" about the house and sometimes out the front door and into the street. Of lesser frequency were Albert's occasional "fits" of crying and/or verbal aggression.

Sophie and the therapist prioritized the target problems and decided to first address those behaviors that placed Albert and/or Sophie in physical danger. The therapist began by making the simple suggestion of removing the control knobs from the stove, except when cooking, and having a dead-bolt installed on the front door which required a key to open it from the inside or the outside. Sophie was encouraged to take any other simple steps to make the house safe. In addition, she was instructed in the basics of functional analysis (i.e., recording antecedents, behaviors, and consequences), provided with several blank monitoring forms (Figure 21.1) and sent home with instructions to monitor Albert's "roaming" behavior.

The following week Sophie noticed that episodes of Albert opening and closing drawers and cabinets coincided with him wandering, and thus she included these behaviors on his monitoring form. This and other information provided through monitoring enabled the therapist and Sophie to complete a functional analysis of Albert's behaviors.

Albert's roaming behaviors were grouped into two categories, based on antecedents, consequences, and topography of the wandering behavior. Episodes 1 and 3 seemed to corresponded with Hussian's (1985) "stimulation-seeking wandering" (see Chapter above). In these episodes, Albert's wandering and associated behaviors (e.g., rubbing hand along wall, touching objects as he passed, flipping light switches, opening cabinets, rattling doorknobs, saying "wo-wo-wo-wo," etc.) seemed to serve the function of providing stimulation. That is, the therapist hypothesized that these behaviors were maintained by the stimulation they provided. Consistency in antecedent stimuli across these episodes was also noted. In episodes 1 and 3, wandering began when Albert was alone, in the dark or near darkness, and relatively inactive.

Episodes 2 and 4 involved Albert leaving through the front door of the house and could be classified as "exit-seeking," according to Hussian's typol-

BEHAVIOR MONITORING FORM

Target *Behavior:* Wandering
General Definition: Wandering behavior = when Albert roams around the house or around a room by himself, sometimes touching things along the way, sometimes exiting out the front door if he's able to do so.

NOTE: Please use as much detail as possible when describing the target behavior and its antecedents and consequences. Write your descriptions so that someone who isn't familiar with the situation could reproduce it exactly.

Date/ Time	Before - what where, with whom?	Target Behavior (vivid description of each incident)	After - what, where, with whom?
2-4/ 5:10 pm	*A was sitting in den, alone, looking out front window ...getting dark outside... S in kitchen preparing dinner...no lights on in den...	A got up & walked from den & into kitchen, roamed into & out of bathroom along the way...Once in the kitchen, he roamed around the room, opened & closed two drawers & three cabinets... rubbed hand along walls, counter tops, & furniture as he walked & repeatedly said "wo-wo-wo".	A knocked bowl of green beans off counter top as he ran his hand across it...S hurriedly picked up beans, seated A in chair at kitchen table, gave him bowl of beans & butter knife... A cut beans into small pieces, eating many of the beans in the process...
2-4/ 8:45 pm	A was watching TV with S ...lights on in den...TV program depicted doorbell ringing	A got up, walked to and opened front door, stood for a moment looking outside, as if confused, then walked outside	S followed A outside, asked A where he's going (he responded "to pick up the kids")...S said" they're already home" and led A back in without resistance
2-5/ 7:00 am	A awoke in bed alone ...no lights on in bedroom...S had been up for about an hour, was in kitchen preparing breakfast	A got out of bed, went into bathroom, placed all items from medicine chest in trash can, walked into den, moved items around on shelves in den, walked into kitchen and began taking items out of pantry and setting them on counter top. Had rubbed hand along wall and was making repetitive, sing-song noises.	S was frustrated when she saw him removing item from pantry, yelled at A, sat him down at table, and gave him a donut, A broke the donut up into small pieces and pressed them flat between his fingers
2-5/ 12:25 pm	On his way back to den from bathroom, *A walked by front door, looked at and touched knob...S was a few steps behind him, having just helped him in the bathroom.	A turned and opened knob, walked out front door, closed it behind him and headed down the street.	S went out door after him, rushed up to him, asked where he was going (he responded "to work"), and led him back to house without resistance.

*A=Albert; S=Sophie

Figure 21.1. Excerpts from Sophie's monitoring of Albert's wandering behaviors.

ogy. In both of these episodes prompts to open the front door (i.e., sound of door bell, sight of door-knob) occurred antecedent to the behavior. The act of opening the door set the occasion for exiting and exiting set the occasion for walking down the street. Albert's responses to Sophie's questions of where he was going were confabulatory. Both episodes of exit seeking were consequated by Sophie rushing out, questioning, expressing concern, providing attention, etc. Thus, maintenance of this behavior could have been a function of antecedent control and attention.

The treatment plan included several components. Sophie and the therapist concluded that wandering was a problem only when it put someone in danger or when it resulted in items being broken, misplaced, etc. Thus, the goal of intervention was to eliminate "dangerous wandering" rather than to eliminate all wandering. To that end, safety latches were placed on the kitchen cabinets, medicine chest, linen closet, dresser drawers, etc. Breakable items (glass candy dishes, etc.) were placed out of easy reach, and picture frames were fastened more securely to the walls so they could not be knocked off as Albert ran his hand over them. In addition, a dead-bolt was placed on the front door to prevent Albert leaving the house unattended.

The dead-bolt on the front door was expected to eliminate the exit-seeking behavior. However, Albert's sight or touch of the door and/or door-knob continued to set the occasion for attempts to exit. When he found the front door locked he often became distressed, even aggressive. Thus, in an effort to decrease to salience of the door as a stimulus to exit, Sophie put a white fabric cover over door-knob and hung a print by Albert's favorite painter on the door. Albert's exit-seeking decreased to near zero at that point, while actual unsupervised exiting was eliminated altogether.

Stimulation seeking was targeted in several ways. First, because darkness seemed to set the occasion for wandering, the lights in the bedroom and den were placed on timers to decrease the chance that Albert would be alone in the dark. In addition, Albert was provided with several items which provided safe stimulation. For example, his harmonica and a xylophone were placed on his bedside table, under the light of the lamp that was placed on a timer. For 2 weeks, Sophie made a point of reinforcing Albert's playing his harmonica or xylophone when he awoke in the morning. Thus, not only did he obtain safe, self-stimulation upon awakening, but the sound of the "music" alerted Sophie that Albert was awake. Finally, Sophie chose to institute a daily habit of going for a walk with Albert, out of doors, just after breakfast and before dinner. This was intended to provide safe stimulation for Albert. It also had the pleasant side-effect of providing Sophie and Albert with some daily, quality time together as well as physical exercise for Sophie and Albert.

Although Albert continued to walk about the house touching things several times each day, episodes of dangerous or destructive wandering were reduced to near zero within a month of the start of treatment. As a result of the changes in Albert's behavior, the increased sense of control she had over her environment, and the increased exercise and quality time with Albert, Sophie reported decreases in stress and increased quality of life. Prior to termination, Sophie and the therapist met for several sessions in which they discussed how Sophie might apply the behavioral principles she had learned to address Albert's future problematic behaviors. She was encouraged to consult further with the therapist if needed.

References

APA (1994). *Diagnostic and statistical manual of mental disorders*, 4th edition (DSM-IV). Washington, DC: American Psychiatric Association.

Azrin, N. H., & Armstrong, P. M. (1973). The "mini-meal"- A method for teaching eating skills to the profoundly retarded. *Mental Retardation, 11*, 9–13.

Azrin, N. H., Schaeffer, R. M., & Wesolowski, M. D. (1976). A rapid method of teaching profoundly mentally retarded persons to dress by a reinforcement-guidance method. *Mental Retardation, 14*, 29–33.

Baltes, M. M., & Zerbe, M. B. (1976). Re-establishment of self-feeding in a nursing home resident. *Nursing Research, 25*, 24–26.

Baltes, M. M., & Werner-Wahl, H. (1987). Dependence in aging. In L. L. Carstensen & B. A. Edelstein (Eds.), *Handbook of clinical gerontology.* New York: Pergamon Press.

Bourgeois, M. S. (1990). Enhancing conversation skills in patients with Alzheimer's disease using a prosthetic memory aid. *Journal of Applied Behavior Analysis, 23*, 29–42.

Bourgeois, M. S. (1991). Communication treatment for adults with dementia. *Journal of Speech and Hearing Research, 34*, 831–844.

Burgio, K. L., & Engel, B. T. (1990). Biofeedback-assisted behavioral training for elderly men and women. *Journal of the American Geriatrics Society, 38*, 338–340.

Burgio, K. L., & Burgio, L. D. (1991). The problem of urinary incontinence. In P. Wisocki (Ed.), *Handbook of clinical behavior therapy with elderly clients.* New York: Plenum Press.

Burgio, K. L., Whitehead, W. E., & Engel, B. T. (1985). Urinary incontinence in the elderly: Bladder-sphincter biofeedback and toileting skills training. *Annals of Internal Medicine, 103*, 507–515.

Carstensen, L. L. (1988). The emerging field of behavioral gerontology. *Behavior Therapy, 19*, 259–281.

Carstensen, L. L., & Fisher, J. E. (1991). Treatment applications for psychological and behavioral problems of the elderly in nursing homes. In P. Wisocki (Ed.), *Handbook of clinical behavior therapy with the elderly client.* New York: Plenum Press.

Cerella, J., Poon, L. W., & Williams, D. (1980). Age and the complexity hypothesis. In L. W. Poon (Ed.), *Aging in the 1980s: Psychological issues.* Washington, DC: American Psychological Association.

Chiverton, P., & Caine, E. D. (1989). Education to assist spouses in coping with AD: A controlled trial. *Journal of the American Geriatrics Society, 37*, 593–598.

Clay, E. C. (1980). Promoting urine control in older adults: habit retraining. *Geriatric Nursing, 1*, 252–254.

Cleary, T. A., Clamon, C., Price, M., & Shullaw, G. (1988). A reduced stimulation unit: effects on patients with Alzheimer's disease and related disorders. *The Gerontologist, 28*, 511–514.

Cohen-Mansfield, J., & Billig, N. (1986). Agitated behaviors in the elderly, a conceptual review. *Journal of the American Geriatrics Society, 34*, 711–721.

Cohen-Mansfield, J., Werner, P., & Marx, M.S. (1989). An observational study of agitation in agitated nursing home residents. *International Psychogeriatrics, 1*, 153–165.

Cohen-Mansfield, J., Werner, P., & Marx, M. S. (1990). Screaming in nursing home residents. *Journal of the American Geriatrics Society, 38*, 785–792.

Cohen-Mansfield, J., Werner, P., Culpepper, W. J., Wolfson, M. A., & Bickel, E. (1998). Wandering and aggression. In L. L. Carstensen, B. A. Edelstein & L. Dorbrand (Eds.), *The practical handbook of clinical gerontology.* Beverly Hills, CA: Sage, in press.

Colenda, C. C., & Hamer, R.M. (1991). Antecedents and interventions for aggressive behavior of patients at a geropsychiatric state hospital. *Hospital and Community Psychiatry, 42*, 287–292.

Craik, F. I. M. (1984). Age differences in human memory. In J. E. Birren & K. W. Schaie (Eds.), *Handbook of the psychology of aging.* New York: Van Nostrand Reinhold.

Craik, F. I. M., & Jennings, J. M. (1992). Human memory. In F. I. M. Craik & T. A. Salthouse (Eds.), *The handbook of aging and cognition.* Hillsdale, NJ: Lawrence Erlbaum.

Craik, F. I. M., Morris, R. G., & Gick, M. L. (1990). Adult age differences in working memory. In G. Vallaar & T. Shallice (Eds.), *Neuropsychological impairments of short-term memory*. Cambridge: Cambridge University Press.

Crook, T. H., & Youngjohn, J. R. (1993). Development of treatments for memory disorders: The necessary meeting of basic and everyday memory research. *Applied Cognitive Psychology, 7*, 619–630.

de Graaf, C., Polet, P., & van Staveren, W. A. (1994). Sensory perception and pleasantness of food flavors in elderly subjects. *Journal of Gerontology: Psychological Sciences, 49*, P93-P99.

Donat, D. C. (1986). Altercations amongst institutionalized psychogeriatric patients. *The Gerontologist, 26*, 227–228.

Duke, L. W., Haley, W. E., & Bergquist, T. F. (1991). Cognitive- behavioral interventions for age-related memory impairment. In P. Wisocki (Ed.), *Handbook of clinical behavior therapy with the elderly client*. New York: Plenum Press.

Engel, B. T., Burgio, L. D., McCormick, K. A., Hawkins, A. M., Scheve, A. S., & Leahy, E. (1990). Behavioral treatment of incontinence in the long-term care setting. *Journal of the American Geriatrics Society, 38*, 361–363.

Fantl, J. A., Wyman, J. F., Harkins, S. W., & Hadley, E. C. (1990). Bladder training in the management of lower urinary tract dysfunction in women: A review. *Journal of the American Geriatrics Society, 38*, 329–332.

Fisher, J. E., Carstensen, L. L., Turk, S. E., & Noll, J. P. (1993). Geriatric patients. In A. Bellack & M. Hersen (Eds.), *Handbook of behavior therapy in the psychiatric setting*. New York: Plenum Press.

Frewen, W. K. (1982). A reassessment of bladder training in detrusor dysfunction in the female. *British Journal of Urology, 54*, 372–373.

Haley, W. E., Brown, S. L., & Levine, E. G. (1987). Family caregiver appraisals of patient behavioral disturbance in senile disturbance. *Clinical Gerontologist, 6*, 25–34.

Hamel, M., Gold, D., Andres, D., Reis, M., Dastoor, D., Grauere, H., & Bergman, H. (1990). Predictors and consequences of aggressive behavior by community-based dementia patients. *The Gerontologist, 30*, 206–211.

Hanley, I. (1986). Reality orientation in the care of the elderly patient with dementia - three case studies. In I. Hanley & M. Gilhooly (Eds.), *Psychological therapies for the elderly*. New York: New York University Press.

Harris, J. E. (1980). Memory aids people use: Two interview studies. *Memory and Cognition, 8*, 31–38.

Hope, R. A., & Fairburn, C. G. (1989). The nature of wandering in dementia: a community based study. *International Journal of Geriatric Psychiatry, 5*, 239–245.

Horgas, A. L.,Wahl, H., & Baltes, M. (1996). Dependency in late life. In L. L. Carstensen, B. A. Edelstein & L. Dornbrand (Eds.), *The practical handbook of clinical gerontology*. Beverly Hills, CA: Sage.

Hunt, T., & Lindley, C. J. (Eds.) (1989). *Testing older adults*. Austin, TX: Pro-ed.

Hu, T. W., Igou, J. F., Kaltreider, D. L., Yu, L. C., Rohner, T. J., Dennis, P. J., Craighead, W. E., Hadley, E. C., & Ory, M. G. (1989). A clinical trial of a behavioral therapy to reduce urinary incontinence in nursing homes: Outcome and implications. *Journal of the American Medical Association, 261*, 2656–2662.

Hussian, R. A. (1981). *Geriatric psychology: a behavioral perspective*. New York: Van Nostrand Reinhold.

Hussian, R. A. (1987). Wandering and disorientation. In L. L. Carstensen & B. A. Edelstein (Eds.) *Handbook of clinical gerontology*. New York: Pergamon Press.

Hussian, R. A. (1988). Modification of behaviors in dementia via stimulus manipulation. *Clinical Gerontologist, 8,* 37–43.

Hussian, R. A., & Davis, R. L. (1985). *Responsive care: Behavioral interventions with elderly persons.* Champaign, IL : Research Press.

Jarman, P. H., Iwata, B. A., & Lorentzson, A. M. (1983). Development of morning self-care routines in multiply handicapped persons. *Applied Research in Mental Retardation, 4,* 113–122.

Keating, J. C. Jr., Schulte, E. A., & Miller, E. (1988). Conservative care of urinary incontinence in the elderly. *Journal of Manipulative and Physiological Therapeutics, 11,* 300–308.

Kegel, A. H. (1956). Stress incontinence of urine in women: Physiologic treatment. *Journal of the International College of Surgeons, 25,* 487–499.

Kikuta, S. C. (1991). Clinically managing disruptive behavior on the ward. *Journal of Gerontological Nursing, 17,* 4–8.

Knapp, M. S., & Shaid, E. C. (1991). Innovations in managing difficult behaviors. *Provider,* November, 17–24.

Laidlaw, R. W., & Hamilton, M. A. (1937). A study of thresholds in apperception of passive movement among normal control subjects. *Bulletin of the Neurological Institute, 6,* 268–273.

Lam, D., Sewell, M., Bell, G., & Katona, C. (1989). Who needs psychogeriatric continuing care? *International Journal of Geriatric Psychiatry, 4,* 109–114.

La Rue, A. (1992). *Aging and neuropsychological assessment.* New York: Plenum Press.

Leibovici, A., & Tariot, P. N. (1988). Agitation associated with dementia: a systematic approach to treatment. *Psychopharmacology Bulletin, 24,* 49–53.

Lemke, H., & Mitchell, R. D. (1972). Controlling the behavior of a profoundly retarded child. *American Journal of Occupational Therapy, 26,* 261–264.

Leventhal, E. A. (1991). Biological aspects. In J. Sadavoy, L. W. Lazarus & L. F. Jarvik (Eds.), *Comprehensive review of geriatric psychiatry.* Washington, DC: American Psychiatric Press.

Lindley, C. J. (1989). Who is the older person? In T. Hunt & C. J. Lindley (Eds.), *Testing older adults: A reference guide for geropsychological assessments.* Austin, TX: Pro-ed.

Mayer, R., & Darby, S. J. (1991). Does a mirror deter wandering in demented older people? *International Journal of Geriatric Psychiatry, 6,* 607–609.

McEvoy, C. L., & Patterson, R. L. (1987). Behavioral treatment of deficit skills in dementia patients. *The Gerontologist, 26,* 475–478.

Meyer, J., Schalock, R., & Genaidy, H. (1991). Aggression in psychiatric hospitalized geriatric patients. *International Journal of Geriatric Psychiatry, 6,* 589–592.

Moak, G. S. (1990). Characteristics of demented and non-demented geriatric admissions to a state hospital. *Hospital and Community Psychiatry, 41,* 799–801.

Morley, J. E., & Reese, S. S. (1989). Clinical implications of the aging heart. *American Journal of Medicine, 86,* 77–86.

Namazi, K. H., Rosner, T. T., & Calkins, M. P. (1989). Visual barriers to prevent ambulatory Alzheimer's patients from exiting through an emergency door. *Gerontologist, 29,* 699–702.

O'Neill, R. E., Horner, R. H., Albin, R. W., Storey, K., & Sprague, J.R. (1990). *Functional analysis of problem behavior.* Sycamore, IL: Sycamore Publishing Company.

Palmstierna, T., & Wistedt, B. (1987). Staff Observation Aggression Scale, SOAS: Presentation and evaluation. *Acta Psychiatrica Scandinavia, 76,* 657–663.

Patel, V., & Hope, R.A. (1992a). A rating scale for aggressive behavior in the elderly-the RAGE. *Psychological Medicine, 22,* 211–221.

Patel, V., & Hope, R.A. (1992b). Aggressive behavior in elderly psychiatric inpatients. *Acta Psychiatrica Scandinavia, 85,* 131–135.

Patel, V., & Hope, T. (1993). Aggressive behaviour in elderly people with dementia: a review. *International Journal of Geriatric Psychiatry, 8,* 457–472.

Patterson, R. L., Dupree, L. W., Eberly, D. A., Jackson, G. W., O'Sullivan, M. J., Penner, L. A., & Dee-Kelly, C. (1982). *Overcoming deficits of aging: a behavioral approach.* New York: Plenum Press.

Pinkston, E. M., & Linsk, N. L. (1984). *Care of the elderly: A family approach.* Elmsford, NY: Pergamon Press.

Poon, L. W. (Ed.) (1986). *Handbook for clinical memory assessment of older adults.* Washington, DC: American Psychological Association.

Poon, L. W., Gurland, B. J., Eisdorfer, C., Crook, T., Thompson, L. W., Kaszniak, A. W., & Davis, K. L. (1986). Integration of experimental and clinical precepts in memory assessment: A tribute to George Talland. In L. Poon (Ed.), *Handbook for clinical memory assessment of older adults.* Washington, DC: American Psychological Association.

Rabins, P. V. (1989). Behavior problems in the demented. In E. Light & B. D. Lebowitz (Eds.), *Alzheimer's disease treatment and family stress: directions for research.* Rockville, MD: US Department of Health and Human Services.

Rapp, M. S., Flint, A. J., Herrmann, N., & Proulx, G. (1992). Behavioural disturbances in the demented elderly: Phenomenology, pharmacotherapy, and behavioural management. *Canadian Journal of Psychiatry, 37,* 651–657.

Rinke, C. L., Williams, J. J., Lloyd, K. L., & Smith-Scott, W. (1978). The effects of prompting and reinforcement on self-bathing by elderly residents of nursing homes. *Behavior Therapy, 6,* 873–881.

Risley, T. R., & Edwards, K. A. (1978). *Behavioral technology for nursing home care: Toward a system of nursing home organization and management.* Paper presented at the Nova Behavioral Conference on Aging, Port St. Lucie, FL.

Rosberger, Z., & MacLean, J. (1983). Behavioral assessment and treatment of "organic" behaviors in an institutionalized geriatric patient. *International Journal of Behavioral Geriatrics, 1,* 33–46.

Ryden, M. B. (1988). Aggressive behavior in persons with dementia living in the community. *Alzheimer's Disease and Associated Disorders: International Journal, 2,* 342–355.

Salthouse, T. A., Babcock, R. L., & Shaw, R. J. (1991). Effects of adult age on structural and operational capacities in working memory. *Psychology and Aging, 6,* 118–127.

Shiffman, S. S., & Warwick, Z. S. (1993). Effect of flavor enhancement for the elderly on nutritional satus: Food intake, biochemical measures, anthropometric measures. *Physiology & Behavior, 53,* 395–402.

Schnelle, J. F. (1990). Treatment of urinary incontinence in nursing home patients by prompted voiding. *Journal of the American Geriatrics Society, 38,* 356–360.

Schnelle, J. F., Traughber, B., Morgan, D. B., Embry, J. E., Binion, A. E., & Coleman, A. (1983). Management of geriatric incontinence in nursing homes. *Journal of Applied Behavior Analysis, 16,* 235–241.

Shepherd, R. J. (1981). Cardiovascular limitations in the aged. In E. L. Smith & R. C. Serfass (Eds.), *Exercise and aging: The scientific basis.* Hillside, NJ: Enslow.

Shepherd, A. M., Montgomery, E., & Anderson, R. S. (1983). Treatment of genuine stress incontinence with a new perineometer. *Physiotherapy, 69,* 113.

Silliman, R. A., Sternberg, J., & Fretwell, M. D. (1988). Disruptive behavior in demented patients living within disturbed families. *Journal of the American Geriatic Society, 39,* 617–618.

Simpson, D. M., & Wicks, R. (1988). Spectral analysis of heart rate indicates reduced baroreceptor-related heart rate variability in elderly persons. *Journal of Gerontology, 43,* M21–M24.

Sisson, L. A., & Dixon, M. J. (1986). Improving mealtime behaviors of a multihandicapped child using behavior therapy techniques. *Journal of Visual Impairment and Blindness, 80,* 855–858.

Smith, W. L. (1988). *Behavioral interventions in gerontology: Management of behavior problems in individuals with Alzheimer's disease living in the community.* Paper presented at the convention of the Association for Behavior Analysis, Philadelphia, PA.

Songbein, S. K., & Awad, S. A. (1982). Behavioral treatment of urinary incontinence in geriatric patients. *Canadian Medical Association Journal, 127,* 863–864.

Spangler, P. F., Risley, T. R., & Bilyew. D. P. (1984). The management of dehydration and incontinence in non- ambulatory geriatric patients. *Journal of Applied Behavior Analysis, 17,* 397–401.

Stimbert, V. E., Minor, J. W., & McCoy, J. F. (1977). Intensive feeding training with retarded children. *Behavior Modification, 1,* 517–530.

Teri, L., & Logsdon, R. (1990). Assessment and management of behavioral disturbances in Alzheimer's disease. *Comprehensive Therapy, 16,* 36–42.

Urinary Incontinence Guideline Panel (1992). *Urinary incontinence in adults: Clinical practice guidelines.* AHCPR Pub. No. 92–0038. Rockville, MD: US Department of Health and Human Services.

Vaccaro, F. J. (1988a). Application of operant procedures in a group of institutionalized aggressive geriatric patients. *Psychology and Aging, 3,* 22–28.

Vaccaro, F. J. (1988b). Successful operant conditioning procedures with an institutionalized aggressive geriatric patient. *International Journal of Aging and Human Development, 26,* 71–79.

Van Hasselt, V. B., Ammerman, R. T., & Sisson, L. A. (1990). Physically disabled persons. In A. S. Bellack, M. Hersen & A. E. Kazdin (Eds.), *International handbook of behavior modification and therapy,* 2nd edition. New York: Plenum Press.

Van Nostrand, J. F. et al. (1979). *The national nursing home survey: 1977 summary for the United States* (DHEW) Publication No. 79–1794). Vital and health statistics. Series 13, No. 43, National Center for Health Statistics. Washington, DC: US Government Printing Office.

Werner, P., Cohen-Mansfield, J., Braun, J., & Marx, M. S. (1989). Physical restraints and agitation in nursing home residents. *Journal of the American Geriatrics Society, 37,* 1122–1126.

Whitbourne, S. K. (1985). *The aging body: Physiological changes and psychological consequences.* New York: Springer-Verlag.

Whitney, L. R., & Barnard, K. E. (1966). Implications of operant learning theory for nursing care of the retarded child. *Mental Retardation, 4,* 26–29.

Wilson, B. A., & Moffat, N. (1984). *Clinical management of memory problems.* London: Aspen.

Winger, J., Schirm, V., & Stewart, D. (1987). Aggressive behavior in long-term care. *Journal of Psychosocial Nursing, 25,* 28–33.

Zarit, J., & Zarit, S. (1987). Molar aging: The physiology and psychology of normal aging. In L. Carstensen & B. Edelstein (Eds.). *Handbook of clinical gerontology.* New York: Pergamon Press.

Zarit, S. H., & VandenBos, G. R. (1990). Effective evaluation of memory in older persons. *Hospital and Community Psychiatry, 41,* 9–16.

Further Reading

Carstensen, L., & Edelstein, B. (Eds.) (1987). *Handbook of clinical gerontology.* New York: Pergamon Press.

Carstensen, L., Edelstein, B., & Dorbrand, L. (Eds.) (1996), *The practical handbook of clinical gerontology.* Beverly Hills, CA: Sage.

Edelstein, B. (Ed.) (1998) *Clinical Geropsychology,* Vol. 7, in A. Bellack & M. Hersen (Series Eds.), *Comprehensive Clinical Psychology.* Pergamon, in press

Espert, R., & Navarro, J. F. (1995). Demencias degenerativas: Enfermedad de Alzheimer. In V. E. Caballo, G. Buela-Casal & J. A. Carrobles (Eds.), *Manual de psicopatología y trastornos psiquiátricos,* Vol. 1. Madrid: Siglo XXI.

Junqué, C., & Jurado, M. A. (1994). *Envejecimiento y demencias.* Barcelona: Martínez-Roca.

Wisocki, P. (Ed.) (1991). *Handbook of clinical behavior therapy with the elderly client.* New York: Plenum Press.

22

Outpatient Treatment for Persons with Mental Retardation

CHRISTINE MAGUTH NEZU, ARTHUR M. NEZU
and LISA DELLICARPINI
Allegheny University of the Health Sciences, USA

Introduction

Despite clear evidence that persons with mental retardation experience a full range of emotional and psychological problems (Matson & Barrett, 1982), people with dual diagnoses of mental retardation and mental illness have historically experienced particular difficulty in receiving mental health services. Several authors have described such individuals as falling in a gap between the mental health and mental retardation service delivery systems, and have further observed an unwillingness on the part of many mental health professionals to bridge this gap (Nezu & Nezu, 1994). As a result, persons who are "dually diagnosed" have remained considerably underserved regarding their psycho-therapy treatment needs. Recently, however, notable attempts have been made to address this oversight. For example, the February, 1994 issue of the *Journal of Consulting and Clinical Psychology* was devoted entirely to the topic of mental retardation and mental illness. However, any attempt to understand how to address the outpatient treatment needs of developmentally disabled persons requires consideration of both intellectual and adaptive behavior.

Mental Retardation and Adaptive Functioning

Since the founding of the American Association on Mental Retardation

(AAMR) in 1876, the concept and definition of mental retardation has changed significantly (AAMR, 1992). The definition of mental retardation presented in the ninth and most current edition of the *Manual on Mental Retardation*, published in 1992, reflects these changes. Specifically, this definition focuses on the interaction between the individual, the environment and the specific adaptive skill areas associated with the disorder (AAMR, 1992).

> "Mental retardation refers to substantial limitations in present functioning. It is characterized by significantly subaverage intellectual functioning, existing concurrently with related limitations in two or more of the following applicable adaptive skill areas: communication, self-care, home living, social skills, community use, self-direction, health and safety, functional academics, leisure and work. Mental retardation manifests before age 18" (AAMR, 1992; p. 5).

In order to confirm a diagnosis of mental retardation, an individual must have an IQ score of approximately 70–75 or below and must exhibit evidence of adaptive skill limitations in at least two adaptive skill areas. The criteria provided in the most recent Diagnostic and Statistical Manual of Mental Disorders (APA; 1994) regarding mental retardation reflects the AAMR definition:

A. Significantly subaverage intellectual functioning: an IQ of approximately 70 or below on an individually administered IQ test (for infants, a clinical judgement of significantly subaverage intellectual functioning).
B. Concurrent deficits or impairments in present adaptive functioning (i.e., the person's effectiveness in meeting the standards expected for his or her age by his or her cultural group, in at least two of the following skill areas: communication, self-care, home living, social/interpersonal skills, use of community resources, self direction, functional academic skills, work, leisure, health, and safety).
C. Onset before the age of 18.

In the United States, the number of adults with mental retardation residing in the community has increased significantly over the past 20 years due to a trend toward national deinstitutionalization. Despite many of the positive consequences provided by this community integration for developmentally disabled adults, the assimilation process has also led to an increase in stressful life experiences. Employment problems, financial difficulties, and interpersonal concerns may be overwhelming for individuals with possible psychological, cognitive, social, and/or biological vulnerabilities. The combination of these vulnerabilities with increased stress may partially explain the high prevalence rates of psychopathology found among individuals with mental retardation (Matson & Sevin, 1994; Nezu, Nezu & Gill-Weiss, 1992) who are living in the community. Actual estimates of comorbidity (mental illness and mental retardation as coexisting problems) have ranged across studies from 10 to 85% (see Borthwick-Duffy, 1994, and Nezu et al., 1992, for reviews of epidemiological studies). The behavioral symptoms associated with comorbidity in the mentally retarded population often results in these individuals losing their new freedom and being moved back to more restrictive environments. Thus, without having access to ways in which they may increase adaptive living skills, many mentally retarded adults cannot sustain their community living arrangements.

Obstacles to Effective Treatment

Despite the need for effective services designed to address the needs of individuals with dual diagnoses, the number of investigations conducted regarding both assessment and treatment is very limited (Nezu et al., 1992; Reiss, 1985). Reasons underlying the lack of scientific investigations regarding development and verification of effective treatments for this population are varied and may be associated with longstanding professional biases (Nezu et al., 1992). For example, many professionals believe that people with mental retardation are somehow immune to mental illness (Fletcher, 1988). Another reason involves the perception that the existence of intellectual deficits takes precedence over the presence of psychiatric symptoms (Reiss, Levitan & Szyszko, 1982). Yet another contributing factor to the lack of empirical focus on psychotherapy evaluation concerning persons with mental retardation involves therapist bias, particularly among psychoanalysts and client-centered therapists. Many such clinicians in the past have viewed clients with mental retardation to be inappropriate candidates for psychotherapy (Rogers & Dymond, 1954). Finally, the dichotomization between mental health and mental retardation in federal and state governmental regulatory bodies has also served to minimize professional interest in developing effective outpatient psychotherapy protocols for persons with developmental disabilities. For example, persons diagnosed with mental retardation who are referred to an office of mental retardation for services rarely have equal access to the mental health system.

Collectively, these factors have led to a paucity of empirical investigations that document the effectiveness of specific strategies for different clinical problems experienced by such individuals. This underscores the importance of redirecting our professional efforts in an attempt to develop better assessment tools and treatment procedures for developmentally disabled adults. This chapter will focus on the theoretical and empirical foundations of the treatment of dually diagnosed individuals. Initially we will present an overview of general assessment considerations, since treatment can not exist in isolation of assessment procedures. Detailed assessment strategies, however, are beyond the scope of this chapter and can be found in alternative sources (e.g. Nezu et al., 1992). Next, we will briefly describe and critique behavioral, and cognitive-behavioral treatment approaches. We believe that the current literature supports the use of cognitive-behavioral strategies, based upon social-learning principles, as an effective treatment alternative for this population. Finally, direction regarding future treatment research will be provided.

Assessment Considerations

Despite the advancements in knowledge within the field of mental retardation in the last few decades, there is still not a wide body of research literature to which a therapist can look for guidance when designing a treatment protocol for an individual with a dual diagnoses. The empirical and applied question posed by Paul (1969) over two decades ago becomes especially difficult to answer concerning this population--"What treatment, by whom, is most effective for this individual with that specific problem, under which set of circumstances?" Unfortunately, there is no easy answer to this question. Even within the general population, there is no "treatment cookbook" to which clinicians refer when attempting an intervention. Each client is treated as an individual with a unique set of circumstances surrounding his/her condition. The same is true of individuals with a dual diagnoses. According to Petronko, Harris & Kormann (1994), use of the term dual diagnoses connotes the presence of two disabilities which often results in assessment and treatment difficulties. These authors conclude that the future of community-based treatment for dually diagnosed individuals will require professionals who are willing to advocate strongly for the rights of this population. The etiology of a mentally retarded individual's emotional difficulties is likely to be complex (Nezu et al., 1992). Therefore, any attempt to explain psychopathology that focuses on a single phenomenon is likely to fall short of clinical reality. Further, those persons such as parents and teachers who would be most likely to refer a mentally retarded individual for an assessment of psychopathology might not do so because of their difficulty in differentiating mental illness from adaptive behavior problems associated with the mental retardation (Borthwick-Duffy, 1994). As a means of optimally addressing client heterogeneity, as well as the complexities involved in the behavior change process of dually-diagnosed individuals, a problem-solving model of clinical assessment and treatment decision making is advocated. Within this framework, both diagnosis and behavioral analysis are parts of the overall assessment process; that is, combining accurate diagnosis and sound behavioral assessment procedures yields a more comprehensive picture.

Multimodal Assessment

An empirical, multimodal assessment includes an evaluation of the individual's strengths and weaknesses on biological, neurological, intellectual, developmental, adaptive, physiological, psychosocial, and behavioral dimensions. However, the presence of phenomena commonly associated with intellectual deficiencies such as concrete thinking or expressive verbal deficits can make differentiation of psychiatric symptoms difficult. There are many obstacles to an accurate psychiatric evaluation of a developmentally disabled person. One involves the diagnosis of mental retardation itself. Regardless of the testing measure used to assess intelligence and adaptive functioning, it is extremely important for the clinician analyzing results to focus on the functions assessed by various test items. This approach allows for a greater understanding of the individual's strengths and weaknesses. A second obstacle to accurate evaluation is the client's own cognitive or developmental limitations. As a result of these limitations, the clinician must be familiar with predictable adaptive deficits associated with various age ranges and levels of intellectual functioning. A third obstacle results from the phenomenon of "diagnostic overshadowing" (Reiss et al., 1982), which may cause clinicians to underdiagnose pathology in mentally retarded adults because the maladaptive behavior is seen as an associated feature of mental retardation rather than as a symptom of diagnostic importance. A helpful way to overcome this obstacle when considering various diagnostic possibilities is to remember to look for disconfirming evidence to clinical hypotheses and to explore fully the context in which symptoms occur. Finally, the presence of multiple etiological factors associated with the pathology can present an obstacle which can best be overcome by addressing assessment variables in the all relevant areas: medical, psychological, familial, social, emotional, and educational. Further, assessment in each area requires the use of reliable and valid diagnostic tools such as pertinent history records, evaluation forms, checklists, behavioral recording forms, and standardized tests.

In keeping with a multiple causality viewpoint, the search for meaningful focal problems should be expanded to include areas beyond the individual. That is, in addition to focusing on the client, assessment and treatment should encompass the caregiving system and the environment as well. The caregiving system includes the members of a client's life space who have direct responsibility for providing support, care, and supervision to the individual on a daily and continuous basis. The broad category of environment encompasses the client's social and physical environment. Social variables include friends, coworkers, roommates, and other individuals who touch a client's life. Physical variables include immediate living quarters and surrounding neighborhood. Any or all variables in the three general categories-client, caregiving system, environment-might serve as causal or maintaining factors regarding the presenting problems. As such, any of these variables may represent viable treatment targets.

Once a thorough and comprehensive assessment has been completed, the next stage of clinical intervention involves designing an overall treatment plan that is individualized to help the client regarding his or her identified treatment target goals. In developing a treatment plan, the therapist needs to choose intervention strategies and identify appropriate training procedures that have some empirical base in the scientific literature.

In summary, the multicomponent assessment procedures described above should direct the clinician to a treatment plan which encompasses the following factors: (1) a clear understanding of the various components of dual diagnosis; that is, knowledge of the definition of mental retardation as well as the comorbidity of mental illness, (2) a comprehensive/multimodal assessment procedure which allows for the understanding of the individual's unique strengths and deficits, and (3) the ability to implement the treatment approach in an environment which will serve the purposes of maximizing success in various settings and over time. These are the ultimate criteria by which to evaluate treatment concerning individuals with dual diagnoses. A fourth factor in developing an effective treatment plan is a thorough knowledge of the various treatment approaches available for this population as well as the advantages of using a combined treatment approach. In an attempt to address this issue, in the following pages we review the literature and attempt to provide a summary of strategies that may be potentially effective in outpatient setting for individuals with dual diagnoses.

Whereas we acknowledge the ambiguity associated with the concept of outpatient psychotherapy, we wish to distinguish such approaches from those conducted primarily in residential or institutional settings. As current worldwide trends in mental health care reflect a continuing policy of deinstitutionalization, the need for community-based services that provide psychotherapy on an outpatient basis becomes very significant (Matson, 1984b).

Behavioral Approaches

Although not necessarily mutually exclusively, we have structurally divided the behavioral literature into approaches primarily based on operant learning, respondent conditioning, and social learning paradigms.

Clinical strategies based upon principles of both operant and respondent learning applied and evaluated in inpatient and residential facilities have been documented to be efficacious therapy protocols for a wide range of problems experienced by adults with mental retardation and concomitant emotional and behavioral disorders. Problems treated include fears and phobias, toileting problems, deficient speech skills, obesity, anxiety disorders, aggression, conduct disorders, sociopathic behaviors, self-stimulation, self-injurious behavior, ruminative vomiting, specific behaviors symptomatic of schizophrenia and major depression, enuresis, encopresis, coprophagy, and specific behavioral deficits associated with autism (see the following for more extensive reviews - Bornstein, Bach & Anton, 1982; Whitman, Scibak & Reid, 1983; Scibak, 1986; Whitman, Hantula & Spence, 1990).

Operant Strategies

Such operant-based behavioral procedures described in the literature include a variety of contingency management strategies such as differential reinforcement, token economies, punishment, time out, prompting, overcorrection, and satiation. In a recent review, Whitman et al. (1990) noted that the treatment outcome literature evaluating such behavioral strategies in general has improved in terms of its methodological rigor. Indeed, an impressive technology for both decelerating maladaptive behavior and increasing adaptive behavior has developed. However, several problems concerning operant-based procedures exist that serve to limit the ease with which such clinical approaches can be utilized in a variety of treatment settings.

First, a major criticism of many of the treatment outcome studies which utilize operant-based, behavioral strategies is that they have been conducted in controlled environments such as institutions, residential placements, and classrooms. Additionally, the interventions require a variety of trained staff who are able to effectively implement contingency management programs. In less restrictive settings such as group homes or in cases where the individual is living with family members, implementing complex contingency management programs becomes more difficult. Training caregivers in behavioral management techniques requires that these individuals be motivated, competent, and resourceful; characteristics that are not always present (Nezu et al., 1992). Second, even when intervention strategies are effective, there are often problems regarding the maintenance of treatment gains and the generalization of these behaviors to new environments (Whitman, 1990). As noted by Matson & Gardner (1991), the use of operant procedures with mentally retarded persons continues to follow the "train and hope" model for generalization and maintenance (Stokes & Baer, 1977). Without the successful learning of the coping skills necessary to impact on various situations in the environment, the use of strictly operant strategies can result in the loss of treatment gains achieved through these strategies (Nezu et al., 1992).

Last, with regard to specific target problems such as aggression, a major theme of the behavior modification literature has been focused on punishment procedures (Gardner, 1988). Such interventions, although potentially effective, offer significant ethical and legal obstacles to clients' rights to least restrictive treatment.

Respondent-Based Strategies

A second general category of behavioral treatment approaches for adults with mental retardation involve those based upon respondent conditioning principles. For example, single case designs such as one conducted by Schloss, Smith, Santora & Bryant (1989) provided initial support for the effectiveness of a respondent conditioning approach (i.e., progressive muscle relaxation and systematic desensitization) in reducing anger responses in one subject. Generalization to natural settings and situations in the client's own milieu was also documented. In addition, Guralnik (1973) combined systematic desensitization with an in vivo procedure when treating fear of heights experienced by a 21-year old male patient with Down's syndrome. Peck (1977) used a group design to replicate studies of desensitization treatments originally developed for patients of normal intelligence regarding individuals with mental retardation. Twenty subjects with fear of rats or heights were identified according to a fear survey and behavioral avoidance test. Four treatment groups (4 subjects per group) were compared and included various desensitization strategies, a placebo group, and a no-treatment control. Although the sample size used in this investigation may have hindered Peck's ability to form firm conclusions, a trend was shown for superior effectiveness of a contact desensitization treatment protocol. In another investigation by McPhail and Chamove (1989), relaxation training was found to be effective in reducing aggression and verbal disruption in a group of six mentally handicapped individuals in comparison to six controls.

These studies, as well as others which support the potential efficacy of respondent-based techniques in addressing the treatment needs of dually diagnosed individuals. Investigators have also used conditioning approaches in combination with operant strategies such as reinforcement schedules, in an attempt to boost overall effectiveness. Interventions such as these may be particularly useful in transferring clinic-based therapeutic gains to the patient's milieu. For example, Waranch, Iwata, Wohl, and Nidiffer (1981) described the use of reinforcement procedures to facilitate homework completion of in vivo counterconditioning trials as important to generalization of socially relevant treatment effects. Despite the potential efficacy of this combined approach, however, finding individuals to carry out these procedures in an outpatient setting is difficult and often unrealistic. Overall, the most effective treatment strategies might be those which allow the individual to learn to regulate his/her own behavior. These strategies apply social learning principles and cognitive-behavioral strategies.

Cognitive-Behavioral Treatment

Whitman (1990) has recently argued that clinical interventions based on social learning and self regulation theory may be more effective than external contingency management systems for learning needed coping skills by individuals with mental retardation. The advantage of these strategies over strictly behavioral approaches is that they more fully address the issues of maintenance and generalization. Social learning theory relies heavily on cognitive processes which play a role in behavior change. By focusing on these cognitive factors, the individual can become better equipped to regulate his/her own behavior in different settings. A recent review of self-management procedures used to facilitate a wide variety of academic and vocational skills indicated that persons with developmental disabilities can learn to successfully implement such procedures (Harchik, Sherman & Sheldon, 1992). Of more clinical relevance, self-management procedures were found to be effective in reducing disruptive verbal ruminations of a mentally retarded adult in a vocational rehabilitation setting (Gardner, Clees & Cole, 1983).

In general, social learning-based approaches would include strategies such as participant modeling, behavioral rehearsal, self-reinforcement, and various other cognitive-behavioral approaches such as problem-solving training, assertiveness training, self-instructional training, and social skills training.

The efficacy of participant modeling as a strategy to decrease the excessive fear of participating in community-based activities was evaluated in a study by Matson (1981). Twenty-four mentally retarded adults were matched into pairs by sex and fear severity and then randomly assigned into either the no-treatment control condition or the participant modeling group. Active treatment first involved having a trainer rehearse going into stores and conducting related activities with the subject at a sheltered workshop. Next, the therapist accompanied the clients to a community grocery store where they performed specific shopping tasks through successive approximations. Treatment was conducted over a 3-month period. Persons involved in the participant modeling condition evidenced significantly greater shopping skills and less fear than untreated clients. In addition to the methodological rigor characterizing this investigation, of particular importance is the fact that Matson addressed a socially relevant target problem, that is, community integration.

Benson, Rice & Miranti (1986) evaluated several different forms of self-control procedures as anger management training for 54 mildly and moderately mentally retarded adults. Specifically, three interventions (progressive muscle relaxation, problem-solving training, and self-instructional coping training) were compared to each other as well as to a combined condition that included all three components. Results after 12 weeks of therapy revealed significant decreases in aggressive responding for all subjects in all four conditions. However, no differences emerged among these treatment protocols.

Although a no-treatment control was not included, thus limiting the conclusions about the actual score of the noted treatment effects, this study does highlight the potential efficacy of self-control procedures with mentally retarded adults.

Other studies which examined the effectiveness of social learning-based approaches with mentally retarded individuals add additional evidence to support the utility of these strategies. The results of these investigations indicated that techniques such as modeling, behavioral rehearsal, and feedback were effective in teaching self-protection skills (Haseltine & Miltenberger, 1990), and employment-related interpersonal skills (Foss, Auty & Irvin, 1989).

Social skills training, as a means of increasing interpersonal functioning and assertive behavior, has been found to be an effective approach with mentally retarded adults (Bregman, 1984; Kirkland & Caughlin-Carver, 1982; Matson & Senatore, 1981; Stacey, Doleys & Malcolm, 1979; Turner, Hersen & Bellack, 1978). More recently, social skills training approaches have been used effectively to improve decision-making skills associated with child-rearing in mothers who have mental retardation (Tymchuk, 1988). Nine mothers with mental retardation received group training in decision making using vignettes describing parenting situations. The results indicated that the use of decision-making skills was significantly improved through this intervention. Teaching social skills to workers with mental retardation has also shown some evidence of being an effective treatment strategy (O'Reilly & Chadsey-Rusch, 1992).

Assertiveness training has also been effective in reducing dually-diagnosed mentally retarded adults' distress, psychiatric symptomatology, and anger-control problems, as well as facilitating their adaptive and assertive behavior (Nezu, Nezu & Arean, 1991).

Within the same study, Nezu et al. (1991) also evaluated the effects of training in social problem-solving skills. More specifically, using a counterbalanced design, 28 dually diagnosed adults were randomly assigned to one of three conditions. Subjects in the first condition (PS/AS) received 5 weeks of problem-solving training (PS) followed by 5 weeks of assertiveness skills training (AS). Members of a second treatment condition, AS/PS, received the same protocol, although in reverse. Ten individuals were included in a waiting list control condition.

Problem-solving training was adapted from the therapy approach previously applied successfully to treat nonhandicapped clinically depressed adults (Nezu, Nezu & Perri, 1989). Results at mid-phase (5 weeks) and posttreatment (10 weeks) indicated significant decreases for subjects in both treatment conditions regarding aggressive responding, psychiatric symptomatology, and feelings of distress relative to the no-treatment control. Problem-solving skills, assertive behavior, and adaptive functioning were also found to increase significantly from pre- to posttreatment. However, no differences between the two skills training protocols emerged regarding these dependent measures. Treatment gains were found to be maintained at a 3-month follow-up assessment.

In a series of methodologically sound single case studies concerning a variety of emotional problems, Matson (1989) used a social learning framework to guide development of an overall treatment package that included modeling, role playing, performance feedback, instructions, and social reinforcement.

Psychological problems included depression (Matson, 1982a), obsessive-compulsive behavior (Matson, 1982b), and psychosomatic complaints (Matson, 1984a). Although it is difficult to ascertain which components served as active ingredients responsible for the resulting positive treatment effects due to the "package" nature of the approach used, these cases probably represent a closer approximation of what therapists actually do in the "real world." Moreover, because of the positive results conveyed by these case studies, clearly the potential viability of social learning strategies was demonstrated.

In a similar package approach, Losada-Paisey & Paisey (1988) describe a comprehensive treatment package to address the skill deficits of mentally retarded sex offenders. The package, which consisted of social skills components such as sex education as well as behavioral components such as a token economy and behavioral psychotherapy, was successful in achieving partial community integration in 5 of the 7 subjects. In another study concerning treatment of deviant sexual behavior, Lund (1992) described a multicomponent behavioral approach with developmentally disabled sex offenders that included social skills training, sex education, and contingency management procedures. Successful outcome, which was partially defined as reduction in offending behavior and increases in independent functioning, was not tied to a specific treatment component. These social skills-based protocols represent a movement away from previous approaches to treatment of sex offenders which included aversive strategies and were based upon classical and operant conditioning principles, and focus more on adaptive skills acquisition.

Obesity in the mentally retarded has also been successfully treated via a social learning approach that included various behavioral self-control and relapse-prevention strategies toward weight loss, such as self-monitoring of caloric intake, reduction of daily food consumption, and self-reinforcement for goal attainment (Fox, Haniotes & Rotatori, 1984; Rotatori, Fox & Switzey, 1980).

Clinical Case Example

The following case example is provided in order to describe an actual intervention with a developmentally disabled individual that utilized strategies that were described in the previous section. We present the case of Henry, a 28 year-old man with mild mental retardation and a concomitant diagnosis of schizophrenia. His group residence staff referred him to one of the authors for treatment because of behavior management difficulties -specifically, aggressiveness toward other residents and staff. Henry was described as "overreactive," "paranoid," and "explosive." For example, he had threatened another resident with a knife because the resident took a long time to finish his laundry. Henry blamed the circumstance on the notion that the other resident did not like him.

Following a thorough assessment, Henry's most salient focal problem was revealed to be impulsivity. The therapist's decision making led to a step-by-step program for shaping Henry's self-control behavior. The individualized program began with basic relaxation strategies and eventually introduced cognitive-behavioral self-control strategies.

Henry was first taught to think before reacting. Initially, he learned to breathe deeply to halt mounting anxiety and counter muscle tension. Next, Henry was taught to count to 10, then breathe deeply. Because this was difficult for him to learn, the therapist added an intermediate step to help Henry redirect himself toward better self-control. Henry would tell himself "Stop" and try to continue relaxation and deep breathing. He would then begin counting to 10 while continuing to breathe slowly and deeply.

Henry practiced this relaxation technique repeatedly during each session; he was also required to practice between sessions. Henry received an index card with pictorial reminders of the techniques, and staff members at his group residence were trained in coaching him to use them. In addition, the rationale for the techniques was explained at the residence so that the caregivers could supplement the treatment by reinforcing Henry's progress. Training the residence staff was also a strategic means of generalizing Henry's new skills, as they would be crucial in providing a positive therapeutic milieu for him in the group home.

When Henry demonstrated the ability to apply the self-control strategies, he was ready for structured role-plays where he could practice the new skills in situations that provoked intense anger. Some of the role-plays were based on actual circumstances. For others, therapist and client together invented scenarios that were likely to produce anger and resentment. Staff members were often included in these sessions, which provided a safe arena where Henry could practice behavioral responses to potentially anger-arousing situations.

Gradually, Henry began to apply these techniques outside of the therapy setting in actual situations that triggered resentment and anger. Because staff members were included in the overall training, they were frequently available to help guide his behavior and reinforce approximations toward more effective self-control.

Several additional cognitive-behavioral interventions were introduced at this point. With some initial success in curbing Henry's tendency to act before thinking, the therapist was able to introduce new coping strategies and develop new cognitive skills. Social problem-solving training (Nezu & Nezu, 1991) was initiated. With this approach, for example, when Henry was feeling rejected, the therapist reviewed with him all possible ways that he could react. One alternative might be to become aggressive, as he had often done in the past. Another alternative might be going to his room, where he could calm down and use relaxation techniques. A third alternative might include talking to his counselor and asking for help in distracting himself, or thinking through the problem. Predictable consequences for each alternative were also reviewed. For example, aggressive acts would predictably be followed by physical restraint, loss of privileges, hospitalization, and shunning by other people.

Henry had initial difficulty learning to anticipate the consequences of his actions. One helpful strategy involved reviewing past incidents as a means of learning to predict possible consequences in the future. Gradually, Henry became quite adept at linking predictable consequences to concrete actions in hypothetical situations. This skill became part of Henry's cognitive-behavioral repertoire for reacting to stressful situations. After breathing deeply and counting to 10, he began to think through different possible actions and predict consequences. He was able to generate alternative courses of action, anticipate their consequences, and choose an alternative on the basis of this information.

Henry was also introduced to stress inoculation training. In this aspect of treatment, he was taught to (a) anticipate difficult situations, (b) picture himself coping in each situation, and (c) reinforce himself for actual attempts at coping with the situation. It was especially helpful for him to rehearse adaptive self-statements such as "I can handle this" when facing a stressful situation or feeling the onset of negative emotions.

Finally, changes were made in Henry's token reinforcement system. Several specific privileges were made contingent on his use of the new self-control skills. For example, by exhibiting self-control, Henry could now earn the opportunity to have his girlfriend visit. This was a potent reinforcer, as these visits had been arranged randomly in the past. Further, Henry meet weekly with his primary counselor to review progress, solve new problems, and schedule his activity reinforcer for the week.

Special Considerations Regarding Application of Social Learning Strategies for Clients with Mental Retardation

Because many cognitive-behavioral strategies are based on clinical approaches developed for use with nonretarded individuals, it may be tempting to apply the same procedures with developmentally disabled clients. However, this translation is rarely simple and the following guidelines regarding use of such strategies may augment treatment efforts.

1. Incorporate strategies for maintaining attention. Because attending to the

stimulus to be learned is central to social learning, it is important to provide skill-building sessions that are entertaining. This may include creative use of video, computer-assisted learning, role-plays, frequent client participation, and instructional games.

2. Because saliency of models is an important variable in social learning, careful consideration should be given to the appropriateness of the model in each learning situation. In one instance, a young male with mild mental retardation helped these authors to develop a videotape that demonstrated specific self-control skills. Other clients later reported that watching a peer succeed at self-control helped them to believe they could also succeed.

3. For an individual with learning disabilities, repetition of material may increase the likelihood that material will be learned. It may be useful to adopt the expectation that protocols may require many more sessions for persons with developmental disabilities than for others. Booster sessions may also be needed during follow-up periods.

4. Individuals vary greatly in their ability to generalize psychoeducational treatment experiences. When implementing treatments based upon self-control and self-regulatory strategies, it may be particularly important to provide concrete examples from a variety of real life situations. This will increase the likelihood that a client may actually use the strategy in real-life settings.

5. Including specific and individualized reinforcement for clients' use of newly acquired adaptive skills may provide increased motivation to use new coping strategies that are difficult to remember.

Conclusions

Despite the conclusion that persons with mental retardation experience a full range of psychiatric disorders at higher rates than non-handicapped individuals and are in great need of treatment services, the literature has responded poorly to their needs (Nezu et al., 1992; Reiss & Trenn, 1984). Although some reports in the literature characterize people with mild to moderate mental retardation as a viable and appropriate treatment population, the professional negative biases against these individuals has unfortunately endured.

Based upon the literature review, it appears that approaches involving social-learning and cognitive-behavioral strategies are clearly the forerunners as potentially effective alternatives concerning outpatient treatment. Treatment packages that are aimed at multiple targets of self-regulation may provide a particularly rich source of alternatives to consider while planning treatment. Additionally, many of these packages may be applicable for use with groups as well as individuals. Because generalized self-control is a core characteristic of people who have adjusted to their environments, further research should continue to explore the application of such treatments for persons with mental retardation.

Future Research Directions

It is clear that more research is necessary that evaluates a variety of clinical strategies for the treatment of persons with a dual diagnosis of mental retardation and mental illness. The following recommendations reflect the specific direction that this research should follow.

1. When possible, group designs with random assignment and adequate control groups should be standard. However, well-designed single case studies using multiple baseline, changing criteria, or alternate treatment designs can provide important information concerning treatment efficacy and should be considered when group designs are not feasible.
2. Samples should be homogeneous with regard to (a) level of retardation, (b) psychiatric diagnosis, and (c) age. Diagnosis of mental retardation and concomitant psychopathology should be consistent across studies and use state of the art procedures.
3. Assessment should be multiple in nature, across types of assessment devices (e.g., direct observation, self-report, clinical interviews), as well as across domains (e.g., cognitive, behavioral, affective, interpersonal, biological).
4. Assessment should incorporate measures that are relevant to a mentally retarded population, as well as reliable and valid.
5. Studies should examine both clinical and practical significance of outcome.
6. Generalization effects, especially with regard to changes in adaptive functioning, should be assessed, as well as maintenance of effects over time.
7. Target problems should be socially relevant (i.e., ones that directly impact on enhancing community integration).
8. Psychotherapy outcome and process studies should be tied to a particular model of psychopathology, especially those specifically relevant to a mentally retarded population.
9. Comparative, integrative, and dismantling studies need to be conducted.

Based on the information presented above, the existence of relevant studies that suggest the potential usefulness of various treatment alternatives for dually diagnosed individuals is evident. Despite this fact, however, only a limited number of strategies have been tested in real psychotherapy settings. It is our belief that efforts to develop a strong body of literature on the treatment of mental health problems of persons with mental retardation have reached a critical turning point. The need for services to this population has never been greater; awareness of the problem is well documented. Yet most clinicians are obliged to make clinical decisions without the security of a comprehensive treatment literature base. With or without more well-designed treatment outcome studies, this population will continue to be treated. As such, an agenda for future research directions has been presented here. The kinds of services people with dual disabilities ultimately receive will depend on the quality and relevance of future research in this area.

Although the number of studies designed to evaluate clinical interventions with mentally retarded adults is small in comparison to treatments for intellectually average populations, there is a growing body of literature which addresses the potential efficacy of some interventions which have been effective with other populations. In addition to this literature, there are a number of studies which provide a comparison of treatment approaches in an attempt to identify those strategies which are most likely to provide positive results. Additionally, as current trends in mental health care reflect a continuing policy of deinstitutionalization, the need for community-based programs that provide treatment on an outpatient basis becomes particularly significant (Matson, 1984b; Nezu et al., 1992; Reiss & Trenn, 1984). Treatment outcome studies, then, have the dual purpose of evaluating not only the effectiveness of a particular intervention, but also of determining its applicability for outpatient purposes.

References

AAMR (1992). *Mental retardation: Definition, classification, and systems of supports*, 9th edition. Washington, DC: American Association on Mental Retardation.

APA (1994). *Diagnostic and statistical manual of mental disorders*, 4th edition (DSM-IV). Washington, DC: American Psychiatric Association.

Benson, B. A., Rice, C. J., & Miranti, S. V. (1986). Effects of anger management training with mentally retarded adults in group treatment. *Journal of Consulting and Clinical Psychology, 54*, 728–729.

Bornstein, P. H., Bach, P. J., & Anton, B. (1982). Behavioral treatment of psychopathological disorders. In J. L. Matson & R. P. Barrett (Eds.), *Psychopathology in the mentally retarded*. Orlando, FL: Grune and Stratton.

Borthwick-Duffy, S. A. (1994). Epidemiology and prevalence of psychopathology in people with mental retardation. *Journal of Consulting and Clinical Psychology, 62*, 17–27.

Bregman, S. (1984). Assertiveness training for mentally retarded adults. *Mental Retardation, 22*, 12–16.

Fletcher, R. J. (1988). A county systems model: Comprehensive services for the dually-diagnosed. In J. A. Stark, F. J. Menolascino, M. H. Albarelli & V. C. Gray (Eds.), *Mental retardation and mental health: Classification, diagnosis, treatment, services*. New York: Springer-Verlag.

Foss, G., Auty, W. P., & Irvin, L. K. (1989). A comparative evaluation of modeling, problem-solving, and behavior rehearsal for teaching employment-related interpersonal skills to secondary students with mental retardation. *Education and Training in Mental Retardation, 24*, 17–27.

Fox, R., Haniotes, H., & Rotatori, A. (1984). A streamlined weight loss program for moderately mentally retarded adults in a sheltered workshop setting. *Applied Research in Mental Retardation, 5,* 69–80.

Gardner, W. I. (1988). Behavior therapies: Past, present, and future. In J. A. Stark, F. J. Menolascino, M. H. Albarelli & V. C. Gray (Eds.), *Mental retardation and mental illness: Classification, diagnosis, treatment, services.* New York: Springer-Verlag.

Gardner, W. I., Clees, T. J., & Cole, C. L. (1983). Self-management of disruptive verbal ruminates by a mentally retarded adult. *Applied Research in Mental Retardation, 4,* 41–58.

Guralnik, M. J. (1973). Behavior therapy with an acrophobic mentally retarded young adult. *Journal of Behavior Therapy and Experimental Psychiatry, 4,* 263–265.

Harchik, A. E., Sherman, J. A., & Sheldon, J. B. (1992). The use of self-management procedures by people with developmental disabilities. *Research in Developmental Disabilities, 13,* 211–227.

Haseltine, B., & Miltenberger, R. G. (1990). Teaching self-protection skills to persons with mental retardation. *American Journal on Mental Retardation, 95,* 188–197.

Kirkland, K., & Caughlin-Carver, J. (1982). Maintenance and generalization of assertive skills. *Education and Training of the Mentally Retarded, 17,* 313–320.

Losada-Paisey, G., & Paisey, T. J. (1988). Program evaluation of a comprehensive treatment package for mentally retarded offenders. *Behavioral Residential Treatment, 3,* 247–265.

Lund, C. A. (1992). Long-term treatment of sexual behavior problems in adolescent and adult developmentally disabled persons. *Annals of Sex Research, 5,* 5–31.

Matson, J. L. (1981). A controlled outcome study of phobias in mentally retarded adults. *Behaviour Research and Therapy, 19,* 101–108.

Matson, J. L. (1982a). The treatment of behavioral characteristics of depression in the mentally retarded. *Behavior Therapy, 13,* 209–218.

Matson, J. L. (1982b). Treating obsessive-compulsive behavior in mentally retarded adults. *Behavior Modification, 6,* 551–567.

Matson, J. L. (1984a). Behavioral treatment of psychosomatic complaints in the mentally retarded. *American Journal of Mental Deficiency, 88,* 639–646.

Matson, J. L. (1984b). Psychotherapy with persons who are mentally retarded. *Mental Retardation, 22,* 170–175.

Matson, J. L. (1989). Social learning approaches to the treatment of emotional problems. In R. J. Fletcher & F. J. Menolascino (Eds.), *Mental retardation and mental illness: Assessment, treatment, and service for the dually-diagnosed.* Lexington, MA: Lexington Books.

Matson, J. L., & Senatore, V. (1981). A comparison of traditional psychotherapy and social skills training for improving interpersonal functioning of mentally retarded adults. *Behavior Therapy, 12,* 369–382.

Matson, J. L., & Barrett, R. P. (1982). *Psychopathology in the mentally retarded.* New York: Grune and Stratton.

Matson, J. L., & Gardner, W. I. (1991). Behavioral learning theory and current applications to severe behavior problems in persons with mental retardation. *Clinical Psychology Review, 11,* 175–183.

Matson, J. L., & Sevin, J. A. (1994). Theories of dual diagnosis in mental retardation. *Journal of Consulting and Clinical Psychology, 62,* 6–16.

McPhail, E. H., & Chamove, A. S. (1989). Relaxation reduces disruption in mentally handicapped adults. *Journal of Mental Deficiency Research, 33,* 399–406.

Nezu, A. M., & Nezu, C. M. (1991). Entrenamiento en solución de problemas. In V. E. Caballo (Ed.), *Manual de técnicas de terapia y modificación de conducta.* Madrid: Siglo XXI.

Nezu, A. M., Nezu, C. M., & Perri, M. G. (1989). *Problem-solving therapy for depression: Theory, research, and clinical guidelines*. New York: Wiley.

Nezu, C. M., & Nezu, A. M. (1994). Outpatient psychotherapy for adults with mental retardation and concomitant psychopathology: Research and clinical imperatives. *Journal of Consulting and Clinical Psychology, 62*, 34–42.

Nezu, C. M., Nezu, A. M., & Arean, P. (1991). Assertiveness and problem-solving therapy for mildly mentally retarded persons with dual diagnoses. *Research in Developmental Disabilities, 12*, 371–386.

Nezu, C. M., Nezu, A. M., & Gill-Weiss, M. J. (1992). *Psychopathology in persons with mental retardation: Clinical guidelines for assessment and treatment*. Champaign, IL: Research Press.

O'Reilly, M. F., & Chadsey-Rusch, J. (1992). Teaching a social skills problem-solving approach to workers with mental retardation: An analysis of generalization. *Education and Training in Mental Retardation, 27*, 324–334.

Paul, G. L. (1969). Behavior modification research: Design and tactics. In C. M. Franks (Ed.), *Behavior therapy: Appraisal and status*. New York: McGraw-Hill.

Peck, C. L. (1977). Desensitization for the treatment of fear in the high level adult retardate. *Behavior Research and Therapy, 15*, 137–148.

Petronko, M. R., Harris, S. L., & Kormann, R. J. (1994). Community-based behavior training approaches for people with mental retardation and mental illness. *Journal of Consulting and Clinical Psychology, 62*, 49–54.

Reiss, S. (1985). The mentally retarded, emotionally disturbed adult. In M. Sigman (Ed.), *Children with emotional disorders and developmental disabilities: Assessment and treatment*. New York: Grune and Stratton.

Reiss, S. A., & Trenn, E. (1984). Consumer demand for outpatient mental health services for mentally retarded people. *Mental Retardation, 22*, 112–115.

Reiss, S., Levitan, G. W., & Szyszko, J. (1982). Emotional disturbance and mental retardation: Diagnostic overshadowing. *American Journal of Mental Deficiency, 86*, 396–402.

Rogers, C. R., & Dymond, R. F. (1954). *Psychotherapy and personality change*. Chicago, IL: University of Chicago Press.

Rotatori, A. F., Fox, R., & Switzey, H. (1980). A parent-teacher administered weight reduction program for obese Down's syndrome adolescents. *Journal of Behavior Therapy and Experimental Psychiatry, 10*, 339–341.

Schloss, P. J., Smith, M., Santora, C., & Bryant, R. (1989). A respondent conditioning approach to reducing anger responses of a dually diagnosed man with mild mental retardation. *Behavior Therapy, 20*, 459–464.

Scibak, J. W. (1986). Behavioral treatment. In J. L. Matson & J. A. Mulick (Eds.), *Handbook of mental retardation*. New York: Pergamon Press.

Stacey, D., Doleys, D. M., & Malcolm, R. (1979). Effects of social skills training in a community-based program. *American Journal of Mental Deficiency, 84*, 152–158.

Stokes, T. F., & Baer, P. M. (1977). An implicit technology of generalization. *Journal of Applied Behavior Analysis, 10*, 349–367.

Turner, S. M., Hersen, M., & Bellack, A. S. (1978). Social skills training to teach prosocial behaviors in an organically impaired and retarded patient. *Journal of Behavior Therapy and Experimental Psychiatry, 9*, 253–258.

Tymchuk, A. J., Andron, L., & Rahbar, B. (1988). Effective decision-making/problem-solving training with mothers who have mental retardation. *American Journal on Mental Retardation, 92*, 510–516.

Waranch, H. R., Iwata, B. A., Wohl, M. K., & Nidiffer, F. D. (1981). Treatment of a retarded adult's mannequin phobia through in vivo desensitization and shaping approach responses. *Journal of Behavior Therapy and Experimental Psychiatry, 12*, 359–362.

Whitman, T. L. (1990). Self-regulation and mental retardation. *American Journal on Mental Retardation, 94*, 347–363.

Whitman, T. L., Scibak, J. W., & Reid, D. (1983). *Behavior modification with the severely and profoundly retarded*. San Diego, CA: Academic Press.

Whitman, T. L., Hantula, D., & Spence, B. H. (1990). Behavior modification and the mentally retarded. In J. L. Matson (Ed.), *Handbook of behavior modification with the mentally retarded*, 2nd edition. New York: Plenum Press.

Further Reading

Matson, J. L., & Barrett, R.P. (1982). *Psychopathology in the mentally retarded*. New York: Grune and Stratton.

Nezu, C. M., & Nezu, A. M. (1994). Outpatient psychotherapy for adults with mental retardation and concomitant psychopathology: Research and clinical imperatives. *Journal of Consulting and Clinical Psychology, 62*, 34–42.

Nezu, C. M., Nezu, A. M., & Gill-Weiss, M. J. (1992). *Psychopathology in persons with mental retardation: Clinical guidelines for assessment and treatment*. Champaign, IL: Research Press.

Reiss, S. (1985). The mentally retarded, emotionally disturbed adult. In M. Sigman (Ed.), *Children with emotional disorders and developmental disabilities: Assessment and treatment*. New York: Grune and Stratton.

Verdugo, M. A. (Ed.) (1995). *Personas con discapacidad: Perspectivas psicopedagógicas y rehabilitadoras*. Madrid: Siglo XXI.

Whitman, T. L. (1990). Self-regulation and mental retardation. *American Journal on Mental Retardation, 94*, 347–363.

Author index

Subject Index